Arms and Armour
of the
Crusading Era, 1050–1350

For my wife Colette
Patience still not returned to her monument

Arms and Armour of the Crusading Era, 1050–1350

Western Europe and the Crusader States

David Nicolle

Greenhill Books, London
Stackpole Books, Pennsylvania

Greenhill Books

This edition of *Arms and Armour of the Crusading Era, 1050–1350* first published 1999 by Greenhill Books, Lionel Leventhal Limited, Park House, 1 Russell Gardens, London NW11 9NN
and
Stackpole Books, 5067 Ritter Road, Mechanicsburg, PA 17055, USA

British Library Cataloguing in Publication Data
Nicolle, David, 1944
Arms and armour of the crusading era, 1050–1350: Western Europe and the Crusader States
1. Military art and science Europe History Medieval, 500–1500 2. Military art and science Middle east History Medieval, 500–1500
I. Title
355'.02'094'09021
ISBN 1-85367-347-1

Library of Congress Cataloging-in-Publication Data
Nicolle, David.
Arms and armour of the crusading era, 1050–1350/by David Nicolle.
p.   cm.
Includes bibliographical references.
Contents: Western Europe and the crusader states.
ISBN 1-85367-347-1
1. Weapons. 2. Armor, Medieval. 3. Crusades. I. Title.
UB10.N5 1999
623.4'41'0902–dc21 98-46532
CIP

Publishing History
Arms and Armour of the Crusading Era was originally published with text and illustrations in separate volumes (Kraus International Publications, New York, 1988). This new, revised and updated edition contains text and illustrations integrated in two volumes, of which this is the first.

Printed and bound in Great Britain by Biddles Ltd, Guildford and King's Lynn

Contents

Preface

This new work is based upon many years of academic study. It forms a reshaped, reorganised and corrected version of my earlier *Arms & Armour of the Crusading Era, 1050-1350*, originally published in a limited edition in 1988. The most obvious change has been to divide the subject into two parts by culture or civilisation rather than having all the text in one volume and all the illustrations in another, as in the earlier work. Hopefully this will enable readers interested in only one of the civilisations to purchase just the volume they require.

Where the illustrations themselves are concerned, some have been redrawn because better sources have become available. Most obviously, however, several oversized pictures which characterised the first edition have now been reduced to average dimensions. Similarly, a smaller number of tiny pictures have been enlarged. In both cases this has been possible because I now have access to more sophisticated equipment than was available in Yarmouk University, Jordan, where I worked during the writing of the first edition.

Finally, a section on China and the Far East has been added to the second book. This is for the simple reason that, since writing the first edition, I have become increasingly convinced that many aspects of military technology seen in the Middle East, Eastern Europe and even Western Europe either had their origins in China or were strongly influenced by developments in Chinese arms and armour.

Introduction

European arms, armour and military technology have been studied for many years in many countries. All too often, however, such studies have focused upon one 'nation', even when that nation did not exist in medieval times, or have assumed too great a degree of uniformity across the whole of western Christendom. The serious study of Byzantine, Islamic, Central Asian, Indian and Far Eastern arms has been a more recent phenomenon but is already suffering from the same parochialism or oversimplification. Nevertheless, it is becoming increasingly obvious that while there was considerable regional variation within each of the great religiously based civilisations of what Europeans call the Middle Ages, there were also varying degrees of stylistic, technological or fashionable influence spreading from one civilisation to another. This seems to have been particularly true of the period under review, which may seem surprising given the fact that this has been characterised as an era of distinct and separate regions. Such varied influences are perhaps more obvious in the early medieval period (5th to 10th centuries), when Byzantium was the main stylistic leader in Europe, than in the Crusading era (11th to 14th centuries) which is the subject of this book. On the other hand the 11th to 14th centuries saw the emergence of greater regional variation across Europe, and indeed Christendom as a whole. Furthermore, such variation reflected both local developments and the influence of neighbouring regions, particularly when the latter did not themselves fall within the medieval Christian world.

One point which will, I hope, become clear is that no single culture or people had a monopoly of technological innovation or even of leadership in fashion. Of course, some peoples had more influence than others, while others were largely the receivers of influence or remained wedded to archaic forms suited to their own military situations. Yet the very fact that the three great cultural blocs of European Christendom, Islam and Turco-Mongol Central Asia came into such violent and widespread contact during the 'Crusading' centuries makes the history of the arms and armour of this period particularly interesting. In turn the study of military technology can throw a useful light on other aspects of a warlike period. In Western Europe the 13th and 14th centuries saw the first phases in the reintroduction of plate armour for body and limbs. Plate armour and its associated technology had, of course, never dropped out of use where the manufacture of helmets was concerned. This fact alone casts doubt on a widely accepted view that the disappearance of plate body-armour during the late Roman and early medieval periods, and its subsequent reintroduction during the High Middle Ages, reflected a decline and revival in European metallurgical technology.

Then there is the question of mere 'fashion' – namely that some changes in arms, armour and other items of military equipment may have resulted from the whims of taste or the demands of fashion rather than a process of supposed technological progress. Nor is fashion a slight or unimportant thing. During the Middle Ages, as today, personal appearance reflected various sociological, political and religious factors. Where military fashion was concerned these pressures were even more obvious. They reflected a rise or fall in the prestige and power of empires or individuals, perceived but not necessarily real military superiorities, actual or desired associations and alliances as well as their negation, plus a whole series of lesser factors. All this affected not only an individual warrior's sense of identity but that of his entire culture. Thus the study of arms and armour can shed light on much more than one facet of the history of technology. It is, as Professor R.P. Lindner described it, 'a wide sea whose currents are largely uncharted; the history of taste, emotional fancy and cultural preference.'[1]

Unfortunately these same currents also swayed the arts. This has been widely recognised where pictorial representations are concerned. Indeed, some scholars are inclined to dismiss medieval art as too unreliable to be taken seriously as a source of information for the history of material culture. I strongly disagree, though any student of this subject must remain aware of those fashions, conventions and archaisms with which medieval art is riddled. Some arts were particularly subject to these cultural pressures and remain exceptionally difficult to interpret. For instance, pictorial arts within, or stemming from, the Byzantine tradition are notorious in this respect. What has, however, been less widely appreciated is the fact that most medieval literary sources, other than technical manuals and inventory lists, also suffer from similar distortions. In fact all aspects of pre-Renaissance civilisation lay under comparable cultural pressures, including fashions in costume, arms, armour, military organisation and tactics. So, of course, did the Renaissance and early modern worlds. Here, however, the pressures were of a different kind, stemming from a different set of cultural preferences and emotional fancies which, as far as parts of Italy were concerned, could already be seen in the first half of the 14th century.

1. R.P. Lindner, 'The Impact of the West on Comnenian Anatolia', in *XVI Internationaler Byzantinistenkongress, Akten* (Vienna, 1982).

Author's Note

The main purpose of this book is to present information in as readily accessible a manner as possible. Such information falls into three main categories: the illustrations themselves; the dictionary of terms; and the bibliography.

The illustrations consist of archaeological, pictorial or other representational evidence. These are combined so as to assist comparison, and are grouped into the main geographical and cultural zones of medieval western Europe. But the order in which these are presented remains an unsatisfactory compromise. There is little reason why northern France should come first, except that it was seen as the 'fountainhead of chivalry' at the time, while England comes next for the simple reason that it was a cultural colony of France. Similarly, the division of the Balkans into two regions, Western and Eastern, is somewhat arbitrary. Essentially this part of south-western Europe was a region of cultural competition between Latin-Catholic western Christendom, and Byzantine-Orthodox eastern Christendom. Nevertheless, my division of the area into Western and Eastern geographical units remains rather unsatisfactory, particularly as this also divides the Balkans between the first and second books.

Within each region the material is generally presented in chronological order. Brief introductory sections describe the region's historical, military and technological circumstances in a very general manner. The following text then endeavours both to describe the archaeological or pictorial evidence and to put it into context. While there is some cross-referencing between items, the reader is recommended to rely on the comprehensive general index for this purpose.

The second main category consists of terminology. This is an enormous but very unevenly studied subject. Some languages, such as Middle English and Old French, have received considerable attention for many years. Others, such as Occitan, remain relatively neglected. Of course, the precise meanings of much medieval technical terminology remains unclear or even unknown. This book hopes merely to suggest some solutions and to present a great many problems. It cannot claim to be an even-handed survey but is intended to juxtapose as many relevant terms as possible in the hope that specialised scholars may note certain interesting linguistic connections, as well as become more aware of both the problems and the potential of comparative terminology.

The third main section is bibliographical. No bibliography on this enormous subject can claim to be comprehensive, but this work is designed to make available as wide a survey of relevant titles as possible, bearing in mind the fact that it deals with the military history and technology of a great many areas. These all too often remain the preserves of specialists who may be unaware of similar situations, events or developments in neighbouring lands. The grouping of titles under 'Arms, armour and art' or 'Military, cultural and social background' is somewhat arbitrary, as there is inevitably a great deal of overlap between these two headings. The reader is, therefore, strongly advised to consult both lists.

Acknowledgements

My thanks are due to a great number of people who helped and encouraged me during the long preparation of this book, both in its first and second editions. Some directed me to sources, made information available, helped in travel and field research or with translations. Any errors in the latter, as in other aspects of the book, remain entirely my own. Nevertheless, I feel bound to offer my particular thanks to the following individuals and libraries: Dr Abdelhadi Tazi (University of Mohammed V, Rabat), Dr M.I. Al Hindi (Damascus), Dr N. Atasoy (Istanbul University), Dr A.S. Atiya (University of Utah), Mr D.S. Begley (Chief Herald, Dublin), Dr J.H. Beeler (Greenboro), Mr Borosy Andras (Budapest), Dr P.E. Chevedden (Salem State College), Dr A.B. de Hoffmeyer (Jarandilla), Dr L. Der Manuelian (Tufts University, Medford), Mrs Ludmila Eltsov (St Petersburg), Dr G. Fehervari (London), Dr M. Gorelik (Moscow), Mrs V. Gyenes (School of Slavonic Studies, London University), Dr A. Halpin (Dublin), Mr H. Harke (Hameln), Mrs Dalu Jones (London), Dr T. Kolias (Ionnina University), Dr Y. Lev (Bar-Ilan University), Prof R. Lindner (University of Michigan), Prof A. Nadolski (Lodz), Dr J.A. Nelson (University of Alabama), Dr H. Nickel (New York), Mrs C.A. Nicolle (always at my side), Mr M.P. Nicolle (London), Mr A.V.B. Norman (London), Mr R.A. Olsen (Kobenhavn), Mr P-R. Royer (Paris), Prof E. Rynne (University College, Galway), Dr M. Scalini (Florence), Prof. G. Scanlon (American University, Cairo), Mr J.K. Schwarzer II (North Carolina), Dr V. Simoniti (Ljubljana University), Dr J. Smith (University of California, Berkeley), Dr J.F. Verbruggen (Vilvoorde), Mrs H.M. Zijistra Zweens (Paterswolde), Yarmouk University Library (Irbid), Nottingham University Library, and Finchley Central Library (Barnet, London).

Finally I want to offer special thanks to Mr Lionel Leventhal, not only for encouraging me to prepare this second edition but also for 'clearing the way' so that it became practical for me to do so.

Maps

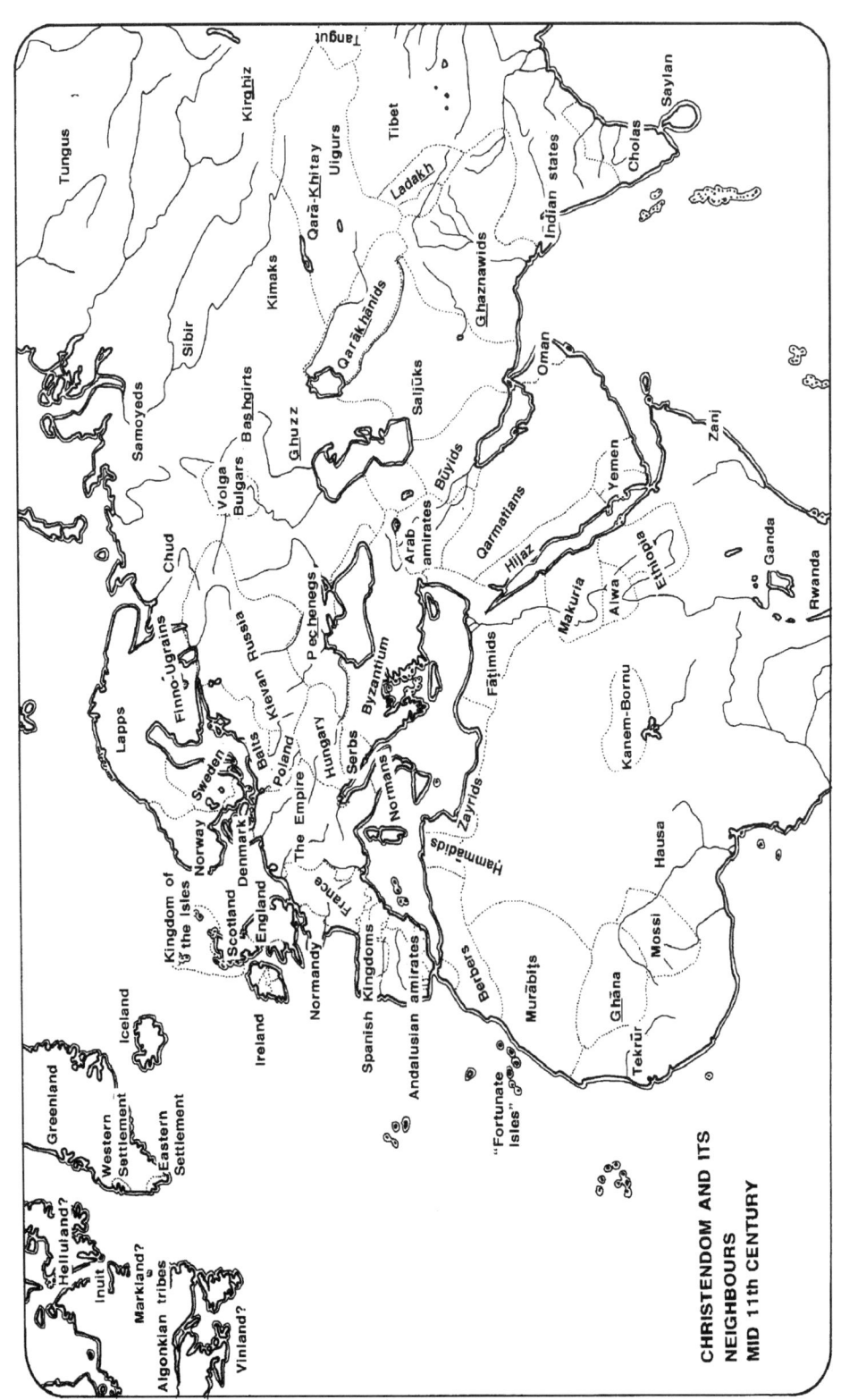

CHRISTENDOM AND ITS
NEIGHBOURS
MID 11th CENTURY

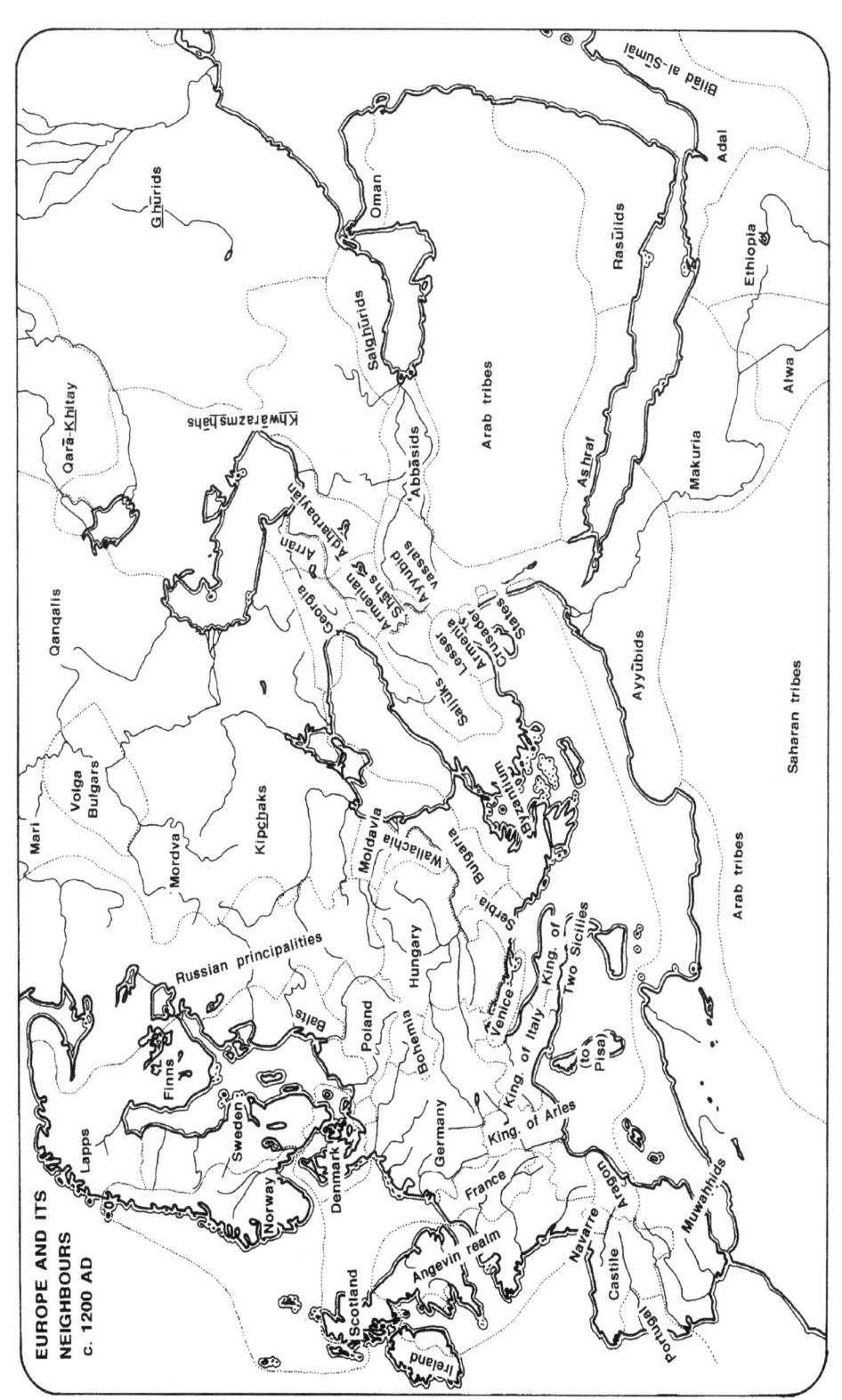

EUROPE AND ITS
NEIGHBOURS
c. 1200 AD

Lapps

Finns

Norway

Sweden

Denmark

Scotland

Ireland

Angevin realm

France

Germany

King of Arles

King. of Italy

Venice

King. of
Two Sicilies

(to
Pisa)

Bohemia

Poland

Balts

Hungary

Moldavia

Wallachia

Serbia

Bulgaria

Byzantium

Crusader
States

Lesser
Armenia

Armenia

Adjabaiyan

Arran

Georgia

Saljūks

Ayyūbid
States
vassals

Abbāsids

Salghurids

Oman

Rasūlids

Ashraf

Ayyūbids

Arab tribes

Arab tribes

Saharan tribes

Muwaḥḥids

Portugal

Castile

Navarre

Aragon

Russian principalities

Mordva

Kipchaks

Volga
Bulgars

Mari

Qanqalis

Qarā-Khitay

Khwarazmshāhs

Ghūrids

Makuria

Alwa

Ethiopia

Adal

Bilad al-Sūmal

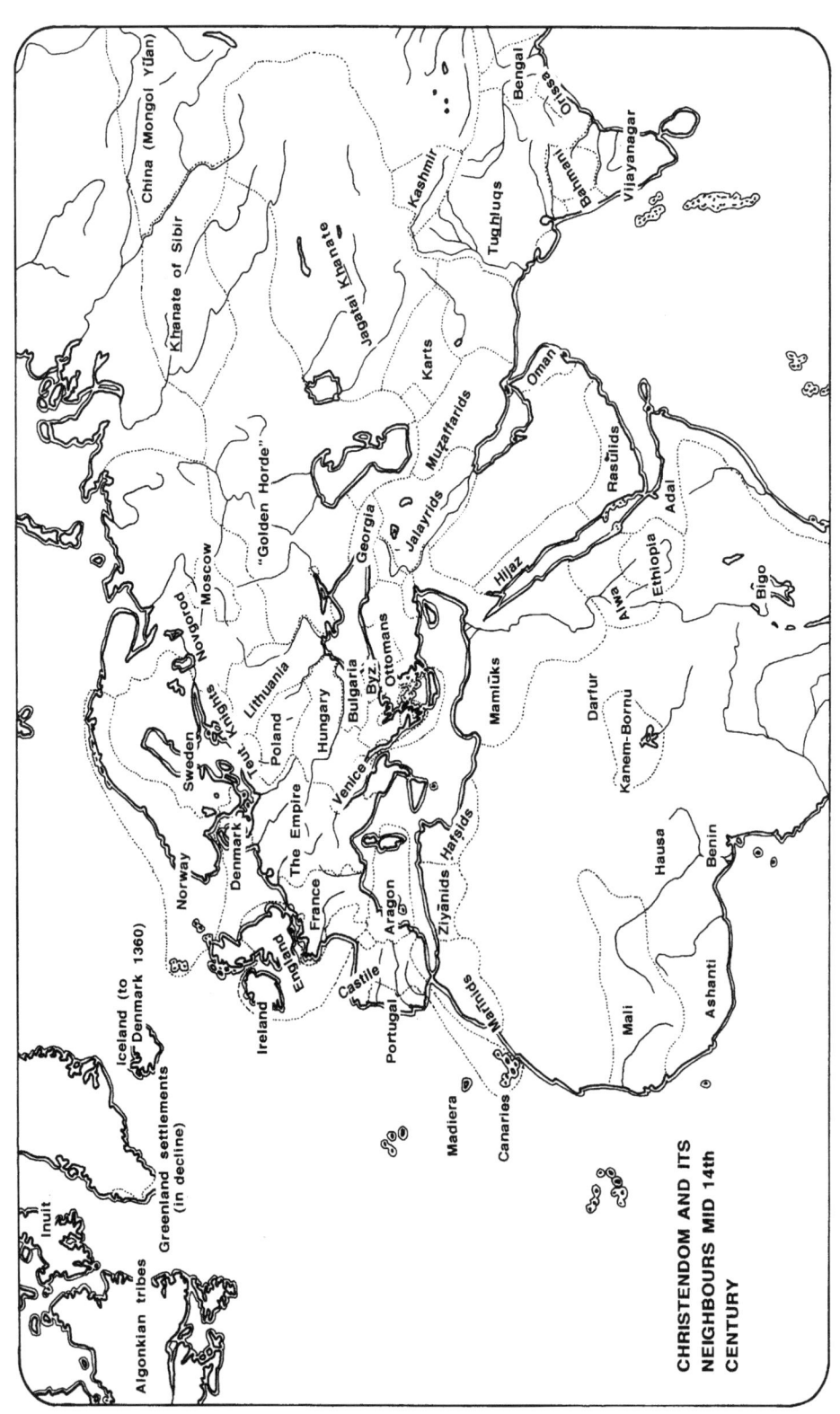

China (Mongol Yüan)

Bengal

Orissa

Kashmir

Bahmanī

Tughluqs

Vijayanagar

Khanate of Sibir

Jagatai Khanate

Karts

Oman

Muzaffarids

Rasūlids

"Golden Horde"

Georgia

Jalayrids

Adal

Hijaz

Moscow

Novgorod

Ethiopia

Alwa

Bigo

Sweden

Teut. Knights

Lithuania

Byz.

Ottomans

Mamlūks

Darfur

Poland

Hungary

Bulgaria

Kanem-Bornu

Norway

Denmark

The Empire

Venice

Hausa

France

Benin

Aragon

Ziyānids

Hafsids

Iceland (to
Denmark 1360)

Ireland

England

Castile

Marīnids

Mali

Ashanti

Greenland settlements
(in decline)

Portugal

Madiera

Canaries

Inuit

Algonkian tribes

**CHRISTENDOM AND ITS
NEIGHBOURS MID 14th
CENTURY**

Chapter 1

Northern France

The frontiers of northern and eastern France during the medieval period were very different from those seen today. For example, in the mid-11th century the County of Flanders, in what is now western Belgium, formed part of the Kingdom of France, whereas Brabant and Hainault to the east, also today forming part of Belgium, then lay within the German Empire. Champagne was within France, though rarely under the control of the French Crown, whereas Alsace and Upper Lotharingia (Lorraine) lay within the Empire. The Duchy of Burgundy around Dijon was part of France whereas the County of Burgundy around Besançon again lay within the Empire. To the south almost all territory east of the rivers Sâone and Rhône formed part of the Empire, while even some districts west of these rivers remained Imperial territory. Little, however, changed along these north-eastern frontiers and the French monarchy's gradual push towards the Rhine had hardly begun by the mid-14th century.

Northern France was also by no means culturally nor militarily homogeneous during this period. Brittany was, of course, still largely Celtic in language and preserved its distinctive military customs well into the late 12th century. In the 11th century Normandy still differed from the rest of the country in certain military matters, though the Normans had by and large learned their extraordinarily successful military techniques from the French. Most distinctive of all were the Flemings; a large proportion of whom spoke Flemish (Dutch) and could not really be described as Frenchmen at all. Infantry also played a much more prominent role amongst them than they did elsewhere in France.

Although northern France was the main source of Western European military styles during the medieval period, this was in terms of fashions rather than technological or tactical innovation. From the 9th to 11th centuries there had been a steady decline in the importance of poorer vassals serving either as infantry or unarmoured cavalry. The term *milites* now came to refer specifically to a horseman, usually with armour,[1] and this was part of a general process of military specialisation which became even more noticeable in the 12th century. These centuries similarly saw a general rise in the power of government, though at a regional rather than national level and being more noticeable in some areas rather than others.[2] The richer and more powerful Counts or Dukes made less use of a general levy or *arrière ban* of all men owing military service, this being yet another indication of growing military specialisation.[3] Nevertheless very large armies, including regional levies, were sometimes seen in the 12th century.[4] However, towns did not as yet have much military significance either as sources of troops or as centres of defence.[5] The 'Peace of God' movement and its regional variations were found in northern France as they were in the south. By limiting the extent of warfare they again contributed to the professionalisation of the warrior class.[6]

By the end of the 11th century full military equipment, particularly for a cavalryman, had become very expensive, and its proper use demanded considerable skill. Men trained as units rather than individuals, while tactics demanded ever more command and control as well as professionalism.[7] The 'feigned retreat' was now an accepted tactic, at least among the Normans and Bretons. The latter may, in fact, never have abandoned it since late Roman times.[8] The development of the 'couched lance' technique with its associated high saddle, straight-legged riding position, very long shield and close formation 'shock' tactics, might be the most noticeable Western European military development of the late 11th and 12th centuries,[9] but heavier and longer swords probably remained the most important weapons, particularly amongst cavalry.[10] On the other hand the origins of the couched lance tactic and its associated *conrois* closely-packed cavalry formation remain a matter of debate. While they are widely assumed to have originated in 11th century Western Europe, evidence for their use in 10th century Byzantium is convincing, while there is also evidence for their use in 9th century Middle Eastern Islamic armies.

Archery similarly increased in importance, though again more so in some areas than in others, Normandy having claim to some precedence in infantry archery.[11] In France, as in most parts of Western Europe, the crossbow would have a bigger military impact than the hand-held bow from the 12th to early 14th centuries.[12] The importance of crossbowmen is indicated by the emergence of crossbow-armed mounted infantry from the late 12th century onwards.[13] Such men were largely professionals, and the first known 'Grand Master of Crossbowmen' in France was recorded in 1230.[14] Furthermore, the crossbow was largely responsible for the reintroduction of plate armour in late 13th and early 14th century Europe.

The process of specialisation was yet more pronounced in the 12th and 13th centuries. A decline in feudal-military service among those members of the knightly class who did not take up the profession of arms accompanied an increasing employment of mercenaries by the King and his leading barons.[15] The forces maintained by the King of France on the Norman border in 1202–3 may be taken as a reasonably typical small professional army of this period.

They consisted of 257 knights, 267 mounted sergeants, 80 mounted crossbowmen, 133 infantry crossbowmen and about 2000 infantry *sergeants*, all of these being Royal troops, supported by 300 unspecified additional mercenaries.[16]

Flanders remained a major source of mercenary troops, both cavalry and infantry, well into the 14th century. Many now came from the cities, which were also developing their own effective guild-based militia systems.[17] Elsewhere in France other towns were growing in importance, both as centres of military organisation and defence, and as sources of military manpower.[18] Infantry continued to play a vital role during the first part of the 14th century, though subsequently declining once again. They included javelin-armed light infantry known as *bidauts*, who seem to have operated in close co-operation with the cavalry.[19] Gunpowder firearms similarly made their first appearance in French hands in 1338, and were often mentioned in the 1340s.[20]

Note that items which have not been specifically linked to southern France are also included in this section on northern France.

Figures

1 Gospel, Duchy of Brittany late 10th/11th centuries
(Bib. Munic., Ms. 8 f.5v, Boulogne, France)

The figure shown here has a great deal in common with those in the
Bayeux Tapestry, which makes an 11th-century date likely for this
manuscript. The shield is, nevertheless, an early example of the large
kite-shaped type.

2 Spearhead from northern France, 11th–12th centuries
(Musée National des Antiquitées, St Germain-en-Laye,
 France)

This almost unique spearhead includes most of the characteristics
associated with a period before a widespread adoption of the couched
lance. Though thick and substantial, it is also broad and includes
flanges or wings. The latter feature was probably not an anti-
penetration device, as sometimes stated, but is more likely to have
reflected a versatile method of both thrusting and fencing with the
spear.

3 Illustrated Bible, north France, early 11th century
(Bib. Munic., Arras, France)

The manuscript is archaic in both style and the military equipment it
portrays. Here a man with an almost Carolingian type of large round
shield thrusts overarm in an old-fashioned manner with a pennoned
spear. His conical helmet might be of segmented construction and,
most unusual of all, it seems to have a mail aventail, the only piece of
mail in the picture. Such a helmet is otherwise unknown in France.
The warrior could reflect an Eastern European – particularly
Magyar (Hungarian) – style, or the manuscript could be partially
based on a Byzantine original.

**4A–B Carved capitals, Normandy, late 11th/early 12th
 centuries**
(*in situ* church, Rucquerville, France)

These warriors are among the earliest surviving Romanesque figure
sculptures in Normandy. They may be based upon conventional
manuscripts, but nonetheless their shields are worthy of comment.
These appear to be of a large round or oval form with bosses fastened
by nails or rivets through lobes rather than a continuous rim.

5 'Fortitude', carved capital from Abbey church of Cluny, Duchy of Burgundy, 1088–1110
(Musée du Farinier, Cluny, France)

Here the figure of Fortitude wears a mail hauberk with a mail coif. Clearly the coif has a very early representation of an unlaced *ventail* hanging down on the wearer's chest, but the damaged carving is unclear in its details.

6 Seal of the City of Soissons, County of Soissons, early/mid-12th century
(Archives Nationales, Paris, France)

The knight symbolising the City of Soissons wears typical northern French equipment of the period, including a conical helmet, a long-sleeved mail *hauberk*, a tall shield on a *guige*, a shield boss, and a broad, tapering, straight-quilloned sword. As no sword-belt is visible the weapon might have been thrust through a slit in the left hip of the hauberk.

7 Sword, France, c.1150–75
(P-R. Royer private collection, Paris, France)

This may be regarded as a typical north-west European weapon of the mid-12th century. Its blade tapers almost to a point, though the lack of a real point indicates that thrusting was still not a normal fencing technique in this part of Europe. Nevertheless, the long, slightly-curved *quillons* and the almond-shaped *pommel* show that considerable changes were taking place in 12th-century European swords.

8 Sword, probably French, c.1130–70
(private collection, ex-Oakeshott, *Archaeology of Weapons*)

Various aspects of this sword suggest a date slightly earlier than the preceding example. Its blade is less tapering and the tip blunter. The *quillons* are straight, although their down-turned ends are decorated with small animal's heads. The blade is also inscribed GICELINMEFECIT ('Jocelin made me').

9A–D Carved capitals, Duchy of Burgundy, c.1120
(*in situ* Church of La Madeleine, Vezelay, France)

A – 'Infidel in combat with a knight'; B–C – 'Goliath'; D – 'David'. Though largely fanciful, the figure of the 'Moorish' or 'Saracen' infidel (A) includes a number of interesting features. His peculiar leaf-shaped sword is clearly meant to be different from normal Christian weapons. On his head he appears to wear a mail cap and he carries a small kite-shaped shield with an angled axis similar to those shown on slightly later carved capitals from the Crusader church in Nazareth. The figures of Goliath and of David are much more straightforward. They wear long-sleeved mail *hauberks* without *coifs* and are armed with broadswords hanging from belts rather than baldrics. Their shields are typically large kite-shaped types. The helmets are, however, distinctive. All are conical, fluted, and have slightly curved lower rims. They also have chin-straps which pass directly through small extensions to the sides of the helmets. Perhaps we have here either an idiosyncratic local variation or an attempt to make the helmets look 'exotic'.

10A–G 'Races of Mankind', carved relief, Duchy of Burgundy, 1120–5
(*in situ* central tympanum, Church of La Madeleine, Vezelay, France)

A – 'Lydian hunter'; B–C – 'Weapons of Italians'; D – 'Lydian hunter'; E–F – 'Saracens'; G – 'Mace of a Saracen'. The slightly later carvings on the tympanum at Vezelay use both similar (E) and dissimilar (F) conventions to indicate mail. The interpretation of this relief as a stylised representation of the Races of Mankind is by no means certain, but if the identification is correct, then the weapons given to each indicate some interesting current opinions about various peoples. A mace (G) would, in fact, be correctly associated with Muslims. The 'Lydians' are shown as simple and uncivilised huntsmen who hold simple rather than composite bows (A and D). One of these would clearly be considered a longbow (D). Note that when unstrung the string of this weapon has slipped down the bow itself. A bag-like quiver hangs from a shoulder-strap. At this time, in almost all parts of Europe, the longbow was regarded as a hunting rather than as a war weapon, though exceptions were found in areas under strong Scandinavian, Byzantine or Islamic influence. Two supposed Italians hold peculiarly hooked spears (C and D). Since the Italians were noted sailors, these may represent militarised 'boat hooks'. On the other hand the northern Italian cities were already famous for effective infantry militias, so these weapons could be seen as exaggerated versions of a type of infantry weapon designed both for thrusting and for pulling horsemen from their saddles. As such it could be regarded as a forerunner of the *halbard*. It is also interesting to note that the designer of this carved relief might have considered the true 'Saracens' as armoured horsemen in the same mould as Crusader knights (E and F).

11 'Flight into Egypt', carved capital, Duchy of Burgundy, c.1120–30
(*in situ* Cathedral, Autun, France)

Joseph's weapon appears to be another example of a large, single-edged blade mounted on a short thick haft. Such a weapon could have evolved out of the single-edged, but long-hafted, so-called 'war-scythe' and may in turn have evolved into the 13th-century *falchion*.

12 **'Life of St Nicholas', carved relief on a font, County of Flanders, 1150–75**
(*in situ* **Cathedral, Winchester, England**)

Fonts carved from hard black stone were a speciality of Tournai and were exported to many places. This example shows what could be regarded as a version of the 'bearded axe', in which the blade extended down and back from a point level with the place where its sleeve went over the haft. Such a style would become popular in central and eastern Europe. In the north and west, however, war-axes developed differently, with an upwards-sweeping edge evolving out of the almost symmetrical 10th and 11th-century so-called 'Danish axe'.

13 **'Visions of Sts Peter and Paul', carved relief on a font, County of Flanders, early/mid-12th century**
(*in situ* **Church of Our Lady, Dendermonde, Belgium**)

St Paul or one of his companions lies prostrate on the road to Damascus. The figure wears a perfectly normal long-sleeved mail *hauberk*, but on his head is a helmet clearly made in two pieces joined along the central comb and reinforced by a band around the rim. Such helmets were more commonly seen in the south but were not normally associated with Northern Europe by the 12th century.

14A–B **'Massacre of the Innocents', carved capital from Abbey of St Georges de Boscherville, Normandy, late 12th century**
(**Musée des Antiquities, Rouen, France**)

The warriors on this very damaged capital wear conical helmets, one of which is clearly fluted (B), over mail *hauberks* with *coifs* and short sleeves. One figure may have an unlaced *ventail* lying across his chest (B). The swords are straight and non-tapering, with pointed (A) or round (B) pommels.

15 **'Martyrdom of Sts Fuscien, Victoric and Gentien', carved relief, County of Vermandois, late 12th/early 13th centuries**
(*in situ* **church, Sains-en-Amiennois, France**)

The late 12th century saw the adoption of a remarkably uniform style of arms, armour and military costume throughout a large part of north-western Europe. This figure is in that style, which consisted of a long-sleeved mail *hauberk* with integral *mittens* and a mail *coif*, plus mail *chausses* on his legs, all worn beneath a simple sleeveless *surcoat*.

16A–C **St Etienne Bible, French, 1109**
(**Bib. Nat., Dijon, France**)

The standard equipment of the early 12th century French, German or Anglo-Norman warrior is illustrated here. It consisted of a long-sleeved mail *hauberk*, a conical helmet sometimes with a forward-angled crown (A), a broad tapering sword and a long kite-shaped shield held by *enarmes* (B). The long-hafted 'Danish' war-axe was still in use, mostly in England, Germany and Scandinavia. Its inclusion here could indicate that this manuscript was made in eastern France or in the Kingdom of Arles.

17 *Winchester Psalter*, 'Massacre of the Innocents', northern French or southern English, c.1115–60
(British Library, Ms. Cotton Nero C.IV.356, London, England)

Most of the military figures in the *Winchester Psalter* are in standard arms and armour but some include unusual characteristics. This man has an interesting type of forward-angled conical helmet in which the *nasal* curves down from the lower rim of the helmet. His sword is hung on his right hip, but this is probably artistic licence. The *hauberk* is, however, a late example of a style which, slit at the sides instead of fore-and-aft, was more characteristic of the 11th century and may originally have been intended for infantry use.

18A–B Manuscript drawing, northern France, late 12th century
(Bib. Munic., Ms. 12/II f.62v, St Omer, France)

Exceptions to the general trend towards uniformity can be found, though usually under special circumstances. The infantry combat shown here is almost certainly an example of trial by battle using specialised non-lethal weapons. Both figures wield mace-like objects and defend themselves with unusual egg-shaped shields. The terminology of 12th-century military equipment shows that a variety of as yet unidentified shields were intended for combat on foot.

19A–E 'Story of Tristan', painted wooden marriage chest, Duchy of Brittany, 1150–70
(Cathedral Treasury, Vannes, France)

The painted chest from Vannes portrays normal as well as unusual arms and armour. The former are seen where two horsemen (A and B) attack a third (C), who is caught while in the act of mounting his horse. A fourth figure hands the startled knight his shield. The helmets are conical, two with *nasals* and one without. One has a straight front profile, another a forward-angled crown. Mail *hauberks* still lack *mittens* but include the usual *coifs*. It is interesting to see how far forward the horsemen thrust their shields. The combat between Tristan (D) and Morhaut (E) portrays much the same sorts of helmet and sword, but it is the shields which demand attention. These are very large and must be designed for infantry combat. They might be termed *mantlets* or *pavises*, or could be *talevas* shields specifically designed to protect foot-soldiers from arrows.

20 Enamelled tomb of Geoffrey of Anjou, County of Maine, mid-12th century
(Museé du Mans, France)

The Count of Anjou is here shown wearing either a painted helmet without a nasal or an embroidered cap. His large kite-shaped shield still has a small boss and a visible reinforcing bar but is of the new flat-topped type. His slender sword tapers but is still shown with a slightly rounded tip.

21 Lost tomb, probably of Count William of Flanders, from Church of St Bertin, St Omer, Flanders, c.1130–75
(from 19th-century drawing, after Nowe)

The disappearance of this tomb must rank with the destruction of some of London's Temple Church effigies as a serious loss for the study of medieval arms and armour. It appears to have portrayed a warrior with a tall, round and rather Germanic helmet having a fixed face-mask. This latter did not, however, cover all the face. Instead it consisted of a *nasal* with cheek-pieces on either side to frame the eyes. Otherwise the man was equipped in standard fashion with a long-sleeved mail *hauberk*, mail *chausses*, a long and surely inaccurately slender sword and a large, flat-topped kite-shaped shield.

22A–B Manuscript marginal illustration, northern France, late 12th century
(Bib. Munic., Ms. 210, f.4v, Avranches, France)

The similarity between this tiny gilded drawing and the other complete illustration of warriors with large shields and peculiarly shaped maces (f. 18) is remarkable. They may come from the same source, and may indicate judicial 'trial by combat'.

23A–T Eighteenth-century drawings of lost early to mid-12th century stained glass windows illustrating the First Crusade, from St Denis, Paris
(ex-*Monuments de la Monarchie Françoise*, Paris, 1729)

A–C – 'Capture of Iznik (Nicea)'; D–F – 'Capture of Antakya (Antioch)'; G–H – 'Capture of Jerusalem'; I–J – 'Defeat of Egyptians at Asqalon'; K–M – 'Turks defeated outside Iznik (Nicea)'; N–P – 'Battle of Dorylaeum'; Q–R 'Egyptians flee into Asqalon'; S–T – 'Defeat of Turks outside Antakya (Antioch)'. These 18th-century drawings of lost 12th-century windows must be treated with great caution. Yet some features can be picked out with some degree of confidence. The Crusaders (A, B, E, F, G, H, I, K, N and T) have symmetrical conical helmets without *nasals*, long-sleeved mail *hauberks* and kite-shaped shields. Their weapons are spears and swords. The Muslims are more varied and the artists seem to have attempted to distinguish between various ethnic groups. The Turks of Anatolia (A and C) are similar to the Crusaders except that they are given round helmets, one of which might correctly have a form of neck extension (A). Elsewhere they are shown with the same equipment (M) except that one of them wears a lamellar *cuirass* (L). Lamellar and mail are again given to the Anatolian Turks at Dorylaeum (O and P) and to other Turks at Antioch (S), although in this latter battle a scale hauberk is also indicated. The Arab-Egyptian troops in Jerusalem and Asqalon (G, H, J, P, Q and R) differ from the Turks in various details. Mail or scale as well as lamellar armours are portrayed, as is an unarmoured man with a small round shield and an apparently shaven head (H). A man whose sword has a tassel or thong from its pommel rides barefooted and perhaps without stirrups (J). In a final scene the Egyptians who flee into Asqalon include a man with what could be a quilted armour (Q) and another with a mail or scale shirt that appears to end at his waist or to go inside a kilt or skirt (R). Almost all these features are seen in Islamic arms and armour of this period. Although few are accurately portrayed in the windows, their presence in pictures of the First Crusade made within relatively few years of the event may indicate either that the artist saw sketches made by clerics who accompanied the Crusade or that the artist heard verbal descriptions from men who took part. One way or another accurate information about Islamic arms and armour had yet to degenerate into the conventionalised 'Moorish' or 'Saracen' forms seen later.

24 'Herod's soldiers', stained glass window, County of Blois, c.1150
(*in situ* west end of Cathedral, Chartres, France)

This is one of the oldest pieces of glass in Chartres Cathedral and the military equipment is virtually the same as that on the lost windows of St Denis. Here two men have long, barely tapering swords with short thick *quillons*. One man also wears a mid- or long-sleeved mail *hauberk* without a *coif*.

25 'Massacre of the Innocents', stained glass window, County of Blois, late 12th century
(*in situ* Cathedral, Chartres, France)

On this slightly later window the sword has longer *quillons*, a heavy *pommel* and a more tapering blade.

26A–C 'Murder of St Thomas Becket', County of Blois, c.1210
(*in situ* Cathedral, Chartres, France)

Considerable differences can be seen by the start of the 13th century. Mail *hauberks* now include *mittens*, while the *coifs* might be separate, though that cannot be identified here. Mail *chausses* are worn and the shields have become shorter and broader, generally with flattened tops. The most striking change is, however, in helmets. These are now flat topped, one or perhaps two with fixed face-mask visors (A and B), one without such a visor (C). None protect the sides or back of the head and so cannot be called *great helms*. They are, in fact, an important transitional form. The absence of a visor on one such flat-topped helmet suggests that some early face-masks may have been removable.

27 'Count Thibault VI of Chartres', stained glass window, County of Blois, c.1217–20
(*in situ* Cathedral, Chartres, France)

On this much obscured window Count Thibault has the same arms and armour as is shown in the 'Murder of St Thomas Becket' except that he has no helmet over his mail *coif* and greater prominence is given to the coat-of-arms on his shield.

28A–M 'Legend of Roland and Oliver', stained glass window, County of Blois, c.1218
(*in situ* Cathedral, Chartres, France)

A – 'Slain Moors'; B – 'Roland'; C – 'Roland'; D–G – 'Moors'; H–J – 'Army of Charlemagne'; K – 'Charlemagne'; L–M – 'Roland and Oliver'. Essentially the same styles are seen in this window as in the 'Murder of Becket' except that the Christians' flat-topped helmets have round edges. This may indicate a slightly later style or simply a variation in construction technique. All such helmets are shown with facial visors (A, C, H–K). Some reach below the chin while others seem a little shorter (C, H and J). One visored helmet looks almost conical (J) but is clearly not the same as the simple conical helmets worn by most of the 'Moors' (A and G). Only once is a defeated 'Moor' shown in a helmet with a forward-angled crown (A). The Christians wear long-sleeved mail *hauberks* with *mittens*, mail *coifs* and mail *chausses*. Most but not all have *surcoats* and carry the newer, broader, flat-topped kite-shaped shields (B, C, H–K). Spears are the favoured weapons while broadswords with straight (J) or curved (I and L) *quillons* are hung from knotted sword-belts (J). The equipment of the 'Moors' is more fanciful and less realistic though it was probably based on a conventionalised reality. Mail or scale *hauberks* and *coifs* are shown (A, D, E and G), as well as mail *chausses* (E–G). Lamellar *cuirasses* are worn over the mail (A, E and G), while shields are round.

29A–J 'Participants in the Crusade of Louis IX' (?), stained glass window, County of Blois, c.1255
(*in situ* choir clerestory window of Cathedral, Chartres, France)

The identification of these figures with men who accompanied St Louis on the disastrous Seventh Crusade is tentative, but various coats-of-arms can be identified, including those of Dreux (A), the Beaumont family (J) and the Royal Arms of France (B). A further figure in intentionally old-fashioned arms and armour represents St George (D). With the exception of the Saint, the supposed Crusaders are in largely uniform equipment except, interestingly enough, for their helmets. They wear mail *hauberks* with, where visible, mail *mittens* and *coifs* (A–C, E, G–I). Some *surcoats* have horizontal and sharply angled shoulders which indicate that substantially padded shoulder protections or even semi-rigid leather *cuiries* are worn beneath the heraldic *surcoats* themselves, but over the mail *hauberks*. All figures have mail *chausses*, and shields are almost triangular with rounded or square upper corners. Only one horse wears a *caparison* (C). All the men save St George carry spears, most of which have large pennons repeating or adding variations to their heraldry. Swords are broad and slightly tapering with decorated *quillons* (A and G), though, again, St George wields an earlier type with a trefoil *pommel*. Is it a coincidence that the man carrying the arms of Dreux (A) appears to be losing his sword over his horse's rump? The supposed pommel of Peter of Dreux's sword captured or found at the Battle of Mansūrah in 1250 subsequently emerged in the Damascus bazaar. It is now in the Metropolitan Museum of Art, New York (fig.33). A second figure (G) has adopted the Muslim fashion of looping a cord or thong from his sword's *pommel* over his wrist while a third figure (H) seems to have a second scabbard on his right hip. The varied helmets in these windows include normal mid-13th-century flat-topped *great helms* (A, B, G, H and J) plus two of an earlier form that does not come so far down the back of the neck (E and F). These also apparently lack vertical strengthening bars at the front. But the two most interesting helmets are flat topped with face-mask visors, one clearly shown (C) and one less clearly so (I). They are closely related to helmets in earlier windows at Chartres and again represent a transitional phase in the development of the true *great helm*.

30 Helmet, French (?), possibly 13th century or a fake
(Musée de l'Armée, Paris, France)

This extraordinary helmet has no parallels in western Europe until the very late 14th and 15th centuries, and even then in Italy and Ireland rather than France. Nor are comparable helmets shown in 13th-century works of art. This does not, however, preclude the possibility that the helmet is an unusual local variation on the *great helm*, although the weight of evidence points towards it being either wrongly dated or being a fake.

31 'A knight of the Clement family receiving the *Oriflamme* from St Dionysius of Paris', stained glass window, County of Blois, mid-13th century
(*in situ* Cathedral, Chartres, France)

This figure has also been tentatively identified as St Maurice of the Theban Legion. He is clearly wearing a long-sleeved mail *hauberk* with *mittens* and mail *chausses*. Presumably his mail *coif* was of the contemporary separate kind. The slightly-raised shoulders of his *surcoat* may indicate padding beneath. His sword with its slightly curved *quillons* hangs from a knotted sword-belt which also has a series of bar-like stiffeners. It is, however, unusual to see such stiffeners on a knotted rather than buckled sword-belt.

32A–C 'Goliath and Philistines', carved reliefs, County of Blois, c.1205
(*in situ* north portal of Cathedral, Chartres, France)

These carvings are good examples of the kind of fanciful and exotic military equipment often given to 'pagan' or 'infidel' figures in early Gothic art. Fanciful as it might be, many of the elements can be traced back to an original source. It is also interesting to see that many pieces which would subsequently be adopted by European warriors first appeared in such imaginary equipment. Here Goliath wears armour based on Byzantine art which was, by the 12th and 13th centuries, often similarly fanciful. It consists in one case (A) of a scale *cuirass* with laminated upper arm defences. In the second example such a *cuirass* seems to be worn over a stylised *hauberk* with *mittens* (B). The leg defences are more interesting. These consist of decorated *poleyns*, *greaves* which seem to lack hinged divisions at sides or back, and either scale-covered or highly stylised mail *sabatons*. Such leg armour is remarkably similar to that of early 14th century Europe. It must also be remembered that the Bible specified Goliath as wearing 'greaves of brass upon his legs' (I Sam., 17.6).

33A–B Enamelled sword-pommel, north French, mid-13th century
(Metropolitan Museum of Art, New York, United States)

One side of the sword-*pommel* is decorated with the arms of Dreux quartered with the ermine of Brittany (A). This almost certainly links it to Peter of Dreux, Duke of Brittany, who fought alongside Louis IX in the disastrous Second Battle of Mansūrah in 1250. The other side of the *pommel* has a shield bearing a red cross on a green ground, a badge often adopted by French Crusaders, and is decorated with vines. This *pommel* must surely come from a sword captured at Mansūrah which then surfaced centuries later in Damascus, perhaps having been the heirloom of a Muslim family.

34 Effigy of Raoul de Beaumont from Étival Abbey, Maine, c.1220
(Archaeological Museum, Le Mans, France)

Although a crude and early effigy, it displays a number of interesting features. The most unusual is the flat-topped but still apparently segmented helmet. This lacks both face-mask and *nasal*, though a remarkably early example of the nose-covering mail flap or *bretache* may hang from the man's chin. The round objects apparently on his shoulders are, in fact, censers swung by attendant angels. Raoul de Beaumont wears a long-sleeved mail *hauberk* with a *coif* and mail *chausses*, and has a large flat-topped kite-shaped shield hanging from a *guige*, and a sword hanging at a peculiar angle across his groin.

35 'Murder of St Thomas Becket', carvings, County of Blois, early/mid-13th century
(*in situ* Cathedral, Chartres, France)

In stark contrast to the fantastic armour of Goliath and the Philistines, the English knights who slay the Archbishop of Canterbury wear simple armour consisting of mail *coifs*, mail *hauberks* with *mittens*, mail *chausses* and unpadded loose *surcoats*. Their swords are equally simple and undecorated.

36 'St Theodore', carving, County of Blois, 1230–5
(*in situ* south transept of Cathedral, Chartres, France)

Slightly more elaborate arms and armour have been given to the warrior saint Theodore, but he still has a basic mail *hauberk* with a *coif* thrown off his head and lying on his shoulders. His mail *chausses* do not go under the soles of his feet. He also wears a *surcoat* slit at the sides to expose another garment beneath. His shield is the newly fashionable, smaller, flat-topped kite-shaped type and his sword has a massive cup-shaped *pommel*.

37 Inscribed tomb slab of Georges de Niverlée, Hainault, c.1262
(*in situ* church, Niverlée, Belgium)

This effigial slab is notable because only one *ailette* is shown, again on the right shoulder, to provide a place for heraldic display comparable to the shield on the man's left side. The warrior on this engraved slab also has a flat-topped *great helm* with a small crest.

38 'Fortitude', carved relief, Isle de France, c.1210–20
(*in situ* west front, Cathedral of Notre Dame, Paris, France)

It is interesting to note how old-fashioned is the equipment given to this figure of Fortitude. The helmet is of a simple conical form and the *hauberk*, which lacks *mittens*, is unusually long. Perhaps the sculptor wanted to indicate that Fortitude was an ancient virtue, which the young should emulate. The round shield and the very loose cloak are likely to be symbolic, though their meaning is now lost.

39 Effigy of Jean d'Alluye from Touraine, c.1250
(Cloisters Museum, Metropolitan Museum of Art, New York, United States)

Although Touraine lay north of the Loire it had much in common with regions to the south. The somewhat fanciful sword may reflect 'exotic' fashions adopted by some members of the supposedly Crusading aristocracy of France, while the scabbard is also laced to the belt in an unusual manner.

40 'King of Sodom', statue, County of Champagne, 1275–1300
(*in situ* inside west front of Cathedral, Reims, France)

This figure is believed to represent the King of Sodom alongside Abraham and Melchizadek, the priest-king of Salem following the defeat of Chedorlaomer (XIV Gen. 12–24). The king is dressed in one of the finest and most elaborate versions of fanciful armour in 13th-century French sculpture. Various features may reflect reports by soldiers returning from Spain or the eastern Mediterranean, or the influence of booty and souvenirs brought back by such men. The fluted helmet and the decoration of the round shield, as well as the waist sash, could be examples of this influence.

41A–C 'Execution of John the Baptist', carvings, County of Champagne, c.1240
(*in situ* west front of Cathedral, Reims, France)

Fanciful pseudo-Byzantine arms and armour similar to that seen a little earlier at Chartres is used to identify certain 'wicked' figures at Reims (A and C). This seems, however, to be reserved for leaders and officers. Ordinary soldiers are shown in the standard equipment of French infantry (B) with mail *coifs* and close-fitting round *cervellière* helmets.

42A–B Effigies, County of Anjou, early 13th century
(*in situ* Abbey of Fontevrault, France)

A – 'Effigy of King Henry II of England'; B – 'Effigy of King Richard I of England'. The effigies at Fontevrault are among the most important early Gothic tombs. Two swords are included in the carvings. Both seem to have unnaturally short *quillons* but this might be a result of inadequate stone carving skills. The sword of Richard I has straight *quillons*, a grip with vertical decorations or anti-slip devices and a small octagonal *pommel*. The sword of Henry II has a diamond-shaped *pommel* and short down-turned *quillons*. One is tempted to see Spanish influence in this latter sword and it should be remembered that Henry was also Duke of Gascony as well as suzerain of the Viscounty of Bearn-Soule in the Pyrenees.

43A–D Carvings, County of Vermandois, c.1230
(*in situ* west front of Cathedral, Amiens, France)

Various allegorical and religious warrior figures decorate the front of Amiens Cathedral. Their equipment is standard, consisting of mail *hauberks* with *mittens*, mail *coifs* and mail *chausses* (A, B and D). Loose *surcoats* are worn, in one case clearly over raised and padded shoulders (D). Significantly this appears to be the only figure to wear another, longer cloth garment beneath his *surcoat*. The rounded or slightly conical helmets lack *nasals*. They are either of segmented *spangenhelm* construction or have been reinforced with metal strips and a band around the brim (A, B and D). Swords are rather massive, tapering but blunt ended, and with trefoil (A and B), squat round (C) or triangular (D) *pommels*. The sword carried by another figure (C) includes a sword-belt of the new buckled type which is here wrapped around the scabbard.

44 Incised monumental brass of Sir Brocardus de Charpignie, France, c.1270
(via Courtauld Institute, London, England)

It would be useful to know more about this monumental brass. Such a style of tomb memorial probably first appeared in northern France around the mid-13th century, Dinant being the main production centre for the copper alloy (latten) of which they were made. Monumental brasses became popular in England from the late 13th century but this early and archaic example may have originated in Flanders or the Rhineland. The warrior appears to have a form of *bascinet*, but even more interesting is the piece of armour that he wears over his long-sleeved mail *hauberk*. This has squared shoulders and is fastened by three laces, buckles or toggles on each shoulder. It probably did not come much below his waist and it is clearly not a form of *surcoat*. This might, in fact, be an early representation of a hardened leather *cuirie* or *quiret*.

45 'The Betrayal', carving probably from area of Amiens, Vermandois, c.1275–1300
(Metropolitan Museum of Art, inv. 17.120.5, New York, United States)

The soldier on the carving of the Betrayal has a close-fitting *cervellière* held by a triple chin-strap over a mail *coif*.

46 Unidentified effigy, Maine, c.1275–1300
(*in situ* Abbey church, Evron, France)

A different sort of mail *coif* and *ventail* made its appearance late in the 13th century. Here it is shown off the head, with the laces of the *ventail* dangling down the right breast.

47 Seal of John de Montfort, France, 1248
(Archives Nationales, Paris, France)

Here the lord of Montfort wears a surprisingly simple form of *great helm* in which the face-mask is made of a separate piece of iron and comes further down the head than do the sides and back of the helmet. The *quillons* of his sword are curved and include a small *langet*. His legs and neck are clearly mailed but no mail appears on his arm. This is probably an artistic error or the result of wear on the seal, or it could indicate an unusual long-sleeved surcoat.

48A–B Enamelled bronze gemellion, France, 13th century
(Cloisters Museum, Metropolitan Museum of Art, inv. 47.101.40, New York, United States)

In addition to a rider carrying a shield (not shown here) two foot soldiers also appear on this piece of French metalwork. They carry convex round shields, a sword (A) and perhaps a spear (B).

49A–AT *Maciejowski Bible*, Paris, c.1250
(Pierpont Morgan Library, New York, United States)

A – 'Amalekites' (f.24v); B – 'Philistines' (f.29v); C – 'Amalekites' (f.9v); D – 'Philistines defeat Saul' (f.34v); E – 'Defeat of Moabites' (f.12r); F – 'Death of Goliath' (f.28v); G – 'Army of Hai' (f.10r); H – 'Death of Cain' (f.2r); I – 'Death of Goliath' (f.28v); J – 'Philistines' (f.14v); K – 'Jacob's covenant with Laban' (f.4v); L–O – 'Defeat of Philistines' (f.29v); P – 'Pharaoh's army' (f.9r); Q – 'Jacob's covenant with Laban' (f.4v); S – 'Goliath and Philistines' (f.27r); T – 'Death of Absalom' (f.45v); U – 'Esau's offering' (f.4r); V – 'Capture of Lot' (f.3r); W–X – 'Philistines' (f.14v); Y – 'King Sisera' (f.12v); Z – 'Saul destroys Nahash' (f.23v); AA–AC – 'Israelites repulsed from Hai' (f.10f); AD–AE – 'Saul's body hung from the walls of Beth Shan' (f.35v); AF – 'Philistines' (f.15r); AG – 'Capture of Hai' (f.12v); AH – 'Israelites repulsed from Hai' (f.10f); AI – 'Abner slays Joab' (f.36v); AJ – 'Death of Absalom' (f.45v); AK – 'Joab pursues Sheba to Abel' (f.46v); AL – 'Capture of Hai' (f.12v); AM – 'Israelites repulsed from Hai' (f.10f); AN – 'Rescue of Lot' (f.3v); AO – 'Israelites repulsed from Hai' (f.10f); AP–AQ – 'Story of the Levite's wife' (f.16r); AR – 'Jonathan' (f.31v); AS – 'Israelites attack Rabbah' (f.42r); AT – 'Absalom's groom' (f.42v). The so-called *Maciejowski Bible* is not only one of the finest European manuscripts of the 13th century but is also an unsurpassed mine of information on arms, armour, military costume and military equipment in general. Basically both 'good' and 'wicked' are equipped in the same manner, the only unusual features of the Philistines and other such groups being decorated or fluted helmets (B, D and J) and their conventional round shields (A, C, D, G and S). Sometimes, though rarely, the 'wicked' are also illustrated using horse-archery (D). Helmets include fully developed *great helms* (M and P), brimmed *chapel-de-fer war-hats* of various round (G, I, L, S, AB and AL) and squared forms (G, V, AC and AN), a wide-brimmed hat which was probably not a helmet (AS) and close-fitting *cervellières* without *nasals*. These could be worn over (B and G) or under a mail *coif* (AO). Such a *cervellière* is seen once hanging from a groom's arm (AT). Older forms of helmet such as tall, conical or rounded helmets with *nasals*, of segmented or one-piece construction are mostly worn by the 'wicked' but are also seen on Israelites (A, C, D, G and AD). Mail *coifs* are all apparently integral parts of a *hauberk* and are worn over padded cloth *coifs* which are also seen worn without mail *coifs* (G, V, AB, AK, AN, AR and AZ). Most mail *hauberks* have long sleeves and *mittens* (A–C, E–G, S, V, Y, AH, AL, AN, AO and AR) but a few have three-quarter length sleeves (D, AF and AL). Mail *chausses* are generally worn by horsemen, some of whom are dismounted (D, E, G, S, AO and AR). Padded *cuisses* appear (S and AN), but the only *greaves* are those worn by Goliath. Though shown in a realistic and practical manner, they might not reflect current usage, as the Biblical text specified that Goliath wore such pieces of armour. It is worth noting that Goliath is illustrated with a shield on his back, the relevant verse stating that he should have a '*target* of brass between his shoulders' (I Sam. 17.6). There is no evidence for rigid or stiffened armours worn beneath the mostly sleeveless *surcoats*, but many quilted *gambesons* are shown which have raised collars buttoned at the side and reach almost to the knees. Some are sleeveless (AL), some short-sleeved (G, V, AH and AN), and some have long sleeves with *mittens* (AB and AN). They can be worn over (AL) or under (AH and AR) a mail *hauberk*, or be worn on their own (G, V, AB and AN). Apart from the probably conventional round shields of the 'wicked' and the isolated round *targe* or *buckler* of an Israelite slinger (AS), shields are kite shaped, either broad and square-edged for the presumed cavalry elite (S) or larger with rounded tops for sappers and infantry (AI and AL). Weapons include a remarkable variety of basic types. Swords are broad with slightly tapering blunted tips, straight bar-like *quillons* and generally round *pommels* (A–C, F, G, O, S, AO and AR). A new feature is the decorated daggers with triangular blades, curved *quillons* and fanciful *pommels* (N and AA). Unfortunately such daggers are not shown in a sheath or belt and so the way of carrying them is unknown. Another type of long-bladed hand weapon is frequently illustrated in the *Maciejowski Bible*. It seems to be an early form of *falchion* and, being seen in the hands of the 'good' more often than the 'evil', may be assumed to represent a real weapon in current use. It can have a simple angled or fancifully decorated back to the blade (A, V, J and AN). A sharply-curved grip is presumably designed to counteract the centrifugal force of swinging such a massive weapon (J). Another example has a lengthened two-handed grip (AN). Comparable weapons with straight backs and curved cutting edges have short hafts (AG, AB and AJ). A smaller single-edged blade may also once be seen on a long spear haft (K). A very long and slender pike-like blade appears on one spear (AB) and once an even thinner, almost needle-like point seems to be thrust into the end of a spear (X). Ordinary spears have diamond or leaf-shaped blades, only that of Goliath having a crossbar, wings or flanges (S). Substantial war-axes are of the old symmetrical 'Danish' type (G, V, AB and AQ), though one has a newer type of socket in which the haft does not protrude beyond the sleeve (A). Maces appear in greater variety. A true spiked mace is put into the hands of an Amalekite (A) and a rather feeble looking version into the hands of a Philistine (AF). Heavier and generally longer-hafted clubs with serried ranks of nail-like lumps are more common and are used by Philistines (W) and Israelites (AB and AP) alike. While crossbows with loading stirrups are shown a number of times (G and AM), bows are only used by Philistines (D) in presumed imitation of Muslim Turks. Naturally Esau the huntsman (U) and the blind man who slew Cain (H) also have bows. The general impression is that the bow, as distinct from the crossbow, was not considered a European weapon of war in mid-13th century northern France. Primitive man-powered mangonels are shown twice (Z and AK), each having three ropes which would have been pulled by the operating team. Another device (AD and AE) is shown elevating the headless corpse of Saul. It seems unlikely that such a machine, here so realistically portrayed, would have been invented by an artist just for this purpose. The detailed locking device and the counterweights on the opposite end of the beam, plus the fact that it is mounted on top of the wall or tower of Beth Shan suggest that it might be the raising mechanism for a drawbridge. Ropes could have led from the crossbar on which Saul's corpse hangs down to a drawbridge below, or it might have been a device for dropping things on the enemy, as mentioned in various written sources.

50A–C 'Goliath', psalter, France, c.1250–75
(Fitzwilliam Museum, Ms. 35–1950, f.7, Cambridge, England)

Despite its date this French psalter gives Goliath archaic equipment. His mail *hauberk* is worn without a *surcoat* and he appears not to wear mail *chausses*, while his helmet is segmented and perhaps slightly conical. His kite-shaped shield is surprisingly long and his sword, though having a strongly tapering blade, also has a trefoil *pommel*.

51A–B *History of Outremer*, Paris, 1295–6
(Bib. de la Ville, Palais des Arts, Ms. 29, f.7v, Lyon, France)

An illustration of a battle outside Antioch shows Crusaders in the round-topped *great helms* that had become standard by the late 13th century (A). The Muslims wield *falchions* (B) but the placing of this unlikely weapon in the hands of 'infidels' was probably an artist's way of interpreting the curved swords that he knew the Turks commonly used.

52A–B Manuscript, northern France or England, late 13th century
(British Library, Ms. Harl. 782, London, England)

The manuscript is in a simple style which is often associated with England. The horsemen have later forms of conical *great helms* which not only protect the wearer against a horizontal thrust but also provide a glancing surface against a downward blow. Body protection still consists of a mail *hauberk* and *chausses* plus a triangular shield which has now shrunk in size. One figure (B) has a tapering sword with a distinct point and slightly decorated *quillons*, while another (A) rides a horse with a full mail *bard*.

53A–B *Le Chevalier du Cygne*, France, early 13th century
(Bib. Nat., Paris, France)

This is an illustration of a siege, including a man with a standard mail *coif*, *hauberk* and *chausses* plus a sleeveless *surcoat*. It also illustrates a simple man-powered *mangonel* in action. The representation of the *mangonel* is garbled beyond recognition but certain features of the operating team demand comment. A pair of hands holds down the sling, perhaps to give a certain spring to the shot, while the team pulling the ropes wear full mail and carry large oval *mantlets*. The only unarmoured man is at the rear of the squad, shielded by those in front.

54 *History of Outremer*, northern France, c.1279
(Burgerbibliothek, Ms. 112 f.110r, Bern, Switzerland)

A substantial war-axe having a very slightly upwards-swept cutting edge and a haft of half a man's height.

55 *Roman de la Poire*, northern France, c.1250–75
(Bib. Nat., Ms. Fr. 2186, f.34v, Paris, France)

In the scene of the 'Siege of the Tower of Love' a flat-topped *great helm* is shown with a concave rear profile. This feature is common enough so that it cannot merely be dismissed as an artistic error. Although almost certainly exaggerated in this and other pictures, it probably reflected some peculiarity of constructional technique.

56 *History of Outremer*, Paris, c.1250–75
(Bib. Nat., Ms. Fr. 779, f.134r, Paris, France)

Here a knight takes part in the siege of S̲hayzar in Syria. His *great helm* seems to have additional triple ventilation holes above the eye-slit and in the rear panels.

57 *History of Outremer*, Paris, c.1290–5
(Bib. Royale, Ms. 9492–3, f.417r, Brussels, Belgium)

An early portrayal of rigid *couters* to protect the elbows which, with *poleyns* for the knees, were the first pieces of true plate armour apart from helmets to be re-adopted in medieval Western Europe.

58 *History of Outremer*, Paris, 1295–1300
(Bib. Munic., Ms. 45 f.22v, Epinal, France)

Knee-protecting *poleyns*, presumably of hardened leather or metal, become increasingly common in manuscripts towards the end of the 13th century. This example might be fastened to thigh-covering *cuisses* worn over mail *chausses*.

59 *History of Outremer*, Paris, 1295–1300
(Walters Art Gallery, Ms. W.137, Baltimore, United States)

Another illustration of a late 13th-century *poleyn* knee-defence seems to show the disc worn directly over, and perhaps attached to, the mail *chausses*.

60 'Pentecost', psalter, France, mid-13th century
(British Library, Ms. Add. 17868, f.29, London, England)

A typical example of the most commonly portrayed sword of the period. It has a regularly tapering blade coming to a not very acute point, plus straight *quillons* and a round *pommel* of modest size.

61A–C *History of Outremer*, Paris, c.1250–75
(Bib. Nat., Ms. Fr. 2630, Paris, France)

A – 'Crusaders besiege Iznik (Nicea)' (f.22v); B–C – 'Crusaders besiege Tyre' (f.111v). In this relatively simple manuscript a crude form of *mangonel* is illustrated tossing enemy heads into the enemy's city (A). Such a device was almost certainly powered by men pulling on ropes, although no ropes are shown here. Or perhaps the thickened ends of the double arms are supposed to act as counterweights. At the siege of Tyre the Crusaders wear early forms of *great helms* (B) with single eye-slits and no central reinforcing bars, while the city's Muslim garrison are provided with curved sabres (C).

62 *Apocalypse of St John*, probably Paris, c.1300
(ex-Oakeshott, *The Archaeology of Weapons*)

The style of this drawing is very close to that of English *Apocalypse* manuscripts dated c.1275–1300. The arms and armour are, however, very interesting. The warrior wields a true *falchion* of exaggerated size. His sword hand is protected by a *gauntlet* with a splinted wrist defence and on his head he wears a brimmed *chapel-de-fer* apparently forged from a single piece of iron. *Gauntlets* would not be widely seen until the early 14th century.

63 *Roman de Tristan*, France, c.1260
(Bib. Nat., Paris, France, after Viollet-le-Duc)

This extraordinary weapon would normally be associated with a slightly later date. It is an early form of *bill* or *bardiche* elongated axe. Such weapons probably evolved out of the earlier war-axe. One line of development led to a thrusting point, as might be shown here, and eventually became the *halbard*. Another feature is that the lower point curves back to rest against or even be attached to the haft of the axe. Such a feature is seen in some 14th-century European and later Islamic war-axes.

64 Manuscript, France (?), 1294
(Bib. Nat., Paris, France; ex-Bib. Richelieu no.938 f.69, after Viollet-le-Duc)

A very similar weapon with both tips of the blade apparently formed into sleeves around the haft. A small spike has also been added at the back.

65 *History of King Arthur*, France (?), c.1260
(Bib. Nat., Paris, France, after Viollet-le-Duc)

The third of these slender-bladed but short-handled axes has a long sleeve joining the blade to the haft, while both ends again curve back to rest against the haft.

66 Manuscript, France (?), 1274
(Bib. Nat., Paris, France; ex-Bib. Richelieu no.342 f.23, after Viollet-le-Duc)

Here a smaller war-axe with a slender blade has both ends resting on the haft.

67 'Goliath', Bible, Paris, c.1300
(Royal Library, Thott Ms. 7, f.1r, Copenhagen, Denmark)

The Philistine once again wears a brimmed *chapel-de-fer war-hat*. This probably enabled an artist to show David's sling-shot embedded in the giant's head. He also wears a mail *coif*, *hauberk* and *chausses* under the broad, smock-like *surcoat* which had come into fashion in some parts of Europe.

68 'Crowning Christ with thorns', France, c.1280
(Bib. Nat., Ms. Lat. 8892, f.29, Paris, France)

The unbelted *surcoat* is again shown worn over the usual items of mail.

69A–F *History of Outremer*, Paris, c.1300
(Walters Art Gallery, Ms. W. 142, Baltimore, United States)

A – 'Siege of Tyre' (f.112r); B – 'Siege of Antioch' (f.28r); C–F – 'Capture of Nicea' (f.21r). Two simple *mangonels* are shown, both with the broad crossbars that normally held ropes pulled by a team of men (A and B). One, however, has a small counterweight added (A). This was hardly big enough to convert the machine into a counterweight *trebuchet* and may instead have had something to do with the loading procedure. Or it could have been a transitional phase in the development of the true *trebuchet*. A broad, tapering sword with slightly-curved *quillons* and a rather surprising trefoil *pommel* is shown (C), along with three rounded *great helms* of complicated construction and with perhaps decorated surfaces. Note that all three *helms* are facing to the right.

70 *Legende de St Denis*, France, c.1317
(Bib. Nat., Mss. Fr. 2090–2, Paris, France)

One of the first clear representations of a separate scale-covered *gauntlet* being worn with a mail *hauberk*. The sleeves of the *hauberk* are visible above the wrist.

71 Broken sword, France, mid-14th century
(Musée de l'Armée, inv. Po.678, Paris, France)

Though broken to less than half its length, this tapering sword with its long curved *quillons* is a typical mid-14th-century weapon. Note that a small reliquary is also set into the *pommel*.

72A–D Carved ivory plaque, France, 1300–50
(Musée Municipal, no.1342, Angers, France)

The plaque probably represents the Siege of the Castle of Love. One figure (A) may carry a mace but is more likely to be throwing a flower. All the warriors wear mail *hauberks* and *chausses* and carry small triangular shields. Their helmets might be round-topped *great helms* but could also be a form midway between a *great helm* and a large *bascinet*, both of which could have large flat visors.

73 Carved ivory box, Paris, c.1325
(Hermitage Museum, St Petersburg, Russia)

The sword shown here seems to be a simple version of the broken sword in the Musée de l'Armée in Paris (fig.71).

74 Lost tomb slab of Guillaume du Breuil from church of St Ouen, Rouen, Normandy, c.1360
(from 17th-century drawing, after *Gazette des Beaux Arts* vol.LXXXIV, 1974)

In many respects this Norman knight wears remarkably old-fashioned armour, particularly when compared to the equipment used in mid-14th-century Germany. Relatively new features include a raised mail *neckguard*, presumably fastened to the padded *gambeson* which is also visible at his wrists. His straight sword has decorated *quillons*, while his legs are protected by *poleyns*, narrow *greaves* with perhaps an added strengthening piece below the knee, and a flap of mail forming a rudimentary *sabaton* on top of his foot.

75 Seal of Count Louis of Flanders, 1322
(Archives Nationales, Paris, France)

Count Louis is shown wearing a *great helm* and mail. On his shoulders are rectangular *ailettes*, which were purely decorative and heraldic. They helped identify a man fully enclosed in armour. The fact that a chain leads from the hilt of his sword to his chest shows that he was wearing some kind of *cuirass* or *coat-of-plates* beneath his *surcoat*; this provided a rigid attachment point for the chain.

76A–E *The Cloisters Apocalypse*, Duchy of Normandy, c.1300–25
(Cloisters Museum, Metropolitan Museum of Art, no.68.174, New York, United States)

A–D – 'Second Horseman of the Apocalypse' (f.8r); E – 'Massacre of the Innocents' (f.2v). This beautiful manuscript illustrates rather old-fashioned arms and armour with a few interesting features. We see close-fitting *cervellière* helmets (A and D), mail *hauberks* with *mittens*, one of the latter pushed back from the wrist (C), and mail *chausses*. The horseman's leg armour includes another kind of foot covering, perhaps with some kind of metallic lining. An acutely-tapering sword (A) and a curved *falchion* (C) are clearly illustrated, while on another page a new way of fastening a scabbard to a sword-belt can be seen. This seems to include a buckle.

77A–C ***Sketch-book of Villard de Honnecourt,* France mid-13th century**
(Bib. Nat., Ms. Fr. 19093, Paris, France, after Verbruggen)

This might be a later copy of de Honnecourt's book. The soldier's *ailettes* (B) certainly suggest a slightly later date. The picture of the counterweight *trebuchet* (B) is one of the earliest and clearest representations of this new siege machine in European art. A highly schematic picture of part of a *trebuchet* (A) is difficult to interpret. It might, in fact, represent a loading mechanism.

78 Manuscript, France, 1350–6
(after Viollet-le-Duc)

This unnamed manuscript is said to have been made for John II, King of France, before his capture at the battle of Poitiers in 1356. It shows several very up-to-date features, including this visored *bascinet* secured by a strap and buckles to the back of a presumably rigid or semi-rigid *coat-of-plates*.

79 *Histoire Universelle,* France, early 14th century
(British Library, Ms. Roy. 20.D.I, f.127, London, England)

It would be wrong to interpret this well-known illumination too literally. There is no evidence for horse-archery being used in 14th-century Western Europe, and, in any case, horse archers would not have been heavily armoured in this fashion. The *great helm* shown here is a good example of the large 14th-century version. Another lies abandoned on the ground showing the untied chin-strap which normally remains unseen.

Notes

1. J.F. Verbruggen, *The Art of Warfare in Western Europe during the Middle Ages* (Oxford, 1977), p.25; P. Van Luyn, 'Les Milites dans la France du XIe Siècle', *Le Moyen Age* vol.LXXVII (1971), pp.7–8 and 16–18.
2. D. Douglas, *The Rise of Normandy* (London, 1947), p.21; D. Bates, *Normandy before 1066* (London, 1982), pp.176–8.
3. R.A. Brown, *The Normans and the Norman Conquest* (London, 1969), p.93.
4. P. Contamine, *La Guerre au Moyen Age* (Paris, 1980), pp.133–5.
5. Contamine, *op.cit.* p.110.
6. Bates, *op.cit.* pp.52–3, 163–4 and 174–6.
7. Contamine, *op.cit.* pp.109 and 126–8; J.F. Verbruggen, 'L'Art Militaire dans l'Empire Carolingien (714–1000)', *Revue Belge d'Histoire Militaire* vol.XXIII (1979–80), pp.396–7; Brown, *op.cit.* p.51; D.R. Cook, 'The Norman Military Revolution in England', *Battle Conference on Anglo-Norman Studies, Proceedings* vol.I (1978), pp.96–102; G. Duby, 'Au XIIe Siècle; "Les Jeunes" dans la Société Aristocratiques',

Annales: Economies, Sociétés, Civilizations vol. XIX (1964), p.839; J.F. Verbruggen, 'La Tactique Militaire des Armées de Chevaliers', *Revue du Nord* vol.XXIX (1947), pp.161–5, 168–9, 172 and 175–80; Van Luyn, *op.cit.* pp.29–30; J. Bradbury, 'Battles in England and Normandy, 1066–1154', *Battle Conference on Anglo-Norman Studies, Proceedings* vol.VI (1983), pp.8–12.

8. B.S. Bachrach, 'The Feigned Retreat at Hastings', *Medieval Studies* vol.XXXIII (1971), pp.346–7; B.S. Bachrach, 'The Origins of Armorican Chivalry', *Technology and Culture* vol.X (1969), pp.166–70; M.J. Swanton, *The Spear In Anglo-Saxon Times* (Ph.D. thesis, Durham University, 1962), p.633.

9. R.A. Brown, 'The Battle of Hastings', *Battle Conference on Anglo-Norman Studies, Proceedings* vol.III (1980), p.12; Swanton, *op.cit.* p.625.

10. Brown, *The Normans and the Norman Conquest, op.cit.* p.169.

11. Swanton, *op.cit.* p.570.

12. Verbruggen, 'L'Art Militaire', *op.cit.* pp.398 and 408–9.

13. Contamine, *op.cit.* p.1165; J. Alm, 'Europeiska Armborst: En Oversickt', *Vaabenhistorisk Aarboger* v/b (1947), p.126.

14. C. Bosson, 'L'Arbalète', *Les Musées de Genève* (February 1956), p.2.

15. J.R. Strayer, 'Knight Service in Normandy in the Thirteenth Century', in *Anniversary Papers in Medieval History by Students of Charles Homer Haskins* (Boston and New York, 1929), pp.315 and 320; Verbruggen, *The Art of Warfare, op.cit.* p.25, J. Beeler, *Warfare in Feudal Europe, 730–1200* (Ithaca, 1971), p.42.

16. Verbruggen, *The Art of Warfare, op.cit.* p.142.

17. W.J. Smith, *Aspects of Military Organization in England under King John* (M.A. thesis, University College of North Wales, 1951), pp.22–6; Verbruggen, *The Art of Warfare, op.cit.* pp.129, 132, 147 and 159–61; J.F. Verbruggen, 'De Goedendag', *Militaria Belgica* vol.III (1977), p.65; J.F. Verbruggen, 'De Ikonografie', in *De Kist van Oxford* (reprint from *De Leiegouw* vol.XXII, Kortrijk, 1980, pp.163–256), pp.205–7.

18. Contamine, *op.cit.* pp.183–4.

19. Contamine, *op.cit.* pp.250–1; Verbruggen, *The Art of Warfare, op.cit.* p.168.

20. Contamine, *op.cit.* p.261.

Chapter 2

England and Wales

Note that this section of the book does not include those parts of France held by the English crown from the 11th to 14th centuries.

The years from 1066 to the end of the period under review saw profound military, social and cultural changes in England as a result of the Norman Conquest in 1066. Nevertheless, the degree of continuity between Anglo-Saxon and Anglo-Norman military institutions remains a matter of debate. Wales saw even more fundamental changes, though these were spread over a longer period and began even before the gradual Anglo-Norman conquest of the country.

Late Anglo-Saxon armies of the mid-11th century were very different from those of early Anglo-Saxon times. In terms of organisation and equipment, though less in tactics, they had a great deal in common with Norman armies. There was also a considerable degree of professionalism. In fact most of the population had been largely demilitarised, while the government now employed mercenaries and used permanent garrison troops.[1] There may even have been the beginnings of a concept of 'knighthood'.[2]

It would similarly be wrong to think of late Anglo-Saxon tactics as primitive. They were, however, still within a Northern European or Scandinavian tradition which emphasised the role of infantry rather than that of cavalry. One of the most hotly-debated questions in the study of medieval warfare is whether or not Anglo-Saxon *cnihtas* ever fought on horseback.[3] Generally speaking it would seem that they did not. On the other hand there is the possibility of a Celtic 'north British' light cavalry tradition surviving in the Anglo-Scottish border regions.[4] If Anglo-Saxon cavalry did exist there is no need to look for a Norman source of inspiration, though, of course, Norman soldiers served in England before the Norman Conquest.[5] The most typical Anglo-Saxon warrior, at least in his most characteristic role, was the highly mobile mounted infantryman.[6] Ranking militarily, though not necessarily legally, below the *cnihtas* and *huscarls* were the *thegns*, who, as part-time warriors, fought in much the same manner.[7] Next came the *fyrd*, a term which referred to various forms of selective local military levy.[8]

Paralleling the professionalisation of late Anglo-Saxon armies were the heavier armour and consequently heavier weapons of the warrior elite.[9] Anglo-Saxon tactics still started battles by using missile weapons such as javelins, throwing axes, possibly thrown maces, and archery.[10] Nevertheless, the question of Anglo-Saxon archery is almost as hotly debated as that of Anglo-Saxon cavalry.

A substantial number of the old Anglo-Saxon military elite, or their sons, left England to seek fortunes in Scandinavia and Byzantium between 1066 and 1100, yet Anglo-Saxons still continued to play an important role in post-Conquest Anglo-Norman armies. Despite this element of continuity, the structure, tactics and equipment of late 11th-century Anglo-Norman feudal forces were generally similar to those of north-eastern France and Flanders.[11] The basic military institution was the *familia* or military household of knights and other retainers, the size of which ranged from the King's *Familia Regis* to the much smaller *familia* of a local lord.[12] Larger armies sometimes incorporated disparate elements, including a barely trained militia which was still known as a *fyrd*.[13] On the other hand the military leadership showed far more planning capability and used wider-ranging strategy, varying its tactics according to conditions to a much greater extent than has generally been recognised.[14] In this the Anglo-Normans were similar to most other European peoples of the period.

Anglo-Norman armies undoubtedly made use of archery,[15] the renewed popularity of which was probably a result of Norman influence. Crossbows were also becoming common,[16] while a widespread use of axes indicated the continuing importance of infantry. The latter seemingly operated in much the same manner as had late Anglo-Saxon troops.[17]

Trends that became apparent in the early 12th-century Anglo-Norman period became much more pronounced in the late 12th and 13th centuries under the Angevin kings. Even under Henry II England was no longer a war-orientated, or at least could no longer be described as a 'war-organised', society.[18] Mercenaries, both local and foreign, increasingly bore the brunt of warfare, much of which extended over long periods and took place outside England.[19] The military role of ordinary people dwindled but remained a legal obligation to be picked up again later.[20] During the 13th century the famous English archer, or more specifically longbowman, was already making his appearance. Most were summoned from the northern counties, or from Kent, Sussex and other forested areas,[21] while other forms of infantry came from counties along the Welsh border.[22] At the same time there was an apparent decline in the popularity of the crossbow; this being contrary to the trend elsewhere in Europe.[23]

Heavier and more extensive mail armour and narrower, more penetrating spearheads characterised 12th and early 13th-century cavalry equipment,[24] while rigid or semi-rigid armour of both iron and hardened leather began to appear in the latter part of the 13th century.[25] The professionalism of the cavalry elite was followed by a comparable professionalisation of the infantry, even of the previously humble bowman.[26] The tactical importance of the archer as a mounted infantryman – though not, of course, as a horse-archer – was to be the most dramatic feature of English warfare in the 14th century,[27] closely followed by an enthusiastic adoption of fire-weapons and gunpowder artillery.[28]

Developments followed a parallel but distinctive course in Wales, which had for many centuries been characterised by a highly stratified warrior society.[29] Unlike the 'Welsh' of early medieval northern Britain, the Welsh of Wales do not appear to have had a cavalry tradition. Instead they had to learn cavalry warfare from the Normans in the late 11th and early 12th centuries. This they did with considerable success, modifying it to their own particular circumstances with the development of light cavalry tactics.[30] Large numbers of Welsh troops served in 13th and 14th century English armies as both allies and mercenaries, presumably also channelling 'modern' military influence back to Wales.[31] Most were spear or javelin men,[32] though some were archers using the so-called flat bow.[33] Only in the mid-14th century did Welsh longbowmen become prominent, by which time there had been considerable English influence on all aspects of Welsh arms, armour, tactics and military organisation.

Another Celtic region of the British Isles, too often ignored, was Cornwall. There is some evidence that early Celtic forms of military organisation survived the conquest of Cornwall by Anglo-Saxon Wessex in 814 and persisted even up to the Norman Conquest.[34]

Figures

80 Sword from Windsor, Anglo-Saxon or Anglo-Norman, 10th–12th centuries
(British Museum inv. 1929.2–6, London, England)

This very corroded sword still has slightly-curved *quillons*. On the top of these lies a decorative plate of some less corroded material which originally acted as a washer between the presumed wood of the grip and the *quillons* themselves.

81 Sword, Anglo-Saxon or Anglo-Norman, 10th–11th centuries
(London Museum, London, England)

An early example of an English sword with quite long, slightly down-turned *quillons* suggesting strong Continental influence.

82 Bronze *quillons*, Anglo-Saxon, Anglo-Danish or Anglo-Norman, 9th–11th centuries
(British Museum, inv. 75.6–17.15, London, England)

Bronze was quite a popular material for sword mounts in certain areas under Scandinavian influence. These presumed *quillons* are also curved, which suggests a later date, perhaps from 11th-century Anglo-Danish England.

83 Spearhead, Anglo-Saxon or Anglo-Norman, 8th–11th centuries
(London Museum, inv. C.786, London, England)

Though probably late Anglo-Saxon, this spearhead represents a very basic type which continued in use for many centuries. Its relatively thick blade was clearly designed to puncture armour and shields.

84 Spearhead from North Weald, Anglo-Saxon, 8th–10th centuries
(after Swanton)

An earlier form provides a contrast to the previous example. Its blade is flatter, broader, and has a much less substantial socket. Such weapons would clearly not be so effective against an armoured foe. They could also have been used laterally to provide a sweeping cut as well as a penetrating thrust.

85 **Spearhead, Anglo-Saxon or Anglo-Norman, 8th–11th centuries**
(University Museum of Archaeology and Ethnology, inv. 34.971, Cambridge, England)

Such a spear is a further development of the narrow type, with a thick, almost diamond-section blade and a long, strong socket. This weapon would seem suitable for cavalry warfare against armoured foes.

86 **Javelin head (?) from Brentford, Anglo-Saxon or Anglo-Norman, 8th–11th centuries**
(London Museum, inv. 0.2080, London, England)

A much smaller spearhead, probably for use on a javelin. Its relatively thin blade suggests a hunting weapon rather than one designed to penetrate armour or shields.

87 **Spearhead from Brentford, Anglo-Saxon or Anglo-Norman, 8th–11th centuries**
(London Museum, inv. 0.2072, London, England)

The flat, broad blade and narrow neck again suggest a weapon for use in hunting or against an unprotected foe.

88 **Spearhead from the River Thames, Anglo-Saxon or Anglo-Norman, 10th–11th centuries**
(London Museum, London, England)

Here is a much more substantial blade with a far stronger, longer socket. The wings or lugs are similar to previous examples, but the emphasis on a powerful thrust indicated by its design suggests an 11th century date or even slightly later.

89 **Spearhead, England (?), 10th–11th centuries**
(Bashford Dean Bequest, Metropolitan Museum of Art, New York, United States)

The proportions of blade, wings and socket, as well as the faceted decoration on the socket, indicate that this weapon dates from the late Anglo-Saxon or early Anglo-Norman period. Nevertheless, the contrast with the following example is striking.

90 **Spearhead from Ely, Anglo-Saxon or Anglo-Norman, late 9th–12th centuries**
(University Museum of Archaeology and Ethnology, inv. 2702B, Cambridge, England)

This spearhead is in the same tradition as that already seen, but it is slightly more substantial and thus, perhaps, later.

91 Spearhead, Anglo-Saxon or Anglo-Norman, 9th–12th centuries
(Museum and Art Gallery, inv. 236.62, Reading, England).

An early version of a spear with wings or lugs beneath the blade. Such a style was common throughout Europe and around the Mediterranean. The example from Reading has a longer, broader and relatively slender blade with a short socket, which either indicates that it is early or that armour was not particularly common in the area where it was used.

92 Spearhead from Walthamstow, Anglo-Saxon or Anglo-Norman, late 8th–11th centuries
(London Museum, inv. C.737, London, England)

This is a larger and broader version of the relatively flat early type of spearhead with a very small socket.

93 Spearhead, Anglo-Saxon or Anglo-Norman, 10th–12th centuries
(after Swanton)

Clearly this weapon, with its decorative strengthening bands around the base of its blade, is within a long Anglo-Saxon tradition, but it is also a more substantial weapon. This probably indicates a later date, which in turn suggests a large degree of continuity between some of the weapons of the Anglo-Saxon and Anglo-Norman periods.

94 'Sigismund and the Wolf', carved relief from the Old Minster, Hampshire, c.1016–35
(City Museum, Winchester, England)

This rare example of late Anglo-Saxon carving might illustrate a Scandinavian-Germanic legend. The warrior probably wears a short-sleeved mail *hauberk*. The lower part of this garment is most unlikely to form mail shorts, as has sometimes been suggested. On the other hand the hems might have been tied around the thighs, which could also be the case in parts of the Bayeux Tapestry. The scabbard of the massive straight sword is equally strange, as it appears to be suspended from a sword-belt by at least one subsidiary strap fastened to a ring around the scabbard. Such a system is not seen elsewhere in 11th-century Western Europe but might indicate eastern influence via Scandinavia.

95 'St Michael', carved relief, Nottinghamshire, mid/late 11th century
(*in situ* tympanum of the Minster, Southwell, England)

Here the Archangel carries a small round buckler with a pronounced boss and a broad sword with down-turned *quillons*.

96 'St Michael', carved relief originally from the church of St Michael, Ipswich, Suffolk, late 11th century
(*in situ* Church of St Nicholas, Ipswich, England)

The Archangel's sword is damaged but his shield is of the normal so-called 'Norman' type. In other words it is a large, kite-shaped shield with rivets to hold the interior *enarmes* or grips.

97A–AQ The Bayeux Tapestry, southern England or Normandy, late 11th century
(Tapestry Museum, Bayeux, France)

A–B – Duke William (left) gives weapons to Harold (right); C–D – Norman archers; E – Fallen Anglo Saxons; F – Norman charging; G – Bishop Odo carrying the *baculus*; H – Anglo-Saxon; I – Norman; J–K – Carpenters' axes; L – Count Guy; M – Count Guy seizes Harold in Normandy; N–O – Harold's sword; P–Q – Normans caught in sands near Mont St Michel; R – Duke William captures Dol; S – Duke William with the *baculus* at Mont St Michel; T–U – Norman weapons being transported; V – Capture of Dol; W – Anglo-Saxons flee after battle of Hastings; X – Anglo-Saxon; Y – King Harold's standard-bearer; Z – Norman scout; AA – Norman weapons aboard ship; AB – Duke William's standard-bearer; AC – Anglo-Saxon; AD – Norman; AE – Norman scout; AF – Norman; AG – Duke William raises his helmet; AH – Duke William's standard-bearer; AI – Anglo-Saxon; AJ – Norman; AK – Norman; AL–AO – Anglo-Saxons; AP – Senior follower of Duke William; AQ – Duke William with the *baculus*. The Bayeux Tapestry is one of the most famous sources for the study of early medieval arms and armour, yet it is still frequently misunderstood. Such misunderstanding usually results from trying to study the embroidery in isolation, without adequate reference to other sources from the 11th and early 12th centuries. The Bayeux Tapestry is in many ways pictorially crude, or at least very stylised, but when other representations of arms, armour and horse-harness are taken into consideration the Tapestry poses few problems of interpretation. The problems that remain may result from the fact that it was probably designed and made in England, and that the people responsible for it did not fully understand certain modern features of Norman, as opposed to Anglo-Saxon, military equipment. Bows, for example, are of medium length with short arrows drawn by the fingers to the chest (C–D). As such they look like self-bows of simple construction but limited size, being closer to hunting weapons than true longbows for use in war. In reality Norman archers at Hastings, particularly the professionals shown here in the main panel of the Tapestry rather than the possible peasant levy or sailors indicated on the lower border, almost certainly used longbows. Such weapons were, however, not in widespread use in late Anglo-Saxon southern England. Spears are used in a number of ways, including the couched style (AD and AJ) on horseback and overarm on foot (X and AN). Some have *gonfanon* pennons (B, AD and AF) which should not be confused with a leader's banner (AB, Y and AH). The latter are shown, perhaps inaccurately, as roughly the same size as *gonfanons*. Javelins are, contrary to some opinions, present but only in the hands of Anglo-Saxon infantry (AC). Swords are straight and broad with straight *quillons* and round *pommels*. Some have their hilts emerging through a slit in the mail *hauberk* (B). Others are more or less clearly worn on a belt over a tunic and sometimes, though not always very clearly, outside the *hauberk* (M, Y, AC, AE, AF, AL and AM). Swords are also shown in their scabbards but unbelted (N and O). Another interesting example has a stored weapon with a loop around its *pommel* (AA). The fearsome 'Danish' axe of the Anglo-Saxons is frequently shown (H, AM and AN), once even in the hands of a Norman nobleman (L). Such weapons are quite distinct from the long-bladed, short-hafted work-axes of carpenters (J and K). Maces appear only rarely, once a knobbed or flanged variety in the hands of a senior Norman (AP) and also being thrown by Anglo-Saxons at the Normans (F). Maces of Mediterranean form could well have reached Normandy from Norman Italy and Sicily, but the supposed Anglo-Saxon maces are harder to explain. The type appears again in the hands of fleeing Anglo-Saxons at the very end of the Tapestry (W). Its form recalls small-headed bronze maces of eastern Europe and the Baltic region. Such a weapon probably reached England via Scandinavia. The wooden club or *baculus* (G, S and AG) must not be confused with a mace. It was almost certainly not a weapon, as it is inconceivable that the most senior figures in the Norman army chose to arm themselves with a wooden cudgel, but may have been a symbolic weapon or staff of office, perhaps descended from a pagan symbol used by the Normans' Norse forebears. Most shields in the Bayeux Tapestry are kite-shaped, including many of those carried by the Anglo-Saxons' armoured elite or *huscarls* (AC, AL, AM, AN and X). This does not necessarily indicate that these armoured Anglo-Saxons were dismounted cavalry, since the large kite-shaped shield may have originated in the eastern Mediterranean as an infantry protection. The Normans all use such shields (I, AE and AJ), many of which are shown from the inside exposing a variety of *enarmes* and *guiges* (F, P–R, Z, AD and AK). Such a variety of straps also accounted for the varied patterns of rivets shown on the outside of shields. It is interesting to note that many kite-shaped cavalry shields do not seem to be supported by *guiges*, perhaps suggesting that the couched lance and all the pieces of equipment and harness associated with it, were still in the process of adoption. Other shields include larger round and considerably convex types (E, Y and AI) and an almost rectangular shield being used by an 'aged', bearded Anglo-Saxon or Anglo-Dane

(H). Such a shield could indicate contact with, or service in, eastern Europe or Russia. Helmets are, by and large, straightforward. Most are tall conical types with long and apparently broad *nasals*. Many have a segmented appearance with a broad band around the rim. This points to a *spangenhelm* construction (A–B, D, U, V, AF, AJ–AL and AQ). Others have a vertical division but no band (G and AC), while one (G) has an apparent button or ring on top. Such helmets could be of the directly riveted segmented type popular in eastern Europe, but are just as likely to represent helmets painted in various colours. Some are of one piece with a broad brow-band (I, X, Y, AB, AG, AH, AM, AN and AP), while others lack the brow-band (E, F and AI). One such (F) seems to be a precocious example of a helmet with a forward-angled crown. Such a helmet is not normally seen in England until the 12th century. Another helmet appears to be round (V). A few senior Normans wear mail *chausses* which either go inside their shoes or are an early type that does not include protection for the foot (AF–AH, AP and AQ). Comparable arm defences are rarer (AG and AH). These might indicate a second, long-sleeved mail *hauberk* being worn beneath the first, but given the fact that long-sleeved *hauberks* are otherwise not shown this seems unlikely. Separate mail sleeves are perhaps a transitional form of armour that was worn before a general adoption of long-sleeved *hauberks* in north-western Europe. As to the *hauberks* themselves, these have been the subject of more controversy than any other piece of military equipment in the Bayeux Tapestry. The varied surface patterns have been explained as the seamstresses' experimenting to find the most suitable way of representing mail, but if so they could be expected to have been concentrated at the start of the Tapestry. Some variations might be explained in this way (A, B, L, T, AD or AF), all of which almost certainly indicate mail. But this still leaves one other very distinctive variation (G and S). In both cases the pattern is not only different but the multiple colouring is quite distinctive. Also note that on one figure (G) the neck and back of the head are given the same stylised mail as most other men in ordinary *hauberks*. The second example (S) wears a long-sleeved garment. One of these figures represents Bishop Odo of Bayeux, who was probably responsible for the Tapestry's manufacture. Perhaps the fact that he has been distinguished in this way suggests specific information concerning the Bishop's costume at the Battle of Hastings, perhaps provided by Odo himself. Neither of these distinctive costumes has the rectangular 'chest piece' which will be discussed below. The most likely interpretation of these two armours is not a scale *hauberk*, as has sometimes been suggested, but a *jazerant* or *jazrain hauberk*. These terms are now known to be European corruptions of the Persian and Arab term *kazāghand*. This in turn referred to a mail-lined cloth garment, usually with some form of padding beneath the mail. Such Middle Eastern garments were held together by stitching, either with or without studs. The horizontal and diagonal lines on the two examples in the Tapestry (G and S) may represent comparable lines of stitching. Most other *hauberks* in the Tapestry have *coifs*, in one case worn without a helmet (Z). Some *coifs* appear to be separate. Others have single or doubled laces at the back (A, AB and AF), which probably had something to do with how the *coif* was tightened around the brow. This leaves one final and most difficult question, concerning the rectangular panels on the upper chests of some warriors. They find their closest parallels in 11th century Catalan manuscripts, where they almost certainly indicate unlaced *ventails*. They probably represent the same feature in the Bayeux Tapestry. Given the crudity of the pictures in this embroidery, and the fact that no Anglo-Saxon warrior has such a rectangle on his *hauberk*, it seems highly likely that the laced *ventail* was a new idea introduced into England by the Normans. As such it may still not have been fully understood by those who made the Tapestry. Finally, and perhaps most significantly, most of the men with these rectangles are not actually engaged in combat. Their uncomfortable *ventails* might therefore have been unlaced. Those in the heat of battle do not have such rectangles on their *hauberks*. It is also worth noting that one *hauberk* 'in store' is shown with such a rectangle (R) though this could represent the empty mail *coif*.

98A–L *Utrecht Psalter*, **Wessex, early 11th century** (British Library, Ms. Harl. 603, London, England)

A – f.69r; B – f.73; C – f.25, D–F – f.68r; G – f.69r; H – f.25; I – f.29v; J – f.73; K–L – f.25. This and similar manuscripts are believed to be copies of a Carolingian psalter. They use the same agitated linear style, but are clearly not following all the details of military equipment shown in the original manuscript. Not only are kite-shaped shields shown (D and L) but so are tall saddles with raised *pommel* and *cantle*, almost exactly the same as seen in the Bayeux Tapestry (I). Another horseman has a straight-legged riding position and a very long cavalry sword (A). Other features are more old-fashioned, including many round shields (B, C, E, F, H, K and L) and the throwing of javelins (A, C, K and H). Such a mixture of old and new would not be surprising in the early to mid-11th century. The angel using a bow (J) is ultimately copied from a southern European original, whereas the armoured figure (B) might reflect the best equipped *huscarls* of the period. He has a conical helmet with a broad *nasal* and a mail *hauberk* without a *coif* but with short, broad, untailored sleeves.

99A–B **Psychomachia, England, early 11th century**
(British Library, Ms. Cotton Cleo. C.VIII, f.24, London,
England)

This late Anglo-Saxon manuscript has often been used in attempted
reconstructions of pre-Conquest English warriors. One figure (A)
simply has an axe and a large round shield. His foeman (B) may
ultimately be based upon a Byzantine original. His hat or helmet
may be fanciful, or indicate an 'alien' helmet based upon
Mediterranean iconography, or simply be a loose woollen hat. Even
his presumed mail shirt with its zigzagged edge could derive from
such a distant source. It is also worth noting that his much obscured
scabbard hangs from a belt or *baldric* underneath this mail shirt.

100 **Pentateuch and Joshua, England, 11th century**
(British Library, Ms. Cotton Claud. B.IV f.41v, London,
England)

A clear representation of a longbow which is, however, being used by
a huntsman rather than a warrior. Note the simple quiver hung from
his neck.

101 ***Bury Psalter*, East Anglia, 1040–50**
(Vatican Library, Ms. Regin. Lat. 12, Rome, Italy)

Once again a figure, here a devil, hangs a simple bag-like quiver for
very long arrows from his neck and shoulder. The large bow is itself
recurved, but is probably a slightly fanciful illustration of a
longbow.

102 **Psalter, Wessex, c.1050**
(British Library, Ms. Cotton Tib. C.VI, London, England)

This illustration probably represents Goliath. He is unarmoured
except for a pointed helmet that was presumably based on a conical
original. It may be of two-piece construction with a rim or simply be a
badly drawn *spangenhelm*. It has no *nasal*. His shield is round with a
rather small boss; his spear has a barbed head which is almost
certainly an artistic convention, and his more realistic sword hangs
from a *baldric*. The sword itself has long curved *quillons*, a domed
pommel, and altogether looks slightly later than the mid-11th century
date normally given to this manuscript.

103 **'Shield of the Archangel Michael', wooden cross,
England (?), c.1070**
(National Museum, Copenhagen, Denmark)

It is interesting to see the Archangel being given a large round shield
with a boss even as late as 1070. On the other hand the shield, if it is in
any way realistic, is not of the convex round type seen in the Bayeux
Tapestry. Rather, it seems to be a curved, wrap-around shield closer

in profile to a kite-shaped shield. It may indeed simply be a badly-drawn kite-shaped shield.

104 Sword from Mileham, Norfolk, 11th century
(Castle Museum, inv. 210.949, Norwich, England)

The *pommel* of this sword seems to be a development of the earlier trefoil type, though it is closer in outline to the dome or nut-shaped *pommels* of the late 11th and 12th centuries. The *quillons*, though relatively short, are highly decorated and slightly curved. Note the very small decorative *langet* extending a short distance down the blade.

105 Sword, England or Germany, c.1050
(private collection, R.E. Oakeshott, England)

The blade of this sword is inscribed INGELRII. Such weapons are believed to have been made in western Germany, then exported throughout Europe and even beyond. It is also possible that 'fake' INGELRII swords were made in other areas, and it is certain that *quillons* and *pommels* were added in those countries to which blades were exported. This example, however, has the long straight *quillons* and large almond-shaped *pommel* of a true INGELRII weapon.

106 Anglo-Danish axe from London, England, 11th century
(London Museum, London, England)

This axe represents the beginning of a development that led from this almost symmetrical blade to the sharply upwards-sweeping war-axes of the 12th and 13th centuries. Even this weapon, which is basically a so-called 'Danish' axe, has the lower tip of its blade closer to the line of the haft than is the upper tip. The upper side of the blade also has a slight upwards sweep.

107 Reverse of Seal of William I, England, 1066–87
(British Library, Dept. of Seals, London, England)

This representation of William the Conqueror is very different from those on the Bayeux Tapestry. He again carries a kite-shaped shield and has a short-sleeved mail *hauberk*, but this latter piece of armour lacks a mail *coif* and does not even reach his knees. If it is of an earlier form it may have remained in use as a lighter style of equipment. William's helmet is probably fanciful and indeed looks like a badly drawn early form of crown.

108 First Great Seal of King Henry II, England c.1154–89
(Seal no.XXXIX.11, British Museum, London, England)

Considered to be one of the finest of 12th-century seals, it shows Henry II in a slightly forward-angled helmet with a small *nasal*, perhaps a long or mid-length sleeved mail *hauberk* plus *coif*, a kite-shaped shield on a *guige*, and a straight sword with slightly-curved *quillons*.

109A–B Carved ivory liturgical comb from St Albans, Hertfordshire, c.1120
(Victoria and Albert Museum, inv. A.27–1977, London, England)

At first glance these tiny carved figures seem typical of their period. They both still wear segmented *spangenhelm* helmets and their mail *hauberks*, though including *coifs*, do not seem to extend below the wearers' waists.

110 First Great Seal of King Stephen, England, c.1135
(Seal no.XXXIX.10, British Museum, London, England)

Here the English king has a forward-angled conical helmet of a typical mid-12th-century form. A streamer or cloth hangs from the back. His shield still includes a boss but his broad sword has the newer type of long, straight *quillons*.

111 Second Great Seal of King Stephen, England, 1137–8
(Collection of Sir Berwick, Lechmere, England)

This seal is not, as has sometimes been thought, a forgery, but is in reality King Stephen's second seal. Once again he has a streamer hanging from his neck, this time apparently wound around his helmet. His sword now has very curved *quillons*.

112 Second Great Seal of King Henry II, England, c.1154–89
(Dean and Chapter, inv. 3. 1. reg. 1a, Cathedral, Durham, England)

The only real difference between this and the king's first Great Seal is that here his helmet is an extremely forward-tilted type. His mail *coif* now covers his mouth and his long shield has a flattened top.

113 Reverse of Seal of William II, England, 1087–1100
(British Library, Dept. of Seals, London, England)

This seal of William II, far from being a mere copy of his father's with a new legend, shows the second William in the latest armour. His shield is still kite-shaped but his *hauberk* is longer, closer fitting, and has full-length sleeves. These lack *mittens* and the seal apparently does not show a *coif*. This could, however, be a result of relatively crude workmanship, plus the fact that the monarch is seen full face.

114 Spearhead from Aldersgate, London, England, late 12th/13th centuries
(Guildhall Museum, inv. 11.406, London, England)

Small broad spearheads of this type seem to be quite rare. Yet the weapon is strongly made with a distinctly expanding socket which perhaps indicates that it was fitted to a very substantial haft. Note that the style of socket with split sides is no longer used, presumably again to increase its strength.

115 Spearhead from Fornham, Suffolk, c.1170
(Moyse's Hall Museum, inv. L.32, Bury St Edmunds, England)

Long, slender, armour-piercing blades with long sockets such as this example were probably the most typical form of cavalry lance in the 12th century.

116 Effigy, England, late 12th to mid-13th centuries
(*in situ* Temple Church, London, England)

Widely differing dates and identifications have been offered for this and other effigies in the Temple Church. Some have suggested that this figure represents Geoffrey, Earl of Essex. The position of the figure strongly indicates an early or mid-13th-century date, whereas some features of the armour look earlier while the curved top of the large shield may be a result of damage. The man wears a mail *hauberk* with *mittens*, mail *chausses* and a mail *coif*. There is no indication of any padded protection beneath the long *surcoat*. His helmet is also particularly interesting, being flat-topped and either of a segmented construction or with vertical reinforcements. The helmet is not, however, a *great helm*. Rather it has what looks like a massive chin-strap around the face, this perhaps forming the foundation of a face-mask or visor, or it might have been part of a special *arming cap*.

117 Carved doorway, Yorkshire, mid-12th century re-used in 1871
(*in situ* Church of St Michael and All Angels, Barton-le-Street, England)

The centaur illustrated on this doorway is based on a manuscript. It has a conical helmet, probably with a forward-angled crown, and a substantial *nasal*. The long-sleeved *hauberk* lacks a *coif* and is only shown as far as the waist because the creature is half horse. The bow is a crudely carved self-bow, probably based on a longbow.

118 Carved stone font, Devon, 1120–40
(*in situ* church, Alphington, England)

There is no doubt that this carving shows a longbow. The huntsman also apparently draws an arrow from his belt.

119A–B Carved font, Northamptonshire, c.1120
(*in situ* St Mary's Church, Wansford, England)

Here two warriors fight with simple maces and a small kite-shaped shields. The motif seems to be based on Byzantine art.

120 Carved stone font, Herefordshire, 1150–5
(*in situ* church, Eardisley, England)

The fighting figures on this font are in the same 'Michelin-man' style as the better known warrior at Kilpeck (f. 122). They wear hats or helmets with forward-angled crowns but no *nasals*. Their striped costumes may represent mail *hauberks* but are just as likely to indicate cloth. One man has a sword with a trefoil *pommel* and *quillons*, the apparent *langet* of which probably results from the deep *fuller* or groove cut down the centre of the blade. The second figure, with his spear thrust through the first warrior's skirt, is remarkably similar to an Islamic Andalusian carving at Jativa (see volume two), though the similarity must be coincidental.

121 'King Herod', carved relief, Anglo-Norman, 1125–50
(*in situ* Church of Our Lady, Aalborg, Denmark)

A considerable amount of English art seems to have been exported to Scandinavia in the 12th century. This carving is one example. The King carries a sword with a large round *pommel*, perhaps curved *quillons*, and what seems to be decoration or writing down the blade.

122 Carved relief, Herefordshire, 1145–50
(*in situ* southern door of church, Kilpeck, England)

Here again the warrior might wear a helmet or a hat. His sword is considerably damaged but his striped shirt may indicate a mail *hauberk* reaching only to the waist. These Herefordshire carvings are, however, a difficult and unreliable source of information.

123A–D Carved relief, Kent, c.1180
(*in situ* Church of St Mary, Barfreston, England)

The carved warriors at Barfreston are much more naturalistic than the earlier examples in Herefordshire. Though badly worn, they include many interesting details. The horsemen, and one man on foot, now have flat-topped but still very large shields (A, B and D), one of which has a substantial boss. All wear conical helmets, only one clearly including a substantial curved *nasal* (D). Mail *hauberks* are long sleeved, lack *mittens* but include *coifs*. Swords are broad and essentially non-tapering, with heavy *pommels* and straight *quillons*. They hang from sword-belts (C and D).

124 'Hercules', carved gaming piece from St Albans, Hertfordshire, 1125–50
(Victoria and Albert Museum, inv. 374–1871, London, England)

Here the ancient Greek hero has a heavy, straight sword with straight *quillons* and an unusually convex kite-shaped shield. In fact the deep profile of this shield may indicate that it is an inaccurately drawn round shield.

125A–F 'St George helping Crusaders outside Antioch' (?), relief carving, Dorset, early 12th century
(*in situ* church of St George, Fordington, England)

There are a number of possible interpretations of this carving, almost all involving Norman troops being aided by St George in battle against Muslims. The presumed Normans (A and B) have spears and kite-shaped shields. They wear forward-angled conical helmets with long *nasals* and long-sleeved *hauberks* with integral *coifs*. The 'infidels' (D-F) are similarly equipped, one even having a kite-shaped shield (F). The others are distinguished by round shields and by the fact that their helmets indicate a possibly segmented construction (D and E).

126 'Patentia flogging Ira', carved stone font, Gloucestershire, 1175–1200
(*in situ* church, Southrop, England)

The female figure of Patience here carries a small round shield, probably based on an earlier Psychomachia manuscript. The carving behind the shield of what appears to be the hilt of some weapon, perhaps a knife, may reflect the survival of earlier styles of combat along the Welsh borders. The Welsh themselves were mostly light infantry and almost certainly used such shields or bucklers.

127A–C 'Virtues', the Troyes Casket, enamelled bronze box, England (?), c.1170
(Cathedral Treasury, Troyes, France)

Though highly stylised and dominated by iconographical convention, the three Virtues shown here carry distinctly different shields. A large kite-shaped shield is used with a spear (A), as is a very small shield (C), while a large round or oval shield is used with a sword (B).

128 'Goliath', psalter from Canterbury, Kent, late 12th century
(Bib. Nat., Ms. Lat. 8849, Paris, France)

Notable features of this illustration include the conical helmet with a *nasal* worn over a mail *coif* with a *ventail*, the very tall kite-shaped shield, and the long-sleeved mail *hauberk* which is either cut away at the sides to make a rectangular slit or, more probably, cut away all round the back. Note that the garment also has a slit at the front. The *hauberk* is worn over another garment which is similarly cut away at the back. This is probably a padded or quilted *gambeson*. The figure wears mail *chausses* laced up the back of his legs and around his ankles. His straight sword has a round *pommel* and thick straight *quillons*.

129A–D *The Great Canterbury Psalter*, Kent, c.1180–90
(Bib. Nat., Ms. Lat. 8846, f.2v, Paris, France)

A – 'Goliath'; B – 'Israelite'; C–D – 'Decapitation of Goliath'. The first picture of Goliath (A) is virtually identical to that seen above, the only difference being that his mail *chausses* are of the kind which fully enclose his legs and that his round helmet has a very broad rim band. Goliath is next shown in almost identical armour (C) except that his *chausses* have reverted to the kind which do not protect the back of his legs. His scabbard and sword-belt are now tied around his waist, and the garment immediately beneath his mail *hauberk* is, like the *hauberk* itself, cut away at the back. It is also given regularly spaced dots or circles. These are again visible at his wrists and almost certainly indicate a padded or quilted construction. An additional figure (B) has the same cutaway *hauberk* with a cutaway garment beneath. These must surely have been designed for cavalry warfare. Swords are straight and slightly tapering, with round or oval *pommels*. Some have straight *quillons* (A and B), one with an apparent *langet* (D), or slightly-curved *quillons* (B and C).

130 'Death of Saul', *The Puist Bible*, Durham, c.1170–80
(Cathedral Library, Ms. A.II.I, f.173, Durham, England)

The chief interest in this little illumination lies in its clear representation of a very large form of kite-shaped shield adopted in some parts of Western Europe in the late 12th century.

131 Embroidered silk, England, c.1180–1210
(St John's Seminary, Wonersh, England)

Here an English source shows the type of very tall, rounded, and perhaps segmented helmet normally associated with Germany. The shield is also of a new broader, shorter kite-shaped type.

132A–B Statues from Hereford, Herefordshire, late 12th/early 13th centuries
(Cloisters Museum, New York, United States)

These two statues stood for some centuries in Hampton Court Palace. They are typical of their period, showing knights in full mail *hauberks* with *mittens*, those of the right arms being slipped off the hand. They also have mail *chausses*. Both wear *surcoats* with raised, squared shoulders which are not repeated in the shape of the *hauberks* beneath.

This is perhaps the clearest representation of a padded *gambeson* worn either beneath or forming an integral part of the *surcoat*. One figure (A) probably has an *arming cap* beneath his *coif*, which gives it a slightly rectangular outline. This was the common means of supporting a flat-topped *great helm*. The second figure (B) wears just such a *great helm*. It probably has two eye-slits and is of the fully developed kind, extended at the rear to protect the back of the head.

133A–C Fragment of a copper-alloy pyx, England, early 12th century
(Burrell Collection, nos.5 and 6/139, Glasgow Museums and Art Galleries, Glasgow, Scotland)

Three sleeping guards at the Holy Sepulchre are shown with typical early 12th century equipment. Their kite-shaped shields are very long with large bosses, and in one case (A) the beginnings of a flattened top. Though heraldry was in its infancy it is worth noting that the central figure (B) seems to have the pattern on his shield repeated on his helmet. The other two warriors also have designs on their helmets which are, at least in one case (C), unlikely to indicate a method of construction and must therefore be painted. The helmets are quite pointed, conical types with large *nasals* broadened towards the base. The mail *hauberks* have long, narrow sleeves but as yet no *mittens*. One man carries a spear (A) and all three have swords, the scabbards of which are visible outside their *hauberks*. This strongly suggests that they are hung from sword-belts, as no *baldrics* are visible.

134 Carved wooden gaming piece, England, late 12th century
(Museum of Fine Arts, no.54, 931, Boston, United States)

The top of this gaming piece consisted of two warriors' heads. Both wear mail *coifs* surrounded by a kind of padded band which could have acted as a rudimentary *arming cap* to support a large helmet.

135 Seal of Aubrey de Vere, Earl of Oxford, England, mid-12th century
(British Library, Dept. of Seals, London, England)

Though damaged, this is a typical early or mid-12th-century seal showing an armoured rider. The long kite-shaped shield still has a boss. The sword appears to taper and the mail *hauberk* has long, close-fitting sleeves.

136 Reverse of the First Seal of King Richard I, England, 1189–99
(British Library, Dept. of Seals, London, England)

By the late 12th century the sword clearly tapers, and has very long *quillons* and a diamond-shaped *pommel*. The helmet seems taller and may have been round rather than conical. The mail *hauberk* also includes *mittens*.

137A–C Wall-paintings, Sussex, c.1100–10
(*in situ* Church of St Botolph, Hardham, England)

A–B – 'St George at Antioch' (?); C – 'Herod's guards'. Probably the oldest Norman wall paintings in England, these include a picture of St George striking down 'infidels', probably referring to the story of this Saint's participation in the Crusaders' battle outside Antioch only a few years before the paintings were made. The Saint (A) may wear a mail *hauberk* and carry a kite-shaped shield. The 'infidels' clearly have such shields with bosses. An even more confused painting of Herod's guards (C) has one of them in a horizontally striped armour or tunic. This is perhaps an attempt, based on verbal reports, to reproduce *lamellar* armour, the vertical divisions of the individual *lamellae* having now become indistinguishable.

138A–B Wall-paintings, Essex, c.1150
(*in situ* church, Copford, England)

A – unrestored figure; B – heavily restored figure. Both figures might represent 'Fortitude'. One has been left in its original state (A), while the second was heavily, though probably accurately, restored many years ago. They wear the same equipment and are virtually mirror images. The low conical helmets have substantial *nasals*. The *coifs* may be separate from the mail *hauberks* and the latter have long but wide and untapered sleeves. The tall shields are supported by *guiges* and neither figure seems to have a sword, although belts are worn.

139A–K Wall-paintings, Shropshire, late 12th/early 13th centuries
(*in situ* Church of All Saints, Claverly, England)

This series of warring figures has sometimes been identified as a *Psychomachia* but there is no evidence that particular figures represent Vices or Virtues. On the contrary, the two forces are almost identical except that conical helmets are only worn by the defeated troops approaching from the right (B, D, F, H and J). All helmets have face-mask visors (A, C, E, G, I, and K) but none are fully-developed *great helms*, as none cover the sides or back of the head. Two of these face-masks appear to be built on or around *nasals* (D and H), while two others have a central reinforcing bar (F and G). All the warriors have long-sleeved *hauberks*, some probably with *mittens* (A and D), others clearly without (E, I and J). A few *surcoats* are seen (C, E and I) but only in the victorious army. One appears to wrap around only one shoulder (G) but this may be a misleading impression due to the damaged state of the paintings. Mail *chausses* are clearly worn by some (A, C, E, and I), perhaps originally by all, figures. Shields are of the newer small, flat-topped kite-shaped type (B–G and I–K) with one exception (H) which has a round top and an apparent boss. Such shields tend to push the paintings into the 13th century. Spears are used, as well as broad tapering swords with long straight, curved or down-turned *quillons* and round *pommels*. In only one case a large domed *pommel* is shown (D).

140A–B 'St Edmund and the Danes', *Life of St Edmund*, Bury St Edmunds, 1125–50
(Pierpont Morgan Library, Ms. 736, f.7v, New York, United States)

A – Dane; B – Anglo-Saxons. A large number of the defeated Anglo-Saxons, particularly those who have been thrown to the ground, lack armour. Lightly-equipped non-noble or barely knightly cavalry still formed part of some armies in early 12th century England. The men who are armoured have almost identical equipment, including conical helmets, mostly with forward-angled crowns, broad rims and no *nasals*. Mail *hauberks* include *coifs* and long sleeves but no *mittens*, and there is no leg armour. Shields all appear to be kite-shaped. Only one spear bears a *gonfanon* and the three visible swords have domed or nut-shaped *pommels*.

141 Psalter, Canterbury or Bury St Edmunds, 1130–50
(Victoria and Albert Museum, inv. 818–1894, London, England)

The figures shown in this miniature of the Betrayal carry a variety of crude weapons, most appearing to be plain wooden cudgels.

142 'Massacre of the Innocents', Northumberland or Yorkshire, late 12th century
(Bodleian Library, Ms. Gough Litung 2.C.S.18343, f.18, Oxford, England)

Not surprisingly, the arms and armour of northern England were more old-fashioned than those of the prosperous south. But these differences are only marginally apparent in works of art. Here a group of soldiers wear conical helmets with *nasals*. *Hauberks* mostly have *mittens* and *coifs*. The *ventails* of the latter are pulled tight and presumably laced, apparently around the back of the neck . In other sources *ventails* are normally pulled to the side of the head and laced at the temple. One figure wears mail *chausses* inside shoes. This was presumably an infantry fashion.

143A–C 'Joshua', *Winchester Bible*, Hampshire, 1160–70
(Cathedral Library, f.209, Winchester, England)

Joshua and a follower are dressed in the height of fashion with very long *surcoats*. The one-piece helmets are now round and only one has a *nasal*.

Long-sleeved mail *hauberks* are worn beneath the *surcoats*, one of which has horizontal heraldic stripes (C). The *mittens* of Joshua's *hauberk* (A and B) appear to be of a transitional type in which the fingers and thumbs are unarmoured, protruding through slits in the glove.

144 *Psalter of St Louis*, England, c.1200
(University Library, Leyden, Netherlands)

In some respects this figure, with his relatively short-sleeved *hauberk* and mail *chausses* covering only the front of his legs and the top of his feet, is rather old-fashioned. But his tall rounded helmet is typical of the late 12th century, as is the massive *pommel* of his sword. His sword-belt is shown without a knot or buckle, which is probably an artistic error.

145 'Massacre of the Innocents', Kent, c.1200
(Bib. Nat., Ms. Lat. 8846, f.4v, Paris, France)

This miniature appears in a psalter that is ultimately based on the Carolingian *Utrecht Psalter* but, like earlier copies, it includes arms and armour in contemporary style. It consists of low, very slightly conical helmets with or without *nasals*, long-sleeved mail *hauberks* with *ventails* drawn tightly across the lower part of the face, and long tapering swords with down-turned *quillons*.

146A–B *Guthlac Roll*, Lincolnshire, c.1200
(British Library, Ms. Harl. Roll Y.6, London, England)

It has been suggested that these drawings illustrating the life of St Guthlac were designs for stained glass windows or enamelled metalwork. These particular figures might refer to the Saint's early life, when he was a soldier fighting for King Ethelred of Mercia. If so, the unusual armour given to the warriors might be an artist's attempt to indicate early Anglo-Saxon origins. The closest parallels to the helmets are found on two of the Scottish or Scandinavian Lewis chessmen. Such helmets, which could also be related to other flat-topped types without face-masks, may have been a feature of various backward regions under Scandinavian influence, such as Scotland, Wales and north-west England. These men wear rather old-fashioned mid-sleeved *hauberks* reaching only to their thighs. One of their spears even has archaic wings or lugs beneath the blade (B). Their small, flat-topped shields are, however, very up-to-date.

147A–B 'Life of David', Hampshire, 1150–75
(Pierpont Morgan Library, Ms. 619, New York, United States)

A – Israelite; B – Goliath. This famous manuscript page was almost certainly illuminated in Winchester. Goliath (A) wears straightforward European equipment with the new high-domed helmet and *nasal*. The pattern on his legs indicates fabric, not mail. No distinction is drawn between Israelites and Philistines except that a minority of the former still have pointed helmets with forward-angled crowns (B).

148A–B 'Massacre of the Innocents', England, late 12th/early 13th centuries
(Emmanuel College Library, Ms. 252/2, f.9, Cambridge, England)

This slightly later version of the Massacre of the Innocents has helmets either of segmented construction, which seems unlikely at this period, or with painted surfaces. Both wear their helmets over *coifs* drawn tight across the mouth. These *coifs* are integral with the *hauberks*. The cross-hatched legs may indicate mail *chausses* or decorated cloth hose.

149A–D Stained glass window, Kent, late 12th century
(*in situ* Cathedral, Canterbury, England)

This scene has variously been interpreted as an episode from the history of Canterbury or from the Old Testament. If the former is true, then the supposed Danes are given old-fashioned equipment consisting of conical helmets with *nasals* (B and C) or round helmets without a *nasal* (A). These are worn over short-sleeved and relatively short-hemmed mail *hauberks*. All three helmets have clearly-drawn chin-straps. Two very large and somewhat archaic kite-shaped shields are also carried.

150A–C Re-used broken tiles, Bedfordshire, late 12th/early 13th centuries
(*in situ* church, Little Kimble, England)

The very damaged and worn tiles at Little Kimble illustrate features of English arms and armour around the year 1200. They include fully-developed flat-topped *great helms* with the face area and eye-slits reinforced by horizontal (B and C) and vertical bars (B). Small flat-topped shields are supported by *guiges* around the neck, and mail *hauberks* include *mittens* (A).

151 'Richard Coeur-de-Lion', tile from Chertsey Abbey, England, late 12th century
(Edward VII Gallery, British Museum, London, England)

Earlier in date but very similar in style and execution are the famous tiles from Chertsey Abbey near Windsor. The arms and armour are also earlier. Here King Richard I wears a *great helm* with a crown around what looks like a slightly domed or even conical top. The helmet does not extend very far down the back of his neck and has no apparent reinforcing bars at the front. As such it is an early example of the true *great helm*. The king's *hauberk* naturally includes *mittens*, but his mail *chausses* are of the lighter type which do not cover the back of his legs. His shield, though flat topped, also looks large and old fashioned.

152A–B *Assize Roll*, England, early 13th century
(Public Record Office, Temp. Henry III, London, England)

This strange little drawing shows judicial 'trial by combat'. The two participants use unusual weapons, double-pointed *war-hammers* or maces and large rectangular shields.

153 'Welsh warrior', manuscript, England, 13th century
(Public Record Office, Chapter House Liber A, London, England)

Although this is a comical sketch of a 'wild Welshman' drawn by an Englishman, a number of features may reflect reality. These include the man's long hair, bare foot, substantial cloak and short bow of simple rough wooden construction.

154A–D Apocalypse from St Albans, Hertfordshire, c.1230
(Trinity College Library, Ms. R.16.2, Cambridge, England)

One of the earliest accurate illustrations of the longbow and its use. Clearly the bow has a much shorter draw (A) than the Asiatic composite bow. Arrows are kept in the belt rather than a quiver (A and C), and the weapon is strung by placing one end against the side of the foot (D).

155 War-axe from Northumberland, England, mid-13th century
(ex-Oakeshott, *Archaeology of Weapons*)

It is interesting to note that one of the best-preserved 13th-century war-axes to be found in England comes from Northumbria. War-axes were also a popular weapon in neighbouring Scotland, where they reflected lingering Scandinavian influence. This example has its blade thrust forward at some distance from the haft, the socket being protected by a diamond-shaped sleeve. What looks like a small hammer has been added to the back. These new characteristics owed nothing to the earlier Scandinavian so-called 'Danish' axe, but might have been partly a result of Central Asian or Islamic influence and partly an internal European development.

156A–B Daggers, English or European, 1250–1300
(private collection, R.E. Oakeshott, England)

These two daggers have hilts similar to those of a *basilard* but the blades are narrower. The weapons are, of course, considerably corroded. Broad *quillons* and an almost equally long crossbar in place of a *pommel* are the normal characteristics of the typical *basilard*, and were clearly also used on other forms of dagger such as these.

157 Sword from the River Witham, England, 1250–1300
(British Museum, London, England)

The similarities between this weapon and that above are obvious, except that the example found in the River Witham has slightly different *quillons*.

158 Conyers Falchion, England, late 13th century
(Cathedral Treasury, Durham, England)

The Conyers Falchion is one of the most famous surviving medieval weapons. Its hilt is similar to that of 13th-century swords, except that in this case the *quillons* are broader, and more decorated, which may reflect the weapon's ceremonial use. They also have a kind of rudimentary *langet* down the blade. The blade itself is that of a typical *falchion*, broadening considerably towards the tip and having a curved cutting edge.

159 Sword, England (?), 13th century
(Wallace Collection, London, England)

A standard 13th-century war-sword. The circular *pommel* is very large, the *quillons* slender, long and slightly curved. The blade tapers to a point but is not yet regularly triangular in outline.

160 Mace head, England, 13th century
(London Museum, London, England)

Though the sleeve or socket of this weapon is corroded, the wings or blades are in excellent condition. It is a typical example of a kind of weapon that became popular in 13th-century Europe after having been adopted from Muslim or other eastern Mediterranean peoples in the 12th century.

161 Effigy of King John, Worcestershire, 1225–30
(*in situ* Cathedral, Worcester, England)

The unarmoured effigy of King John grasps a sword with a decorated, diamond-shaped *pommel*, and *quillons* inlaid with apparent stones. Such a design might be fanciful or might reflect a highly decorated ceremonial weapon.

162 Twin effigies of knights, Lancashire, c.1225–50
(*in situ* Abbey, Furness, England)

The effigies in Furness Abbey are primitive in style and were presumably made in an isolated part of northern England. The helmets, though crudely carved, are straightforward flat-topped *great helms* with cross-shaped reinforcements across the face and eye-slits.

163A–C Unidentified effigy, London, early 13th century
(ex-Temple Church, London, England, now destroyed)

The tragic destruction of several of the monumental effigies in London's Temple Church during the Second World War was a serious blow to the study of arms and armour. Yet surviving drawings and photographs indicate a number of interesting features. Most of the early effigies are dressed in the same kind of armour, consisting of mail *hauberks* with *coifs* and *mittens*, some padded *gambesons* being indicated by raised and squared shoulders. They also have flat-topped kite-shaped shields of the large early kind. Much of this armour might even suggest a date at the very end of the 12th century. It is, however, the headgear of these figures that makes them so special. All seem to be versions of substantially padded *arming caps*. Two are clearly to support flat-topped *great helms* (A and C). The third (B) may have had the same function. It lacks the padded squab around the crown but does include an apparent padded neck extending down as far as the *surcoat*.

164A–C Effigy of De Lisle, Devon, early/mid-13th century
(Bampton Church, England; after Stothard)

Another early effigy was that of De Lisle at Bampton. The head and face are considerably worn but the *coif* appears to have a roughly square outline suggesting an *arming cap* to support a *great helm* worn beneath the mail. The band around the outside of the *coif* could have been a decorative *circlet* or a padded squab to keep the helmet clear of the mail. De Lisle's sword also seemed to have a decorated, almost trefoil-shaped *pommel*.

165 Effigy of Sir Robert de Vere, Essex, 1250–1300
(*in situ* Church of St Mary, Hatfield Broad Oak, England)

There is still debate about the date of this effigy. It was certainly made several years after the death of its subject in 1221. The style of carving could indicate the end of the 13th century, but the arms and armour could push the date back almost as far as mid-century. Perhaps a sculptor, aware that his subject died many years earlier, attempted to portray old-fashioned equipment, which consists of a separate mail *coif* held tight by a strap or lace around the brow, though this latter feature could be a decorative *circlet* indicating the man's rank. The mail *hauberk* still has *mittens* rather than individual fingers. The mail *chausses* are worn beneath padded *cuisses*, these having a very early example of knee-plates. These are not yet domed *poleyns* but appear to be simple plates of iron or hardened leather fastened directly to the *cuisses*. The flat-topped, almost triangular shield is held by *enarmes* around the upper arm, plus a *guige*. The scabbard is supported by a sophisticated series of straps which form an integral part of the buckled sword-belt. This is, in fact, one of the clearest carvings of such a system.

166 Effigy of Sir Arnaud de Gaveston, England, mid-13th century
(after Stothard)

The lost carving of Sir Arnaud de Gaveston was essentially the same as most other mid- or late 13th-century military effigies. It did show a buckled *guige* for the shield plus lacing of the sword-belt to the scabbard, and what looked like broad decorative *quillons* similar to those on the Conyers Falchion.

167 Wooden effigy of Duke Robert of Normandy, Gloucestershire, c.1250–75
(*in situ* Cathedral, Gloucester, England)

This wooden effigy has been considerably damaged and restored. The left hand and lower arm are not original, while the figure almost certainly had a shield on this arm. Duke Robert wears a *coif* beneath his crown, this having a *ventail* fastened on the right side to a strap across the brow. The strap may also have served to tighten the *coif* around the temples. His mail *hauberk* has long sleeves and *mittens*, his mail *chausses* being reinforced by smooth but probably padded *cuisses*, which would have covered his thighs as well as his knees.

168 Effigy, Worcestershire, c.1270
(*in situ* Abbey, Pershore, England)

This very famous effigy includes one of the earliest, and certainly one of the clearest, representations of a *cuirie* or *coat-of-plates* worn over a mail *hauberk* but beneath a *surcoat*. Its exact construction is unclear but it obviously opened at the sides where at least three of its buckles can be seen. The spacing of these buckles might suggest a laminated construction of iron strips or semi-hoops fastened to a leather or canvas cover. It clearly does not extend below the groin. Note the man's hunting horn slung from his sword-belt in much the same manner as a dagger would later be hung. His mail *coif* also hangs loose around his face, though no *ventail* is visible. The striped padding of a probable *gambeson* is visible on his right wrist where the mail *mitten* has been thrown back.

169 Effigy, Lincolnshire, late 13th/early 14th centuries
(*in situ* church, Gosberton, England)

The Gosberton effigy, which probably dates from the first years of the 14th century, includes a detailed representation of the hanging of a scabbard. The sword has slightly curved *quillons* and an unusual pointed *pommel*. Of even greater interest are the *poleyns* to protect the knees. These are no longer simple small plates fastened to *cuisses* but appear to be built up of pieces of hardened leather or metal fastened to a presumably metallic frame. The whole structure goes around much of the knee.

170 Effigy, County Durham, mid-13th century
(*in situ* church, Whitworth, England; after Stothard)

The crude style could indicate a date prior to 1250, as might the size of the shield. The most interesting feature is the *great helm*, which has reinforcing strips going across the top of the helmet in both directions, one presumably being an extension of a vertical strip running up between the eye-slits.

171A–C Effigy of Robert de Ros, London, late 13th/early 14th centuries
(*in situ* Temple Church, London, England; also a cast in the Victoria and Albert Museum, London)

An early 14th-century date is more likely for this effigy, which includes a number of new features. The framed knee-protections or *poleyns* (B) have been seen before, but the method of hanging the scabbard is new. Here the top of the scabbard is enclosed by a decorative metal collar (A) to which the belt is fastened by rings. The belt itself is stiffened with metallic medallions rather than the vertical bars seen earlier. The effigy also includes a particularly detailed representation of a spur and its fastening straps (C).

172 Effigy, London, mid/late 13th century
(Temple Church, London, England; also a cast in the Victoria and Albert Museum, London)

This effigy is said to represent Gilbert Marshal. Its most interesting feature is the method of supporting the scabbard by cords running from the sword-belt which, unusually, runs outside the scabbard itself. Such a system has something in common with Andalusian and Spanish sword-belts. It can also be seen as a transitional, perhaps experimental, stage between the earlier system with its complicated straps and laces and the simpler 14th-century system of rings attached to either side of the scabbard.

173 Effigy of William Longspée, Wiltshire, c.1230–40
(*in situ* Cathedral, Salisbury, England)

The effigy of William Longspée is one of the earliest datable monumental effigies in England. Its military equipment is correspondingly simple, consisting of mail *chausses* tightened below the knees with small straps, a mail *hauberk* with *mittens*, and a mail *coif* worn over a substantially-padded *arming cap*. The *coif* may have a line up the left side indicating a *ventail* and it certainly has a tightening strap or lace around the brows. The shield is of the large, early form, and the sword hangs from a belt.

174 Effigy, London, early/mid-13th century
(Temple Church, London, England; after Stothard)

This effigy, said to represent William Marshal the Elder, who died in 1219, shows a squared *coif*, which would be worn beneath a *great helm*. A *ventail* is fastened to the left side of the head.

175 Effigy, London, mid-13th century
(*in situ* Temple Church, London, England; also a cast in the Victoria and Albert Museum, London)

A sword suspended in traditional style from a sword-belt. The *chape* is decorated with two holes.

176 Effigy, Worcestershire, c.1225
(*in situ* Abbey, Malvern, England; after Stothard)

This extremely unusual effigy can be interpreted in at least two ways. A small round shield and double-headed war-hammer could indicate the influence of light infantry tactics along the Welsh border, or the man could have been a professional 'champion', as his peculiar weaponry was normally associated with trial-by-combat.

177 Effigy of William Longspée the Younger, Wiltshire, c.1270–80
(*in situ* Cathedral, Salisbury, England)

The smaller shield and shorter *surcoat* indicate this effigy's later date. The sword also has long slender *quillons*. The appearance of a decorated circular and presumably metallic *poleyn* on his knee would confirm such a period, while the almost identical *couter* to protect his elbow suggests a date closer to the end of the 13th century.

178A–B Wooden effigy, Norfolk, late 13th/early 14th centuries
(*in situ* church, Fersfield, England)

The painted wooden effigy at Fersfield has aspects of armour normally associated with the 14th rather than the 13th century. His helmet (B) is an early, tall form of *bascinet* in which the sides and rear of the helmet do not extend very far down the head. It would probably be worn with an *aventail* rather than a *coif* even at this date. The man has separate *gauntlets* (A), though they show no evidence of being strengthened with scales or rigid material. Such early *gauntlets* may simply have provided padding to protect the fingers and may have been worn over mail. The figure clearly wears fully developed bulbous *poleyns* to protect his knees, a feature which tends to suggest a date early in the 14th century. Carbon dating of some of these rare but distinctive wooden effigies might help confirm the dating of the appearance of certain features also seen on carved stone effigies.

179A–E Effigy, London, mid-13th century
(Temple Church, London, England; also a cast in the
  Victoria and Albert Museum, London)

Abundant minor details of armour are visible on this effigy, which is
said to represent William Marshal the Younger. The mail *coif* (A)
appears to be lined, and it has a *ventail* hooked rather than laced to
the left side of the face, plus a presumably padded band to support a
helmet. The legs have padded *cuisses* or stiffened leather knee
protections which are tied by laces over the mail *chausses* (C). The
sword (D) has an octagonal grip and *quillons* which, though probably
exaggeratedly broad in the carving, clearly include a rudimentary
langet. Given the flat rather than pyramidal top of the scabbard one
may assume that such a *langet* went outside the scabbard. This system
of sealing the scabbard and protecting the blade from the elements
was probably adopted during the Crusades as it had been seen many
centuries earlier on Islamic swords.

180A–B The Great Grimsby Seal, Lincolnshire, c.1300
(Corporation Archives, Grimsby, England)

This fine seal (B) probably shows Havelock the Dane carrying a
sword and a round, probably archaic shield with a massive boss. He
could wear a long-sleeved mail *hauberk* without *mittens* or *coif*, while a
minor figure carries the long-hafted 'Danish' axe associated with this
hero.

181A–C Statues, Somerset, 1230–40
(*in situ* west front of Cathedral, Wells, England)

Most of the armoured figures on the facade of Wells Cathedral wear
standard mail *hauberks* and *chausses*. One, or perhaps two, figures (B
and C) have the angled shoulders that suggest padded *gambesons*
beneath the *surcoats*. The possibility that some padding or even
stiffening formed an integral part of the *surcoat* is reinforced by the
raised and clearly stiffened collars that protect the throats of two
figures (B and C). One figure (C) has a mail *hauberk* and *coif* beneath
these padded elements, while another does not (B). Both, however,
wear cloth *coifs* with large padded squabs around the head which are
obviously intended to support *great helms*. One such *great helm* is
present in the Wells carvings (A). It is of an early form with a single
broad eye-slit reinforced at the edges by an additional piece of metal
which also runs down the front of the helmet. The top plate is turned
over the edge and riveted.

182 Ivory chessman, England, mid-13th century
(Ashmolean Museum, Oxford, England)

This tiny carving is equipped with typical mid-13th-century arms
and armour. It has a flat-topped *great helm*, a sword with straight

quillons, a long-sleeved mail *hauberk* with *mittens*, mail *chausses*, probably padded *cuisses*, and an almost triangular shield.

183A–B 'Massacre of the Innocents', *Abingdon Apocalypse*, Canterbury (?), 1250–75
(British Library, Ms. Add.42.555, f.34, London, England)

There are one or two strange features in the arms and armour of this illumination. The sword (A) has very short *quillons* and an elongated *pommel*. One soldier appears to wear a heavy coat with mid-length sleeves and an almost raised collar. Under this he might wear a mail *coif* and *hauberk*. On his head is a brimmed *war-hat* of peculiar form. The manuscript is one of a group showing many French characteristics and it is possible that this unusual warrior ultimately derived from a Byzantine original via the exotic 'infidel' armours of 13th-century French art.

184 Bestiary, England, late 12th/early 13th centuries
(British Library, Ms. Harl 4751, f.8, London, England)

A little-known manuscript includes a clear illustration of the same kind of single eye-slit early *great helm* as is portrayed on Wells Cathedral. By now the crossbow has a loading stirrup and since the man presumably represents a humble crossbowman or sergeant he only has a mid-sleeved mail *hauberk*. The pattern on his chest is almost certainly a heraldic *surcoat*, but the possibility of it indicating the rivets of a *cuirie* or an early *coat-of-plates* cannot be ruled out.

185 Wooden effigy, Northamptonshire, c.1280–90
(*in situ* church, Woodford, England)

Separate but unplated *gauntlets* appear on this effigy, which has been considerably damaged and somewhat patched. The shield is very knocked about and the sword has lost its *quillons*. The head has a deep *bascinet* but the outline of the mail suggests that it formed part of a *coif* worn beneath the *bascinet* rather than being an *aventail* hanging from its rim or sides. There also appears to be some inexpert restoration to the back of the head and neck.

186A–B 'Easter Sepulchre' carved reliefs, Lincolnshire, 1290–1300
(*in situ* Cathedral, Lincoln, England)

The Sleeping Guards are here shown in very fashionable costume of long loose-fitting *surcoats*, one with slit sleeves (B). Their only armours are mail *hauberks*, *coifs* and *chausses*. One has a sword-belt with vertical stiffeners (A).

187 'Goliath', *The Peterborough Psalter*, **Huntingdonshire, 1222**
(Fitzwilliam Museum, Ms. 12, f.78, Cambridge, England)

A singularly vigorous portrayal of Goliath has him wearing a mail *hauberk* with the *mittens* thrown back from the wrists, plus an integral *coif*. His helmet is a very clear representation of a flat-topped *helm* with a *nasal* but no face-mask, a type from which the *great helm* had almost certainly derived but which was still apparently in use in the early 13th century. The shield is of a short but broad flat-topped, almost triangular variety with a small boss. This latter feature is something of an anachronism by the 13th century. The blunt-ended sword would also soon disappear.

188A–B 'Massacre of the Innocents', *Oscott Psalter*, **England (?), mid-13th century**
(British Library, Ms. Add. 50.000, f.13, London, England)

This simply-drawn manuscript shows a fully developed *great helm*, apparently with a single eye-slit (A). The mailed warrior (B) also wears domed *poleyns* on his knees.

189A–B 'Massacre of the Innocents', **England, late 13th century**
(St John's College Library, Ms. K.26, f.15v, Cambridge, England)

One of the 'wicked' soldiers in this scene (B) is given a decorated round helmet very similar to those worn by some Philistines and other 'enemy' figures in the *Maciejowski Bible*. The design may ultimately derive from the fluted helmets of the Middle East. The sword (A) is, however, a typical tapering late 13th-century European weapon, with slightly decorated *quillons* and a large *pommel*.

190 *Westminster Psalter*, **St Albans or Westminster, c.1225–50**
(British Library Ms. Roy. 2.A XXII, London, England)

The figure shown here illustrates a Knight of Christ. He is equipped in a very up-to-date fashion. His *great helm*, here in the hands of an angel, is highly decorated and might even have some kind of brocaded cloth covering over its upper part. The chin-straps can also be seen hanging down. The man's mail *coif* is tightened with a horizontal lace to which the *ventail* is apparently tied. His mail *cuisses* cover thighs and knees, but below these he appears to have shin and foot-covering *chausses* of a different material. This could also represent mail, but the border around the edges where the armour is tied behind his calves tends to distinguish them from other items of mail. The multiple circles could indicate rivets holding some scale or mail-lined cloth or leather, as would be seen more than a century later. The *surcoat* has a tie under the left arm. Such a loose garment would hardly need a laced opening at the sides, so this little lace could be fastened to some *gambeson* or semi-stiff armour worn inside the *surcoat*. The little cross on the knight's shoulder could be a purely iconographic symbol but it does recall the shoulder-mounted *ailettes* of half a century later. If it is in any sense realistic, this little cross appears to be mounted on, or fastened to the shoulders of the man's apparently padded *surcoat*. His sword is a typical mid-13th-century weapon, with long straight *quillons* and a decorated but essentially round *pommel*. A complicated system of straps and laces attaches the belt to the scabbard, which has a large decorated *chape*.

191A–C 'Martyrdom of St Thomas Becket', psalter, Canterbury (?), early 13th century
(British Library, Ms. Harl 5102, f.32, London, England)

The style of the miniatures in this psalter are unlike the rest of the manuscript and may reflect strong French influence. The armour also includes some interesting features, the most important of which are, of course, the helmets (A and C). Though one is round and the other flat topped, both appear to have bands around the face similar to those seen on one of the Temple Church effigies. These could be mistaken for the edges of a lined mail *coif*, except that no such edge is shown on the *coif* worn without a helmet (B). Two of the mail *hauberks* have *mittens* (A and C) and one man wears mail *chausses* down the front of his legs (A). The swords are broad, slightly tapering, and with almost blunt tips.

192A–C *Life of the Two Offas*, St Albans (?), c.1250
(British Library, Ms. Cotton Nero D. 1, London, England)

The illustration of Offa being made a knight shows him first given spurs and a sword (B) and subsequently being helped into a mail *hauberk* with *coif* and *mittens* (C). Another picture illustrating a battle (A) includes an unique piece of armour, apparently a face-mask worn directly on the front of a mail *coif*. I know of no other representation of such a headpiece. The idea could be simply fantasy or could be artist Matthew Paris' attempt to visualise some lost reference in a written text. It could also be a very unusual case of a detachable face-mask, normally fastened to a helmet with a face-frame, being worn without a helmet.

193 *L'Estoire de St Aedward*, England, c.1250–75
(University Library, Ms. Ee.3.59, Cambridge, England)

An interesting variety of infantry weapons here includes axes, spears, a narrow-bladed weapon somewhat like a pike, and what might be regarded as a militarised pitchfork.

194A–D **'Battle outside Antioch',** *History of Outremer,* **London, c.1250**
(British Library, Henry Yates Thompson Ms. 12, f.29r, London, England)

This interesting English copy of the *History of Outremer* includes standard *great helms* (A and B), one of which has a heraldic bird painted on the side. Some of the Muslim foes are armed with winged maces (C) and have round helmets of apparent two-piece construction (D).

195A–I ***Roman de Toute Chevalerie,* England, mid-13th century**
(Trinity College Library, Ms. O. 9.34, Cambridge, England)

The horsemen in one miniature (H and I) are equipped with standard mid-13th-century arms. The horse-armour does, however, demand comment. It is of mail and is clearly made in two separate pieces, one for the head, neck and foreparts of the animal, and one to protect the rump. It seems most unlikely that a man would go into battle with only half a horse-armour (I). On the other hand representations of horses wearing only the rear part of a caparison, though not necessarily an armoured bard, were seen in Spain. Elsewhere an armourer is shown carrying the front part of a mail *bard* or horse-armour (A). Others test the symmetry of a pointed *great helm* (B), make a flat-topped *great helm* (C), and probably inspect the positioning of *quillons* on a sword (D). Another man puts on a mail *hauberk* that includes *coif* and *mittens* (E), presumably to be followed by the *great helm* at his feet. Elsewhere a horseman's sword (F) breaks against the mailed shoulder of his foe (G). The latter figure rides a horse with a full mail *bard*.

196A–E ***Historia Anglorum* by Matthew Paris, England, c.1255**
(British Library, Ms. Roy. 14.c.VII, London, England)

Here a naval attack on a coastal castle shows two short bows (B and C), two *staff slings* (D and E) and a kind of *war-flail* (A). The latter may be for knocking down the defences.

197 **'Martyrdom of St Thomas Becket', Ramsey Abbey, East Anglia, c.1300**
(Pierpont Morgan Library, Ms. 302, New York, United States)

Here again the basic equipment consists of mail *coifs, hauberks* with *mittens* and mail *chausses.* One figure also appears to have knee-covering *poleyns* with scalloped edges, while a warrior in the background has a partially obscured round-topped *great helm.* This man appears to be wielding a double-curved *falchion.*

198A–E   Apocalypse, Canterbury, c.1270
(Bodleian Library, Ms. Douce 180, Oxford, England)

A–F – 'Defeat of Satan's army before Jerusalem', f.88; E – 'The Devil leads Gog and Magog against Jerusalem', f.87. This splendidly decorated Apocalypse was made for the future King Edward I. It clearly includes some fantastic elements, but the bulk of its arms and armour are real enough. The Devil's army is equipped in standard fashion but with a clear emphasis on infantry rather than on aristocratic cavalry. This probably reflected current opinions about the uncivilised 'hordes' of Gog and Magog. Almost all figures wear relatively short mail *hauberks* with integral *mittens*, only one lacking these (E). Mail *coifs* also seem to form an integral part of these *hauberks*. Mail *chausses* are shown in a number of conventional ways, most but not all being worn inside shoes. One interesting example (B) clearly lacks foot-covering mail. This could indicate that some of the other mail *chausses* ended just below the ankle and did not go inside the shoes. Most figures have knee and thigh-covering *cuisses*, most but not all of which (B) have round *poleyns* attached. Some of these *cuisses* may also be scale-covered (E) though this seems unlikely. Short sleeveless *surcoats* give no indication of being padded or lined, but two figures do seem to have stiffened collar defences (D and E), one of which has Magog written on it. Such collars inevitably recall those on the padded soft-armours of the *Maciejowski Bible*. Shields are small and flat-topped, some being quite pointed (A and B), others less so (C). Some have almost round bases (E). Helmets are mostly of the *chapel-de-fer war-hat* variety with relatively small brims (A and E). One even has an incongruous and probably fanciful *nasal* (E), brimmed helmets with *nasals* not otherwise being seen until the late 14th century, in Italy. Others are simply round (C and E). Weapons include normal swords, some worn in 'sinister' fashion on the right hip. Spears, war-axes of exaggerated size (E), a kind of pickaxe (E), and an apparent pitchfork (E) are also seen.

199   'Battle of Stamford Bridge', *L'Estoire de Seint Aedwald le Rei* by Matthew Paris and his school, St Albans, c.1245–60
(University Library, Ms. Ee.III.59, f.32v, Cambridge, England)

Almost lost amid the carnage of this picture are a number of interesting pieces of arms and armour. They include flat-topped *great helms* with riveted upper rims, others with what look like decoratively shaped strengthening pieces at the back, simple domed helmets, some with decorated rims, as well as *war-hats*, one of which seems to have a square top (first warrior from the left with raised sword). Weapons include a large axe which is naturally held by the Norse leader, spears, spiked and flanged maces, and swords with various decorated *pommels* and down-turned, in one case bifurcated, *quillons*. The picture even includes a very early illustration of a *basilard*-style dagger being used during the struggle on the ground (lower right of picture). There is, however, no indication of any other form of armour for the body or limbs other than mail. Two horses wear *caparisons*. The head of one has a design around the muzzle and eye suggesting that a stiffened *chanfron* may be worn beneath.

200A–D *Chanson d'Aspremont*, England, c.1250–75
(British Library, Ms. Lansdowne 782, f.12v, London, England)

The *Chanson d'Aspremont* is in the same style as seen earlier, but the armour is slightly more advanced. Two *great helms* are shown, both of the round-topped variety. The mail *hauberks*, *chausses* and horse-armour are the same. One figure (C) might also have padded *cuisses* over his knees. The *surcoats* stand higher on the shoulders, suggesting that a padded *gambeson* or semi-rigid *cuirie* might be worn beneath. A domed helmet that looks like a *war-hat* with a minimal brim is also seen (A). It has an unexplained knob on top which might be a carrying ring.

201 Monumental brass of Sir Robert de Bures, Suffolk, c.1300
(*in situ* church, Acton, England)

Although some of the finest early English monumental brasses are believed to have been made, or at least to have had their outlines cut, in Flanders, there is little reason to doubt that the arms and armour they portray were used in England at the time of their manufacture. It is often shown in considerable detail (this drawing has been simplified). Sir Robert wears a separate mail *coif* tightened around the temples with a lace. Under a close-fitting *surcoat* he has a mail *hauberk* with *mittens* which are again tightened around the wrists with a lace. His thighs are protected by probably padded *cuisses* decorated with flowers and fleurs-de-lys. Laced over his knees are highly decorated, perhaps metal, *poleyns*. These are, in fact, the only pieces of plate armour to be seen. His legs and feet are enclosed by mail *chausses*. His flat-topped shield is presumably strapped to his upper arm as well as being supported by a broad *guige* which runs partly under the lower part of his *coif*. His large sword is supported in an old-fashioned way, with the sword-belt attached at two separate points around the scabbard. This meant that the weapon hung at a slightly sloping angle which made it easier to draw when on horseback.

202A–B **Lost wall-paintings of the 'Painted Chamber' in Westminster Hall, England, late 13th century (ex-Hewitt)**

The medieval wall-paintings in Westminster Palace were considerably damaged even before they were destroyed in the 19th-century fire. They showed a horseman with a *great helm* and mail *hauberk* with *mittens* and *coif* (A). His legs were also probably mailed. One slightly unusual feature was what looked like mail *cuisses* over his *chausses*. It is, of course, possible that many of the apparently quilted or padded *cuisses* seen in other works of art were in reality lined with mail. The horse carries a full mail *bard*, including either an extra flap of mail below the sides of the saddle or a flap extending over this vulnerable area from the front or back portions of the *bard*. Another part of the wall-painting illustrates a warrior in segmented or framed *war-hat* wielding a curved *falchion* with double-curved *quillons* (B).

203 **Mail *coif*, probably England, 1300–50 (Royal Scottish Museum, Edinburgh, Scotland)**

One of the best preserved of medieval mail *coifs*. It is typical of the 14th century in having no *ventail* across the chin. Instead it was tightened by being laced up the back. This was now possible because mail makers were able to tailor the shape of a *coif* to fit comfortably over the head, chin and throat.

204 **Sword, England (?), 1300–50 (Guildhall Museum, London, England)**

During the early part of the 14th century one popular form of sword-blade became narrower in profile, more regularly tapering towards a point, and thicker in section. One reason for such a trend was the gradual adoption of a fencing and thrusting style of sword-play such as had been seen in the east for some centuries. This in turn was related to the adoption of more plate armour, which was better able to withstand the bludgeoning style of swordsmanship normal throughout Western Europe since early medieval times.

205A–B **Effigy of Thomas de Sheffield, Yorkshire, c.1330–50 (*in situ* St Gregory's Church, Bedale, England)**

The otherwise typical mid-14th-century effigy of Thomas de Sheffield has quite early forms of plated arm defences (A). The *rerebrace* on the upper arm appears to be hinged. The elbow is protected by a *roundel* and the *gauntlets* seem to consist of simple, perhaps padded, gloves with small plates protecting each joint of the fingers. The material covering the wrist and back of the hand seems to be slightly flexible, perhaps indicating some form of heavy leather. The man's legs are clearly protected by *poleyns*, which probably consist of a decorative iron frame with a scalloped edge, the sides consisting of hardened leather.

206A–F Effigy of Brian Fitzalan, Yorkshire, 1300–10
(*in situ* Church of St Gregory, Bedale, England)

The effigy of Brian Fitzalan is a particularly fine example of early 14th-century styles. Basically his visible armour still consists of mail, including a *hauberk*, a mail *coif* thrown off his head onto his shoulders (A), *mittens* tightened at the wrists by small straps (A and D), and full mail *chausses* reinforced by *poleyns* (B, C, and E). These *poleyns* are of an early form, probably built up on an iron frame to which rectangular plates of *cuir-bouilli* (hardened leather) have been riveted. These plates are in turn decorated with heraldic shields. Brian Fitzalan's typical sword hangs in a scabbard supported by two rings to the sword-belt (C and F). These rings are positioned non-symmetrically so that the weapon hangs at a convenient angle (F). The buckled *enarmes* holding the knight's damaged shield to his arm are also just visible (D).

207 Effigy, Berkshire, c.1320–30
(*in situ* church, Aldworth, England)

This effigy is only slightly later than that of Brian Fitzalan but already considerable developments can be seen. A loose *surcoat* is still worn, plus an unusual floppy hat-like object over the *bascinet*. The helmet itself has a mail *aventail* fastened to its rim, an additional flap of this *aventail* apparently hanging down as far as the neck. Such a style is seen in Italy and Germany but is rare in England. The arm and leg armour is also unusual, being highly decorated and possibly consisting largely of *cuir-bouilli* reinforced with a metal edging. Perhaps this man had served in Italy or even further east.

208 Effigy, Shropshire, early 14th century
(*in situ* St Mary's Church, Shrewsbury, England)

The dating of this effigy is difficult. The style is stiff and provincial. The short, tight *surcoat* indicates a date after 1330, but the very simple armour looks earlier. The unnamed subject might have been a relatively poor knight wearing old-fashioned equipment. The *bascinet* comes far down the sides and back of the head and seems to be worn over a mail *coif* rather than having an *aventail* fastened to its rim. Note that he has no plate armour on his arms and wears no *gauntlets*, his elbows simply being protected by a flexible sleeve of some semi-stiff or padded material.

209 Effigy of John of Eltham, Middlesex, c.1340
(*in situ* Abbey, Westminster, England)

John of Eltham, younger brother of King Edward III, naturally wears the most up-to-date and fashionable armour of his day.

Beneath a Prince's crown he has a *bascinet* and an *aventail* with a decorated fastening. His arms are protected by a plated *rerebrace* for the upper arm and a *vambrace* for the lower arm, the elbow being defended by a cup-like *couter* and a *roundel*. His *gauntlets* are still essentially heavy leather gloves, the backs of which are partially covered by a flexible series of plates. A *coat-of-plates* would have been worn beneath the tight-fitting *surcoat*, although nothing is visible on the surface. A mail *hauberk* with tight-fitting sleeves but probably no *mittens* would be worn beneath the plate armour and *surcoat*, the V-shaped hem of this being visible below the surcoat and the decorated scalloped hem of the presumed *coat-of-plates*. The prince's legs are protected by shaped metal *greaves*, decorated *poleyns* for the knees, and laminated *sabatons* for the feet. Note that his highly-decorated sword, apparently already pulled a few centimetres from its scabbard, hangs at an angle because the sword-belt is attached to the scabbard at two asymmetrical points.

210 Effigy of Sir Oliver Ingham, Norfolk, c.1340
(*in situ* church, Ingham, England)

A similarly dated but damaged effigy shows that the equipment of a fully armoured knight differed from that of a royal prince mainly in its degree of decoration. The only real difference is in the style of the helmet, which was probably a matter of fashion. Oliver Ingham also wears the short sleeves of his mail *hauberk* outside the plated upper-arm *rerebraces*. This indicates that the mail seen inside his elbow is a small separate piece, probably laced to an *arming coat*. His *poleyns* are worn over, or attached to, *cuisses*. In the mid-14th century most such *cuisses* seem to have been dotted with studs or rivets, strongly suggesting some laminated, splinted or scale protection beneath the outer cover. This knight has *greave* plates over his shins, the back of his legs being protected only by his mail *chausses*. His feet are, however, again protected by laminated *sabatons*.

211 Effigy of Hugh Despenser, Gloucestershire, c.1350–75
(*in situ* Abbey, Tewkesbury, England)

In contrast to the early *bascinet* worn over a *coif* at Shrewsbury (f. 208), the later effigy of Hugh Despenser has a *bascinet* with a mail *aventail* suspended in the normal manner from a series of *vervelles*. These were pierced lugs which normally followed a line at some distance from the rim of the helmet. The *aventail* was then hooked over these lugs. A strip of pierced leather covered the untidy edge before a cord or lace was threaded through the pierced *vervelles* to hold both the leather strip and the mail aventail in place. Such a system was presumably developed from the earlier Middle Eastern and Asiatic way of fastening a mail *aventail* to the rim of a helmet.

212 Effigy of Sir William Baggily, Cheshire, c.1320–30
(*in situ* church, Bowdon, England)

The dagger carried by Sir William Baggily is shaped like a small sword and appears to be suspended from the man's belt by a tassel, the knot of which stops the thong from slipping out from beneath the belt.

213 Unidentified effigy, Yorkshire, early 14th century
(*in situ* church, Goldsborough, England)

The main importance of the Goldsborough effigy lies in the detailed representation it provides of the inside of a shield. This is clearly covered by one or more sheets of leather held in place by a series of small nails.

214 Effigy, Herefordshire, mid-14th century
(*in situ* church, Clehonger, England)

The effigy at Clehonger is again in almost the same style but is in some respects slightly more advanced. On the other hand the *bascinet* appears to be worn over a mail *coif* as no *vervelles* can be seen. The lower edge of the *coif* also has a decorated fringe. The shoulders are now protected by small laminates as well as a *roundel* and hinged tubular *rerebrace*. A structurally similar system protects the elbows, where a small amount of mail is also visible. The tubular *vambrace* is again hinged and buckled but the *gauntlets* are now beginning to look more like the all-metal *gauntlets* of later years rather than the plated gloves worn by previous generations. Note that the man grasps a dagger in his left hand. This is almost certainly hung from his sword-belt but is one of the earliest appearances of such a weapon on a carved effigy. The decorative hem of a presumed *coat-of-plates* is visible at his thighs between his *surcoat* and his mail *hauberk*. The leg-armour consists of fully-developed iron *poleyns* and shaped tubular *greaves*.

215 Relief carving on monument to William de Staunton, Nottinghamshire, c.1326
(*in situ* church, Staunton, England)

This simple relief illustrates a typical early 14th-century *great helm* of the rounded, almost pointed variety. Although sometimes still used in warfare, such heavy cumbersome helmets were fast being relegated to the tournament field and even to symbolic ceremonial and heraldic purposes. This example has a suspension ring on top, a feature that might have been the reason for many apparent knobs or buttons shown in less detail elsewhere.

216 'Sleeping Guard at the Holy Sepulchre', Nottinghamshire, c.1330
(*in situ* on the Easter Sepulchre, church, Hawton, England)

A sleeping soldier wears an interesting mixture of new and old-fashioned military equipment. On his head is a close-fitting *bascinet* with what appears to be a loose *aventail* suspended from *vervelles*. His armour consists of a simple mail *hauberk* and *chausses*. Even his heavy sword is slung in the old way by a complicated series of straps which form part of the sword-belt.

217 Carved canopy of the Percy Tomb, Yorkshire, c.1342–5
(*in situ* Minster, Beverley, England)

Much of this almost unique carving is obscured by an exaggeratedly large heraldic shield. On his head the warrior has an early example of a visored *bascinet*, the visor being raised. On his legs are *poleyns* with wing-like extensions to protect the sides and backs of his knees. *Greaves* cover only the front of his legs and he has no *sabatons*, only the mail of his *chausses*.

218A–D *Holkham Picture Bible*, East Anglia, c.1320–30
(British Library, Ms. Add. 47.682, London, England)

A – 'Sickness of Herod', f.16v; B–C – 'Questioning of the Sower', f.14v; D – 'Murder of Nobles', f.17. One figure (D) is clearly an 'exotic', his headgear probably being based on conventional images of Asiatics. Other pictures show men in mail *hauberks* and *chausses* (A and D). A very large *bascinet* with a neck extension that almost qualifies as a *salet* (A) looks more Italian than English. The wearer seems to be wielding a long-headed mace. Another infantry warrior (B) has a helmet that appears to be midway between a *great helm* with a movable visor and a visored *bascinet*. He also leans on a long-hafted, long-bladed weapon with a substantial spike at the back. Such a weapon might be a *guisarme* or a very early form of *halbard*. Another long-hafted weapon is the axe (D) with a swept back blade and a small spike at the back.

219 Manuscript illumination, England (?), early 14th century
(British Library; ex-Austin Lane Poole *Medieval England*)

An infantryman wields a *goedendag*, which is normally only associated with the Netherlands and Belgium. If it is indeed an English manuscript, then it indicates a previously unsuspected spread of a short-lived weapon which was a specialised anti-cavalry mace with a spike at the end.

220A–B **Manuscript, England, early 14th century**
(British Library, Ms. Roy. 16.G.VI, f.172, London, England)

An apparent *bascinet* made in two pieces (B) is again seen in this manuscript. So is a large helmet with a movable visor (A). The warriors are otherwise almost identically armoured in long-sleeved mail *hauberks* with *mittens*, mail *chausses*, plus *poleyns* and *greaves*. One figure also has a *roundel* on his shoulder (A) and wields an axe, whereas the second figure has a sword (B).

221 ***The Luttrell Psalter*, East Anglia, c.1340**
(British Library, Ms. Add.42130, London, England)

The famous *Luttrell Psalter* includes a particularly fine picture of a knight. It also shows how relatively simple and backward was England's military equipment when compared to that of Germany. The knight has a conical *bascinet* with an *aventail* to be worn beneath the visored *great helm* that is handed to him by his wife. He wears a long-sleeved mail *hauberk* with *mittens*, plus *ailettes*, but there is no indication of a *coat-of-plates*. His legs are protected by mail *chausses*, *poleyns* and *greaves*. The horse has a heavy and perhaps armoured *bard* or *caparison* and clearly wears a large rigid *chanfron* on its head. The crest on this *chanfron* echoes that on the man's helm.

222 ***St Omer Psalter*, East Anglia, c.1330**
(British Library, Ms. Yates Thompson 14, f.7, London, England)

This weapon appears to be midway between an European *falchion* and an eastern sabre. If it ever existed in reality it could be regarded as a development of the normal *falchion*.

223A–M **Treatise of Walter de Milemete, London, c.1326**
(Christ Church Library Ms. E. 11, Oxford, England)

The early illustration of a cannon in Walter de Milemete's treatise on *Nobility, Wisdom and the Prudence of Kings* has tended to divert attention away from other interesting pieces of armour and weaponry in this manuscript. The picture of a gun (A) is perhaps slightly more accurate than has sometimes been thought. Small bottle-shaped bronze hand-guns of more elongated form than the object shown here were apparently mounted on shafts about a metre long. The large cannon in the Milemete illumination seems to be based on such small guns. Perhaps these were the only firearms with which the artist was familiar. In reality, larger early cannon were generally tubular in shape, being built up of strips and hoops of iron. Nor were they, of course, mounted on flimsy trestles as shown here. All firearms were almost certainly fired by a red-hot metal *touche*, as shown in this manuscript. Other interesting pieces of arms and armour in Walter de Milemete's treatise include a round-topped *great helm* with a movable visor (B). Such helmets may, at least as far as their visors are concerned, be seen as a transitional stage leading to the later visored *bascinet*. Other helmets include a large and almost pointed *great helm* with a crest (C), a tall and broad-brimmed *chapel de-fer war-hat* of somewhat Germanic form (D), and many close-fitting *cervellières* or early *bascinets* (E–G and I–M). Another figure (D) also has an early example of a throat-covering *barbote*. Such a piece of armour would become popular in various parts of 15th-century Europe but at this period seems mostly to have been limited to Italy and the Balkans. Mail *hauberks* with *mittens* and *coifs* are seen (E, F, H and J–M). *Roundels* protect some shoulders (C–G and M) while rectangular *ailettes* are seen twice (H and I). One or two men have *roundels* at their elbows (D and E) and tubular arm defences are shown in a somewhat rudimentary manner (E–G), as are *greaves* (E, H, M and K). A series of small circles might indicate a *coat-of-plates* worn by a figure without a *surcoat* (I). This figure also shields himself with a large round-based infantry *mantlet*. Spears are widely used, but another foot soldier also carries a spiked weapon with a hook at the back (K).

224A–F *Carlisle Charter*, **Cumbria, 1316**
(City Library, Carlisle, England)

A highly-decorated initial illustrates the siege of Carlisle by the Scots in 1315. The Scots are, of course, shown in an unfavourable manner but nevertheless this is one of the earliest and most accurate representations of Scottish costume made by an artist who presumably knew what he was drawing. The Scots (A, B, E and F), or perhaps more accurately Scots Borderers and Galwegians, lack armour, wear capes, are apparently bare legged and have large floppy hats that bring to mind the 'blue bonnets' of later centuries. These Scots have a modern *trebuchet*, although one figure (B) seems uncertain how to operate it. Another figure (A) carries a relatively short bow while a group of sappers (F) includes a man with a pick. A final figure on a scaling ladder (E) wields a battle-axe. The garrison of Carlisle include a fully armoured figure with a small flat-topped shield, a perhaps visored *great helm*, mail *hauberk*, and perhaps *gauntlets* (C). Next to him a mailed figure with a broad *war-hat* and squared shoulders suggesting padded armour or a *cuirie* beneath the *surcoat*, winds a winch to load a very rarely illustrated siege-crossbow (D). The devastating impact of this large, frame-mounted *great crossbow* is seen in the large arrow or bolt that has transfixed the Scots archer. Other defenders of the citadel (E) include a man with a spear and another with a *falchion*.

225 Jesse Window, Shropshire, early 14th century
(*in situ* St Mary's Church, Shrewsbury, England)

The supporting donor figures in this early 14th-century window illustrating the Tree of Jesse are largely equipped in traditional style. They could, in fact, have stepped out of the late 13th century. Their armour consists of a mail *coif*, mail *hauberk* perhaps with individual fingers to the *mittens*, and mail *chausses*. Another garment is just visible beneath the long *surcoat* on the right knee. Though far from clear this is probably part of the man's padded, lined or mailed *cuisses*.

226 'St George', wall-painting, Bedfordshire, early 14th century
(*in situ* church, Little Kimble, England)

This somewhat worn painting is of interest chiefly because it illustrates *ailettes*. These normally rectangular pieces worn on the shoulders are now generally agreed to have been made from light material such as wood or leather, and to have been purely for recognition and heraldic purposes. It is, however, still unclear how they were attached, but laces to the shoulders of a padded *surcoat* or a quilted *gambeson* would seem likely.

227 Monumental brass of Sir John de Creke, Cambridgeshire, c.1325
(*in situ* church, Westley Waterless, England)

The brass of Sir John de Creke shows some of the most decorated and detailed armour of the early 14th century. His helmet is particularly splendid, consisting of a fluted *bascinet* with a decorated finial. The *vervelles* to fasten the mail *aventail* are also decorated. The closest parallels to such a helmet are found in the eastern Mediterranean region and it would be interesting to know if Sir John ever aspired to be a Crusader. His arms are protected by animal-headed *epaulettes* and half of a tubular *rerebrace* worn over a mid-sleeved mail *hauberk*. A hinged *vambrace* is worn under the mail to protect his lower arms. An animal-headed *roundel* protects his elbows and he would almost certainly have worn *gauntlets*, though they are not shown here. His shield, sword, scabbard and sword-belt are standard for the period. He wears a *coat-of-plates* over his *hauberk*, the decorated hem and lowest row of rivets being visible below the cutaway front of his *surcoat*. Part of this *coat-of-plates* may also be visible on the front of his right shoulder. His leg harness is straightforward, consisting of *poleyns*, *greaves* for the front of his legs and laminated *sabatons* worn over mail *chausses*.

228 Monumental brass of Sir John de Bacon, Suffolk, c.1320
(*in situ* church, Gorleston, England)

The simpler and more damaged brass of Sir John de Bacon illustrates armour in a slightly earlier fashion than that worn by Sir John de

Creke. *Ailettes* are still present, as is a full mail *coif*. Some garment, perhaps a *cuirie* or *coat-of-plates*, is worn over the long-sleeved mail *hauberk* and is visible where the *surcoat* opens at the groin. Arm defences over the mail sleeves include *roundels* for the insides of the elbows and shoulders, half-tubular *rerebrace* and *vambrace*, plus perhaps domed *couters* for the elbows. His legs are protected by mail *chausses*, some form of *cuisses* over the thighs and *greaves* for the shins. The knee defences are harder to interpret as they look more like close-fitting and flexible extensions to the *cuisses* than rigid metallic *poleyns*. Perhaps they are, indeed, of semi-rigid leather but have been decorated in the same manner as the plate armour for arms and legs. Note that his sword is suspended in the old-fashioned way with straps, to a sword-belt that apparently lacks a buckle. Altogether this monumental brass includes a number of odd features suggesting that its designer was not fully familiar with the details of armour and its construction.

229 Monumental brass of Sir William Fitzralph, Essex, c.1325
(*in situ* church, Pebmarsh, England)

The brass of Fitzralph illustrates highly decorated armour (here simplified), but the basic forms are relatively simple. The separate mail *coif*, long sleeved mail *hauberk* with *mittens* and mail *chausses* are all traditional. The sword is also suspended in the old manner, with split straps and a belt. A padded garment may just be visible below the hem of the *hauberk* and *cuisses*. These latter might also be quilted. Plate armour, though not necessarily all of metal, consists of *roundels* for shoulders and elbows, a domed *couter* for the outside of the elbow, half-round *rerebrace* and *vambrace* for the outsides of the arms, and highly decorated *poleyns* for the knees. These have rudimentary wing-like extensions on the outside to protect the back of the knee. Added to these are *greaves* and laminated *sabatons* for the shins and the tops of the feet. The back of the calf and sides of the feet are still protected only by mail *chausses*.

230 Monumental brass of Sir Hugh Hastings, Norfolk, c.1350
(*in situ* church, Elsing, England)

Certain important developments had taken place by the time this brass was made. The figure shown here is, in fact, one of seven surviving minor supporting figures, five of whom are armoured warriors. An eighth figure represents St George. New features include a *bascinet* with a hinged visor, this latter being of domed form with a long extension to protect the throat. *Roundels* have disappeared from the elbows to be replaced by small wing-like extensions to the domed, elbow-covering *couters*. The mail *hauberk* lacks *mittens*, as the hands would now be protected by plated *gauntlets*. Apparent studs on the thigh-covering *cuisses* suggest some rigid elements inside their decorative cloth covering. The domed *poleyns* are still fastened to a sleeve-like knee covering but now have wing-like extensions to protect the back of the knees. *Greaves* have both front and back plates, but the laminated *sabatons* seem to cover only the tops of the feet.

231A–B Effigy of Patrick de Barton, Cheshire, c.1340–50
(*in situ* church, Farndon, England)

Two features of this very worn effigy demand comment. The first is the helmet, which is a very tall affair, apparently made of two pieces joined along the comb. Such an old-fashioned type of helmet may reflect the relative backwardness of north-western England and neighbouring Wales. This effigy might also illustrate a raised mail collar worn outside a mail *aventail* or *coif*.

232 Effigy of Sir Richard de Venables de Newbold, Cheshire, c.1335–50
(*in situ* church, Astbury, England)

A very rare representation of a deep *bascinet* with its mail *aventail* apparently pulled up and twice fastened to the sides of the helmet. This itself may be of a local two-piece construction and might extend down to cover the side of the jaw.

Notes

1. F. Barlow, *Edward the Confessor* (London, 1970), p.170; M. Powicke, *Military Obligation in Medieval England* (Oxford, 1962), pp.2–5; P. Contamine, *La Guerre au Moyen Age* (Paris, 1980), p.139.
2. Powicke, *op.cit.* p.3.
3. Barlow, *op.cit.* p.170; R. Glover, 'English Warfare in 1066', The *English Historical Review* vol.LXVII (1952), pp.5–9; M.J. Swanton, *The Spear in Anglo-Saxon Times* (Ph.D. thesis, Durham University, 1966), p.572; E. John, 'The End of Anglo-Saxon England', in *The Anglo-Saxons*, ed. J. Campbell (London, 1982), p.237.
4. Glover, *op.cit.* pp.8–9; D.C. Nicolle, *Arthur and the Anglo-Saxon Wars* (London, 1984), p.18.
5. Barlow, *op.cit.* pp.93–4, 175 and 206.
6. J.F. Verbruggen, *The Art of Warfare in Western Europe during the Middle Ages* (Oxford, 1977), p.100; Swanton, *op.cit.* pp.618–20 and 636; W.A. Seaby and P. Woodfield, 'Viking Stirrups from England and their Background', *Medieval Archeology* vol.XXIV (1980), pp.87 and 102.
7. Powicke, *op.cit.* pp.4–7.
8. Powicke, *op.cit.* pp.8–9 and 18; H.L. Turner, *Town Defences in England and Wales* (London, 1971), pp.28–9.
9. Swanton, *op.cit.* pp.301–2, 328 and 610–12.

10. Swanton, *op.cit.* pp.580–2.
11. S. Harvey, 'The Knight and the Knight's Fee in England', *Past and Present* vol.XLIX (1970), p.27.
12. D.C. Douglas, *William the Conqueror* (London, 1964), p.274; M. Chibnall, 'Mercenaries and the Familia Regis under Henry I', *History* vol.LXII (1977), pp.15–17; F. Barlow, *William Rufus* (London, 1983), pp.22–3.and 152–3.
13. J. Beeler, 'The Composition of Anglo-Norman Armies', *Speculum* vol.XL (1965), pp.404, 409 and 412–13.
14. J. Beeler, 'Towards a Re-evaluation of Medieval English Generalship', *Journal of British Studies* vol.III (1963), pp.5–6; Barlow, *William Rufus, op.cit.* pp.3–7 and 370–1.
15. J. Beeler, *Warfare in Feudal Europe, 730–1200* (Ithaca, 1971), p.274; E.G. Heath, *Archery, a Military History* (London, 1980), pp.103–11; G. Rausing, *The Bow, Some Notes on its Origins and Development* (Lund, 1967), p.133.
16. Rausing, *op.cit.* p.159; J. Alm, 'Europeiska armborst, En översickt', *Vaaben-historisk Aarboger* v/b (1947), p.126.
17. N. Hooper, 'Anglo-Saxon Warfare on the Eve of the Conquest: A Brief Survey', *Battle Conference on Anglo-Norman Studies, Proceedings* vol.I (1978), p.92; A. Borg, 'Gisarmes and Great Axes', *Journal of the Arms and Armour Society* vol.VIII (1974–6), p.338.
18. F. Barlow, *The Feudal Kingdom of England, 1042–1216* (London, 1961), p.320.
19. Barlow, *The Feudal Kingdom, op.cit.* pp.320–1 and 336; Harvey, *op.cit.* p.31; S. Painter, 'Castle Guard', *The American Historical Review* vol.XL (1934–5), p.459.
20. Contamine, *op.cit.* pp.190–2.
21. R.F. Walker, *The Anglo-Welsh Wars, 1217–1267; with Special Reference to English Military Developments* (Ph.D. thesis, Oxford University, 1954), pp.29–31.
22. Walker, *op.cit.* pp.94–5.
23. Alm, *op.cit.* p.127.
24. Swanton, *op.cit.* pp.105–6 and 329–30.
25. A.V.B. Norman, 'An Early Illustration of Body Armour', *Zeitschrift für Historische Waffen- und Kostümkunde* vol.XVIII (1976), pp.39–40.
26. Contamine, *op.cit.* p.250.
27. A.E. Prince, 'The Strength of English Armies in the Reign of Edward III', *The English Historical Review* vol.CLXXXIII (1931), pp.355–7 and 362.
28. A.Z. Freeman, 'Wall-Breakers and River-Bridgers: Military Engineers in the Scottish Wars of Edward I', *Journal of British Studies* vol.X (1971), p.15; Contamine, *op.cit.* p.260.
29. L. Alcock, *Arthur's Britain* (London, 1971), p.321.
30. Barlow, *The Feudal Kingdom, op.cit.* p.212; Beeler, 'The Composition of Anglo-Norman Armies', *op.cit.* p.405; Giraldus Cambrensis, 'Description of Wales', in *The Itinerary through Wales and the Description of Wales*, ed. and trans. M. Llewelyn Williams (London, 1908), pp.198–200.
31. Walker, *op.cit.* p.26; Prince, *op.cit.* p.362; A.D. Carr, 'Welshmen and the Hundred Years War', *The Welsh History Review* vol.IV (1968), pp.22–3; D.C. Douglas, *The Norman Fate 1100–1154* (London, 1976), p.73.
32. Verbruggen, *op.cit.* p.106; Rausing, *op.cit.* p.133; Carr, *op.cit.* pp.22 and 29; Giraldus Cambrensis, *op.cit.* pp.166–7 and 192–3; Heath, *op.cit.* pp.111–14; Walker, *op.cit.* pp.38–9; R. Hardy, *Longbow, a Social and Military History* (Cambridge, 1976), pp.36–7; C. Oman, *A History of the Art of War in the Middle Ages* (London, 1924), vol.II, p.69.
33. A.T.E. Matonis, 'Traditions of Panegyric in Welsh Poetry; the Heroic and the Chivalric', *Speculum* vol.LIII (1978), pp.671–3 and 686–7; C. Blair, 'The Pre-

Reformation Effigies of Cheshire' (part two), *Transactions of the Lancashire and Cheshire Antiquarian Society*, vol. LXI (1949), pp.95–8.

34. I am grateful to Mr C. Thomas of the Institute of Cornish Studies (University of Exeter) for this information.

Chapter 3

Scotland

The Kingdom of Scotland was theoretically under English suzerainty throughout the period under review. During the late Anglo-Saxon and Norman era it was also under considerable military influence from England. When, in the late 13th and early 14th centuries, influence and interference was succeeded by attempts at direct political control the Scottish Wars of Independence began, culminating in England's defeat on the field of Bannockburn in 1314.

At the same time Scotland had embarked upon a process of cultural, political and military unification that would not be completed until the 18th century. The heartland of the kingdom had been the Pictish-Scottish state which, known as the Kingdom of Alba, dominated Scotland north of a line between the Firths of Forth and Clyde. This area had subsequently been divided once again by Scandinavian colonisation of the Western and Northern Isles plus certain neighbouring coasts. The decline of Anglo-Saxon Northumbria led to a Scottish conquest of the Lothians and eastern Lowlands as far south as the present English border by the early 11th century. The British or Welsh Kingdom of Strathclyde, with its substantially Scandinavian sub-kingdom of Galloway, was only drawn into Scotland in 1034. This created an Anglo-Scottish border which cut through present-day Cumbria, far to the south of the existing frontier.[1] Almost inevitably the centre of the Scottish kingdom now gravitated southwards towards Edinburgh and Glasgow. The existing military aristocracies of the Anglo-Saxon ex-Northumbrian eastern, and the Celtic-Welsh-Scandinavian western Lowlands remained, and they retained their own military traditions. Scottish monarchs also began a policy of feudalisation, using late Anglo-Saxon and Anglo-Norman institutions as their model. They even encouraged Normans to settle in Scotland, where these newcomers eventually had a profound military influence.[2] Nevertheless, 12th century Scotland was still a deeply divided land, between the Lowlands of the east and south and the Highlands of the north and west.[3]

In the 11th century the military organisation, tactics and equipment of the Scottish Lowlands was very like that of northern England, in particular Northumbria, with cavalry playing a minor role before the year 1000.[4] The

favoured infantry weapons were axes,[5] swords and spears, though the warriors
of regions such as Galloway remained notably poorly equipped throughout
this era.[6] Despite the emergence of a small feudal armoured elite in the 12th
to 14th century, Lowland Scottish warfare still relied primarily on infantry,
armed at first with swords and javelins, and later with long spears or pikes.[7]
Unlike the situation in England, where war was now largely the business of
professionals, the Scottish peasantry continued to play an important role,
raiding, booty and plunder were the prime objectives.[8] Nevertheless, by the
late 13th and 14th centuries the Scots were using much the same siege engines
as the English, and there had been a moderately widespread adoption of
archery amongst Lowland communities.[9]

By contrast, warfare in the Highlands and Islands preserved many archaic
features, though even these changed gradually. War fleets and the need to find
crews for ships had been fundamental to the military organisation of the old
Scots-Irish Kingdom of Dalriada (present-day Argyll)[10] and a feudalised
development of this form of 'ship service' could still be seen in 12th and 13th
century western Scotland.[11] Generally speaking, Highland warfare remained
a matter of raiding and skirmishing, for both of which lightly-equipped
infantry and a few lightly-armoured cavalry were most suited. Their
equipment generally reflected Viking origins or Scandinavian influence.[12]
Even as late as the 14th century the arms and armour of the Highlands
remained lighter than that of the Lowlands, which in turn was old-fashioned
when compared to neighbouring England.[13]

Figures

233 War-axe from Caerlaverock, Dumfriesshire, 1050–1100
(Burgh Museum, Dumfries, Scotland)

An excellent example of the early development of the medieval axe from the 10th and 11th century 'Danish axe'. Here the blade already has a very slight upwards sweep.

234 Seal of King Alexander I, Scotland, 1107–24
(British Library, Dept. of Seals, London, England)

Here the King of Scotland is equipped in the same style as his English neighbours except that his armour looks slightly old-fashioned. Alexander has a large kite-shaped shield, and a conical helmet of apparent segmented construction with a forward-angled crown and a *nasal*. His mail *hauberk* has long, rather broad sleeves without *mittens*. Judging by the line of an apparent shoe around his ankle but well above his spurs he also lacks mail *chausses* for his legs.

235 Sword, Scotland, c.1250
(Royal Scottish Museum, Edinburgh, Scotland)

This fine sword of the mid-13th century was probably made in Germany, although so little is known about arms manufacture in medieval Scotland that it is impossible to say for certain whether or not top-quality weapons were made there.

236 War-axe from Lumphanan, Aberdeenshire, 12th century
(National Museum of Antiquities, inv. 727, Edinburgh, Scotland)

The next stage in the development of the Scottish axe can be seen in this weapon, where the upwards sweep of the blade is more pronounced.

237 Effigy of Hugo de Arbuthnot, Fife, c.1300
(*in situ* church, Arbuthnot, Scotland)

The equipment worn by Hugo de Arbuthnot, including the large shield, was definitely old-fashioned by the year 1300, at least when compared to that seen in most of Western Europe.

238A–B Effigy of Malise, Earl of Strathearn, Perthshire, c.1271
(*in situ* Cathedral, Dunblane, Scotland)

A number of interesting monumental effigies survive in Scotland but they are generally much more damaged than those in England. Some might have been made south of the border and as such might not accurately reflect Scottish military equipment. On the other hand, their normally crude carving and old-fashioned style could indicate that, although inspired by the effigies of England, they were local products. The considerably worn effigy of the Earl of Strathearn shows a man with mail *coif* tightened around the brows with a lace, a mail *hauberk*, and mail *chausses*. His shield is large and old-fashioned, hinting that plate armour or even a hardened leather *cuirie* were not worn beneath his *surcoat*. He also carries a relatively short straight sword.

239A–B Effigy of Walter Stewart, Earl of Menteith, Perthshire, late 13th century
(*in situ* Priory, Inchmahone, Scotland)

The twin effigy of Walter Stewart and his wife is an interesting and romantic variation on a traditional theme. The knight again wears only a mail *coif*, *hauberk* with *mittens* apparently thrown back from the wrist, and mail *chausses*. Note that his wife's hand is visible beneath his neck. Walter Stewart also carries a large, flat-topped though considerably worn shield, and has a sword-belt across his hips.

240 Unnamed effigy, Aberdeenshire, late 13th/early 14th centuries
(*in situ* church, Bourtie, Scotland)

This is one of the simplest, crudest and most worn in Scotland. Once again the man wears only a mail *coif*, *hauberk* and *chausses*, while his shield is notably large. The thick band around his head may form a kind of *arming cap* to support a heavy helmet such as a *great helm*.

241 Effigy of Lord Alan of Galloway, Kirkcudbright, mid-13th century
(*in situ* Abbey, Dundrennan, Scotland)

The effigy of the Lord of Galloway may be very broken but it is not as worn as most other Scottish effigies. The workmanship is also fine, perhaps reflecting the influence of Yorkshire masons to the south-east. His equipment is again rather basic, consisting of a mail *hauberk* and *coif* under a loose *surcoat*. His head is damaged, but he seems to have worn a close-fitting fluted or segmented *cervellière* over his mail *coif*. Across his chest is the *guige* of his unseen shield, while around his waist is a broad sword-belt with vertical stiffeners.

242 Effigy of Sir James Douglas, Lanarkshire, c.1335
(*in situ* St Bride's Church, Douglas, Scotland)

The Earl of Douglas was one of the great barons of Scotland but again he appears in simple, almost rudimentary military equipment consisting of a mail *coif* with a *circlet* or *arming-band* to support a helmet, a mail *hauberk*, probably with fingered *mittens*, and mail *chausses*. There might be a padded *gambeson* visible below the hem of his *hauberk* and he certainly has a splendidly-decorated sword-belt. His shield is, however, still very large considering the date of the effigy, and probably reflects his lack of plate armour.

243A–C Unnamed effigy, Dunbartonshire, late 13th/early 14th centuries
(*in situ* church, Old Kilpatrick, Scotland)

One of the most interesting effigies in Scotland is, unfortunately, very worn. It is located on the west coast close to the Highland border. Later 14th and 15th century effigies in the Western Isles indicate that a distinct style of arms and armour persisted in this region; a style that finds some parallels in Ireland. A few characteristics of this later style might already be present here, though the eroded state of the carving makes positive identification difficult. The man wears a mail *coif* with a lace or circlet around the brows. Under his loose sleeveless *surcoat* is what appears to be a short-sleeved mail *hauberk*. Such a fashion is unknown among the knightly class of England, as it probably was in the Scottish Lowlands. Yet it may result from both the isolation, poverty in iron resources, and traditional infantry and light cavalry tactics of the far west. The man clearly wears separate *gauntlets* and he probably also has mail *chausses*. On his hip is a long broadsword with large curved or angled *quillons* having bulges at their tips. The scabbard is supported in the old-fashioned way. The design of this hilt is remarkably similar to the earliest known representations of the famed Scottish *claymore*, which date from the late 14th or 15th centuries.

Notes

1. G.W.S. Barrow, *The Kingdom of the Scots* (London, 1973), pp.142–4 and 149–54; G. Menzies, *Who are the Scots?* (London, 1971), p.85; J.G. Scott, 'An 11th century War-Axe in Dumfries Museum', *Transactions of the Dumfriesshire and Galloway Natural History and Antiquarian Society* vol.XLIII (1966), p.120.
2. Barrow, *op.cit.* p.161; F. Barlow, *The Feudal Kingdom of England, 1042–1216* (London, 1961), p.158; F. Barlow, *William Rufus* (London, 1983), p.317; D.C. Douglas, *The Norman Fate, 1105–1154* (London, 1976), p.74; W.C. Dickinson, *A New History of Scotland, vol.1: Scotland from the Earliest Times to 1603* (London, 1965), pp.83–91.

3. Dickinson, *op.cit.* p.39.

4. Barrow, *op.cit.* pp.39–44 and 280; G. Donaldson, *Scottish Kings* (London, 1977), pp.12–13.

5. Scott, *op.cit.* p.120; A. Borg, 'Gisarmes and Great Axes', *Journal of the Arms and Armour Society* vol.VIII (1974–6), p.338.

6. J. Bradbury, 'Battles in England and Normandy, 1066–1154', *Battle Conference on Anglo-Norman Studies, Proceedings* vol.VI (1983), p.2.

7. C. Oman, *A History of the Art of War in the Middle Ages* (London, 1924), vol.I, p.392, and vol.II, pp.73, 80 and 102–3; J.F. Verbruggen, *The Art of Warfare in Western Europe during the Middle Ages* (Oxford, 1977), pp.147 and 159–60.

8. P. Contamine, *La Guerre au Moyen Age* (Paris, 1980), p. 169; D. Hay, 'Booty in Border Warfare', *Transactions of the Dumfriesshire and Galloway Natural History and Antiquarian Society* vol.XXXI (1954), pp.149–50 and 158–9.

9. H.L. Turner, *Town Defences in England and Wales* (London, 1971), pp.78–9.

10. J. Bannerman, *Studies in the History of Dalriada* (Edinburgh, 1974), p.148.

11. Dickinson, *op.cit.* pp.37 and 90.

12. Oman, *op.cit.* vol.I, pp.392 and 407; J.T. Dunbar, *History of Highland Dress* (London, 1962), pp.23–4; A. Mahr, 'The Galloglach Axe', *Journal of the Galway Archaeological and Historical Society* vol.XVIII (1938–9), p.67.

13. R. Brydall, 'The Monumental Effigies of Scotland, from the Thirteenth to the Fifteenth Century', *Proceedings of the Society of Antiquaries of Scotland* vol.XXX (1895), pp.330 and 335–6.

Chapter 4

Ireland

In the mid-11th century Ireland was still recovering from the Viking attacks of the preceding century. These had a profound effect on the country's military and political institutions. In particular they led to some consolidation of royal authority. Nevertheless, prior to the Anglo-Norman invasion of the later 12th century Ireland was still divided into five kingdoms, some of which had already begun to adopt Norman court ceremonial.[1] The Anglo-Norman invasion was not complete, occupying no more than half of the island. Thereafter a local Norman-Irish aristocracy evolved within the conquered area while a Gaelic nobility continued to rule the rest of the country. By 1300 the Norman-Irish effectively dominated the island and had come to terms with their Gaelic opposite numbers, while both recognised the increasingly ineffective suzerainty of the English Crown.

Traditional Irish warfare had been a relatively restrained affair compared to conflicts on the mainland of Europe. It largely seems to have consisted of cattle-raiding and combats between champions.[2] The Viking invasions changed the character of war and the numbers of people involved but had less impact on military organisation and technology. The only probable exception were swords and axes.[3] Archery remained extremely primitive and was reserved almost entirely for hunting, where flint arrowheads were still used. The descendants of the Viking settlers in eastern Ireland may, however, have made greater use of the bow.

The new military structures established in eastern and southern Ireland in the latter part of the 12th century owed much to Anglo-Norman systems,[4] though there was also a substantial Flemish element amongst the invaders and settlers. These men played a very important military role, both in the initial conquest and in subsequent wars.[5] Meanwhile Scandinavian influence could still be seen in Gaelic regions of western Ireland, even after the Anglo-Norman invasion.[6] Whether these were residual survivals from an earlier period or reflected continuing contact with the largely Scandinavian regions of north-western Scotland is unclear.

A form of guerrilla warfare proved to be the most effective defence against Norman-Irish attack, and here traditional Irish weapons such as the javelin and sling remained effective.[7] The efficacy of Gaelic-Irish military styles is further indicated by the fact that they survived even within supposedly more advanced Norman-Irish areas.[8] On the other hand Norman-Irish mercenaries were soon recorded serving Gaelic lords.[9]

In the late 13th century the Norman-Irish cavalry elite went into a military decline as the Gaelic aristocracy enjoyed a political revival.[10] During the 14th century a form of warfare almost unique in western Europe developed in Ireland, though it did find remarkable parallels in Islamic Spain and other parts of the Muslim world.[11] Such later medieval Gaelic-Irish tactics primarily relied on light cavalry as a main striking force,[12] supported by light infantry archers or javelin-throwers known as *kernes*.[13] These were in turn strengthened by an elite of armoured axe-wielding infantry known as *gall óglaich*, a term which originally meant 'foreign warriors'. The first such *gall óglaich*, or *galloglas*, of the late 13th century appear to have been mercenaries from the Hebridean islands off the western coast of Scotland.[14] Scottish military influence continued to be important in early 14th century Ireland, most noticeably in the forms of Irish war-axes.[15] In return, a form of Irish light cavalryman known as a *hobelar* served in 14th century Scotland, in England, and eventually in France under English colours, though what influence he might have had on the military styles of these countries remains unknown.[16]

Figures

244 Longbow from Balinderry, Viking or Hiberno-Scandinavian, 10th century
(after Rausing)

The longbow seems to have been introduced into Ireland by Scandinavian invaders and settlers. It remained in use, primarily as a hunting weapon, among the Hiberno-Scandinavian coastal community but did not become widespread as a weapon until after the Anglo-Norman invasion of the late 12th century.

245A–D Spear and javelin heads, Viking or Hiberno-Scandinavian, 10th–11th centuries
(National Museum, Dublin, Ireland)

These three relatively light weapons (A, C and D) were almost certainly javelins; a weapon which remained popular in many Celtic areas long after largely being abandoned elsewhere in the British Isles. Such a survival almost certainly reflects a lack of body armour and even helmets in Ireland.

246A–D Cross of the Scriptures, Ogaly, Meath, 10th century
(*in situ* Clonmacnois, Ireland)

A–B – Two chiefs; C – Warrior; D – Sleeping Guards at the Holy Sepulchre. The bishopric of Clonmacnois was one of the main ecclesiastical centres of the old Gaelic kingdom of Midhe. Though the carvings are simple and stylised they do shed light on 'native' Irish military styles. Here two chiefs, their cloaks held by pairs of massive shoulder brooches, carry short but broad swords. Traditional Irish swords were, in fact, described as having been remarkably short. The weapons appear to have dome-shaped *pommels* and, in one instance quite clearly (A), to have been suspended from *baldrics* attached to their scabbards at two separate points. Ireland and the Iberian peninsula were in cultural and religious contact, probably by sea, during the early Christian and early medieval periods, and various aspects of military styles in Ireland, particularly swords, suggest that such contacts may have been maintained on a much reduced scale even after the Islamic conquest of Spain and Portugal. Another carving of a warrior (C) shows a similarly short sword, probably on a *baldric*, though here the *pommel* is a large round type. The simple carving of the Guards at the Tomb (D) is almost certainly based on an unrealistic manuscript illumination.

247A–B 'The Betrayal', Cross of Muiredach, Uladh, 10th century
(*in situ* Monasterboice, County Louth, Ireland)

The more worn carvings on the Cross of Muiredach again show relatively short non-tapering swords.

248 Shrine of St Maedoc, gilt bronze casket, Ireland, 11th century
(National Museum, Dublin, Ireland)

St Maedoc, otherwise known as Aidan of Ferns, is probably not the subject of this small figure, which carries a sword and a scourge. The weapon has a blade with almost parallel edges which turn at a sharp angle to meet at the tip. Such weapons have been found in Ireland but are normally dated from the 7th to 9th centuries. The broad bar-like *pommel* of the weapon is also distinctive. The discs on either side of the man's face are rivets forming part of the structure of the casket.

249A–B *Cumdach* of the *Stowe Missal*, Ireland, 11th–12th centuries
(Royal Irish Academy, Dublin, Ireland)

This *cumdach* or gilded bronze book-container shows two 'native' or Gaelic Irish warriors armed in traditional style. Neither wear armour or helmets. One is armed with a remarkably short sword with a somewhat conical *pommel* (A) while the other holds a small round convex *buckler* with a large boss while wielding a broad-bladed spear.

250 Arrowhead, Ireland, 12th–15th centuries
(British Museum, no.1867.7 20.4, London, England)

The dating of medieval arrowheads is notoriously difficult. This example may be later than the 12th century, as its head is clearly designed to penetrate armour.

251 Arrowhead from Dublin, 11th–13th centuries
(National Museum, Dublin, Ireland)

This elongated arrowhead probably served as part of a specialised incendiary arrow. Its length would originally have been around 19 cm, the long iron socket being wrapped in inflammable material.

252 Sword, probably from England or the Continent, 11th–12th centuries
(Bunratty Castle, inv. 213, County Clare, Ireland)

This weapon is almost certainly not of Irish manufacture as it reflects neither the native Gaelic nor Scandinavian traditions. Its exact provenance is unknown but if it was, in fact, found in Ireland then it may have been brought in during the late 12th century Anglo-Norman invasions, or could have arrived earlier as an exotic import from England.

253 Axehead, probably from Ulster, 12th/early 13th centuries
(Ulster Museum, no.181–1952, Belfast, Northern Ireland)

A series of axes found in Ireland clearly illustrate the development of this weapon in the Celtic west and north-west of the British Isles. From the almost symmetrical blade of the 11th century, a distinctly upwards-curving form had evolved by the 12th or 13th centuries. The hole in the base of this blade is probably the result of corrosion.

254 Sword from Derrymore, Westmeath, late 13th/early 14th centuries
(National Museum, no.Wk.3:F341, Dublin, Ireland)

A large and typical Western European sword, again probably not made in Ireland. The similarity between its curved *quillons* and those on the Movilla carving depicted in fig.256 are clear. Such weapons should probably be associated with the Anglo-Norman or, by this date, the Anglo-Irish aristocratic elite, though some may also have been acquired by the native Gaelic-Irish elite of western Ireland.

255 'Centaur', relief carving, Ireland, 12th century
(*in situ* Cormac's Chapel, Cashel, Ireland)

The centaur is shown using an accurately represented simple bow with the kind of barbed arrow widely used in warfare by Western European warriors. He also wears a conical helmet with a slightly forward-angled crown and a substantial *nasal*. This may be taken as evidence for the spread of normal Western European military technology into the previously somewhat isolated world of Gaelic Irish arms and armour.

256 Relief carving on a coffin lid, County Down, 12th–13th centuries
(*in situ* Movilla, Northern Ireland)

The carvings at Movilla are very simplified but even here some features can be identified. The blade is straight, with the *quillons* distinctly down-curving in 13th-century European style, while the *pommel* seems to be a development of earlier Scandinavian styles which are believed to have survived for a long time in Ireland. The weapon looks, in fact, like a mixture of new and traditional influences.

257A–B War-axes, Ireland, 13th century (?)
(National Museum, Dublin, Ireland)

A – from Ballina, County Mayo, inv. 1936:1879; B – from County Donegal, inv. 1939:3633. These two very similar weapons are decorated with silver inlay in Scottish style. Given their provenance in the far north-west and west of Ireland – well inside the 'native' Gaelic area – they may be seen as early examples of the so-called 'Gallóglaich axe'. The gall óglaich, or 'foreign warriors', who were to become famous as infantry axemen in Irish service, were originally recruited as mercenaries from western Scotland and the Hebrides. First recorded in Ireland around 1290, they had probably been serving there for at least fifty years before this date. The weapons shown here, though they have a distinct upwards-sweep to their blades, have evolved along different lines from another style of medieval war-axe in which the upwards-sweeping blade was developing a thrusting point.

258 War-axe from Derryhollagh, County Antrim, late 13th/ 14th centuries
(National Museum, Dublin, Ireland)

Popularly known as a 'Gallóglaich axe', it is, however, within a wider 14th-century European and particularly Scandinavian or Central European tradition. Such weapons may well have been used by later gall óglaich, but by then these troops would seem to have been absorbed into a general Northern European infantry tradition.

259 War-axe from Coleraine, County Derry, 13th century (?)
(National Museum, no.Wk.ll, Dublin, Ireland)

Though related to similarly-dated silver-inlaid axes, this weapon has its upwards sweep culminating in a point. Similar but more developed weapons subsequently became characteristic of southern Scotland as well as of various other areas far removed from Ireland.

260 Arrow or crossbow-bolt head from Stokestam Crannog, County Roscommon, late 13th–15th centuries
(National Museum, Dublin, Ireland)

The presence of such an obviously armour-piercing weapon in an early medieval crannog or lake dwelling is an anachronism. It probably got there at a later date.

261 Arrowhead from Dublin urban site, early 13th century
(National Museum, inv. E 71: 15491, Dublin Ireland)

This much more straightforward arrowhead was probably for use in the defence of Dublin city.

262 **Hunting arrowhead, Ireland, early 13th century (?)**
(National Museum, no.Wk.79, Dublin, Ireland)

This is an apparently unique find since it is in a style of broad arrowhead common among the Turks and Turkish-influenced peoples of the East but very rare in Europe. Such lateral blades were designed to kill animals rather than to be used in warfare.

263 **Arrowhead from Waterstown, County Westmeath, 13th–16th centuries**
(National Museum, inv. 1934:488, Dublin, Ireland)

This massive arrowhead, perhaps 7 cm across, might have been used for hunting large animals such as deer. Large barbed arrowheads of this type are, however, seen in some manuscripts illustrating battles.

264 **Seal of William de Braosa, Ireland, 1210**
(National Library, deed no.27, Ormond College, Dublin, Ireland)

This simple seal shows an armoured knight of the new Anglo-Norman aristocracy whose equipment is slightly old-fashioned by French or English standards. He probably wears a full mail *hauberk* with a *coif*. His helmet is not clear but would seem to be a close-fitting *cervellière*. He rides with a slightly-bent knee, indicating either that the maker of this seal was not familiar with the knightly riding style or that some of the new elite were already adopting aspects of Ireland's indigenous light cavalry tactics.

265A–B **Bronze *pommel*, Ireland, c.1300 (?)**
(National Museum, no.1956.361, Dublin, Ireland)

A number of bronze sword pommels have come to light in Ireland. They are generally without provenance and their dating is more a matter of intuition than historical evidence. They were probably made in Ireland, perhaps in the Gaelic regions. As such they are likely to have represented a continuation of a tradition introduced from Scandinavia. They were probably attached to blades imported without hilts from Europe.

266 **Spearhead (?) from Clough Castle, County Down, 13th century**
(Ulster Museum, Belfast, Northern Ireland; after Swanton)

This slender but very strongly-made spearhead is clearly designed to penetrate armour. It may have been part of a pike or a javelin or it might be from a large bolt to be shot from frame-mounted crossbow.

267 Javelin head (?) from Cork, County Cork, mid-13th century
(Public Museum, no.E 146:30006, Cork, Ireland)

Too large to be an arrow and too small to be an ordinary spearhead, this may come from a javelin or a bolt to be shot from a heavy siege-crossbow.

268 Javelin head (?) from Wood Quay, Dublin, 13th century
(National Museum, no.E 132:98263, Dublin, Ireland)

The slightly more slender blade of this weapon may indicate an earlier date than that in the preceding figure.

269 Arrow or crossbow-bolt head from Wood Quay, Dublin, 13th century
(National Museum, no.E 132, Dublin, Ireland)

The small size of the blade and the fact that it has a tang rather than a socket suggest that it is from a crossbow bolt.

270 Spearhead from Cork, County Cork, 1250–1300
(Public Museum, no.E 146:12001, Cork, Ireland)

The relative abundance of medieval weapon fragments found in eastern Ireland compared to their rarity in the west must reflect the comparative wealth in both weapons and iron of the Anglo-Norman eastern counties. The poverty in iron of the 'native' Gaelic west is equally notable. The weapons of the east, like this small spearhead, are virtually identical to those seen in England and the rest of Western Europe.

271 Spear or pike head from Muckamore Priory, County Antrim, late 13th century
(Historical Monuments and Buildings Branch, no.78/465, Dept. of the Environment, Belfast, Northern Ireland)

A substantially-made blade, being diamond-shaped in section. The socket is similarly almost rectangular, to stop the blade turning on its haft.

272 Spear, pike or javelin head from Clough Castle, County Down, 1250–1300
(Ulster Museum, Belfast, Northern Ireland)

Like the other blade from Clough Castle (fig.266), this is rectangular in section with a long socket. A late date is indicated by the strength of this weapon, which was clearly designed to penetrate armour.

273 **'Irish foot-soldier', English manuscript, late 13th century**
(Public Record Office, Chapter House Liber A, London, England)

A fanciful and mocking picture of the 'wild Irish' made by their foes. Nevertheless, it does include some interesting elements based upon verbal or perhaps even lost pictorial evidence about Irish costume and equipment. The man's 'fool's cap' forms part of a cloak comparable to that worn by the Scots shown in the Carlisle Charter. He wears baggy hose, has bare feet, and wields the axe associated with the most effective of Irish warriors.

274A–B ***De Topographia Hiberniae of Giraldus Cambrensis, England, c.1250–75***
(Bodleian Library, Ms. Laut. Misc. 720, Oxford, England)

Although this is an unflattering caricature of Irishmen drawn by an English artist, probably based only on verbal reports, it correctly emphasises the axe as a typical Irish weapon during this period.

275 **'Dermot McMurrough', Anglo-Irish manuscript (?), 13th/early 14th centuries**
(National Library, Dublin, Ireland)

Similar costume and weaponry are here given to this representation of a 'native' Irish leader.

276 **Dagger, Ireland, early 14th century (?)**
(National Museum, R.S.A.I. 162, Dublin, Ireland)

A beautifully-decorated dagger related to the 14th-century so-called 'Burgundian knife'. Despite a superficial resemblance to the early medieval *scramasax* or *seax*, it is, in fact, completely different to such Scandinavian and Anglo-Saxon weapons. Whereas the *seax* had a curved or angled back and a straight edge, this weapon has a broad, straight and considerably decorated back, and a curved or angled cutting edge.

277 **Dagger from Drumdarragh, County Fermanagh, 14th century (?)**
(Ulster Museum, no.7–3, Belfast, Northern Ireland)

This weapon may be related to the previous example, although it has a triangular outline and a straight cutting-edge.

278 **Wooden bow from Desmond Castle, County Limerick, 14th century (?)**
(City Museum, Limerick, Ireland)

A relatively short bow, probably used as a hunting weapon, though its outline and section are similar to the war-bows of the period.

279 Crossbow-bolt head (?) from Trim Castle, County Meath, 14th century (?)
(Office of Public Works, National Monuments Branch, no.E 94:4184, Dublin, Ireland)

This strange little object is probably a removable bolt head.

280 Crossbow-bolt head from Trim Castle, County Meath, early/mid-14th century (?)
(Office of Public Works, National Monuments Branch, no.E 94:2046, Dublin, Ireland)

Though obviously an arrow or bolt head, it is unusual in that the barbs appear to have been bent back to rest against the sides of the socket. Perhaps this happened when it burst through a piece of armour or might have been done intentionally to improve its armour-piercing capability.

281 Seal of unknown member of the Le Botiller family, Ireland, mid-14th century
(National Library, Ormond College, Dublin, Ireland; after drawing supplied by D.S. Begley, Chief Herald, Dublin Castle)

This heraldic shield portrays a very simplified sword of a typical 14th-century type with a tapering blade and large round *pommel*.

282 Unnamed seal, Ireland, 1364
(National Library, Ormond College, deed no.1.078, Dublin, Ireland; after Begley)

An heraldic shield bears a *great helm* with a substantial crest. Such helmets had largely been relegated to the tournament-field in England and had probably never been popular in Ireland, where warfare was largely a matter of raid and ambush.

283 *Magauran Duanaire* manuscript, Ireland, early 14th/ 15th centuries
(ex-*Journal of the Galway Archaeological and Historical Society*, vol.XVI (1936), p.84)

Although the manuscript in which this drawing is found dates from the early 14th century, the illustration itself may be a later addition, perhaps from as late as the 15th century. The rider's sword certainly looks later than the 14th century. He also wears a mail *hauberk*, possibly a large *bascinet* with a *nasal*, and he carries a heavy, broad-bladed spear.

Notes

1. F. Barlow, *The Feudal Kingdom of England, 1042–1216* (London, 1961), p.333; J.F. Lydon, *The Lordship of Ireland in the Middle Ages* (Dublin, 1972), p.82.
2. M. and L. De Paor, *Early Christian Ireland* (London, 1958), pp.77–9 and 84–5.
3. De Paor, *op.cit.* pp.158–61; G.A. Hayes-McCoy, *Irish Battles* (London, 1969), p.19; E. Rynne, 'The Impact of the Vikings on Irish Weapons', in *Atti de VI Congresso Internazionale delle Scienze Preistoriche Protostoriche* – Roma 1962 (Rome, 1966), p.182.
4. Lydon, *op.cit.* pp.83–4; G.H. Orpen, *Ireland under the Normans* (London, 1911–12), pp.338–40.
5. Orpen, *op.cit.* pp.396–8.
6. Rynne, *op.cit.* pp.182–4; E. Rynne, 'An Irish Sword of the 11th century?' *Journal of the Royal Society of Antiquaries of Ireland* vol.VIIC (1962), pp.208–9; T.E. McNeill, *The History and Archaeology of the Anglo-Norman Earldom of Ulster* (Ph.D. thesis, Belfast University, 1973), p.255.
7. M.J. Swanton, *The Spear in Anglo-Saxon Times* (Ph.D. thesis, Durham University, 1962), p.594; P. Contamine, *La Guerre au Moyen Age* (Paris, 1980), p.356.
8. Orpen, *op.cit*, p.328.
9. K. Simms, 'Warfare in the Medieval Gaelic Longships', *The Irish Sword* vol.XII (1976), p.106.
10. Hayes-McCoy, *op.cit.* p.41.
11. P. Harbison, 'Native Irish Arms and Armour in Medieval Gaelic Literature, 1170–1600', *The Irish Sword* vol.XII (1976), p.280; Hayes-McCoy, *Irish Battles, op.cit.* pp.36 and 42.
12. Harbison, *op.cit.* pp.176–7; Lydon, *op.cit.* pp.100–1.
13. Harbison, *op.cit.* p.281.
14. Hayes-McCoy, *op.cit.* pp.40 and 48–9; Harbison, *op.cit.* p.282; G.A. Hayes-McCoy, 'The Gallóglach Axe', *Journal of the Galway Archaeological and Historical Society* vol.XVII (1937), pp.103 and 113.
15. Hayes-McCoy, 'The Gallóglach Axe', *loc.cit.*; A. Borg, 'Gisarmes and Great Axes', *Journal of the Arms and Armour Society* vol.VIII (1974–6), p.341.
16. Contamine, *op.cit.* p.165; C. Oman, *A History of the Art of War in the Middle Ages* (London, 1924), vol.II, pp.101 and 119; S.J. Burley, 'The Victualling of Calais, 1347–65', *Bulletin of the Institute of Historical Research* vol.XXXI (1958), p.51; J.F. Lydon, 'The Hobelar: An Irish Contribution to Medieval Warfare', *The Irish Sword* vol.II (1954), pp.13–16.

Chapter 5

Southern France

This region is taken to include all the old Kingdom of France south of the River Loire and most of what is now known as the French Midi. Regions east of the Rhône are excluded because they formed part of the Kingdom of Burgundy or Arles, which will be dealt with as a section of the Empire. The area under consideration consisted of the enormous Duchy of Aquitaine, the lesser Duchy of Gascony, and various smaller counties or marquisates. By the mid-11th century these had their own distinctive culture, language (Occitan) and military traditions.

During the mid-12th century almost all this region, except for the County of Toulouse, fell under the control of the Count of Anjou. Henry Count of Anjou then became King Henry II of England, as a result of which most of the Midi soon formed part of a huge Angevin (Anjou) empire spreading from Scotland to the Spanish border. Perhaps inevitably the French monarchy felt bound to break this realm, a large part of which was, in feudal-legal terms, theoretically subject to the French crown. Between 1180 and the outbreak of the Hundred Years War in 1337, the kings of France succeeded in reducing southern French territory controlled by English monarchs to the southern Saintonge and western Gascony. Meanwhile the reduction of 'English' control in northern France was even more dramatic.

Meanwhile southern France, and above all the County of Toulouse, had suffered the full effects of the Albigensian Crusade. The Albigensians were a heretical, partially Manichaen, sect similar to and influenced by the Bogomils of the Balkans, who had in turn emerged as an offshoot of the Paulicians of eastern Anatolia. The Albigensians' activities made them the target of a savage Crusade in the early 13th century, one result of which was to greatly increase northern French military influence in southern France.

The military styles of the Midi were not fundamentally different from those of the north. Nevertheless, the extreme fragmentation characteristic of the southern French feudal system had earlier led to an excess of 'private war' amongst a large and anarchic military class. This in turn prompted an early development of the 'Peace of God' movement among the non-noble classes.[1] The turbulent *milites* or knights of the Midi also played a leading role in the

Iberian *Reconquista*,[2] and many of their own military styles mirrored those of northern Spain. On the other hand the success of the 'Peace of God' movement and the diversion of the Midi's military energies southwards seem to have led to relatively peaceful conditions and a neglect of urban fortifications during the 12th century.[3]

Even after the Albigensian Crusade, or perhaps in some ways because of it, mercenaries from the French Midi were still widely recorded in the 13th century. Amongst the most highly-regarded were Gascon infantry.[4] Bordeaux may, meanwhile, have grown in importance as a centre of arms production, and there is plenty of evidence to suggest that southern France, like Italy, was one of the first regions to adopt new types of sharply-pointed thrusting sword. These were designed to counter newly-adopted forms of armour such as the mid- or late 13th-century *coat-of-plates*.[5]

Further militarisation of the Midi was characteristic of the 14th century, particularly after the outbreak of the Hundred Years War in 1337. This was most noticeable in the cities, where there was a great expansion of urban militias and an increase in their military significance.[6] There also seems to have been some degree of militarisation in rural areas.

Figures

284A–D Carved capitals, County of Toulouse, c.1100
(*in situ* Cloisters, Abbey of St Peter, Moissac, France)

A – Sacrifice of Isaac; B – St Martin; C–D – Crusaders (?). Once again a clear distinction is drawn between a general purpose knife (A) and a sword (B). The down-turned *quillons* of the latter are early and suggest Spanish influence in this part of southern France. The placing of so broad-bladed a spear (C) and a war-axe with a spike at the back (D) in the hands of Crusaders similarly shows a link with Spain, where such weapons would in turn probably reflect Arab-Andalusian influence.

285 'Demon', carved capital, County of Toulouse, late 11th century
(*in situ* Cathedral of St Sernin, Toulouse, France)

The placing of an early form of crossbow in the hands of a Demon probably resulted from Papal attempts to control and limit the use of this devastating new weapon. The carving also provides an interesting illustration of how these early crossbows were spanned. Note the bulge at the base of the stock, which is similar to those on crossbows seen in the late 12th-century Egyptian manuscript by al-Ṭarsūsi.

286A–C Carved capitals, County of Toulouse, 1087–1119
(*in situ* Cloisters, Church of Ste Foy, Conques, France)

The lack of visible armour worn by these three warriors again provides a link with Spain. Their sword-belts are crudely carved but are of the normal 12th-century knotted type. During the late 11th and early 12th centuries many northern French warriors still hung their swords from baldrics. Two forms of shield are shown: a standard European kite-shaped form (B and C) and a flat-topped kite-shaped shield (A) of a style not normally seen until the mid- or even late 12th century. Three forms of helmet are present. One (A) is unclear, but the second (B) is simply a conical type without a *nasal*. The third is more interesting as it appears to include a very early representation of the forward-angled crown, as well as a *nasal* coming down from rounded brows. The wearer has, of course, pushed his helmet onto the back of his head, perhaps for greater comfort.

287A–B *Beatus Commentaries on the Apocalypse* from St Sever, Duchy of Gascony, 1028–72
(Bib. Nat., Ms. Lat. 8878, Paris, France)

A – Sacrifice of Isaac, f.8; B – Horseman of the Apocalypse, f.148v. The *Beatus* of St Sever is a rather primitive and crudely-illustrated manuscript, yet it is relatively easy to interpret as it uses many of the same iconographic conventions as carvings from south-western France. Warriors wear mail *hauberks* and conical helmets with *nasals* (B). One of the unusual features is, however, an early version of a *falchion*, a single-edged sword with a curved cutting edge and, often, an angled back. This early type has no *quillons* or *pommel* and in some respects looks like a cut-down *glaive* or *bill*. Yet it does have the main characteristic of a *falchion*, namely that the blade broadens rather than tapers from the hilt.

288A–I *The Atlantic Bible*, southern France, late 11th century
(Biblioteca Medicea-Laurenziana, Ms. Edili 125–126, Florence, Italy)

A – Expulsion of Moses' mother, f.27r; B–C – Soldiers of Holofernes, f.42v; D – f.212r; E – Expulsion of Moses' mother, f.27r; F – f.99r; G – f.88v; H–I – f.99r. Simple maces or clubs are illustrated twice in this manuscript (D and E). Otherwise the military equipment is straightforward, consisting of spears, kite-shaped shields, and short-sleeved, short-hemmed mail *hauberks*. One such *hauberk* has slightly longer sleeves (G) while others lack *coifs* (A, B, H and I). None are shown with *ventails* across the face or hanging unlaced on the chest. These *hauberks* do, in fact, seem to be of a simpler, earlier form than those illustrated in other late 11th-century southern French sources. But the helmets are of basically the same variety as seen in various carvings. These include round forms with rims but no *nasals* (C, F, H and I), slightly-pointed forms with rims but no *nasals* (H-I), and tall conical types with integral *nasals* (A and B).

289A–H Carved capitals, County of Auvergne, late 11th/early 12th centuries
(*in situ* church, St Nectaire, France)

A–D – Flagellation; E – Oppressive knight; F – Guards at the Holy Sepulchre; G – The Betrayal; H – Horseman of the Apocalypse. The region of the Auvergne is rich in Romanesque carvings illustrating military equipment. These indicate that the area was a kind of cultural frontier between north and south and that the late 11th and early 12th centuries were a time of technological change. This is most clearly illustrated in the helmets, of which there are quite a variety. Low-domed types, apparently of two segments joined along a central comb and strengthened by a wide rim, are almost certainly descended from late-Roman forms (A, B and G). Conical segmented or fluted helmets with *nasals* seem to mirror the slightly simpler conical helmets of northern France (C, E and F). A similar form, though lacking a *nasal*, is worn by the unarmoured Horseman of the Apocalypse. Most mail *hauberks* have mid-length sleeves and reach only to the upper or mid-thighs. A very interesting feature of these mail armours is their integral *coifs* with *ventails* across the lower part of the face. All would be laced at the left temple and are twice shown laced in this manner (C and E). Elsewhere they hang down from the chin (A, B, F and G), forming a roughly rectangular shape which probably explains the square shapes shown below the throats of mail-clad warriors in two Catalan Bibles and in the Anglo-Norman Bayeux Tapestry. Shields are basically kite-shaped. Swords are broad and straight with round (A), quatrefoil (C) and nut-shaped (F) *pommels*. One is carried beneath the *hauberk* with its hilt protruding through a slit in the mail (A). Another is carried from a knotted sword-belt (F). Two war-axes are shown, both with half-moon blades (F and G). One has a substantial spike at the back which makes it closer to the weapon seen at Moissac and others in Spain. Such a feature was not characteristic of Northern European weapons at this time. Another figure (G) also illustrates a substantial but rather mysterious *glaive*-like hafted weapon. It has a long, apparently single-edged blade but the haft is mostly obscured.

290 'Entry into Jerusalem', carved capital, County of Toulouse, 1100–50
(Musée des Augustins, Toulouse, France)

A turbaned figure holds this short-hafted axe with a half-moon blade. Such weapons are not characteristic of Northern Europe but were seen in Spain. The idea, if not the weapon, could similarly have reached the County of Toulouse from Sicily or the Middle East – where such weapons were also common – via the Crusades.

291A–B Relief carving, County of Poitou, c.1140
(*in situ* west front, Notre Dame de la Couldre, Parthenay, France)

The carved warriors at Parthenay are extremely damaged, but a number of interesting and even surprising features can be distinguished. Sleeveless *surcoats* are worn over mail *hauberks*, the former not being widespread in France until later in the 12th century. The *hauberks* clearly have very wide sleeves. This cumbersome style can no longer be a result of technological backwardness and perhaps reflects the wide sleeves of contemporary civilian costume. Instances of civil dress influencing armour are not unknown and this could be an early example. One shield (B) appears to have an indented, almost kidney-shaped, upper edge which is again most unusual outside Spain.

292A–D **'Soldiers of the High Priest', carved capital, Notre Dame de la Couldre, Parthenay, County of Poitou, c.1140**
(Isabella Stewart Gardner Museum, Boston, United States)

The same very wide sleeves are shown on the tunics worn by these apparently unarmoured soldiers. They also wear peculiar fluted helmets (C and D) or pointed caps, while the *quillons* of their otherwise normal swords are seemingly asymmetrical or reverse-curved (A and B). All these features may be a sculptor's attempt to identify them as 'wicked' by drawing on garbled reports concerning the military equipment of Muslim al-Andalus.

293 **Relief carving, facade of Notre Dame de la Règle, Viscounty of Limousin, early 12th century**
(Musée des Beaux Arts, Limoges, France)

This early 12th-century carving probably owes much to manuscript painting. The mail is crudely represented but clearly includes a *hauberk*, probably with short sleeves, and a *coif*. The helmet is conical and perhaps segmented. It might have a broad rim, though this could equally represent a cloth wound around the helmet. The end of a head cloth is clearly hanging down the man's back. In western European art such a feature usually indicates a 'Moor' or other 'infidel', but it was apparently also adopted by some Crusaders. The warrior's shield is a normal kite type with a cross-shaped riveted iron reinforcement. His sword, with down-turned *quillons*, is carried in a scabbard worn on the outside of the *hauberk*, probably on a *baldric*.

294 **'Moor slain by a Christian knight', carved frieze, County of Angoulême, c.1125**
(*in situ* west door of Cathedral, Angoulême, France)

Both Christian victor and defeated 'Moor' wear the same kind of armour on this relief. It is almost certainly not intended to show scales but is one of many current conventional ways of indicating mail. A scale *hauberk* would be most unlikely to include a *coif* and could not have had scales beneath the armpits. In fact almost all known scale armours have flap-like sleeves in which the scales only protect the outer part of the limb. As such they are closer in form to lamellar armours than to mail. This man's *hauberk* has a slit at the side through which the hilt of his sword protrudes, the weapon being supported beneath the *hauberk*. As a 'Moor' or 'Saracen', the warrior also carries a conventional round shield, but his helmet is of a very interesting form. It has a slightly forward-angled crown, an apparently fluted surface, and may also be extended at the back to protect the neck.

295 **'Guard at the Holy Sepulchre', carved capital now sited at ground level, County of Auvergne, c.1160**
(*in situ* church, Mozat, Puy-de-Dôme, France)

This relatively crude carving shows, once again, a mail *ventail* hanging unlaced across the wearer's chest. The conical helmet has a long *nasal* and the sword hilt protrudes through a slit in the side of the *hauberk*.

296A–B **'Christian and Moor in combat', wall-painting, County of Toulouse, 12th century**
(*in situ* Château Comtal, Carcassonne, France)

Perhaps illustrating an episode from the *Song of Roland*, a Christian warrior approaches from the left armed with a couched lance, a long, kite-shaped shield and a conical helmet without a *nasal*. He might also have a mail *hauberk*. The Muslim warrior approaching from the right uses his lance, here shown breaking, in the same manner. He also seems to be identically equipped apart from his conventional round shield and a cloth hanging from his helmet.

297A–B **Carved capitals, County of Saintonge, 12th century**
(*in situ* church, St Pierre de l'Île, France)

The chief interest of these carvings lies in the association of a sword with a clean-shaven warrior holding a kite-shaped shield, and of maces with whiskered warriors carrying small round shields. These latter figures could represent 'infidels' of some kind.

298A–B **Relief carving, County of Toulouse, c.1145**
(*in situ* entrance steps to the Church of St Gilles, St Gilles du Gard, France)

A – Goliath; B – Huntsman. The carvings at St Gilles are in many respects closer in style to those of northern Italy. Some of the military equipment is also unlike that seen elsewhere in the County of Toulouse. There is a bow of obvious composite construction with angled ears (B) and an armour (A) which, from the care taken by the sculptor to indicate strengthening ribs down each individual scale, can be regarded as a genuine scale *hauberk* rather than conventionalised mail. Its fabric or leather base is seen hanging slightly below the last row of scales at the hem. Unfortunately the right arm is damaged so that it is impossible to see how the artist represented the underneath of Goliath's shoulder and arm. There is some indication of an edging or stitched band around the damaged neck but this is far from clear. The existence of such a scale *hauberk* on a carved relief does not necessarily mean that such armours were used in 12th-century southern France. The armour is here worn by Goliath, one of the 'wicked' who were often given alien or exotic equipment. Many seem to have been based on barely understood verbal reports from the Islamic world or Byzantium. The rest of the Philistine giant's weaponry is also interesting in its own right. Here we have a clear and detailed view of the straps on the inside of a kite-shaped shield, while his short, broad-bladed spear may have some kind of binding around its lower end to improve the grip.

299A–B 'Arrest of St Aventin', carved relief, Duchy of Gascony, late 12th century
(in situ south door of church, St Aventin, France)

This relief carving illustrating the life of St Aventinus includes some remarkable and probably accurate representations of the Muslims of al-Andalus. It was such 'Moors' who originally arrested the Bishop. The artist clearly drew upon his own or local knowledge of those Muslims who ruled territory about 300 kilometres away. The warriors have appropriately baggy trousers and in one case a head cloth recalling the *lithām* or 'veil' still worn by troops of Berber Saharan origin in the Iberian Peninsula. One has a small round shield (B), the other a single-edged sword without *quillons* (A). This latter feature was commonly associated with North African weapons. Both men also appear to wear a relatively stiff garment over their loose trousers. This falls down the front of one man's hips (B) but is divided down the front on the other warrior (A). Perhaps it represents a form of soft or semi-rigid leather or felt protection such as might be seen in Spanish *Mozarab* manuscripts.

300A–C Carved tympanum, County of Toulouse, 1120–30
(in situ west front, Church of Ste Foy, Conques, France)

The falling horseman (A) probably represents the Fall of Pride. He wears a mail *hauberk* with mid-length sleeves and an integral mail *coif*. This *hauberk* is also slit at the sides in a rather old-fashioned style for the date of this carving. The two devils (B and C) carry suitably 'horrifying' weapons: a pickaxe and a rare illustration of a ball and chain. Such a device was almost certainly not a common or even normal weapon in the mid-12th century and, in association with a pick, was probably an instrument used in sieges rather than in combat.

301 Carved capital, County of Auvergne, mid-12th century
(in situ choir of Notre Dame du Port, Clermont Ferrand, France)

Ira, personification of the Sin of Anger, commits suicide with a large dagger or knife. At this date such daggers were essentially the same as everyday knives, with long grips and no *quillons*. Not until the 13th century, amid a notable spread of influence from the East, did daggers in the form of small or short swords apparently reappear.

302A–C 'Struggle of Vices and Virtues', carved capitals, County of Auvergne, c.1155
(*in situ* Notre Dame du Port, Clermont Ferrand, France)

A–B – Generosity fighting Avarice; C – Charity. Almost exactly the same equipment is shown in Notre Dame du Port as in the slightly earlier carvings at St Nectaire. The later date does, however, suit the longer tunics worn beneath mail *hauberks*. The *hauberks* themselves might have mid to long sleeves (B and C) and *ventails*, either drawn across the face (A) or unlaced and hanging beneath the throat. A sword protrudes through a slit at the side (C) as at Mozat, but a large and much broader shield has now appeared. This looks suitable for infantry combat rather than for cavalry and is also seen in the hands of foot-soldiers in a Norman carving of a slightly earlier date. The non-tapering sword (B) is a broad Mediterranean form, as distinct from the tapering and pointed sword current in Northern art. A fluted conical helmet with a *nasal* and a lower rounded form without a *nasal* are present, as they are at St Nectaire. One of the latter has, however, become so stylised that one doubts whether the sculptor had ever seen such a helmet.

303A–J 'Siege of a city – Carcassonne (?)', relief carving, County of Toulouse, late 12th/early 13th centuries
(*in situ* church of St Nazaire, Carcassonne, France)

No distinction is drawn between the defenders and besiegers of this city and all look very European. The panel probably represents the siege of Carcassonne during the Albigensian Crusade. Mail *hauberks* are now long-sleeved and can include *mittens* (A, B and E). The lack of any *surcoats* even at this late date is perhaps surprising. Flat-topped *great helms* are shown (A and C), as are a variety of shields including large kite-shaped types with possible reinforcing bars (1). Swords are quite varied, from pointed and tapering (B, C and J) to blunt-tipped and almost non-tapering (E and F). The continued presence of such early forms of sword is interesting, as is the appearance of a weapon with acutely down-turned *quillons* and a long *langet* (J). This particular sword looks almost Islamic and could be an import from al-Andalus, or have been included symbolically to indicate the 'wickedness' of its user. A crossbow is also illustrated, but most attention has been focused on the *mangonel* (G). This carving provides one of the earlier representations of the *mangonel* in Western European art. The device shown here is the simple man-powered type which had been in common use all around the Mediterranean since at least the early 12th century, and probably much earlier.

304 'Guards at the Holy Sepulchre', carved relief, County of Toulouse, 12th century
(*in situ* west front, church of St Gilles, St Gilles du Gard, France)

The carved frieze on the church of St Gilles illustrates standard military equipment, although the detailed illustration of how a *guige* may be attached to the inside of a shield is interesting. The confusing object in the hand of a warrior behind the damaged front figure could be an early carving of a winged or flanged mace.

305 Ivory chessman, southern France, 12th century
(Bargello Museum, Florence, Italy)

A late 12th-century date is suggested by the knight's *surcoat*, his large flat-topped shield, and the fact that his horse might wear a limited form of *caparison*. His helmet is rounded and low-domed with a substantial rim. It seems to be constructed as a sort of *spangenhelm*, with segments beneath a large cross-shaped frame. The purpose of the button on top is unclear, but the overall outline of this helmet is so similar to that of other helmets with 'buttons' on top that these latter might also have been constructed in the same manner. Almost exactly the same system is shown in much greater detail in mid-13th-century sources like the *Maciejowski Bible*. The structural similarity is such that one might suggest that the helmet worn by this little chessman and by some figures in carvings from the Auvergne are early forms of *chapel-de-fer*, and that the rim is really a brim that the carvers were unable to show sticking out as much as it would in reality.

306A–B Ivory chessmen, southern France (?), 12th century
(Bargello Museum, Florence, Italy)

These warriors are carved in relief on the sides of a chess piece and their equipment is so unlike that which is normally found in 12th-century France that they might either represent 'Moors' or 'Saracens' or they might not have been made in France at all. Italy seems a more likely candidate. The length of one man's tunic (A) and the finger-draw used by the horse-archer (B) makes a Middle Eastern origin unlikely. The first warrior (A) uses a spear, perhaps as a javelin, and a large round shield whose spiral decoration recalls the silk-bound spiral cane shields of the Middle East. The horse-archer has a recurved bow of probable composite construction and a quiver which, as he is turning in his saddle to shoot over his horse's rump, hangs rather peculiarly on his left hip. Altogether these unusual little relief carvings seem to show Sicilian, eastern Mediterranean or Byzantine warriors.

307A–D **Wall-painting (now lost), church at Poncé, Sarthe,**
County of Maine, mid-12th century
(from records in the Services des Monuments Historiques,
Paris, France)

Although this lost wall-painting comes from a region just north of the
Loire, its character and style are very close to existing paintings in
areas on the other side of the river. The 'Moor' or 'Saracen' (A) wears
a long-sleeved mail *hauberk*, while at least one of his compatriots seems
to have a helmet with a rectangular neckguard (B) such as those seen
in late 12th and early 13th-century Iran. The victorious Christian
knight (C) has a conical helmet with a forward-angled crown and a
large, flat-topped kite-shaped shield.

308A–D **Wall-painting, County of Auvergne, c.1150**
(*in situ* Cathedral, Le Puy, France)

Four round shields placed in the hands of 'infidels'. Their decorations
are remarkably similar to those seen in Islamic art and may
ultimately have been copied from war-souvenirs brought home by
returning Crusaders.

309A–H **Wall-painting, County of Angoulême, mid-12th century**
(*in situ* ex-Templar church [now Protestant Church],
Cressac, France)

The splendidly preserved wall-paintings at Cressac may, at least in
part, illustrate Templar knights and the followers of the brother of
the Count of Angoulême, participating in the defeat of Nūr al-Dîn in
1163. On this occasion the Christian army was a united force of local
Crusaders from Tripoli and Antioch, pilgrims from the Lusignan and
Angoulême area of France, and Byzantine troops under Constantine
Coloman. The Byzantines took a leading and particularly effective
role in the battle, which could make a more detailed study of the
paintings at Cressac worthwhile. The pictures are in two distinct
styles. Those along one register (A–E) are in a somewhat
impressionistic and not very detailed hand, those along another
register (F and G) being both more normal in style and easier to
interpret. The typical mid- to late 12th-century painting (F–H)
shows Christian warriors in tall domed helmets with substantial
nasals, one of which seems to even cover the wearer's chin (F). They
have long-sleeved *hauberks* without *mittens*, worn over fashionably
long tunics. Their large kite-shaped shields have flat (G and H) or
rounded tops (F), and in combat their lances are clearly couched
(H). The second distinct style includes probable Turks in flight
carrying round shields (B). But it is the other figures in this second
picture who pose some problems. They are probably mostly
Christians and their shields are large and either kite shaped (D) or
almost triangular with sharp corners (A, C and D). This could

indicate a later date for the picture. The helmets are pointed (A and C), and though many are partially obscured by the edge of the painting, most have *nasals* (A, C, D and E). Some helmets even have swept-back crowns.

310 *La Charité Psalter*, Counties of Bourg or Nevers, end of 12th century
(British Library, Ms. 2895, f.51b, London, England)

Here Goliath is shown with simple military equipment. This is not, however, necessarily old-fashioned, as many warriors, infantrymen and sergeants as well as some knights, still used relatively short-hemmed, short-sleeved mail *hauberks*. His helmet is quite tall and rounded with a *nasal*. Such a style seems to have been as popular as the conical type in many parts of late 12th-century Europe. His large kite-shaped shield may hang from a *guige* though the decorated strap across his chest might be part of a *baldric* for a sword.

311A–G *The Souvigny Bible*, Counties of Bourg or Nevers, late 12th century
(Bib. Munic., Moulins, France)

A–D – David armed by Saul; E–G – Goliath and the Philistines. The extraordinary illuminations in the *Souvigny Bible* are in a westernised Byzantine style. If it is an almost direct copy of a lost Byzantine original then it could shed light on Byzantine equipment of the day. Setting aside the conventionalised and almost certainly unrealistic *cuirasses* (C, D and G), the manuscript includes a normal mail *hauberk* with an integral *coif* (B) and helmets with extended neckguards (C, D and E–G), a few of which have some kind of stylised *aventail*.

312 Seal of Roger IV, Count of Foix, County of Foix, 1241
(Archives Nationales, Paris, France)

This simple and rather worn seal shows a flat-topped *great helm*, perhaps with a small crest attached, the raised shoulders of a probably padded *gambeson* worn beneath a *surcoat*, a straight non-tapering and again blunt-tipped sword with an enormous *pommel*, and a very wide shield with a flat top and a rounded base. The count's horse is also covered by a *caparison*.

313 Unidentified effigy, Pout, c.1250–75
(Musée Antiquaries de l'Ouest, Poitiers, France)

This otherwise typical mid-13th century effigy is interesting because it includes an extreme example of the raised shoulders of an otherwise ordinary *surcoat*. There can be little doubt that such an outline indicates either substantial padding or some form of semi-rigid *cuirass* or shoulder protection worn beneath the *surcoat* but over the mail *hauberk*.

314A–B Wall-painting (now lost?), church of St John the Baptist in the Château Gontier, Duchy of Guienne, 1250–1300
(from Service des Monuments Historiques, Paris, France)

Two distinct forms of helmet were shown in the wall-paintings of the Château Gontier. These included a very tall domed type (A), perhaps of segmented construction that was more typical of Germany than of France. A second form, worn probably by a member of Pharaoh's army (B), may be a crudely-drawn wide-brimmed *chapel-de-fer*, or it might indicate a conical *spangenhelm* with something wound decoratively around it.

315A–E 'Roman de Tristan et Iseult', wall-paintings, County of Auvergne, mid/late 14th century
(*in situ* ex-Templar Chapel in the castle, St Floret, France)

These provincial but vigorous wall-paintings have sometimes been described as early 15th century. If this is so then the arms and armour worn by the Arthurian knights are remarkably old-fashioned. Helmets are the last form of pointed *great helm* before such helmets were abandoned in favour of *bascinets*. One might have a movable visor (C). Elsewhere actual *bascinets* may be shown (B and E). Splinted arm defences (A and E) with plated elbow protections (A–C and E) and possibly mail *gauntlets* (B, C and E) are all in 14th-century style. Body armour is hidden by relatively tight-fitting *surcoats*, but legs are fully plated with *poleyns*, *greaves* and *sabatons*. Swords are typical of the mid- or late 14th century and spears are the only other weapons shown. Some horses wear *caparisons* but there is no evidence to indicate that these were protective *bards* (A, B and D).

Notes

1. D. Bates, *Normandy before 1066* (London, 1982), pp.52–3.
2. A.R. Lewis, *The Development of Southern French and Catalan Society, 718–1050* (Austin, 1965), pp.382–3.
3. R.P.R. Noel, *Town Defences in the French Midi during the Hundred Years War, c.1337–1453* (Ph.D. thesis, Edinburgh University, 1977), pp.231–2.
4. P. Contamine, *La Guerre au Moyen Age* (Paris, 1980), p.206.
5. A.B. De Hoffmeyer, *Arms and Armour in Spain: A Short Survey*, vol.II (Madrid, 1982), p.73.
6. Noel, *op.cit.* pp.97, 100–2, 110, 115–19, 132, 143–7, 170–1 and 176.

Chapter 6

Aragón, Navarre and Catalonia

The string of tiny states that emerged on the southern slopes of the Pyrenean mountains in what had been the old Carolingian Spanish March were different from the Iberian kingdoms to the west in several ways. The first to play a major role was Navarre. By the mid-11th century it had, in fact, reached its ultimate frontiers by capturing the Muslim city of Tudela in 1046. Thereafter Navarre's military efforts were aimed at assisting other Christian states beyond its frontiers and in preserving its independence from these same Christian neighbours.

By the beginning of the 12th century the Kingdom of Aragón already existed in what had been the western part of the French County of Barcelona. Unlike Navarre, Aragón continued to drive southwards after achieving a common frontier with Castile in 1118. A century later Aragón completed its part of the Spanish *Reconquista* by seizing the Balearic Islands (1229–35) and the Denia peninsula (1248). This, plus Aragón's absorption of Catalonia in 1162, led the Aragónese to turn their attention seaward. As a result they soon came to rival the French House of Anjou for control of Sicily and southern Italy.

In the first half of the 11th century Catalonia was divided into no less than eight counties, all theoretically under the French Crown. By the time of the First Crusade these had largely united to take part in the *Reconquista* by pushing south as far as Tortosa in 1148. Thereafter Catalan military history was linked to that of the Kingdom of Aragón. Generally speaking, all these sub-Pyrenean states were under increasing southern French military influence from the 11th century onwards.[1] Nevertheless, there were clear differences between these various regions. Navarre, being almost entirely a land of mountains and valleys and never breaking out into the great plains of central Iberia, remained an infantry area.[2] Navarrese javelin-armed infantry were, however, highly regarded, and were employed as mercenaries in many parts of 12th-century Western Europe. The same was true of the neighbouring and militarily similar Basques[3] and Gascons,[4] though the latter often used bows instead of javelins. Navarrese infantry were still in demand during the 14th century,[5] at which time the Kingdom of Navarre was itself employing Muslim troops, possibly from the Tudela area and probably serving as light cavalry in the style known as *a la jineta*.[6]

In Aragón, light cavalry soon played a major role as the kingdom spread across the Ebro plain.[7] Meanwhile, most Aragónese mercenaries outside the Iberian peninsula still seem to have been infantry.[8] The most famous and characteristic of such Aragónese troops were the *almogavers* (Arabic *al-mughāwir*, 'raiders'). These light infantrymen specialised in guerrilla warfare and rapid manoeuvre.[9]

Very similar military traditions evolved in Catalonia following a wave of strong Islamic influence in the 10th century.[10] Catalan cavalry still served as mercenaries in Muslim *Murābiṭ* forces in the early 12th century,[11] but by the 13th century it was crossbowmen who were the most highly-regarded of professional Catalan soldiers.[12] The crossbow was, of course, now the main weapon in Mediterranean naval warfare, a field in which both Catalans and Aragónese were becoming expert.[13] Firearms had yet to take to sea, but as early as 1359 Aragón was using *bombards* in defence of a harbour.[14]

Figures

316A–B **Tomb of Doña Sancha from the Convent of Santa Cruz de la Séros, Aragón, mid-12th century**
(Benedictine Convent, Jaca, Spain)

Originally thought to date from the late 11th century, this carved sarcophagus is now considered mid-12th century. It portrays two horsemen in combat, both identically equipped although one (A) may represent a moustached 'Moor'. The other figure (B) holds his lance tightly couched beneath his arm and also has a straight, tapering sword. The lack of armour on both figures is noteworthy.

317 **Carved capital from the Spanish or French Pyrenees, late 11th/early 12th centuries**
(Metropolitan Museum of Art, no.21.21.2, New York, United States)

This carving includes one of the earliest representations of a winged or flanged mace in European art, probably indicating Andalusian influence.

318 **Carved capital, Aragón, c.1110**
(*in situ* Cathedral, Jaca, Spain)

The story of 'Balaam and the Angel'. The sword has clearly down-curved *quillons* and a large round *pommel*.

319A–B ***Beatus Commentaries on the Apocalypse*, Spain, 1086**
(Cathedral Library, Burgo de Osma, Spain)

A – Sword of Nebuchadnezzar; B – Sword of a Horseman of the Apocalypse. Nebuchadnezzar's sword (A) is essentially the same as that on the carved capital in Jaca Cathedral (fig.318), having down-turned *quillons* and a massive round *pommel*. The crossbow (B) is interesting for a number of reasons. The bow is painted blue and although weapons having steel bows are unknown for several more centuries it is possible that either an artist imagined such a device in the late 11th century, or the advanced metallurgy of Islamic al-Andalus made experimentation with a steel crossbow stave possible. The crossbow has a shorter stock than most early crossbows (as would also be characteristic of late-medieval steel-armed crossbows) and lacks a stirrup in which an archer might put his foot. This form was spanned or drawn back by placing the feet on the arms of the bow itself. The artist also shows the arrow or bolt without feathered flights, which makes it the same as those used with the late-Roman crossbow and some late 12th/early 13th century Middle Eastern crossbows.

320A–B 'Spears of Castor and Pollux', astrological treatise from Santa Maria de Ripoll, Catalonia, 11th century
(Vatican Library, Reg. Lat. 123, f.177, Rome, Italy)

Here two otherwise identical spears are distinguished by their sockets. One has a bulge at the base in Bedouin Arab style (A) while the other does not.

321A–AH Roda Bible, Catalonia, 11th century
(Bib. Nat., Ms. Lat. 6, Paris, France)

A–G – Siege of a city; H–I – f.83r; J–L – f.134r; M–N – f.144r; O–P – f.?; Q–T – Death of Saul, f.21; U – f.?; V – Death of Saul, f.21; W – Defeat of Sisera, f.99v; X–Y – Babylonians besiege Jerusalem, f.145; Z – The attack on Bathzakaras, f.145; AA–AC – The attack on the Sabbath, f.144; AD – The expedition of Holofernes, f.134; AE–AG – The attack on Bathzakaras, f.145; AH – Defeat of Israel, vol.III f.5. Two extremely important 11th-century manuscripts survive from Catalonia: the *Roda Bible* and the *Farfa Bible*. One feature that has drawn the attention of armour scholars to these manuscripts is that they seem to show rectangular shapes on the breasts of normal mail *hauberks* (P, U, V, W, Z, AA and AG). This is otherwise only seen in the 11th-century Anglo-Norman Bayeux Tapestry and a handful of other isolated illustrations. Here, however, they almost certainly represent unlaced mail *ventails* that hang below the wearers' chins. Such unlaced *ventails* are frequently shown in 12th-century sources, and the square outline of those in the Catalan Bibles might indicate either that they were a new feature with which the artists were not fully familiar, or that early forms of unlaced *ventail* from the 11th century did tend to fall into a roughly rectangular shape rather than into the triangular shape seen in the fully developed 12th-century version. The figure of Judas Maccabbeus or perhaps King Eupator (Z) has sometimes been interpreted as wearing a *coat of scales*. This is unlikely in the 11th century and may simply be the manuscript artist's attempt to make this important figure more splendid. Most helmets appear to be of segmented construction (B, C, E, F, H, L, N, U, Y, Z, AA, AE and AG), either of two pieces joined along the comb in sub-Roman style or true *spangenhelms* with the segments fastened to a frame. One-piece helmets might also appear (G, I, P, R, V, W and AH). Some helmets have *nasals* (H, N, P, Q, S, U, W, AA, AE and AG) but most do not. Some even appear to have extended neckguards (AE and AG), while others are shown with brims or partial brims like *chapel-de-fer war-hats* or even early *salets* (G and Z). One helmet might include a rudimentary representation of the decorative brow plate seen in later Andalusian helmets (S). The manuscript clearly reflects a period of experiment and change before the almost universal adoption of conical one-piece helmets with *nasals* in the late 11th and 12th centuries. The traditions and influences seen in the helmets of this transitional period seem to include late-Roman, north European, Islamic, and perhaps even Byzantine elements, none of which should be surprising given Catalonia's geographical and political position. Other features of interest are the variety of shields, which range from the large convex round forms for cavalry (H and I) to smaller round ones for infantry (P and AH). The whole early history of the kite-shaped shield seems to be illustrated in this one manuscript, from almost oval forms (L and V), through round-based kite-shaped types (J) to the fully kite-shaped variety for both horsemen and foot-soldiers (G, N, Y, Z, AA and AG). Apart from spears, mostly with wings or flanges, and swords with straight, curved and down-turned *quillons*, round, nut and a remarkable bar-like (AC) *pommel*, the *Roda Bible* includes other interesting weapons. Large staff-slings are shown no less than three times (F, K and AD). Such weapons were used in siege or naval warfare and should be seen in the context of other beam-sling devices, from the smallest man-powered *mangonel* to the largest counterweight *trebuchet*. Almost as surprising are the differently shaped long-hafted axes. The simpler types have similarities with Northern European war-axes (L, T and AB), but a second variety (D and X) has a half-moon blade and a long sleeve down the haft. It seems to be connected with the *ṭabarzîn* war-axes of Iran and the Middle East.

322A–M *Farfa Bible*, **Catalonia, 11th century** (**Vatican Library, Cod. Lat. 5729, Rome, Italy**)

A – Pharaoh's Guard, f.6v; B – Defeat of the Amalekites, f.94v; C–D – Pharaoh's army, f.82; E – Army of Nebuchadnezzar, f.227; F – Holofernes, f.327; G–K – Battle of Bethhoron, f.342; L–M – Battle against Nicanor, f.235. The *Farfa Bible*, though in much the same style as the *Roda Bible*, is stylistically freer and includes more obvious references to Muslim or specifically North African costume. It may, in fact, be a slightly later manuscript, the clearer Islamic elements resulting from the *Murābiṭ* invasion of al-Andalus in the late 11th century. It is worth noting that all 'wicked' figures are dressed to some degree in the more obviously Islamic costume. Pharaoh's guard (A) has his sword slung in a manner not unlike that of southern France, while the defeated Amalekites (B) and Holofernes, captain of the army of Assur, are European in their equipment to the extent of even having unlaced mail *ventails*. Only Holofernes' mace-like weapon sets him apart. His slightly forward-angled conical helmet is a bit of an enigma, further suggesting a late 11th or even early 12th century date for the manuscript. On the other hand the *Roda Bible* could indicate that this form originated in the Mediterranean area, in Spain, Provence, Italy or even al-Andalus. Elsewhere in the *Farfa Bible* turbaned figures are associated with men wearing very tall hats, helmets or headcloths (E and H). These may be garbled versions of the face-covering fashions of the original Saharan *Murābiṭīn*.

323A–E *Beatus Commentaries on the Apocalypse of King Sancho of Navarre*, Mozarab, 11th century
(Biblioteca Nacional, Madrid, Spain)

The *Beatus of King Sancho* is one of the most stylised of *Mozarab* manuscripts, yet it still illustrates a number of identifiable pieces of military equipment. Here the Babylonians are perhaps shown in Andalusian costume. They seem to wear small turbans, and tunics that have buttons or toggles down the front. They are armed with spears or bows, while two figures appear to be throwing rocks (A and B). Shields are small and, in the case of the horse-archer (E), can be hung on the front of the saddle or from the horse's breast strap.

324 'Demon', painted panel from the apse of Sant Quirze de Pedret, Catalonia, 1075–1100
(Diocesan Museum, Solsona, Spain)

This damaged painting might show a javelin with arrow-like flights at the rear end. Such weapons seem to be mentioned in written sources and are shown in 14th or 15th century Egyptian manuscripts but do not appear elsewhere in 11th or 12th century European art.

325 'St Martin and the Beggar', painted altar front from Puigbo, Catalonia, late 11th/early 12th centuries
(Diocesan Museum, Vich, Spain)

Once again a horseman with a spear, sword and kite-shaped shield of otherwise European style wears no apparent armour. This could indicate that a large number of northern Spanish and southern French cavalrymen chose not to wear, or could not afford, expensive mail armour. Or it could be evidence that they, like their Muslim opposite numbers in al-Andalus, North Africa and the Middle East, often chose to hide their armour under another garment.

326A–I Carved doorway, San Miguel de Uncastillo, Aragón, 12th century
(Museum of Fine Arts, no.28.32, Boston, United States)

This beautifully carved arch may be responsible for one of the greatest popular fallacies in arms and armour, one that Hollywood continues to perpetuate despite massive evidence to the contrary. Namely that the 'ball and chain' was a typical knightly weapon. The doorway from San Miguel de Uncastillo includes one of a small number of representations of this device which is here shown in association with an apparent crowbar (H). Both were probably wall-breaking or demolition tools rather than weapons. Other true weapons carved on the doorway are tapering straight swords (B and G), one having *quillons* with slightly down-turned tips, a curved knife or dagger (A), a bull-headed mace (C), two bows of apparently simple construction

(E and F), and a spear with a very broad leaf-shaped blade. The persistence of such broad spearheads may reflect Arab influence and the use of light cavalry tactics *a la jineta*. Similar spears also appear around the same date on the 'Triumph' arch in Ripoll (next figure).

327A–J Arch of the Triumph of Christianity, Catalonia, c.1150 (*in situ* Monastery of Santa Maria, Ripoll, Spain)

A–B – Battle against the Amalekites; C–E – Joshua fights the Amalekites; F – Battle against the Amalekites; G – Guards of Gad; H – Imprisonment of Paul; I – Saul incites the Jews; J – Spear of David. The splendidly carved Arch of the Triumph of Christianity provides some of the most convincing evidence that on the battlefield Spanish Christians and Muslim Andalusians – though not North African Berber newcomers – looked almost identical. Here no distinction is drawn between Jews and Amalekites except, perhaps, for some of the latter having cloths wound around their helmets (E). Most horsemen carry long oval or kite-shaped shields (A and C–E) and have mail *hauberks*. It is also interesting that while the presumed Jews (A, C and D) have short-sleeved *hauberks*, it is their Amalekite foes (B and possibly F) who wear the heavier, long-sleeved styles. Spears are generally broad-bladed, sometimes very broad, and are not shown couched beneath the arm. A single club is shown (I) and swords are of the broad, non-tapering, essentially Mediterranean or Arab form. Infantry carry small round shields (F–H) while horsemen and perhaps dismounted armoured cavalry (A–E and F) have long shields. The helmets are the most interesting feature of all. One seems to be a standard conical type with a *nasal* (E). Though damaged, another has what looks like a face-mask built around a broad *nasal* (A). Most remarkable is the third helmet, with a clear extension to protect the neck (B). A fourth helmet worn by a warrior in the back row of a group of men on foot (F) may be of segmented construction.

328 'Moor fighting Faragut', carved capital, Catalonia, late 12th/early 13th centuries (*in situ* Cathedral Cloisters, Tarragona, Spain)

In contrast to the Castilian illustrations of the Faragut story in Estella and Salamanca, the 'Moorish' champion is here shown without armour, with a round shield and perhaps a rudimentary turban. This might be more accurate and could reflect the proximity of Islamic Valencia and the Balearic Islands.

329A–B Carvings, Navarre, c.1155 (*in situ* south door, Santa Maria la Real, Sangüesa, Spain)

Though crudely and simply carved, these little figures are amongst the clearest representations of a helmet with a fixed visor or oversized nasal. The bowl of the helmet also extends some way down the backs of the wearers' necks.

330A–D Carved capitals, frontier of Castile and Aragón, mid-12th century
(*in situ* Cloisters of the Colegiata de San Pedro, Soria, Spain)

The carvings in San Pedro, Soria, have some features in common with *Mozarab* art, and the weapons they portray also include various Andalusian characteristics. The bow (A and B) is, however, of apparently simple rather than composite construction. The sword (C) is of the blunt-ended non-tapering type and even seems to have a form of *langet* from the *quillons* down the blade. The style of another figure (D) recalls small huntsmen on carved ivory boxes from Cuenca a short distance to the south. Both Soria and Cuenca lay in the mountainous region between Castile and Aragón and both retained large, culturally influential Muslim communities throughout the Middle Ages.

331 Carved tympanum, Aragón, late 12th century
(*in situ* west door, Ermita Santiago, Agüero, Spain)

By the late 12th century representations of winged or flanged maces had become quite realistic, but such weapons were still more widespread in the Iberian peninsula than in most other parts of Western Europe.

332 *Homilies of St Augustine*, Aragón, 12th century
(Archivo de la Corona de Aragón, Barcelona, Spain)

A great many Spanish sources portray swords with curved or down-turned *quillons*, but this picture has a more delicately-drawn representation of such a weapon . The slender *quillons* on this sword are probably much closer to reality than the chunky *quillons* seen in most other sources.

333 'Martyrdom of St Thomas of Canterbury and the monk Edward Grim', wall-painting, Catalonia, c.1175–1200
(*in situ* Church of Santa Maria, Egara-Tarrasa, Spain)

Here an artist has chosen to show the saint and monk being slain by a curved sword. The weapon is inaccurately drawn and the artist must have known that St Thomas was martyred in England. Presumably, therefore, he chose to include a curved weapon for symbolic reasons, such swords having already become associated with the 'wicked', with 'pagans' and with Muslims. The association seems to have been based on verbal tradition or written sources as the artist did not base the weapon on a realistic sabre. As sabres were not normally used by the Muslims of al-Andalus or the Maghrib the idea must have reached Catalonia from the Middle East, probably via the Crusades.

334A–B Goliath, wall-painting from Santa Maria de Tahull, Catalonia, c.1123
(Museum of Ancient Art, Barcelona, Spain)

The somewhat archaic wall-paintings from Tahull illustrate Goliath in a style of *hauberk* that is more common in Northern Europe than in the south. This type has a slit at the side through which the hilt of a sword and the top of a scabbard protrude. These were in turn hung from a belt or a *baldric* beneath the *hauberk*.

335A–C Wall-paintings from the Ermita de San Baudilio, Berlanga, Aragón, early 12th century
(Prado Museum, Madrid, Spain)

The late *Mozarab*-Romanesque paintings from Berlanga reflect the mixed culture of an area which was, at the start of the 12th century, within a few miles of the Muslim frontier. The huntsmen (A and B), who appear to be monks judging from the tonsure of one and the habit of the other, use a massive crossbow (B) and, almost unique in 12th-century European art, a trident (A). Such a weapon appears later in the art of the Middle East, where it is associated with invaders from Central Asia. Its presence here in Spain is unexplained. A third figure (C) is also something of an enigma, but his weapons are straightforward enough. He carries a broad-bladed spear and a large round shield with tassels hanging from the rivets which hold the *enarmes*. Such tassels would be seen in a Castilian manuscript of a century later and would subsequently become a feature of Islamic Andalusian *adarga* shields.

336 'Horseman of the Apocalypse', Polinya, Catalonia, c.1122
(Diocesan Museum, Barcelona, Spain)

Here a Horseman rides with bare feet and appears to wear baggy trousers, while slaying a man who appears to carry an oval shield. The Horsemen of the Apocalypse were occasionally shown as Muslims in Spanish art and it seems likely that this figure is also dressed as an 'infidel'. Bedouin Arabs rode bareback or with non-metallic loop-stirrups as late as the 11th century, and this picture might reflect either a misunderstood version of this habit or a transitional phase when some poorer tribal horsemen still rode without boots or shoes.

337A–AQ *Bible of King Sancho*, Navarre, 1197
(Bib. Munic., Ms. 108, Amiens, France)

A–B – The Betrayal, f.184r; C – Abraham pursued by his brother's captors; D – Israelites flee to Sucoth, f.46v; E – The army of David fighting Saul, f.99r; F–G – The Betrayal, f.184r; H – Pharaoh's army, f.49r; I – Slaughter of the priests of Baal, f.111v; J – Companion strikes Prophet, f.113v; K–N – Lot and the Sodomites taken prisoner, f.6v; O – Abraham pursued by his brother's captors; P – Lot and the Sodomites taken prisoner, f.6v; Q – Goliath f.86v; R – Death of Simon and Jude, f.211r; S–V – Gog and Magog, f.249v; W – Goliath, f.85v; X – Sacrifice of Isaac, f.12r; Y – Death of Ahab, f.119r; Z – Table knife, Joseph invites his brothers to eat, f.33r; AA – Moses kills an Egyptian, f.40v; AB – Philistines defeat Saul, f.91r; AC–AE – Guards at the Holy Sepulchre, f.193v; AF–AG – Israelites fight Amalekites, f.50v; AH – Saul defeats Amonites, f.82v; AI – Goliath, f.84v; AJ–AK – Guards at the Holy Sepulchre, f.191v; AL – Saul throws a spear at David, f.87v; AM – David cuts the hem of Saul's coat, f.89v; AN – Massacre of the Innocents, f.169v; AO–AQ – Pharaoh's army, f.46v. Though it is not a particularly rich or splendidly decorated manuscript, the illustrated *Bible of King Sancho* is full of interesting details of arms and armour, as well as some unusual features rarely seen elsewhere. Its subjects are probably based upon the Pyrenean warriors of Navarre itself and their Muslim foes of the Upper Ebro valley. Mail *hauberks* and *coifs* are rarely shown (O, P, AE, AN and perhaps AH, AO and AP) which may reflect the relative poverty of Navarre. Nevertheless, two *hauberks* do include mail gloves with individual fingers rather than the mail *mittens* which were themselves still quite rare in the late 12th century. It is, of course, possible that mail *mittens* were so new in Navarre that the artist did not realise that they did not have individual fingers. Some figures who wear this latest form of *hauberk* are also the only ones clearly wearing mail *chausses*. It is remarkable that a figure such as Goliath (Q, W and AI), who is otherwise so fully equipped, should lack a mail *hauberk*. Since he is probably based on a Muslim warrior he might be wearing mail under a tunic or his tunic may itself be lined with mail. Note that in one representation (W) the Philistine giant wears a short-sleeved garment over a tight-fitting, long-sleeved tunic. The outer one might be a form of *kazāghand* or *jubbah*. Helmets are more common than body armour and almost all are conical with a forward-angled crown (Q, W, AE, AH, AO and AP). Most have substantial *nasals*. Shields are varied and little attempt is made to link one shape with any particular group or nation. Large round shields are used by horsemen (H, W, AB, AH and AI) as well as by infantry (AG). An almost oval form is also used by both (S–V and AK). Kite-shaped shields are similarly seen in the hands of various warriors. They include forms with pointed bases, with or without metal reinforcing bands, plus others with more rounded outlines (C, K–N, P, O, AA, AB, AF, AH and AK). Some shields are also decorated with heraldic devices. Swords are broad and generally blunt-tipped, slightly-tapering or non-tapering (O, P, Q, X, AG, AH, AJ and AN). Daggers or short swords of substantial proportions, lacking *quillons* or *pommel*, are shown, a clear distinction being drawn between weapons (I and J) and smaller table knives (Z). Spears are of standard types but an interesting form of javelin also appears (R, AL and AM). This clearly has a grip or lug approximately midway down its haft. A similar but not identical grip is shown on a spear or javelin in an early 13th-century Sicilian source. Other weapons seen in the *Bible of King Sancho* are a wooden club (AA), a spherical-headed mace (L), two narrow-bladed axes with spikes at the back (A and B), and an unclear weapon or agricultural tool with a curved blade and hook. Since most of these unusual weapons are seen in the illustration of the Betrayal they should be treated with some caution, as the Betrayal traditionally incorporated an exotic variety of weapons in Byzantine, Romanesque and even Gothic illustrations. If any reality is to be found in such pictures it is probably that of the varied, sometimes home-made, weaponry of a peasant levy despised by the aristocratic warrior elite.

338 *Usatges de Berenguar I*, Catalonia, late 12th century (Library, Monastery of San Lorenzo de Escorial, Spain)

Here an unarmoured 'Moor' is slain by Berenguar. Though crudely drawn, the Moor clearly wears a turban, carries a kidney-shaped *adarga* shield with tassels, and wields a straight sword that would be carried in a scabbard hung on a *baldric*.

339A–F *Beatus Commentaries on the Apocalypse*, Catalonia, 1190–1225 (Bib. Nat., Nouv. Acq. Lat. 2290, Paris, France)

A–B – f.106v; C – f.141; D–F – f.106v. This manuscript is believed to have been made in northern Spain, probably Catalonia, and most of the military equipment that it illustrates is relatively straightforward. This includes long-sleeved mail *hauberks* (A–B and F), round and conical helmets with and without *nasals* (A, B, D and E), flat-topped shields (A, B and D), straight swords (A, B and F), a war-axe (E) and two apparent wall-breaking pickaxes (A and B). Two knobbed or spiked maces are also shown (C and D), but most interest focuses on a figure with an early form of *great helm* (D) with what appears to be a single eye-slit. The figure also seems to wear another form of armour over his mail *hauberk*. This could be interpreted as a sleeveless padded *gambeson*, but this is unlikely to have been worn over a long-sleeved mail *hauberk*. Instead it seems more likely to be a very early representation of a scale-lined or splint-lined *coat-of-plates*. Note the form of lacing or buckles which appears under the right arm. If it is indeed a *coat-of-plates* then its appearance in Catalonia could be significant. Such a style might have come from north of the Pyrenees, but there is little evidence for *coats-of-plates* in France at this time. It could be a result of Catalonian trade and cultural contacts around the Mediterranean, although such contacts were more characteristic of 13th-century Catalonian history. This leaves the possibility of direct influence from Muslim al-Andalus, where the similar lamellar *jawshan* was known though not apparently widespread. In the absence of further evidence this possibly precocious appearance of a *coat-of-plates* in north-eastern Spain remains a mystery.

340A–B 'Martyrdom of Santa Lucia', painted panel, Catalonia, late 13th century
(Bosch Collection, Barcelona, Spain)

No obvious 'Moorish' features have been given to the soldiers slaying Santa Lucia, despite their being among the 'wicked', unless the hanging of a sword on a *baldric* indicated such an association. One figure is quite straightforward, although he is interesting because he wears a mail *coif* that is now separate from the *hauberk* (A). The second figure also has a mail *coif* but no apparent *hauberk*. Could his tunic be a mail-lined *kazāghand* or *jubbah* such as that believed to have been worn by some Andalusian soldiers? The series of triple dots on the garment are probably decorative but could indicate stitches to hold some inner reinforcement.

341 'Arrest of Santiago', wall-painting, Aragón, early/mid-13th century
(*in situ* Ermita San Juan, Uncastillo, Spain)

The mail *coif* is an odd shape which might indicate a skull cap or *cervellière* worn beneath. The short-hafted axe is remarkably Northern European in form, but the kilt that the man seems to wear over his mail *hauberk* is unlike anything seen this far west. Instead it recalls certain Middle Eastern fashions.

342A–B 'Muslim troops in Valencia', wall-painting, Aragón, late 13th/early 14th centuries
(*in situ* Castle, Alcañiz, Spain)

Relatively few Spanish wall-paintings specifically illustrate Muslim Andalusian warriors. Here, however, the garrison of Valencia is seen surrendering to James I, King of Aragón, in 1238. They are shown wearing conical helmets and mail *coifs*, one of which (B) covers most of the face. This figure might also wear some stylised form of lamellar or scale *cuirass*.

343 'Herod's soldiers', stone *retable*, probably Catalonia, c.1320
(Museum of Fine Arts, no.24.249, Boston, United States)

A small and damaged carving portraying warriors in mail *coifs* and close-fitting *cervellière* helmets, one of the latter having a broad decorative rim.

344 Ceramic plate from Paterna, *Mudejar*, Aragón, c.1300
(González Marti Ceramic Museum, Valencia, Spain)

On this plate made by a potter from a *Mudejar* or Muslim Andalusian community under Spanish rule, a member of the De Luna family, lords of Paterna, again uses his spear overarm. Another interesting feature is the horse's *caparison*, which only includes the rear part covering the animal's rump. Presumably such half *caparisons*, which are seen elsewhere in 14th-century Spain, were purely heraldic and included no protective layer.

345A–B Painted wooden panel, Barcelona, Catalonia, c.1300
(Museum of Ancient Art, Barcelona, Spain)

On this panel a Christian knight (A) and a 'Moor' (B) are in combat. The former has normal European arms and armour, a painted round helmet with a *nasal*, a mail *hauberk* with *coif* and *mittens*, mail *chausses*, and a large, flat-topped shield. His horse wears a *caparison* made in two pieces divided by the saddle. The only unusual feature is his manner of using a spear, which is here thrust overarm in a light cavalry manner *a la jineta*. His turbaned Muslim opponent similarly wears a mid- or long-sleeved mail *hauberk* beneath his tunic, though this lacks a *coif* or *mittens*. He also has mail *chausses* on his legs, while his shield is of a form that suggests a variation of *adarga*.

346 Wall-painting, Catalonia, late 13th century
(Museo de Historia de la Ciudad, Barcelona, Spain)

Here three crossbowmen carry early forms of the weapon with long bow-staves of apparently simple construction and no loading stirrups. The short crossbow bolts are held in quivers attached to their belts. One man seems to carry a dagger (A) as well as a sword, while another clearly has a sword at his belt (C). No mail is shown but the raised and broad collars worn by at least two of the men (B and C) indicate a kind of stiffly-padded soft armour which is more clearly illustrated in the slightly earlier French *Maciejowski Bible*. One man seems to have a *coif* (A) though this need not have been a form of armour. The second (B) has a similar and apparently padded *coif*, while the third wears a small round helmet (C) with a substantial *nasal* over a *coif* or *arming cap*.

347A–F 'Conquest of Majorca by James I of Aragón', wall-painting, Catalonia, late 13th century
(Museo de Artes de Cataluña, Barcelona, Spain)

A – Islamic flag; B–E – Islamic garrison and army of Majorca; F – Aragónese warriors. Various details indicate that this wall-painting provides an accurate representation of both Islamic and Christian troops. The latter is only to be expected but the reliability of the pictures of the 'Moors' is strongly suggested by the inclusion of the 'Hand of Fatima' as a totemic device on one shield (D) and by the form of three Islamic flags (A and E) which correspond to surviving specimens from the 13th century. In fact, the 'Moors' are more varied in their equipment than might at first appear. Their shields are round and small or middle-sized rather than being the expected kidney-shaped *adargas*. Foot-soldiers are unarmoured and use sword and buckler (D), staff-sling (C), or spear and buckler (B). The sword-armed cavalry are, however, almost as heavily armoured as their

Christian foes, having long-sleeved mail *hauberks* with *mittens*, and mail *chausses* beneath their tunics. The only major difference between such horsemen and the knights of Aragón is that the latter wear mail *coifs* and round helmets with or without *nasals* (F). Their short-sleeved *surcoats* may be padded or even be lined with some form of metal armour, a possibility suggested but not proved by the fact that heraldic devices are repeated on the sleeves but not on the chests and skirts of these garments. Instead, the body of the *surcoat* is marked with rows or circles of dots which could indicate stitching or even small rivets.

348 'Vilardell and the Dragon', carved relief, Catalonia, 1329
(*in situ* north door, Cathedral, Barcelona, Spain

The Catalan folk hero Vilardell slays the dragon before raising his sword in triumph and dying from the beast's poisonous blood which drips from his blade. Since the story is essentially concerned with the sin of vainglory, the knight is shown in the best and most up-to-date equipment. He wears a long-sleeved mail *hauberk* which now clearly includes mail gloves with individual fingers. His *coif* is a separate piece of mail and is worn beneath a wide-brimmed *chapel-de-fer war-hat*. The shape of his perhaps damaged scabbard suggests a single-edged sword, but there is no indication of this in the weapon itself. Vilardell also has a half-round *rerebrace* on his upper arm and perhaps a half-round *vambrace* on his lower arm, plus *roundels* on his elbows and shoulders. He wears full *greaves* on his legs and laminated *sabatons* on his feet.

349 Effigy of Ugo de Cervellon, Catalonia, c.1335
(*in situ* Basilica of Santa Maria, Villafranca del Panadés, Spain)

A fine carving showing a broad war-sword in the normal European style. The way of supporting the scabbard is, however, not the usual system seen in 14th-century Europe. The rings and decorated metal bands around the scabbard are similar to the Arab system as seen both in Granada and in the Middle East.

350 Carved gargoyle, Catalonia, early 14th century
(*in situ* exterior of apse, Cathedral, Barcelona, Spain)

A little-known carving portraying a horseman in typical Catalan equipment. By northern French standards he would be relatively lightly armoured, but history shows that Catalan light cavalry were well able to cope with northern foes. This man wears a brimmed *war-hat* of a type that would later evolve into the typical 15th-century Spanish *cabacete*. He probably has a mail *hauberk* without *mittens*, a large flat-topped shield, and a heavy sword whose hilt is visible above his saddle. In his right hand he may originally have held a spear.

351 **Effigy of a member of the Cardona family, Catalonia, c.1330**

(*in situ* Montserrat Monastery, Barcelona, Spain)

This interesting effigy well illustrates the differences between Spanish and northern French military equipment of the period. The man's sword is hung in a rather unusual manner and he is relatively lightly armoured. Beneath a long-sleeved but unpadded *surcoat* we wears a mail *hauberk*. His head is covered with a mail *coif* and he also has mail *chausses*, which are visible at his feet. *Greaves* of a rather simple form, perhaps of hardened leather as seen in early 14th-century Italy, cover his legs.

352 **Effigy of a member of the Castellet family, Catalonia, c.1330**

(*in situ* Basilica of Santa Maria, Villafranca del Panadés, Spain)

The similarity between this effigy and the Christian warriors shown on the wall-painting of 'The Conquest of Majorca by James I' (fig.347) is clear; the most obvious parallel being the padded or lined *surcoats* with mid-length sleeves and decorated with heraldic devices. By 1330, however, the Catalan knight wears plated *gauntlets* and apparently plated *greaves*.

353 **Effigy of Bernado de Minoris, Catalonia, c.1330**

(*in situ* Church of Santa Maria de la Seo, Manresa, Spain)

In contrast to the preceding similarly-dated effigy, that of Bernardo de Minoris wears the latest European arms and armour. In fact he seems to have more in common with the knights of eastern France and Germany than with his Spanish compatriots. His *coif* is worn over a padded *arming cap*, giving it an almost square outline so as to support a flat-topped *great helm*. He has no plate armour on his arms, and the only indication that he might wear anything other than a mail *hauberk* is the fact that there is another garment, perhaps a *coat-of-plates*, under his *surcoat*. This is visible where the *surcoat* is slit at the sides. He has *greaves* on his legs and laminated though rudimentary *sabatons* over his mailed feet. He holds a very large sword, while at his side a substantial *basilard* dagger hangs by thongs from a belt under his *surcoat*.

354A–E **Effigy of Don Alvaro de Cabrera the Younger from the Church of Santa Maria de Bellpuig de las Avellanas, Lérida, Catalonia, mid-14th century**

(Cloisters Museum, Metropolitan Museum of Art, New York, United States)

Again, a number of distinctive features seen in 14th-century Spanish, Italian and perhaps Byzantine-Balkan arms and armour appear here. The most obvious is the raised *bevor* to protect the neck (B–D). Here it is shown attached to a collar around the shoulders. The collar is decorated with the same flower motif that appears on the upper part of the tunic or *surcoat* and on the feet (C–E). In all cases it almost certainly indicates some kind of metallic or hardened leather lining consisting of scales, laminae or splints. On the man's body the pattern probably indicates a local version of the *coat-of-plates*. This effigy also wears a mail *coif* (B–D), which appears to have a small rectangular medallion on the brow (B). Other features of interest include *gauntlets* with remarkably long arm pieces (A, C and D) which, to all intents and purposes, serve as *vambraces*. Although these elongated *gauntlets* seem to be of metal, such a substance would have made it virtually impossible for the wearer to flex his wrists, so perhaps this part of the *gauntlet* was of semi-stiff leather or even flexible buff-leather. The *greaves* (D–E) are hinged and probably pinned or buckled, thus almost certainly being of iron. The *sabatons* (D–E) may have been of laminae or scales, the rivets forming a floral pattern comparable to that of the probable *coat-of-plates*.

355 Effigy of Roderigo de Rebolledo, Catalonia, early/mid-14th century
(*in situ* Monastery of Santa Maria de Poblet, Lérida, Spain)

The similarity between this effigy and others in Spain from the same period is obvious. The man's head is damaged, but he probably wore only a cloth *coif*. Around his neck is a raised rigid *bevor* of a type also seen in 14th-century Italian art. It may be attached to the triangular chest piece which covers his shoulders and comes to a point above his solar plexus. This triangular object is richly decorated, as are the sleeves of his *surcoat* or tunic, though in a different pattern. The mail *mittens* form integral parts of an otherwise hidden *hauberk*. Iron or leather *greaves* may be worn on the legs, though this is far from clear.

Notes

1. J. Beeler, *Warfare in Feudal Europe, 730–1200* (Ithaca, 1971), p.158
2. Beeler, *op.cit.* p.165.
3. J.F. Verbruggen, *The Art of Warfare in Western Europe during the Middle Ages* (Oxford, 1977), pp.119–21; C. Oman, *A History of the Art of Warfare in the Middle Ages*, vol.I (London, 1924), p.379.
4. M.J. Swanton, *The Spear in Anglo-Saxon Times* (Ph.D. thesis, Durham University, 1966), p.570.
5. P. Contamine, *La Guerre au Moyan Age* (Paris, 1980), p.251.
6. P.F. Russell, *The English Intervention in Spain and Portugal in the Time of Edward III and Richard II* (Oxford, 1955), pp.262–4.
7. Beeler, *op.cit.* p.166; Contamine, *op.cit.* p.165; Russell, *op.cit.* pp.128–9.
8. Verbruggen, *loc.cit.*

9. Contamine, *op.cit.* p.168.
10. A.R. Lewis, *The Development of Southern French and Catalan Society, 718–1050* (Austin, 1965), p.191.
11. E. Lévi-Provençal, *Histoire de l'Espagne Musulmane* (Paris, 1950–67), pp.71–6.
12. Contamine, *op.cit.* p.206.
13. C.-E. Dufourcq, *L'Espagne Catalane et le Maghrib aux XIIIe et XIVe Siècles* (Paris, 1966), pp.50–2.
14. A.B. De Hoffmeyer, *Arms and Armour in Spain: A Short Survey*, vol.II (Madrid, 1982), p.218.

Chapter 7

León and Castile

The Kingdom of León-Castile eventually became the largest state in the Iberian peninsula. For many years the territory between the river Douro and the Sierra de Gredos had been a largely depopulated zone separating León-Castile from Islamic al-Andalus, but by the mid-11th century it had been repopulated and incorporated into the Christian kingdom.

A more vigorous thrust southwards by Alfonso VI culminated in the capture of Toledo in 1085, which in turn prompted the *Murābiṭ* take-over of al-Andalus a few years later. The next stage of the *Reconquista*, or 'reconquest' of Islamic territory, thereafter proceeded in small steps whenever Muslim weakness permitted. By defeating the *Muwaḥḥidîn* at Las Navas de Tolosa in 1212, a united Castilian, Leónese and Navarrese force suddenly opened the whole of al-Andalus to invasion. Within fifty years the Muslims had lost all save the *Amîrate* of Granada. Thereafter, for more than two centuries, the Castilians were preoccupied with relations with neighbouring Christian states within Iberia as well as their involvement in the Anglo-French Hundred Years War.

The military developments that accompanied the Castilian *Reconquista* began with a rise in the importance of cavalry in the 9th century,[1] but at the same time there was a continued reliance on large numbers of often unarmoured light horsemen.[2] Mail armour of typical western European form had, of course, long been used by an elite minority of cavalry.[3] There is also a possibility that some Castilian light horsemen were archers, though in the early Islamic rather than Turkish style.[4] Traditional Castilian cavalry tactics of *turna fuoya* were also identical to, and almost certainly based upon, the Arab-Andalusian tactic of *karr wa farr*, repeated attack and withdrawal.[5] Another characteristic of Leónese-Castilian military organisation was the survival of very wide military obligation among the population and of cavalry service by men of non-noble background.[6] Urban militias also provided a large element of both infantry and cavalry, although militia infantry seem to have been more prominent in Castile than in León.[7]

The next phase in Castilian military development overlapped these archaic survivals. It was characterised by an adoption of French styles of arms, armour and combat techniques, though there was less copying of French military organisation.[8] By the 13th century heavier armour, helmets and weapons, the use of the couched lance and some use of horse-armour were very apparent.[9] As Castilian power grew relative to neighbouring states, so Castilian military influence spread.

Heavily armoured infantry and the use of the crossbow were another part of this trend,[10] but the appearance of crossbow-armed cavalry in the 14th century and the re-adoption of light cavalry fighting *a la jineta* reflected the influence of the small but militarily significant Islamic Andalusian *Amîrate* of Granada.[11] Nevertheless, Castilian military organisation and general tactical concepts were regarded as old-fashioned by the French and English in the 14th century, probably because of the internal nature of Iberian warfare and the necessity of facing Islamic forces on their own terms.[12] Perhaps as a result of this the later 14th century saw the imitation of Anglo-French systems in northern or Old Castile.

Military developments on the Iberian peninsula are illustrated in a number of very important pictorial manuscripts. Although Andalusian manuscripts are extremely rare, those made by the Christian community under Islamic rule, and by their descendants who retained the same artistic style, are abundant. This community and its associated art are known as *Mozarab*, meaning 'those who became Arab' or 'Arabised'. Most surviving *Mozarab* manuscripts were made within the now expanding Christian states, but their artistic style and origins are almost entirely Andalusian. As such they probably illustrate the traditional military technology and costume of the Iberian peninsula, both Christian and Muslim, before the latter came under strong Maghribi (North African) influence and the former under even stronger French influence. *Mozarab* manuscripts are highly stylised and lack pictorial detail, but although they are often difficult to interpret they contain a wealth of information. In addition to the *Mozarab* manuscripts, those sources not linked to a specific Christian-Iberian kingdom have also been included here.

Figures

356A–B *Mozarab* missal, Castile, 10th–11th centuries
(Archivo de la Real Academia de la Historia, Madrid, Spain)

Though *Mozarab* manuscripts are highly stylised and lack pictorial detail they contain a wealth of information. This particular example shows a spear-armed, turbaned warrior with baggy trousers but no apparent armour (A). A second figure (B) holds a spear of clearly exaggerated dimensions with 'lugs' projecting from beneath the blade. He also has a small round shield and a straight, slightly tapering sword with a trilobate *pommel*.

357 Carved capital, León, late 11th century
(*in situ* southern arcade of the nave, San Isidoro, León, Spain)

Here a rather simple carving seems to illustrate another turbaned warrior with a straight, non-tapering but possibly single-edged sword. The crudity of the workmanship might be misleading but the *quillons* of this weapon and the length of its grip hint at something similar to a form of short-hafted weapon, perhaps a *fausar*, which is seen in French art. It also has similarities with oversized daggers or short swords seen in Navarre.

358A–B 'Leovigildo the Visigoth captures the capital of Cantabria', ivory panel from San Millan de la Cogolla, late 11th/early 12th centuries
(Archaeological Museum, Madrid, Spain)

Although sometimes described as 11th century, the carved ivory and the arms and armour it portrays seem slightly later. If the earlier date is correct then it may be taken as evidence that the long-sleeved mail *hauberk*, round helmet and oversized *nasal* seen in Muslim al-Andalus were also known in northern Spain. This would place Christian Spain technologically in advance of France or even Italy and it might, in fact, have been the area from which such styles spread to much of the rest of Europe. Since the bow and the crossbow seem to have played a more prominent role in 11th-century Iberian warfare than they did in areas north of the Pyrenees, these weapons may have been partially responsible for the adoption of more extensive armour. This could have been particularly true of the broad *nasal*, which may have later developed into the face-mask, which in turn preceded the all-enveloping *great helm*. The shields in this ivory panel (B) include both an early round-based version of the kite-shaped shield and a small round buckler.

359 Shield of an angel, Spanish ivory box, 1059
(Treasury of San Isidoro, León, Spain)

This shield on a dated mid-11th century source is very similar in outline to the preceding example and might support an earlier date for the ivory box from San Millan de la Cogolla. The shield is shown as being half a man's height and is used by a figure on foot who is armed with a spear.

360A–L *Beatus Commentaries on the Apocalypse* written for the Monastery of Santo Domingo de Silos, *Mozarab-Castilian*, 1091–1109
(British Library, Ms. Add. 11695, London, England)

A – Horsemen of the Apocalypse, f.102; B – Angel, f.198; C – f.202; D – Destruction of Jerusalem, f.143; E – Angel fighting the Beast, f.133; F – Spear of an Angel, f.2; G – f.239; H – Soldier of Nebuchadnezzar, f.143; I–J – Babylonians attacking Jerusalem; K – Sword of Nebuchadnezzar, f.232; L – Goliath, f.194. This is perhaps the most famous of all *Mozarab* manuscripts. It is generally thought to illustrate Castilian warriors in essentially typical European military equipment, but this could be misleading. Written and other evidence suggests that the warriors of Islamic al-Andalus, as distinct from men of North African origin, used styles very similar to those of their northern Christian-Spanish foes. Close inspection of the manuscript also reveals a number of clear differences between its arms and armour and that of, for example, France. Not only is the artistic style *Mozarab* but the manuscript was made within a few kilometres of the frontier between Castile and the Islamic state of Saragossa. Added to this is the fact that many of the figures shown here are representatives of the 'wicked', who are normally shown in Christian art as aliens, pagans or Muslims. All the shields are round (H, I and L). Mail *hauberks* of the Babylonians and of Goliath are long-sleeved (I and L), while that of an angel is short-sleeved (A). A form of apparently stitched soft armour is shown once (B) and perhaps twice (H). This could be a crude representation of a defence made from sheets of felt which is said to have been used in the Iberian peninsula. The figure of Goliath (L) may have a yellow-coloured quilted *aketon* beneath his mail *hauberk*. One feature of considerable interest is the fact that Goliath wears a mail *chausse* on only one leg. This feature is also seen a little later in Verona, in Italy, where it indicates an infantry warrior who would kneel in the ranks behind a large shield with his armoured leg thrust forward. Its association with a small round shield here in

Spain seems incongruous and might indicate that the artist was illustrating a feature that he did not fully understand. Helmets include conical and perhaps segmented types (L), plus versions with forward-angled crowns (I and J). This latter style would become popular throughout much of Europe in the 12th century. Both these forms of pointed helmet have relatively small *nasals*. A very unusual third form (C) appears to have an advanced shape, but might be the product either of the artist's imagination or a confused reference to an ancient or classical prototype. With the exception of a large wall-breaking crowbar (D) the only weapons are bows (not shown here), spears and swords. The spears are straightforward if stylised, and generally have single or doubled flanges or wings beneath their blades. This strongly suggests that the couched lance technique was not yet commonly used in Iberia. The swords show some interesting features. All have trilobate or, as in the case of Goliath's weapon, even more decorative *pommels*. Such a style was fast going out of fashion in the rest of Europe. Nebuchadnezzar's sword (K) is shown without any form of *quillons* or guard. This might be taken as an artistic error were it not for the fact that he is illustrated a second time holding exactly the same kind of weapon. Swords without *quillons* are seen in North African and Sicilian sources and even in southern French representations of Moors.

361A–B Beatus Commentaries on the Apocalypse by Facundus, León, 1047
(Biblioteca Nacional, Ms. B.31, Madrid, Spain)

Another *Mozarab* manuscript showing the same spear, round shield and baggy trousers (A). A club presumably all of wood (B) is also illustrated.

362 Homilies from Santo Domingo de Silos, Mozarab-Castilian, 11th century
(British Library, Ms. 30.853, London, England)

Here an angel holds a spear with perhaps fanciful down-curved wings beneath the blade.

363A–B Beatus Commentaries on the Apocalypse, Mozarab, late 11th century
(Archivo de la Real Academia de la Historia, Ms. 33, Madrid, Spain)

Though essentially a *Mozarab* manuscript, this particular copy of the *Beatus Commentaries* is clearly under considerable influence from the Romanesque art of northern Spain or France. The shield (A) is of a pointed kite-shaped type while the horseman wears a full mail *hauberk* with broad sleeves (B). The width of such sleeves added nothing to the hauberk's defensive qualities and must have been a tiring inconvenience when wielding a weapon. In fact they probably reflect the inability of Northern armourers as yet to make tailored tapering sleeves from mail. This would be further evidence that, until the early decades of the 12th century, European arms and armour technology lagged behind that of the Muslims and Byzantines. The horseman's helmet is also interesting. It seems to be made of three sections, the bowl being of two pieces joined along the crown and then reinforced by a broad lower band. Similar helmets seem to have been standard in Southern Europe since at least Carolingian times, and probably derived from similarly-constructed late-Roman helmets.

364 *Psalter of San Millan de la Cogolla*, Castile, 11th century (Archivo de la Real Academia de la Historia, Madrid, Spain)

The horsemen in this miniature seem to be 'Moors', or at least men equipped in a largely Islamic fashion. Their costumes, with head-cloths around their chins, and their apparent bamboo-hafted spears look distinctly North African. Yet their pointed shields, high saddles and straight-legged riding position do not fit such an interpretation. Perhaps these men represent Murābiṭîn who have settled in al-Andalus and been influenced by Andalusian military styles. A late 11th or early 12th century date may therefore be more suitable for this manuscript.

365 Arca Santa, decorated metal plaque, Asturias, 1075 (Cámera Santa, Oviedo, Spain)

The axe, held by a demon, is quite unlike the war-axes of 11th-century Northern Europe and seems to have features in common with the Middle East, particularly with Armenian and Iranian weapons. As such its association with a devil might indicate that comparable weapons were used by the Muslims of Iberia.

366 La Tizona del Cid, Spanish sword-blade from the Royal Treasury of Segovia, early 12th century (Real Armeria, no.G.180, Madrid, Spain)

This weapon, traditionally associated with the hero El Cid, is of typical European form except for its blunt tip, which might be a relic of Arab-Islamic influence.

367A–B Carved relief, León, early 12th century (*in situ* Church of Santiago, Carrión de los Condes, Spain)

The little church in Carrión de los Condes provides one example of the numerous fine pieces of Romanesque sculpture to be found along the old Pilgrims' Road to Santiago. Here two men fight with maces, weapons that were as yet rare north of the Pyrenees and which almost certainly reflect Islamic influence. Two types of shield are shown, kite-shaped and large round, but there is nothing else to suggest that one warrior represents a Christian, the other a Muslim.

368A–C 'Martyrdom of Sts Sabina, Cristela and Vicente', carved relief, Castile, early/mid-12th century
(*in situ* Church of San Vicente, Avila, Spain)

In this martyrdom scene the unarmoured slayers of the three saints are given unmistakable Islamic costume. The armoured slayers, however, are shown in long-sleeved mail *hauberks* and *coifs* the same as those used by northern Spanish or French warriors. Only the fact that two of the *coifs* cover the lower part of the wearer's face (A and C) makes these figures slightly unusual, but even this feature was sometimes seen to the north.

369 Relief carving, León, c.1120
(*in situ* south door, Church of San Isidoro, León, Spain)

Much of the early sculpture in León seems to be related to *Mozarab* art. The style of the carving and some of the military equipment illustrated is unlike that of normal Romanesque sculpture. Here a turbaned horse-archer attempts a 'Parthian shot' over the rump of his horse. There is no evidence of such techniques being used in Iberia in the 12th century or earlier. The sculptor was probably working from a manuscript illustration or a lost original. It is worth noting that the archer uses a simple bow with a regular curve, that his arrow passes to the left of the bow, and that he is using a finger draw rather than a thumb-draw. All this strongly suggests that the kind of archery with which the artist was personally familiar was with a self-bow or longbow of simple construction. Such weapons have never been associated with the kind of Turkish horse-archery techniques illustrated in this carving.

370 'St Vincent', relief carving, León, c.1120
(*in situ* east portal, Church of San Isidoro, León, Spain)

Again recalling characteristics of *Mozarab* art, the man carries a relatively small kite-shaped shield and a remarkably tapering, almost triangular, short sword.

371 'St James', relief carving, Galicia, 12th century
(*in situ* west door, Church of Santiago, Betanzos, Spain)

The church of Santiago was restored in the 15th century, which might make this surprising carving suspect. It includes a very rare representation of a tunic fastened at the front with buttons or toggles. Such tunics are shown in certain *Mozarab* manuscripts and were probably in use before the spread of French fashions. Such a method of fastening clothes would remain virtually unknown elsewhere in

Europe for many years. In addition, this carving of St James shows him wielding a very early representation of a broad sword with sharply down-turned *quillons* of a type associated with combat *a la jineta*.

372 'Templar fighting a Moor', carved capital, Castile, early 13th century
(*in situ* west door, Church of Vera Cruz, Segovia, Spain)

A rather old-fashioned carving is of interest because a distinction is now made between the Christian knight on the left and the Muslim on the right. The former has a helmet with a long *nasal*, a long, flat-topped kite-shaped shield, and a full-length mail *hauberk* extending to his knees. The Muslim, however, is distinguished by his small round shield and a mail *hauberk* which, though it seems to have long sleeves, only reaches his waist. It might, of course, have continued inside his skirt or kilt as was seen in the 13th-century Middle East.

373A–F 'Guards at the Holy Sepulchre', carved relief, Castile, 1135–40
(*in situ* cloisters, Monastery of Santo Domingo de Silos, Spain)

Once again a remarkable Spanish carving in late-Romanesque style includes features of military equipment unlike anything seen outside the Iberian Peninsula. Given the identity of these warriors, their peculiar arms and armour are likely to reflect either Islamic Andalusian equipment or Andalusian influence on Castilian equipment. Their large, kite-shaped shields, mail *hauberks* with mid-length sleeves, straight swords, scabbards and sword-belts are essentially the same as those seen in 12th century France. Their headgear, however, is different. Once again, great attention has been given to protecting the face by drawing the *ventail* of a mail *coif* across the nose (B–C). Some *ventails* are even fastened to the pointed brow of the helmet (C), a fashion not normally seen outside the Middle East or Byzantium. The helmets themselves are distinctive. Not only do they appear to have reinforced crowns and pointed brows (A, C and F) but they extend downwards to protect the sides of the head and the back of the neck. As such they look like very early versions of a *salet*, a helmet not normally seen until the 14th century.

374 'Guards at the Holy Sepulchre', wall-painting from Hermitage of San Baudelio de Berlanga, Castile, late 12th century
(Museum of Fine Arts, Boston, United States)

The soldiers have conical helmets of apparently segmented *spangenhelm* construction with broad *nasals*. They are worn over mail *coifs* which cover the lower parts of their faces. Also, one helmet has a slightly forward-angled crown which would not usually be associated with a segmented construction. This may originally have indicated that the front part of the helmet was thicker than the sides and rear; the whole being forged from a single piece of iron. Note also the very wide sleeves of the *hauberks*.

375 'Massacre of the Innocents', carved capital from Santa Maria de Aguilar de Campo, Castile, late 12th/early 13th centuries
(Archaeological Museum, Madrid, Spain)

The crudely carved capitals from Aguilar de Campo include one warrior in a helmet unlike anything else seen further west than Russia. It might be purely fanciful, or it might represent a similar defensive response in an area where archery played a more prominent role than in most of Europe. If so, it must be seen in the same context as the 12th-century development of helmets with rigid face-masks and ultimately the *great helm*. The helmet is also fastened with a chin-strap.

376 Carved relief, Castile, 1176
(*in situ* south door, Church of Soto de Bureba, province of Burgos, Spain)

This small carving probably represents typical Castilian equipment of the late 12th century. The top edge of the shield has been damaged and the helmet once again appears to have a curved edge forming an extension to protect the neck.

377 Carved capital from the Palace of the Dukes of Granada in Estella, Castile, late 12th century
(private collection)

This carving could, in fact, date from the early 13th century. It shows a warrior with a shield having metal reinforcing bars, a straight sword, a mail *hauberk* with an integral *coif*, and a high-domed round helmet. The helmet may have a *nasal* below its narrow rim, but this is not clear.

378A–B 'Roland and Faragut', carved capital, Castile, late 12th century
(*in situ* Old Cathedral, Salamanca, Spain)

Both Roland (A) and the 'Moor' Faragut (B) are shown with almost identical equipment except for certain distinct differences. Roland is armed with a couched lance, while Faragut holds a sword with a *langet* extending a short way down the blade from its *quillons*. Roland has a large, kite-shaped shield, Faragut a decorated round shield. Most interesting of all are the different helmets. That of Roland is a typical 12th-century tall, conical type with a forward-angled crown and a chin-strap. That of Faragut is a low, round-domed helmet, either segmented or fluted, with a very large *nasal* extending down the face and seemingly disappearing inside the *coif*.

379A–B 'Roland and Faragut', carved capital, Castile, late 12th century
(*in situ* Palace of the Dukes of Granada, Estella, Spain)

Here Faragut (A) is slain by Roland's lance and is followed by a second 'Moor' (B). Their mail *hauberks* and *coifs* are typically European, with only their round shields and the cloth around Faragut's head to distinguish them as Muslims.

380A–B Carved sarcophagus, Castile, late 12th/early 13th centuries
(Monastery of Nuestra Señora de Irache, Estella, Spain)

Once again figures in a martyrdom scene are shown in turbaned Islamic costume. One figure (A) holds a mace, the second (B) a sword. Both are severely foreshortened in this illustration.

381 Carved capital, Castile, c.1200
(*in situ* Monastery of Las Huelgas, Burgos, Spain)

Here an unarmoured figure of no specific religious association carries a mace and a small shield of the kite-shaped type. Perhaps he represents the peasant levy employed by most Iberian states.

382 Carved ivory plaque, Spain, mid-12th century
(Louvre Museum, Paris, France)

The jousting knights may be taken as representatives of the French-influenced military elite of Spain, as their equipment is indistinguishable from that of their Northern neighbours. Each wears a conical helmet, apparently without a *nasal*, plus a short-sleeved mail *hauberk*. Both carry very large kite-shaped shields, one with a small boss and one without, and they are armed with couched lances.

383A–E *Beatus Commentaries on the Apocalypse*, Spain, early 12th century
(Archaeological Museum, Madrid, Spain)

Once again the helmet distinguishes an Iberian warrior from a Frenchman of the same period. The style of this later *Mozarab* example is, however, strongly influenced by Spanish Romanesque art, which leads to a much more detailed and realistic illustration. The warrior wears a mid-length sleeved mail *hauberk* over a padded *aketon* or *gambeson*, and carries as kite-shaped shield plus a broadsword with slightly-curved *quillons*. But it is his helmet which demands attention. This is of a low-domed variety forged from a single piece of metal, with a broad rim and a large face-mask or fixed visor. This is one of the earliest illustrations of such facial protection and its appearance in Iberia is probably significant. Other helmets in this copy of *Beatus* (B and C) are more straightforward, though they both have clearly broadened *nasals*. Weapons also include a substantial axe (D) and a crudely-drawn mace (E) with a spiked or knobbed head.

384A–F Liber Testamentorum Regium, Asturias, 1126–9
(Library of the Cathedral, Oviedo, Spain)

A – Guards of Alfonso II of Asturia; B–D – Guards of Alfonso III of Asturia; E – Guards of Alfonso II of Asturia. It seems as if earlier styles might have survived in the isolated Asturias while French influence penetrated Castile. Here soldiers carry broadswords with down-turned *quillons* (B and D), and in one case recurved *quillons* (E). Two large, kite-shaped shields are shown. Generally such large shields seem to be associated with spears; and small round shields or bucklers with swords. If this is a survival of Arab-Islamic influence then the sword and buckler might indicate cavalry, the large shield and even larger bladed spear indicating infantry as in the iconography of Fāṭimid Egypt. Without further evidence, however, they might also indicate light infantry with sword and buckler and heavy, European-style cavalry with lance and tall shield.

385 Libro de Privilegios, Spain, c.1130
(Cathedral Archives, Tumbo A, Santiago de Compostella, Spain)

In complete contrast to the local style of miniature painting seen in the previous manuscript, the famous *Libro de Privilegios* is almost entirely French Romanesque in style. So is the horseman with his large, kite-shaped shield supported by a *guige*, and his lance couched firmly under his armpit.

386A–B Book of Matins from Santo Domingo de Silos, Castile, 12th century
(Bib. Nat., Ms. Nouv. Acq. Lat. 2176, Paris, France)

Here the guards at the Holy Sepulchre are illustrated in an indigenous style which has similarities with *Mozarab* art. Their equipment is, however, unremarkable, consisting of rather tall conical helmets, no apparent armour, tall kite-shaped shields on *guiges*, straight swords, and long spears.

387A–F Biblia Segunde de San Isidoro de León, Spain, 1162
(Real Colegiata Basilica de San Isidoro, León, Spain)

Here Goliath and the Philistines noticeably lack kite-shaped shields. They are otherwise equipped much like Northern European warriors except for some of the helmets. That of Goliath is a conical type with a typically 12th-century forward-angled crown. However, another figure (D) has the down-curved rim and neckguard seen elsewhere in northern Spain. Another (F) appears to be simply a mail cap over some kind of presumably padded hat. Though rare, such a form of protection is seen elsewhere in Spain, though not very clearly; also in France being worn by a Saracen, and in Iran.

388A–G *Avila Bible*, *Mozarab*-Castilian, late 12th/early 13th centuries
(Biblioteca Nacional, Ms. ER., Madrid, Spain)

A–F – Betrayal and Crucifixion, f.324r; G – Guards at the Holy Sepulchre, f.324v. The *Avila Bible* is a very late example of *Mozarab* art. It illustrates warriors in long-sleeved mail *hauberks* with mail *coifs*, in one case perhaps worn over a padded *aketon*. They carry flat-topped kite-shaped shields, indicating the later date of this manuscript, and broad, non-tapering, blunt-tipped swords of Mediterranean-Arab form. Their helmets are conical with forward-angled crowns and they have substantial fixed face-masks or visors.

389A–F 'Charlemagne's Army leaves for Spain', Spain or France, mid/late 12th century
(Cathedral Archives, *Codex Calixtinus* f.162v, Santiago de Compostella, Spain)

This manuscript may have been illustrated by a French hand, and most of the arms and armour are straightforward. One helmet has an apparent button or suspension ring on top (B) and a second (D) is of the archaic southern French, pseudo-Roman, two-piece type. The same warrior (D), an infantryman, also carries an unusual though far from unknown weapon with a long asymmetrical blade and a short haft, which is also seen in French sources and might be a *fausar*. One spear (F) is shown with a split socket, a rather old-fashioned system normally associated with the British Isles.

390A–H Carved doorway from Church of San Vincente Martyr, Frias, Castile, mid/late 12th century
(Cloisters Museum, Metropolitan Museum of Art, New York, United States)

These carvings show combat scenes, some probably between Spaniards and North African Moors (A–C) and others probably between Spaniards and Muslim Andalusians (E–F). The Spaniards, who come from the right, are armed in round helmets, one clearly (E) and one probably (A) having rigid face masks. They also have mail *coifs* and long-sleeved mail *hauberks* (E), and carry flat-topped kite-shaped shields, one with a prominent boss (E). The Muslims include a man wearing a small turban and a long-sleeved mail *hauberk* without a *coif* (B and C). This rider may also have a sleeveless quilted or padded garment reaching to his thighs. He thrusts with a broad-bladed spear and carries a straight sword, probably from a *baldric* (C). The presumed Andalusian infantryman is shown as 'alien' or 'barbarous' by his bare feet (F). Otherwise he is given basically the same arms and armour as his foe: the scabbard of a tapering sword hanging from a sword-belt, a flat-topped but round-based shield, and a round helmet with a fixed face-mask, secured by a chin-strap over a mail *coif* which forms part of a long-sleeved mail *hauberk*. Three other swords are also shown, all straight. Two have broad, straight *quillons* and rounded *pommels* (D and G), while the third is thrust like a dagger (H). It lacks *quillons* and also has no apparent *pommel*.

391 Sword of Sancho IV, Castile, 1280–95
(Capilla Major, Toledo Cathedral, Spain)

A number of very well-preserved medieval swords, with scabbards and even sword-belts, survive in Spain. This example belonged to King Sancho IV of Castile. Although it is essentially a normal European sword of its time, its flattened, relatively-broad and slightly-curved *quillons* probably represent a particular Iberian style developed from earlier Andalusian patterns. The *quillons*, *pommel* and enamelled roundels on the grip are decorated with Arabesque patterns and pseudo-Kufic inscriptions of obvious Islamic inspiration. The method of attaching the sword-belt to the scabbard is also an interesting example of a relatively early simple style which is typically European.

392A–D Sword of Fernando de la Cerda from his tomb, Castile, early 13th century
(Museum of the Monastery of Las Huelgas, Burgos, Spain)

The sword of Fernando de la Cerda provides an interesting contrast to and a parallel with the sword of Sancho IV. The hilt of the weapon (A) is much more typically European, as is the scabbard (B). However, the sword-belt (C and D) has similarities with the Islamic Middle East. The basic design with its vertical stiffeners, decorative plaques and rigid end-pieces is akin to French examples, although the decoration does include 'Moorish' Arabesques. The metal loop to support the scabbard is different and recalls aspects of Mamlūk Egyptian equipment.

393 Carved altar column from church of San Benito, Sahagún, Castile, early 13th century
('Elmwood' private collection, Cambridge, United States)

An interesting little carving showing a sword with a massive trapezoid *pommel* and *quillons* with a slightly triangular shape. This latter feature might also indicate residual Islamic influence.

394 Statue of a converted 'Moor' adoring the Virgin, Castile, late 13th century
(*in situ* Monastery of Santo Domingo de Silos, Spain)

The sculptor clearly had some knowledge of Islamic Andalusian swords, perhaps based on unclear manuscript illustrations, but he did not fully understand his sources. The result is a confused representation of a light sword of the *jineta* type. It hangs from a *baldric* which seems to be attached to the *quillons* or guard of the weapon in an obviously impossible manner.

395 Ivory plaque, *Mudejar*, Spain or Sicily, early 13th century
(Museo Nazionale, Ravenna, Italy)

Mudejar art, the art of the Muslims who continued to live in the Christian kingdoms after large areas of Islamic al-Andalus had been conquered, includes a few representations of warriors. This example may be from Spain or may have been made by Muslims in Hohenstaufen southern Italy. It shows a huntsman, perhaps in a mail *hauberk*, being devoured by a lion. He carries a short, tapering sword with apparently non-symmetrical *quillons*.

396 Ivory plaque, *Mudejar*, Spain (?), 13th century
(Hermitage, St Petersburg, Russia)

Another illustration of the same subject. The prostrate huntsman again wears a mail *hauberk*, and might hold a sword.

397A–G Bible from San Millan de Cogolla, Castile, early 13th century
(Archivo de la Real Academia de la Historia, Mss. II and III, Madrid, Spain)

A – Goliath, I.f.49; B–D – Pharaoh's Guards, I.f.40v; E – Sons of Levi slay 3000, I.f.54r; F–G – Hebrews besiege Jericho, I.f.123. Again the warriors have basically European equipment with certain interesting variations. Goliath's small round shield may simply be a way of identifying him as a 'pagan', but the swords with non-symmetrical *quillons* used by Pharaoh's Guards surely reflect some kind of real weapon. The *quillon* is extended only on the priority cutting edge, although the blades themselves appear to be double-edged. The pointed profile of one shield in this picture (D) seems unlikely and might have been an artist's attempt to combine a deeply convex leather *adarga* with a normal kite-shaped shield. The oversized dagger or short sword used by the Sons of Levi (E) may just be an enlarged illustration of an ordinary knife. Both sides in the siege of Jericho use crossbows (F and G); these probably having bows of composite construction judging by their shape and surface pattern.

398A–Y *Beatus of Liébana,* Spain, c.1220
(Pierpont Morgan Library, Ms. 429, New York, United States)

A–B – Destruction of Jerusalem, f.18r; C–D – Victory of the Lamb over the Beast, f.128; E – Guard of King Darius, f.162; F – Punishment of the False Prophet, f.138v; G–H – Horseman of the Apocalypse, f.72v; I–P –Army of Nebuchadnezzar; Q–S – Guards of Nebuchadnezzar; T – Spear of an angel, f.6r; U – Spear of an angel, f.1v; V–Y – Horseman of the Apocalypse. The *Beatus of Liébana* is one of the finest of medieval Spanish manuscripts, containing a number of interesting features. These include clubs or maces (C and F) and large round shields with tassels attached to their external rivets (A, I, J, M, N, Q and R). Such tassels are more commonly associated with the 'Moorish' kidney-shaped leather *adarga* shields of the late 13th to 15th centuries. Here they might be used to identify 'pagans' and may, in fact, have been a feature of Islamic Andalusian shields even before the appearance of the kidney-shaped *adarga*. A variety of helmets are illustrated, including round types of which one is of apparent segmented construction (G). Two figures (I and P) have such broad *nasals* that they might almost be considered face-masks. Other helmets are round, conical, or with forward-angled crowns. The similarity between the pointed hats of two Babylonian archers (K and L) and those of some archers in a late 12th or early 13th century Sicilian manuscript is intriguing but perhaps coincidental. In one of two illustrations of the Four Horsemen of the Apocalypse the figures are all given unmistakable turbans (V–Y). Bows are of a double-curved type, perhaps of composite construction (H, K and L), swords are broad and straight, while one large axe with an apparent hammerhead at the back is placed in the hands of an infantryman (O). Spears are straightforward, mostly having leaf-shaped blades. None have wings or lugs. A smaller spear of half the height of a man has a decorated haft and is held by King Nebuchadnezzar. As such it is probably a symbol of authority rather than a weapon and very likely reflects the long-standing influence from the Islamic Middle East. Armour consists of long-sleeved and mid-length sleeved mail *hauberks* with or without mail *coifs* (E, I, J, N–R and V–Y). Mail *chausses* are common (I, J and N–R). Two figures also wear apparently quilted *aketons* or *gambesons* (Q and R) of a style very similar to that seen in the slightly later French *Maciejowski Bible.*

399A–AG *Chronicle of Alfonso X,* Castile, late 13th century
(Library, Ms. T. 1.1, Monastery of San Lorenzo del Escorial, Spain)

This profusely and magnificently illustrated manuscript is not only one of the great treasures of Spanish art but is also an invaluable source of information for both Christian and Islamic arms and armour. The artists who made it took care to distinguish between various groups of warriors, be they Christian Spaniards, Muslim Andalusians or Muslims from North Africa. The former two groups, Spaniards and Andalusians, have a great deal in common but are usually distinguished by relatively minor features, while the North African Muslims are easy to identify. Nevertheless, it must be remembered that the rapidly-shrinking area of al-Andalus, which by now consisted of little more than the Amîrate of Granada, was itself under very strong military influence from North Africa. Andalusian warriors were, in fact, in the process of changing from military styles which they had shared with the Castilians and other Christian states, to new fashions largely based on Maghribi traditions. Warriors who can be identified as Andalusians include figures A, M, T, U, X, Y, the more heavily-armoured individuals in Z, AC and AB, plus possibly D, E, J, L, O–Q, AB and AD. Some of these warriors might, of course, include Christian mercenaries in Muslim service. Specifically Christian are figures B, C, F and N, whereas a North African identity can be offered for figures I, possibly W and AA, plus the more lightly armoured men in Z, AB and AC. The basic difference is that drawn between heavily armoured cavalry and more lightly equipped troops, particularly those wearing turbans or riding with shortened stirrups (W and AA). These latter are early versions, or predecessors of, cavalry fighting *a la jineta*. All the infantry appear to be well armoured and thus to be from the Iberian peninsula; whether Christian or Islamic. Another feature which seems to distinguish Muslim Andalusians are fanciful curved crests or brow-plates attached to many helmets (D, E, O–Q, T, AC and AG). These most commonly appear on light conical or round helmets but they are even seen on *great helms*, once on a helmet of such magnitude that it looks like a predecessor of the 15th-century *great bascinet* (T). Such crests might be considered fanciful but for their persistence in other late 13th and 14th-century Spanish art and for their probable appearance in Andalusian Islamic art. One of the most commonly illustrated helmets is, in fact, a *chapel-de-fer* or *war-hat* with a brim of various widths (B, I, N, U, V, Z, AB, AC and AE). These are often painted. The plain, close-fitting *cervellière* without a brim is shown, but less frequently (A, M, X and Y). Other interesting features in this manuscript are the great variety of shields, from large flat-topped kite types for infantry (B and AE), small round-based flat-topped types for horsemen (J, L–N, Z and AC), kidney-shaped *adargas* (K, W, Z, AB and AC), and a very large mantlet to protect pioneers (X). These pioneers also wear a form of scale *cuirass* that was appearing in various parts of Europe in the late 13th and early 14th centuries. It was probably part of a general trend towards the readoption of plate armour. The development was almost certainly in response to a widespread use of the crossbow, which also appears here (F and X). These weapons now have regularly curved bows instead of the recurved outline seen earlier. Two figures who wear the scale *cuirass*, this time over a mail *hauberk*, are a siege engineer (Y) and a heavily armed infantryman (AE). *Surcoats* with raised and acutely-angled shoulders (M and Z) are again seen elsewhere in Europe and almost certainly indicate considerable padding or even a semi-rigid lining, perhaps of hardened leather. Horse-armour is illustrated, always with a rigid *chanfron*, but both with and without a cloth covering (N, AF and AG). Swords are straight and generally slightly tapering, with curved *quillons* and either round or 'tear-drop'-shaped *pommels*. The spears of North African warriors or those riding *a la jineta* generally have much larger blades than those of the heavily-armoured horsemen. These large blades also seem to have various, often multiple protuberances beneath the blade itself (V, W, Z and AB).

400A–H *Gran Conquistas de Ultramar*, Castile, early 14th century
(Biblioteca Nacional, Ms. 195, Madrid, Spain)

A – Crusader; B–H – Saracens defending a city. This early 14th century manuscript is a later product of the school which produced the *Chronicle of Alfonso X*. It illustrates virtually the same arms and armour, even to the extent of giving a few warriors on both sides short-sleeved scale *cuirasses*. That of the attacking Crusader (A) is clearly worn over a mail *hauberk* with a mail *coif*. That of the Muslim defender is worn alone and may be an artist's attempt to reproduce the Middle Eastern lamellar *cuirass*, a form of armour he may never have seen. Other features of interest are the Christians' almost triangular shields, which look remarkably like a 14th-century Byzantine form. It is worth noting that a company of Spanish and other mercenaries, known as the Catalan Great Company, was already playing a major role in early 14th century Byzantine affairs. Meanwhile, the Kingdom of Aragón now ruled Sicily and was in continuous rivalry with the Angevins of southern Italy and Greece. The Saracens in this miniature are, however, basically portrayed as western Muslims, Moroccans or Andalusians. They have kidney-shaped *adarga* shields, brimmed *war-hats*, round or conical helmets with, in two cases, those still-unexplained frontal plumes or decorative plaques.

401 Effigy of a member of the Centellas family, Castile, early 14th century
(*in situ* Church of San Juan, Talamanca, Spain)

Written sources indicate that in many respects the majority of Castilian soldiers were equipped in old-fashioned styles compared to the troops of 14th-century France or even Catalonia. This effigy is evidence of the simple character of much early 14th-century Castilian arms and armour. The knight has a full mail *hauberk* with *mittens* and an apparently integral mail *coif*. He wears no plate armour, no *surcoat*, and lacks any form of leg protection. He looks, in fact, like a soldier from a hundred years earlier.

402A–H *Libra de los Juegos de Alfonso X*, Castile, 1283
(Library, Ms. T, J.6, Monastery of San Lorenzo de Escorial, Spain)

A–C –Berber? f.11v; D – Moor? f.43v; E–F – Orientals? f.52r; G – Berber or Moor? f.43v; H – Guard of a Moorish King, f.17v. King Alfonso's *Book of Chess* is virtually the same in style as his more famous *Chronicle* and *Cantigas*. Similar costumes are shown, though with perhaps a greater emphasis on various Islamic and exotic eastern figures. Western Islamic individuals, whether Ma<u>gh</u>ribis or Andalusians, are shown with straight swords hung from *baldrics* in traditional Arab style (C, G and H). Easterners seem to be based on verbal descriptions and inadequate pictorial sources which contribute both to impractical curved swords (E) and more realistic sabres (F). The latter is also hung, albeit inaccurately, from a sword-belt. Such curved swords were unlikely to have been used in Morocco or Granada at this time. Other weapons in the manuscript include spears with very long sockets (A) and a recurved, perhaps composite, bow (B). A helmet with a brow-plate or crest is also shown, this time with a headband or cloth wound around its rim.

403A–L *Haggada Resach*, Jewish-Spanish, late 13th/early 14th centuries
(British Library, Ms. Or. 2884, London, England)

A–B – Maces of Israelites; C – People coming to Joseph for Judgement; D –Pharaoh in the Red Sea; E – Egyptian soldiers; F – Joseph as governor of Egypt; G – Joseph's brothers; H – Esau's dagger; I – Joseph in the fields; J – Cain and Abel; K – Joseph's father; L – Joseph's brother. The *Haggada Resach* is an interesting pictorial source as it can be considered 'neutral' in its portrayal of figures based on Christian or Islamic types. Generally speaking it is, however, in northern Spanish style, and is difficult to date. The weapons seem to indicate an early 14th-century origin. They include numerous maces of rather simple form (A, B and I), one having a very long haft. A heavy axe is shown (K), as is a broad-bladed dagger of the *basilard* type (H). Swords are straight and mostly tapering (C, E, F, G and K), though one seems to reflect a slightly-curved sabre of almost Mamlūk Middle Eastern form with asymmetrical *quillons* (L). One scabbard is clearly hung from two straps, probably from a *baldric* (C). Infantry spears have broad but somewhat exaggerated blades (E). Shields include small round bucklers (C and E), a small hand-held kite type (E) and a larger flat-topped cavalry shield (D). A horseman, the Pharaoh, wears a full mail *hauberk* and rides a *caparisoned* horse, while the foot-soldiers have mail *coifs* or conical helmets (E).

404 'St George', *Mozarab*-Spanish drawing, late 13th/early 14th centuries
(Archivo de la Real Academia de la Historia, Madrid, Spain)

A late example of *Mozarab* art showing a horseman wearing a pointed and brimmed *chapel-de-fer*, a mail *hauberk*, mail *chausses*, and a flat-topped shield, perhaps with reinforcing bands and a small boss. He holds his broad-bladed spear in the couched style. The continued representation of spears with quite large blades is a feature of 14th-century Spanish art. It probably reflects a style of weapon which might have remained in use because many Spanish horsemen – and, of course, their Andalusian foes – made little use of body-armour while fighting *a la jineta*.

405 Carved wooden panel, *Mozarab*, from Toledo, Castile, 14th century
(Archaeological Museum, Madrid, Spain)

An extraordinary little carving apparently showing a foot-soldier behind an enormous round shield.

406 *Libro de la Coronaciones de los Reyes de España*, Castile, early 14th century
(Library, Monastery of San Lorenzo de Escorial, Spain)

The two warriors shown here are attendants of King Alfonso VII of Castile and León. They wear tall, pointed and wide-brimmed *war-hats* over mail *coifs*. The surface decoration seems to recall the crests or brow-plates of late 13th and early 14th-century Andalusian warriors.

407 Effigy of a member of the Guzman family, Castile, c.1360
(*in situ* Convent of San Isidoro del Campo, Santiponce, Spain)

In contrast to the Centellas effigy in Talamanca (fig.401), here a member of the illustrious and warlike Guzman family is still relatively lightly-equipped by Northern European standards, with more mail and less plate than would be seen in France. But plate *greaves* and tubular *vambraces* of a modern type are present. The overall lightness of the armour may be a matter of climate, local tactics and personal choice. The effigy is located in the south of Spain, in what had now become the Christian province of Andalusia. The main enemy would have been lightly-armoured Muslims fighting *a la jineta*, and the climate of the area probably made any heavier armour impractical.

408 Sword, Spain, 1300–50
(Cathedral Treasury, Toledo, Spain)

Typically European, betraying none of the lingering Islamic characteristics seen in some 13th-century Spanish weapons.

Notes

1. J. Beeler, *Warfare in Feudal Europe, 730–1200* (Ithaca, 1971), p.166.
2. Beeler, *op.cit.* p.172; C. Sánchez-Albornoz, 'El Ejécito y la Guerra en al Reino Asturleónes, 718–1037', in *Ordinamenti Militari in occidente nell'alto Medioevo, Settimane di Studio del Centro Italiano di Studi sul'alto Medioevo* vol.XV, no.1 (Spoleto, 1968), pp.334–5; L. Lourie, 'A Society Organized for War: Medieval Spain', *Past and Present* vol.XXV (1966), pp.57 and 68–9.
3. Al-Ṭurtūshî, Muḥammad Ibn Walîd, *Sirāj al Mulūk* (Cairo, n.d.), pp.303 and 309, and *Lámpara de los Principes*, trans. M. Alarcón (Madrid, 1931), pp.321 and 334.
4. Sánchez-Albornoz, *op.cit.* p.333.
5. W.S. Hendrix, 'Military Tactics in the "Poem of the Cid"', *Modern Philology* vol.XX (1922), p.46.
6. Lourie, *op.cit.* p.60; P. Contamine, *La Guerre au Moyen Age* (Paris, 1980), p.169.
7. J.F. Powers, 'The Origins and Development of Municipal Military Service in the Leónese and Castilian Reconquest, 800–1250', *Traditio* vol.XXVI (1970), pp.91–2, 97 and 109; J.F. Powers, 'Townsmen and Soldiers: The Interaction of Urban and Military Organization in the Militias of Medieval Castile', *Speculum* vol.XLVI (1971), pp.641–5 and 652–4.
8. Beeler, *op.cit.* pp.158 and 168; A.B. De Hoffmeyer, *Arms and Armour in Spain: A Short Survey*, vol.I (Madrid, 1972), p.140.
9. A.B. De Hoffmeyer, *Arms and Armour in Spain: A Short Survey*, vol.II (Madrid, 1982), pp.33–4 and 82; C. Oman, *A History of the Art of War in the Middle Ages* (London, 1924), vol.II, p.181.
10. Hoffmeyer, vol.II, *op.cit.* pp.84 and 87.
11. Hoffmeyer, vol.II, *op.cit.* p.212; Oman, vol.II, *op.cit.* p.180; P.E. Russell, *The English Intervention in Spain and Portugal in the Time of Edward III and Richard II* (Oxford, 1955), pp.98–9.
12. Russell, *op.cit.* pp.4–5 and 98–9.

Chapter 8

Portugal

French influence gradually spread from the east to the west of the Iberian Peninsula. It was not, however, a steady infiltration of ideas but rather a gradual adoption of various Northern European military styles and tactics in different places at different times. As a result the process which started in Catalonia before the Crusading era only really reached Portugal in the 14th century.

In the early 11th century the County of Portugal extended as far as the river Douro and still formed part of the Kingdom of León. Culturally and militarily it had much in common with Galicia to the north, both areas being largely free of French military influence. By the 12th century Portuguese autonomy was effectively complete, and the southern frontier of what had now become an earldom reached beyond the Mondego river. In 1143 Portugal achieved the status of a kingdom, and in 1249 the reconquest was completed with the capture of the Algarve (Arabic al-Gharb, 'the west'). Thereafter Portuguese efforts focused on securing the eastern frontier with Castile and ensuring independence. Portugal's interest in maritime expansion began in the 14th century, but at the same time the country could not escape the threat of Castilian intervention and, by extension, involvement in the quarrels between England and France.

Medieval Portuguese military history remains a largely neglected subject. While it is generally agreed that the country's military styles and organisation were very old-fashioned until the 14th century, there is disagreement on the degree of survivals from the pre-Islamic Visigothic era in culturally isolated areas such as the Asturias, Galicia and what became Portugal.[1]

The role of cavalry clearly rose in importance as the Christian offensive against Islamic al-Andalus gathered momentum, raids aimed at the destruction or seizure of enemy property being the main form of warfare.[2] The role of infantry meanwhile declined as Spanish campaigns spread into the central Iberian plateau. In Portugal the situation may have been a little different, as most of the country consists of rugged mountains and valleys. The longbow was also popular in the 14th century, although this might have been a result of English influence.[3] It may, in fact, have replaced composite bows of Arab form. Meanwhile slings remained widespread, particularly at sea.[4] On the other hand one of the first, though unclear, European references to counter-weight *mangonels* was found in an account of the siege of Lisbon in 1147.[5] However, this probably reflected Islamic Andalusian military technology rather than that of the Christian Iberian states.

Prior to the late 14th century, Portuguese military organisation and tactics reflected the Islamic Andalusian tradition.[6] A conscious, government-sponsored adoption of 'modern' Anglo-French military styles began in 1372 as a direct result of the battle of Najera (1367).[7] Some changes do, however, seem to have occurred earlier, particularly in arms and armour.

Figures

409 Carved relief, Portugal, early 12th century
(*in situ* portal of the church of Villar de Frades, Portugal)

Relatively little is known about the appearance of early Portuguese armies, although they were likely to have been similar to those of neighbouring León and Galicia. This crude carving shows a warrior in a mixture of European and Islamic Andalusian equipment. His shield is a typical 11th or early 12th-century large, kite-shaped variety, held both in the hand and by straps around the forearm. He might wear a conical helmet, but his broad, non-tapering, blunt-tipped sword is of a form unlike that used in the north. Such blades were in the Byzantine and early Islamic tradition but were also seen in other parts of Arab-influenced Mediterranean Europe. The man seems to be riding with a bent knee and shortened stirrups, these latter probably having a broad triangular profile. Such stirrups remained characteristic of Islamic Andalusia and the Maghrib until modern times and were probably introduced into the Iberian Peninsula from North Africa in the 11th century.

410A–C Statuette, Portugal, 1325–50
(*in situ* Capela dos Ferreiros, Oliviero do Hospital, Portugal)

By the early 14th century even Portugal was feeling strong French influence. Naturally the aristocratic elite of heavy cavalry was the first affected. The small carving of a knight in the Capela dos Ferreiros shows a heavy *great helm* with an unusual type of hinged *bevor* to protect the knight's throat. He also wears a mail *hauberk* under his *surcoat*, plus *greaves* and *sabatons*, probably of iron, to protect his legs and feet. His shield is typical of the mid-14th century, as is the *chanfron* with its pierced eye cups which the horse wears under a cloth *caparison* (C). The knight is armed with a large, typically European sword and has a winged or flanged mace (B) on his right shoulder.

411A–B 'St James fighting the Moors', relief carving, Portugal, 14th century
(*in situ* Church of Matriz de Santiago, Cacém, Portugal)

Here St James (A) appears to be dressed almost like a Moor, though this is probably a result of an artist's attempt to give the saint 'ancient' or quasi-Roman dress. He wields a straight sword which is clearly longer than those of his foes (B) and he carries a rather confused representation of a flat-topped, probably triangular, shield on a *guige*. The 'Moors', North Africans or Andalusians, are far more interesting for they are shown in apparently realistic detail. They are armed with light but broad swords of the type associated with light cavalry tactics *a la jineta* and carry similarly light *adarga* shields. One of these is shown from the inside, exposing the handgrip. Armour and helmets are not visible, which probably identifies these riders as Moroccans rather than men from Granada. They ride with very short stirrups of typically North African type. This carving may, in fact, celebrate the defeat of a mixed Granadan and Moroccan army by a combined Christian force at the battle of Salado in 1340.

412A–D 'Guards at the Holy Sepulchre', relief carving, Portugal, late 13th/early 14th centuries
(Museu de Machado de Castro, Coimbra, Portugal)

This source again indicates the mixed character of the Portuguese army. One figure (A) is a typical European knight with his *great helm* (B) lying beside him, while another (C) has an ordinary sword. A third figure (D), though shown here in a confused manner because of inadequate photographic evidence, seems to be rather different. He has a small round shield similar to those used by the light infantry of early 14th-century Italy, and wears a full mail *hauberk* plus mail *chausses* but no *surcoat*. The lack of a *surcoat* makes him look very old-fashioned by normal European standards. His headgear is also unusual, as he seems to wear a mail *coif* over a small, close-fitting *cervellière* helmet.

Notes

1. C. Sánchez-Albornoz, 'El Ejécito y la Guerra en al Reino Asturleónes, 718–1037', in *Ordinamenti Militari in occulente nell'alto Medioevo, Settimane di Studio del Centro ltaliano di Studi sull'alto Medioevo* vol.XV, no.I (Spoleto, 1968), pp.331–2, and J. Beeler, *Warfare in Feudal Europe, 730–1200* (Ithaca, 1971), p.158, both emphasise the degree of continuity, while P. Contamine, *La Guerre au Moyen Age* (Paris, 1980), p.147, denies such continuity.
2. Contamine, *op.cit.* pp.117–8.
3. A.B. De Hoffmeyer, *Arms and Armour in Spain: A Short Survey*, vol.II (Madrid, 1982), p.212.
4. Hoffmeyer, *op.cit.* p.213.
5. Hoffmeyer, *op.cit.* p.102; D.R. Hill, 'Trebuchets', *Viator* vol.IV (1973), p.102.
6. P.E. Russell, *The English Intervention in Spain and Portugal in the Time of Edward III and Richard II* (Oxford, 1955), pp.129 and 202.
7. Russell, *op.cit.* p.333.

Chapter 9

The Empire – Germany

The Empire will be discussed in four sections. These approximate the 12th/ 13th-century Imperial subdivisions of: (a) the Kingdom of Germany; (b) the Kingdom of Bohemia plus Moravia; (c) the Kingdom of Burgundy or Arles; and (d) the Kingdom of Italy including the Patrimony of St Peter. Such general divisions of that most complicated and rapidly-changing of medieval states, the German Empire, are bound to be potentially misleading. However, some form of division is necessary as there were clear differences in the military traditions, arms and armour of, for example, Germany and Italy.

The Kingdom of Germany evolved out of the Kingdom of Louis the German, which was itself created by the Carolingian Treaties of Verdun (843) and Mersen (870). It consisted of present-day western Germany, the Netherlands, eastern Belgium, Luxembourg and large parts of north-eastern France. On the eastern frontier the Marks or Marches of the Billungs, Nordmark and Thuringia in eastern Germany had been incorporated into the Empire by the year 1100, as had the March of Austria. To the south the Kingdom of Germany also included eastern Switzerland, the rest of modern Austria and much of Slovenia.

These frontiers remained largely unchanged, apart from the addition of Pomerania, Polish Silesia and, temporarily, some Baltic regions ruled by the Teutonic Knights in the 13th century. From the mid-12th century, however, the central authority of the Emperor, as King of Germany, declined sharply. This in turn had profound political and military consequences.[1]

The concept of knighthood had, in fact, been slow to develop in Germany, dating from the late 11th and early 12th centuries. Nor did the associated term *rîter* necessarily apply only to a horseman.[2] The general *ban* or levy of all free vassals also survived longer in Germany than in France or England. This led to large but often ill-trained and inadequately armed forces.[3] The military role of the peasantry was another feature of parts of Germany long after it had been abandoned further west. Many such peasant warriors were of un-free serf origin yet still served as cavalry.[4] While the Emperor-King's authority declined, so the military obligations of the feudal military elite similarly decreased, particularly those of the leading aristocracy.[5] As in England and

France, mercenaries came to play an increasingly important role in the late 12th and 13th centuries. Most of them were recruited from within the Empire, particularly from Brabant, the Netherlands or neighbouring Flanders.[6] A large proportion of such men were infantry. Foot-soldiers armed with spears, hooked pikes and other interesting infantry weapons continued to play a very important tactical role even in the early 13th century.[7] The precocious development of plate armour for cavalry may have been partly a response to the threat from such infantry, particularly from crossbowmen.[8]

Rural militias were another feature of some parts of Germany, but more directly associated with the continuing role of infantry was the growing importance of German towns, both as strategic centres and as sources of men and money.[9] The urban militias soon became well armed,[10] their effectiveness being indicated by the success rate of Flemish urban forces against French royal armies in the 14th century (three victories and three defeats out of six major battles between 1302 and 1382).[11] Furthermore the early utilisation of gunpowder artillery in Germany was directly linked to the military role of cities such as Metz, Aachen, Deventer, Soest, Frankfurt-am-Main and Köln (Cologne) as well as neighbouring cities just inside French-ruled Flanders.[12] All these early references to firearms stem from the Rhineland, the Meuse basin or neighbouring provinces. The only exceptions are from Styria in the far south-east of the German kingdom. Although the latter are among the earliest such references, they inevitably bring to mind even earlier but very obscure references to firearms in Friuli, just across the border in Italy though still, of course, within the Empire.[13]

There was considerable variation between the military systems of different parts of the Kingdom of Germany. The western regions were highly urbanised while others were more primitive. The survival of infantry forces in areas such as the Swiss mountains, the Frisian islands, and the Dithmarschen marshes, or among the eastern Weser River settlements, reflected their isolation rather than the development of urban militias.[14] The emergence of crossbow-armed mounted infantry in parts of southern Germany[15] might have reflected eastern European, Hungarian or Balkan influence. On the other hand the military styles, equipment and tactics of largely Slav areas in the south-eastern corner of the kingdom, such as the Duchies of Styria, Carinthia and Carniola, were identical to those of neighbouring Germanic provinces.

Figures

413 Sword and scabbard, Saxony, 11th century
(Cathedral Treasury, Essen, Germany)

The filigree decoration on the *pommel* and *quillons* of this ceremonial sword are here shown simplified. The basic weapon represents a typical product of a rapidly expanding Rhineland armaments industry. From this region swords and other weapons were exported all over Europe and beyond.

414 Helmet from Lake Lednikie (restored), Germany, 11th century (?)
(Directorate of Archaeological Monuments, Poznań, Poland)

A much-restored helmet of typical 11th-century Western European form, believed to have been made in Germany.

415 War-axe from Lutomiersk, probably imported from the Rhineland, early 11th century
(Centre for the Archaeology of Central Poland, Łódź, Poland)

If this axehead was indeed imported from Germany, then it indicates that the burgeoning Rhineland arms industry was catering for specialised markets, as such weapons do not appear to have been popular in western Germany itself.

416 'Herod's Guards', *Golden Gospels of Echternach*, Lower Lotharingia, c.1040
(Germanisches National Museum, Nuremberg, Germany)

This famous manuscript betrays a number of Byzantine influences, which are particularly apparent in helmets which seem to have *aventails*. The sword, spear and large kite-shaped shield are, however, more western. The short-hemmed, short-sleeved mail *hauberk* might have a slit at the side, although this slit actually appears to be over one hip. *Hauberks* slit at the sides were originally an infantry rather than cavalry style but they seem to have persisted in the Empire for longer than in, for example, France. It is worth noting that the Byzantines, when recruiting western mercenaries in the late 11th and early 12th centuries, considered Germans to excel as infantry, Frenchmen as cavalry.

417 'Guard of King Herod', carved wooden door panel, Lower Lotharingia, c.1065
(*in situ* north transept, Church of S. Maria im Kapitol, Köln, Germany; also a cast in the Victoria and Albert Museum, London)

Here a warrior holds a spear with wings or lugs below the blade, and a round or oval shield.

418 Sword from Lutomiersk, probably imported from the Rhineland, early/mid-11th century
(Centre for the Archaeology of Central Poland, Łódź, Poland)

This is much more old-fashioned in the design of its hilt than the previous but similarly dated example. It may indicate that the mounts were added in Poland or that traditional styles continued to be made in the main German armaments centres for export to the east.

419 Ivory plaque, Franconia, late 11th century
(University Library, Würzburg, Germany)

If we assume that the *quillons* have been broken, the warrior appears to be using a sword similar to one of those shown above. If, however, the missing *quillons* never existed, then the weapon is the most northerly, and one of the earliest, European representations of a sword with non-symmetrical *quillons*.

420 Manuscript from the Abbey of St Evre-les-Toul, Upper Lotharingia, late 11th century
(Staatsbibliothek, Ms. 10.293, Munich, Germany)

In a manuscript decorated in an archaic style, a warrior wears a stylised form of headgear that virtually defies interpretation. He also has a short-sleeved *hauberk* or mail shirt that apparently only reaches his waist. His weaponry consists of a large round shield and a short spear with prominent flanges below the blade. Although such styles should have disappeared by the 11th century they might have persisted in isolated areas among infantry levies. Toul, on the borders of the Duchy of Upper Lotharingia and the French County of Champagne could not, however, be considered an isolated or backward region.

421 'Martyrdom of St Felix of Aquileia', decorated portable metal altar front, Germany, c.1100
(*in situ* church, Abdinghof, Germany)

In this martyrdom scene a good deal of military equipment is illustrated in detail. The slayers on the left have helmets with forward-angled crowns of a type normally associated with the early

12th century. Their shields are tall and kite-shaped with rivets to hold the *enarmes* but no bosses. Their mail *hauberks* have *coifs* and long sleeves and are now slit at the front. The swords, which appear to hang from typically 12th-century knotted sword-belts, have straight *quillons* and some form of decoration on their blades. The martyrs, who have disarmed themselves, had spears without wings or flanges, plus swords and shields identical to those of their persecutors.

422 'Christ Triumphant', Reliquary of St Hadelin, Lower Lotharingia, c.1046
(Treasury of Church of St Martin, Visé, Belgium)

Christ Triumphant here wears one of the clearest representations of an 11th-century mail *hauberk* slit at the sides rather than at the front and back. Although such a style was worn by both foot soldiers and horsemen, its persistence in a region which was otherwise very advanced in metal technology and arms production reinforces the view that infantry continued to play a leading role in the warfare of this area.

423 Gilt bronze figure on a candlestick from Abbey Church of St Nicholas, Gross-Comburg, Swabia, c.1140
(Landesbildestelle, Stuttgart, Germany)

The figure on the candlestick is clearly based very closely on a Byzantine original. His scale or lamellar *cuirass* even has the opening across the belly seen in the best Byzantine sources, though these are of a somewhat earlier date. German art was, for a number of reasons, under Byzantine influence at this time, and in some ways this figure might shed more light on early 12th-century Byzantine arms than on German arms.

424 Sword, Germany, c.1200
(Wallace Collection, London, England)

A more damaged and considerably simpler sword which is basically the same as that of the Sword of St Maurice depicted in the next figure.

425 Sword of St Maurice, Germany, 1198–1215
(Treasury, Kunsthistorisches Museum, Vienna, Austria)

A magnificent weapon, here shown slightly simplified, is decorated with engraving and enamel-work. However, its form is again typical of late 12th and early 13th-century German swords.

426 Fragment of a bronze *aquamanile* (metal ewer for ablutions at altar or table) from Hildesheim, late 12th century
(present location unknown)

The helmet worn by this figure appears to be a later development, or a more accurate representation, of the rounded conical helmet with the crown thrust forwards, but this example also includes a *nasal*. He wears a mail *coif* and *hauberk*, plus a presumed *guige* for a missing shield.

427 Engraved copper altar front from Hildesheim, Saxony, c.1120
(Victoria and Albert Museum, London, England)

The helmet worn by this warrior is very similar to those seen on the Abdinghof altar. So is the sword, although the *pommel* is much larger. The flat-topped shield, though it has a small boss, also indicates a later date.

428A–B Engraved copper altar front, Rhineland, 1118
(Cathedral Treasury, Paderborn, Germany)

Swords with two distinct types of *pommel* appear on the Paderborn altar front. These are the oval, almost 'cocked-hat' forms (A), and the more normal flattened nut shape (B).

429A–G Carved reliefs, Upper Lotharingia, c.1130–40
(*in situ* exterior of Abbey church, Andlau, France)

A – Hunter; B–C – Theodoric the Goth and Hildebrand save Sintram from the Dragon; D–G – Warriors. The carvings at Andlau provide some of the best illustrations of early 12th century German military equipment. Conical (D, F and G) and forward-angled (E) helmets are shown, though only one appears to have a *nasal* (F). The armoured men wear short-sleeved *hauberks* with *coifs* (B–G), one of them clearly slit at the side (D). Horsemen carry kite-shaped shields (B–E), while infantry still use large round shields (F and G). Spears have plain heads without wings or flanges (A, D and E). Swords are straight and non-tapering with straight or slightly curved *quillons* (B, F and G).

430 Woven textile, Saxony (?), c.1150–1200
(Cathedral. Treasury, Halberstadt, Germany)

This figure might represent the Archangel Michael. He wields a long spear and carries a later form of short but broad and flat-topped, deeply-curved shield, supported by a *guige*.

431A–C 'Story of St Hadelin', Reliquary of St Hadelin, Lower Lotharingia, c.1150–75
(Treasury of Church of St Martin, Visé, Belgium)

The later gilded panels on the Reliquary of St Hadelin portray military equipment which is a later version of that seen in the earlier panel of 'Christ Triumphant' (fig.422). A mail *hauberk* is still slit at the side (A), which is somewhat surprising given the date. The *hauberks* are also short-sleeved, with presumably integral *coifs* (A–C). The fact that the mail twice appears to be fastened to the sides of low-domed *cervellière* helmets (A and C) is probably a misleading detail of embossed metalwork. Other items of military equipment include round-topped, presumably kite-shaped shields (A and B), a knotted sword-belt (A), and a spear with apparent flanges below its blade (C).

432A–B Engraved stone funerary slab of Nicola III de Rumigny, Lower Lotharingia, c.1175
(now lost)

A – after a drawing by Joseph van dun Berg, c.1900 (Ms. B.1642 p.49, Bibliothèque de l'Université, Liège, Belgium); B – after a drawing by Roland (*Annales, Société Archéologique de Namur* vol.XIX, 1891, p.131). Although these two drawings of the lost tomb slab of Nicola de Rumigny differ considerably, they also show basically the same kind of equipment. The most important feature is, of course, the *great helm*. The slab was inscribed 1175, the year of Nicola III's death. If it was made in or shortly after this year then these are among the earliest known representations of true flat-topped *great helms*. Other features support an early date. The *hauberk* has no *mittens*, the man wears no *surcoat* and the shield is clearly large and flat-topped. The crudity of the carving, even taking into account the apparently unskilled draughtsmanship of the two late 19th-century antiquarians, is equally apparent. The slab represents the beginning of a tradition that ultimately led to the superb monumental brasses of the late 13th and early 14th centuries. The sketch by Joseph van dun Berg (A) is probably more reliable as it was done from life in a small notebook. That by Roland (B) was engraved and then published in a journal, increasing its unreliability. The peculiarities of the *great helm*, as illustrated by Van dun Berg, could indicate that the man who made the original tomb slab was unfamiliar with this form of helmet. This itself could show that they were still rare even in a technologically advanced area such as Namur, which lies between the two metalworking centres of Dinant and Liège.

433A–B Ivory jewel case from Köln, Lower Lotharingia, late 12th century
(British Museum, Forrer Collection, London, England)

The shields carried by these warriors are similar, though larger, to that seen in the previous figure. They also wear long-sleeved mail *hauberks*, probably with *coifs*, and wield broad swords with straight (B) or down-turned (A) *quillons*. Their helmets are particularly interesting as they are to some degree flat-topped, though with rounded edges and large *nasals*. As such they are comparable, though not identical, to some early 13th-century examples shown in the Chartres Cathedral windows in France. They may also be the presumed predecessors of a typically German form of early *great helm*.

434A–C 'Totila's Army', *Book of Dialogues of St Gregory*, Germany (?), c.1175–1200
(Bib. Royale, Ms. 9916–9917, f.86, Brussels, Belgium)

There is considerable similarity between this source and manuscripts from England. The most obvious parallel is found in the way in which mail *ventails* are pulled towards the back of the wearers' heads. Mail *hauberks* have mid-length sleeves. Only one helmet is shown and this is tall, with a broad rim band and a curved *nasal*. Swords are straight with straight *quillons* and round *pommels*. An interesting kite-shaped shield seems to have an indented top but this might be an artist's attempt to indicate that the shield was curved.

435 'David and Goliath', Germany, 1148
(British Library, Ms. Add. 14789, f.10, London, England)

In this manuscript Goliath is armed and armoured in a very basic style that indicates no particular regional or German variation. His helmet is a conical *spangenhelm* with a long curved *nasal*. This is worn over a mail *coif* that forms part of a long-sleeved mail *hauberk*. On his legs and feet are *chausses* which, though given a different pattern, are almost certainly of mail. His long kite-shaped shield has a *guige*, and his spear lacks wings or flanges but has a fringed *gonfanon*. His sword, shown somewhat schematically, has short broad *quillons* and a round *pommel*. It would be carried in a scabbard hung in traditional manner by split straps from a sword-belt.

436A–E *Hortus Deliciarum*, Germany, c.1180
(ex-Library of Strasbourg; from a facsimile made a few years before the destruction of the original in a fire in 1870)

Nineteenth-century copies of some of the illuminations in this lost manuscript might be unreliable in detail but they do show certain major features. One is the very tall, perhaps segmented or painted helmet with a *nasal* (A). This is worn by a figure who otherwise uses standard equipment comprising a long-sleeved mail *hauberk* with *coif* and *mittens*, mail *chausses* on the front of his legs, a sword with straight *quillons*, and a tall, distinctly curved, flat-topped kite-shaped shield. A longbow of just under a man's height (C) and a simple quiver in which the arrows are placed points uppermost (B) are seen in the hands of a presumed hunter. An interesting variety of *gonfanons* or banners are shown (D), as well as another certainly segmented tall, round-topped helmet with a *nasal* (E).

437A–C 'Passion scenes', *Antiphony*, Austria, c.1160 (Library of the Abbey of St Peter, Codex A.XII. 7, p.629, Salzburg, Austria)

Once again a piece of German art shows considerable Byzantine or Eastern European influence. Whether this was from copying a Byzantine manuscript or resulted from Austria's position on the eastern frontier with Hungary is unclear. The Centurion at the Crucifixion (A) is clearly based on a Byzantine original, with his headcloth, small round shield and traditional attitude. He seems to wear a peculiar mixture of a short-sleeved mail shirt with a lamellar *cuirass* or skirt. This could indicate some knowledge of *lamellae* on the part of the artist, or could simply be his misunderstood version of the Byzantine original. The Centurion also wears typical Western European mail *chausses*. Another warrior with a small round shield or buckler (B), has a mid-length sleeved mail *hauberk* with a *coif*, plus mail *chausses* on his legs. His helmet is slightly unusual for the period, being a segmented conical affair, perhaps of two-piece construction, and no *nasal*. The Salzburg *Antiphony* also includes one of the earliest representations of a curved sword in German art (C). It is a moderately realistic portrayal which may reflect the curved sabres still used by some warriors in neighbouring Hungary.

438A–Q *Eneid of Heinrich von Veldeke*, Germany, c.1145–1210 (Deutsche Staatsbibliothek, Ms. Germ. 20282, Berlin, Germany)

This is one of the most interesting of 12th or early 13th-century German manuscripts, particularly for the helmets that it portrays. These include flat or almost flat-topped types with or without *nasals* (F and G). Others are either proto-*great helms* consisting of little more than flat-topped helmets with face-masks (C and D), or early forms of true *great helm* (E and L–Q). An archer is also shown in a kind of narrow-brimmed *chapel-de-fer war-hat* (J). The figures with flat-topped *great helms* lacking face-masks seem to have mail *coifs* covering the entire face save for eye holes (F and G). Such a style seems to be almost unique outside Central Asia and the Islamic world. If it really was seen in late 12th-century Germany it is likely to have reflected Eastern European or even steppe influences. Three figures have some kind of turban wound around their helmets (D, O and P), while others carry substantial crests (L–N and P). Another unusual but not unique feature for Europe is the wrist-strap around the *pommel* of one sword (H). The swords themselves are much more conventional. Mail *hauberks* now include *mittens* (I, L, M, O and P), and mail *chausses* are worn (A, I, N, P and Q). Shields are kite-shaped but shorter, held by *enarmes* (D and I) and sometimes supported by *guiges* (I, L, P and Q). Two horses wear *caparisons* or *bards*, the decorations of which are clearly not heraldic and probably indicate padding, quilting, or even mail linings (L and N).

439A–B *Jungfrauenspiegel*, Germany, c.1200
(Kestner Museum, Hannover, Germany)

Comparable and presumably typically-German equipment appears in the similarly-dated *Jungfrauenspiegel*. It is also shown in greater detail. Again the warriors wear early forms of *great helm* with rounded edges and not much protection for the back of the neck. One example has a single eye-slit (A), while the second has a vertical reinforcing piece up the centre of the face-mask (B). The warriors carry large, curved, kite-shaped shields on *guiges*, and wear presumed mail *hauberks* with *mittens*, plus *chausses*. The swords are typical of the time and place.

440A–C 'Massacre of the Innocents', *Ingeborg Psalter*, Germany, France or England, c.1195
(Musée Condé, Ms. 1695, f.18v, Chantilly, France)

This manuscript may have been made in a French-speaking area of the Empire, in France, or in Anglo-Norman England. It portrays rather old-fashioned mid-sleeved mail *hauberks*, with mail *coifs* having *ventails* laced on the right side. One such *coif* lies on the wearer's shoulders (C). The straight swords have large round *pommels* which look more French than German.

441A–E *Das Rolandslied des Pfaffen Konrad*, Franconia, 1170
(University Library, Codex Palatinus Germanicus 112, Heidelberg, Germany)

The spare and linear style of drawing seen in certain 12th-century German manuscripts means that some assumptions have to be made when interpreting their arms and armour. No surface pattern is given to the mail but these figures must certainly wear long-sleeved mail *hauberks* with (E) or without (B and C) *mittens*. They have integral mail *coifs* drawn across the lower part of their faces under tall, domed helmets with substantial *nasals*. The shields are extremely large kite-shaped types. The two visible swords have tapering blades and either almond (C) or flattened nut-shaped (E) *pommels*.

442 **'Gideon',** *Bible d'Averbode,* **Lower Lotharingia (?),**
   c.1170
(**Bib. de l'Université, Ms. 363B, f.16v, Liège, Belgium**)

The main interest of this picture of Gideon is the rectangular line
below his throat. This could be seen as another example of the
otherwise mysterious rectangles depicted on *hauberks* in the Bayeux
Tapestry and the *Roda Bible*. Here, however, it probably represents
an early example of a separate mail *coif*. The other broad line across
his chest may reflect the influence of Byzantine iconography in which
many warrior-saints are given a kind of sash around the body. The
man otherwise has a conical helmet, short-sleeved mail *hauberk*,
sword, and large kite-shaped shield with a boss.

443A–E **Painted ceiling, Swabia, late 12th century**
(*in situ* **church of St Martin, Zillis, Switzerland**)

A–C – Magi (?); D–E – Massacre of the Innocents. The almost unique
painted ceiling at Zillis is naturally crude in style and old-fashioned in
content. The region where it was painted, though on the road to the
Little St Bernard and Splüge Passes, was located in a distant southern
part of the Duchy of Swabia. The swords are standard (D and E) but
the axe, knobbed mace and probably sheathed sword (A–C) given to
the Three Wise Men are likely to reflect the array of weapons carried
by pilgrims and other travellers as they made their way to or from the
southern passes.

444 **Sword from Brunau, Germany, c.1250**
(**present whereabouts unknown**)

The *pommel* on this sword seems to be of a 'cocked-hat' form which was
particularly popular in 13th-century Germany.

445 **Sword, Swabia–Switzerland, c.1250**
(**Landesmuseum, no. A.G.2765, Zurich, Switzerland**)

The thin curved *pommel* shown here seems to have been a development
of the 'cocked-hat' type. It was also popular in many parts of the
Empire, as well as being seen on daggers.

446 **Sword, Germany, c.1250–1300**
(**Zeughaus, Munich, Germany**)

This later sword has slightly longer *quillons* than that from Brunau
(fig.444) but its simpler *pommel* is presumably related in style.

447 **Sword, Germany (?), c.1200–50**
(**Museum and Art Galleries, Glasgow, Scotland**)

This sword might be German. Its long slender *quillons* suggest a date
well within the 13th century but its somewhat blunt-tipped blade and
nut-shaped *pommel* point to an earlier period.

448 Sword, Swabia, 13th century
(Musée Oeuvre Notre Dame, no.22.980.4, Strasbourg, France)

Clearly in the same basic family as the sword in the Munich Zeughaus (fig.446).

449A–E Crossbow-bolt heads from the Castle of Birkenfels, Obernai, Swabia, 13th–14th centuries
(Musée Oeuvre Notre Dame, no.XLVI.98, Strasbourg, France)

These undated crossbow bolts indicate the variety of types which were presumably used by garrisons and militias. All are strongly made and are designed to penetrate armour.

450 Ceremonial Imperial Sword of the Holy Roman Empire, Germany or Sicily, c.1200–20
(Treasury, Kunsthistorisches Museum, Vienna, Austria)

This splendid Imperial Sword may have been made, or at least decorated, in Sicily or southern Italy when these regions were under Hohenstaufen rule. Swords with small round *pommels* seem, in fact, to have been more popular in Italy than in Germany, which might in turn reflect differing styles of sword-play in these two regions of the Empire.

451 *Great helm* from Schlossberg bei Dargen, Pomerania, c.1250–75
(ex-Berlin Zeughaus; present whereabouts unknown)

A very good example of a strongly-built early form of fully-developed, flat-topped *great helm*. As such it may be regarded as a kind of archetype.

452 Unidentified effigy, Westphalia, early 13th century
(*in situ* church, Marienfeld, Germany)

Here a *coif* falls into two sections when taken from the head, which suggests that a new style was introduced in the 13th century. Note that the flap-like objects hanging over the mail of his sleeves are part of a cloak.

453A–B 'St George', carving, Franconia, c.1219–37
(*in situ* tympanum of Gnadenpforte, Cathedral, Bamberg, Germany)

The beautifully-carved early Gothic statue of St George in Bamberg Cathedral portrays a warrior in rather old-fashioned equipment for the early 13th century. This was presumably done intentionally for iconographic reasons. The saint has a mid-length sleeved mail *hauberk* with an integral *coif*, the *ventail* of which is unlaced and hanging from his right cheek. His sword-belt is of the early knotted variety.

454 **Statue of Count Dedo von Wettin, Saxony, c.1240**
(*in situ* Cathedral, Wechselburg, Germany)

Count Dedo's sword is virtually identical to certain surviving
examples, while the statue is also very similar to the better known
examples in Naumberg Cathedral.

455A–C **Carved relief, Swabia, early 13th century**
(*in situ* Cathedral, Freiburg im Breisgau, Germany)

The stylised and in some ways fanciful figures in this late-
Romanesque carving carry both kite-shaped (A) and small round
shields (C). The swords have straight *quillons* and either pointed (A)
or 'cocked-hat' (C) *pommels*.

456 **Carved choir-screen, Franconia, c.1220–30**
(*in situ* Cathedral, Bamberg, Germany)

This carving of an angel provides an interesting three-dimensional
view of the inside of a large kite-shaped shield.

457 **Carved head, Franconia, c.1230**
(Museum des Historischen Vereins, Bamberg, Germany)

This carved head, said to represent St Maurice, might have come
from the Cathedral or from the medieval city bridge. It almost
certainly mirrors the patron saint as seen in the city's medieval seal
(fig.459). The helmet in the carving is, however, unusual. It is a
simple conical affair, made in two pieces joined by a single comb-like
strip and reinforced by a rim band. The helmet also has a chin-strap.
Whether it is supposed to look archaic or whether it represents a real
style of helmet influenced by Eastern European fashions is unknown.

458A–C **'Massacre of the Innocents', carving, Lower
Lotharingia, c.1240**
(*in situ* west front, Liebfrauenkirche, Trier, Germany)

The soldiers are equipped in standard mid-13th century fashion and
are almost indistinguishable from their fellows in northern France.
They have mail *coifs*, mail *chausses*, and mail *hauberks* with *mittens*,
worn under sleeveless *surcoats*. However, a distinctive and perhaps
German feature is the almost crescent-shaped pommel of the sword
in the second figure's scabbard (B and C).

459 **Seal of the City of Bamberg, Franconia, 1230**
(Museum des Historischen Vereins, Bamberg, Germany)

The seal matrix, which shows a warrior in reverse, portrays the same
helmet as in the carving depicted in fig.457, which must have had
some iconographic significance at the time. This warrior also has
what appears to be a separate mail *coif*. His mail *hauberk* includes
mittens and he has mail *chausses*. He is armed with a spear and a

straight-*quilloned* sword having an apparently diamond-shaped *pommel*. The *surcoat* is also slightly peculiar in having squared shoulders and because it is very cut-away beneath the arms. This could indicate that it was supposed to be an early *coat-of-plates*. Indeed the row of dots which looks like the lower part of a mail *coif* could be intended as a line of rivets as it is placed at a slight distance from the adjacent row of dots.

460 Statue from the Cathedral, Swabia, c.1290
(Musée Oeuvre Notre Dame, Strasbourg, France)

The carving of an elderly warrior saint includes a number of interesting features, the most important of which is his mail *coif*. It is almost certainly worn over a padded *arming-cap*, which gives it a bulbous, almost square, outline. A *great helm* would presumably be worn over such a *coif* and *arming-cap*. The lower part of the *coif* also falls loosely below the throat. There is no *ventail* as such, but this part of the *coif* does appear to have an edging. Presumably a lace passed through here which could be pulled tight, thus drawing the *coif* over the chin or mouth. Such a simple system may provide an alternative interpretation for the much earlier rectangular shapes seen on the upper chests of some figures in the Bayeux Tapestry and elsewhere. This warrior also has a padded *gambeson* beneath his mail *hauberk*, this being visible at his right wrist. A massive sword has broad but slightly-curved *quillons*, one of which is missing.

461 'St Maurice', carved figure, Brandenburg, c.1250–1300
(Cathedral Museum, Magdeburg, Germany)

Since St Maurice was referred to as 'the Egyptian', he has been given African facial features. This particular carving has, however, attracted attention because it portrays an early example of a *coat-of-plates*. Over his long-sleeved mail *hauberk* the saint wears a cloth-covered garment in which the hidden metal splints or *lamellae* are indicated by two rows of rivets plus additional rivets near the shoulders. Note that this armour lies beneath a separate mail *coif*. Such an armour would have been laced or buckled at the back. The lower part of the garment consisted of non-protective flaps hanging down at the front and back. The similarity in outline of at least the upper part of this *coat-of-plates* and the garment seen on the slightly earlier Bamberg Seal (fig.459) is striking. St Maurice's sword is also worthy of comment, being a very short, perhaps broken, weapon with a large polyhedral *pommel*. It is, however, surely no coincidence that most of the earliest clear and less clear representations of German *coats-of-plates* are found in or near the eastern half of the country. These regions might have been under Slav or Hungarian influence, but more importantly they had more immediate experience of the armour worn by invading Mongol armies.

462A–C 'Massacre of the Innocents', carving, Thuringia, c.1255–60
(*in situ* Cathedral, Naumberg, Germany)

The swords are very similar to those seen on monumental statues in the same cathedral (f.463).

463A–E Statues of donors, Thuringia, c.1250
(*in situ* Cathedral, Naumberg, Germany)

A – Count Hermann von Wettin; B – Count Eckhart; C – Count Konrad; D – Count Timo; E –Dietrich von Brehna. The statues of the counts in Naumberg Cathedral all have the same large, flat-topped kite-shaped shields. None wear armour but each carries a sword with a different hilt. These presumably represent a range in use during the mid-13th century.

464 'Sleeping Guard at Holy Sepulchre', painted carving, Saxony, 1250–1300
(**Provincial Museum, Hannover, Germany**)

This little carved warrior is best known for his *coat-of-plates*, which consists of vertical splints riveted to the inside of an otherwise normal *surcoat*. The man also wears a mail *hauberk* with *mittens*, apparently over a padded *gambeson* which is visible at his neck. On his legs are normal mail *chausses*. His helmet is a flat-topped *great helm*. The carving seems to show this to be of the fully developed type with protection for the back and sides of the neck. But the curved outline of the face-plate or face-mask may indicate that in reality the helmet was closer to being a flat-topped helmet with a face-mask than a fully developed *great helm*.

465A–D Carving, Swabia, c.1270–1300
(*in situ* tympanum west door, Cathedral, Freiburg im Breisgau, Germany)

A–B – Crucifixion; C–D – Betrayal. Similar swords are shown on the west front of Freiburg Cathedral, including a clear example of a large 'crescent-shaped' *pommel* (C). Other interesting features include close-fitting *cervellière* helmets, one of which appears to be carried by its chin-strap over a man's left arm (B). Another man carries a very substantial axe with a sort of triple socket for the haft (D).

466A–E 'Sleeping Guards at the Holy Sepulchre', carving in St Mauritius Rundkapelle, Swabia, c.1300
(*in situ* Cathedral, Constance, Germany)

The most important feature of the arms and armour on these three small armoured figures is remarkably difficult to see, but includes the laces or buckles that fasten a *coat-of-plates* (E). Two warriors probably have such *coats-of-plates* (B, C and E), judging from the wide cut-away sides of their *surcoats*, which are themselves worn over the sword-belts. The third figure has short cap-sleeves with scalloped edges (A and D), which might indicate another form of soft armour or *coat-of-plates* being worn beneath the *surcoat*. Other features of interest are a relatively small *great helm* (C), typical almost-triangular shields, a sword with a small round *pommel* but a ribbed grip (B and E), and two broad *war-hats* (A, B and D). Both of these have had their brims damaged. One is also shown with a split chin-strap.

467A–C Shrine of Charlemagne, silver reliquary, Lower Lotharingia, c.1200–7
(*in situ* Cathedral, Aachen, Germany)

A number of very interesting early forms of *great helm* are shown on the embossed silver Shrine of Charlemagne. They are basically flat-topped helmets with face-masks, but in two cases (A and B) they clearly have additional plates added at the back. This might represent the transitional stage between the helmet with a face-mask and the true *great helm*.

468 *Goslar Evangeliar*, Saxony, c.1230
(Rathaus Library, f.10, Goslar, Germany)

An early form of almost crescent-shaped *pommel*, which was to become very popular in Germany, appears in this manuscript.

469 'St Matthew' on Chasse de Sainte Gertrude, silver gilt reliquary, Lower Lotharingia, c.1272
(*in situ* Church of St Gertrude, Nivelles, Belgium)

The axe held by Matthew seems to show the blade fastened to the haft at two points, on a long sleeve which encloses the upper part of the haft.

470 Bronze *aquamanile*, Lower Saxony, c.1250–1300
(Metropolitan Museum of Art, inv. 64.101.1492, New York, United States)

A vigorous little sculpture showing a man in relatively simple equipment consisting of a flat-topped *great helm* with a small horned crest, a long-sleeved mail *hauberk* with *mittens*, and mail *chausses*. No plate armour or even weapons are shown. The lump or protuberance behind his shoulder was part of the hinge mechanism for the lid of the *aquamanile*.

471A–F *Psalterium B. Elisabeth*, Thuringia (?), early 13th century
(Museo Archeologico Nazionale, Cividale Ms. CXXXVII, Cividale, Italy)

A–B – f.139v; C – f.lv; D – f.6; E–F – f.4v. This particular psalter illustrates a number of features that are interesting not only for the weapons they show but for the light they might shed on warfare in Thuringia and neighbouring Saxony. This region has been known for its effective levy of peasant archers in the early medieval period. An archer using either a longbow or a large form of flat-bow (C) appears in the *Psalterium B. Elisabeth*. The quiver that hangs at his belt is slightly more sophisticated than normally seen in 13th-century Western Europe. This, plus the crescent-bladed arrows that are held points uppermost in the quiver, might point to a large degree of eastern influence on Thuringian archery via the Slavs. Two armoured figures are unlike most other 13th-century German warriors since they wear short, tight-fitting tunics with decorative lower edges (A and B). These might be padded *gambesons*. The men certainly have padded *cuisses* over their thighs and knees with mail *chausses* worn beneath. Their mail *coifs* appear to be separate from their long-sleeved *hauberks* and to have squared lower edges. One man (B) also wears an early form of decorated *great helm*. Swords have long straight *quillons* and are carried from knotted sword-belts.

472A–D 'Parzival and Feirefiz', *Parzival*, Germany, c.1250 (Staatsbibliothek, Ms. Germ. 19, f.49v, Munich, Germany)

Here two warriors fight and subsequently discuss the combat; perhaps wondering why the hero's sword broke (A and C). Their weapons are straight and non-tapering, with long straight *quillons* and oval *pommels*. Their helmets are early flat-topped *great helms*, and they wear long-sleeved mail *hauberks* with *mittens*, and mail *chausses*, but no apparent pieces of plate armour. Their shields are of the distinctly triangular form popular in Germany. From here the style may have spread to Byzantium as large numbers of German mercenaries are known to have served in Byzantine and other Balkan armies in the 13th century.

473 Oak statue of King Louis IX of France by the 'Strasbourg Master', Swabia, c.1290 (private collection; after Müller-Wiener)

Although this carving represents the canonised French king St Louis, who died a generation before the statuette was made, the carver is believed to have been from the Imperial city of Strasbourg. The armour it portrays is very traditional and even old-fashioned with the exception of the plated *greaves*. This is, in fact, one of the earliest clear representations of such *greaves*. The rest of the king's armour consists of a mail *hauberk*, *coif* and *chausses*. The *coif* clearly lacks a *ventail* and may be of the type that is tightened around the face by a draw-string. His sword, sword-belt, shield and *guige* are traditional.

474 Engraved stone funerary plaque of the knight Antoine, Lower Lotharingia, early 13th century
(Curtius Museum, Liège, Belgium)

This simple tomb-slab shows a knight in normal mail armour plus a flat-topped *great helm*. It is interesting to compare this with the lost Belgian tomb slab of Nicola III de Rumigny (fig.432).

475 Seal of John de Werd, Swabia–Upper Lotharingia, 1297
(Archives Departmental, Strasbourg, France)

Large and sometimes extravagant crests mounted on *great helms*, as shown here, were more popular in late 13th and early 14th century Germany than in most other parts of Europe. It is, however, far from certain that such crests were used in battle.

476 Seal of Frederick of Lorraine, Upper Lotharingia, 1264
(Archives Departmental, Strasbourg, France)

This seal, from the same region as the preceding, shows an earlier form of shield and a flat-topped *great helm* without a crest. The horse wears a *caparison* which appears to include a raised ridge down the animal's nose. This is probably part of a *chanfron*.

477 Seal of John of Lichtenberg, Upper Lotharingia, 1284
(Archives Departmental, Strasbourg, France)

John de Lichtenberg is here shown in a perhaps round-topped *great helm* beneath a very fanciful crest. He wields a sword with down-turned *quillons* and an apparent *langet*. His armour is of mail but there is a suggestion of early *poleyns* on his knees.

478 Seal of Count Louis II of Looz, Lower Lotharingia, 1216
(City Archives no.13.714, Brussels, Belgium)

A most interesting seal. It shows the count in a mail *hauberk*, *coif* and *chausses* but no *surcoat*, which is an early fashion. He also wears an early type of flat-topped *great helm* which does not provide much protection for the sides and back of the head. The pointed piece on top may indicate a slightly conical outline to the helmet or be a plume holder. His sword has down-turned *quillons* and his long shield wraps around his body. His horse wears only the front section of a *caparison*.

479 Seal of Jan van Harnes, Lower Lotharingia, 1288
(ARA Zegalafgietsel no.7083, Antwerp, Belgium)

On his seal Jan van Harnes looks more French than do the figures on the preceding seals. This may reflect the strength of French influence in Brabant, Hainault and Flanders. His crest is relatively small and his *great helm* is of a transitional form between the flat-topped and later round-topped types. The only visible armour is of mail.

480 Seal of Nicola V de Rumigny, Lower Lotharingia, c.1244
(after Roland)

This member of the De Rumigny family wears an old-fashioned long-sleeved mail *hauberk* without *mittens*. His helmet is a standard flat-topped *great helm* and his long sword again has a rather old-fashioned nut-shaped *pommel*.

481 Seal of Jacques de Rumigny, Lower Lotharingia, c.1270
(after Roland)

So little has changed during the years between the seals of Nicola V and Jacques that a large degree of family iconographic tradition seems inevitable. Both men are shown without *mittens* to their *hauberks*, which is unusual for the 13th century.

482 *Roman de Saint Graal*, Flanders, late 13th/early 14th centuries
(British Library, Ms. Add. 10.292, f.266, London, England)

This manuscript may have been made in French or Imperial Flanders. It shows a mailed warrior with at least one *ailette* on his shoulder and a large domed *poleyn* on his knee. This appears to be fastened directly to his mail *chausses*.

483 *Histoire de Bon Roi Alexandre*, Flanders (?), c.1300
(Bib. Royale Albert I, Ms. 11040, Brussels, Belgium)

If the dating of this manuscript is correct, then it includes some early representations of important pieces of armour. All the horsemen have pointed *great helms*, that of Alexander being topped by a crown. At least four riders, including the king, have side-hinged visors attached to these helmets. The figure on the furthest right has his helmet turned towards the viewer. Three of these visors seem to suggest that only the part of the helmet below the eye-slit is movable. Perhaps this was, in fact, the earliest attempt to make a movable visor by dividing the helmet at its most obvious point, across the eye slit. *Ailettes* are seen twice and Alexander also appears to have *greaves* around his shins with possible *poleyns* over his knees. Otherwise the armour is all of mail. In two cases laces are apparently drawn around the mail sleeves to stop them flapping uncomfortably, not only at the wrist but also at the elbow.

484 'Maccabean Army', *Bible de Leau*, Lower Lotharingia (?), 1248
(Bib. Grand Séminaire, Ms. 243, Liège, Belgium)

A simple illustration showing almost the maximum possible amount of mail armour, consisting of a long-sleeved mail *hauberk* with *mittens*, and a mail *bard* for the horse. Only mail *chausses* are missing . The man also wears a flat-topped *great helm*.

485A–B **'Thieves at the Crucifixion', *Liège Psalter*, Lower Lotharingia (?), c.1250**
(Bib. de l'Université, Ms. 431, f.188v, Liège, Belgium)

A very rare example of an artist making an unmistakable distinction between armour of mail (B) and armour of scale or lamellar (A). The former includes a *coif* and *mittens*. The latter seems to be short-sleeved and clearly lacks a head protection. Both of these features are correctly associated with armour of scale or lamellar. What is even more interesting is the fact that the man in scale or lamellar is the thief whose soul is being taken by angels while the thief in a mail *hauberk* is counted among the damned, his soul being seized by a devil. This is in clear contradiction to normal 13th-century iconography where armour of scale or lamellar is almost always associated with the 'wicked', Muslims, or other 'infidels'.

486 **Manuscript, Flanders, late 13th century**
(British Library, Ms. Sloane 2435, f.85, London, England)

Once again the illustration could have been made in Imperial or French Flanders. It shows normal equipment for the 13th century, consisting of a flat-topped *great helm*, mail *hauberk* with *mittens*, mail *chausses*, sleeveless *surcoat* and an almost-triangular shield.

487A–C ***Somme le Roi*, manuscript, Upper Lotharingia, c.1280**
(British Library, Ms. 2862, f.8v, London, England)

A–B – David and Goliath; C – Sword of Proesse. Goliath (B) has here been given somewhat rudimentary equipment of a mail *hauberk* with *coif* and *mittens*, mail *chausses*, and a sort of narrow-brimmed *cervellière*. The Sword of Proesse (C) is, however, a fine weapon with decorated *quillons*. It is worth noting that the forefinger over the *quillons* indicates knowledge of a more advanced fencing technique than was generally seen in the early 13th century and might indicate Italian influence.

488A–D ***Vita Caroli Magni*, manuscript, Swabia (?), late 13th century**
(Cathedral Library, St Gallen, Switzerland)

The relatively rare flat-topped *chapel-de-fer war-hat* (A) appears in this manuscript, as do flat-topped *great helms* with apparent reinforcing pieces at the back (B and D).

489A–D ***World Chronicle of Rudolf von Ems*, manuscript, Swabia (?), late 13th century**
(Cathedral Library, St Gallen, Switzerland)

An almost identical type of *great helm* again appears (B) in this similarly dated and stylistically comparable manuscript. Whether such helms would have been worn by crossbowmen is open to doubt.

Other aspects of the picture seem equally incongruous, such as the apparent sapper (D) with an axe and a very small shield. Sappers would normally have used larger *mantlets*, presumably like the one held by a warrior in a deep-brimmed *war-hat* (C). The various forms of *enarmes* and internal grips given to these shields are, however, worth noting (A, C and D).

490A–E   Shrine of St Odilia, painted wooden chest, Lower Lotharingia, 1292
(Museum, Monastery of Kolen-Kerniel, Belgium)

This martyrdom scene portrays the standard late 13th-century equipment for sergeants and other non-noble warriors in both France and the neighbouring provinces of the Empire.

491A–C   'Massacre of the Innocents', manuscript, Germany, c.1280
(British Library, Ms. Add. 17.687, London, England)

An artist has here used a variety of patterns to indicate mail, but there is little reason to doubt that they all refer to a perfectly ordinary form of mail construction. All three warriors have separate mail *coifs* with rectangular flaps hanging down the front, and probably down the back as well. One has a short-sleeved mail *hauberk* (B) worn over a tunic, another a long-sleeved mail *hauberk* with *mittens* (C) worn under a *surcoat*. One man has ordinary mail *chausses* (A) while a second has mail *chausses* under probably padded *cuisses* which reach to mid-calf (C). These also seem to have *poleyns* attached to protect the knees. A third figure (B) has almost identical probably padded *cuisses*, this time certainly with *poleyns* attached, but apparently he wears them without mail *chausses*. All three men have tapering swords with large, almost crescent-shaped, *pommels*.

492   *Great helm* from Küssnacht Castle, Swabia, c.1320–50
(Schweizerisches Landesmuseum, Zurich, Switzerland)

These corroded remains are from a late form of helmet that was popular in many parts of the Empire. *Great helms* seem to have continued to be used in war in Italy for longer than in Germany, where they had largely been relegated to the tournament field.

493A–Q   Arms and armour fragments from Schönenwerd in Limmattel, Swabia, before 1344
(Schweizerisches Landesmuseum, Zurich, Switzerland)

These fragments from a castle near Zurich include a spear (A) and either arrow or crossbow-bolt heads (B–D). Far more important, however, are the corroded remains of a presumed *coat-of-plates* (E–G). The sizes and shapes of the elements differ considerably and were clearly intended for different parts of the body.

494 *Hauberk* and *bascinet*, said to have been made for Rudolf IV, Austria, 1339–65
(Royal Armouries Museum, Leeds, England)

This *bascinet* with its associated mail *aventail* is of an early close-fitting type; the *aventail* clearly being drawn tight by a lace around the face. The mail *hauberk* is of a short-hemmed, mid-sleeved cut. It would normally be worn with plate armour such as a *coat-of-plates* and arm defences.

495 *Great helm*, Germany, late 13th/early 14th centuries
(Museum für Deutsche Geschichte, Berlin, Germany)

A fine specimen of a flat-topped *great helm* similar to the example found in Pomerania (fig.451). It could, in fact, date from the mid-13th century.

496 *Great helm*, Germany or Italy, mid-14th century
(Waffensammlung, Kunsthistorisches Museum, Vienna, Austria)

This helmet belonged to a member of the Prankh family. It was probably for use in tournament rather than war and could have been made on either side of the Alps.

497 *Bascinet*, Germany (?), c.1330
(Metropolitan Museum of Art, New York, United States)

The *vervelles* are modern. The original helmet could have had some similar means of supporting an *aventail* but may also have been worn over a *coif*. It is, in fact, something of a cross between an early *bascinet* and a close-fitting *cervellière*. The smaller holes around the rim are to fasten a lining.

498 *Great helm*, Germany, 14th century
(Germanisches Museum, Nuremburg, Germany)

A fine decorated helmet which belonged to a member of the Kornburg family and was probably used for tournaments. The additional mail collar to protect the throat seems to have been an unusual feature.

499 *Great helm*, Germany, 14th century
(private collection; ex-Berlin, present whereabouts unknown)

The origins of this *great helm* are unclear. It could date from the mid-14th century and have been for tournament use. It is also a late type with a deep pointed 'beard' jutting down to protect the throat.

500 *Basilard* dagger, Bavaria (?), 14th century
(Zeughaus Museum, Munich, Germany)

A typical *basilard*, having a double-edged, almost-triangular blade plus a hilt in which the *quillons* or guard and the upper part of the grip form an H-shape.

501 Dagger, Burgundy (?), 14th century
(Boissonas Collection, Geneva, Switzerland)

An example of a dagger with a single-edged blade, known as a 'Burgundian' dagger.

502 Dagger, Upper Lotharingia (?), 14th century
(Boissonas Collection, Geneva, Switzerland)

This form of dagger, while similar to the *basilard*, also has parallels with the later *rondel* dagger. Its double-sided blade was narrower than that of a *basilard* but seems to have been thicker in section.

503 *Basilard* dagger, Germany, 14th century
(Boissonas Collection, Geneva, Switzerland)

This particular *basilard* seems to have been made from one piece, to which grips of bone or wood could have been attached.

504 *Bascinet* with *bretache*, Swabia, c.1350
(Schweizerisches Landesmuseum, Zurich, Switzerland)

An excellently-preserved helmet complete with the removable visor that became a popular feature in 14th-century Germany. Such a *bretache*, attached to the chin of the mail *aventail*, would have given protection from all but the most powerful lateral blow. At the same time it allowed easier breathing and far better visibility than a full visor.

505 Sword, Germany (?), 14th century
(Boissonas Collection, Geneva, Switzerland)

This is unusual for the 14th century, having a parallel-sided blade. It might have been a lighter weapon to be carried in time of peace.

506 Crossbow, Swabia, 14th century
(Schweizerisches Landesmuseum, Zurich, Switzerland)

This appears to have been of a heavy type with a very long stock. Such crossbows would have normally been used from behind a fortified wall.

507A–B Sword and scabbard, Germany (?), 14th century
(Boissonas Collection, Geneva, Switzerland)

A standard 14th-century *sword-of-war*, though the survival of its scabbard makes it rather special.

508A–B Bascinet from Schmalenstein, Swabia, c.1350
(Badische Landesmuseum, no.C.7349, Karlsruhe, Germany)

A – original condition; B – restoration. The contrast between this fully developed and rather deep *bascinet* and the earlier bowl-like example (fig.497) illustrates the development of the type. This *bascinet* would have had a substantial visor attached to the hinges on each temple. A mail *aventail* would also have been fastened to the *vervelles* on the side of the facial opening and around the lower edge.

509 Pikehead, Switzerland, 14th century
(Boissonas Collection, Geneva, Switzerland)

The attribution of this pikehead to the 14th century is far from certain, though long spears or pikes of this period probably had blades of a similar sort.

510 Ivory chess piece, Germany, early 14th century
(Staatliche Museen, Berlin, Germany)

This chess 'knight' presumably represents a horseman leading a troop of crossbowmen. The horseman wears a brimmed *war-hat* over a *coif* and is armed with a broad, tapering sword and a flat-topped shield. His followers carry crossbows with loading stirrups. Some of them might also wear close-fitting helmets, but this is not clear.

511 Sword, Germany (?), 14th century
(Boissonas Collection, Geneva, Switzerland)

A large so-called *great sword*. Such weapons were used from horseback by men who sometimes also carried a normal-sized sword.

512A–F Effigy of Heinrich Otto, Landgraf of Hessen,
Franconia–Saxony, c.1320
(*in situ* Church of St Elizabeth, Marburg, Germany)

This effigy, on the borders of Franconia and Saxony, includes a number of very interesting minor details. Basically, however, the man wears a long-sleeved mail *hauberk* with *mittens* slit at the palm and slipped back over the wrist (A). The mail *coif* (A and C) appears to be integral with the *hauberk* and is clearly lined with some material such as fabric or soft leather to protect the face and head from chaffing. Mail *chausses* are worn (A), these being fastened to a sole for ease of walking (E). It is most unlikely that the mail went inside this sole, or that mail was ever worn under the feet as this would make walking almost impossible. Perhaps the most important features on this effigy are the *ailettes* (A and B). On this highly-detailed three-dimensional carving they are shown as vertical pieces with fringed edges, fastened to the shoulders with knots or tassels. As such they would have provided almost no protection even if made of steel. *Ailettes* were, in fact, for heraldic recognition purposes only. The detailed carving of the sword-hilt (D) shows a weapon with, perhaps, a wire-bound grip, and some kind of flap over the *quillons*. This clearly cannot be fixed to the scabbard and must be a sort of hood or washer to keep damp and dirt out of the scabbard. It is possible that many apparent short *langets* protruding down a blade from otherwise normal *quillons* in less-detailed pictorial sources are the same kind of 'weather-proofing' hood, cap or washer. The Landgraf has a dagger on his right hip. This is of a simple form like a miniature sword and is held in a decorated sheath which seems to be hung from the sword-belt by thongs.

513A–E 'Sleeping Guards at the Holy Sepulchre', carved relief, Swabia, c.1345–50
(*in situ* Cathedral, Freiburg im Breisgau, Germany)

A number of superb 14th-century Easter altars with scenes of the Resurrection on their front panels survive in south-western Germany, Alsace and Lorraine. This example includes a wealth of detailed information about the presumably non-noble soldiers who formed the bulk of contemporary armies. The only obviously fanciful feature is the tall helmet of one figure (E) which, with its curled crown, stems from contemporary representations of Central Asiatic 'pagans'. The lower part of the helmet is based on a *bascinet*. More realistic features include tall, brimmed *chapel-de-fer war-hats* made from one piece (A and D), an all-mail *bretache* (B), an old-fashioned mail *hauberk* with integral fingered *mittens* (A), various *basilard*-style daggers (A and C–E), a sword with a crescent-shaped *pommel* (A), and *gauntlets* of plate (B and C) or flexible leather plus segmented fingers (E). Other mail *gauntlets* either have a single plate to protect the back of the hand or are the *mittens* of a mail *hauberk* being worn under a *vambrace* with an additional plate for the hand. A small buckler with a large boss is shown (B), as well as a possibly unstrung crossbow (C). Armour for the limbs includes mail *chausses* (B and C), one with an apparent slit in the leather sole (E), half-round *rerebraces* and *vambraces* (C) and fully tubular *rerebraces* and *vambraces* (D), *poleyns*, *greaves*, and laminated *sabatons* (C). A *great helm* is also shown (C). Soft armour is present in the form of horizontally (E) and perhaps also vertically-quilted *gambesons* worn beneath mail. A quilted garment or perhaps a laminated collar is visible around one man's neck (D). Various figures may have *coats-of-plates*. One quite clearly does so (D), and this armour probably includes shoulder-pieces or *epaulettes*.

514A–D Effigy of Ulrich de Werd, Landgraf of Lower Alsace, Swabia, c.1345
(*in situ* Church of St William, Strasbourg, France)

The magnificently detailed effigy of Ulrich de Werd is one of a large number of mid-14th century carvings that illustrate German arms and armour during the years of transition from the 'age of mail' to the 'age of plate'. Beneath his head lies a *great helm*, which shows the internal support consisting of split leather laced at the crown. His *bascinet* with mail *aventail* would have been worn under this. The Landgraf wears a mail *hauberk* with mid-length sleeves over arm defences of which the lower-arm *vambrace* is visible. On his hands are gloves over which he would presumably have put the plated *gauntlets* which lie on top of his sword (A–C). From the chest of his *hauberk* run a series of chains to which *great helm*, sword, dagger and any other important weapons would be attached. Their presence virtually proves that some form of rigid or semi-rigid *coat-of-plates* is worn beneath the *surcoat*, though this is not visible at the shoulders or armpits. An additional garment between the *surcoat* and mail *hauberk* is, however, visible on his hips below the point where the *surcoat* is fastened by three buttons. Mail *chausses* are worn on the legs. *Poleyns* cover his knees and are laced behind, over apparently padded *cuisses* (A and D).

515 Carved relief of an Elector of Bavaria from the Kaufhaus, Mainz, Franconia, 1318
(Museum of Antiquities, Mainz, Germany)

This much cruder relief carving portrays a man in equipment similar to that of Ulrich de Werd. A *great helm* with a crest hangs from his shoulder, and he has a *bascinet* with an *aventail*. Over the mail *hauberk*, this time with old-fashioned mail *mittens*, he wears a *surcoat* with chains from the chest indicating a *coat-of-plates* beneath. These chains run to the hilt of his *basilard* dagger and his sword, which appears to have some kind of flap over the top of the scabbard. Over his legs are mail *chausses* and over his knees are *poleyns*.

516 'Sleeping Guards at the Holy Sepulchre', relief carving, Franconia, mid-14th century
(*in situ* Church of St Nicholas, Haguenau, France)

The leg-harness worn by this warrior is of the fully-developed mid-14th-century form with laminated *sabatons*, shaped *greaves* for the front of the legs, hinged *poleyns* with doubled wings at the sides to protect the back of the knee, and even a plated *cuisse* for the front of the thigh, all this being worn over mail *chausses*. Other aspects of the man's equipment are remarkably old-fashioned. His mail *hauberk* might include fingered *mittens*, although the substantially padded wrist bands might form part of separate mail *gauntlets*. He even has a flat-topped *great helm* to wear over his *bascinet* and mail *aventail*. A thong rather than a chain holds his dagger. It presumably runs to some point on his chest where it would be fastened to a *coat-of-plates*. The small plate on his shoulder may form part of such an armour. Indeed, the entire *surcoat*, which is laced tightly at the side of his chest, may be part of a *coat-of-plates*.

517 **Effigy of Rudolfs IV, Markgraf of Baden, Swabia, c.1348**
(*in situ* Fürstenkapelle, Lichtental bei Baden-Baden, Germany)

The armour of Rudolfs IV seems to stand at a point in development between that of Ulrich de Werd and that of the Elector of Bavaria. He wears a *bascinet* and *aventail*, to which has been added a most interesting plate chin-piece or *bevor*. In addition to a mail *hauberk* with long sleeves and separate *gauntlets* he has a kind of rudimentary arm protection consisting of single splints for the upper and lower arms which meet at a *roundel* laced on the side of the elbow. Like the Elector, the Markgraf has a place to which he might attach a chain to retain his *basilard* dagger. This might pass through a hole in the tight jerkin which is laced up his chest. On the other hand this jerkin, with its fringed lower edge, might itself be the covering of a *coat-of-plates*. The scalloped cap sleeves visible at his shoulder may form part of this armour or could more likely be part of a relatively short *surcoat* reaching almost to his knees, similar to that worn by the Elector. Also like the Elector, he carries a small flat-topped shield and wears mail *chausses*, beneath *poleyns* which may be of splinted or fluted construction and be fastened to or over padded *cuisses*.

518 **Engraved funerary slab of Gilles de Hamal, Holland, c.1354**
(*in situ* church, Heeren-Elderen, Netherlands)

Similar cap sleeves and short jerkin are seen on this funerary slab. However, this example has a flap down the back and is clearly worn over a *coat-of-plates*, the lower part of which is visible from the solar plexus to the upper groin. Chains again retain a *basilard* dagger and a heavy sword. Other interesting features are the splinted *rerebraces* for the upper arms, which are worn outside a relatively long-sleeved mail *hauberk*, and the splinted *vambraces* for the lower arms, which are worn beneath the sleeves of the *hauberk*. Over his thighs he wears probably padded *cuisses* to which very bulbous domed *poleyns* are attached. Below these are full *greaves*, which appear to be laced. This might simply be a form of decoration, or might indicate that they are made of splints, perhaps even of leather. His feet are protected by the lower flaps of mail *chausses*, or perhaps simply mail attached to the *greaves*.

519 **So-called effigy of Berthold V, last Duke of Zahringen, Swabia, c.1350–75**
(*in situ* Cathedral, Freiburg im Breisgau, Germany)

This oversized effigy clearly dates from considerably later than the death of Berthold V early in the 14th century, and it includes many of the features already seen in other effigies. The tall domed *bascinet* has its removable *nasal* unfastened and hanging from the chin. He wears a tight *surcoat* with decorated cap sleeves over a presumed *coat-of-plates* and a short-sleeved mail *hauberk*. Heavy plated *gauntlets* appear to include padded wrist protections, although this is not clear. On his legs are extremely bulbous fluted *poleyns* and mail *chausses*. The *quillons* of his sword have been damaged, but on his right hip he carries an early version of an 'ear dagger'. This should not be confused with the later 'ballock dagger', in which the 'testes' form the guard or *quillons* rather than, as here, the *pommel*.

520 'City militiaman', carved corbel, Upper Lotharingia, early 14th century
(Musée Oeuvre Notre Dame, Strasbourg, France)

In this crude little carving a member of the Strasbourg militia is armed with a spear and a broad-bladed dagger. His armour consists of a *bascinet* which seems to have a fastening point for a *bretache*, visor or mail flap, though neither is shown. He also has a mail *aventail*, and a shield which he appears to hold almost upside down. No other armour is visible.

521 Effigy of Gunther von Schwarzburg, Franconia, c.1350
(*in situ* Cathedral, Frankfurt-am-Main, Germany)

Once again a mid-14th-century German knight uses basically the same arms and armour as are depicted in the earlier figures, but with certain variations. His *bascinet* is pointed and apparently slightly fluted, with the *nasal bretache* hanging loose. A heavy *great helm* with a large crest is clearly shown. This time his arm defences are all worn over the mail of the *hauberk*, the *rerebraces* and *vambraces* being of a splinted and riveted construction. Since German armourers were clearly quite capable of making sophisticated plate armour, the most logical reason for such a splinted and riveted construction, which is also seen on his *greaves*, is for lightness or cheapness. Such armour for the limbs was probably of leather reinforced with iron splints. The plated *gauntlets* now have funnel-shaped wrist coverings which permitted easier movement of the hands. A dagger, basically of the *basilard* form, hangs at his waist while his *surcoat* seems to have a decorated lining. He has fluted *poleyns* over his knees, while his *sabatons* are of a different construction yet again. Given the accurate representation of mail on his *aventail* and arms, his feet are unlikely to be covered by the same material shown in a more stylised form. The random pattern of dots might indicate rivets holding scales on the inside of decorative *sabatons*.

522A–B 'Guards at the Holy Sepulchre', carved relief, Franconia, c.1350–5
(*in situ* Church of St Nicholas, Haguenau, France)

Two infantry soldiers are here shown in much the same equipment as seen elsewhere. The crossbowman (A) has a *bascinet* and *aventail*, a long-sleeved mail *hauberk* with *gauntlets*, and a possible *coat-of-plates*, the shoulder protecting *epaulettes* of which are visible. His full leg-harness consists of plated *cuisses, poleyns* and *greaves*, while his feet seem to be protected by riveted *sabatons*, perhaps scale-lined. His massive sword has a cap or flap which goes over the top of the scabbard, while the bolts for his crossbow are held in a bag-like quiver on his hip. The axeman (B) differs in having removed his helmet, thus exposing the upper part of a stiffened jerkin or *coat-of-plates* which has been laced up the front. His leg protection is much the same except that the scales of his *sabatons* are now visible. His hand defences are most interesting, consisting of mail or mail-covered *gauntlets* with a small plate to protect the back of the hand and substantially padded or perhaps splinted wrist coverings.

523A–C 'Sleeping Guards at the Holy Sepulchre', carved relief, Swabia, c.1320–30
(*in situ* Cathedral, Strasbourg, France)

Here an earlier version of the same subject illustrates the considerable developments that took place in western German armour from 1325 to 1350. These men are primarily protected by mail, including a *coif* (A), full *hauberk* with *mittens* (A–C), and mail *chausses* (A). A possibly close-fitting *cervellière* (B) and a late form of *great helm* (C) both appear, as do presumably padded *cuisses* (A). The most modern piece of equipment is, of course, the *coat-of-plates* (A), which seems to be fastened at the shoulders.

524A–I Guards at the Holy Sepulchre', carved relief, Swabia, c.1345
(Musée Oeuvre Notre Dame, Strasbourg, France)

Perhaps the most detailed of the series of reliefs showing soldiers at the Holy Sepulchre is that in Strasbourg. It is also one of the most varied in content. Helmets include round and pointed fluted *bascinets* with mail *aventails* (A and H). Another larger apparent *bascinet* lies on the ground (D). This might, in fact, be a visored *bascinet* seen from the back. Such a visored *bascinet*, though without an *aventail*, is also worn by another figure (G), while a visored *great helm* lies beneath the elbow of a third figure (H). The final figure has a brimmed *war-hat* resting on his knee (B). Body armour includes long and mid-sleeved mail *hauberks* (A, B and G) and at least one laminated *coat-of-plates* worn beneath a jerkin which laces up the front and has very wide sleeve openings (A). Leg-harnesses consist of simple mail *chausses* (A), splinted *greaves* with *poleyns* and padded *cuisses* (B), and *greaves* plus *poleyns* and riveted, probably splint or scale-lined *cuisses* (H). Arm defences consist of similarly-constructed *vambraces* (B, G and H), plus *gauntlets*. These are basically leather gloves with plates to cover the back of the hand

and fingers (A, E, F–I). Two shields are shown; round (B) and oval (G). The former is an infantry shield but the second is held on a *guige* by a man in apparent riding boots (G). Perhaps this latter figure represents the specialised light cavalry who made their appearance in many parts of 14th-century Europe. Only a few weapons are shown. The axe (A) is a modern restoration. A *basilard* dagger (A and F) is shown in considerable detail. It is apparently suspended behind a kind of small purse (E). A *falchion* appears at first sight to be straightforward, but on closer inspection poses some difficult questions (B and E). While the weapon itself is a typical *falchion* with a blade that broadens towards the tip, the scabbard does the same. How might the weapon be drawn from such a scabbard? Presumably the scabbard was slit down the side for some distance, so perhaps the otherwise apparently redundant buckle (E) on the outside had something to do with closing such a slit.

525 Statue of a member of the Gent levy, Flanders, c.1340 (Stonework Museum, Gent, Belgium)

Only one of the original statutes representing the Gent city militia survives. It originally stood on the belfry, where it has now been replaced by a reproduction. The carving is quite simple but clearly shows a man equipped in a style similar to that seen in Strasbourg (fig.520). He has a *bascinet* with an *aventail*, *epaulettes* which probably form part of a *coat-of-plates*, and the short sleeves of a mail *hauberk* over *rerebraces*. A *roundel* can be seen at his elbow, while his lower arms are protected either by splinted *vambraces* or the extended cuffs of large *gauntlets*. His sword seems, rather surprisingly, to be suspended from a *baldric* unless this is a very long *guige* leading to his flat-topped shield. On his right hip is an early example of a true 'ballock dagger'. This form is sometimes more delicately, but less accurately, called a 'kidney dagger'. No armour is discernible on his legs.

526 Bronze *aquamanile*, Lower Lotharingia (?), early 14th century (Rijksmuseum, Amsterdam, Netherlands)

The knight shown here with his extravagantly-horned crest wears a late form of flat-topped *great helm* and a full mail *hauberk* with *mittens*. The only 'modern' features are the *poleyns* and apparently plated *cuisses*, which are worn over mail *chausses* to protect his knees and the front of his thighs.

527 Seal of Anselme de Ribeaupierre, Upper Lotharingia, 1310 (Archives Departmental, Strasbourg, France)

Another *great helm* with the massive crest favoured throughout much of the Empire appears on this seal. The figure otherwise seems to wear mail *hauberk* and *chausses*, perhaps having *ailettes* on his shoulders, while his horse has a full *caparison* or *bard*.

528 Seal of Ulrich de Werd, Landgraf of Lower Alsace, Swabia, 1325
(Archives Departmental, Strasbourg, France)

Here Ulrich de Werd is shown in a slightly earlier style of equipment than appears on his effigy (fig.514). His *great helm* has a large horned crest and he has an *ailette* on his right shoulder. The possibility that a single *ailette* was sometimes worn alone cannot be dismissed, for if such shoulder-pieces were solely for heraldic purposes they would have been largely redundant on the left side, where a shield with its own heraldic device would be far easier to see.

529 Seal of Jan van Namen, Flanders, 1302
(City Archives, Politieke Charters reek I, nr.170, Brugge, Belgium)

This early and very specifically dated seal (1 August 1302) is almost unique in portraying a man wearing at the same time both *ailettes* and, judging from the chain which runs from his sword to his chest, a presumed *coat-of-plates*. He also has a round-topped *great helm* with a crest and cloth streaming to the rear. Mail is visible on his arms but not on his legs, which could indicate that he is wearing *greaves* and *poleyns*. There is nothing to indicate whether or not his horse's *caparison* was lined with mail.

530 Seal of Adalard IV of Bourghelles, Lower Lotharingia, 1300
(Zegalafgietsel nr.11642, Antwerp, Belgium)

On this seal the rider is almost certainly armoured in mail only, and wears a pointed *great helm* of a relatively early type, offering little protection to the neck and throat.

531 Effigy of Kuno von Falkenstein, Swabia, c.1343
(*in situ* church, Kirchzarten, Germany)

The most interesting feature of this effigy is the evidence of a scale-covered or partly covered *coat-of-plates* worn beneath his loose *surcoat*. These presumed scales are visible around his shoulders and over his groin. Otherwise he wears a *bascinet* with a mail *aventail* and *bretache*, mailed *gauntlets*, probably plated *vambraces*, a short-sleeved mail *hauberk*, mail *chausses*, and unusual fluted *poleyns*. His armament consists of a 'ballock dagger', a long sword and a small, flat-topped shield.

532A–C 'Nequambuch IV', *Soester Nequambuch,* Saxony, early 14th century (?)
(City Archives, Soest, Germany)

Some features in this manuscript illustration may be consciously archaic. Nevertheless, they deserve comment. The main figure (B) has a visored helmet that seems halfway between a deep *bascinet* and a late form of visored *great helm.* He also has what looks like a flower-shaped *ailette* and mail *chausses,* while a padded *gambeson* is visible above his knee. Rather surprisingly the long and mittened sleeves of such a garment are also visible on his arms. Other figures (A and C) wear mail and in one case a simple *bascinet* (C).

533A–G Album, Flanders (?), early 14th century
(Bib. Royale Albert I, Ms. 9245, Brussels, Belgium)

A – f.450v; B–D – f.258v; E–G – f.254r. The origins of this manuscript fragment are not clear. It does, however, illustrate some important transitional features. Ordinary *great helms* are pointed (A and E–G), while others have large visors (G). A *bascinet* (B) and *cervellière* (D) are both shown, as are *ailettes* (A). Full mail *hauberks* with *mittens* are standard equipment, as are mail *chausses.* But to this have been added *poleyns, greaves* (A and G) and a *coat-of-plates* with chains to attach sword and dagger (D). This *coat-of-plates* may also be worn with *roundels* to protect the armpits (D), unless these latter are uncharacteristically round *ailettes.* One crossbowman clearly wears a sleeveless scale *cuirass* over his normal *hauberk* (E). One horse's *bard* is lined with mail (A).

534A–D *Grands Chroniques de France,* manuscript, Flanders (?), c.1321
(Bib. Royale Albert I, Ms. 5, Brussels, Belgium)

Again the origins of this manuscript are not clear. The style is basically French, but the very accurate representation of a *goedendag* spiked club or mace make a Flemish origin likely; this being the most characteristic weapon of Flemish urban militias in the early 14th century. Other equipment is straightforward, consisting of mail *hauberks* with *mittens* (A–C), *ailettes* (A), *greaves, poleyns,* perhaps rudimentary *sabatons* (A and B), and *cervellières* (B) or early *bascinets* (C). The foot-soldier's sword is relatively short, with curved *quillons* and an almost oval *pommel* (C).

535A–C 'Martyrdom of St Catherine of Alexandria', window of the Baker's Guild, Swabia, c.1320
(in situ Cathedral, Freiburg im Breisgau, Germany)

The swords shown in the Bakers' Window look old-fashioned (A and B), though this is almost certainly a result of the crudity of the workmanship. Of greater interest is a soldier who wears a scale *cuirass* over his mail *hauberk* (C). The presence of scale armour in other 14th century sources means that this picture cannot simply be dismissed as fanciful. Yet the story of St Catherine, a martyred noblewoman of Egypt, leaves open the possibility that the artist is attempting to show Islamic or at least 'eastern' lamellar armour. Note that this figure also wears *poleyns* and *greaves* over his mail *chausses*.

536A–B 'Boarhunt', manuscript, Lower Lotharingia (?), c.1300–50
(Bib. de l'Université, Ms. 137.C, f.251, Liège, Belgium)

This illumination is of interest as it shows a long-bladed and barbed boarspear being used in conjunction with a small hand-held buckler (B). The second figure (A) has wrapped a cloak around his arm to provide a rudimentary shield in a manner seen in art since at least Roman times. He also has one finger over the *quillons* of his relatively short sword, indicating knowledge of a southern and eastern style of fencing that was now spreading across much of Western Europe.

537A–D 'Mordred beseiges London', *Roman de Saint Graal*, Flanders, early 14th century
(British Library, Ms. Add. 10292, f.81b, London, England)

A counterweight *trebuchet* is here shown with considerable accuracy, though no great detail. It is operated by a man in an early *bascinet* or *cervellière*.

538A–F *Codex Balduini Trevirensis*, Germany or northern Italy, c.1315–30
(City Archives, Inv.I.C.i, Coblenz, Germany)

A–B – Henry VII captures Montevarchi, f.27; C–D – Knights jousting; E – Henry VII lifts the siege of Florence, f.29; F – Henry VII burns the castle of S. Giovanni Valdarno, f.2. This manuscript seems to portray mixed German and Italian styles, as would be expected in such a subject. The triple-pointed lance-blades used by the two figures (C–D) show that they are jousting peacefully. They are protected by conical *great helms* and small flat-topped shields. The only visible armour appears to be mail, but the figure on the left is also wearing a separate *gauntlet* on his spear hand. Most warriors wear *bascinets* with *aventails*; the exception having a wide-brimmed *chapel-de-fer war-hat* (E). Separate but apparently unplated *gauntlets* are worn (A, B and F), and while horsemen carry normal small, flat-topped kite-shaped shields, a man storming a castle wall has a much larger shield on his back (B). This indicates that the supposedly old-fashioned kite-shaped shield remained in use for siege warfare.

539A–C Wall-painting of the Gent levies from the Leugemetefries, Gent, Flanders, 1346
(now lost; after Verbruggen)

These wall-paintings only survive in 19th-century sketches. Each troop of militiamen seems to have been led by a standard-bearer wearing a visored *bascinet* (A). Like the rest of the men he has a mail *aventail* and a long mail *hauberk*. These *hauberks* could have long tight sleeves (A and C) or looser mid-length sleeves (B and C), with *roundels* to protect the elbows (A–C). Some men seem to have *gauntlets* or heavy gloves (B and C), while one figure (B) may have a second mail sleeve below the first. Other men carry flat-topped shields (C) and are armed with long-hafted weapons, one of which is clearly a *goedendag*. Another troop have crossbows and swords (C), while a third have *goedendags* and possibly a *falchion* (B).

540 'St George', wall-painting, Swabia, early/mid-14th century
(*in situ* church, Bergheim, France)

Though said to date from the mid-14th century, the armour suggests an earlier date. Here the saint has a round-topped *great helm* surmounted by a large *lambrequin* or trailing cloth. Otherwise his armour is all of mail.

541A–G The Courtrai Chest, Flanders, c.1305
(New College, Oxford, England)

The Battle of Courtrai in 1302 was one of the most remarkable in early 14th century Western Europe. A French army, in which heavy cavalry played the leading role, was defeated by an army largely consisting of infantry militiamen from the cities of Flanders. This victory, so astonishing to the contemporary world, was celebrated on this carved wooden chest now in Oxford University. Here the *goedendag*, to which the Flemings attributed much of their victory, is given pride of place (A, C, D, E and F). The *goedendag* is a rather mysterious weapon but appears to have been a very long-hafted mace with a spike or blade at the end. It had a devastating effect on the French cavalry at Courtrai when used by ranks of disciplined infantry supported by pikemen and crossbowmen. Both pikes and crossbows are also shown on the Courtrai Chest (D and F). Other armament used by the Flemish infantry are swords and bucklers (B) and heavier *falchions* (G). The only armour visibly worn by ordinary infantry are *cervellières* or early forms of *bascinets*, mail *coifs* which often cover much of the shoulders, and mail *mittens* which were probably part of long-sleeved mail *hauberks*. Some men in the front ranks (F) also wear mail *chausses*. Two even have *ailettes* on their shoulders, probably indicating that they are men from the knightly class who led the ordinary militia (F). Flemish cavalry (A) have *ailettes* and mail *chausses*. Most also have rounded or pointed *great helms* as well as normal flat-topped cavalry shields. Their horses wear *caparisons*. The French cavalry are identically equipped (D, F, and G). A large counterweight *trebuchet* can be seen inside a besieged French castle (E).

542 'St Maurice', stained glass window from Mutzig, Franconia, early 14th century
(Musée Oeuvre Notre Dame, Strasbourg, France)

Once again an early 14th century figure is shown armoured only in mail. However, his *coif* appears to have a very bulbous outline. This probably means that a rounded *arming-cap* is worn beneath the mail to support the rounded *great helm* which is seen behind him. If this is the case, then the square-outlined *arming-caps* which supported earlier flat-topped *great helms* had, to some extent, been replaced by round *arming-caps*.

543A–F 'Soldiers at the Crucifixion', alabaster statuette from Notre Dame de Huy, Lower Lotharingia, c.1350
(Metropolitan Museum of Art, inv. 26.101.7, New York, United States)

This beautiful piece of Mosan alabaster carving shows three differently-equipped warriors. The leader (A and D) wears a *coat-of-plates* beneath a very wide-sleeved *surcoat*. On his legs are *poleyns* and *greaves*. The hilt of a *basilard* is just visible on his right hip (D) and a relatively short sword with a truly massive hilt hangs on his left hip. A figure at the back has a type of *chapel-de-fer* which looks almost like a bowler hat (B and E). A third figure (C and F) has a pointed *bascinet* with a large mail *aventail* that covers most of his shoulders. Below this a kind of splinted *rerebrace* can be seen. He also has *poleyns*, *greaves*, and another sword with a massive *pommel* (C).

544 *Romance of Alexander*, Flanders, 1338–44
(Bodleian Library, Ms. 264, Oxford, England)

An exceptionally fine manuscript sheds considerable light on a number of pieces of arms and armour. The tall *bascinets* worn by all the figures have mail *aventails*, one of which seems to have the extra mail flap seen in some Italian sources. More important, however, are the *coats-of-plates*, one of which is shown from the back so that the lacing system in clearly visible. Both splinted and laminated upper-arm *rerebraces* are illustrated, while one figure seems to have a *couter* laced over a mail sleeve, which in turn probably partly covers a *vambrace*. *Gauntlets* are shown, two of which are clearly plated. Leg-harness includes perhaps splinted *cuisses*, normal early forms of *poleyns*, plus presumed *greaves*. One horse has a *caparison* while another has a plate *chanfron* and a most interesting piece of armour to protect the upper part of its neck behind the ears.

Notes

1. P. Contamine, *La Guerre au Moyen Age* (Paris, 1980), p.159.
2. P. Van Luyn, 'Les Milites dans la France du xie siècle', *Le Moyen Age* vol.LXXVII (1971), pp.5–6.
3. Contamine, *op.cit.* pp.117–19.
4. Contamine, *op.cit.* pp.117 and 119–20.
5. Contamine, *op.cit.* p.175.
6. J.F. Verbruggen, *The Art of Warfare in Western Europe in the Middle Ages* (Oxford, 1977), pp.120–l and 124; J. Boussard, 'Les Mercenaires au XIIIe siècle', *Bibliothèque de l'École des Chartres* vol.CVI (1945–6), p.193; C. Oman, *A History of the Art of War in the Middle Ages* (London, 1924), vol.I, pp.376–7.
7. Oman, *op.cit.* vol.I, pp.476 and 484–7.
8. Oman, *op.cit.* vol.I, pp.499–502.
9. C. Gaier, 'L'Évolution et l'usage de l'armament personel defensif au Pays de Liège du XIIe au XIVe siècle', *Zeitschrift für historische Waffen- und Kostümkunde* vol.IV (1962), p.66.
10. Contamine, *op.cit.* p.182; Gaier, *op.cit.* pp.65–6; A. Joris, 'Remarques sur les Clauses Militaires des Privilèges Urbains Liegèois', *Revue Belge de Philologie et d'Histoire* vol.XXXVII (1959), pp.298, 301 and 306.
11. J.F. Verbruggen, 'Vlaamse Gemeentelegers tegen Franse Ridderlegers in de 14de en 15de Eeuw', *Belgisch Tijdschrift voor Militaire Geschiedenis* vol.XXIV, no.4 (1981), p.382.
12. Contamine, *op.cit.* p.260; A.V.B. Norman, 'Notes on Some Early Representations of Guns and Ribaudekins', *Journal of the Arms and Armour Society* vol.VIII (1974–6), p.236; H. Rothert, 'Wann und wo ist die Pulverwaffe erfunden?', *Blätter für deutsche Landesgeschichte* vol.LXXXIX (1952), pp.84–6.
13. Rothert, *loc.cit.*
14. Verbruggen, *The Art of Warfare, op.cit.* pp.100–1.
15. Contamine, *op.cit.* p.165.

Chapter 10

The Empire – Bohemia

This section covers the Kingdom of Bohemia and the March of Moravia. Both areas had been under Polish rule early in the 11th century but were then drawn into the Empire. Early in the 14th century they came under the rule of the House of Luxemburg, and as such Bohemia was the occasional administrative, though by no means the cultural or economic, centre of the Empire.

Bohemia was under strong, almost overwhelming, German military influence throughout the Middle Ages, this being particularly apparent among the cavalry élite,[1] which even adopted some mailed horse-armour by the late 13th century.[2] This was, however, later than such armour had been seen in Germany, and Bohemian military equipment remained old-fashioned compared to that of neighbouring German provinces well into the 14th century.[3] There also seems to have been little use of archery until the 14th century, when the crossbow became a popular infantry weapon.[4] Firearms also came late to Bohemia, not being mentioned until the early 15th century, though surviving examples in Czech museums might date from the 14th century.[5]

Figures

545 Helmet from Olmutz in Mähren, Moravia, 11th–12th centuries
(Waffensammlung, Kunsthistorisches Museum, Vienna, Austria)

Perhaps the most typical of surviving so-called 'Norman'-style helmets. Its dating is far from certain and might even be 10th century. The helmet has a slight keel or comb running fore and aft but is also slightly pointed. It is thicker at the crown than around the rim, indicating sophisticated iron working techniques in which the helmet was beaten from a single piece of metal.

546A–B So-called Helmet of St Wenceslaus, Bohemia, 10th–11th centuries
(Cathedral Treasury, Prague, Czech Republic)

The famous helmet associated with St Wenceslaus of Bohemia is earlier in form than the helmet from Olmutz. It lacks the keel or comb, is low domed, and may even have originally had a rounded or only slightly pointed top. The helmet appears to be far less strongly made and may be closer in style to the Byzantine or Islamic *baydah* helmets from which it probably derived. Rim and *nasal* decorations (B) were, however, a feature that persisted well into the 12th century, particularly in Eastern Europe.

547 'Guards at the Holy Sepulchre', *Vyšehrad Codex*, Bohemia, c.1086
(University Library, Prague, Czech Republic)

The sleeping soldiers in this early Bohemian manuscript may have conical helmets without *nasals*, but such headgear could also be interpreted as pointed hats. They wear no other apparent armour but carry round-topped kite-shaped shields characteristic of the period. Their spears have clear wings or flanges, while a typical 11th-century sword has an early form of perhaps trefoil *pommel*.

548 'Massacre of the Innocents', *Lectionary of Arnold of Meisen*, Bohemia, c.1290
(State Library, Ms. 76, Prague, Czech Republic)

The soldier shown here is equipped in essentially German fashion, as would be expected by the late 13th century. He has a long-sleeved mail *hauberk* with *mittens*, a separate mail *coif* with a squared lower edge, no leg armour, and a straight sword with a large round *pommel*.

549 Seal of John of Luxembourg, King of Bohemia, Bohemia, c.1310–19
(State Archives, Prague, Czech Republic)

This early seal, dating from just after the House of Luxembourg's inheritance of the Crown of Bohemia, shows a *great helm* with a flowing *lambrequin* and a massive feathered crest representing a wing.

550 Seal of John the Blind of Luxembourg and Bohemia, Bohemia, early/mid-14th century
(State Archives, Prague, Czech Republic)

John the Blind died at the Battle of Crécy in 1346. Judging from its relatively old-fashioned military equipment the seal probably dates from early in his reign. He wears a *great helm* with a *lambrequin*, plus the feathered crest of his family. On his shoulders are *ailettes*, and his visible armour consists of a mail *hauberk* with *mittens* and mail *chausses*. The chain leading from his tapering sword to his chest indicates the presence of a *coat-of-plates*. The elaborate decoration on his horse's head also suggests that the animal's *caparison* includes a rigid *chanfron*, if no other armoured element.

551A–F *Velislav Bible*, Bohemia, c.1345–50
(State Library, Prague, Czech Republic)

A–B – Esau and followers, f.34; C – after Warner; D–F – Pharaoh's army, f.70. The *Velislav Bible* is important because it shows the limitations of German influence in Bohemia. The troops shown here are not only equipped in rather old-fashioned style but they carry some distinctive pieces of equipment. They clearly ride with bent knees as light cavalry (B and E) and such troops were probably closer to those of Slovakia and Hungary than to the typical heavy cavalry of Germany. Their basic armour consists of mail *hauberks* with *mittens* and mail *chausses* but with no evidence of *coats-of-plates*. Apart from the *poleyns* worn by Esau directly over his *chausses* (B) there is, in fact, no plate armour in these illustrations other than helmets. The latter include an apparently riveted two-piece *bascinet* (A), a *chapel-de-fer* worn over a mail *coif* (B), and ordinary *bascinets* with *aventails* (E and F), one of which seems to be worn beneath a wide-brimmed floppy hat. A sword (C) and scabbard are hung in the old-fashioned manner and the spears seem to have very archaic wings or lugs beneath their blades. This all supports the theory that the horsemen were light cavalry who would not normally engage an armoured foe head on, couched lance against couched lance. Their shields are distinctive, two being of a tall oval (B) or almost rectangular (A) form, while the third (E) seems to have features in common with the trapezoid shields of the later Hungarian *hussar* and the Ottoman *deli*, both of whom were to become the typical light cavalry of south-eastern and Central Europe.

552 Drawing on paper, Bohemia or Italy, c.1350–60
(Library, Christ Church College, Oxford, England)

This drawing remains something of a mystery. Its style is Italian, the provenance probably Bohemian, and the subject Central European or Balkan. The archer may, in fact, represent a type of light infantryman seen in many areas on the fringes of the medieval Hungarian state. His bow appears to be of a simple rather than composite construction; his small quiver for long arrows finds no parallel in Western Europe and his curved sword with its single asymmetrical *quillon* looks distinctly Turkish.

553A–C Vyšši Brod Altar, Bohemia, c.1347–59
(after Warner)

Three basic forms of helmet are shown on this altar: a *chapel-de-fer* (A), a crudely-drawn *great helm* (B), and a *bascinet* with a peculiar sort of flap at the front (C). The flap remains unexplained, while the inaccurate drawing of the *great helm* may also indicate that such helmets were barely known in Bohemia.

Notes

1. B. Warner, *Slavonic Terms for Weapons and Armour in the Middle Ages: A Lexico-Historical Study* (MA thesis, London University, 1965), p.137.
2. C. Oman, *A History of the Art of War in the Middle Ages* (London, 1924), vol.I, p.519.
3. Warner, *op.cit.* pp.144–5 and 149.
4. Warner, *op.cit.* pp.137 and 144–5; K.Cs. Sebestyén, 'Bogen und Pfeil der Alten Ungarn', *Dolgozatok* vol.VIII (1932), p.254.
5. W. Wilinbachow, 'Poczatkowy Okres Rozwoju Broni Palnej w Krajach Slowiańskich (Note on the Initial Period of the Use of firearms in Slavonic Countries)', *Kwartalnik Historii Techniki* vol.VIII, no.2 (1963), pp.234 and 245.

Chapter 11

The Empire – The Kingdom of Arles

The Kingdom of Arles, which was also known as the Kingdom of Burgundy, was created in the 10th century out of the states of Burgundy and Provence, which were in turn relics of the old Kingdom of Lothair created by the Carolingian Treaty of Verdun in 843. By the end of the 11th century the kingdom – consisting of what is now western Switzerland, France east of the Rhône and Sâone, plus a few districts west of these rivers – had been drawn into the Empire. During the 13th and first half of the 14th centuries much of the southern part of the kingdom was gradually absorbed by France. The Kingdom of Arles seems to have had no distinctive military features, except for the persistence of peasant infantry forces in the Swiss mountains. It was otherwise under considerable French, some German, and some Italian influence.

The feudal levy remained important throughout the 11th and into the 12th century. As in other western parts of the Empire and in Italy, such feudal troops still had to be paid if sent beyond their own locality.[1] As elsewhere in the Empire the feudal host declined in the 12th century, with greater reliance being placed on mercenaries, but still survived as a genuine part of the army.[2] The mounted crossbowmen who made their appearance in the 13th century were presumably paid professionals. Crossbows were also vital weapons in Provençal fleets,[3] but were not recorded among the Swiss until the early 13th century.[4]

The mountain peasantry of what is now Switzerland, both those living in the German Duchy of Swabia and in the Burgundian north of the Kingdom of Arles, were to become some of the most effective and famous crossbowmen of the later Middle Ages. Many Swiss served as mercenaries in northern Italy during the 13th century, where they learned advanced infantry tactics.[5] By the time they burst upon an astonished Europe, first in successful defence of their mountainous homeland against knightly cavalry and later as the most effective mercenary infantry of the 14th century, the Swiss had developed their own highly-disciplined tactics. In the early 14th century these relied primarily on the *halbard*, with the long *pike* being added in the mid or late 14th century.[6]

Figures

554 Seal of the Abbey of St Maurice, Savoy, late 11th/early 12th centuries
(Abbey of St Maurice, Valais, Switzerland)

The acutely forward-angled crown of the helmet on this seal strongly suggests an early 12th-century date, as does the slightly-flattened top of the long shield.

555 'Cutting Samson's hair', carved capital, Provence, 12th century
(*in situ* Cathedral of Notre Dame des Doms, Avignon, France)

The axe shown here in the hands of a Philistine looks more like a work tool that a weapon.

556A–B Reliquary of St Candide, Savoy, early 12th century
(Treasury, Abbey of St Maurice, Valais, Switzerland)

This embossed silver reliquary shows soldiers typically equipped, except that an unusual convention is used to indicate the mail of the *hauberks*. It is, in fact, possible that a convention normally used to indicate 'infidel' lamellar has here been inappropriately used to show 'infidel' mail in this martyrdom scene. Swords and sword-belts are otherwise typically European.

557A–D Relief carvings, Provence, early 13th century
(*in situ* southern side of cloisters, Church of St Trophime, Arles, France)

The craftsmen who made these very damaged carvings seem to have gone to considerable lengths to indicate scale rather than mail armour. A number of other features also suggest that the *hauberks* were indeed of scale-covered fabric or leather. They lack *coifs* (A and D), have short sleeves, and appear to have some kind of strap, perhaps to tighten a flap-like sleeve, around the upper arms. Whether or not such scale armours were used in Provence is unclear. They could be stylised and based upon the lamellar *cuirasses* of the 'infidels'. Other points of interest are the helmets of apparent two-piece construction joined along a low comb (D). The shields are large and rather old-fashioned kite-shaped types, while the sword and scabbard are within the normal Western tradition.

558A–C **'Massacre of the Innocents', carved capital, Provence, 12th century**
(*in situ* east side of Cloisters, Church of St Trophime, Arles, France)

Here the warriors wear perfectly normal mail *hauberks* with integral *coifs* and long sleeves. Two of the swords have tapering blades while one has parallel sides.

559A–D **Relief carvings, Provence, early 13th century**
(*in situ* west front, Church of St Trophime, Arles, France)

The carvings on the facade of St Trophime include some of the earliest Provençal illustrations of separate mail *coifs* of the early type with squared lower edges (A and B). Otherwise the warriors wear ordinary mail *hauberks*, but their swords are of the almost parallel-sided non-tapering form seen in many Mediterranean sources. Scabbards are decorated (B–D).

560 **Reliquary of the Children of St Sigismond, Savoy, c.1130**
(Treasury, Abbey of St Maurice, Valais, Switzerland)

The warrior is an almost archetypal knight of the early 12th century except that his helmet is of a decorated fluted type without a *nasal*. His mail *hauberk* has long sleeves and a *coif*, and his shield is of the long kite-shaped type, supported by a *guige*. His scabbard is clearly worn under the *hauberk*; the hilt of the sword presumably emerged through a slit on the left hip as in the Bayeux Tapestry.

561A–D **'Story of St Maurice', Reliquary Chest of the Abbé Nantelme, Savoy, 1225**
(Treasury, Abbey of St Maurice, Valais, Switzerland)

This particular piece of decorated metalwork provides some of the clearest illustrations of an early German form of *great helm*, which is flat-topped but relatively close-fitting without extending far down the neck (B–D). All the figures wear mail *coifs* and *hauberks* with *mittens*, one clearly slit horizontally across the palm (A). Mail *chausses* are worn, one pair of which are of the early type laced up the back of the leg (C). Two figures have padded *cuisses* with some form of *poleyn* to protect the knee (C and D). The figure of St Maurice himself (A) wears a *surcoat* with shoulders that are so raised that some form of rigid or semi-rigid *cuirie* may be worn beneath.

562A–F **Wall-paintings, Provence, mid/late 13th century**
(*in situ* Tour Ferrande, Pernes-les-Fontaines, France)

A–D – War between Angevins and Hohenstaufens; E – Iaiar, the infidel; F – War between Angevins and Hohenstaufens. The wall-paintings at Pernes-les-Fontaines are very simple in style but they contain many interesting features. The figure of an 'infidel' (E) is largely stylised and is equipped in European style except that he has no head protection, wears a headcloth, and carries a small round buckler, all features associated with the stereotyped Muslim. The warriors shown in various scenes of the Angevin–Hohenstaufen struggle in neighbouring Italy are clearly based on contemporary military styles. Some of the warriors in these battles wear conical *great helms*, some with plumes or streamers. Others have close-fitting *cervellières* (A and D), while one seems to wear a form of slightly-pointed *bascinet* (D). The only clearly visible armour is of mail, being full *hauberks* with *mittens*, *coifs* and *chausses*, although some form of knee defence may also be present (B). Shields are of the small flat-topped type, and all horses have *caparisons*. Spears are the dominant weapon, but tapering swords with slightly down-turned *quillons* also appear (D and F).

563A–C Carved capitals, Provence, early–late 13th century
(*in situ* cloisters, Church of St Trophime, Arles, France)

A–B – south side of cloisters; C – east side of cloisters. Among the 13th century carvings in the St Trophime cloisters is a man who wears a helmet that has a decorated central comb (C), perhaps indicating a two-piece construction, and is secured in place by a chin-strap over a mail *coif*. The man's *hauberk* seems to have long sleeves which have been pulled back to the elbows. He carries an axe which, given the context, should be a weapon despite its similarity to a work axe. Some other figures (A and B) are somewhat later. One of these represents an obviously North African 'Moorish' horseman (B). He has such features as a loosely-wound turban and a primitive rope-loop stirrup, which are so accurate that some degree of personal or at least second-hand knowledge of such 'Moors' can be assumed. The round object on the otherwise unarmoured man's back might be a shield or a water flask. A further figure (A) carries a winged mace and seems to have no armour save for his mail *coif*. It is, of course, possible that the *coif* forms part of a mail *hauberk* worn beneath a long-sleeved tunic.

564 Effigy of Othon de Grandson, Burgundy, c.1330
(*in situ* Cathedral, Lausanne, Switzerland)

On his effigy Othon de Grandson is portrayed in essentially old-fashioned arms and armour. Perhaps the effigy was made considerably before his death, since he lived to an unexpectedly great age for the 14th century. Although not visible in this drawing, the curvature of his coif, which is separate, over the sides of his head clearly indicate that a padded *arming cap* not only covered the top of his head but also extended around his temples and chin. Behind this the bulges formed by his ears equally clearly indicate that nothing other than the mail itself lay over these, which would be quite logical as the wearer would not wish to have his hearing impaired by a layer of padding. His long-sleeved mail *hauberk* with *mittens* is worn under a *surcoat*. What at first glance appear to be tassel-like objects on his shoulders have sometimes been interpreted as decorative items functioning like *ailettes*, whereas in fact they are the heads of two small lions who lie beneath the recumbent knight, supporting his shoulders.

Notes

1. P. Contamine, *La Guerre au Moyen Age* (Paris, 1980), pp.120–1.
2. Contamine, *op.cit*. pp.175–6.
3. Contamine, *op.cit*. p.169.
4. V. Maglioli, 'La balestra', *Armi Antiche* (1955), p.99.
5. J.F. Verbruggen, *The Art of Warfare in Western Europe during the Middle Ages* (Oxford, 1977), p.103.
6. C. Oman, *A History of the Art of War in the Middle Ages* (London, 1924), vol.II, pp.239–40, 245 and 254–5; Contamine, *op.cit*. p.255; Verbruggen, *op.cit*. pp.147 and 159–61.

Chapter 12

The Empire – The Kingdom of Italy

As part of the Empire, the Kingdom of Italy included all the present Italian state north of the Abruzzi, plus part of the Campagna south of Rome. Its northern borders were roughly those of modern Italy excluding the northern parts of the Trentino and Trieste. Venice, strictly speaking, lay outside the Empire, but it has been included in this section of the book for the sake of simplicity. By the mid-14th century the Papal States, consisting of Rome, Latium, Umbria, Spoleto, the Marches and much of Emilia-Romagna, had also drifted out of the Empire.

Three main themes dominate the history of northern and central Italy from the 11th to 14th centuries. These are the decline of Imperial feudal authority and the rise of the cities as centres of both regional government and power (wars of the Lombard League and the League of Verona), the growing territorial power of the Papacy, and political strife between Pope and Emperor. The latter struggle passed through various phases, from the Investiture Contest (1075–1220) and German invasions in the 12th and 13th centuries, to the rivalry between *Guelph* and *Ghibelline* – pro-Papal and pro-Imperial factions – within the bounds of Italy. Early in the 14th century the Papacy went into its 'Babylonian Exile' in the city of Avignon on the frontier between France and the Imperial Kingdom of Arles, where it remained until 1377.

Although the 11th-century Kingdom of Italy theoretically consisted of relatively few Duchies, Marches and such subdivisions, in reality the country was extremely fragmented and full of castles built by almost all levels of local authority.[1] Feudal military obligations to a distant German Emperor were light, while most of Italy's cities had already slipped out of feudal aristocratic control, being either directly responsible to the Emperor or lying under local ecclesiastical authority.[2] On the other hand Italian military styles and technology were quite advanced, early forms of couched lance technique having already been seen in 9th-century cavalry training.[3]

The decline of feudal obligation and of a rural-based military aristocracy continued during the 12th and 13th centuries, the cities meanwhile extending their authority over surrounding territory. These now formed a city's *contado*, a source of food, revenue and military manpower. Cavalry and foot-soldiers were drawn from both city and *contado*, although the best-equipped and disciplined infantry seem to have been urban.[4] Such developments were more characteristic of Lombardy and Tuscany than of the rest of central Italy, where feudal forces persisted longer. Here, in what became the Papal States, mercenaries also made an early appearance.[5]

The discipline of infantry forces within northern Italian urban militias was something new in medieval Western European warfare, as was the degree of co-operation between cavalry and infantry.[6] Only in the Crusader States could anything comparable yet be seen, although plenty of examples might be found in Byzantium or the Islamic regions. Specialised naval versions of this form of military organisation existed in Italian coastal cities.[7] During the 13th century cavalry remained the decisive, offensive element in urban forces while infantry remained a defensive element even in open battle. Tactics were sophisticated by the standards seen elsewhere in Europe, as was the equipment of all classes of warrior.[8] A very widespread use of the crossbow and of crossbow-armed mounted infantry certainly contributed to the further effectiveness of 13th century Italian foot-soldiers. It also made them much in demand outside Italy.[9]

The importance of the rich, highly-civilised cities of Italy, as well as their close commercial contact with the eastern Mediterranean, must have contributed to the rapid development and adoption of sophisticated military devices such as the counterweight *trebuchet*, fire weapons and, in the 14th century, firearms.[10] Nevertheless, the late 13th and early 14th centuries saw few major changes in tactics or types of troops. The 'citizen knight' was still the most important warrior even in the early 14th century,[11] but one very significant development was the increasing employment not only of individual mercenaries but of entire mercenary 'companies'. These were the famous *condottieri*, who were drawn from all over Italy, the Empire, and even beyond. Such 'companies' included both cavalry and infantry.[12]

The employment of professionals tended to make late 13th and 14th-century Italian warfare more extended, while the growing wealth of the cities led to a great strengthening and elaboration of fortifications. Sieges and the devastation of enemy territory were the main strategies, with relatively few full-scale battles. Cavalry armour was now becoming elaborate and scientific, providing excellent protection while still allowing freedom of movement. This probably reflected the threat from crossbows and other infantry weapons.[13] Much such armour was also of hardened leather, perhaps indicating a degree of Byzantine,[14] or Islamic influence via southern Italy. Infantry rose in tactical importance during the early 14th century, though declining again later.[15] This was particularly apparent in a new form of light infantry, some of whom were archers, who often adopted an offensive role in collaboration with the heavily-armoured cavalry.[16] Closely associated with the infantry, though more so with surviving urban militias than with professional foot-soldiers, was the early use of firearms in Italy. The earliest but far from clear reference comes from Florence in 1326, then from Friuli in 1331, and more certainly from Lucca in 1341. Earlier and much more problematical is a record of *sclopeti* or *sclopi*, meaning hand-held guns, being used at Forli in 1284. *Bombards* or field-pieces were, however, still much more common, even in such an isolated mountainous region as Savoy and in otherwise backward areas such as the Papal States.[17]

Figures

565   Sword, Italy, c.1100
(Museum of Art, no.1977.167.529, Philadelphia, United States)

This sword certainly looks 11th or early 12th century, but its peculiar spiked *pommel* sets it apart from other Western European weapons of the period.

566A–B   Ivory box from Farfa, Latium, c.1071
(Treasury of S. Paolo fuori le Mura, Rome, Italy)

The simple figures on this Crucifixion scene include some unusual features. One man (A) seems to wear a hat or helmet with a knob on top while the second, holding the vinegar sponge, has a sword with a horizontal, almost crescent-shaped *pommel*, curved *quillons*, and a tapering blade. All these features would be associated with a later period north of the Alps but here perhaps reflect Byzantine or Middle Eastern influence.

567   'Martyrdom of Abdon', carved relief, Lombardy, late 11th century
(*in situ* Cathedral, Parma, Italy)

The 12th-century carvings at Parma, though simplified, are remarkably consistent in their accuracy. The same is probably true of the few late 11th-century reliefs in the cathedral. The sword shown here, with its broad almost non-tapering and round-tipped blade, is in the old Mediterranean tradition. This suggests that, in some respects, early medieval Italian arms and armour had more in common with Byzantium and the western Islamic world than with the rest of the Empire.

568   'Merman', wall-painting, northern Italy, 11th century
(*in situ* S. Jacopo, Termeno, Italy)

These relatively simple weapons probably represent a self bow rather than one of composite construction. The archer is clearly using a finger draw rather than the thumb draw favoured in Byzantium and the Middle East.

569A–B 'Crucifixion', mosaic, Venice, late 11th century
(*in situ* Cathedral of S. Marco, Venice, Italy)

The mosaics in San Marco Cathedral are so completely Byzantine in style that they can probably be discounted as a source of information on Italian arms and armour. Yet it has to be borne in mind that Venice had itself been involved in the Byzantine army until the 9th century. For many years subsequently, it seems to have had more in common with Byzantium and the Balkans than with the rest of Italy. The helmets shown here are probably fanciful but might reflect some aspects of Byzantine military technology.

570A–H 'Legend of King Arthur', carved relief, Lombardy, 1106–10
(*in situ* north door, Cathedral, Modena, Italy)

The famous relief carvings over the Porta Pescheria of Modena Cathedral show northern Italian military equipment to have been basically the same as that of Germany or France. Here all but one of the warriors wear long-sleeved mail *hauberks*, as yet without *mittens* but including *coifs*. These, with one exception (B), go across the lower part of the face. No leg armour is shown but the helmets are conical with substantial *nasals*. Shields are long and kite-shaped, mostly held on a *guige* (B and D–F). All the horsemen, including one unarmoured individual, carry heavy lances, some with large decorated and fringed *gonfanons*. The men seen from the left have remarkably short swords, the scabbards of which are apparently outside their *hauberks* (D). One small and rather demoniacal infantryman wields what could be a pickaxe or an early form of war-hammer (H).

571 Genesis frieze, carved relief, Lombardy, c.1106–10
(*in situ* west front, Cathedral, Modena, Italy)

The blind huntsman seen here slaying Cain clearly uses a simple bow, although long enough to be considered a longbow.

572A–C Relief carving from church at S. Giovanni-in-Borgo, Lombardy, 1125–50
(Museo Civico, Pavia, Italy)

The simple carving shows tall forms of fluted conical helmets, of a type apparently favoured in Italy. Two have acutely forward-angled crowns (B and C) but none have *nasals*. They are worn over mail *hauberks* and *coifs*.

573A–F Carved reliefs, Lombardy, c.1200
(*in situ* west front, Cathedral of S. Donnino, Fidenza, Italy)

Various scenes are illustrated on the facade of Fidenza Cathedral, including the story of the Knight Milo (D). The military equipment shows considerable development compared to early 12th century

Italian sources. Mail *coifs* are now separate (C); mail *hauberks* have long sleeves though they still lack *mittens*; mail *chausses* are worn (A, B and E); but swords are still of the broad, blunt-ended type with large round (A) or nut-shaped *pommels* (D). A large bow seems to be of composite construction judging by its complicated recurved shape (F), but arrows are simply thrust into a belt.

574A–B 'The Betrayal', relief carving, Tuscany, 12th century (*in situ* crypt of Cathedral, Pistoia, Italy)

Apart from their distinctly forward-angled conical helmets with *nasals*, one of which seems to be a separate piece of metal (B), the infantrymen are protected only by their shields. Two shields are particularly tall and have slightly-flattened tops (B). The only visible weapons are spears of various lengths. The men on this carving probably illustrate the typical urban militia infantry of northern Italian cities.

575A–G Relief carvings, Tuscany, early 12th century (*in situ* west front of Cathedral, Lucca, Italy)

These shallow relief carvings show two warriors and a number of interesting pieces of equipment. Both men have round helmets with short *nasals* and cloths wound around them. One helmet also includes an apparent partial comb or crest (G). One *hauberk* (D) appears to be of scale or lamellar but this also seems to have a scale or lamellar *coif*. Such a piece of equipment is virtually unknown and could be dismissed as the stereotyped armour of a conventional 'infidel'. On the other hand a similar *hauberk* is seen elsewhere worn by a supposed member of the Milan city militia. The second figure (G) has a straightforward long-sleeved mail *hauberk*. Both carry kite-shaped shields with large bosses. One wields a sword with a massive *pommel* (D) while the weapon of the second figure (B) defies interpretation. Other weapons on the cathedral facade include a probable composite bow (F), two maces with fluted or winged heads (B and C), and a broad-bladed spear with long flanges (E).

576A–D 'Roland and Faragut', carved relief, Lombardy, c.1138 (*in situ* west front of Church of S. Zeno, Verona, Italy)

With the exception of the cloth wound around Faragut's head (A and C) both warriors are almost identically equipped. Their forward-angled conical helmets may have face-masks attached, thus making them among the earliest representations of such face-masks in Western Europe. But the faces on the carving are so damaged that they could just as well illustrate very substantial *nasals*. The two men wear mail *coifs* and *hauberks*, which in the case of Faragut is clearly short-sleeved. Roland is also once shown wearing mail *chausses* (D). They both carry long, flat-topped, kite-shaped shields and are armed with lances, plus straight tapering swords with straight *quillons* and a large tear-shaped *pommel* (C). An interesting but far from clear feature might be the strap or belt that seems to pass around Faragut's waist (A) from his cantle to his saddle pommel. Such a means of fixing a man in his saddle is mentioned, though very rarely, in documentary sources. It also appears much later in the 14th century, though interestingly enough again at Verona.

577 'Roland', carving, Lombardy, c.1139
(*in situ* west front of Cathedral, Verona, Italy)

This unusually detailed mid-12th century carving is of considerable importance where Italian communal weaponry is concerned. The fact that the warrior clearly has a mail *chausse* on his left leg shows him to represent a man who would fight on foot in disciplined ranks, probably kneeling on his right leg and forming a shield wall with comrades to right and left. He has a slightly decorated conical helmet with a forward-angled crown, a slightly-curved lower rim and no *nasal*. His helmet is secured by a chin-strap and is worn without a *coif*. The rest of his equipment is straightforward, consisting of a large, flat-topped, kite-shaped shield with a boss, and a straight pointed sword with straight *quillons* and a nut-shaped *pommel*. The apparent curvature of the sword is a result of high relief carving.

578A–F Carved relief from Porta Romana, Lombardy, 1167
(Sforza Castle Museum, Milan, Italy)

The Porta Romana carvings are believed to show the Milanese militia. Most are unarmoured infantry (I–O) but some wear full armour. Two of the latter (G and H) might represent the city's aristocratic cavalry. The differences in their armour probably result from various ways of indicating mail *hauberks*, but the fact that the *coif* of one figure (G) bulges considerably beneath the helmet could indicate a padded garment or even some very unusual form of scale armour. This figure also has a slightly peculiar helmet, perhaps of segmented construction, with a splayed *nasal*. The other mailed man has an ordinary conical helmet with a *nasal*. Both have large kite-shaped shields and spears or lances. The less well-equipped presumed infantry also include interesting features. All save the bearded leading man have helmets with peculiarly small *nasals*. Some are segmented (I, J and L), others clearly not so (A–C, M–N). Most are pointed but a few are round. Most figures have spears and very large flat-topped, and in some cases round based, shields, just as are described in the written sources. Those nearer the head of the column have swords (N and O). One clearly has an early form of *falchion* (M) similar to a weapon on a comparably dated carving from Burgundy. A knobbed mace is also shown (E).

579 Relief carving, Lombardy, 12th century
(*in situ* Baptistry, Parma, Italy)

An 'alien' archer, supposedly indicating a Turk with his long flowing hair. The composite bow has angled ears and the hat or helmet is largely fanciful.

580 'St George', relief carving, Lombardy, c.1135
(*in situ* west front of Cathedral, Ferrara, Italy)

A splendid carving of the warrior-saint shows him wearing a form of conical helmet with a decorated rim and no *nasal*. Such a style seems to have been popular in early 12th century Italy. He has no *coif* and his short-sleeved mail *hauberk* is slit at the sides in a style originally designed for combat on foot. His shield would probably have been kite-shaped but his sword seems more up-to-date than the rest of his equipment, being quite pointed with long slender *quillons* and a large *pommel*.

581A–L Carved capitals, Lombardy, 1150–70
(*in situ* Cathedral, Parma, Italy)

The carvings in Parma Cathedral are among the finest examples of Romanesque sculpture in Italy. They also illustrate important details of arms and armour. Here two bows are shown (B and L), both probably of the recurved composite type. Spears lack flanges or wings, whether in the hands of a huntsman representing the month of May (E), of foot-soldiers (C and I) or of horsemen (F, J and K). Swords are similarly straightforward, being of two distinct forms with tapering (A, G and J) or non-tapering (D) blades, straight *quillons*, and round (A, D, G and J) or nut-shaped (E) *pommels*. The helmeted horsemen presumably wear long-sleeved *hauberks* with *coifs* (D, F, G, J and K). Two forms of helmet are shown. Most are conical types, some with forward-angled crowns, plus *nasals* of various sizes (D, F, G, J and K), but a quite different helmet is worn by an infantryman. This is tall, round, either fluted or segmented, and lacks a *nasal* (I). It even seems to have a slightly angled or curved lower rim like an exceptionally early *bascinet*. It is worth noting that this foot-soldier also carries a distinctive form of tall, flat-based *mantlet* of a type known in the Middle East as a *januwîyah* ('Genoese') shield. Such shields are quite common in Italy but are otherwise virtually unknown outside the Middle East. All other shields are normal kite-shaped cavalry types with or without rivets. One is seen from the inside (J), showing a system of three straps, one for the fist, one across the elbow and one linking the former two.

582A–B Carved column bases, Lombardy, late 12th century
(*in situ* beneath altar, Cathedral, Modena, Italy)

These two recumbent figures, both being devoured by animals, support the altar platform above the cathedral crypt. They may represent the defeated foes of Modena. One (A) is perfectly straightforward, wearing a long-sleeved mail *hauberk* with an integral *coif* and holding a tapering sword with long straight *quillons* and a nut shaped *pommel*. The other figure (B) has a similarly unremarkable *coif*, *hauberk* and shield on a broad *guige*. His sword is of the non-tapering, blunt-ended type, though it also has very long curved *quillons*. But it is the man's helmet which demands attention. The rear has been extended to protect the neck. It has a forward-angled crown, the angle of which seems only to affect the long comb which divides the helmet. It also has a broad *nasal*. Except for this *nasal* one might regard it as a very early form of *salet*. Comparable helmets are to be found in later Italian sources and they find rough parallels in Byzantine art. Perhaps this style of helmet represents a transitional stage between the pseudo-Roman two-piece helmets of the Carolingian era and the true *salets* of the 15th century.

583A–F 'Betrayal', wall-painting, Tuscany, 1138
(*in situ* Cathedral, Sarzana, Italy)

All the figures in this painting are dressed in typical, early 12th-century, short-sleeved mail *hauberks* with *coifs*. Their helmets appear to be conical types without *nasals*, but while one is surprisingly pointed (D) another is almost certainly supposed to be of two-piece construction joined along a central comb (A).

584 'Sleeping Guards at the Holy Sepulchre', carved ivory panel, Venice, late 12th/early 13th centuries
(Victoria and Albert Museum, no.2951867, London, England)

Once again a work of art from Venice betrays strong Byzantine influence. Here, however, Byzantine archaisms are less obvious. The men carry large round shields. One has a sword at his belt and both have simple conical helmets with *aventails* or neckguards.

585A–O Carved stone candlestick made by Nicola d'Angelo and Pietro Vassalletto, Rome, c.1170
(*in situ* S. Paolo fuori le Mura, Rome, Italy)

A–J – Soldiers of the High Priest; K–L – Sleeping Guards at the Holy Sepulchre; M–O – Soldiers of the High Priest. The basic equipment of the numerous warriors shown on this enormous stone candlestick reflects current usage in central and southern Italy. It consists of long-sleeved (C, G, K and L) and short-sleeved (D, H, J and N) mail *hauberks*, most with integral *coifs* but some without. A few figures appear to wear padded *gambesons* beneath their mail (C, G and N) but this could just represent a pleated or creased garment. Shields are relatively small and kite-shaped (K and L), although one has a flattened top and a series of probably iron reinforcing straps across the front (F). The helmets are far more varied and may include some fanciful examples. The most ordinary has a forward-angled crown, is fluted, and is held by a chin-strap (M), but even this seems to have a cloth wound around its rim. Simple round or conical types are shown (A, D, H, J and L), though again some appear to be fluted and to have cloths wound around them. One helmet seen from an awkward angle (K) has a raised comb or ridge across it. This odd feature is also seen in Castile at around the same period. A final and more difficult helmet clearly has a button on top (C, F and N). Two are fluted and one seems to have an elaborate surface decoration or to be of segmented construction. These could be dismissed as fanciful except for the fact that exactly such an outline and associated system of construction was found in early medieval Turkish helmets from the Crimea and neighbouring regions. Perhaps such helmets were still used by the Turkish nomads of southern Russia, the Balkans or even Hungary and thus have entered the repertoire of exotic 'alien' headgear worn by such figures as the High Priest's soldiers on a 12th-century Italian carving. The weaponry on this candlestick is simpler but is still very interesting. It consists of spears (C, D, F, H and M), a sword (K) and varied axes (F, H and I). A kind of mace may also be seen (E) as well as a hooked and spiked hafted weapon (O). Such hooked weapons seem to have been associated with the Italians elsewhere, so it is interesting to note that they also appear in Italian sources. Three men are given daggers (H, L and M); the two that are out of their sheaths clearly having one straight and one curved side, presumably being single-edged. Daggers or knives are not normally shown as weapons in 12th-century Europe, so their appearance here probably indicates a knowledge of the Islamic *khanjar* or its possible Byzantine equivalent.

586A–C 'Pharaoh's army', carved font, Tuscany, late 12th century
(*in situ* Church of S. Frediano, Lucca, Italy)

With the exception of the ruler's perhaps fanciful hat or helmet (A) the military equipment carved on the S. Frediano font seems to be very realistic. Yet it still includes some unusual features, the most obvious being a sleeveless mail *hauberk* (B) and another which might have only one short sleeve (C). Such a system would seem suitable for archers, if it actually existed. Otherwise the carving illustrates a *hauberk* with a *coif* (C), another without (A), and mail *chausses* (A and C). The leading figure also has his scabbard hanging from a decorated sword-belt.

587A–B 'Guards at the Crucifixion', wall-painting, Rome, 12th century
(*in situ* S. Paolo fuori le Mura, Rome, Italy)

The two soldiers in this scene are clearly based on Byzantine originals, perhaps drawn from a manuscript. Their flat-based shields, though seen in some Eastern Christian art, are more typical of 12th century Italy.

588 'Martyrdom of Sts Ermacora and Fortunato', painted ceiling, Friuli, late 12th century
(*in situ* crypt of Massenzio, Basilica, Aquileia, Italy)

Another example of the blunt-tipped blade in the late 12th century. This sword has slightly curved *quillons* and a small *pommel*.

589 'Saul at the stoning of Stephen', wall-painting, Tuscany, late 12th/early 13th centuries
(*in situ* Church of S. Frediano, Lucca, Italy)

This wall-painting indicates that blunt-tipped swords, with almost parallel-sided blades, remained in use or at least in the artistic repertoire for a considerable period in Italy. The example shown here has a massive *pommel*.

590A–I Wall-paintings, Friuli, late 12th/early 13th centuries
(*in situ* crypt of Massenzio, Basilica, Aquileia, Italy)

The damaged wall-paintings in the crypt of Massenzio are made in imitation of decorative wall-hangings. They portray some unusual pieces of military equipment which, because of Aquileia's geographical position, may shed light on otherwise obscure parts of 12th and 13th century Europe. The pictures have sometimes been regarded as illustrating combat between Italians and invading Hungarians, this part of Italy having suffered severely at the hands of raiding Magyars in the 10th century. If so, then the peculiarities of the armour might reflect the military equipment of a cultural frontier zone where Italian Friuli, Byzantinised Venice and its northern Adriatic possessions, German-ruled Slovenia, and Hungarian-ruled Croatia, all came together. The similarity between the brimmed *chapel-de-fer war-hats* at Aquileia (B and H) and some helmets seen in 12th and 13th century Byzantine and Balkan art is obvious. Other helmets include that of a presumed Italian horseman (B and E) which looks like a proto-*salet* as seen earlier at Modena (fig.582). An ordinary forward-angled conical helmet is worn by a possible Hungarian-Magyar horse-archer (A). Others wear ordinary round helmets (C and H). Mail *hauberks* are short-sleeved with *coifs* (B, C, F and G). The only shield fully visible (B) is an ordinary, flat-topped, kite-shaped cavalry shield with a rather old-fashioned boss. Most men are armed with ordinary cavalry spears, but one is being used in a most unusual two-handed technique (F). Such a style is virtually unknown elsewhere in Western Europe, although it was normal in the Middle East and Central Asia. It must therefore reflect an artist's effort to indicate the different fighting technique of other nations, perhaps Hungarians or Balkan Slavs.

591A–B **'Combat between Fel and the Christian warrior', stone mosaic, Lombardy, c.1148**
(Museo Leone, Vercelli, Italy)

A – Christian knight; B – Fel. This crude piece of floor mosaic makes a clear distinction between the tall kite-shaped shield of the Christian (A) and the small, round, highly-decorated shield of the bare-footed 'infidel' (B). Both, however, have been given long straight swords of European form.

592A–D **Frontispiece of a Bible, Tuscany, c.1125–50**
(Museo Diocesano, Trent, Italy)

This Bible, illustrated in Florence, shows helmets with angled crowns and *nasals* (B–C), one of which seems to be attached to the rim rather than the bowl of the helmet. A mail *hauberk* has long but very wide sleeves (B), and a sword has an acutely-tapering blade. This was still an unusual feature so early in the 12th century. Two peculiarly short spears or javelins are also shown (A and D).

593 ***Annales Januenses* of *Caffaro*, Liguria (?), late 12th/early 13th centuries**
(Bib. Nat., Ms. Lat. 10136, Paris, France)

A simple man-powered *mangonel* is illustrated in this simple sketch in a manuscript that is probably from Genoa.

594 ***Great helm* from Bolzano, Trentino, c.1300**
(Castel Sant Angelo Museum, Rome, Italy)

The helmet may have been cut down at a later date, or it could have been of a relatively early flat-topped style which gave little protection to the neck and throat.

595 **Second Sword of St Mauritius, Italy, mid-13th century**
(Royal Armoury, Turin, Italy)

The similarity between this surviving sword with its slightly-tapering blade, blunt tip, and curved *quillons*, and weapons illustrated in the best pictorial sources, indicates that many of the latter were done in a realistic and trustworthy style.

596A–B **'Martyrdom of St Regulus', carved relief, Tuscany, c.1233**
(*in situ* Church of S. Martino, Lucca, Italy)

A – Arian heretic; B – Beheading of St Regulus. The broad-bladed, blunt-ended type of sword (B) still appeared in 13th century Italian art. By this time it had almost certainly become an unrealistic archaism. It is shown here with equally unlikely reverse-curved *quillons*. The Arian heretic wields a long-headed, perhaps fluted, mace (A).

597 Seal of the Ferrarese Guild of St George, Lombardy, c.1290
(Dept. of Seals, British Library, London, England)

If this seal from the city of Ferrara has been correctly dated, then it again indicates the presence of certain items of armour in Italy long before they are seen elsewhere in Europe. The most obvious of these are the full-plate *greaves* and possible *sabatons* worn with a fluted, pointed *poleyn*. The rider almost certainly also wears a *coat-of-plates* with a scalloped lower edge of a type not normally seen until well into the 14th century. The apparently laminated or scale-covered skirt around his hips seems likely to have been an archaism adopted from Byzantine art, as would be his flowing cloak and bare right arm. Otherwise he is protected by an ordinary flat-topped shield and a fully developed *great helm*.

598A–B Carved reliefs, Venice, c.1240
(*in situ* facade of Cathedral of S. Marco, Venice, Italy)

These carvings, probably of warrior-saints, are clearly based directly on Byzantine originals and might even be booty brought back from Constantinople following the Fourth Crusade. Although largely archaic and stereotyped, they might include some realistic details of Byzantine military equipment. By the 13th century the scale or lamellar *cuirass* can probably be discounted, except perhaps in a ceremonial context. The swords, sword-belt, spear and shield may, however, reflect some reality.

599 Effigy of Peter, Earl of Richmond (lost), Savoy, late 13th century
(ex-*Archaeologia* vol.XVIII, 1817)

The effigy of Peter, Count of Savoy and Earl of Richmond, used to lie in the Church of Aiguebelle (Agua Bella) but seems to have been destroyed during the first half of the 19th century. Peter was an international figure who played an important role in English, French and northern Italian politics. In his effigy he appears in typical late 13th-century equipment: a mail *coif*, long-sleeved mail *hauberk* with *mittens*, and almost certainly mail *chausses*. He is armed with a sword having a large round *pommel*, and he carries a broad, flat-topped kite-shaped shield.

600 Carved fragment from the back of the ivory throne of Frederick II, Romagna, c.1212–50
(Museo Nazionale, Ravenna, Italy)

Here a simple little carving shows one very unusual, perhaps unique, feature, which looks like the broad and very long *nasal* of a helmet which is otherwise invisible beneath a mail *coif*.

601   Wall-painting, Rome, c.1243–54
(*in situ* Chapel of St Sylvester, Church of Quattro Coronati, Rome, Italy)

A very clear illustration of a long, slender, mid-13th-century sword, with a pointed *pommel* and long, narrow, slightly-curved *quillons*. The narrow straps would presumably attach the scabbard to a sword-belt.

602A–B   Wall-painting, Lombardy, early 13th century
(*in situ* former City Hall, Novara, Italy)

This wall-painting is quite primitive for its date and location, showing knights leaving a castle or city gate. They wear round helmets with *nasals*. One is clearly painted in the same heraldic pattern as the man's kite-shaped shield (B). The riders also wear mail *hauberks* and *coifs*, apparently without *surcoats* or any leg armour.

603   Carved relief on tomb of Guilelmus Beraldus, Tuscany, c.1290
(*in situ* Convent of the Annunziata, Florence, Italy)

This is perhaps one of the most important sources for the arms and armour of late 13th century Italy. It shows a horseman wearing a conical, perhaps fluted helmet with a very small brim. This is an unusual helmet which has features in common with both the *cervellière* and the early *bascinet*. It is probably worn over a *coif* rather than having its own *aventail*. The rider has a long-sleeved mail *hauberk* with fingered *mittens*, mail *chausses*, and perhaps laminated or scale-lined *sabatons* on his feet. His legs are also protected by sheets of *cuir-bouilli* (hardened leather) forming *greaves*, a specialised type of *cuisse*, and a *poleyn*, the last perhaps being of metal. The fleurs-de-lys on the upper part of his *surcoat* are not repeated on the lower section. They are probably decorations surrounding and to some extent hiding the outer rivets of a *coat-of-plates*. The rider carries a typical late 13th-century sword and shield. At his hip, however, he has a large dagger, a feature not normally seen elsewhere in Western European art until the 14th century. The precocious presence of this weapon probably resulted from Italy's close contacts with Byzantium and the eastern Mediterranean.

604   Stone mosaic, Rome, early 13th century
(*in situ* Church of S. Giovanni Evangelistica, Rome, Italy)

The mosaic pavement is better known for the two-masted ship that it also portrays, but the warriors that are shown on the crudely executed pavement are also of interest. The scene is likely to represent the capture of Constantinople by the Fourth Crusade. The soldiers are given remarkably primitive equipment, apparently consisting only of kite-shaped shields and mail *hauberks* without *mittens* or *coifs*, but no helmets. One man wields a simple sword (A) while the others raise spears (B).

605A–B 'Betrayal', wall-painting, Central Italy, 1263
(*in situ* Church of S. Maria ad Cryptas, Fossa, Italy)

This peculiar wall-painting shows two warriors in what look like flat-topped helmets. Similar helmets are known elsewhere, but generally a bit earlier and mostly with face-masks attached. These examples also have uniquely sloping tops. One man has a separate mail *coif*, a *hauberk* and a flat-topped shield (B).

606 'Massacre of the Innocents', wall-painting, Abruzzi, early 13th century
(*in situ* Church of S. Maria Ronzano, Castel Castagna, Italy)

This man's peculiar *hauberk* and *coif* might be assumed to be of mail, but other figures in the same wall-painting are shown wearing ordinary sleeved *hauberks*, the mail of which is indicated in a normal way using horizontal lines. Perhaps the armour shown here really is of scale, which could account for its lack of sleeves and its very broad arm holes. The mountainous Abruzzi region was, of course, a backward and isolated frontier district, almost a no-man's-land between the Neapolitan kingdom to the south and the Papal States. Here some communities may have had to make their own armour as best they could.

607 Wall-painting, Rome, early 13th century
(*in situ* Church of S. Giovanni in Porta Latina, Rome, Italy)

This sword, wielded by an angel, is clearly exaggerated, but even taking this into account it remains a heavy, broad-bladed weapon. It has normal long, curved *quillons* but the *pommel* is of an unusual almond-shaped form.

608A–I Embossed silver altar front of *antipendium* by Andrea di Jacopo d'Ognabene, Tuscany, late 13th century
(*in situ* Cathedral, Pistoia, Italy)

A–B – Martyrdom of St James; C – Condemnation of James; D–G – Massacre of the Innocents; H–I – The Betrayal. The silver altar in Pistoia Cathedral consists of panels made at different periods, of which this is the oldest. Some of the figures are clearly based on Byzantine traditional archaisms – for instance, the pseudo-Roman *cuirasses* with splinted arm and thigh defences (E–G). Other figures do not appear to be so archaic. They wear a variety of helmets, including simple round *cervellières* (A, D and H), brimmed two-piece proto-*salets* (B), and a form of similar two-piece helmet which, though it sometimes has fanciful decorative additions, is probably rooted in Italian, Byzantine or Balkan arms (C, E–G and I). One man has a mail collar without any other apparent armour (A). Such a *collière* appears again in Italian art relatively few years later. Other figures, including those with conventionalised Byzantine 'classical' armour, also have full mail *hauberks* but without *mittens* (D–H). Two men wear mail *chausses*, perhaps inside ordinary shoes, plus *greaves* of iron or hardened leather (H and I). Most shields are small round bucklers (A, C and D), though this need not necessarily be an archaism at a time when light infantry were becoming increasingly important in Italian warfare. One shield is of the much larger kite-shaped variety (I). Swords and scabbards are typical of the late 13th century (A–C, H and I). Large daggers or small-swords (E–G) are common. Some have almost triangular blades and hilts which are in one instance quite clearly those of a *basilard* (E). Again, this kind of weapon makes its appearance earlier in Italy than in most other parts of Europe.

609 'Apostles at the Last Judgement', wall-painting by Pietro Cavallini, Rome, c.1290
(*in situ* Church of S. Cecilia, Rome, Italy)

In most ways this painting is typical of the late 13th century. Only its nut-shaped *pommel* looks rather old-fashioned.

610 'Story of Job', wall-painting by Taddeo Gaddi, Tuscany, mid-14th century
(*in situ* Camposanto, Pisa, Italy)

An accurate representation of the infantryman who would become increasingly important in 14th century Italian warfare. He might wear a helmet, though this is unclear. Otherwise he has only his large oval shield, a broad-bladed spear, a sword on his left hip and a substantial dagger on his right hip.

611A–B 'Byzantines attack Shayzar', *History of Outremer*, Lombardy, c.1291–5
(Bib. Nat., Ms. Fr. 2631, f.205-7, Paris, France)

Three interesting features are apparent in this illustration of Byzantine troops: a spear with a bamboo shaft (A), which would be correctly associated with eastern Mediterranean warriors; separate mail *gauntlets* (A), which are also seen in Byzantine-style manuscripts; and rowel spurs worn over mail *chausses* (B). This is one of the earliest representations of such spurs and it would be interesting to know whether they reflect an Italian or Byzantine original.

612A–B Wall-paintings, Duchy of Spoleto, c.1280–90
(*in situ* Upper Church of St Francis, Assisi, Italy)

A – Betrayal; B – Sacrifice of Isaac. A number of interesting weapons are illustrated in the wall-paintings of the Upper Church, including a long-bladed, long-hafted axe which might be termed a *guisarme* (A), as well as a curved form of *falchion* (B).

613A–I Wall-painting, Latium, c.1250–5
(*in situ* crypt of Cathedral, Anagni, Italy)

A – Abraham; B–C – Saracens (?), transfer of the Relics of St Magnus from Veroli to Anagni; D–I – Philistines capture the Ark, and slay Hophni and Phinehas. The wall-paintings at Anagni were painted under strong but far from overwhelming Byzantine influence, which is more apparent in some pictures (B–I) than others. But even the picture of Abraham (A) betrays some unusual features, such as a fluted conical helmet, a kind of neck-cloth or *coif* which is apparently not of mail, and perhaps two *hauberks* worn one over the other. His sword, though short, is otherwise straightforward, as is his shield. Similarly short, straight and non-tapering swords are placed in the hands of some Philistines (E and I). Perhaps the most Byzantine features are the brimmed *chapel-de-fer war-hats*, some of which are round (B–C, F and H–I), others pointed (D, E and G). The round shields would equally suit a Byzantine origin (B, G and I) but other figures have normal Western kite-shaped shields (D and E). No armour is apparent, but the head-cloths worn beneath helmets are also reminiscent of some Byzantine art.

614A–D Wall-paintings, Tuscany, c.1280–92
(*in situ* Dante Hall, Town Museum, San Gimignano, Italy)

The wall-paintings in San Gimignano are crude but very important in the history of Italian arms and armour. Three types of helmets are present: a small brimmed *chapel-de-fer* with a *coif* or probable *aventail* (D); a pointed *great helm* (B); and a large helmet with a movable visor (A). A similar type is probably worn by the fourth figure (C). Mail *hauberks* are worn beneath *surcoats*, two of which are slit down the front (A and C). A third has a decorated upper edge and a somewhat pronounced chest, perhaps indicating that a *coat-of-plates* or some form of *cuirie* was attached to the inside (D). All four horsemen have mail *chausses*, but the most important features are the plate arm and leg defences. Their highly decorated surfaces and their clear similarity with such defences shown in more detail in other sources indicates that they are of hardened, perhaps decoratively tooled leather. These pieces of armour include shoulder *roundels* (C and D), as well as *rerebraces* and *vambraces* (A and C). The hands are unclear but might be covered by padded *gauntlets* (A and C). Comparable leg defences include *greaves* (A, C–D), and in all cases presumed rounded *poleyns*. The latter are attached to some kind of more flexible *cuisses*, which also extend some way below the knees (A–C). Two men fight with lances (C and D), the other two with heavy tapering swords having long *quillons* and large round *pommels*. One figure (A) clearly has a large *basilard* dagger on his hip. All four shields are large, flat-topped and kite-shaped, with a distinct curvature. Three horses wear *caparisons*, one of which does not go over the animal's head (D). In another case the horse is also protected by a *chanfron* (C).

615 'Inferno', wall-painting by Orcagna, Tuscany, mid-14th century
(Museo dell'Opera di Santa Croce, Florence, Italy)

It would be interesting to know the identity of the figures in this part of the painting. The female (B) may be a horned demon. The male is naked except for his mail collar or *collière*. He also wears an early and very typically Italian *bascinet*, and carries a large *basilard* and perhaps an oval shield.

616A–D *History of Outremer*, Rome, 1295
(Bib. Nat., Ms. Fr. 9082, Paris, France)

A–C – Crusaders attacking Antioch, f.75v; D – Fulk's men, f.171r. Late 13th-century Italian manuscripts tend to show arms and armour in a very stylised manner. Nevertheless, two distinct forms of helmet can be identified here: low domed *great helms* (A–C) and a two-piece *chapel-de-fer* over a mail *coif* (D).

617A–E 'Romans', *Faits des Romains*, Rome, 1293
(Bib. Royale, Ms. 10168-72, f.168v, Brussels, Belgium)

As this manuscript includes no obvious archaisms, one may assume that the warriors reflect late 13th-century Roman or at least central Italian warriors. Oval shields (B and C) are seen in various late 13th century sources so they need not be regarded as an anachronism. The men wear full mail *hauberks* with *mittens*, plus mail *coifs*. A round helmet with an old-fashioned *nasal* is shown (A), but the remaining warriors wear a variety of somewhat simplified *great helms* with round or pointed tops. A tapering sword has a diamond-shaped *pommel* and down-turned *quillons* (A).

618A–B 'Crucifixion', panel painting, Tuscany, c.1260–70
(Yale University Art Gallery, no.1871.2, New Haven, Connecticut, United States)

Paintings such as this, in the so-called 'Greek manner' of 13th century Italy, are naturally very much under Byzantine influence. The most realistic elements include a raised collar of a mail shirt (B) which is presumably stiffened by being attached to some arming garment. The scabbard is probably realistic (A) and even the small round bucklers could have been used by light infantry.

619 'Crucifixion', *Missale Romanum*, Friuli or Styria, 13th century
(Museo Archeologico Nazionale, Ms. LXXXVI, Cividale, Italy)

This manuscript was made in a cultural frontier zone where Italian, Balkan and German influences were all at work. Although the style is basically Byzantine, the raised collars of presumed mail *hauberks* probably indicate Western armour. The sword, small round buckler and *chapel-de-fer* helmet with an apparent feather thrust into its brim looks distinctly Byzantine. Perhaps the styles of Slav areas like Croatia or Slovenia are reflected in this illustration.

620 ***Address from the City of Prato to King Robert of Naples, Tuscany, early 14th century***
(British Library, London, England)

This detailed representation of an early 14th century helmet shows a type which could be described as a visored *great helm*. It seems as if the hinged visor was first used on this kind of helmet and shortly afterwards appeared on the much smaller *bascinets*.

621 ***Bombardella*, from Val di Susa, Savoy, c.1325–75**
(Historisches Museum, Bern, Switzerland)

This middle-sized early cannon might also have been carriage mounted. It weighed 45.6 kg and was 38.7 cm long.

622 ***Bombardella*, from Morro, The Marches, c.1325–75**
(Artillery Museum, Turin, Italy)

This larger cannon was found near Ancona. It weighed 41 kg, was 58 cm long, and was almost certainly mounted on a carriage.

623 ***Bombardella*, from Verrua Savoia, c.1357**
(Bottega dell'Armarolo, Turin, Italy)

This is one of the earliest surviving cannons to be cast in one piece. It weighed 10 kg and was 29 cm long. As such it might have been a 'hand cannon' of the kind mounted on a long shaft and supported by a rest or a wall when fired.

624 ***Bombardella*, from Issogne, Savoy, c.1325–75**
(Historisches Museum, Bern, Switzerland)

The Val d'Aosta cannon weighed 60.5 kg and was 40 cm long.

625 ***Bascinet*, Italy, c.1350, cut down and re-used in the 15th century**
(Metropolitan Museum of Art, inv. 29.158.44, New York, United States)

One of the earliest pieces of armour in a large collection of weaponry found on the island of Evvoia (Euboea-Negroponte). The tall fluted *bascinet* originally had longer sides and back, as well as a straight brow (here indicated by dotted lines). At some time later it was cut down, had eye-slits added and was clearly worn lower on the head.

626 Effigy of Giovanni di Castruccio Castracane, Tuscany, c.1343
(*in situ* Church of S. Francesco, Pisa, Italy)

This is a better preserved effigy than some. It shows a knight with his head protection removed. This, consisting of a *bascinet* and a mail aventail which would seemingly gave left only his eyes uncovered, lies beneath his feet. His mail *hauberk* has small plated *couters* added to protect the elbows and is worn under a *coat-of-plates* with chains leading to a sword and a dagger. Over this is worn a *surcoat* with the fashionable cap sleeves favoured in Italy. *Poleyns* and *greaves* protect his legs and the feet of mail *chausses* are visible.

627 Effigy of Gherarduccio de Gherardini, Tuscany, c.1331
(*in situ* Church of S. Appiano Barberino d'Elsa, Italy)

The effigy of Gherarduccio de Gherardini illustrates quite advanced armour. The *bascinet* and *aventail* clearly include a flap-like *bretache* which would be fastened at the brow of his helmet. His mail *hauberk* has large *couters* attached to it, or strapped over it, to protect his elbows. Rectangular plates form rudimentary *rerebraces* to protect his upper arms. A *coat-of-plates* is worn beneath his *surcoat* and he is armed with a sword and very large *basilard* dagger, both fastened to chains linked to the *coat-of-plates*. Studded *cuisses*, probably lined with scales or splints, can be seen on his thighs, while the rest of his legs and feet are covered by *poleyns, greaves* and laminated *sabatons*.

628 Tomb slab of Luigi de Chamenet, Tuscany, c.1348
(*in situ* Church of SS. Vincenzo and Anastasio, Siena, Italy)

This particularly worn tomb slab illustrates a deep *bascinet*, the lower third of which could be the additional flap of mail sometimes favoured in Italy, while a *bretache* clearly hangs from his chin. The large *couters* on his elbows have most unusual spikes and on his right hip is a large *basilard* dagger with a curved *pommel*.

629 Tomb slab of Johann Spirer de Gleyspalsen, Tuscany, c.1345
(*in situ* Church of S. Romano, Lucca, Italy)

Johann Spirer was one of the many German knights who served in early 14th-century Italy. His effigy is very worn but shows what could be a low-domed *bascinet* and *coif*, perhaps with a *bretache* face-guard hanging from the chin. His relatively small *great helm* has a *lambrequin* and crest. Large cap sleeves covering his shoulders probably included some form of shoulder plates attached to a *coat-of-plates*. The probable presence of the latter is indicated not only by the chains running from his chest to a *basilard* dagger and a massive sword, but also by the scalloped hem of the garment worn beneath the *surcoat* and over the mail *hauberk*. Glove-like *gauntlets* are worn, probably with scales and small plates to protect the back of the hands and the fingers. *Poleyns* and *greaves* cover the legs and, though very worn, there seem to be traces of lacing on the inside of his left leg.

630 Tomb slab of Filippo dei Desideri, Romagna, c.1315 (Museo Civico, Bologna, Italy)

A large number of early 14th-century engraved tomb slabs and effigies survive in Italy. Many, like this one, are very worn, but they show a style of armour distinct from that worn in either France or Germany. This man clearly wears a *bascinet* which wraps around to protect the sides of his face, plus a mail *aventail*. His mail *hauberk* has moderately long sleeves which seem to go over splinted *vambraces*, while his separate *gauntlets*, though too damaged to be interpreted with certainty, were probably thickly padded and either lined or covered with scales. Over the mail *hauberk* there is a *coat-of-pates* with shoulder pieces. From this *coat-of-plates* chains run to a *basilard* dagger (probably hung from the sword-belt) and a sword with straight *quillons* and a large round *pommel*. His legs are fully covered with bulbous *poleyns* and *greaves*. There seem to be the remains of lacing on the inside of these greaves, suggesting that they were of hardened leather rather than iron. The front part of his feet are protected by scales, which could either be part of separate *sabatons* or have been added to mail chausses.

631 Effigy of Lorenzo di Niccolo Acciaiuoli, Tuscany, c.1353 (*in situ* Certosa di Valdema, Florence, Italy)

Perhaps the most elaborate mid-14th-century effigy in central Italy. It portrays highly decorated costume and armour and finds its most obvious parallels in southern Italy. Niccolo Acciaiuoli was a loyal servant of the Angevin Kings of Naples and spent much of his career in Greece. The close, though far from friendly, contact between the Angevins and various Balkan States – including the remnants of the Byzantine Empire – may account for the popularity of hardened leather armour in southern Italy. Such armour is shown in considerable detail on this effigy. The mail *hauberk* has a raised collar, perhaps attached to the garment beneath. A lion-shaped *epaulette* hangs from the *coat-of-plates*, which appears to be covered in rich brocade. Splinted *vambraces* protect his lower arms and he has plated *gauntlets* on his hands. A long dagger with a decorated hilt hangs on his right hip, while his sword has an even more decorative hilt with an elongated *pommel* and angled *quillons*. Splinted *cuisses* seem to be worn above *poleyns* which, like the *epaulette*, are shaped like lions' heads. Small flaps of mail protect the vulnerable joints between *poleyns* and probably tooled-leather *greaves*. Another flap of mail hangs below the *greaves*, overlapping the upper part of the laminated *sabatons*.

632 Tomb slab of Bernardino dei Baranzoni, Lombardy, c.1345–50
(Museo Lapidario Estense, Modena, Italy)

The tomb slab of Bernardino dei Baranzoni, though broken, is still in a remarkable state of preservation, and provides a number of details unseen elsewhere. These include the extra flap from the mail *aventail*, which hangs like a curtain around his neck. His mail *bretache* is clearly visible, as are details of his sword-belt and sword-hilt, and – of greatest interest – his arm defences. The mail of a long-sleeved *hauberk* can be seen at his armpits and around his lower arms. A decorated *couter* is visible on his elbow, while a tubular *rerebrace* goes around his upper arm. The rivets on this piece of armour strongly suggest that it is of splinted construction with a decorative fabric or leather covering. The flap of mail hanging from the *rerebrace* over his elbow could simply be an additional piece fastened to the *rerebrace*, or indicate that either two mail *hauberks* or a *hauberk* and a shorter *haubergeon* are both worn beneath the *coat-of-plates*. His *gauntlets* appear to have no pieces of plate attached, although the wrist area might be made of stiffened leather.

633 Carved relief, Tuscany, c.1322–6
(Bargello Museum, Florence, Italy)

This rider seems to represent the might of Florence itself. He has a late pointed form of *great helm*, a small flat-topped shield, a mail *hauberk* and mail *chausses*. Over these he seems to wear a scale *cuirass* with very short sleeves, plus scale-covered *gauntlets*. The *cuirass* is shown with such realism that it probably reflects a fashion that was actually current in Italy, even if only for a short time, before being ousted by the *coat-of-plates*. Over his legs he seems to wear a form of rigid or semi-stiff *poleyn* and *greaves*, perhaps of *cuir-bouilli* (hardened leather) reinforced with metal strips. His sword is a heavy tapering weapon with straight *quillons* and a round *pommel*, while his horse's very decorated *caparison* almost certainly incorporates a rigid *chanfron* to protect the animal's head.

634A–G Carved capitals, Venice, c.1309
(*in situ* Doge's Palace, Venice, Italy)

The allegorical and other figures carved above the lowest register of columns on the Doge's Palace are partly fanciful but largely realistic. Even the most imaginative figure, that of 'Pride' (G), seems to reflect certain aspects of late Byzantine armour. Perhaps the now shrunken Byzantine Empire was still being taken as the epitome of the sin of Pride. The horns can perhaps be ignored, though it is worth noting that the *salet* of Skanderbeg (Iskander Bey), the mid-15th-century hero of Albanian resistance to the Ottomans, had antlers attached as a form of crest. In Middle Eastern folklore Alexander the Great, from whose name Skanderbeg's own was derived, was known as _Dhū al-Qarnayn_, 'He of the Two Horns'. Here, 'Pride's' helmet is a decorated early _salet_ made in two pieces and worn over a mail _coif_. His splinted neck and shoulder-covering collar clearly have parallels in Byzantine and Balkan art while his flowered _cuirass_ seems to be an uncovered _coat-of-plates_ with apparent _epaulettes_. He might have a _vambrace_ under the sleeve of his mail _hauberk_, while his hand is protected by a simple mail _gauntlet_. The sword is clearly fanciful but he seems to have a straightforward dagger on his hip. Other figures have more orthodox equipment, including _bascinets_ with mail _aventails_ and with or without _bretache_ nose-guards (A, E and D). One figure has an early _salet_ (C) like a simplified version of that worn by 'Pride'. Another figure has an old-fashioned long-sleeved mail _hauberk_, perhaps over a padded _gambeson_ but worn with modern plated _poleyns_ and _greaves_ plus laminated _sabatons_ (A). Yet another has a mail _hauberk_ under a possible _coat-of-plates_ (D). He, too, has up-to-date leg defences of plate, and seems to have his shield slung across his back. The man's weapon looks like a massive mace, club or iron staff (D). If it is such a specialised mace, then perhaps the comparable object wielded by 'Pride' should not be dismissed as merely fanciful (G). Other weapons include broad swords with long _quillons_ and large round _pommels_ (A–B), an ordinary infantry spear (C), and a probable composite bow with angled ears (F).

635 'Marriage of St Catherine', panel painting, Tuscany, 14th century
(Museum of Fine Arts, no.15.1145, Boston, United States)

This painting from Siena provides a nice illustration of the inside of a small round infantry shield. Even if the form of the shield reflects Byzantine tradition, the internal arrangement of straps probably represents a system commonly used in Italy. There are two horizontal straps, one for the fist and one across the elbow, while the inside of the shield seems to have a fabric-covered padded squab.

636 Carved head from the tomb of Guido Tarlati, Tuscany, c.1330
(Museum, Arezzo, Italy)

This finely carved head of a worshipping knight clearly shows the low-domed _bascinet_ with its mail _aventail_ and the additional doubled flap of mail popular in mid-14th century Italy.

637A–T Relief carvings on the tomb of Guido Tarlati, Tuscany, c.1330
(_in situ_ Cathedral, Arezzo, Italy)

A–G – Siege of Laterina; H–N – Siege of Chiusi; O–T – Siege of Bucine. Some details of these relief carvings were restored in the 17th century, but no items stand out as being obviously anachronistic. Their chief importance is the light they shed on infantry equipment rather than that of the cavalry elite, which is well served by surviving effigies and tomb slabs. The cavalry are shown wearing various types of *great helm* (A and P–S), a *bascinet* and *aventail* (C), mail *hauberks* (B and O), plated leg defences, *poleyns* and *greaves* (B, O and S). Some ride horses with heavy *caparisons* or *bards* (O and T). A few dismounted men have the same heavy armour, plus shoulder pieces, elbow-covering *couters* and, probably, *coats-of-plates* (H–K). One foot-soldier with a massive rectangular *mantlet* also appears to wear *poleyns* and possible shoulder-pieces (M), while a crossbowman has similar shoulder-pieces (N). Note the loading hook on a belt worn by another crossbowman (L). Otherwise the crossbowmen have *bascinets* with or without *aventails* (L and N), while the humble sappers or pioneers have only *bascinets* without any other apparent armour (D–G).

638 Statue of Can Grande della Scala, Lombardy, c.1330 (Castelvecchio Museum, Verona, Italy)

This massive statue once stood on the top of Can Grande's tomb outside the Church of S. Maria Antica in Verona. Though rather crudely carved, it shows a man wearing a *bascinet*, *aventail* and *bretache*. The *great helm* slung so uncomfortably on his back has probably been moved from another location, perhaps the saddle, during previous restoration. He wears a mail *hauberk* and light *gauntlets*, almost certainly a *coat-of-plates*, and full leg-harness of *poleyns*, *greaves* and *sabatons*. The horse's *caparison* or *bard* may have included a protective layer and the animal clearly wears a *chanfron* with semi-domed eye cups.

639 Statue of Mastino II della Scala, Lombardy, c.1351 (*in situ* outside Church of S. Maria Antica, Verona, Italy)

The statue shows Mastino II wearing perfectly normal mid-14th-century armour. However, one unusual and extremely interesting feature is also present. This is the broad strap leading over his thighs from the *cantle* to be fastened to the *pommel* of his saddle. A few sources refer to heavily-armoured 14th-century horsemen being 'tied' to their saddles, and this is probably the system to which such allusions refer.

640A–B La Madonna del Rocciamelone, metalwork, Savoy, 1358 (*in situ* Church of S. Giusto, Susa, Italy)

A – St George; B – donor's helmet. Once again the arms and armour of Italy's far north-west shows strong French influence. The donor's helmet (B) is a straightforward *great helm* with a massive crest. The rings on the bottom rim may be to hold a chin-strap or an additional mail flap. St George (A) has a tall visored *bascinet* and a mail *aventail*. The riveted elements of a *coat-of-plates* are visible on his shoulders and around his waist. Mail is visible below this. On his arms are a fully-plated *rerebrace*, *couter*, *vambrace* and *gauntlet*. The rivets of his *cuisses* are seen above his plate *poleyns* and *greaves*, below which are his laminated *sabatons*. On his hip is a relatively small dagger, and his spear has a *roundel* to cover his hand, although this appears to have been reversed. Like Mastino II, he is secured in his saddle by a strap from *cantle* to *pommel*. His shield seems to have a rounded base and an almost rectangular top. The horse clearly has a *chanfron* over its head and what looks like a small *peytral* to protect its chest.

641 Carved relief, Tuscany, c.1342–7
(*in situ* Campanile of Church of S. Maria de Fiore, Florence, Italy)

This detail of a carved relief on a bell tower illustrates leg-harness with considerable accuracy. Under a cut-away *surcoat* the horseman has a *coat-of-plates*, identified by its rows of rivets. Beneath this is his mail *hauberk*. His thigh is protected by a *cuisse* which also covers his knee; a domed *poleyn* is fixed directly to this. A plated iron or hardened-leather thigh defence is laced over the *cuisse*. Around his lower leg is a *greave*. The lack of a joint or hinge even on such a detailed carving as this suggests that it was made of a flexible material such as hardened leather. This was probably also true of his foot-covering *sabaton*, under the toes of which a mailed shoe or the end of a mail *chausse* can be seen.

642 Bronze *aquamanile*, Italy, c.1340
(Bargello Museum, no.R.372, Florence, Italy)

The crosses on the knight's shield, *surcoat* and *ailettes* might identify him as St George. They could also link him with Florence, Savoy or Genoa, all of which had crosses on their flags. The armour points to northern Italy and perhaps to French influence. The horseman has a *bascinet* with a mail *aventail*, a mail *hauberk* which is visible at the armpit and elbow, heraldic *ailettes*, and full arm defences of *rerebrace*, *couter* and *roundel* for the elbow, *vambrace*, and *gauntlets*. His spear also has a small circular addition both to protect the hand and to stop the weapon sliding through his fist at the shock of impact. His shield has a cut-out lance-rest in one corner. There is no sign of a *coat-of-plates* and his legs are defended only by early-style *poleyns* and mail *chausses*.

643 Carved relief on the tomb of the *Gonfaloniere* Giovanni d'Medici, Tuscany, c.1351
(*in situ* Church of S. Reparata, Florence, Italy)

By the mid-14th century, *great helms* such as that shown here were probably reserved for parades and tournaments, rather than the battlefield. The helmet has a large crest and a long flowing *lambrequin*.

644 'Betrayal', *Maesta* panel painting by Duccio, Tuscany, c.1308–11
(Museo dell'Opera del Duomo, Siena, Italy)

A number of long-bladed, long-hafted axes appear in 14th century Italian art. They are probably to be identified as *guisarmes*.

645 'Betrayal', wall-painting by Giotto, Lombardy, c.1303–6
(*in situ* Arena Chapel, Padua, Italy)

This is a somewhat smaller-bladed axe or *guisarme* than that which appears on Duccio's *Maesta*.

646A–B 'Crucifixion' by Simone Martini, Italy, c.1320
(Koninklijik Museum voor schone kunsten, Antwerp, Belgium)

While leading figures like the Centurion are almost invariably archaised in early 14th century art, the lesser soldiers are given many pieces of contemporary equipment. Here such equipment includes a number of interesting helmets: a tall *bascinet* (A), a wide-brimmed *chapel-de-fer* (B), a similar helmet with a mail *aventail* (C), a partially obscured helmet with a single antler as a crest (D), a round *bascinet* with an *aventail* (F), a helmet of apparent two-piece construction (G), and an early form of *cabacete* or *salet* with a *barbuta* neckguard.

647A–D 'The Way to Calvary', polyptych of the Passion by Simone Martini, painted in Avignon, c.1340
(Musée du Louvre, Paris, France)

Once again Simone Martini mixes archaism and contemporary realism in one picture, though whether the realistic arms and armour reflects that of Avignon or his native Italy is unclear. A dagger, basically a *basilard*, hangs by cords from the wearer's belt (A). Pointed (B) and rounded *chapel-de-fer war-hats* are worn over probable mail *coifs* which are elsewhere seen on their own (D). One man has a rigid *barbuta* or collar.

648A–B 'Crucifixion', wall-painting by Pietro Lorenzetti, Umbria, c.1329
(*in situ* Lower Church of St Francis, Assisi, Italy)

Here two visored *bascinets* are somewhat crudely drawn.

649A–E 'Lives of Sts Peter and Paul', wall-painting attributed to Deodato Orlandini, Tuscany, c.1300–5
(*in situ* Church of S. Pietro a Grado, Pisa, Italy)

If correctly dated, this is one of the earliest representations of helmets with movable visors. They are almost certainly developed from a late form of pointed *great helm* but could not yet be referred to as *bascinets*.

The painting also shows a *basilard* with a broad triangular blade, and leg defences consisting of a *poleyn*, *greave* and mail *chausse*.

650 Seal of Count Amadeo IV of Savoy, Savoy, early 14th century
(Archives Nationales, Paris, France)

Compared with sources of a similar date from central Italy and even Lombardy, this Savoyard seal illustrates remarkably old-fashioned armour. The style is essentially French, consisting of an almost flat-topped *great helm*, a long-sleeved mail *hauberk* with one *mitten* apparently dangling from the wrist, probable mail *chausses*, and a flat-topped kite-shaped shield. Even the massive sword tapers only slightly. The horse, however, clearly wears a *chanfron*, apparently over the front of its cloth *caparison*.

651 'Crucifixion', panel painting, Italy, c.1355
(Musée du Louvre, Paris, France)

The unknown artist of this Crucifixion scene provides us with an exceptionally detailed picture of the back of a *coat-of-plates*. Rivets hold the internal plates and the sides of the garment are drawn around the back, where they are laced not only to each other but vertically to the upper part of the back-plate. The man wears a rather simple *bascinet* with an *aventail* plus the additional flap sometimes seen in Italy. A *bretache* is just visible on his chin. A laminated *gauntlet* can be seen, but otherwise his arms seem to be protected only by the sleeves of a mail *hauberk*. The padded squab and *enarmes* on the inside of his almost triangular shield are clearly visible, and he is armed with a fluted mace.

652A–D 'Old Testament scenes', wall-painting, Tuscany, c.1356
(*in situ* Collegiata, San Gimignano, Italy)

A – Slaughter of Job's family; B–C – Slaying of Job's shepherds; D – Arrest of Joseph's brothers. This sequence of pictures has a number of unusual features, including an apparent *falchion* with a hooked grip but no *quillons* or guard (A). A massive *basilard* dagger is more than one-third of a man's height in length (B). A riveted *bascinet* has either a small neckguard or an additional flap of mail (C), and a somewhat fanciful but certainly very slender-bladed sword is slung from a sash-like belt in clear imitation of normal Middle Eastern style (D). This latter feature probably reflects some knowledge of Mamlūk Egyptian or Turkish fashion rather than reflecting current Italian usage.

653A–D 'St Martin renouncing the sword', wall-painting by Simone Martini, Umbria, c.1317
(*in situ* Montefiore Chapel, Lower Church of St Francis, Assisi, Italy)

A – German; B–D – Romans. It is interesting to note that it is the German or 'barbarian' warrior rather than the Italianate Romans who has been given the rigid neckguard (A). Such a neck piece is so often given to 'barbarian', 'wicked' or 'infidel' warriors in 14th century Italian art that one may assume that it was generally associated with aliens or foreigners. This piece of armour is in some respects similar to the raised neck defences seen in late Byzantine and Balkan art, where it is generally given to warrior saints. This coincidence seems to suggest that rigid or semi-rigid neck defences were indeed characteristic of the 14th century Balkans. The German also has a wide-brimmed *chapel-de-fer* or early *cabacete*. The Romans have slightly different but equally wide-brimmed helmets (B), while one man has a simple pointed helmet hanging from his belt by its chin-strap (D). He and another warrior meanwhile wear fashionably tall hats rather than helmets (C and D). The most obvious armour of these Romans is a *coat-of-plates* (B and D). This particular form, however, has a long hem hanging below the knees. Both men wear *greaves*, but whereas one has riveted cloth-covered *sabatons* (B) the other has laminated *sabatons* (D). This latter figure also carries a lance with a *roundel* ahead of the grip.

654A–K 'Crucifixion', wall-painting by Orcagna and others, Tuscany, c.1360
(*in situ* Church of S. Spirito, Florence, Italy)

Warriors whose 'infidel' or 'alien' status is indicated by their beards are given a number of unusual features. These include feathered crests (D and I), old-fashioned long kite-shaped shields (G and H), and some Byzantine archaisms such as splendid upper-arm defences (K). A large number have rigid neckguards (A, E, G, and H). All save one have varied types of wide-brimmed *chapel-de-fer war-hats*, while the last wears a form of *bascinet* (I).

655 'Life of St James', wall-painting by Buonamico Buffalmacco, Italy, 1315
(*in situ* church, Badia a Settimo, Savoy, Italy)

A very wide and deep-brimmed *chapel-de-fer* seems to have been popular in Italy and some neighbouring regions during the first half of the 14th century. One, and perhaps two, are shown in this painting, both apparently being of a two-piece construction.

656A–B 'Guidoriccio da Fogliano', wall-painting by Simone Martini, Tuscany, 1328
(*in situ* Palazzo Publico, Siena, Italy)

This famous wall-painting portrays one of the best-known of early *condottiere* commanders. In the background are a number of scenes of siege warfare including a large infantry *mantlet* (A). The horseman himself has discarded much of his armour. What remains includes a mail *hauberk* with long, broad sleeves and a raised stiffened collar. His leg-harness is complete and consists of: bulbous *poleyns* – probably attached to the lower part of his *cuisses* – to which short mail fringes have been added; metal *greaves* made in two sections, probably hinged up the outside; and mail *chausses* which extend to cover his feet. His sword is hung in the new way, with the sword-belt fastened to a pair of asymmetrically placed rings. The horse's *caparison* is highly likely to have been lined with mail or at least thick felt, and a rigid *chanfron* with semi-domed eye defences is clearly worn beneath the *caparison*.

657A–AB Wall-paintings, Lombardy, c.1330–50
(*in situ* Church of Sant'Abbondio, Como, Italy)

A – Way to Calvary; B–F – Betrayal; G – Way to Calvary; H–K – Betrayal; L–O – Crucifixion; P–T – Way to Calvary; U–Y – Accusation of Peter; Z–AB – Massacre of the Innocents. Most of the figures in the Sant'Abbondio cycle appear to be heavily-armed infantry, perhaps reflecting the successful militia forces of Milan, under whose rule Como now lay. A number of archaisms may be present, the most obvious being the splinted pendant upper-arm defences and skirts worn by various leading figures (A, E and G). These stem from Byzantine art and are presumably intended to reinforce the 'Roman' identity of the troops. The rest of the arms and armour are straightforward. Most men wear *bascinets*, some with *aventails* (A, D, I and P), others apparently without (B, G, J, K, R, T, U–Z and AB). Some of the latter are worn above stiff mail collars which are high enough tŏ meet the rim of the helmet. Only the men's long hair indicates that helmet and collar are not joined. An unfastened mail *bretache* face protection is shown once (I). Angled and clearly hinged *nasals* also appear, once with a fastening point on the *aventail* (D), once on a *bascinet* without an *aventail* (T), and twice on a helmet that might be described as an early form of *salet* (Q and AA). These helmets have central combs and a neckguard clearly made from a separate piece of metal. A similar helmet is also shown without the *nasal* (C). Other helmets include brimmed *chapel-de-fers* (E and H) and a partially obscured visored helmet worn with a massive *barbuta*. Such *barbutas* also appear with a *war-hat* (E) and a *bascinet* (G). The fact that the raised stiffened and clearly thickly-padded mail collars form part of mail *hauberks* is indicated, though not proved, by figures wearing only such mail *hauberks* and no plated body armour (H, I, K and AB). These *hauberks* are clearly worn over substantially-quilted *gambesons* which reach below the knees. Their sleeves are much more thickly padded above the elbow than on the lower arms (B, D, E, G, O, Q, X, Z and AB). One garment, with comparably puffed sleeves and probably worn over a *gambeson*, is worn by a man holding the nails for the Crucifixion (T). Various figures have been given separate mail *gauntlets* (A, B, E, G, O, Q, Z and AB), while a few have leg armour of *greaves*, once clearly buckled on the inside of the calf (A). Elsewhere such armour can only be assumed because of the different shape around the wearer's ankles (E, G, H, Q and T). Two types of *sabaton* are seen, the normal laminated type (G) and a pair apparently made of linked scales (T). *Rerebraces* for the upper arms are probably of hardened leather (B, O, Q and Z). A strange form of *cuirass* that appears to be of segments, perhaps of leather, is given to a few leading figures and is not always associated with fanciful archaised 'Roman' splinted armour (G, O, Q and Z). Shields are equally varied and interesting, ranging from the ordinary flat-topped kite-shaped variety (K) – one of which appears to have a metal butt fixed to it (N) – to a larger round-topped kite-shaped shield with a clear spike attached to its base (I). This latter form of shield may be a kind of *mantlet* which could be thrust into the ground to create a shield-wall behind which infantry could crouch. A third form of shield seems to be a small sausage-shaped buckler fastened to a man's lower right arm (O). Varied weaponry includes daggers ranging from small knives (A) to full-size *basilards* (E, Q, T, Z and AB), which are worn normally on the right hip. Swords are more rarely shown (I, K, N, O, T and AB) while maces, some clearly winged or flanged, are obviously popular (D, G, I, O and Q). Various spearheads are seen in the background, as well as a heavy single-edged blade mounted on a long haft (L).

658A–BG 'Battles of *Guelphs* and *Ghibellines*', wall-paintings, Lombardy, c.1340
(*in situ* Castle of Sabbionara, Avio, Italy)

A–D–*Guelphs*; E–St George; F–I–*Ghibellines*; J–K–Training duel (?); L–Y–*Ghibellines*; Z–AC–*Guelphs*; AD–*Ghibellines*; AE–AJ–*Guelphs*; AK–AW–*Ghibellines*; AX–AY–*Guelphs*; AZ–BG–'Oriental' allies of *Guelphs*. The very detailed wall-paintings at Avio are even more important than those in Como. They were painted for the Veronese Castelbarco family, who were staunch supporters of the *Ghibelline* (Imperial) faction, and appear to illustrate their struggle against the Bishops of Trento, who were equally committed supporters of the *Guelph* (Papal) cause. The figure of St George (E) is unlike other mounted figures and may be copied from a more conventional source. He wears a round *bascinet* and *aventail*, and a mail *hauberk* under a *coat-of-plates*, part of which is visible at the shoulder beneath his *surcoat*. His arms are protected by *rerebraces* and *vambraces* but no visible *couters*. His legs are fully encased in plate *cuisses*, *poleyns*, *greaves* and *sabatons*. His sword is a long tapering weapon with straight *quillons* and a round *pommel*. The object hanging from his sword-belt on his right hip might have been to hold a dagger. The other pictures in Sabbionara Castle reflect northern Italian and possibly southern German arms and armour. Some cavalry wear *great helms* with *lambrequins* and massive crests (B, D and S), but most seem to have tall or low rounded *bascinets* with large movable visors and mail *aventails* (A, C, Q, R, T and U). Some clearly, and the rest probably, wear *coats-of-plates* (D, S and U). Various forms of plate or splinted and riveted arm defences, *vambraces* and *rerebraces*, plus *couters*, are worn (C, D, Q, S and U). *Gauntlets* are shown, but not in sufficient detail for their construction to be analysed. Leg-harness is only clearly visible on two figures, where it consists of *poleyns* and probably *cuisses*, plus *greaves* which mirror the clearly splinted (Q) and probably fabric-covered (S) construction of the wearers' arm defences. The only cavalry weapons are lances with (D) or without (S) hand-protecting *roundels*, large swords (D and T), and large daggers (S). Some horses wear *caparisons* or *bards*, one of which clearly has the eye protections that betray a *chanfron* beneath the fabric (S). It is, however, the infantry who make these wall-paintings so important. They are shown in considerable detail and even greater variety. Most men wear tall *bascinets*, some of which come right down the neck (G, I and W), but most of which have elongated sides covering the ears (H, M, O, V, AE, AK, AO, AQ, AU, AW and BB). A few of these *bascinets* have decorative caps or coverings over them (AF, AH, AS, AU and AW). Other men shown in plain cloth *coifs* (J and K) are probably engaged in training or mock combat. A few helmets might be simple conical types, without the extensions around the ears which would make them into *bascinets* (N, AF, AV, AZ and BE). Some of the 'Oriental' allies of the *Guelphs* are identified by very tall hats with upturned brims. These seem to be a largely conventionalised headgear based upon Mongol prototypes. As such they may identify the troops as Cumans, Hungarians or Balkan troops. This is not, of course, to deny that similar or comparably tall hats were worn by various south-east European warriors of Central Asian or Turco-Mongol origin. Most of the infantry have only padded or quilted *gambeson* or *aketon* jerkins (F, I, J, K, L, P, V, X, AD, AR, AU and BC). These have various patterns of stitching, with a clear distinction being drawn between the arm above and below the elbow. This has already been seen in Como. All have raised stiffened collars, and while some are buttoned down the front others are not. They also have scalloped lower hems reaching to mid-thigh. Two of these quilted garments may be worn together (P). Over such soft armours, a small mail *hauberk* or *haubergeon* could be worn (G and AC). Elsewhere another but shorter cloth-covered garment forms a top layer. These reach only to the hips, generally with short sleeves, and often have apparent rivets spaced across them. They are probably simple forms of *coat-of-plates* or early versions of the scale-lined *jack* (J, AM, AN, AO, AS, AT, AW and BD). No other arm or leg defences are shown. Shields and their internal arrangements of straps and padded squabs are shown in detail and range from small hand-held bucklers (J and K), through medium-sized oval shields held on the arm (M, P, Y, AC, AE, AO and AV–AY), to extremely large rectangular *mantlets* which are also worn on the arm (F, G, V, AF, AM, AP, AQ, AI and AU). The most common weapon is a long spear which could almost be called a pike. A few long, straight swords with large, round *pommels* and straight or down-turned *quillons* (J, K and Y) are seen, plus a long, curved sabre held by an 'Oriental' (AZ). This latter weapon is not very realistically shown and is probably based on rough sketches or verbal reports. Its lack of *quillons* is interesting but unexplained. Many men carry daggers of apparent *basilard* form on their right hips (J, V, AD, AV and AW) while others fight with large daggers or short swords the bar-like *pommels* of which indicate that they are probably *basilards* (M and AX). Crossbows, rather surprisingly, are of an early form without loading stirrups and are once clearly seen being loaded by placing a foot on the weapon and pulling the cord back with both hands (N, AR and AS). Bows are placed in the hands of some 'Orientals'. These are of a slightly recurved form with extravagantly curved ears (AZ and BC). They are of such an unusual form that one may speculate that such bows are also based upon verbal reports concerning Eastern military equipment.

659 'Court of Justice', Romagna, c.1356
(Nationalbibliothek, Ms. 2048-9, f.149, Vienna, Austria)

This manuscript was made in Bologna. Judging by his complete lack of leg armour it probably shows an infantryman, who is otherwise fully protected by a deep *bascinet, rerebraces, couters, vambraces* and *gauntlets* for his arms. He may even have a one-piece *breastplate* beneath his tight-fitting *surcoat*.

660 'Sagittarius', *Book of Stars*, Venice or Padua, mid-14th century
(Museum of National Literature, Prague, Czech Republic)

This is a direct Latin translation of Al-Sufi's Arabic *Book of Fixed Stars*. The illustrations also follow their Islamic prototype quite closely. It was probably from sources such as this that images of the fully-developed Turkish curved composite bow entered Italian iconography. Not until some years later were such bows actually used in Italy, particularly in Venice and her overseas possessions.

Notes

1. P. Contamine, *La Guerre au Moyen Age* (Paris, 1980), pp.122–3.
2. Contamine, *op.cit.* pp.119–21 and 123.
3. M.J. Swanton, *The Spear in Anglo-Saxon Times* (Ph.D. thesis, Durham University, 1966), pp.624 and 627.
4. J. Beeler, *Warfare in Feudal Europe, 730–1200* (Ithaca, 1971), pp.195–8; F. Cardini, 'La Guerra nella Toscana bassomedievale: Aspeti e dimenioni in un presenza storica', in *Guerre e assoldati in Toscana, 1260–1364*, ed. L.G. Boccia and M. Scalini (Florence, 1982), pp.21–35.
5. D.P. Waley, 'Papal Armies in the Thirteenth Century', *The English Historical Review* vol.CCLXXXII (1957), pp.1–2; P. Partner, *The Lands of St Peter* (London, 1972), pp.144, 195 and 278–9.
6. Beeler, *op.cit.* pp.208–9 and 238; J.F. Verbruggen, *The Art of Warfare in Western Europe in the Middle Ages* (Oxford, 1977), pp.125–6; C. Oman, *A History of the Art in the Middle Ages* (London, 1924), vol.I, pp.448–9.
7. E. Jamison, *Admiral Eugenius of Sicily* (London, 1957), p.114; G. Rausing, *The Bow, Some Notes on its Origins and Development* (Lund, 1967), p.160; F.C. Lane, 'The Crossbow in the Nautical Revolution of the Middle Ages', in *Economy, Society and Government in Medieval Italy* (Kent, Ohio, 1969), pp.161–71.
8. M. Giuliani, 'L'organizazzione militare a Firenze fra XIII e XIV secolo, forme di aggregazione e carattari generale d'esercito fiorentino', in *Guerre e assoldati in Toscana, 1260–1364*, ed. L.G. Boccia and M. Scalini (Florence, 1982), pp.37–49; H.L. Oerter, 'Campaldino, 1286', *Speculum* vol.XXXIII (1968), p.434; E. Oakeshott, *The Archaeology of Weapons* (London, 1960), pp.279–80.
9. Contamine, *op.cit.* pp.165–6 and 206; Waley, *op.cit.* pp.4–5; J. Alm, 'Europeiska armborst; En översickt', *Vaaben-historisk Aarboger* v/b (1947), p.127; V. Maglioli, 'La balestra', *Armi Antichi* (1955), pp.98–9; P. Pieri, 'I Saraceni di Lucera nella Storia militare medievale', *Archivio Storico Pugliese* vol.VI (1954), p.96.
10. D.R. Hill, 'Trebuchets', *Viator* vol.IV (1973), p.104; J.-F. Finó, 'Machines de jet médiévales', *Gladius* vol.X (1972), pp.28–9 and 321; U. Barlozzetti and M. Giuliani, 'La Prassi Guerresca in Toscana', in *Guerre e assoldati in Toscana, 1260–1364*, ed. L.G. Boccia and M. Scalini (Florence, 1982), pp.51–65.
11. Cardini, *loc.cit.*
12. Barlozzetti, *loc.cit.*; Waley, *op.cit.* pp.15–20; D.P. Waley, 'Le origini della Condotta nel Duecento e le Compagnie di Ventura', *Rivista Storica Italiana* vol.LXXXVIII (1976), pp.533–5; D.P. Waley, 'Condotte and Condottieri in the Thirteenth Century', *Proceedings of the British Academy* vol.LXI (1975), pp.339–40, 344, 348 and 350; Guiliani, *loc.cit.*
13. L.G. Boccia, 'HIC IACET MILES: Immagini guerriere da sepolcri toscani del Due e Trecento', in *Guerre e assoldati in Toscana, 1260–1364*, ed. L.G. Boccia and M. Scalini (Florence, 1982), pp.81–99.
14. L.G. Boccia and E.T. Coelho, 'L'armemento di cuoio e ferro nel trecento Italiano', *L'illustrazione italiani* vol.I, no.2 (1972), p.245.
15. Contamine, *op.cit.* p.251.
16. Barlozzetti, *loc.cit.*; Contamine, *op.cit.* p.167; Giuliani, *loc.cit.*; Pieri, *op.cit.* pp.100–1.
17. Barlozzetti, *loc.cit.*; Contamine, *op.cit.* pp.260–1; General A. Gaibi, 'Un raro cimelio piemontese del trecento', *Armi Antiche* (1965), pp.29 and 32; S. Pasquali-Lasagni, 'Note di Storia dell'Artiglieria della Stato della Chiesa nei secoli XIV e XV', *Archivio della R. Deputazione Romano di Storia Patria* vol.IX (1937), p.150.

Chapter 13

Southern Italy and Sicily

The south of Italy and Sicily were politically and to some extent culturally separate from the rest of the country throughout the period under review. During the first few years Sicily remained under Islamic rule and parts of the mainland under Byzantine. The arms and armour of these areas during that time are consequently found in the second of these two volumes, being included in the chapters on the Islamic Ma<u>gh</u>rib and Byzantium respectively; the independent and semi-independent cities and duchies of 11th-century southern Italy, however, are covered here. After the Normans completed their conquest of southern Italy (the Mezzogiorno) and Sicily in 1076 and 1088 the area could be treated as a whole. Naples was not formally taken over until 1140, but had been effectively dominated by the Normans for many years. This was despite considerable cultural differences between ex-Islamic Sicily, ex-Byzantine Calabria, Apulia, Gaeta, Naples and Amalfi, and ex-Lombardic Salerno, Benevento and Capua. The cultural and military-technological identity of the south survived subsequent dynastic changes and the political separation of Sicily from southern Italy following the famous 'Sicilian Vespers' of 1282. The two regions would not be reunited until 1442.

The Lombardic duchies that ruled large parts of southern Italy before being conquered by the Normans had their own distinctive military systems. In some ways these were archaic, going back to Byzantine, early medieval Germanic and even late-Roman prototypes. Military service was normally a personal matter, not being linked to the holding of land. Generally speaking, in fact, the local aristocracy was city or town-based rather than living in country castles like Northern European élites. The church was also involved in the supply of troops from the later 10th century.[1] The Lombards are generally assumed to have been weak in cavalry, but this might be an oversimplification applying only to certain areas which were in revolt against Byzantium when the Normans arrived.[2] Elsewhere, as in Naples, Bari and perhaps other cities, a class of *milites* and 'burgess knights' already existed, being enfiefed by the Normans shortly after the Norman conquest.[3] In contrast infantry garrison troops often seem not to have been of free origin.[4]

The military heritage of the south also reflected Islamic influence from neighbouring Sicily and North Africa, many earlier Arab or Berber invaders and mercenaries having settled in the area. These gradually converted to Christianity and became absorbed into the local population.[5] It should also be remembered that coastal cities like Amalfi still had close political as well as trade connections with the Islamic world. On the other hand, it is possible that the Christian community within Islamic Sicily retained some form of military role.[6] Local troops were similarly available in the ex-Byzantine areas after these were conquered by the Normans, the defence of such provinces having already passed to local forces after the Byzantine *theme* armies were disbanded around 1040.[7]

Although Normans naturally played the dominant role in the Norman conquest of southern Italy and Sicily, other Northern warriors were also involved. These included Bretons, Flemings, Poitevins and men from Anjou,[8] but their military styles and tactics would have been virtually identical to those of the Normans. After the conquest there was considerable feudalisation of the countryside while towns were garrisoned by government troops.[9] In theory the entire male population had a military role but in reality only a minority were called upon.[10] This seems to have been even more true in Sicily, where the indigenous Islamic population in the west of the island also played a vital role. Such Siculo-Muslim warriors became, in some respects, the most loyal and reliable troops in the Norman army, as well as being among the most effective. They included cavalry, some of whom were armed with the bow, plus infantry, the most famous of whom were, again, archers.[11] The Normans, Italians, and other Christian communities probably provided the bulk of heavily-armoured cavalry and infantry forces, these being recruited from knightly classes, urban militias and northern Italian mercenaries.[12] The important role of Italian troops in both the initial conquest and in subsequent Italo-Norman armies has, in fact, only recently been recognised.[13] Mercenaries from these and other sources became increasingly important in royal armies during the 12th century,[14] just as they did elsewhere in Europe. Nevertheless, militias – urban and rural – seem to have survived as vital elements in most such armies, though many were apparently of serf origin, unlike the militias of northern Italy.[15]

The subsequent Hohenstaufen and Angevin take-overs of the southern Italian-Sicilian state had little impact on the military structures created by the Normans. This was particularly apparent in the continuing, though gradually declining, military role of Sicilian Muslims into the late 13th century. The transferral of the last Muslims to Lucera on the mainland was, in fact, essentially the enforced relocation of a military community.[16]

The possession and carrying of arms was strictly controlled in the mid-13th century Hohenstaufen Kingdom of Sicily which, of course, also included southern Italy.[17] At the same time a number of interesting technical developments were seen in southern Italian arms and armour in the 13th and early 14th centuries. Many seem to have reflected Islamic or Byzantine influence, while others might have done so. Whether the last generations of originally Sicilian Muslims had any direct influence is, however, unclear. Relatively short stabbing swords and large *basilard* thrusting daggers were characteristic of the 13th century,[18] as were mounted crossbowmen, though these were almost certainly serving as mounted infantry,[19] while extensive use of hardened-leather armour appeared in the early and mid-14th century.[20]

Figures

661A–B **'Crucifixion',** *Exultet Roll,* **southern Italy, 10th–11th centuries**
(John Rylands Library, Ms.2, Manchester, England)

The *Exultet Rolls,* so characteristic of southern Italian Romanesque art, are a useful source of information but are difficult to interpret. Here a man wields a spear with obvious wings or flanges beneath its blade (A). He also carries what looks like a straight sword with a single, slightly-curved edge (A). Such a weapon is also held by a second figure (B) and probably reflects Byzantine influence or even influence from Islamic Sicily or North Africa. Both weapons have simple nut-shaped *pommels.*

662 **'Arrest of Jesus', carved relief, Apulia, mid-11th century**
(*in situ* Tomba di Rotari, Monte San Angelo, Italy)

Armed only with a spear, the man shows considerable Byzantine and Islamic influence in both his costume and the style of carving.

663 **Carved figure on the episcopal throne, Apulia, 1098**
(*in situ* Cathedral, Bari, Italy)

It is impossible to state with certainty whether this otherwise unarmoured and unarmed figure is wearing a hat or a fluted helmet. The headgear clearly has a cloth or turban wound around it and is similar to helmets seen in other sources.

664A–B **Carved altar, Campania, late 11th/12th centuries**
(*in situ* Church of S. Maria in Valle Porclaneta, Magliano de Marsi, Italy)

Two interesting weapons are seen here. Whereas the composite recurved bow with angled ears was common throughout the central and eastern Mediterranean (A), the winged or flanged mace (B) almost certainly shows strong Islamic influence, perhaps via the nearby seaport and major trading centre of Amalfi.

665A–C **Carved relief, Apulia, late 11th century**
(*in situ* south portal of Church of S. Bernadetto, Brindisi, Italy)

This frieze representing huntsmen is perhaps the most Islamic-influenced of 11th century southern Italian carvings. One man not only has a tall helmet with a probable *nasal* (A), but he wields a broad-bladed spear with an apparent bamboo haft. His coat or tunic appears to be padded or quilted. All these features suggest strong Islamic, or more particularly North African, influence. The other two figures also have short spears, one with wings or flanges (B), but their main interest lies in the distinction drawn between their apparently ordinary tunics and that of the first figure.

666 'Crucifixion', ivory plaque, southern Italy, 11th century (?)
(Staatliche Museen, Berlin, Germany)

Compared with the chessmen illustrated next, this little figure looks typically European. Yet his short spear, short tunic and cross-gartered legs can also be seen throughout the eastern Mediterranean and even in the Islamic regions beyond. There was, in fact, a considerable degree of similarity in peasant costume over a vast area during the 11th century.

667A–E Ivory chessmen, southern Italy or Sicily, 11th century
(Bib. Nat., Cab. des Medailles, Paris, France)

These chessmen are certainly the most important single source of information about 11th century southern Italian military equipment. They probably portray the traditional styles of equipment used in the Lombardic duchies, the Byzantine provinces or even in Islamic Sicily, rather than that of the Norman newcomers. These fashions have little in common with 11th century Northern Europe but a great deal in common with Byzantium and western Islam. The fact that one horseman carries a kite-shaped shield (A and D) in no way indicates Norman influence, since such shields were widely used and may even have been developed in Byzantium. This figure seems to wear a kind of pointed hood which goes right around his head and chin. At this early date it is most unlikely to have been an all-enveloping helmet and probably represents either a mail *coif* or a fabric-covered hood or hat worn over a small helmet. Such headgear is seen in early Islamic areas and in parts of Central Asia adjacent to the Islamic world. It may also be the answer to some Byzantine and southern Italian sources which are otherwise hard to interpret. The horseman seems to hold a broad, non-tapering sword of early medieval Mediterranean form but has no scabbard. He wears a short, perhaps sleeveless, *cuirass* or *hauberk* that reaches only to his waist. Its surface patterning is so stylised that one cannot say whether it is meant to be mail or lamellar, though its shape tends to indicate the latter. Such small lamellar *cuirasses* were probably a typical 11th century form of Byzantine armour. A second horseman (B and C) carries a round shield, a broad sword in his right hand and a scabbard on his left hip. This is clearly worn outside a *hauberk*, though no sword-belt is visible. The *hauberk* itself includes a *coif*, though its surface patterning looks remarkably like lamellar. A lamellar *cuirass* and a lamellar *aventail* are not inconceivable, but are unlikely in the 11th century central Mediterranean region. It is more likely to be a crude representation of an ordinary mail *hauberk*. He clearly wears a low-domed helmet, perhaps fluted, with some kind of separate rim, the curved lower edge giving it an outline different from that of normal European helmets. It has similarities with much later *bascinets*, which might indicate that the *bascinet* did, in fact, originate in the Mediterranean, more specifically in Byzantine or Islamic regions. The foot-soldier (E) is in several respects even more interesting and unusual. He has a slightly pointed helmet with a *nasal*. The helmet appears to come down over the sides and back of his head, in common with the later *bascinet*. The lower rim seems to indicate that the mail is attached. This could refer to an *aventail*, although a helmet worn over a mail *coif* and *hauberk* would seem more likely at this early date. The man almost certainly wears a short-sleeved mail *hauberk* which comes to his waist but has a flap down the front. It is worn over a sash and has much in common with various other Sicilian and Middle Eastern sources. His sword is of the broad Mediterranean form and his shield is a very tall kite-shaped *mantlet*, perhaps with the flattened base seen elsewhere in Italy and the Middle East.

668 **'Centaur', carved oliphant, Campania, 11th century**
(Museum of Fine Arts, no.57.58L, Boston, United States)

This oliphant is believed to have been carved in Salerno. The mace is crudely portrayed, but the presence of such weapons in 11th-century southern Italy shows influences from Byzantium or Islamic regions.

669 **Carved oliphant from Chartreuse de Portes, Campania, mid-11th century**
(Bib. Nat., Paris, France)

This carved tusk is considered to be of Saracenic workmanship but to have been made in Amalfi. The horseman holds a short spear. The long cloth that he appears to wear across his chest and which billows out behind his shoulder is, however, more typical of the 12th-century Middle East, though it is also seen on the Cappella Palatina in Sicily.

670 ***Leges Langobardorum*, Campania, 11th century**
(Archives of Badia della Santissima Trinita, Co. 4, f.192, Cava, Italy)

This 11th-century manuscript from Benevento may illustrate the considerable degree of Islamic influence seen in some parts of pre-Norman southern Italy. The man appears to have a *ṭirāz* band around the arm of his tunic. His broad but slightly tapering sword is of a type seen throughout the eastern Mediterranean and beyond,

finding echoes and maybe even origins in the art of India, from which
the Arab world imported the highly-prized *sayf al-hind* or 'Indian
sword'. His small round or oval shield, with its pattern of multiple
rivets holding the internal straps, seems to have more in common with
North Africa and al-Andalus than with northern Italy or the rest of
Europe.

671 Carved oliphant, southern Italy or Sicily, late 11th century
(Private collection, on loan to Victoria and Albert Museum, London, England)

A 17th-century silver mount obscures the upper part of the ivory
figure but a number of features are still clearly visible, most of which
indicate Islamic inspiration. The figure wears a short-sleeved,
probably mail, shirt which is likely to have continued inside his
waist-sash and skirt. He holds a deeply convex shield in his fist and
wields a sword without *quillons*. Such features were typical of Sicily
and North Africa.

672 'Guard at the Holy Sepulchre', *Exultet Roll* from Monte Cassino, Campania, 11th century
(Cathedral Archives, Capua, Italy)

A damaged and confused drawing which appears to show a soldier in
a *hauberk* with an oval or inverted kite-shaped shield and a conical
helmet. An unclear weapon could be an axe. With the exception of
this obscure weapon, such a figure may be much more typical of
Western Europe, perhaps indicating a late 11th century date.

673A–X *Encyclopedia of Maurus Hrabanus*, Campania, 1023
(Abbey Library, Ms. 132, Monte Cassino, Italy)

A–C – De Bellis, f.474; D–E – De Paganis, f.383; F – De Theatro,
f.489; G – Labarinthis, f.348; H–I – De Jus Gentium, f.387; J – De
Martyribus, f.66; K – De Magis, f.379; L–X – De Repositorii (On
Weapons), f.363. The *Encyclopedia of Maurus Hrabanus* is potentially a
very useful, though difficult and largely ignored, source of
information about traditional arms and armour in the pre-Norman
Mezzogiorno. Shields are round or oval and deeply convex (B, D, J
and L). Mail *hauberks* are short-sleeved and slit at the sides or front,
and are seen with and without *coifs* (A–D and J). One may have a
crudely-drawn *ventail* (B). Helmets are more of a problem. All seem
to have rings or buttons on top. Three may either be mail *coifs*, or
have been confused with Byzantine or Turco-Iranian-style hoods or
caps worn over possible helmets (B, D and J). Elsewhere a helmeted
head is probably a very degenerate echo of a Roman original
reflecting no current reality (M). Two other helmets are slightly more
straightforward. One just appears to be a conical type worn without a

coif (A) while the second seems to be of two-piece construction as seen elsewhere in early medieval Southern Europe (C). Weapons include spears with or without wings or flanges (A, B, D, E, J and K) plus a probable javelin (V). Various spears or javelin heads are illustrated as part of a survey of weapons (O, S, T and U). Swords are all of the broad early medieval Mediterranean form, normally with short straight *quillons* (C, F and R). They have curved (G and N), round (C and R) and typical early medieval European trefoil *pommels* (F, G and N). A bow and arrow appear once in a section concerned with law (H and I). The daggers are more interesting. One work-knife is shown with a narrow curved blade (X). The other three have tapering, almost triangular blades. One has a rounded tip and a tear-shaped *pommel* (P). The others (Q and W) look very much like southern Italian, or perhaps more accurately central Mediterranean, prototypes of the later *basilard*. Their long bar-like *pommels*, which give them almost H-shaped hilts, are very distinctive. If this is a correct interpretation then it pushes the history of the *basilard* back by two-and-a-half centuries.

674A–B 'Pharaoh's army', *Exultet Roll*, Campania, 11th century (Cathedral Archives, Roll 2, Gaeta, Italy)

In complete contrast to the previous manuscript, this *Exultet Roll* made in Gaeta shows warriors dressed in supposedly more typical European style. Yet the subject of Pharaoh's army drowning in the Red Sea is one in which 'alien' or 'infidel' features might have been expected. The two horsemen both wear full mail *hauberks* with long, close-fitting sleeves. This latter feature was not normal in Western Europe until well into the 12th century and either indicates that southern Italy was technologically in advance of the north or that such *hauberks* were associated with the enemy, perhaps Islamic or Byzantine. Both riders carry spears and wear round helmets of two-piece construction riveted to a central comb with a band around the rim. One also has a large round shield (A).

675A–C *Exultet Roll*, southern Italy, 11th century (Museo Civico, Pisa, Italy)

A picture dedicated to Duke and Emperor. This suggests that it was made in an area within, or closely associated with, the Empire yet also within the south Italian cultural zone where such *Exultet Rolls* were used. Part of the Duchy of Spoleto or the rump of the Duchy of Benevento, which fell under Papal control in the 11th century, fit such a scenario. The style of the crudely drawn figures is unlike most other sources and seems to reflect, however distantly, Byzantine art. The main figure (B) has a small round shield and a spear with wings below the blade. An identical spear is seen elsewhere (C). He seems to wear a hood or *coif*, perhaps the former judging from the floppy headgear of the second figure (B). The cloth or cloak across the first figure's chest (A) is also seen elsewhere in the Mezzogiorno. Both figures also wear some form of sleeveless armour on the upper parts of their bodies. This is rendered in such a stylised form that its construction can only be guessed at, though its lack of sleeves and its length, reaching only to the waist, does suggest a small lamellar *cuirass*.

676 'Centurion at the Crucifixion', *Exultet Roll* from Monte Cassino, Campania, c.1075
(British Library, Ms. Add. 30337, London, England)

The style of this *Exultet Roll* is almost entirely traditional Byzantine, as is the military equipment it illustrates. As such it largely consists of conventional archaisms, although some features of current Byzantine weaponry may be present.

677 'St Benedict frees a prisoner', manuscript from Monte Cassino, Campania, c.1070
(Vatican Library, Ms. Lat. 1202, f.72, Rome, Italy)

All the details of the rider's equipment and the horse's harness point to strong Northern influence, almost certainly resulting from Norman penetration and domination of southern Italy. The rider carries a large kite-shaped shield slung across his back on a *guige*. He has a long lance without wings or flanges and his saddle is of the tall type with raised *cantle* and *pommel*, associated with the couched style of lance play.

678A–C 'Pharaoh's army', *Exultet Roll* from Monte Cassino, Campania, c.1075
(British Library, Ms. Add. 30337, London, England)

These short-sleeved lamellar *cuirasses* are probably conventional, although they may still have been used in some areas of Byzantium. The helmets are conical, some having *nasals* and most having decorative plumes or feathers. Three background figures (A) have *coifs* or *aventails*, two of which cover the lower part of the wearer's face. One spear with a typically Western European *gonfanon* is shown (A) while both large round (A and C) and kite-shaped (A and B) shields appear. It is worth noting that the visible saddles seem to be of the Western European type, with raised *cantle* and *pommel*.

679A–C 'The Betrayal', *Breviarium Casinense* from Monte Cassino, Campania, c.1099–1105 A D
(Bib. Mazarine, Cod. 364, Paris, France)

An ordinary spear (C) and two less common weapons appear in this manuscript. One is an axe (A) that seems to have more in common with a work tool than a weapon. The other appears to be a form of scythe (B), perhaps again a work tool rather than a weapon.

680A–M 'Siege of a city', carved reliefs, Apulia, early 12th century

(*in situ* north door, Church of S. Nicola, Bari, Italy)

A–E – Defenders; F–M – Attackers. Various interpretations have been suggested for this carving which shows horsemen attacking a city, four from each side, while the defenders emerge on foot to challenge them. It could represent the Norman capture of Bari in 1071, in which case the defenders would be Byzantine, or the Norman capture of Palermo in 1072, in which case the defenders would be Muslim. It could also portray the capture of Antioch in 1098, in which case the attackers would include Italo-Normans and other Crusaders; the defenders, of course, being Turks. Finally it could portray the Crusaders' capture of Jerusalem in 1099, in which case the defenders would be Fāṭimids. It is a pity that the identity of the subject, and thus of the participants, cannot be more precise, as a number of unusual pieces of military equipment are included on the carving. The defenders are obviously shown as 'aliens' or 'infidels'. Four seem to wear small turbans (A and C–E), one over a probable mail *coif* (C). The fifth defender has a normal conical helmet which, in common with all the other helmets on the carving, lacks a *nasal*. It is also worn over a mail *coif* which may be a separate piece of armour, as a mail *hauberk* without a *coif* is worn by another defender (A). Three figures (B, D and E) wear long *cuirasses* of scale or lamellar construction with short sleeves. The likelihood of strong Byzantine influence in Apulia and the probable Islamic identity of the figures in question make lamellar more likely. Large, kite-shaped shields are used by the defenders (A–D), who are also armed with a broad, non-tapering sword (A), spears (B and D), a rock or possibly a fire-grenade (C), and a remarkably inaccurately-carved bow (F). Whatever the exact identity of these figures, local prototypes were probably used by the artists. These could be the Byzantines themselves, if the scene shows the fall of Bari, or the Muslims of Sicily if the collapse of Palermo, Antioch or Jerusalem form the subject. The attackers are divided into two distinct groups. The men dressed in short-sleeved mail *hauberks* and *coifs* attack from the left (G, H, J and M), men wearing mail (F) or presumed lamellar (K and L) or a mixture of both (I) attack from the right. The reason for this distinction is unknown. One man wearing a presumed lamellar *cuirass* does so over an apparently long-sleeved mail *hauberk* (I), the only such long-sleeved armour seen on the carving. His lamellar *cuirass* also seems to have a kind of flap to protect the side of his head. The two other *cuirasses* also include lamellar to protect the sides and back of the head (K and L). This must indicate a form of *aventail*, as a helmet could hardly be worn over a lamellar coif even if such a piece of armour existed. Two of these *cuirasses* have half-length sleeves (I and K), while the third appears to be sleeveless (L). Helmets include the simple pointed conical type (K and L) and a rounder form, perhaps fluted or segmented, with a slight forward tilt to its outline (G, H, I and M). The spears have no flanges or wings. One bears a *gonfanon* (G) while another may do so (H). Swords are broad and non-tapering and have varied *quillons*, though these are generally rather difficult to see (E, I and L). It is also worth noting that the men attacking from the left all use spears, while three of the four on the right wield swords, only one handling a lance. Those shown with shields all carry typical early 12th-century kite-shaped forms with bosses (F, G, I, K and L).

681 'Centaur', carved relief, Apulia, 1153
(*in situ* west front of Cathedral, Bari, Italy)

This little carving of a centaur seems to draw upon images of Islamic warriors and weaponry, perhaps the famous Siculo-Muslim archers. The beast has a stylised turban and wears a mail *coif*, which is probably part of a *hauberk* worn beneath his tunic. He has a recurved bow and a quiver on his belt similar to that seen on one of the Monreale capitals (fig.690Z).

682 'St George', carving, Campania, late 12th/early 13th centuries
(*in situ* Cathedral, Benevento, Italy)

Many southern Italian representations of warrior-saints draw upon Byzantine iconography. This is usually apparent in their stylised lamellar or scale *cuirasses* which are unlikely to reflect reality. Beneath the *cuirass* this saint wears a mail *hauberk* and mail *chausses*, though different conventions are used to indicate these two pieces of armour.

683A–F 'Demons', carved relief, Apulia, mid/late 12th century
(*in situ* exterior of Cathedral, Barletta, Italy)

In the series of carvings bordering the windows, maces (A, C and D) and small round shields (A, B and D) are given to demons rather than 'infidels'. Other weapons include ordinary spears (B) and two very unusual forms of axe (E and F).

684 'Merman', relief carving, Apulia, c.1175–1200
(*in situ* nave of Cathedral, Bitonto, Italy)

This relief carving inside Bitonto Cathedral again draws upon Islamic arms; namely a highly-decorated round shield and a fluted or winged mace. This combination of weapons seems to have been widely associated with Muslims and other 'infidels' in southern Italian art.

685A–B Painted ivory box, Sicily, 12th century
(Bargello Museum, Florence, Italy)

Later ivory boxes from Sicily or southern Italy, which are generally regarded as examples of Islamic art made under Christian domination, are generally painted rather than carved. This example shows considerable influence from Middle Eastern Islamic art, particularly where the horse trappings and harness are concerned. The only weapons shown are simple spears.

686A–C Painted ivory box, Sicily, 12th century
(Cappella Palatina Treasury, Palermo, Italy)

This second painted box shows warriors or huntsmen, one of whom (A) has a long, straight sword, the almost semicircular *quillons* or guard of which recalls earlier Ma<u>gh</u>ribi as well as 13th and 14th century Andalusian weapons. A broad-bladed spear (B) and a recurved bow with, perhaps, angled ears (C) can also be seen.

687A–C Relief carvings, Apulia, early 12th century
(*in situ* west front, Church of S. Nicola, Bari, Italy)

A–B – Christian slays infidel; C – Pharaoh's army (?). Less well-known and almost certainly later than the carvings over the north door of S. Nicola di Bari are the warriors shown on the facade. In one scene a Christian warrior with a round cap or fluted helmet, long kite-shaped shield on a *guige* and a broad non-tapering sword, slays two naked 'infidels', only one of whom is shown here. They carry round shields. Elsewhere on the facade is a possible representation of Pharaoh's army in the Red Sea. Here a bareheaded or possibly turbaned warrior (C) wears a short sleeveless scale or lamellar *cuirass* over a long-sleeved mail *hauberk* which is not, however, visible below the hem of the *cuirass*. He wields a straight, non-tapering sword.

688 'Geste de Floovant', carved relief, Molise, c.1148
(*in situ* facade of church, S. Maria della Strada, Italy)

Relatively few 12th-century sources are known from the isolated and mountainous Molise region. This carving illustrates the story of Floovant, a popular 12th century romance. The knight has a tall, fluted helmet with a distinct extension to protect the back of his neck. He holds a very large kite-shaped shield of the newer flat-topped variety, and he uses his lance in the couched manner.

689A–B 'Huntsman', carved relief, Sicily c.1140
(*in situ* over north door, Church of La Martorana, Palermo, Sicily)

This is one of the earliest carved representations of arms and armour in Norman Sicily . It shows an archer in a long-sleeved mail *hauberk* without a *coif* (A). He has a pointed one-piece helmet without a *nasal* and he uses an early form of composite bow with distinctly angled ears. The three-pointed object apparently on his belt is unexplained but might indicate that the belt was knotted. A second figure (B) is naked save for a kilt and he uses a heavy spear, the blade of which recalls those of certain Islamic weapons.

690A–AU **Carved capitals, Sicily, late 12th century**
(*in situ* cloisters of Cathedral, Monreale, Italy)

The costumes, arms and armour portrayed on the Monreale cloister capitals are remarkably varied, ranging from virtually naked infantry to fully-armoured horsemen. The subjects appear to be drawn from various traditions, including Western European, Byzantine and Mediterranean Islamic, which in turn probably reflected the very mixed armies of Norman Sicily and southern Italy. Helmets and headgear include the kind of pointed *coif*, hood or cap seen in other south Italian sources (H and I), a possible cap or helmet (Q) that might have parallels in Spain, a probable loose turban (R and AR–AT) and a turban wound around a helmet (AD). A rounded helmet with a crest and possible neck extension (Y) could reflect a ceremonial Byzantine type or simply echo a barely understood Roman original. Other helmets are more straightforward. These include a conical form with a forward-angled crown and a face-mask (X), a similar style without a face-mask (AF), a simple conical helmet with a decorative rim (AB), a slightly conical form with an apparent comb or crest up the front (AI), and round helmets of apparent two-piece (AE) or fluted (AD) construction. Several helmets have single or doubled chin-straps (X, Y, AF and AI). Mail *coifs* are only seen as part of *hauberks* (AF and AI), these *hauberks* themselves being short-sleeved and thigh-length (AD, AF and AK). A lamellar or scale *hauberk* of probable Byzantine or Islamic inspiration is worn by one of two sleeping Guards at the Holy Sepulchre (AE). Sleeveless and much shorter scale or lamellar *cuirasses* of similarly Byzantine or Islamic origin are quite common, though almost invariably worn by 'infidel' or 'wicked' figures (R and AR–AU). The only possible exception to this is a horse-archer (AJ) who might represent a warrior-saint. Shields are shown in considerable detail and variety, including small round types (G, T, V, AL and AN), most of which are held by men whose other attributes suggest North African or Islamic origins. A larger round shield is also held by a Guard at the Holy Sepulchre (AD). Other shields are kite-shaped, some round-topped and plain (J, AF and AH), some round-topped but with bosses or strengthening straps across the front (H, I, X, AC, AI, AK and AM), others kite-shaped but virtually flat-topped (Q, AB and AG). A final and most interesting shield (Y) almost has a vertical 'keel' and an indented top, recalling the later leather *adargas* of Iberia which were themselves of North African origin. Another and even closer parallel is to be found in a carved capital from Crusader Nazareth. Weapons are varied, including a short, very broad-bladed spear (B) as well as more ordinary spears (D, K, Z, AM and AP). Bows are mostly in the traditional pre-Turkish Mediterranean form with angled ears (A, O and AJ) although a simple, regularly curved bow is also shown (AA). A simple quiver is fastened to one man's belt (Z).

Axes with curved blades (P and S), a complicated mace (C) and simple club-like weapons (F, V, W and AQ) are all seen. Another mace may also be carried on his right arm by the horse-archer (AJ). Swords are the most varied of all, most being of a non-tapering or very slightly tapering form (E, H–J, Q, R, U, AC, AE, AG, AR, AT and AU). Some of these have rounded tips, others have points. Weapons with almost triangular blades (X, Y and AB) are unlike any other 12th-century European swords but may be the originals from which the later Italian triangular-bladed *cinquedea* developed. The swords have round (H, I, U, Y, AK and AT), oval (AE), or tear-drop-shaped (X, AB, AR and AU) *pommels*. Others appear to have straight, curved or angled and apparently flared hilts without *pommels* (E and L). This would indicate similarities with some Middle Eastern, Central Asian or perhaps Byzantine weapons. *Quillons* are straight (J, L, R, X, AB and AE), curved (U, Y and AG), peculiarly reverse-curved (E, H and I), apparently flared (AR and AU) or down-turned (AC and AT). Among the strangest weapons is a curved sabre with a plain hilt lacking *quillons* or *pommel* (G). This is almost certainly an artist's attempt to show an 'infidel' sword based upon North African types. Straight blades without *quillons* (AL and AO) similarly reflect North African styles, which might also have been used by the Muslims of Sicily. A large curved dagger hangs at one man's belt (AL) while another warrior holds a single-edged dagger in his hand (M).

691A–M **Ivory altar-back, Campania, c.1100–50**
(Cathedral Museum, Salerno, Italy)

A–E – Massacre of the Innocents; F–G – Soldiers at the Crucifixion; H–I – Sleeping Guards at the Holy Sepulchre; J – Sacrifice of Isaac; K–M – Herod's soldiers. Though highly stylised and based to some extent on both Byzantine and western Islamic art, most features of the arms and armour in the Salerno ivory altar can be readily identified. The most problematic elements are the headgear worn by soldiers at the Massacre of the Innocents (A–E). These are clearly related to other obscure forms of hood, *coif* or helmet in southern Italian art. The body armour, though looking like scales, is probably taken from a much smaller, perhaps Byzantine, manuscript illustration which in turn is likely to have portrayed a mail *hauberk*. This must, however, remain conjectural. While the spears of these men (A and C) are straightforward, their swords or daggers (D and E) also seem to be based on a lost and probably largely misunderstood original. Another dagger (H) is more intelligible and realistic. Herod's soldiers (K–M), with their close-fitting pointed helmets and mail *coifs* or *aventails* across the lower parts of their faces, are clearly related to previously discussed ivory chessmen. Unarmoured figures have decorative *ṭirāz* bands of obvious Islamic inspiration around their upper arms (F–I). They carry short spears and an ordinary

European-style sword with a trefoil *pommel* and curved *quillons* (G), hung on a *baldric*. They also have large round shields with pronounced bosses (H–I).

692 Carved wooden column, Calabria or Sicily, c.1150–1200
(Victoria and Albert Museum, inv. 269L1886, London, England)

A roughly carved and rather damaged piece of wood clearly showing a man carrying a straight sword with down-turned *quillons* and a round *pommel*. He wears a fur-lined cloak and the garment beneath may be a very crude representation of mail.

693 Relief carving on wooden episcopal throne, Campania, late 12th/early 13th centuries
(Abbey Museum, Montevirgine, Italy)

It has been suggested that some of the motifs carved on the Abbot's Throne at Montevirgine were copied from a Persian manuscript. This is unlikely to be true of this horseman, with his broad sword, high saddle and large spurs. On the other hand his peculiar helmet, which seems to have features in common with an early *bascinet*, does recall certain 12th and 13th century Islamic sources.

694A–E Bronze door panels, Apulia, late 12th century
(*in situ* Cathedral, Trani, Italy)

The famous bronze doors of Trani Cathedral illustrate contemporary infantry plus one horseman, St Eustace, who may also reflect current fashions. The saint (A) is apparently unarmoured as he is out hunting, but he carries a sword, as would be expected of one of Emperor Trajan's supposed generals. This weapon has acutely down-turned *quillons* and appears to hang on slender straps, presumably leading to a sword belt. As such it could reflect Byzantine rather than Western European styles. The other figures are two infantry archers (B and C). One wears a possible fluted conical helmet with a turban wound around it and both draw early forms of composite bow with angled ears and an angled grip. The second archer (C) has the same loose leggings as St Eustace, plus what might be a mace hanging from his right hip . Two other figures (D and E) have simple club-like maces and hold small round bucklers.

695A–J The Rome Casket, carved ivory box, Sicily or southern Italy, late 12th century
(Palazzo di Venezia Museum, Rome, Italy)

A–C – Philistines; D – Goliath; E – Martyrdom of a saint; F–I – Israelites; J – Goliath. The arms and armour on the Rome Casket consist almost totally of conventional archaised weaponry based on Byzantine prototypes; probably from a manuscript. Some features are, however, worthy of comment. One is an interior view (J) of a helmet which is presumably intended to be the same or similar to others seen from the outside. These latter are virtually identical to many helmets seen in Byzantine art. If this source is to be trusted at all, then it indicates that such helmets consisted of a normal iron bowl, probably conical, plus a scale or lamellar *aventail*, the whole then being covered in a layer of fabric or other such decorative material. Some Middle Eastern written sources could also be interpreted in the same way. Two presumed swords lack guards or *quillons* (E and J) and as such may be related to other weapons of perhaps Maghribi origin. All the figures except one have stylised lamellar *cuirasses*, indicated by horizontal lines across the body. Here it is worth noting the construction of some recently discovered late 12th/early 13th century hardened leather armours from the Middle East. They also consisted of horizontal bands around the body, though the bands were made of continuous strips of hardened leather rather than laced lamellae. One exception (A) appears to have a semi-circular breast-plate or *plackart* across his abdomen. The origin of this is unknown and seems to have no parallels elsewhere.

696A–O Mosaics, Sicily, c.1180–90
(*in situ* Cathedral, Monreale, Italy)

A–D – The Betrayal; E – Martyrdom of Sts Castus and Cassius; F–I – The Betrayal; J – Esau; K – Esau; L – Pilate's Guard; M–N – Crucifixion; O – Martyrdom of St Peter. The mosaics in Monreale Cathedral, though made for the Norman rulers of Sicily, are regarded as both typical and particularly fine examples of 12th century Byzantine art. The arms, armour and costume that they portray are similarly Byzantine and suffer from the usual conventional archaisms associated with that school of art. The most obvious example of this is found on the figure of one of Pilate's guards (L). The subject is a Roman soldier, who is given the usual lamellar *cuirass* with splinted skirt and upper arm defences. His helmet is, however, interesting, because it shows a simple round type with a plume or crest on top. The spear is straightforward, as are other examples in this mosaic. The sword, with its straight, barely tapering and blunt-tipped blade, round *pommel* and slightly curved *quillons*, is also similar to others in the mosaic (E and O). Both these other swords are shown in slightly greater detail and have down-turned tips to their *quillons*. The two pictures of Esau the hunter show him with a recurved bow, once unstrung (J) and once drawn (K). Other weapons include a mace with an almost spherical head (F), two substantial half-moon bladed axes (A and M) and three unusual hafted weapons. Two might be so-called war-scythes, both of which have hooked blades, one with a thrusting point (I) and one without (N). A third weapon has a blunt point and presumably only one cutting edge (C).

697 'Guard during St Paul's escape from Damascus', mosaic, Sicily, mid-12th century
(*in situ* Cappella Palatina, Palermo, Italy)

The archaisms which can be seen in the Monreale mosaics become completely dominant in those at Cappella Palatina. It is also possible that the archaised figures on the carved ivory Rome Casket (fig.695) were based on sources such as these.

698 *Exultet Roll* from Troia, Apulia, 12th century
(Cathedral Archives, Roll 3, Troia, Italy)

Made in a city originally founded by the Byzantines as a frontier fortress to defend Apulia, the manuscript includes a simple but naturalistic representation of a fully-armoured warrior. He has a long-sleeved, very long-hemmed mail *hauberk*, and the mail *coif* may be separate.

699A–F *Exultet Roll* from Benevento, Campania, 12th century
(Biblioteca Casanatense, Ms. 724, Bl.13, Rome, Italy)

A–B – The King and his people; C–D – The Emperor's Guard; E – Crucifixion; F – The Emperor's Guard. The two armed figures (A and B) represent a *Protospathius*, a title of Byzantine origin. One man wears a tall helmet (D) with an extended neckguard that looks like an early *salet* or *bascinet*. Once again a Southern European or even eastern Mediterranean origin might be indicated for these later forms of helmet. Both guardsmen have ordinary kite-shaped shields but hold swords with broad triangular blades, curved *quillons* and large round *pommels*. As has already been suggested, such weapons may be the ancestors of the later medieval *cinquedea*. The soldier at the Crucifixion (E) has a broad-bladed spear with multiple flanges or one set of wings and two securing rivets. His sword seems to taper to a point, judging from the shape of its scabbard, but its *pommel* looks like a fanciful development of the earlier trefoil type.

700A–G *Exultet Roll* from Fondi, Campania, early 12th century
(Bib. Nat., Ms. Nouv. Acq. 710, Paris, France)

A – Betrayal; B–F – Pharaoh's army; G – Crucifixion. This Roll comprises a mixture of archaism, stylised convention and current reality. The soldier at the Betrayal (A) wears a simplified lamellar *cuirass* of Byzantine inspiration which is unlikely to have been widely used in 12th century southern Italy, unless a few such armours survived from earlier Byzantine times. His headgear might represent a cap or a simple conical helmet with a rim-piece. The 'infidel' character of Pharaoh's army as it tries to cross the Red Sea is indicated solely by very stylised turbans (C and D). The rest of its equipment – consisting of long-sleeved mail *hauberks* with *coifs* covering the lower part of the face (C and D), probably large kite-shaped shields (C), spears (B), couched lances (C) and heraldic *gonfanons* (E and F) – would be among the standard equipment of Italo-Norman cavalry. A pointed helmet with a decorative finial (G) seems to recall certain 11th century sources and may reflect an earlier, or Byzantine, type of helmet.

701 *Petri Lombardi Sententiae*, south Italian, 12th century (Biblioteca Guarneriana, Ms. 42, S. Daniele del Friuli, Italy)

The bow shown in this simple south Italian manuscript represents a composite form with an angled grip but without angled ears. Whether such a type was actually used in Italy remains unclear.

702A–AA Painted wooden ceiling panels, Sicily, c.1140 (*in situ* Cappella Palatina, Palermo, Italy)

The Cappella Palatina ceiling is painted in Islamic early Fāṭimid style, though dating from the mid-12th century and executed for the Christian ruler King Roger II. Most of the military figures portrayed on the panels are dressed and equipped in western Islamic style, perhaps that of Sicilian Muslims who fought for the Norman kings. Only one figure clearly represents a Christian warrior (T). He may be one of the new Norman aristocracy of Sicily. Other figures are obviously Muslim or specifically Arab (E, C, F, M, P, Q, W and Z) and most wear turbans. Some of these are worn over pointed helmets or tall caps (C, P and Z). Elsewhere, pointed headgear might be helmets or hats (B, K, S, Y and AA) but are probably the former. Only one helmet clearly has a broad *nasal* (O) although others may do so (S and Y). Round helmets are present, but are less common (J, T and X). Body armour, in common with the military fashions of most Islamic areas outside Iran and al-Andalus, is rarely seen but was presumably worn by some warriors beneath other clothes. Those that are visible are worn by horsemen and consist of mid-length or long-sleeved mail *hauberks* with or without *coifs* (T, X and Y). Shields are as varied as one would expect in such a culturally mixed area as Norman Sicily. With one exception they are all carried by horsemen. An example of a flat-based kite-shaped *januwîyah* (B) should still be regarded as an infantry shield although it has incongruously been given to a horseman or mounted infantryman. Other shields include small round bucklers (E, S, U and V) and normal 12th-century kite-shaped shields (A, K, L, O, T, X-Z and AA). The bases of some of these shields are obscured by later restoration and may well have been flat, this making them *januwîyahs* (Z and AA). Two figures also use cloaks over their arms as rudimentary shields (H and I). Some weapons are easy to identify. For example, a spear carried by a camel-riding Arab is clearly related to those used by Arab Bedouin in an early 13th century *Maqāmāt* manuscript. Some of the others have the fanciful or at least more complicated blades which are similarly seen in the Middle East (A, J and X). There might be a problem of interpretation with some objects having half-moon apparent blades attached to them (C and D). These could be the *nāchakh* axes of a ruler's élite guard or could simply be light fans to cool the ruler's brow. One other long-hafted axe (F) has an unmistakably upwards-sweeping blade and as such is a typically north European weapon descended from the 11th century 'Danish axe'. Its appearance in Palermo is interesting and might suggest the presence of Anglo-Norman infantry. Only one mace is shown, with a broken haft and in the hands of a fleeing warrior, the same man who carries a *januwîyah*. Perhaps he represents a defeated infantryman who has seized a horse. Swords are by far the most common weapon on the Cappella Palatina ceiling. Most are straight, barely tapering, with blunt or only slightly pointed tips. Most have thick but short bar-like *quillons*. Other variations have broad-curved *quillons* with a *langet* (M) and what could be the non-symmetrical *quillons* of a slightly curved weapon (Y). *Pommels* are generally obscured, although that of a clearly visible, narrower-bladed weapon (H) seems to be round. Others might also be (F, R and W), while another might be nut-shaped (P). Some blades have central ridges clearly indicated (I and S). One of these (E) lacks *quillons* or guard. As such it is another example of a type of sword associated with North Africa. A much shorter and perhaps more tapering weapon (V) that is, however, held like a sword rather than a dagger, is placed in the hands of an infantryman. A final interesting figure holds a long-hafted object in a kind of waist sling that hangs almost to his ankles (N). This might be a means of supporting a large banner or perhaps the ruler's ceremonial parasol although a short, pointed, mace-headed or sword-like object seems at present to be held in the sling.

703A–AV *Liber ad honorem Augusti of Peter of Eboli*, Sicily or southern Italy, c.1200–20
(Burgerbibliothek, Ms. Cod. 120/II, Bern, Switzerland)

A–F – Sicilian troops, f.131; G–I – Constantine besieged in Salerno, f.117a; J – Richard of Acerra captures Capua, f.124a; K – Defender of Salerno, f.111a; L–M – Siege of Naples, f.109a; N – Frederick's soldiers cut down a forest, f.143a; O–P – Richard of Acerra captures Capua, f.124a; Q–R – Villagers fighting Diopuldo, f.130a; S – Guard of Henry VI, f.137a; T–V – Imperial Bohemian troops besiege Naples, f.15a; W – *Mangonel* in Castrum Maris, f.98a; X – Corrado at Capua, f.122a; Y – f.118a; Z – Frederick Barbarossa on Crusade, f.107a; AA–AC – Constance flees from Salerno, f.119a; AD – Traveller, f.101a; AE–AJ – Siege scene, f.132a; AK–AM – Siege of Salerno, f.116a; AN – Henry VI's entry into Palermo, f.134a; AO – The people acclaim Tancred, f.99a; AP–AQ – Siege scene, f.132a; AR – Slaughter of Muslim child, f.127a; AS–AU – Triumph of

Tancred, f.102a; AV – Surrender scene, f.131. The *Chronicle of Peter of Eboli* probably dates from the early 13th century rather than from the very late 12th century as is sometimes believed. It illustrates a considerable variety of military equipment. Most of the obvious Christian European warriors wear full mail *hauberks* with long sleeves and almost certainly integral *coifs*. Most do not include *mittens*, though some apparently do (S and N). Mail *coifs* cover the chin and mouth (N, X and Z). Where visible, all the mailed figures also have mail *chausses*. Helmets are more varied, although all save one have substantial *nasals*. The exception is likely to be an artist's error (J). The most common form of helmet is conical. Some have a peculiarly backwards-tilted crown (E, P, AM and AN). Another form is basically round but with a button or finial on top (D, H, AK and AL), which is presumably in the same tradition as other Italian helmets with such buttons. These helmets are also associated with the Italo-Normans rather than with the invading Imperial troops and may therefore represent a real south Italian tradition rooted in the Byzantine past. A third form of helmet is also round but is much taller and bulbous (T and Z). Worn by Imperial troops of specifically German or Bohemian origin, it is clearly the same as the tall round helmets seen in some German sources. Shields are all of the round-topped kite-shaped type. Two are shown from the side, which makes them appear more flat-topped (S and AN). The only real exception may be a small round buckler hung from a traveller's waist (AD). This man is also armed with a simple club having a thong or strap at the end. A spiked or knobbed mace may be shown elsewhere (Y) but this is far from clear. Other rarely illustrated weapons are two axes (AB and AC) plus a third possible axe (AA), all of which are carried aboard the ship in which Constance flees Salerno. A further axe (R) is more likely to represent a work tool placed in the hands of a peasant as he defends his fields. A second peasant wields a knife (Q), the size of which has probably been exaggerated for artistic reasons. A similar simple knife is also seen elsewhere (AR). Simple slings (I and AP), as well as staff-slings (K) and man-powered *mangonels* (T–W), are used in siege warfare. Bows range from large weapons which might almost rate as longbows (B and C) to recurved bows of composite construction. Some have angled ears and/or grips (A, G and AS) while others do not (U). Crossbows lack loading stirrups and are used by both ordinary infantry and by men wearing turbans or tall pointed hats. These are presumably to be identified as Sicilian Muslims (D–F, L and AT). The quivers of archers and crossbowmen are identical (A–C, G, M, AS and AT). Long cavalry lances include some very large flags or *gonfanons* (O and P), while shorter infantry spears include examples with (H) and without (AU) wings or flanges. Swords are invariably straight, and mostly broad and blunt-tipped, though a more pointed form is also seen (AH). They have large round *pommels* and straight, generally flared *quillons*, and are slung from belts rather than *baldrics*.

704A–D *Book of Stars*, Sicily, c.1220–50
(Bibl. de l'Arsenal, Ms. 1036, Paris, France)

A – Orion, f.36; B – Sagittarius, f.29v; C – Perseus, f.10; D – Ursa Minor, f.1r. This is another Latin translation, and probably an even more direct copy, of the Arabic *Book of Fixed Stars* by al-Sūfī. The hunter's spear (D) has a kind of grip or plug near the end of its haft, similar to that seen somewhat earlier in Navarre. Such a feature could suggest that this manuscript was made after the Aragónese conquest of Sicily in 1282, though all other features point to an earlier date. One sword with its flared *quillons* and blunt-tipped blade is related to weapons in the *Chronicle of Peter of Eboli*, whereas the other, with its very down-turned *quillons* (A), is probably much closer to a western Islamic original. The bow (B) is so stylised that one may assume that it was simply copied from a previous manuscript and does not reflect bows in current use.

705A–AJ *Skylitzes Chronicle*, Sicily, 12th/early 13th centuries
(Biblioteca Nacional, Cod. 5-3, N2, Madrid, Spain)

A–B – Arabs, f.116v; C – Byzantines besiege Mopsuestia (Mamistra), f.151v; D–E – Siege of Amorium by al Ma'mun, f.59v; F–H – Fleeing Saracens, f.54v; I–J – Arabs defeat Michael III outside Samsat, f.72v; K – Andalusian Muslim ruler of Crete, f.39r; L – Arab ruler defeated by Bardas Phocas, f.136v; M – Arabs in naval battle near Crete, f.41r; N–O – Andalusian Muslims in Crete, f.39v; P – Arabs attack Urfa, f.208; Q–S – Muslims defeated by Petronas in Armenia, f.73v; T – Byzantine warship, f.34v; U–X – Saljūk troops, f.234; Y – Al-Ma'mun retreats from Amorium, f.60v; Z–AA – Defenders of Benevento, f.97; AB–AD – Arabs attack Benevento, f.97; AE – Battle outside Dorustolon, f.169r; AF – Arabs sack Thessaloniki, f.111v; AG–AI – Arabs defeat Procopius, f.99v; AJ – Byzantines besiege Preslav, f.166r. Considerable debate centres on the date and origin of this splendid manuscript. My personal opinion is that it was probably made by Greek artists in Sicily during the late 12th or early 13th centuries, and was probably copied from a lost Byzantine original of the *Skylitzes Chronicle*, with a few additions and alterations. Various different hands can be identified. The Madrid *Skylitzes* is, however, remarkable for the accuracy with which one or more of its artists portrayed Islamic troops, particularly Arabs. This suggests personal familiarity with the subject, which would not be surprising if the manuscript were made in Sicily at that time. The most realistic figures wear loose head-cloths and are equipped with round shields, straight non-tapering or slightly-tapering swords, and spears or javelins (A–B, L, P, Y, AB–AD and AF–AI). Two of these men seem to wear lamellar *cuirasses* (L and P), one of which is clearly sleeveless. One of their shields (L) has tassels from its rivets, reminiscent of certain 13th century Andalusian styles. Another artist dresses the Muslims either in archaised or stylised Byzantine armour of mail or lamellar, but identifies them with stylised turbans (E, G–K, N, O and Q–S). This latter artist or group of artists gives his subjects a wider range of swords, from straight types which, judging by their scabbards, are non-tapering (K and Q–S), to very curved sabres (M) and curved or single-edged weapons without *quillons* (N and O). These last two swords are wielded by Hispano-Arabs; men specifically identified as coming from the western part of the Islamic world. Weapons lacking *quillons* have already been tentatively identified with North Africa and Sicily. Saljūk and other possibly Turkish troops (D and U–X) are identified firstly by their long hair, secondly by a bow (D) which is otherwise a weapon that appears rarely in this manuscript, and finally by a form of hat or helmet which consists of a small dome set on a larger one (D and V). Helmets with such an outline were certainly used by early medieval Turks in the Eurasian steppe regions and may still have been correctly associated with Turkic peoples. Such helmets are, of course, given to 'alien' warriors in other Italian sources. Byzantine troops (C) are given long lamellar *cuirasses* and pointed helmets, one of which appears to be a form of early *bascinet* with a possible mail *aventail* (C). Specifically Western troops (Z and AA) have similar pointed or rounded helmets and kite-shaped shields. Other features of interest are two distinct forms of man-powered *mangonel*, one small (AE and AJ) and the other larger (C). The Madrid *Skylitzes* may also include one of the very few representations of a 'Greek Fire' siphon from this period (T). This simple and slightly damaged picture seems to indicate a small projection, almost like a fore-sight, on top of the siphon tube. Perhaps this was intended to show a means by which the inflammable liquid was ignited as it shot from the mouth of the siphon. A single apparent horse *chanfron* is also illustrated (F). No other horse-armour is present and this isolated piece is given to the mount of a leading Muslim warrior, perhaps the defeated leader 'Abuzachar' himself. A comparable *chanfron* is worn by the horse of an Egyptian religious figure in a manuscript from the Fāṭimid period, but both these pieces of equipment may well have been ceremonial rather than really protective.

706 Carved and painted ivory box, Sicily, late 12th/early 13th centuries
(Staatliche Museum Dahlem, Berlin, Germany)

Clearly the workmanship of the Muslim ivory workers of Sicily had declined by the end of Norman rule, but the subjects they illustrated remained the same. Here a lion-hunter carries a long spear and a deeply convex shield while wearing a short-sleeved mail *hauberk* which probably continued inside his kilt.

707 'St Demetrius', wall-painting, Basilicata, early 14th century
(*in situ* Grotto of S. Biagio, San Vito dei Normanni, Italy)

A number of painted grotto churches almost completely Byzantine in style survive in certain parts of southern Italy. Most of the representations of arms and armour which they contain are completely stylised and archaised. This example, however, shows a horseman with a typical 14th-century Byzantine triangular shield hung on his shoulder by a *guige*.

708A–B 'Murder of Becket', wall-painting, Spoleto, late 12th century
(*in situ* Church of SS. Giovanni e Paolo, Spoleto, Italy)

Although this painting was made just north of the Norman kingdom of southern Italy and Sicily it may be taken as showing some typical aspects of Southern military equipment. Both warriors wear mail *hauberks* with long sleeves. *Mittens* are worn only on the sword hand. Three conventions are probably used to show mail, a different cross-hatched technique appearing on the mail *chausses* (B). The only real doubt cast on this interpretation stems from the fact that the artist uses two separate conventions to distinguish the feet and legs of the presumed mail *chausses*. The first figure has a mail *coif* beneath a pointed helmet with a fixed face-mask (A). The helmet itself is of a common form with a forward-angled crown. The second figure is more damaged around the head but appears to wear a simple domed helmet over a separate *coif*. This latter is depicted plain gold in the wall-painting, which might indicate that the *coif* had been given a decorative cloth covering. Such a fashion would become popular in Italy and some other parts of Europe 200 years later. Both swords have tapering but clearly blunt-tipped blades, one clearly straight pair of *quillons*, and round or oval *pommels*

709A–C *Tales of King Arthur* from Naples, Campania, c.1300–25
(Bib. Munic., Ms. 951, Tours, France)

A – f.154v; B – f.250r; C – f.361r. In the late 13th and early 14th centuries southern Italian arms and armour were under considerable French influence, largely because the French Angevin dynasty now ruled the country. Here two flat-topped *great helms* are shown, one with a crest (A), the other with a flowing *lambrequin* (C). A third helmet is a one-piece *chapel-de-fer* with a rather angular outline, worn over a mail *coif* (B).

710 Unnamed effigy, Campania, c.1325
(*in situ* Cathedral, Salerno, Italy)

This effigy is almost certainly earlier than that of Niccolà Merlotto (fig.711). Here similar sheets of *cuir-bouilli* form both *rerebraces* for the arms and *greaves* for the legs. *Roundels* are laced to the elbows and a mail *hauberk* is worn. The impression that a broad, elbow-length sleeve is worn over another tighter sleeve is probably the result of an inferior style of carving. A padded *surcoat* with somewhat raised shoulders is worn over the *hauberk*, and simple mail *chausses* are worn beneath the hardened-leather *greaves*. A very long but otherwise straightforward sword with straight *quillons* and a round *pommel* hangs at his left side.

711 Effigy of Niccolà Merlotto, Campania, c.1358
(*in situ* Church of S. Chiara, Naples, Italy)

Despite strong French influence, the armour of the 14th century Mezzogiorno developed a strongly individual character that was soon to influence other parts of Italy, such as Tuscany. What made this style of armour so distinctive was a widespread use of decorated pieces of *cuir-bouilli* (hardened leather). Quite how and where the style originated is unclear but, given the Angevins' close involvement in Greek, southern Balkan and Byzantine affairs, some kind of Eastern influence seems likely. This seems even more probable given the recorded reliance of 14th-century Turkish Anatolian warriors and perhaps other Turks on armour of hardened leather. Such Turkish troops were often recruited as mercenaries and allies by the enfeebled Byzantine Empire, which frequently sent them against the Angevins in Greece. Nor was this contact invariably hostile in the confused political situation which prevailed in the 14th century Balkans. The effigy of Niccolà Merlotto provides a rather late example of such leather armour. Here it only forms *rerebraces* on his upper arms. The rest of his armour consists of a long-sleeved mail *hauberk* with *roundels* laced at the elbows, probably worn beneath a *coat-of-plates* with large pendant *epaulettes* to protect the shoulders. He has mail *chausses* under smooth *greaves* and *poleyns* which may be of iron. On his right hip hangs a *basilard* dagger.

712 Unidentified effigy, Campania, c.1300–50
(*in situ* Church of S. Lorenzo Maggiore, Naples, Italy)

This is an early example of the peculiarly south Italian style of armour that included pieces of highly decorated *cuir-bouilli*. The man's basic armour consists of a long-sleeved mail *hauberk* with *mittens*, which are here thrown back at the wrists. Beneath these, splinted or fluted *vambraces* can be seen. The upper part of his *surcoat* probably covers, or forms the outer layer of, a *coat-of-plates* or a *cuirie*, to which the zoomorphic *epaulettes* are presumably attached. *Cuir-bouilli rerebraces* and *roundels* of unknown material are laced to the upper arms and elbows respectively. *Greaves*, probably of metal, are worn over his mail *chausses*. His weapons consist of a 'ballock dagger' hung from his belt, and a relatively short sword with straight *quillons*.

713 Effigy of Perotto Cabano, Campania, c.1300–50
(*in situ* Church of S. Chiara, Naples, Italy)

Probably slightly earlier than the preceding example, the warrior shown here differs in wearing a full mail *coif* and larger *cuir-bouilli rerebraces* but no *epaulettes*. He has the same splinted *vambraces* but apparently no mail *mittens* on his *hauberk*. His *greaves* also look simpler and earlier, perhaps being of undecorated hardened leather. Like the previous effigy, he is armed with a 'ballock dagger' which hangs from his first belt, not from his sword-belt, by long laces or thongs.

714A–B Effigies of members of the Barrile family, Campania, c.1300–50
(*in situ* Church of S. Lorenzo Maggiore, Naples, Italy)

These two relatively early effigies are virtually identical except for their leg protections. They wear long-sleeved mail *hauberks* without *mittens*. The tightly-pleated skirts of their *surcoats* are remarkably reminiscent of later Epirote ('Evzone') folk costume. At their shoulders are flower-shaped *roundels* or *epaulettes*. Their arms are also protected by decorated *cuir-bouilli rerebraces* and simple *roundels* on their elbows. Both men wear mail *chausses* but one (B) also has barely visible *poleyns* and perhaps *cuisses*, plus decorated *cuir-bouilli greaves*. The two men are identically-armed with *basilard* daggers attached to their sword-belts, and long straight swords, one of which has straight *quillons* (B), the other slightly curved *quillons* (A).

Notes

1. G.A. Loud, 'The Church, Warfare and Military Obligation in Norman Italy', *Studies in Church History* vol.XX (1983), pp.32–3; L.S.G. Matheson, *The Norman Principality of Capua (1058–1095) with Particular Reference to Richard I (1058–1078)* (Ph.D. thesis, Oxford University, 1974), p.6.
2. J. Beeler, *Warfare in Feudal Europe, 730–1200* (Ithaca, 1971), p.66.
3. E. Curtis, *Roger of Sicily* (London, 1912), pp.356 and 358.
4. C. Cahen, *La Régime Féodale de l'Italie Normande* (Paris, 1940), p.74.
5. F.E. Engreen, 'Pope John the Eighth and the Arabs', *Speculum* vol.XX (1945), p.320; J. Gay, *L'Italie Méridionale et l'Empire Byzantin* (Paris, 1904), p.137.
6. C. Cahen, 'Un texte peu connu relatif au Commerce oriental d'Amalfi au Xe Siècle', *Archivio Storico per la province Napoletane* n.s. vol.XXXIV (1955), pp.64–5.
7. A. Guillou, 'L'ltalia bizantina, douleia e oikeîsis', *Bolletino dell'Istituto Storico Italiano per il Medio Evo* vol.LXXVIII (1967), pp.11–12; Matheson, *op.cit.* p.21; A. Guillou, 'Italie méridionale byzantine ou Byzantins en Italie méridionale?' *Byzantion* vol.XLIV (1974), p.175.
8. G.A. Loud, 'How "Norman" was the Norman Conquest of Southern Italy?' *Nottingham Medieval Studies* vol.XXV (1981), p.20.
9. E. Jamison, 'The Norman Administration of Apulia and Capua', *Papers of the British School at Rome* vol.VI (1913), pp.266 and 268.

10. Beeler, *op.cit.* pp.72–4.
11. M. Amari, *Storia dei Musulmani di Sicilia* (Catania, 1933), vol.III, no.2, p.547; L.-R. Menager, *Amiratus-L'Emirat et les Origines de l'Amirauté (XIe-XIIIe siècles)* (Paris, 1960), p.88; C. Fitz-Clarence, 'Mémoire sur l'emploi des mercenaries mahométans dans les armées chretiens', *Journal Asiatique* vol.XI (1827), pp.46–7; A. Guillou, 'Inchiesta sulla popolazione greca della Sicilia e della Calabria nel Medio Evo', *Rivista Storica Italiana* vol.LXXVI (1963), pp.63–4; Beeler, *op.cit.* pp.74–5; F. Gabrieli, 'La Politique Arabe des Normands de Sicile', *Studia Islamica* vol.IX (1958), pp.87 and 92–3.
12. Beeler, *op.cit.* pp.74–7; G. Buckler, *Anna Comnena: A Study* (London, 1929), p.376; Curtis, *op.cit.* pp.371–2; Cahen, *La Régime Féodale, op.cit.* pp.62–5; D.P. Waley, 'Combined operations in Sicily, AD 1060–78', *Papers of the British School at Rome* vol.XXII (1954), p.121.
13. Waley, *loc.cit.*; E. Jamison, *Admiral Eugenius of Sicily* (London, 1957), p.114.
14. Cahen, *La Régime Féodale, op.cit.* pp.76 and 118; Matheson, *op.cit.* p.273.
15. Curtis, *op.cit.* pp.356–7 and 365; Jamison, *Admiral Eugenius, op.cit.* p.39; F. Chalendon, *Histoire de la Domination Normande en Italie et en Sicile* (Paris, 1907), p.535.
16. P. Pieri, 'I Saraceni di Lucera nella Storia militare medievale', *Archivio Storico Pugliese* vol.VI (1954), pp.94–101; C. Oman, *A History of the Art of War in the Middle Ages* (London, 1924), vol.I, pp.499 and 502; E. Lévi-Provençal, 'Une héroine de la Résistance Musulmane en Sicile au début du XIIIe Siècle', *Oriente Moderno* vol.XXXIV (1954), p.286; J.F. Verbruggen, *The Art of Warfare in Western Europe during the Middle Ages* (Oxford, 1977), p.128; A.B. De Hoffmeyer, *Arms and Armour in Spain: a Short Survey*, vol.I (Madrid, 1982), pp.102–3.
17. J.M. Powell, trans., *The Liber Augustalis* (Syracuse, 1971), pp.15–18.
18. L.G. Boccia, 'HIC IACET MILES: Immagini guerriere da sepolcri toscani del Due e Trecento', in *Guerre e assoldati in Toscana, 1260–1364*, ed. L.G. Boccia and M. Scalini (Florence, 1982), pp.81–99.
19. Oman, *op.cit.* vol.I, p.497.
20. L.G. Boccia and E.T. Coelho, 'L'armamento di cuoio e ferro nel trecento Italiano', *L'Illustrazione italiani* vol.I, no.2 (1972), p.25.

Chapter 14

The Latin East

This section includes the Crusader States in Syria and Palestine, Cyprus following its conquest by Richard I of England, and the Latin 'Empire' of Constantinople plus its successor principalities in Greece. The history of the Crusader States in Syria, Palestine and the Lebanon began with the arrival of the First Crusade in the Middle East in 1098, and ended with the fall of Acre and the remaining Crusader-held coastal cities to the Mamlūks in 1291, although the Templars remained in possession of the offshore island of Arwād until 1303. The Crusader 'Empire of Romania', based upon Constantinople (Istanbul), lasted only from 1204 to 1261, but Crusader principalities in southern Greece survived into the fifteenth century. The Kingdom of Cyprus was annexed by Venice in 1489.

The small, vulnerable character of all Crusader States, with the possible exception of Cyprus, clearly had an effect on their military development.[1] However, it would be wrong to think that only the leading knights among the First and later Crusaders were well equipped.[2] Nevertheless, a shortage of horses was clearly a problem in the early years[3] and may have remained a source of weakness later. A shortage of manpower, though serious, seems to have been exaggerated by earlier generations of historians, who misunderstood the figures for Crusader military personnel and grossly overestimated the numerical strength of their Islamic foes. On the other hand the numerical problem was exacerbated following the establishment of Crusader States in Greece in 1204, when large numbers of men saw a more promising future in this new 'Romania'.[4]

Crusader tactics and military organisation have been studied in some detail,[5] though greater attention has been given to the initial conquest and the first expansionist century than to the second, defensive phase. Two interesting features of these later years were, however, the vital role of Military Orders such as the Templars and Hospitallers[6] and that of the town-based military 'confraternities'.[7] Generally speaking, the Crusaders had little to teach the warriors of the eastern Mediterranean region. On the contrary, they adopted much that was to be seen in Byzantium, though possibly through a parallel response to similar military situations rather than by learning directly from the experience of a long-established regional rival. The Crusaders also adopted ideas and items of equipment from their Islamic foes, though these could again be parallel responses rather than conscious copying. The most noticeable examples of this phenomenon were light cavalry[8] using light spears with reed or bamboo hafts,[9] extensive use of mounted infantry for high-speed raiding, and perhaps the vital role given to infantry archers.[10] The last were needed to combat enemy horse-archers, and as such possibly mirrored Fāṭimid-Arab or Armenian practice. Even the more sophisticated later cavalry formations associated with the Crusaders' famous couched lance 'shock' tactics are, through their close co-operation with disciplined infantry, remarkably similar to Byzantine and Fāṭimid-Arab systems. On the other hand they had nothing in common with Turkish practice.[11]

Pieces of military equipment having Middle Eastern origins included the *jazerant*, a lined or padded mail *hauberk*, and the counterweight *trebuchet*. Other possible candidates for Islamic, Byzantine or Central Asian origins are the scale-lined or laminated *coat-of-plates*, the *bascinet* helmet which protected the back and sides of the head, movable visors on a helmet, and separate *gauntlets*, though these last two items are more problematical. The Armenians may have been a vital channel for the spread of such advanced military technology. Their role as occasional allies and as a source of mercenaries for the Crusader States in Syria is clear and far more important than that of any other eastern Christian group.[12]

Perhaps the most interesting military development seen in the Crusader States was the emergence of the *turcopoles*. These were not a homogeneous group, as they included both cavalry and infantry, archers and non-archers, though the majority appear to have been light horsemen, the archers among them using bows in a Byzantine or Mamlūk style but certainly not in the harassing style of the Central Asian Turks.[13] It is also worth noting that *turcopoles* appeared in Crusader Cyprus,[14] Balkan or Greek 'Romania', and perhaps even in Normandy after the return of the Crusading King, Richard I of England.

Figures

715 Coin of Baldwin II, Count of Edessa, 1100–18
(Bib. Nat., Cabinet des Medailles, Paris, France)

The coins of the Latin East often used a mixture of earlier indigenous designs plus new Western European forms. This may be reflected in the military equipment crudely illustrated on many such coins. Those of the County of Edessa are very varied and in some respects more useful than those of the other states, which was probably a result of lingering Armenian and Artuqid Turkish influence. On this coin Count Baldwin has a very European form of helmet with a forward-angled crown. A distinction is, however, drawn between the body of his armour and the sleeves. This could be just an accident of design, but is equally likely to indicate the mail sleeves of a *hauberk* and the lamellar of a sleeveless *cuirass* in typical Middle Eastern style.

716 Coin of Baldwin II, Count of Edessa, 1110–18
(Bib. Nat., Cabinet des Medailles, Paris, France)

On a second coin, Count Baldwin wears a short-sleeved garment, the body of which has no particular emphasis on horizontal or vertical patterns and may thus be assumed to represent a mail *hauberk*. His shield is surprisingly small for the early 12th century and probably reflects Byzantine-Armenian influence. The tall object on his head finds no parallels in the armour of the period and is probably a hat.

717 Coin of Raymond of Poitiers, Prince of Antioch, 1136–49
(Bib. Nat., Cabinet des Medailles, Paris, France)

The coins of Antioch normally used a simple helmeted head, the helmet having a *nasal* and a cross painted on the side. Here the wearer is also shown wearing a mail *hauberk* which ends at his shoulders. The helmet itself is a round, low-domed type.

718 Coin of Baldwin II, Count of Edessa, 1100–18
(Bib. Nat., Cabinet des Medailles, Paris, France)

Here, Count Baldwin has some kind of *hauberk* or *cuirass*, perhaps sleeveless, with what appears to be a broad tapering sword in his hand. On his head he might have a brimmed *war-hat*, a type of helmet later common in Armenian, Crusader and some Byzantine art.

719 Coin of Baldwin I, Count of Edessa, 1098–1100
(Bib. Nat., Cabinet des Medailles, Paris, France)

The earlier coins of Crusader Edessa, including those minted for Baldwin I, are harder to interpret. This example clearly shows a man with a sword, a kite-shaped shield and a conical helmet. Why a pattern is put on his skirt but not on his chest is, however, unexplained.

720 Coin of Richard, Lord of Marash, Principality of Antioch, early 12th century
(Bib. Nat., Cabinet des Medailles, Paris, France)

Minted for one of the great northern vassals of the Principality of Antioch, this coin reflects the same Armenian and Byzantine influences as are seen in the coins of Edessa. The figure wears a conical helmet, carries a sword, and holds a relatively small kite-shaped shield. The sharply angled upper corners of this shield make is unlike early 12th-century Western European shields and could indicate that later European forms with flat tops were at least partially a result of Byzantine or other eastern influences.

721 Seal of Geoffrey de Bouillon, *Advocatus Santi Sepulchri*, Palestine, 1099–1100
(after Prawer, *Histoire du Royaume Latin de Jerusalem*)

Seals, which are bigger than coins, can show considerably more detailed military costume. Here Geoffrey wears a conical helmet with an interesting extension to protect his neck. He is armed with a spear and a presumably kite-shaped shield.

722 Seal of a Count of Tripoli, Syria–Lebanon, 12th century
(after Schlumberger, *Sigillographie de l'Orient Latin*)

The peculiarly angled, seemingly broken, spear and banner shown on this shield was probably an artistic device to fill a limited space. The horseman wears a tall helmet and carries a normal kite-shaped shield.

723 Seal of a Viscount of Nablus, Palestine, 12th century
(after Schlumberger, *Sigillographie de l'Orient Latin*)

The most interesting feature here is the large round helmet worn by the horseman.

724 Seal of a Prince of Galilee, Palestine, 12th century
(after Schlumberger, *Sigillographie de l'Orient Latin*)

Much closer to the standard forms of Western Europe, this horseman wears a tall conical helmet, probably with a *nasal*, and carries a spear and a large kite-shaped shield.

725 **Seal of the Templars, Syria–Palestine, 12th century**
(after Schlumberger, *Sigillographie de l'Orient Latin*)

An early example of the Templars' 'poverty' symbol of two men riding a single horse. The warrior-monks carry spears, wear conical helmets with apparent rims, and are wrapped in cloaks.

726 **Seal of a Lord of Marash, Principality of Antioch, 12th century**
(Bib. Nat., Cabinet des Medailles, Paris, France)

Once again the designs from northern Syria show greater individuality and variety than those of Crusader areas further south. Here a bareheaded man with a spear may wear an armour that covers only his chest. The most obvious source for such an armour would be the limited chest and abdomen covering lamellar *cuirasses* of Byzantium, Cilician Armenia and the neighbouring Islamic states.

727 **Carved relief, Palestine, 12th century**
(Museum of the Greek Orthodox Patriarchate, East Jerusalem, Palestine)

A bow of obvious recurved composite construction with angled ears is clearly shown on this very damaged carving. Such bows were in common use all around the Mediterranean and were not a specifically Middle Eastern weapon.

728A–C **Carved capitals from Nazareth, Palestine, late 12th century**
(Historical Museum, Nazareth, Israel)

The slightly later carved capitals from Nazareth are considered to be in southern French style, yet they include some 'demons' who use non-French military equipment. One shield (A) has an angled front and an indented top which to some extent recalls the later Spanish *adarga*. A similar but more straightforward shield (C) is used by a demon who also thrusts with a broad-bladed spear. Another demon shoots a recurved composite bow (B) using the Western finger-draw rather than the Middle Eastern or Turco-Iranian thumb-draw.

729A–C **Ivory cover of *Queen Melisende's Psalter*, Palestine, early 12th century**
(British Museum, London, England)

A – Goliath; B – Pride slain by Humility; C – Fortitude slaying Avarice. An interesting variety of arms and armour is shown on this ivory book cover, and it might be possible to guess why particular styles are given to particular figures. Both Goliath (A) and Pride (B) seem to wear armour in Byzantine style, perhaps reflecting a current coolness in Crusader-Byzantine relations. These two armours are probably very stylised, even archaised, and seem to consist of mail jerkins with splinted upper-arm protections. Pride is the most Byzantine of all, having a splinted skirt, a helmet with some form of non-mail *aventail*, a sword hung from a *guige*, and a small round shield. Goliath is less Byzantine in appearance and may be an attempt to show certain Middle Eastern Islamic fashions. His mail shirt includes a *coif* and could be intended to extend beneath his kilt. His large kite-shaped shield, however, looks Western European. The figure of Fortitude (C) is a paradox. One would have expected him to be shown as a typical Western European Crusader, but here he almost certainly wears a substantial lamellar *cuirass*. Similar but far from identical armours are seen in Norman southern Italy at roughly the same date. Could the giving of lamellar to Fortitude betray a reluctant admiration for the 'infidel' Turks on the part of the artist? (The high regard in which these warriors were held by their Crusader foes is clear in many historical accounts of the First Crusade.) Or perhaps he is dressed as an Armenian warrior. Melisende, the original owner of this psalter, was the daughter of an Armenian princess, Morphia, who was in turn daughter of Gabriel of Malatya and wife of King Baldwin of Jerusalem. She also did a great deal to improve relations between the Catholic Crusaders and the local Armenians and other Christian communities.

730A–B Paintings on columns, Palestine, early 12th century
(*in situ* Basilica of the Nativity, Bethlehem, Palestine)

The painted decorations on the columns of the Church of the Nativity appear to have been made quite soon after the Crusader conquest. At least two warriors are shown. One (B) is in purely Byzantine style with a deeply convex round shield and archaised conventional 'saintly' armour. Another, perhaps representing Cnut of Denmark or St Olaf of Norway, is more Western in style, with a decorated kite-shaped shield.

731 'Centurion at the Crucifixion', icon from the Crusader states, 12th century
(St Catherine's Monastery, Sinai, Egypt)

Large kite-shaped shields were not, of course, only seen in Western European art. They were also found in 12th century Byzantine sources and in the strongly Byzantine-influenced religious art of the Crusader states.

732A–K *Queen Melisende's Psalter*, Kingdom of Jerusalem, 1131–43
(British Library, Ms. Egerton 1139, London, England)

A–H – The Betrayal, f.7v; I – Guards at the Holy Sepulchre, f.10r; J – Sagittarius, f.18v; K – decorated initial, f.23v. *Queen Melisende's Psalter* was probably one of the earliest products of a school of illumination at Acre (in the Kingdom of Jerusalem) that would subsequently produce many distinctive manuscripts. It is largely Byzantine in style and has some similarity to local Middle Eastern manuscripts plus a small amount of Western European Romanesque influence. The mixture of extraordinary weapons seen in the 'Garden of Gethsemane' (A–H) reflects Byzantine, Armenian and Syriac styles. Seen here are a knife or dagger (A), round-headed and spiked maces (B and E) which were as yet rarely seen in the West, spears (D and F), and a long-bladed axe with a hammer at the back (G). Two very unusual infantry weapons are also illustrated. One appears to be a kind of pointed war-hammer (C), the other a war-flail (H), a weapon which would not become widely popular until the 14th and 15th centuries. It is worth noting the presence of such an infantry weapon, which was most effective against the legs of horses, Crusader Palestine being, of course, an area where the foe consisted primarily of horsemen. The sleeping guards (I) outside the Holy Sepulchre are almost entirely Byzantine in style, partly realistic and partly archaised. The two archers (J and K) use early forms of composite bows with angled grips. Both the bows and one man's quiver (K) on a strap over his shoulder have echoes in Mediterranean Europe rather than in the Middle East.

733A–E *Syriac Gospel*, **Principality of Antioch (?), late 12th century**
(University Library, Ms. 01.02, Cambridge, England)

A – Guard of Cyrus, f.199r; B–D – Judas Maccabeus and his army, f.208v; E – Joshua, f.63v. This manuscript, which might have been made within one of the northern Crusader states, shows an interesting mixture of military styles. Joshua's body-armour and legs (E) are depicted in conventional Byzantine style and probably have little relevance to contemporary fashion. His sword is of a broad, non-tapering, round-tipped style which, though seen in Byzantine and Mediterranean European art, is more characteristic of the Arab Middle East. The scabbard is similarly Byzantine or eastern Mediterranean. The one-piece helmet is, however, almost entirely European, with its conical shape and slightly forward-angled crown. A second helmet (A) may be of the same style but could also fit the local Middle Eastern pattern. The same might be said of the axe (B), spear (C), and a second sword (D).

734A–I **Armour fragments from Qurayn (Montfort) Castle, Kingdom of Jerusalem, c.1270**
(Metropolitan Museum of Art, New York, United States)

Various fragments of arms and armour have been found in ruined Crusader castles. Those from Montfort are among the most interesting. One small fragment has many small holes pierced in it and this is sometimes identified as part of a *great helm* (A). It could, however, just as well be part of a filter bucket or some other domestic device. Three pieces of metal (B–D) are almost certainly scales from a *coat-of-plates*, an early form of *jack*, or a scale *cuirass*. In many respects they have more in common with Eastern European or Russian armour than with surviving Western European fragments. If this is the case, then the logical intermediary stage or location would be Byzantium. The largest fragment is approximately 8 cm long. Other finds from Qurayn include the head of a javelin, or more likely of a bolt shot by a large frame-mounted crossbow (E), which is approximately 12 cm long, plus four other smaller crossbow heads. Two are of the tang type which are not in the normal European tradition (G and I), while others are even more unusual, apparently being designed to slip directly over the ends of an arrow or bolt (F and H). Here it is worth mentioning that most of the late 12th century crossbow bolts recently found in the Middle East seem designed to take such sleeve-like heads as these.

735 Enamelled sword *pommel*, Syria or Palestine, 13th century
(Metropolitan Museum of Art, no.29.153.685, New York, United States)

This *pommel* is made and decorated in basically Middle Eastern style with the obvious exception of a heraldic shield at its centre. It was probably made by a Syrian craftsman, inside or outside the Crusader States, for a European customer.

736A–E Weapons from ͨAthlîth (Pilgrim's) Castle, Kingdom of Jerusalem, late 13th century
(after Johns, *Quarterly of the Dept. of Antiquities of Palestine*, vol.V, no.1 (1935), fig.15, p.50)

A superb spearhead was found in the ruins of the Templar castle at ͨAthlîth on the Palestinian coast (A). Three small tang-type arrowheads were also recovered (B–D) although the flatter two (B and C) look more Mamlûk than Crusader. A substantial axehead (E) was, judging from the thickness of its blade, a work-axe rather than a weapon. Nevertheless, its presumed original outline had a characteristic half-moon shape.

737A–B Carved marble tympanum from Larnaca, Cyprus, 1200–50
(Victoria and Albert Museum, inv. A2-1982, London, England)

The small and somewhat worn reliefs on this carving show perfectly straightforward European military equipment. The only slightly unusual feature is that none of the armoured figures wear *surcoats*.

Two sleeping guards outside the Holy Sepulchre (A) have tall conical helmets without *nasals*, plus long-sleeved mail *hauberks*, *coifs*, and in one case mail *chausses*. Two other soldiers at the Crucifixion (B) have the same armour, though they lack helmets and their *hauberks* lack *mittens*. Swords are straight and in one case apparently non-tapering. A lack of *surcoats* seems to reflect current Byzantine styles and there is no reason why the Larnaca sculptor should not have chosen to use Byzantine models for these men. After all, the Byzantines regarded themselves as descendants of the Romans (and, indeed, called themselves Romans) and were often seen as such by their allies, rivals and foes.

738A–B Engraved monumental slabs of the Lusignan family, probably from Aya Sofia Mosque (former Cathedral), Famagusta, Cyprus, late 13th/early 14th centuries (soon to be in the Limasol Historical Museum, Cyprus)

These two little-known tomb slabs shed important light on the arms and armour of the later Latin East. Both men wear mail *hauberks* with integral mail gloves, these having individual fingers. The necks are raised, perhaps being fastened to a stiff undergarment, but the *coifs* were clearly separate. Their heraldic *surcoats* seem to have squared shoulders, suggesting substantial padding or some semi-rigid *cuirass* worn beneath. One figure still has his plated leg-harness (B), consisting of knee-covering *poleyns* and *greaves* that only cover the front of his shins. Mail *chausses* are worn under these. Their swords, interestingly, distinguish these figures from their Western European contemporaries. One figure (B) clearly has his weapon slung from a *baldric* rather than a sword-belt. The sword itself appears to be a straight non-tapering weapon unlike the very pointed blades of the West. With these exceptions the figures are armoured in a style very reminiscent of Italian arms and armour, which is not surprising given the growing influence of the maritime republics and of southern Italy in Crusader affairs.

739A–D Coins of Bohemond IV, Prince of Antioch, 1201–33 (Bib. Nat., Cabinet des Medailles, Paris, France)

Thirteenth-century coins from Antioch still portray a helmeted head bearing a cross. By the 13th century, however, these pictures had become slightly more detailed, showing a variety of hemispherical helmets with sometimes substantial *nasals* (D) and riveted rims. These are worn over mail *coifs* that seem to cover the lower part of the face and may even be joined at the brow to cover the face (B).

740 Coin of Raymond-Roupen, claimant to the Principality of Antioch, 1216–19 (Bib. Nat., Cabinet des Medailles, Paris, France)

It would be hazardous to see Armenian influence behind the slight differences in this similarly dated helmet. Raymond-Roupen was, of course, supported by Cilician Armenia in his unsuccessful struggle for Antioch. The helmet is almost square in outline and seems to have a bulge and perhaps a dangling lace at the back.

741A–K *Histoire Universelle*, Kingdom of Jerusalem, c.1287
(Bib. Nat., Ms. Fr. 20125, Paris, France)

A – Oedipus, f.91v; B – Polyneices and Tydeus, f.96r; C – Death of Hector, f.133v; D–F – Muslims (?); G–H – Crusaders (?); I – Army of Alexander, f.235r; J – Holofernes, f.205v; K – Army of Holofernes, f.207v. This manuscript from the school of Acre includes some more up-to-date pieces of military equipment as well as traditional items. Oedipus (A), for example, has a round helmet with a small *nasal* and his limited mail *chausses* cover neither the calf of his leg nor his heel. Polyneices and Tydeus (B), on the other hand, have two forms of *great helm*, one a very early picture of a round-topped type and the other a traditional flat-topped variety. Both have crests, presumably in the kind of plume-holders seen in the previous manuscript. The flat-topped *great helms* in this manuscript are, incidentally, a transitional form in which the top plate is itself quite domed (B, G and H). Note that horsemen (B) also wear padded or perhaps scale-covered *cuisses* with round, knee-covering *poleyns* attached. In the death of Hector at the hands of Achilles a rather gruesome picture shows the victim being slain by a spear thrust into the upper thigh above the top of his mail *chausses* (C). Elsewhere presumed Muslims are given very curved sabres (D) and two peculiar objects which do not seem to be maces (E and F). Could they be the long-necked 'fire-pots' full of *naft* (Greek Fire) that were used by Mamlūks and other troops as grenades? A soldier in Alexander's army (I) who could be expected to appear as a Westerner is dressed in full mail armour but carries a small round buckler, which might have been a local infantry fashion in the Crusader States. These and oval shields are certainly put in the hands of Crusaders in other Acre manuscripts. Such shields were also used by Muslim, Byzantine, Balkan and Italian foot-soldiers. This warrior in Alexander's army wears what appears to be a broad-brimmed hat over his mail *coif*. It could be a *chapel-de-fer* but its irregular lower edge makes this unlikely. Such presumed sun-hats also appear in Islamic sources of the same period. They were, after all, a practical idea in the Middle Eastern climate. Holofernes (J) seems to wear *poleyns* on his knees, while a soldier in his army (K) has a helmet with a broad chin-strap worn over a separate mail *coif*.

742A–F *History of Outremer*, Kingdom of Jerusalem 1286
(Bib. Nat., Ms. Fr. 9084, Paris, France)

A – Crusaders massacre Muslims of Antioch, f.64; B – Bohemond and Raymond before Jerusalem, f.307v; C – Crusaders besiege S̲h̲ayzar, f.182v; D – Siege of Tyre; E – Siege of Antioch; F – Siege of Damietta.

In another manuscript made by the school of Acre, Crusaders are clearly and quite deliberately shown with round (C) or oval (B) shields. This seems to indicate that, far from the Muslims adopting some of the supposedly more advanced military technology of the West, the reverse might have been happening to a limited degree in response to specific military circumstances. The Crusader States were by now little more than a string of castle-bound garrisons. Ventures into open battle were rare and usually disastrous. Any local military fashions that distinguished the troops of the Crusader States from those of Western Europe are, therefore, likely to reflect purely defensive warfare of ambush and siege. One warrior has a brimmed *chapel-de-fer war-hat* (A) which is of almost exactly the same size and form as the supposed sun-hat in the previous manuscript. Muslims are accurately portrayed with turbans (D and E), maces (E), and small round shields (D and E). One archer has a hat or an iron *war-hat* with a square top (D), while others have pointed helmets, tall, short or with angled crowns (F), as well as mail and perhaps in one instance lamellar armour (F).

743A–E *History of Outremer*, Kingdom of Jerusalem, 1290–1
(Biblioteca Laurenziana, Ms. Plu. LXI. 10, Florence, Italy)

A – Crusader crossbowman, f.162v; B – Crusaders massacre Muslims of Antioch, f.61; C – Crusaders besiege Antioch, f.42r; D – Crusaders attack Acre by sea, f.63; E – Crusaders attack Nicea, f.33. No flat-topped *greathelms* are seen in this manuscript, only a very round-topped version (B). Most troops wear *chapel-de-fer* war-hats, which would presumably have been more suited to the climate (C and E), or mail *coifs* alone (D). Shields are mostly oval (B) or round (C and D), with a few flat-topped triangular ones attached to the side of a galley (D). Mail is the only other armour shown, but crossbows are common (D and E) with two clear pictures of loading hooks hung from a belt (A and E). An axe is used to undermine a fortress (E), while a solitary archer takes part in naval warfare (D). This manuscript also includes a very clear illustration of a counterweight *trebuchet* (C).

744A–C *History of Outremer*, Kingdom of Jerusalem, 1287
(Bib. Munic., Ms. 142, Boulogne, France)

A – Defenders of S̲h̲ayzar, f.153v; B – Standard-bearer of Godefroy de Bouillon, f.16r; C – Crusaders slaughter Muslims of Antioch, f.49v. The sabres given to the Muslim defenders of S̲h̲ayzar (A) are among the most accurate Christian portrayals of such weapons. The thickening of the blades towards the tips is exaggerated but the lack of *pommels* and one curved hilt show a genuine knowledge of Islamic sabres. Godefroy's standard-bearer during the First Crusade (B) seems to wear a *war-hat*, while two of the Crusaders in Antioch (C) clearly carry oval shields.

745A–L *Histoire Universelle*, **Kingdom of Jerusalem, c.1286**
(British Library, Ms. Add. 15268, London, England)

A – Scythian women besiege their enemies, f.101v; B – Club of Joseph's brother, f.48r; C – Mace of Goliath, f.104; D–E – Soldiers of Nimrod, f.16r; F–G – Frontispiece, f.1v; H – Bow of Amazon, f.123r; I – Soldiers of Nimrod, f.71r; J – Trojan or Greek warrior, f.105v; K – Athenian in sea battle, f.136v; L – Soldier of Alexander, f.208r. Another manuscript from the school of Acre shows an interesting mixture of Western European, Byzantine and Islamic influences in both the style of painting and the military equipment it illustrates. The siege by Scythian women and their menfolk (A) portrays the latter as heavy cavalry with round or flat-topped *great helms*, swords, and normal kite-shaped shields. The women, plus one man, are shown as sappers or infantry with an axe and three pickaxes. The defenders have bows, crossbows, an axe, and assorted rocks. They wear mail *hauberks* with or without *mittens* and have brimmed *chapel-de-fer war-hats* or close-fitting round helmets, both made of two pieces joined along the crown. One defender also has what looks like a stiffened or scale-covered collar of a type seen elsewhere in the manuscript (E and J). Such collars were to become a feature in late 13th and 14th century Byzantine and Balkan art. They may also represent Byzantine influence in this manuscript. Two forms of club (B) or mace (C) are portrayed, the latter perhaps having a knobbed iron head. The followers of Nimrod (D, E and I) also seem to indicate strong Byzantine influence. Two guardsmen (D and E) even have splinted upper-arm protections, in one case apparently fastened to a *coat-of-plates* (D) which has rivets on the chest. In a second case they are fastened to a second mail jerkin (E). Another figure (D) also has an archaic splinted skirt and a long-sleeved mail *hauberk* with *mittens* under his perhaps fanciful *coat-of-plates*. His mail *coif* is likely to have been separate, while the second guard (E) has a *coif* and a collar which is not of mail. Both men wear mail *chausses* and carry small round shields. Their brimmed helmets are similar but not identical in construction. The second guard carries a sword which is barely tapering, blunt-tipped, and somewhat archaic. Many of these features are shown, in a simpler form, being worn by others of Nimrod's soldiers (I). A simple mail *coif* and brimless helmets of two-piece construction, some with a raised comb, are also seen. A Greek or Trojan (J) is in a similar mould, with a perhaps scale-covered or splinted collar. Such collars are unlikely to have been totally fanciful as similar systems would appear in early 14th century Europe. An Athenian warrior (K) has a strange mixture of influences in his armour. His upper-arm protections are a Byzantine convention but his long-sleeved mail *hauberk*, small shield, acutely tapering sword and either flat-topped helmet or *coif* worn over a squared *arming cap*, are all typically Western European. A small degree of Islamic influence may be seen in the archer who uses a thumb-draw (F), in a recurved bow (H), and in the open bag-like quiver on the right hip of a horse-archer, whose tunic also appears to be buttoned (L).

746A–L *Histoire Universelle*, Principality of Antioch (?), 1250–87
(Vatican Library, Ms. Pal. Lat. 1963, Rome, Italy)

A–D – Muslim defenders of Antioch, f.40r; E–F – Crusaders, f.31v; G–H – Crusaders massacre Muslims of Antioch, f.49r; I–K – Siege of Antioch, f.40r; L – f.188r. Very few Crusader manuscripts are believed to have survived from anywhere except the school of Acre, with the possible exception of this one. It may also be rather earlier than most other manuscripts from the Latin East. Though stylised, it shows arms and armour without apparent archaisms or conventions, and may cast a useful light on some current Islamic styles. These latter include a round helmet with, perhaps, a full face-covering *aventail* (A), pointed hats of Turkish or Mongol inspiration (B and D), a round helmet with a *nasal* (C), a possible helmet and *aventail* (H), and very clearly triangular shields of a type normally associated with the Byzantines. Crusader equipment includes round helmets with *nasals* (E and G) as well as various forms of *great helm*, including a very early representation of a round type (J), and early flat-topped types which do not come very far down the neck (F, I and K). Long-sleeved mail *hauberks* are seen (I–K), as well as a *surcoat* with distinctly square or padded shoulders (J), and flat-topped shields (K and G). A damaged illustration of a horse's *caparison* seems to have it extending beneath the saddle in Islamic style rather than consisting of two separate sheets divided by the saddle. It may in reality have been a mail-lined *bard* of Islamic style or even Islamic origin.

747A–E *Arsenal Bible*, Kingdom of Jerusalem, 1275–91
(Bib. de l'Arsenal, Ms. 5211, Paris, France)

A – Sacrifice of Jephthah's daughter; B–D – Amalekites; E – Army of Holofernes. Though full of the most peculiar archaisms, the *Arsenal Bible* also includes some interesting pieces of arms and armour. These find very few parallels in the military equipment of the Crusader States or Western Europe but may reflect Byzantine forms. The manuscript is, in fact, very Byzantine in style. The most realistic-looking helmets are brimmed *war-hats* with (C–D) or without (E) raised crests. A straightforward knife or dagger is illustrated (A), as are spears and large kite-shaped shields (E). The men may wear mail *hauberks* with *coifs*, separate *mittens* being shown (C). It is also worth noting that the horsemen use relatively low saddles and ride with short stirrups (E).

748 'Goliath', *Book of Psalms*, Crusader States, 1275–91
(Biblioteca Capitolare, C.12, f.27b, Padua, Italy)

The only features that make the figure of Goliath unusual are his tall, pointed helmet and small round shield. His mail *coif, chausses*, and *hauberk* with *mittens* are otherwise typically European.

749A–K Histoire Universelle, Kingdom of Jerusalem, late 13th century
(Bib. Munic., Ms. 562, Dijon, France)

A – Army of Porus of India, f.190; B–C – Army of Porus of India, f.172v; D–E – Spears of Amazons and of Alexander, f.86v; F–G – Soldiers of Joseph in Egypt, f.57; H – Story of Troy, f.89v; I–K – Soldiers of Alexander (?). Most of the figures in this manuscript are dressed and equipped in European style. The exceptions are the 'Indians' (A–C) who, with their maces (A), small convex round shields (A–C), *ṭirāz* bands around some sleeves (B) and an emphasis on archery (B–C), are clearly based on Muslim prototypes. The same might be true of the spear pennons or streamers of the Amazons (D), which are in clear contrast to the triangular pennons of Alexander's men (E). A mounted knight (K) is in up-to-date European style, even including plate *poleyns*. Two other *great helms* have plumes or streamers attached (I–J). Infantry are in heraldically-striped helmets and *surcoats* (F and H). Both also have raised and presumably stiffened collars on their mail *hauberks*. One shield appears to be a foreshortened oval type (F). The second infantryman has an extremely interesting and very early representation of a *basilard* dagger on his hip. No belt is shown, but such a dagger would presumably have been hung from a belt by cords, as commonly seen in early 14th century European sources.

750A–O History of Outremer, Kingdom of Jerusalem, c.1280
(M.E. Saltykov-Shchredin State Public Library, Ms. Fr. fol.v.IV.5, St Petersburg, Russia)

A – Siege of Damietta, f.166r; B – Attack on S̲h̲ayzar, f.129r; C–E – Siege of Maarat al-Numan, f.45r; F – Siege of Tyre, f.103r; G – Siege of Antioch, f.18v; H–I – First Crusade, f.10v; J – Siege of Antioch, f.27r; K–O – Capture of Antioch, f.36r. The Leningrad copy of the *History of Outremer* is one of the earliest and finest of late 13th century manuscripts from the school of Acre. It shows considerable knowledge of Islamic arms and armour, even to the extent of showing a kind of large saddlecloth of a type which found no parallel in 13th-century Western Europe (B). Muslim troops correctly wield heavy, winged maces (B), carry round shields (B and J), and have turbans wound around presumed conical helmets (C and L). Elsewhere they have possibly fluted helmets (D), brimmed hats or *war-hats* (D), low or tall conical helmets without turbans (J and K), and mail *coifs* (C and K). The Crusaders use mail *hauberks* with integral *mittens* (B, H and J), mail *coifs* (H and M), and mail *chausses* (B and H–J). Some have presumably padded *cuisses* over their mail *chausses* (B, I and J). Skull-cap *cervellières* or low-domed round helmets appear (H and M), but the most common helmet is the fully developed *great helm* (A, B, J and O), usually with an angled front profile. Most of these also have a clearly defined plume holder or ventilation hole on top, though no plumes are actually shown. Swords are tapering with curved *quillons* (B and N), and a crossbowman is shown with what looks like an early example of a loading-hook on his belt (H). Two interesting siege machines are illustrated. One is a small, man-powered *mangonel* mounted on a pole with attachments for three ropes (G). A second is an extraordinary device mounted on a substantial frame, with what looks like a loading winch in the front (F). Given the accuracy of other pictures in this manuscript, it seems unlikely that the artist has simply forgotten to draw the other end of the beam sling, so perhaps this machine is operated by torsion power in some way which was either unclear to him or is unclear to the modern observer. The closest equivalent to this device seems to be an engine somewhat crudely drawn on an Iranian ceramic plate some fifty years earlier.

751 Seal of Baldwin I, Latin Emperor of Constantinople 1204–5
(now lost, after Schlumberger, *Sigillographie de l'Orient Latin*)

Various features of this otherwise typical European seal are worthy of note. Attached to the symbolic crown-helmet is a face-covering visor, while the sword is of the new thrusting and regularly tapering type. Although the *mittens* appear to be separate, such a feature is not normally seen in the early 13th century and might simply be the artist neglecting to add stylised 'squiggles' to indicate mail.

752 Seal of Henry I, Latin Emperor of Constantinople, early 13th century
(Bib. Nat., Cabinet des Medailles, Paris, France)

At first glance this seal seems very similar to that of Baldwin I (fig.751). The sword similarly tapers to a point and the hand is either unmailed or has a glove made of a different material. The shield appears to be of a small, somewhat Byzantine kite-shaped variety, but it is the helmet which demands attention. It clearly has a crest or plume. Such an idea is unknown in Western Europe at this time and probably reflects Byzantine or archaic Roman symbolism. The helmet also appears to have a form of chin-guard around the face. This could be a frame to support a face-mask or it could be another unrealistic artistic convention. Somewhat similar frames around the face are occasionally seen in 13th-century Western Europe but even here their interpretation and real purpose remain uncertain. If it was not for the plume or crest such a piece of headgear could be regarded as an *arming cap*.

753 Seal of John II of Ibelin, Lord of Beirut, County of Tripoli, 1261
(Archivio di Stato, Venice, Italy)

This seal from the Crusader States is completely European in style. The rider's helmet is either a flat-topped *great helm* with a single eye-slit or perhaps a flat-topped helmet with a rectangular face-mask. His *surcoat* has pointed shoulders indicating either padding or a semi-rigid *cuirie* worn beneath. His sword is tapering with a relatively acute tip.

754A–D Icon of St George, Crusader (?) Greece, 13th century
(Byzantine Museum, inv. 89, Athens, Greece)

A–C – Soldiers in Passion scenes; D – St George. The warriors on this icon are probably dressed in 13th century Byzantine style, although the icon itself may have been made either in one of the Crusader States in Greece or in an area under strong Western European influence. Byzantine troops in Greece were reportedly more lightly equipped than their Crusader foes. The minor figures (A–C) wear round or slightly pointed *chapel-de-fer war-hats* and short-sleeved mail *hauberks*. In one instance (A) a sleeveless mail jerkin, painted gold in the original, is worn over the sleeved *hauberk*. The larger figure of St George (D) has a standard European type of shield and a blue-painted short-sleeved mail hauberk. Over this, but under his cloak, he has a shorter, brown-painted garment with split sleeves. This could indicate a leather-covered *coat-of-plates*, a stylised piece of 'Roman' armour, or some other unidentified garment.

755 Icon of St Nicholas from Church of St Nicholas tis steyis, Crusader Kingdom of Cyprus, late 13th century
(Makarios Foundation, Nicosia, Cyprus)

St Nicholas' armour consists of a mail *hauberk* with fingered *mittens*, mail *chausses*, and maybe a padded *surcoat* with squared shoulders. A small and perhaps symbolic *great helm* is added just ahead of the figure, while on his head he might wear a round helmet with a *nasal*. The face has, of course, been disfigured.

756A–B Icons, Crusader States (?), 13th century
(Monastery of St Catherine, Sinai, Egypt)

These saints are dressed in traditional and even archaic armour. One may be identified as St Theodore Tyro 'the Recruit' (B), the third of the great soldier saints of the Middle East after Sts George and Demetrius. The equipment of another (A) can almost certainly be dismissed as fanciful, but that of St Theodore (B) has a new splinted or scale-covered 'collar' which was not seen in earlier Byzantine art. His *cuirass* may also be intended as a quilted form of armour.

757 Icon of the Virgin Mary, Crusader Kingdom of Cyprus, c.1300
(Makarios Foundation, Nicosia, Cyprus)

The story of the Dominican or Carmelite Order is illustrated on the smaller panels of this icon. The arms and armour are typically European except that the shields are either very small kite-shaped types of early Byzantine form or small round bucklers.

758 Icon of St Sergius, Crusader States, late 13th century
(Monastery of St Catherine, Sinai, Egypt)

This well preserved icon of the Syrian warrior St Sergius is believed to have been made in one of the Crusader States. It is basically Byzantine in style but includes very accurate representations of Middle Eastern military equipment. In this context it should be noted that the nomads of the Middle East traditionally regarded Sergius as their patron saint. Here he wears a short-sleeved mail *hauberk* without any head or leg protection. His shield is round and he rides in the bent-leg position, despite having a Western-style high saddle with a raised *cantle* and *pommel*. His archery equipment is an accurately shown mixture of Turkish, Mamlūk Egyptian and possibly Mongol styles, but it does not appear to have been fully understood by the artist, who neglected to include the straps that would have led from the upper-rear side of the quiver to the belt. A smoothly recurved bow is in a bowcase on the saint's left hip.

759 Fragment of a sgraffito-ware ceramic dish from al-Mina, Principality of Antioch (?), early 13th century
(Hatay Museum, Antakya, Turkey)

The style is Arab-Islamic but the dish's provenance suggests that it might have been made within the Crusader States. It could, however, equally well have been imported. Its subject appears to be a mailed horseman, probably hunting with a hawk on his wrist. His horse appears to be covered with an Islamic style one-piece *caparison* or *bard*, with a portion cut out behind the stirrups.

760 Fragment of *Aldrevandini*-style enamelled glass, Crusader States, Cyprus or Venice, late 13th/early 14th centuries
(Museum of London, inv. 134-190-1982, London, England)

The origins of the pieces of a glass beaker in a style known as *Aldrevandini*, excavated in London in 1982, remain unclear. One fragment shows a man on horseback with a flat-topped shield and probably a lance. On his head is a hat, turban or helmet with a long plume. Both the technique and the subject are very similar to early 14th century Mamlūk enamelled glass but the pictorial style is, of course, very different.

761 **Incised monumental stone slab from Kastiliotis,
Kingdom of Cyprus, 14th century**
(**Historical Museum, Nicosia, Cyprus**)

This worn and damaged stone slab almost certainly dates to the 14th
century. It shows a round helmet of two-piece construction, probably
with an *aventail* or, less likely, worn over a *coif*. The two-piece
construction with a slightly raised comb clearly remained popular in
the eastern Mediterranean for many years.

762 **Seal of Guy de la Tour, titular king of Thessaloniki,
1314**
(**Bib. Nat, Cabinet des Medailles, Paris, France**)

Although Guy de la Tour, son of Humbert I of Viennois, never went to
the East this seal was attached to a charter drawn up by the mercenary
Catalan Company in Greece, offering him the crown of the Kingdom
of Salonika, which itself no longer existed. As such it is likely to reflect
the military styles of the Catalans and other 'Franks' in Greece and the
Balkans. The rider wears a round-topped *great helm*, apparently with a
single broad eye-slit. Mail is visible on his neck and arm. He carries a
large, flat-topped shield, and his horse wears a *caparison*.

763A–C **Wall-painting, Venetian province of Crete, early 14th
century**
(***in situ* Church of Panaghia Kera, Kritsa, Crete, Greece**)

A–B – Sword and scabbard of a warrior saint; C – Warrior with club.
The sword is quite straightforward, but the scabbard has two unusual
features which might indicate Byzantine influence. The first is its flat,
broadened top instead of the usual cone-shaped pyramidal outline
common to most European scabbards. The second is its very large
chape. Another figure (C) carries a primitive club but wears a broad
belt with stiffeners, which was the belt of a knight.

764 **Funerary carving from Famagusta, Kingdom of
Cyprus, mid-14th century**
(**present whereabouts unknown, after photographs from
Mrs T. Stylianou**)

A number of 14th century funerary stelae or reliefs have survived in
Cyprus, mostly in an Italian style. This example shows a tall crest,
probably of leather stuffed with wool, fastened to a *great helm* with a
single broad eye-slit.

765 **'St George', wall-painting, Principality of Achaia, 14th
century**
(***in situ* church of St George, Geraki Castle, Greece**)

This kind of sword was now used by Western Europeans, the 'Franks'
in the Crusader states of Greece, and the Byzantines, as well as in

many Balkan states. Most of the swords would probably have been exported to these areas from the main arms manufacturing centres of Germany and northern Italy.

766 'St George', wall-painting, Crusader Kingdom of Cyprus, 14th century
(in situ Church of Panagia Phorbiotissa, Asinou, Cyprus)

Once again, a painting in Cyprus, though made under a Crusader ruler, is purely Byzantine in style. The rider's legs are covered by some kind of riding boots or *greaves*. The former seem more likely, but the two apparent rivets to hold a leather hinge tend to indicate that these leg coverings were made of a stiff material. Almost identical, and more clearly metallic *greaves* appear in a late 14th or 15th century Georgian psalter (Manuscript Institute, Georgian Academy of Sciences, Ms. No.A.1665, Tbilisi, Georgia). Similar types also appear in later 14th century Iranian manuscripts. Perhaps their inclusion here indicates that the Byzantine originals that lay behind this wall-painting were already under very strong Islamic influence via the Ottomans and other Turks.

767A–B 'Way of the Cross', wall-painting, Crusader Kingdom of Cyprus, 14th–15th centuries
(in situ Church of Panagia Phorbiotissa, Asinou, Cyprus)

Other paintings in the Church of Panagia Phorbiotissa are in a more traditional artistic style but are also much more difficult to date. Here, soldiers (B) in short-sleeved but variously represented mail *hauberks* carry maces and spears. Their helmets have hanging *aventails* in the Turkish or Islamic manner and are conical or have slightly forward-angled crowns. They also have small brims. The officer (A) differs in that his armour is shown as a lamellar *cuirass*. His helmet again has a mail *aventail* but also has a wider brim, making it a type of *chapel-de-fer*. His shield is a large round type. Even though this wall-painting may date from as late as the 15th century, the style of relatively light armour that it portrays was probably common in 14th century Byzantium.

Notes

1. P. Contamine, *La Guerre au Moyen Age* (Paris, 1980), p.156; J. Richard, *The Latin Kingdom of Jerusalem* (Oxford, 1979), p.256.
2. F. Duncalf, 'The Peasants' Crusade', *American Historical Review* vol.XXVI (1921), pp.441–2.
3. Richard, *op.cit.* pp.16–17.
4. Richard, *op.cit.* p.210.

5. R.C. Smail, *Crusading Warfare, 1097–1193* (Cambridge, 1956), pp.120–3, 130–3, 156–7 and 201–2; J. Prawer, *The Crusaders' Kingdom* (New York, 1972), pp.327 and 341–2; J. Beeler, *Warfare in Feudal Europe, 730–1200* (Ithaca 1971), p.144, Contamine, *loc.cit.*

6. R.C. Smail, 'Crusaders' Castles in the Twelfth Century', *The Cambridge Historical Journal* vol.X (1951), p.148; J. Riley-Smith, *The Feudal Nobility and the Kingdom of Jerusalem 1174–1277* (London, 1973), pp.28–9.

7. Richard, *op.cit.* pp.284–5.

8. Smail, *Crusading Warfare, op.cit.* pp.110–11.

9. N. Elisseeff, *Nūr al Dīn: un Grand Prince Musulman de Syrie au temps des Croisades* (Damascus, 1967), p.732.

10. J.F. Verbruggen, *The Art of Warfare in Western Europe during the Middle Ages* (Oxford, 1977), pp.115–16.

11. Verbruggen, *op.cit.* p.93.

12. Prawer, *op.cit.* p.219; Smail, *Crusading Warfare, op.cit.* pp.52–3; Richard, *op.cit.* pp.140–2 and 366; D.C. Douglas, *The Norman Fate, 1100–1154* (London, 1976), p.184; J. Laurent, *Études d'Histoire Arménienne* (Louvain, 1971), pp.145–6; C.J. Yarnley, *Byzantine Relations with the Armenians in the Eleventh Century, with Special Reference to Cilicia* (B.Litt. thesis, Oxford University, 1972), p.149.

13. Smail, *Crusading Warfare, op.cit.* pp.111–12, Prawer, *op.cit.* pp.109 and 140.

14. H.E. Mayer, *The Crusades* (Oxford, 1972), p.164.

Chapter 15

The Western Balkans

The medieval Balkans were as fragmented as they are today. Most of the region's inhabitants were Slavs, including Bulgarians, Macedonians, Serbs, Bosnians, Dalmatians, Croats and Slovenes. Of these, the last four groups were largely Catholic until the Ottoman conquest, and as such they will be discussed in this volume, as will be the non-Slavic Albanians. After the Ottoman conquest the majority of Bosnians gradually converted to Islam, but interestingly enough there was already a substantial non-Christian minority within medieval Bosnia long before this. These were the Bogomils, followers of a version of the Manichaean faith which had earlier been seen in eastern Anatolia (where its adherents were known as Paulicians), and which would also emerge in southern France, where historians generally refer to its followers as Albigensians. The inhabitants of medieval Dalmatia were also partly Italian in culture and speech. The Greeks of the Aegean and Ionian Sea coasts are not dealt with here (see the section on Byzantium in the second volume for these), nor are the Vlachs. Although these semi-nomadic ancestors of the modern Rumanians were found across a large part of the Balkans, including some western and southern parts of the peninsula, they too will be covered in book two.

Early in the 11th century most of the western Balkan peninsula, except parts of Slovenia and Croatia, formed part of the Byzantine Empire. By the time of the First Crusade the Croats, after a period of independence, were falling under Hungarian rule. With the Fourth Crusade's capture of Constantinople (Istanbul) in 1204, the whole Balkan region fragmented once again. Northern and western Greece was itself divided between minor Crusader principalities and the Byzantine Despotate of Epirus. Even the Albanians soon won a brief independence, but by the mid-14th century Serbia had conquered a large though ephemeral empire from the Danube to the Gulf of Corinth. The southern Italian Kingdom of Naples was also deeply involved in Albanian and Greek affairs. The Crusader principalities held a small part of southern Greece, while Venice and Genoa struggled for control of most of the Greek islands.

Culturally and even politically Byzantium had, of course, been the main influence on most of the Balkan peninsula. However, during the period under consideration western and central Europe had an increasingly important impact on the western parts of the region, particularly in military matters.[1] In terms of military technology Western influence came via the expanding Hungarian kingdom and the Republic of Ragusa (Dubrovnik), which was a major channel for the import of Italian arms and armour. This was then passed on to Bosnia and areas further east.[2] In fact the military élites of the western side of the Balkan peninsula looked to the West not only for military supplies but also in broader political terms, which tended to isolate them from the bulk of the Orthodox population, which remained basically 'anti-Frank' or 'anti-Catholic'. Such alienation was to be of profound importance before and during the Ottoman conquest of the Balkans.[3]

The Bosnians, being closer to the Adriatic coast and to Italy, were under greater Western influence than the Serbs, whom they otherwise mirrored in military matters. To all intents and purposes Bosnia was independent from the early 12th century to 1253, when it fell under Hungarian rule before being incorporated in Stefan Dushan's ephemeral 14th-century Serbian Empire. This was, however, a relatively poor, isolated and certainly rugged mountainous area, in which archaic forms of warfare survived and distinctive equipment seems to have evolved. An example of the latter might be the large triangular *scutum bosniensem* cavalry shield of the mid-14th century.[4]

Croatia, having been united with the Hungarian kingdom on terms of near equality in 1091, remained a part of the Hungarian state until modern times. Unsurprisingly, Croatian military equipment therefore echoed that of Hungary, though it generally lacked the horse-archery element of Eurasian steppe origin which distinguished Hungarian military styles from those of other Western countries.[5]

More is known about Dalmatian arms and armour than most other Balkan regions because more documentary sources survive and the art is less influenced by Byzantine archaism. Cavalry seem to have been almost identical to those of the West, and particularly of Italy.[6] Infantry, above all archers with simple and composite bows but later also with crossbows, played a very important role in this urbanised and maritime region.[7] In fact infantry increased in importance from the early 14th century because of greater pressure on the Dalmatian cities by their inland Balkan neighbours.[8] Even as early as 1351 Ragusa (Dubrovnik) was importing firearms from Venice to defend itself from Hungarian attack.[9]

Most unreservedly Westernised of all the Balkan peoples, in terms of military equipment, were the Slovenes. They inhabited the provinces of Carniola, Styria and, until the area was Germanised, parts of Carinthia. All of these had lain within the medieval German Empire since they had been recovered from the invading Hungarians in the 10th century. Only western Istria fell outside the Empire, being ruled by Venice.

Like so many other Balkan peoples, the Albanians were dominated by their neighbours throughout most of the Middle Ages. The coastal cities of Albania had survived the urban decline of the early Middle Ages, remaining large as well as commercially and militarily important until the end of the 11th century.[10] The lowlands were in some respects feudally organised under Byzantine rule, with local warriors already serving as *stradiotes* under various categories of Byzantine leadership. The Albanian military role seems to have been quite significant, but a sense of national identity was hindered by the fact that some Albanians were Catholic (*Arbanite*) while others were Orthodox (*Epirote*).[11] Nevertheless, independence was won around 1190 during a general period of Byzantine decline, only to be lost again to the Despotate of Epirus in 1216. The next phase came with an invasion by the Angevins of southern Italy who, in 1272, established another Albanian kingdom under Angevin patronage. This was followed by a considerable wave of southern Italian and French military influence which was at first eagerly accepted by the local military élites. Angevin control, however, never extended far beyond the coastal plains and cities, while the highlands continued to be dominated by local, sometimes almost nomadic peoples.[12] In the 14th century Albanian nomads had spread as far south as Thessaly[13] and they had long dominated the wild highlands of Epirus. When Albania, both Angevin and Despotate, fell under Serbian control in the early 1330s the area was said to support no less than 15,000 cavalry,[14] almost all being lightly-armed tribesmen fighting with spear and sword. Such troops would later make a dramatic impact – normally under the Venetian flag – in 15th century Italy, where they were again known as *stradiotti*.

Figures

768 **Carved relief on a choir-screen from Biskupija, Dalmatia, c.1070**
(Museum of Croatian Archaeological Monuments, Split, Croatia)

Although coming from a Slav area, this carving has much in common with Romanesque Italian art, which in turn reflected the high degree of Italian influence in Dalmatia. The man's sword is straight, barely tapering, and has prominent *quillons* and a round *pommel*.

769A–V **Arrow, javelin and small spear heads from Biskupija, Dalmatia, 9th–12th centuries**
(Museum of Croatian Archaeology, Split, Croatia)

This extraordinary collection of weapon fragments was excavated at the turn of the 20th century. Their dating is very unreliable, but the collection does include an interesting variety of types. There are only three tanged arrowheads (C, N and V), almost certainly introduced by outsiders from Hungary, the southern Balkans, or even Central Asia. The rest are of the socket type, many being barbed (K and P-U). Armour-piercing crossbow bolts may be present (D, E, J and M), perhaps betraying Italian influence. Two peculiar objects (I and O) may not be arrow or bolt heads at all, while some of the large objects are more likely to have come from javelins or small spears (G, H, L, P, R and S).

770A–G **Spearheads from Biskupija, Dalmatia, 9th–12th centuries**
(Museum of Croatian Archaeology, Split, Croatia)

Like the other objects from Biskupija, the dating of these spearheads is uncertain. An assortment of types can again be seen, perhaps showing a variety of influences. In particular, one (A) appears to be single-edged, while another (B) might either be damaged or could be a local form of hafted infantry weapon, of a type known in Western Europe as a war-scythe.

771A–K **Axes from Biskupija, Dalmatia, 9th–12th centuries**
(Museum of Croatian Archaeology, Split, Croatia)

Some of these axeheads may be work tools rather than weapons (A, G and K). The narrow blades of many of the remainder (D–F and H–J) place them in the Eastern rather than the Western tradition of war-axes.

772A–E **Arrowheads, Dalmatia, 11th–14th centuries**
(**Archaeological Museum, Split, Croatia**)

Most of these varied arrowheads were chance finds from around
Vrgorac, a few miles from Split. At the very least they indicate the
variety of bows and crossbows used in Dalmatia during the medieval
period.

773A–E **Mace heads from Biskupija, Dalmatia, 11th–13th
  centuries**
(**Museum of Croatian Archaeology, Split, Croatia**)

These weapons are clearly in the same tradition as those found in
Hungary. They appear to have been popular in many parts of
Eastern Europe in both Slav and non-Slav areas.

774A–F **Spear and javelin heads, Dalmatia, 11th–14th centuries**
(**Archaeological Museum, Split, Croatia**)

These varied weapons were all found in the bed of the River Cetina,
at a ford near Trilj, near Split. The most distinctive (B and C) are
such broad but thin weapons that an unarmoured foe was presumably expected. A third blade (E) looks very Hungarian, or
perhaps even earlier Avar.

775A–B **Bronze mace-heads, Dalmatia, 11th–14th centuries**
(**Archaeological Museum, Split, Croatia**)

These were again found in the bed of the River Cetina, at a ford near Trilj,
near Split. The first, spiked example (A) is so small that its identification
as a weapon remains debatable. The second (B) is flimsy and hollow, and
would presumably originally have been filled with lead.

776 ***Patristica of Gregorius Magnus*, Croatia, early 12th
  century**
(**Metropolitan Library, Ms. MR-138, Zagreb, Croatia**)

Here a fully-armoured warrior is shown in purely Western European
style. In fact his acutely forward-angled conical helmet and *nasal* look
distinctly Italian.

777A–G **Carvings, Dalmatia, c.1240**
(***in situ* west door of Cathedral, Trogir, Croatia**)

These carvings may be rather old-fashioned in style but they are known
to have been made by a Slav Dalmatian mason, Master Radovan, and
are likely to reflect what he saw around him. The archer-huntsman (C)
uses an early form of composite bow similar to that seen in southern
Italy, Byzantium, and the pre-Turkish Islamic Middle East. The sword
and shield carried by a figure in unrealistic Roman armour (A) is again
old-fashioned, but more realistic than the man himself. Two other
warriors (B and D) appear as lightly-armed infantrymen, though the

apparently padded headgear of one (B) is unusual. Most interesting of all, however, are the three Guards at the Holy Sepulchre (E–G). They have wide-brimmed *chapel-de-fer* helmets with buckled chin-straps, separate mail *coifs*, and long-sleeved mail *hauberks* without *mittens* but worn beneath lamellar or scale *cuirasses*. The nearest parallel to the last, both stylistically and geographically, seems to be the effigy of Guido Pallavicino at Fontevivo in northern Italy, though this was made some sixty years later.

778A–D Undated swords from Dalmatia
(Museum of Croatian Archaeology, Split, Croatia)

Most of these weapons were found in river crossings. They are almost certainly of the same date and type as the better-preserved Sword of the Ban Nikola Banić of Lendava (fig.779).

779 Sword of the Ban Nikola Banić of Lendava, Croatia, 14th century
(Museum of Croatian History, Zagreb, Croatia)

This fine sword belonged to an important *Ban*, or Governor. Its light weight and virtually non-tapering shape suggest either that it would have been worn for personal protection in peace-time, and not while wearing full armour, or that lightly-armoured light cavalry tactics were already a feature of the eastern Balkans. If the latter is the case, then this may be seen as a forerunner of the later medieval Balkan cavalry sword known in Italy as *a la stradiotta*.

780 *Zagreb Cathedral Bible*, Croatia, early 14th century
(Metropolitan Library, Ms. MR-159, Zagreb, Croatia)

Once again soldiers in a Croatian source appear completely Western European, even down to their horses' *caparisons*. Only their lack of helmets or any rigid limb defences other than *poleyns* makes them look lightly equipped and old-fashioned. One head at the far left rear might have a slightly decorated, close-fitting *cervellière*.

781 St Krševan, wall-painting, Dalmatia, 13th century or later
(from Zara, now lost; after V. Brunelli, *Storia della citta di Zara*, Venice, 1913)

The saint is portrayed in an essentially Byzantine manner, but his thick lance with its more slender grip looks more 14th than 13th century.

782 Armorial bearing of Charles Thopia, bas-relief, Angevin Albania, mid-14th century
(*in situ* Church of St John Vladimir, near Elbasan, Albania)

Charles Thopia was lord of the Kruja and Petrela regions. His support for the Angevin Kingdom of Naples in its efforts to dominate

Albania are reflected in his adoption of the *fleur-de-lys* as part of his coat-of-arms. Whether pro-Angevin local rulers actually used such Western armour as the *great helm* shown above Thopia's equally Italian shield must remain doubtful.

783 **Seal, Bosnia, mid/late 14th century**
(National Museum, Sarajevo, Bosnia)

This seal is totally within the Western European, and more specifically Italian, tradition. The accuracy with which the mid to late 14th century armour and horse-harness is portrayed suggests that either the seal-maker was himself Italian, or that the ruling élite of Bosnia did indeed equip themselves in this manner.

Notes

1. G.A. Škrivanić, 'Armour and Weapons in Medieval Serbia, Bosnia and Dubrovnik', in Serbian with English summary, *Posedna Izdania* vol.CCXCIII (Belgrade, 1957), pp.203–4; V. Subotić, *Guide, Military Museum* (Belgrade, n.d.), pp.12–13.
2. D. Petrović, *Dubrovako Oružjie u XIV veku (Weapons of Dubrovnik in the 14th century)* with English summary (Belgrade, 1976), pp.278–9.
3. S. Shaw, *History of the Ottoman Empire and Modern Turkey, vol.1, 1280–1808* (Cambridge, 1978), pp.50–1; H. Inalcik, *The Ottoman Empire: The Classical Age 1300–1600* (London, 1973), p.11.
4. Petrović, *op.cit.* p.268.
5. D. Pribaković, 'O srednjovekovnom oružju na umetnikim spomenicima Hrvatske (Les Armes du Moyen Age sur les Monuments des Arts de la Croatie)', *Vesnik Vojnog Muzeja* vol.II (1955), pp.70–1.
6. Škrivanić, *op.cit.* p.204.
7. Petrović, *op.cit.* pp.263–4.
8. Petrović, *op.cit.* p.268.
9. D. Petrović, 'Fire-arms in the Balkans on the eve of and after the Ottoman Conquests of the fourteenth and fifteenth centuries', in *War, Technology and Society in the Middle East*, ed. V.J. Parry and M.E. Yapp (London, 1975), p.165.
10. K. Lako, 'Rezultatet e gërmimeve arkeologjik në Butrint në vitet 1975–76 (Fouilles archologiques 1975–76 dans la cit de Butrint)', *Iliria* vol.XI, no.l (1981), pp.32–5.
11. S. Pollo and A. Puto, *A History of Albania from its Origins to the Present Day* (London, 1981), pp.35–9.
12. Pollo and Puto, *op.cit.* pp.45–8.
13. P. Magdalino, *The History of Thessaly, 1266–1393* (Ph.D. thesis, Oxford University, 1976), p.67.
14. Pollo and Puto, *op.cit.* pp.48–50; J.F. Verbruggen, *The Art of Warfare in Western Europe during the Middle Ages* (Oxford, 1977), p.263.

Chapter 16

Hungary

The medieval Hungarian state was very large, and included many provinces inhabited by non-Magyar peoples, though some of these latter areas did have substantial Hungarian minorities. Many cities also included German minorities or could even be described as Germanic islands set in a Hungarian sea. In fact the Hungarian state had many of the characteristics of an empire. The most important non-Magyar regions were Transylvania (which had a mixed Hungarian, Romanian and German population), and Zips (Slovakia-Ruthenia), Croatia, Bosnia, Temesvar (northern Serbia), and northern Dalmatia, all of which were essentially Slav. Croatia, Bosnia and Dalmatia have already been discussed separately, as part of the Western Balkans (see chapter 15). To the east, Wallachia and Moldavia were for some time under Hungarian suzerainty, but this was relatively short-lived, and as a result these two Vlach-Rumanian principalities are considered part of the Eastern Balkans, covered in volume two.

The original Hungarians, or Magyars, were a nomadic people of basically Finno-Ugrian origin, though incorporating a large Turkic or Khazar element. After an era of intense warfare, in which the Magyars raided across much of Central Europe and the Germans tried to destroy the nascent Magyar state, the Magyars suffered a major military defeat at Lechfield in 955. Part of their military aristocracy was slaughtered by the victors following this battle, and from then on the Magyars were gradually integrated into Christian European civilisation.

Hungary officially became Christian in 1001 with the accession of its first king, Stefan. Previously it had been a duchy or principality. Western European feudal institutions were introduced and most of the élite came to adopt Western military systems and styles. While remaining on the defensive along its western frontier, the new Christian Kingdom of Hungary started to press against its northern, southern and eastern neighbours. Following the Magyars' first occupation of the Central Danubian Plain, their boundaries had rested on the crests of the Carpathians to the north, east and south-east, though there is some doubt about the effectiveness of Magyar control over eastern Transylvania. This was probably inhabited by semi-nomadic Vlach tribes.

To the south the Danube and Save rivers formed a frontier between Hungarian and Croatian, Serbian, Bulgarian and Byzantine territories. From the mid-10th century the western frontier incorporated Slovakia but not Moravia. It then ran slightly west of the present Hungarian-Austrian frontier, where it remained throughout the period under review. By the mid-13th century Croatia and Dalmatia had been drawn into the Hungarian kingdom by marriage alliance. Bosnia was conquered from the Serbs and western Wallachia lay under Hungarian suzerainty. Hungary next felt the full effect of the Mongol assault in 1241, but the country was never incorporated into the Mongol world empire. In fact Hungary recovered quite quickly, and during the 14th century developed into a powerful centralised state modelled almost entirely along Western lines. Bosnia was retaken, temporarily, in 1328, both Wallachia and Moldavia remaining under Hungarian suzerainty until the 1360s.

Traditional Magyar military styles had relied on a small tribal élite of cavalry; mostly lightly equipped horse-archers though a minority might have used heavier armour. Tactics were basically in the Eurasian steppe tradition,[1] though in the version characteristic of the western rather than eastern steppes. In addition early-medieval Hungary had many characteristics in common with Iran rather than with the Central Asian Turks. Bows were also closer to the Sassanian, Caucasian, Byzantine or early Islamic style than to the Turkish form,[2] as were several aspects of arms and armour.[3] There is also evidence to suggest that Magyar horse-archery tactics were closer to those of the Middle East than to those of Central Asia. In addition the early Magyars used quite sophisticated siege engines. Cultural as well as trade contacts with the Islamic world were, in fact, very important in 10th and 11th century Hungary.[4]

The first phase of 'Westernisation' from the 10th to 12th centuries probably only affected the royal household, mercenary troops, and the leading barons. Some sections of Magyar society, particularly in the Great Plain, remained tribal and at least transhumant if not strictly nomadic well into the 12th century.[5] But the majority of the population, especially in the Slav areas, had always been agricultural. Many Magyars also settled down, which in turn led to increasing feudalisation of the country and of the army. Light cavalry did not disappear but they declined in importance, while arms and armour became largely, but not entirely, Western European.[6]

The process of military 'Westernisation' was apparently more characteristic of the Slav provinces of the Hungarian kingdom. Here arms, armour and military traditions had never ceased to be within the wider European tradition. By the 12th century Hungary was making use of Balkan troops drawn from areas which had been under Western European influence since Carolingian times.[7] Despite a considerable Magyar impact, the military traditions of the northern Carpathian mountains also remained essentially Western.[8]

The same process could be seen in the 13th and 14th centuries. By then the traditional or steppe elements had been revived or reinforced by the migration of large numbers of Cuman (Kipchak) refugees into Hungary at the time of the Mongol invasions. Nevertheless, the dominant feudal nobility were almost indistinguishable from their German or Italian counterparts,[9] as were, of course, German settlers and German Teutonic Knights in such areas as Transylvania.

Hungary's long experience of warfare against nomads from the steppes just across the Carpathian mountains probably accounted for a continued employment of quantities of relatively lightly-armed horse-archers of various origins. The 13th century Hungarian army had, in fact, many characteristics in common with Byzantine forces.[10] Infantry crossbowmen played some part, though most such troops came from Slav areas such as Slovakia.[11] The crossbow then rapidly became popular throughout the kingdom, though even by the 15th century it had not completely ousted the composite hand-bow.[12] The Hungarians used other tactics associated with the peoples of the western steppes, such as wagons drawn up to form field fortifications,[13] although this particular idea may never have been abandoned since early Magyar times. Many so-called oriental features seen in late Hungarian armies are sometimes explained as betraying Ottoman influence, but the Hungarians hardly met the Ottomans face-to-face until the late 14th century. Meanwhile various features of late 14th and early 15th-century Ottoman military practice, such as the use of wagons as field fortifications and the adoption of firearms, could correspondingly be seen as examples of Hungarian influence.[14]

Figures

784 **Lance blade from Pécs-Üszog, Hungary, 10th–11th centuries**
(Archaeological Museum, Budapest, Hungary)

Many lance blades of extremely Central Asian form have been found in Hungary. This example has been associated with the Magyars, but similar types seem to have been used by the Avars in the 7th and 8th centuries. The Avars were, however, even more typical representatives of Eurasian steppe culture than were the Finno-Ugrian Magyars.

785 **Spearhead, Slovakia, 11th–12th centuries**
(location unknown; after Ruttkay)

This spear, which is clearly within the Western European tradition, comes from a Slav part of the Hungarian state and provides a clear contrast to the preceding weapon.

786 **Spearhead, Slovakia, 10th–12th centuries**
(Krajske Museum, Trnava, Slovakia)

This is in the same Western tradition as the previous example and comes from a similar region. Its form, with pronounced wings or flanges, suggests a fencing style of lance-play that might have been more suited to infantry warfare, in contrast to the more specifically cavalry weapon from Pécs-Üszog.

787 **Spearhead, Hungary, 9th–11th centuries**
(Military Museum, Budapest, Hungary)

It is possible that the Western European style of this weapon dates from the period of Slav revival under Carolingian rule that filled the interval between Charlemagne's crushing of the Avars at the end of the 8th century and the Magyar invasions of the 10th century. On the other hand subordinate Slav peoples retained their cultural identity within Hungary until absorbed by the Magyars many centuries later. Hence this weapon could date from as late as the 11th century.

788 **Spearhead, Slovakia, 10th–12th centuries**
(Okresné Museum, Topolcany, Slovakia)

Apart from the three decorative bands around the socket, this is a normal early medieval weapon probably designed for infantry use.

789 Spearhead, Slovakia, 12th–14th centuries
(Stadtausschuss, Myjava, Slovakia)

Like most weapons from Slovakia, this is typically European and shows no particularly Hungarian or Eurasian steppe characteristics.

790A–C Spearheads, Hungary, 11th–13th centuries
(National Museum, Budapest, Hungary)

These three spearheads illustrate the gradual Westernisation of Hungarian weapons. One example (A) still has some features associated with the Eurasian steppe style used in the early Migration Period, the second (B) is almost Western European in form, while the third (C) seems to have something in common with weapons from Eastern Europe and the Baltic States. There is, however, no reason to put these spearheads in any particular chronological order as it is clear that some Magyars retained their semi-nomadic way of life and their steppe culture long after tribes in other parts of the country had settled down.

791A–B Spearheads, Slovakia, 10th–12th centuries
(Krajske Museum, Trnava, Slovakia)

The similarity between one of these large broad-bladed spears (A), with its relatively small and feeble socket, and certain weapons from the Baltic States and Poland is obvious. The other (B) is more typically Western European and, with its stronger socket, seems to anticipate a more heavily-armoured foe.

792 Spearhead, Slovakia, 11th–12th centuries
(Archaeological Institute, Nitra, Slovakia)

This comes from an area close to the Moravian frontier. Its relatively-small size could indicate that it was a cavalry weapon, perhaps for use with the new couched style of lance-play.

793 Spear or pike head, Hungary, 11th–13th centuries
(National Museum, Budapest, Hungary)

The socket of this slender and long-bladed weapon is gilded. It was probably an infantry weapon, most likely from the 13th century.

794 Sabre from Székes-Fejérvar, Hungary, 10th–11th centuries
(National Museum, Budapest, Hungary)

This beautiful sabre has a non-tapering blade with an angled tip. In many respects it recalls some fine, and very much later, Japanese swords. The origins of both groups of weapons almost certainly lay in Central Asia. The bulbous *quillons* are of an unusual and probably early form.

795 **Sabre from Esztergom, Hungary, 10th–11th centuries**
(**Museum of Balassa Bálint, Esztergom, Hungary**)

Esztergom, which was founded as a bishopric in the year 1001, is not far
from Visegrád, the first capital of Hungary. Not surprisingly, some
magnificently decorated weapons have been found in the area, this sabre
being perhaps the finest. Curved *quillons* with bulbous ends, similar to
those depicted here, continued to be made for many years, and they were
clearly related to those on some of the earliest Islamic sabres.

796 **Sabre, Hungary, 11th–12th centuries**
(**replica, Military Museum, Budapest, Hungary**)

A simpler and probably slightly later weapon still has *quillons* related
to those of the magnificent Esztergom sabre. The blade is, however, of
a later form with a broadened tip and angled back, designed to
deliver a more powerful blow. Such weapons were characteristic of
the Middle East from the 12th century onwards and were presumably
developed in response to a wider use of armour.

797A–C **Bronze mace heads, Hungary, 11th–13th centuries**
(**National Museum, Budapest, Hungary**)

Relatively small bronze mace heads appear to have been popular in
many parts of Eastern Europe. Such weapons would not have been very
effective against a heavily-armoured foe, and as such are likely to have
been used by poorer warriors, ordinary tribesmen among the Magyars
of the Hungarian plains, or peasant villagers in the Slav areas.

798 **Sabre, Hungary, 11th century**
(**National Museum, Budapest, Hungary**)

The cultural connection between medieval Hungary, the Turkic
nations, and the world of Islam is demonstrated by this sabre. Not
only is it a typical weapon of nomadic steppe peoples but its
asymmetrical *quillons* and the short sleeve covering part of the blade
below them are features seen, either together or separately, in
surviving weapons and in art from Western Asia and the Middle East.

799 **Sword, Hungary, 10th–11th centuries**
(**Archaeological Museum, Pécs, Hungary**)

Coming from the south of Hungary where the population remained
mixed for many years, this type of sword is normally associated with
Slavs, but may also have been adopted by some Magyars.

800 **Sword, Hungary, 10th–11th centuries**
(**Military Museum, Budapest, Hungary**)

Like the previous example, this weapon may be seen as evidence of
the gradual Europeanisation, and more specifically Germanisation,
of Hungarian arms, armour, armies and military organisation.

801A–C Swords, Hungary, 11th–13th centuries
(National Museum, Budapest, Hungary)

The gradual spread of German and Slav influence across Hungary is again confirmed by these slightly later swords. Their generally straight, relatively long *quillons*, and their nut-shaped or oval *pommels*, are all in the Western European tradition. One weapon is, however, basically single-edged (C) or has priority given to one edge. This might reflect the survival of a sabre style of sword-play among Hungarian horsemen. It could also be seen as evidence of Scandinavian influence, as such weapons were also seen in the far North in the 10th century. More likely, however, the presence of such weapons in Scandinavia reflects Magyar or Eastern European ideas, or even weapons brought back to Norway and Sweden by returning Vikings.

802 Sword, Slovakia, 11th–12th centuries
(Vlastivedné Museum, Bojnice, Slovakia)

A very typical Western European sword, perhaps made in Germany, although there was also a flourishing iron industry in neighbouring Bohemia.

803 Sword, Slovakia, late 11th–12th centuries
(Danubian Museum, Komárno, Slovakia)

This sword appears to be slightly later than the previous example, having curved *quillons* and a more tapering blade.

804 Sword, Slovakia, 11th–12th centuries
(Stadtausschuss, Myjava, Slovakia)

Although broken, this is a fine example of the INGELRII swords found over much of Central and Eastern Europe. The other side of the blade has a more worn inscription which appears to consist mostly of patterns.

805 Sword from Zipser Komitat area, 11th–12th centuries
(National Museum, Budapest, Hungary)

Although almost certainly having a similar date to the preceding swords, this weapon has a shorter grip and a less tapering, blunter-tipped blade. As such it seems to have features in common with swords in medieval art from Italy and other Mediterranean regions.

806 Helmet, Hungary, 10th–11th centuries
(Archaeological Museum, Pécs, Hungary)

This helmet is made of directly riveted segments, some of the joints being decorated with copper or gilt filets placed between the iron segments. Such helmets had a finial or plume holder on top and would have had a mail *aventail*. They are clearly related to the so-called 'Great Polish' style of helmets, as well as to other eastern European and Russian examples. The origins of all such helmets are to be found in Central Asia.

807 Arrowheads, Hungary, 11th–13th centuries
(National Museum, Budapest, Hungary)

All the arrowheads in this varied collection are of the tanged rather than the socket type. Clearly the Central Asian traditions of the Magyars survived longer in archery equipment than in most other aspects of Hungarian military technology. Some of the blades are very broad and almost identical to arrowheads from the Eurasian steppes. Others are square or diamond-shaped in section and are clearly designed to penetrate shields or armour.

808 Arrowhead, Slovakia, 11th–12th centuries
(Okresne Museum, Topolčany, Slovakia)

Arrowheads from the Slav region of Slovakia are very different from those of Magyar areas to the south. They are of the socket instead of the tang type and often have broad barbed heads.

809 Sword, Hungary, 12th century
(Military Museum, Budapest, Hungary)

The later form of typically European sword is in complete contrast with the Kun sabre described below (fig.810). Such swords were, by the 12th century, the normal weapons of the Hungarian military aristocracy, who had almost totally adopted Western feudalism and its associated military systems.

810 Sabre, Hungary, 12th–13th centuries
(Military Museum, Budapest, Hungary)

This was used by one of the Kun, which was the name given to those Turkish Pecheneg tribes which fled into Hungary and then settled there. For several centuries they retained a separate identity and maintained a transhumant pastoral way of life comparable to that of the original Magyars. This long, slender sabre is a typical Turco-Mongol type of weapon, although the uncharacteristically long *quillons* may be a local development following the Kuns' settlement in Hungary.

811 Relief carving on a gravestone from Vranjevo, Vojvodina, 11th century
(National Museum, Budapest, Hungary)

Probably dating from the early part of the 11th century, this is one of the oldest surviving pieces of Hungarian carving. It portrays a nobleman wearing a fluted cap or helmet, perhaps with a cloth wound around it. Such fashions are unlike those of neighbouring peoples and might reflect Hungary's persistently strong cultural contacts with the Eurasian steppes and beyond.

812 **Arrowhead from Keszthely, Hungary, 11th–13th centuries**
(location unknown; after Hampel)

This large socket-type arrowhead comes from the western end of Lake Balaton, an area that retained a Slav character and Slav minority well into the Middle Ages. Generally speaking such minorities survived in hillier areas, while the originally nomadic Magyars dominated the wide plains.

813 **Axehead, Hungary, 11th–13th centuries**
(National Museum, Budapest, Hungary)

Relatively light, narrow-bladed axes are found in many parts of Eastern and Central Europe. The fact that comparable weapons are equally common in the Eurasian steppes suggests that they were introduced into Europe by nomadic conquerors such as the Huns, Avars or Magyars.

814A–B **Helmet of possible Iranian or Mongol origin, Hungary, 12th–13th centuries**
(National Museum, Budapest, Hungary)

A – present condition of helmet; B – engraved surface decoration of the helmet. The exquisite surface decoration on this helmet seems to combine motifs from Islamic metalwork with fanciful birds of Central Asian origin. The complete lack of Arabic inscriptions makes an Islamic origin unlikely unless the helmet was made specifically for export. Otherwise the decoration and, above all, the small peak at the front suggest an early 13th century Mongol origin.

815 **Helmet, Hungary, 12th–13th centuries**
(National Museum, Budapest, Hungary)

This helmet is basically a *cervellière*. Its construction is very similar to that of many *chapel-de-fer war-hats*, except that it lacks a brim.

816 **Possible fragment of a helmet from Ducové, Slovakia, 12th/early 13th centuries**
(Archaeological Institute, Nitra, Slovakia)

This iron object looks too massive to be a helmet since its plume or crest would have been almost 3 cm across. It could, however, have been the top of an early form of *great helm*. Its construction is directly riveted, and in some ways recalls the so-called 'Great Polish' type of helmet. This object could also have been part of a lantern.

817A–C **Spearheads, Slovakia, 12th–14th centuries**
(Local Museum, Trenčín, Slovakia)

These weapons are normally regarded as spearheads. This is almost certainly true of one example (A) and may be true of a second (B).

However, the third (C) is different in form. Whereas the first two look like infantry weapons, the third has the appearance either of a cavalry lance head or perhaps another example of a large bolt head, to be shot from a siege bow.

818 Sword, Hungary, 12th century
(National Museum, Budapest, Hungary)

A typical European sword of the type which, like the previous example (fig.809), was adopted by the Hungarian knightly class.

819 Sword, Hungary, mid-13th century
(National Museum, Budapest, Hungary)

The similarity between this weapon and some from Slovakia is clear. All were probably made in Germany.

820A–B Parts of two knife sheaths, Slovakia, 12th/early 13th
centuries
(Archaeological Institute, Nitra, Slovakia)

These metal stiffeners also served to protect the sheath from the single cutting edge of the weapon. They are, however, too small to be from dagger sheaths and almost certainly were for a kind of working knife.

821 Sword from Dehá nad Váhom, Slovakia, late 12th/early
13th centuries
(Archaeological Institute, Nitra, Slovakia)

The many 13th-century swords found in Slovakia provide an interesting survey of Central European types. Many were probably made in the Rhineland for export. Their blades are now longer, more slender with thrusting points and much narrower *fullers*, or grooves, down their blades. Such *fullers* often extended for two-thirds of the weapon's length, as in this example.

822 Sword from Kostolná-Zárieĉie, Slovakia, 12th century
(Local Lore Museum, Trenĉín, Slovakia)

In most respects identical to the previous example, its bent hilt is a result of damage.

823 Sword from Skýcov, Slovakia, late 12th/13th centuries
(private collection of E. Ĉerňanský, Nitra, Slovakia)

This type of sword has a groove running the full length of the blade. Its later date is also indicated by long curved *quillons* and rather unusual hat-like *pommel*.

824 **Arrow or crossbow bolt head, Slovakia, 12th–13th
  centuries**
(**Archaeological Institute, Nitra, Slovakia**)

This weapon was clearly designed to penetrate armour. The fact that
it has a tang rather than a socket could indicate Magyar influence,
but such bolt heads were also seen elsewhere in Europe by the 13th
and 14th centuries.

825 **Arrowhead, Slovakia, 12th–14th centuries**
(**Bezirksmuseum, Hlohovec, Slovakia**)

The dating of the arrowhead is conjectural. It is, however, of the
Western socket type, but has a narrow blade to penetrate armour or
shields.

826A–D **Arrowheads, Slovakia, 12th–14th centuries**
(**Považské Museum, Žilina, Slovakia**)

These weapons come from Central Slovakia, from a region of
mountains and narrow valleys that was never effectively settled by
Magyars. Nevertheless, two of the arrowheads (B and C) are of the
tanged type with diamond-shaped heads which place them firmly
within the steppe horse-archery tradition. They might, of course,
have been used by a local Hungarian Magyar or even a Kun garrison.
Or they could indicate the spread of Hungarian archery technology
into Slav areas such as Slovakia. The other two arrowheads (A and
D), with their sockets and barbs, are within the Western archery
tradition.

827A–C **Arrowheads, Slovakia, 13th–15th centuries**
(**locations unknown, after Ruttkay**)

These arrowheads probably represent the end of the influence of
steppe archery techniques in Slovakia. One (A) is a well-made and
typical tang-type armour-piercing arrowhead, but the other two (B
and C) are rather degenerate forms with feeble tangs.

828 **Head of a javelin or a large crossbow bolt, Slovakia,
  12th–14th centuries**
(**Local Museum, Trenčín, Slovakia**)

An unusually large barbed head which might have been used on a
javelin, if such weapons were still in use, or which could have formed
part of a large crossbow bolt to be shot from a frame-mounted siege
bow.

829A–B **Bronze *aquamanile*, Hungary, 12th century**
(**National Museum, Budapest, Hungary**)

Aquamaniles of this kind, particularly having stylised hunting cats
behind the rider's saddle, are clearly based on Islamic prototypes.

This example, based on an Iranian-Islamic original, has lost its lid and handle and thus the rider appears without a helmet. His right arm is also missing, but his tall kite-shaped shield with its central boss is clearly displayed.

830 Bronze *aquamanile*, Hungary, 12th century
(National Museum, Budapest, Hungary)

Though the figure is crudely portrayed, the rider clearly has a conical helmet. Its very pointed outline and vertical divisions strongly suggest a directly riveted helmet of the so-called 'Great Polish' type. His tunic might be a long-sleeved *hauberk*, and on his left arm he carries a large, kite-shaped shield.

831 Helmet, Cuman–Kun, 13th century
(National Museum, Budapest, Hungary)

This low-domed helmet, which is basically made from one piece of iron plus a plume holder or finial and a deep reinforcing rim, was used by one of those warriors who fled into Hungary from the Ukraine ahead of the Mongols. It is clearly related in style and structure to various Iranian helmets.

832A–B Carved capitals from Pécs Cathedral, Hungary, mid-12th century
(Stonework Museum, Pécs, Hungary)

Relatively little representational carving survives from early medieval Hungary. These fragments show weapons which are in typically Western European style, and the stonemasons themselves may well have been non-Hungarian. The axe (A) is held by a Centaur, while the tapering sword with its straight *quillons* and flattened nut-shaped *pommel* is carried by an angel during the expulsion of Adam and Eve from Paradise.

833 Carved capital, Hungary, late 12th century
(*in situ* south portal of the Royal Chapel Palace of Bela III, Esztergom, Hungary)

This left-handed infantry archer might have been balanced by another lost figure. The bow might be of a recurved composite form.

834 'Huntsman', carved capital, Slovakia, c.1170–90
(*in situ* Praemonstratensian Church, Biňa, Slovakia)

The archer, who seems to be in danger of shooting his own thumb, uses a finger-draw. There is no indication of a recurved shape and thus of composite construction in his simple bow. As such there is no evidence of influence by the Magyars or any other nation of steppe nomads or horse-archers.

835A–H ***Gebhard Bible*, Hungary or Germany, mid-12th century**
(**Church of St Petrus, Csatar; after Gerevich**)

A – Israelites; B–D – Philistines; E – King Saul; F–H – Israelites. The *Gebhard Bible* seems to reflect a small degree of Byzantine influence. This is most apparent in the archaised armour of some Philistines (C and D), which seems to include splinted upper-arm defences. These might be dismissed as fanciful were they not to appear again in a later and generally more reliable Hungarian manuscript (fig.888). The *Gebhard Bible* otherwise shows standard European equipment of conical helmets with *nasals* (B, F and G), long-sleeved *hauberks* (A, B, E, G and H), kite-shaped shields with or without large decorative bosses (B, D, E and H), straight, barely tapering swords with straight *quillons* (C, E, G and H), and a couched lance with a *gonfanon* (A). The only slightly unusual features are a number of helmets, both conical and round, which appear to be of two-piece construction joined along a comb with a broad rim band (A, D and H). Such helmets are, of course, also known elsewhere in 12th century Western Europe.

836 Donor wall-painting, Slovakia, c.1200
(***in situ*** **church, Dechtice, Slovakia**)

This donor figure appears to have a broad, flat-topped kite-shaped shield hanging below his left shoulder.

837 Sword, Slovakia, 13th century
(**Danubian Museum, Komárno, Slovakia**)

A typical mid or late 13th century sword, except for its peculiar flat *pommel*.

838 Gold mountings of a sword belt, Kipchak, 13th century
(**National Museum, Budapest, Hungary**)

Though found in a Kipchak site, this belt is entirely European in design. The fact that such belts were used by the Kipchak may indicate a gradual adoption of Western techniques, or simply show that the owner had accepted the status of 'knight' and was probably regarded as such by his Hungarian overlords.

839 Sword, Slovakia, late 13th/early 14th centuries
(**Gemerské Museum, Rimavská Sobota, Slovakia**)

The spread of essentially German military influence throughout the Hungarian state is shown by the presence of a modern form of very pointed thrusting sword with long *quillons*, long grip, and a highly-decorated *pommel*, which appeared even in the mountainous east of Slovakia.

840 Sword, Slovakia, late 13th century
(Danubian Museum, Komárno, Slovakia)

The fertile Danube valley was in some respects the heartland of the medieval Hungarian state, particularly after the adoption of Western European feudal political and military systems. This is a typical European sword from the area.

841 Sword from Trenčín, Slovakia, late 13th/early 14th centuries
(Local Museum, Trenčín, Slovakia)

Though longer and narrower than other similarly dated weapons, this sword has a relatively thick blade clearly intended for thrusting, designed to counter newly adopted plate armour.

842A–C Swords, Hungary, 13th/early 14th centuries
(National Museum, Budapest, Hungary)

These swords from Hungary itself show the same variety of forms as those found in Slovakia, thus illustrating a high degree of military uniformity across the central and northern parts of the medieval state. Two probably date from the late 13th or early 14th centuries (A and B), while the third (C) might date from the early or mid-13th century.

843 Sword from Ploštin, Slovakia, c.1250–1300
(Slovak National Museum, Martin, Slovakia)

This sword, although damaged, is in most respects identical to one of the above examples.

844A–B Swords, Slovakia, c.1250–1300
(Danubian Museum, Komárno, Slovakia)

The *quillons* of one of these swords appear to have been reversed (B). Otherwise they are remarkably similar to examples found on the Hungarian side of the frontier.

845 War-axe from Vršatské Podhradie, Slovakia, late 13th/14th centuries
(location unknown; after Ruttkay)

Narrow-bladed axes of this type, though known elsewhere in Europe, seem to have been particularly popular in the Slavonic east. This example is a late development of a long-lived traditional form and was probably for use on horseback.

846 Sword, Slovakia, 13th century
(Danubian Museum, Komárno, Slovakia)

This broken blade, which also lacks a hilt, is exactly the same type as the example depicted in fig.844.

847 Sword from Husiná, Slovakia, 13th century
(Gemerské Museum, Rimavská Sobota, Slovakia)

Basically the same form again, though with a slightly wider *fuller*. Its *pommel* is different and unusual.

**848 Sword from Kálna nad Hronom, Slovakia, late
   13th/early 14th centuries**
(Tekov Museum, Levice, Slovakia)

The narrow, tapering and relatively short blade of this weapon indicates a later date. The grip is also longer, and the round *pommel* larger.

849 Sword from Myjava, Slovakia, mid-13th century
(Slovak National Museum, Martin, Slovakia)

The *pommel* of this sword is reminiscent of some seen on statues in Naumberg Cathedral in Germany. Like many Slovakian swords it was probably imported from Germany.

850 Sword from Červenik, Slovakia, 13th century
(Okresne Museum, Hlohovec, Slovakia)

The outline and wide *fuller* of this broken blade suggest a date in the first half of the 13th century.

851 Sword, Hungary, 13th century
(Military Museum, Budapest, Hungary)

Though very similar to the preceding example, this sword has an ordinary round *pommel*.

852 Sword, Hungary, late 13th/early 14th centuries
(National Museum, Budapest, Hungary)

Many of the swords of the late 13th and 14th centuries tended to have longer grips. This does not indicate that they could be used with two hands, but might have something to do with the introduction of the plated *gauntlet*.

**853 Sword from Mužla, Slovakia, late 13th/early 14th
   centuries**
(Archaeological Institute, Nitra, Slovakia)

Another example of the later style with a longer grip.

854A–B Axes, Hungary, 13th–14th centuries
(National Museum, Budapest, Hungary)

These two axes seem to stem from very different traditions, both of which are unlike the narrow-bladed form seem above (fig.845). The first example finds parallels in the northern European 'Danish' axes of an earlier period, while the second (B) has similarities with some Polish weapons.

855A–C **Spear or pike heads, Hungary, 13th–14th centuries**
(**National Museum, Budapest, Hungary**)

Three very different types of spearheads, probably from infantry weapons. Two are quite traditional (B and C). Another may be an echo of the Magyars' steppe nomadic past or have been introduced by the Kun.

856A–B **Swords from Dlhá and Váhom, Slovakia, late 13th/early 14th centuries**
(**Archaeological Institute, Nitra, Slovakia**)

One figure (A) is probably earlier than the other (B). The main differences are in the increased length of later *quillons*. The fact that so many of these swords have lost the lower parts of their blades, but are otherwise largely undamaged, suggests that in battle such weapons often broke against the increasingly strong armour of the period.

857 **Sword from Trenčín, Slovakia, c.1250–1300**
(**Local Museum, Trenčín, Slovakia**)

In most respects this is a typical late 13th century sword. The *quillons* are, however, shorter and thicker than normal. Perhaps they were a locally-made replacement following damage to the original *quillons*.

858A–F **Spear-heads, Kipchak, 13th century**
(**National Museum, Budapest, Hungary**)

These weapons clearly betray the Kipchaks' background in the Eurasian steppes, although the fact that four of them (B–E) have long, strong sockets and in some cases very narrow blades indicates that an armoured enemy was expected.

859A–E **Mace heads, Kipchak, 13th century**
(**National Museum, Budapest, Hungary**)

These relatively small mace heads are to all intents and purposes identical to examples found in non-Kipchak sites across much of the medieval Hungarian state. Whether they were adopted by the Kipchaks from the Magyars, or whether their spread was encouraged by the Kipchak newcomers, is unclear.

860A–B **Spearheads, Slovakia, 12th–14th centuries**
(**Local Museum, Trenčín, Slovakia**)

The dating of these spearheads is conjectural. Clearly one (A) is strongly built, presumably being designed to penetrate armour. The other (B) is decorated with inlay and may have had an heraldic or ceremonial function. It is similar to certain weapons from the Baltic regions.

861A–H Bronze mace heads, Hungary, 13th–15th centuries
(Military Museum, Budapest, Hungary)

No full study has yet been made of the relatively small maces, usually of bronze, that were so widely used throughout Eastern Europe. The dating of these examples remains doubtful. They do, however, seem to have remained in use for many centuries and to have been popular among the horse-raising semi-nomadic peoples of the Great Hungarian Plain.

862A–H Arrowheads, Hungary, 13th–14th centuries
(National Museum, Budapest, Hungary)

All these arrowheads appear to be of the tanged variety. This places them in the Eurasian steppe tradition. Yet the majority have very narrow heads with sharply-angled blades. None is of the leaf-shaped variety so popular among the true steppe nomads. As such they probably indicate that the horse-archery techniques of the Magyars and Kun had been modified in the face of heavy Western European plate armour.

863A–D Crossbow-bolts, Hungary, 13th–14th centuries
(National Museum, Budapest, Hungary)

These bolts have heavy heads of diamond section, clearly designed to puncture armour. The bolt flights are of wood. Such weapons would have been used by troops from settled village areas or cities, but not by the semi-nomadic peoples of the plains.

864A–G Gold mounts of a sword-belt, Hungary, 13th century
(National Museum, Budapest, Hungary)

A–F – engraved gold plate attached to the buckle; G – part of the belt showing buckle, engraved plate, one decorative stud and one stiffener-fastening eyelet. This magnificent sword-belt is not only interesting in its own right, but it also provides one of the most detailed pictures of 13th-century Hungarian warriors from the new feudalised aristocracy. There seem to be no representatives of the traditional semi-nomadic Magyar way of life on this piece of metalwork even though some sections of Hungarian society apparently clung to these old ways. However, three fully-armoured knights are shown (B, D and F). They wear flat-topped *great helms*, two with large crests. They have long-sleeved mail *hauberks*, probably with integral *coifs*, as does a fourth unhelmeted figure (A). The goldsmith seems to indicate that their *mittens* are of a different substance (A, B, D and F), and although these might be of padded or leather construction the distinction between *mittens* and sleeves is probably merely a result of the artist trying to avoid visual confusion. Mail *chausses* are worn (B, D and F), perhaps beneath padded or leather *cuisses* for the thighs and knees. Shields are relatively small, flat-topped, and kite-shaped, supported by *guiges*. Two of the three swords are clearly tapering (D and F), while the third, though pointed, has more parallel sides. The *pommels* may be round (B and F), while one seems to be diamond-shaped (D). Two horses have *caparisons* or *bards* (B and F). In the background are a trumpeter and a drummer. The presence of the latter may be a survival from the Magyars' past, as war-drums were a typical feature of almost all Turco-Mongol and other armies from the steppes.

865 Fragments of a mail shirt with shoulder plates, plus a gold mounted sword-belt, Kipchak, 13th century
(National Museum, Budapest, Hungary)

The original shape of this completely fused and smashed mail shirt is impossible to determine but the amount of surviving mail suggests that it was quite small, perhaps being similar to examples from the Ukraine. The fact that it also included a pair of shoulder-protecting plate *epaulettes* is potentially very important. Such pieces of plate were not seen on Western armour until the 14th century, which may be taken as further evidence that the European *coat-of-plates* with which such *epaulettes* are normally associated was inspired by, if not directly copied from, various forms of Turco-Mongol body-armour. The gold belt mounts found with this mail *hauberk* are from a typically European sword belt.

866A–U Arrowheads, Kipchak, 13th century
(National Museum, Budapest, Hungary)

The mixture of arrowheads in this collection indicates that the Kipchak Cumans took some ideas, or at least some available arrows, from their predecessors in Hungary. At least ten are of the typically Western or Slav socket type (A–D, N–R and U). The remainder are of the tanged type (E–M, S and T). Two arrows, one with a tang (F) and one with a socket (P), are also of the broad barbed type generally associated with Western styles of archery.

867 Seal of Istvan Király, Hungary, c.1270–2
(Budapest Historical Museum, Budapest, Hungary)

On his seal this Hungarian prince is shown as a typical European knight. Only the knotting of his horse's tail in Turkish fashion sets him slightly apart. He has a flat-topped *great helm* and a mail *coif* is visible at his neck. He carries a flat-topped almost triangular shield and holds his lance in the couched manner.

868 Axe, Slovakia, 14th century
(Krajske Museum, Trnava, Slovakia)

The long narrow blade of the axe suggests a late development of a typical Eastern European weapon, but the thickness of the blade makes it look like a work-tool. Perhaps the latter feature was in response to the increasing strength of armour.

869 Axe from Zemianske Podhradie, Slovakia, 14th century
(Slovakian National Museum, Martin, Slovakia)

This axe also has a very thick blade, but the magnificence of its decoration points to it being a weapon, and a ceremonial one at that.

870A–I Axes, Slovakia, c.1300–50
(Danubian Museum, Komárno, Slovakia)

The majority of these war-axes are within the long, narrow-bladed East European or Slav tradition (A, B, E, G and I). Two appear to have war-hammers on the back (B and E). Other axes are developments of the late-medieval Western European type, ranging from an extreme example (D) to weapons with lesser 'beards' (C, F and H). None of this latter form have hammers at the back.

871A–C War-axes, Hungary, 14th century
(Budapest Historical Museum, Budapest, Hungary)

These three axes are typical Central or even Western European infantry weapons. This is particularly true of the example with an upwards-swept blade and a thrusting point (C). One axe is unusual in having a hammerhead on the back (B).

872A–B Javelin heads (?), Slovakia, 14th century
(Slovak National Museum, Bratislava, Slovakia)

These large heads with their extended sockets may come from javelins, perhaps to be used in siege warfare, or from bolts to be shot from large, frame-mounted siege crossbows.

873A–C Arrow or crossbow-bolt heads, Slovakia, 14th century
(Slovak National Museum, Martin, Slovakia)

These crude, rather peculiar objects, may have come from crossbow bolts and have been designed to puncture armour.

874A–B Arrowheads, Slovakia, c.1300–50
(Danubian Museum, Komárno, Slovakia)

Of these arrowheads of the socket type, one is probably for use in war (A), the second probably for hunting (B).

875A–G Arrowheads, Slovakia, 14th century
(Local Museum, Smolenice, Slovakia)

The survival of early Eurasian steppe-style tanged arrowheads into 14th century Slovakia is in some ways remarkable. It is also worth noting that the tanged type (A–C) are very much smaller than the socket variety (D–G). The latter are so large that they are likely to have been used on crossbow bolts.

876A–G Spearheads, Slovakia, c.1300–50
(Danubian Museum, Komárno, Slovakia)

A varied collection of spearheads includes conventional types (A and F), a very narrow-bladed form (B), and narrow but substantially built types with very strong sockets, perhaps for use by cavalry (C and D). An unusual spindle-like blade (E) may have been part of a larger weapon, while an equally unusual broad blade has a tang instead of a socket (G). Perhaps this latter was for use with a haft of reed, such plants being common in certain parts of the Danube basin.

877 Caltrop, Slovakia, c.1300–50
(Tekov Museum, Levice, Slovakia)

A rare surviving example of a device scattered around an army's encampment or in front of a rank of infantry to impede an enemy attack, particularly if a mounted enemy was expected.

878A–B Mace heads, Slovakia, c.1300–50
(Tekov Museum, Levice, Slovakia)

Two further examples of the light mace heads popular throughout much of the medieval Hungarian state.

879 Arrowhead, Slovakia, 14th century
(Slovak National Museum, Bratislava, Slovakia)

Another late example of the slender armour-piercing tang-type of arrow or a crossbow-bolt head. Such heads may well have been interchangeable even during battle.

880 Relief carving, Hungary, early 13th century
(*in situ* Praemonstratensian Church, Jánoshida, Hungary)

A very damaged carving forming part of a once collapsed and now rebuilt door. It shows a warrior in a full mail *hauberk* and mail *chausses*, with a long straight sword hung from a broad sword-belt.

881 Enamelled bronze plate, Hungary (?), 13th century
(National Museum, Budapest, Hungary)

It is not clear whether this plate was made in Hungary or was imported from the West. It shows a huntsman holding a large round shield with a single central grip.

882A–F Wall-painting, Hungary, early 14th century
(from Homoradszentmarton, now destroyed; after Ruttkay)

The figures in this wall-painting were all armoured in Western

European fashion, with pointed helmets (C–F). Their mail *hauberks* have *coifs*, one of which partly covered the face (E), plus long (B) or short (E) sleeves. A broad, straight sword was also shown (F), but a second sword (B) seems to have been very slender and slightly tapering. Two figures also have bowcases – accurately drawn and correctly angled – on their left hips (A and C). The horse-harness also accurately reflects that of the Eurasian steppes.

883 Kipchak Cumans, 'Legend of St Ladislas', wall-painting, Slovakia, c.1370
(*in situ* Evangelical Church, Rimavská Baňa, Slovakia)

Here a portrayal of horse-archers shows considerable familiarity with such troops, except that their composite recurved bows are being used left-handed. This may be an example of artistic licence resulting from the composition of the picture. The front archer has an accurately drawn box-type quiver on his hip.

884 Coin of King Andrew II, Hungary, 1205–35
(after Ruttkay)

The coin is both simple and worn. Nevertheless, it clearly shows a man with a long, flat-topped kite-shaped shield and a straight sword.

885 Coin of King Bela IV, Hungary, 1235–70
(after Ruttkay)

Bela IV holds a spear rather than a sword and his shield, in common with the changing style of those found in mid and late 13th century Europe, is shorter and more triangular in shape.

886A–C 'The Betrayal', wall-painting, Slovakia, c.1370
(*in situ* church, Zehra, Slovakia)

In an east Slovakian painting two warriors wear almost late-Byzantine style pointed and brimmed *war-hats* with mail *coifs* (B–C). The third figure (A) has a mail *hauberk* and mid-length sleeves, perhaps with plated *epaulettes*.

887A–I 'Legend of St Ladislas', wall-painting, Slovakia, c.1300
(*in situ* church, Velká Lomnica, Slovakia)

The story of St Ladislas, King of Hungary (1077–95), was a popular subject for wall-paintings throughout the medieval Hungarian state (see also fig.883), but most surviving examples are found outside the boundaries of modern Hungary, in Slovakia and Romanian Transylvania. The subject depicted here shows the royal saint rescuing a maiden from a Kipchak invader. The young lady then assists her hero in slaying the unfortunate Turk. The presence of whole tribes of Kipchak refugees in 13th and 14th century Hungary means that the invaders in these wall-paintings are almost inevitably based upon such nomads. Ladislas himself is shown with a couched lance and flat-topped kite-shaped shield (A). He wears a long *surcoat* over probably mailed *chausses* having plated *poleyns* (C), and with a 'ballock dagger' on his right hip (C and F). The Kipchak is naturally shown as a horse-archer with a recurved composite bow and the box-type quiver normal among Eurasian steppe peoples (B). He wears a peculiar, almost winged hat, with a *coif* (B and D). The construction of this headgear is a bit of a mystery, for when it is removed in the last scene (I) the *coif* comes off with it. The spirited maiden contributes to her own rescue by striking the Kipchak in the ankle with an axe (E) and subsequently helps to decapitate him with his own curved sabre (H).

888A–S *Hungarian National Chronicle*, **Hungary, c.1360** (**National Széchényi Library, Ms. Clmae 404, Budapest, Hungary**)

A–B – Subjects of King Louis I, f.1; C–E – Huns arrive in Pannonia, f.4a; F – Mongols defeat King Bela, f.63b; G–I – Ladislas and the Cuman abductor, f.36a; J – Kund, the fourth Magyar champion, f.13a; K – Another Magyar champion, f.13a; L – Arpad and the champions of the Magyar Conquest, f.12a; M – Carol Robert, Governor of Bessarabia-Moldavia; N – King Stephen; O – Battle of Rozgony; P – Hungarians oppose the Crusaders of Conrad III and Louis VII; Q – Axe of Prince Geza; R–S – Arpad arrives in Pannonia, f.11. The *Hungarian National Chronicle*, though painted in a very Italian style, is an invaluable source for the arms and armour of 14th century Hungary, including various subject and tributary regions. The eastern origins of the Magyar people are emphasised by giving some of the figures slightly oriental or Byzantine military equipment. Basically, however, the Hungarians are shown in typical mid-14th century arms and armour. This normally includes a *bascinet* and mail *aventail* (A, G, I, L and S), once also shown with a large visor (O). Variations include decorations and crests (A) or a hat worn over the *bascinet* (S). A long-sleeved mail *hauberk* is generally worn with *gauntlets*, under a *coat-of-plates* (A, G, I, J, L–O, R and S). Many figures also wear full Western European leg-harness of mail *chausses* and plate *cuisses*, *poleyns*, *greaves* and *sabatons* (A, I, M, O and S). One figure (N) appears to have laminated *sabatons* and some other form of *chausses* which are shown in a different colour. He also has a different surface texture to his mail *hauberk*. Also note that the horizontal lines on this man's *surcoat* are heraldic and are not concerned with the structure of his *coat-of-plates*. Another typically mid-14th century Western feature are the roughly square shields with lance rests in the top corner (A, G, K, L, N, O and S). These are not only carried by men in typically Western armour, but also by others (K). Most swords are characteristically straight, tapering, long-hilted and long-*quilloned*

European weapons (A, J, K, L–N and S). Spears are similarly unremarkable, while daggers are notably absent. A large, long-hafted axe (Q) is probably more symbolic than real, but reflects the *guisarmes* of the 13th century. Non-Western features include curved sabres which are specifically associated with people of Turkic origin, either the Kipchak–Kun subjects of Louis the Great (B) or the Mongols who defeat King Bela (F). Horse-archery and recurved composite bows are also associated with such peoples, but not invariably so (B, G and P). The artist seems to make it clear that horse-archers were regarded as a normal part of the Hungarian army. People whose culture was still within that of the Eurasian steppe tradition, whether they are enemies or allies of the Hungarians, are distinguished by such costume features as ankle-length double-breasted coats (B, F, I and J), abundantly long sleeves (R), and various pointed, fur, upturned, brimmed and otherwise exotic hats (B, F, G, H, J, K, R and S). The central chest medallion, which remains a largely unexplained feature, seems to have been adopted from the Mongols, amongst whom it might have had an heraldic function (B, K, R and S). It was similarly adopted in many regions of the Islamic world in the post-Mongol period. The unusual or non-Western European armour may shed light on some of the fringes of the Hungarian state, particularly those in the Byzantine-influenced east and south. These variations include helmet crests (A), pointed helmets of Asiatic form (E), helmets with *aventails* that hang like curtains on the sides and back of the head rather than also covering the wearer's throat (E and L), *chapel-de-fer war-hats* (E) and other helmets with broad rims (D, J and L). The presence of splinted arm protections hanging from shoulder *roundels* or *epaulettes* is a bit of a problem (A, E, R and S). Some examples might be unrealistic Byzantine archaism, but here they are worn by the contemporary Hungarian nobility (A), by 'Huns' (E), perhaps by Arpad the Conqueror himself (R), and by his early Magyar followers (S). Perhaps such pieces of military costume survived in the Balkans even into the 14th century as marks of rank or status. As such they would have continued the old Byzantine tradition of coloured *pteruges* as military identification marks. A number of men carry large oval shields (A, E and J). Although these are also seen in Italy and elsewhere, their presence in Hungary, where they are carried by a fully armoured élite, may similarly set this area slightly apart from most of its Western neighbours.

Notes

1. J.F. Verbruggen, *The Art of Warfare in Western Europe during the Middle Ages* (Oxford, 1977), p.92; K. Leyser, 'The Battle of the Lech, 955: A Study in Tenth Century Warfare', *History* vol.I (1965), pp.2–3.

2. G. Fabian, 'The Hungarian Composite', *Journal of the Society of Archer. Antiquaries* vol.XIII (1970), pp.12–15; G. Rausing, *The Bow, Some Notes on its Origins and Development* (Lund, 1967), pp.69–70.

3. J.F.E Haldon, 'Some Aspects of Byzantine Military Technology from the Sixth to the Tenth Centuries', *Byzantine and Modern Greek Studies* vol.I (1975), p.29; Gyala Laszlo, *The Art of the Migration Period* (London, 1974), pp.65–70.

4. Gyala Laszlo, *loc.cit.*; C. Meredith-Jones, 'The Conventional Saracen of the Songs of Geste', *Speculum* vol.XVII (1942), p.201 note 2.

5. P. Contamine, *La Guerre au Moyen Age* (Paris, 1980), pp.113–14; Leyser, *op.cit.* pp.4, 14 and 19–23; J. Kalmár, 'A Történeti Múzeum Fegyvértárának Középkori Sisakjai', *Archeologiai Ertes'tö* vol.LXXXV (1958), p.195; J. Csemegi, 'Az Aracsi Kö', *Archeologiai Ertes'tö* vol.LXXXV (1958), pp.188–9.

6. A.N. Kirpicnikov, 'Russische Helm aus dem frühen Mittelalter', *Zeitschrift für Historische Waffen- und Kostümkunde* vol.XV (1973), p.89; Leyser, *loc.cit.*

7. R.-J. Lilie, 'Die Schlacht von Myriokephalon, 1176', *Revue des Études Byzantines* vol.XXXV (1977), p.274; V. Subotić, ed., *Guide, Military Museum* (Belgrade, n.d.), pp.12–13.

8. A. Ruttkay, 'Waffen und Reiterausrüstung des 9. bis zur ersten hälfte des 14. Jahrhunderts in der Slowakei' (part one), *Slovenska Archeologia* vol.XXIII, no.1 (1975), pp.125–6.

9. J. Von Kalmar, 'Der Ungarische Säbel im 16. und 17. Jahrhundert', *Zeitschrift für Historische Waffen- und Kostümekunde* (1937), p.164.

10. J. Richard, 'Les causes des victoires Mongoles d'après les historiens occidentaux du XIIIe siècle', *Central Asiatic Journal* vol.XXIII (1979), p.104; C. Oman, *A History of the Art of War in the Middle Ages* (London, 1924), vol.I, pp.517 and 525, and vol.II, p.330.

11. K.Cs. Sebestyén, 'Bogen und Pfeil der Alten Ungarn', *Dolgozatok* vol.VIII (1932), p.254.

12. Contamine, *op.cit.* p.239.

13. H. Inalcik, *The Ottoman Empire: The Classical Age 1300–1600* (London, 1973), p.21.

14. Inalcik, *op.cit.* pp.15–16 and 21.

Chapter 17

Poland

Great Poland around Poznań and Little Poland around Kraków to the south-east were united at the end of the 10th century. Mazovia north-east of Warsaw, Silesia to the south-west and Lausitz in what is now eastern Germany were all drawn into the Polish state in the early 11th century. Pomerania on the Baltic coast was also occupied for a while before falling under German domination, as, briefly, were what are now the Czech Republic and Slovakia plus parts of Ukraine further east. By the year 1100 Poland occupied much the same territory as it does today, with the exception of Pomerania on the Baltic coast and the southern Prussian lands. These frontiers remained relatively unchanged, though Lausitz and Silesia were lost to Germany in the 13th century. Such losses were partially compensated by eastern gains. In the 1340s, for example, Ruthenia and Galicia were acquired from the Grand Duchy of Lithuania, which had itself only recently taken them from a fragmented and weakened Russia.

During the period when the Polish state was being formed, the north-western Slavs appear to have had few cavalry. The Poles may have had rather more than other Slav tribes such as the Wends, Wiltzes or Obodrites,[1] and they also seem to have been moderately well armed. By the early 12th century the coastal Slavs possessed war-fleets which raided as far as Norway and had also developed effective light cavalry tactics similar to those of the neighbouring Prussians and Lithuanians. By the early 13th century the Slav princes of what are now the Baltic coastal provinces of Germany were Christian members of a German warrior aristocracy. They joined in Crusades against their pagan neighbours and fought in typical European style.[2]

The Polish Slavs never, of course, became German, but they remained under considerable German military influence. An armoured cavalry élite emerged in the 10th century, although the majority of Polish horsemen still fought as unarmoured light cavalry like their pagan neighbours to the north-east.[3] The question of Polish archery is less clear, though on balance it would appear that the simple bow or longbow was an important weapon among Polish infantry from the 10th to 12th centuries.[4]

In the south-east of the country Central Asian influence, which might have come via Kievan Russia or from Hungary,[5] was apparent in horse-harness and some weapons. Elsewhere 10th to 12th-century Polish military equipment was closer to that of Germany, from where most swords seem, in fact, to have been imported,[6] as too may have been some spearheads and other weapons. However, arms such as long-hafted light axes, and helmets of the directly-riveted form, were a specifically Slav feature.[7]

In the mid-12th century the Polish kingdom began to disintegrate into a series of petty principalities,[8] but this did not halt the process of 'Westernisation'. Crossbows began to replace bows as an important infantry weapon,[9] while cavalry equipment became virtually identical to that of Germany or Bohemia, but somewhat more old-fashioned. Nevertheless, cavalry tactics still showed some Eastern features.[10]

As in so many parts of Eastern Europe, not least among the Poles' Baltic neighbours, the Mongol invasions led to considerable military and technological changes in the later 13th and early 14th centuries. This applied to light cavalry tactics, which began to betray yet more Eastern influence;[11] to armour, where lamellar might have become more common in the east of the country;[12] and to the limited introduction of horse-archery in the south-east of Poland, which might date from the 14th century.[13] Nevertheless, even in the 14th century Polish forces still included large numbers of infantry. For example, the army led by Władyslaw Łokietka in 1330 reportedly consisted of 2100 heavily-armoured cavalry, 20,000 light cavalry and some 30,000 assorted infantry.[14]

Figures

889A–B Helmet from Gierz, Poznań, Great Poland, 10th–11th centuries
(Archaeological Museum, Poznań, Poland)

A – present condition; B – reconstruction of original state (after Warner). This helmet is very similar in construction to the example from Gorzuchy (fig.890). The decorative fillet of copper between the riveted iron plates is a feature of many such helmets and is particularly apparent here.

890A–B Helmet from Gorzuchy, Kalisz region, Great Poland, 10th–11th centuries
(National Museum, Kraków, Poland)

A – present condition; B – reconstruction of original state (after Warner). This was found in the heartland of the first medieval Polish state, as a result of which this form of helmet has sometimes been called the 'Great Polish' style, named after the Great Poland area. This example consists of gilded copper decoration on directly riveted iron segments strengthened by an iron rim. The remains of a mail *aventail* were also found. Helmets with basically this same form of construction were found throughout early medieval Eastern Europe and continued to be used in Russia long after being abandoned in Poland. The method is ultimately of Central Asian origin and was almost certainly introduced by invaders from the steppes, such as Huns, Avars or Magyars.

891 Helmet from Eastern Europe, Poland (?), 11th–12th centuries
(Merseyside County Museum, Liverpool, England)

A once-magnificent helmet consisting of four directly riveted, gilded iron segments. It is of the so-called 'Great Polish' type but may, however, have come from the Baltic states, Slovakia, Hungary, Russia or even the Balkans, as well as Poland. If it is, indeed, Polish then it would illustrate a later survival of Eastern European military styles in that country.

892 Helmet from Lake Orchowskie, Bydgoszcz, Cujavia, 11th–12th centuries
(Collection of S. Pijanowski, Głucha Puszcza, Poland)

This is a typical Western European type of one-piece conical helmet with a relatively small *nasal*. It might have been imported into Poland, and certainly reflects the spread of Western European influence in the 11th and 12th centuries. During this period, Polish arms, armour and military traditions shifted away from earlier styles, which were similar to those of Russia and the eastern Slavs, towards forms which were in most respects identical to styles from Germany and Bohemia.

893 Helmet from Lake Lednikie, Poznań, Great Poland, 11th–12th centuries
(Museum of the First Piasts, Lednica, Poland)

The upper part of this helmet has been inaccurately restored. It is basically a typical Western European helmet of the so-called 'Norman' type. The only unusual feature is a hook at the base of the *nasal*. This would have supported a *ventail* or the upper part of a mail *hauberk* to protect the lower part of the face. Such hooks might have been used in Western Europe but the evidence for this is unclear. On the other hand it might be an Eastern European fashion reflecting the armour styles of the Eurasian steppes as well as the importance of archery.

894 Sword from Grzebsk, Ciechanów, Mazovia, 12th century
(probably lost in Second World War)

The blade of this typical, and probably originally German, sword is inscribed IN NOMINE, the remainder of the Latin inscription apparently having been lost.

895 Sword from Brześć Kujawski, Włocławek, Mazovia, 11th century
(State Archaeological Museum, Warsaw, Poland)

A far more typical 11th century sword still has distinctive angled *quillons*, which might have been an Eastern European fashion. The blade is, however, inscribed ULFBERHT, which indicates that it was made in the Rhineland. On the other hand a number of blades made in the East might have been fake 'Ulfberhts'.

896A–B Daggers or knife blades, Poland, 11th century
(after Warner)

A – from Młodzikowo; B – from Blichowa. These were probably domestic knives rather than weapons. One (A) still has part of its wooden grip.

897 **Spearhead from Buszek, Sieradz, Great Poland, 11th century**
(Archaeological and Ethnological Museum, Łódź, Poland)

This long, pointed spear-blade has similarities with examples from the Baltic States.

898 **Spearhead from Krośniewice, Płock, Mazovia, 11th–12th centuries**
(J. Dunin-Borkowski Collection, Krośniewice, Poland)

It has been suggested that this was re-forged from a broken sword-blade. It is certainly of a very unusual form.

899 **Spearhead from Łubówko, Posnań, Great Poland, 11th century**
(Archaeological Museum, Posnań, Poland)

One of the most decorated 11th-century spear-blades from Poland is similar in outline to weapons made in Götland and other parts of Scandinavia.

900A–F **Spearheads, Poland, 11th century**
(after Warner)

A – from Turowo; B – from Buczek; C – from Siemianice; D – from Turowo; E – from Ciepłe; F – from Lutomiersk. This collection of spearheads indicates the great variety seen in 11th-century Poland. One (A) seems to be an extreme example of a type in which the blade narrows almost to a 'waist' below its point. The second (B) seems to be similar to certain Götlandish weapons. A third (C) also finds parallels in Baltic weapons. The fourth (D) has a small blade in comparison to the size of its socket; so much so that it looks like a cut-down version of a previously damaged weapon. The final two examples (E and F) are basically leaf-shaped and also have similarities with weapons from neighbouring areas.

901 **Lead weight or mace head, Młodzikowo, Posnań, Great Poland, 11th century**
(Archaeological Museum, Posnań, Poland)

This large, solid lead object is a bit of a mystery. It is probably a mace head, but as such is almost unique.

902 **Axehead from Lutomiersk, Great Poland, 11th century**
(Centre for the Archaeology of Central Poland, Łódź, Poland)

This appears to have been a development of the typical Polish and western Slav war-axe.

903 **Axehead from Lutomiersk, Sieradz, Great Poland, 11th century**
(Institute for the History of Material Culture, Łódź, Poland)

The war-axe has less of a downwards-sweep to the blade than usual.

904 **Axehead from Witonia Płock, Mazovia, 11th century**
(State Archaeological Museum, no.V/1340, Warsaw, Poland)

In contrast to the previous axe, this example has a very long 'beard' or extension to the blade.

905 **Axehead from Niewiarowo-Sochy, Poland, 12th century**
(after Warner)

This axe appears to be a later development of a typical Slav form.

906 **Sword from Ostrów Lednicki, Poznań, Great Poland, 10th–11th centuries**
(Museum of the First Piasts, no.257, Lednica, Poland)

A large number of medieval swords have been found in Poland and their survival may reflect the persistence of pre-Christian folk rituals. Most such swords, particularly those of the 10th to 12th centuries, were probably imported from Germany. This might be one such example.

907A–B **Spearheads from Lake Ledniki, Poznań, Great Poland, 10th–11th centuries**
(Museum of the First Piasts, nos.236 and 237, Lednica, Poland)

The presence of these spear blades in a lake strongly suggests the survival of ancient 'weapon-sacrificing' rites. They are very well made, with pointed blades, suggesting a widespread use of armour.

908A–B **Axeheads from Lake Ledniki, Poznań, Great Poland, 10th–12th centuries**
(Museum of the First Piasts, nos.203 and 204, Lednica, Poland)

These weapons were also probably thrown into the lake intentionally. Their form suggests a relatively late date, perhaps into the 12th century, by which time Poland had supposedly been converted to Christianity. They are also from a different tradition to that of the Scandinavian 'Danish axe', since their blades are thrust out from the haft on a sort of extended arm. As such they have something in common with the war-axes of nomadic steppe peoples, from which they may ultimately have derived. By the 12th century, however, such war-axes had become a popular weapon among many western and southern Slavic peoples.

909 **Sword from Czersko Polskie, Bydgoszcz, Cujavia, 11th century**
(lost in Second World War)

This sword may originally have been Polish, Pomeranian or even Prussian. The blade could be a German import, but the *pommel* and *quillons*, carved from horn in obvious imitation of metal sword mounts, were made locally.

910A–B **Swords from Lutomiersk, Great Poland, 12th–14th centuries**
(Academy of Sciences, Łódź, Poland)

These swords are sometimes ascribed to the 11th century but are almost certainly later. Their long slender *quillons* and the almost nut-shaped *pommel* suggest a 13th century date and a German origin

911 **Sword from Winiary, Płock, Mazovia, late 11th–early 14th centuries**
(Diocesan Museum, Płock, Poland)

The *pommel* and *quillons* of this sword look late but the blade seems early. The weapon might have been cut down and re-used. Such a practice is likely in an area that had a relatively small domestic arms industry and in which backward peoples such as Pomeranians, Prussians and Lithuanians would naturally have tried to re-use captured weapons, however damaged.

912 **Scabbard from Gdańsk, Pomerania, 11th century**
(Archaeological Museum, Gdańsk, Poland)

This scabbard is made of wood around a hide inner sleeve; the whole being covered by linen. Pomerania, where the scabbard was found, was ruled by Poland from c.980 to 1033. Thereafter it was independent until conquered by Germans in the 12th and 13th centuries.

913 **Sword from Katowice, Little Poland, 11th–12th centuries**
(after Warner)

This is a typical late 11th or 12th century weapon. The southern area of Little Poland seems to have been under Moravian, Slovakian and even Hungarian influence.

914 **Sword from Czersko Polskie, Bydgoszcz, Cujavia, 11th century**
(after Warner)

The curvature of this otherwise typical 11th or early 12th-century sword is the result of damage. The blade would originally have been straight.

915 Sword from Dołubowo Białystok, Mazovia or Volhynia, 1150–1200
(State Archaeological Museum, no.73/75, Warsaw, Poland)

This sword, which was certainly imported from Western Europe, was found in a frontier region of the medieval Polish state where the borders of Polish Mazovia, the Russian Principality of Volhynia, the German Order of Teutonic Knights and the pagan Prussians and Lithuanians came close. In this war-torn area military equipment must have changed hands frequently, so it would be misleading to guess at the nationality or religion of the last user of this sword.

916 Sword from Pokrzywica Wielka, Olsztyn, Prussia, mid-12th century
(State Archaeological Museum, Warsaw, Poland)

Found amid the Masurian Lakes, the heartland of Prussian resistance to conversion and conquest by both Teutonic Knights and Poles, this is a much earlier form of weapon than that seen above (fig.915), and may have been locally made. The hilt has the unusual mixture of thick but short *quillons* and what look like the remains of a more up-to-date nut-shaped *pommel*.

917 Sword from Bydgoszcz, Cujavia, 12th–13th centuries
(after Warner)

A rather unusual local variation on the basic European 12th or 13th century sword. The blade tapers to a point, which is more characteristic of the 13th century. The unusually shaped *quillons* may, however, have been damaged, or may be a local addition to an imported weapon.

918A–D 'St Adalbert of Prague lands in Prussia', bronze panel, Great Poland, 12th century
(*in situ* doors of Cathedral, Gniezno, Poland)

The similarity between the shields on the Gniezno Cathedral doors (C and D) and those in an unnamed Polish manuscript (fig.929) are obvious. None of the figures on the doors have apparent armour or helmets. They are armed only with spears (A and B) and swords (C and D).

919 Coin of Prince Jacza of Köpenick, Pomerania, c.1150
(Zentral Institut für Alte Geschichte und Archäologie, Berlin, Germany)

Prince Jacza seems to have been one of the last native Slav princes of the Berlin area, which was divided between the German Nordmark and independent Pomerania in the mid-12th century. The prince appears in a strange mixture of Eastern and Western styles. His spear and banner look somewhat German and he might have a large kite-shaped shield hung rather incongruously on his right arm. He also seems to wear a stylised or inaccurately rendered lamellar *cuirass*.

920 Bronze mace head room Gorzyce, Tarnów, Little Poland, 12th–14th centuries (?)
(Archaeological Museum, Posnań, Poland)

This undated medieval mace head came from an area close to Hungarian-ruled Slovakia and the Slav Principality of Ruthenia which was culturally close, if not always actually part of, the Ukraine. The weapon is similar in style to a number of relatively light mace heads from Hungary and regions incorporated into the medieval Hungarian state.

921 *Szczerbiec*, the Polish Coronation Sword, Poland, c.1225–50
(Wawel State Art Collection, Kraków, Poland)

This magnificently decorated ceremonial sword was probably made for Prince Boleslaw of Mazovia and Sandomierz in Little Poland. Its form is typical of mid-13th century European weapons, except that the blade has a rather unusual hole now partially covered by a decorative shield bearing the Polish eagle. Perhaps it originally contained a sacred relic.

922 Sword from the River Odra, Szczecin, Pomerania, 1250–1350
(National Museum, no.1701, Szczecin, Poland)

This is almost certainly of German manufacture and dates from the period when the area where it was found formed part of the German Duchy of Slavinia.

923 Sword from Chrustowice, Kielce, Little Poland, 13th century
(National Museum, no.3365, Kielce, Poland)

The *quillons* may have been reversed. It is otherwise a typical European weapon of its period.

924A–H Arrowheads from Tum, Płock, Mazovia, 11th–13th centuries
(Institute for the History of Material Culture, Łódź, Poland)

This remarkable collection of arrowheads indicates the many varied influences at work in medieval Polish military styles. The majority are, or were, socket types (A–D, G and H). Of these, three were barbed hunting or war-arrows of typical Western or Northern European form (A–C). The other three (D, G and H) might have been from armour-piercing crossbow bolts, and as such probably date from the 13th century. All can be seen as essentially European. Two arrowheads are, however, of the tanged variety (E and F) and are much closer in style to those used by the horse-archers of the Eurasian steppes.

925 Bow made of yew, from Opole, Brzeg, Silesia, 14th century
(Piasts Museum, Brzeg, Poland)

The length of this bow is 119.5 cm, which makes it a short bow rather than a longbow. It was almost certainly a hunting weapon but the carefully carved ears show it to be relatively sophisticated, perhaps even indicating the influence of composite bows from nomadic peoples to the south-east.

926 Crossbow nut of horn from Tum, Płock, Mazovia, 12th–14th centuries
(Institute for the History of Material Culture, no.2142/50, Łódź, Poland)

The crossbow was introduced into Poland no earlier than the 12th century, probably from Germany or Scandinavia. This piece of a release mechanism is of an advanced type. Earlier forms seem to have had wooden release nuts.

927 Mace head from Szcepankowo, Poland, 12th–13th centuries
(after Warner)

Maces of knobbed rather than winged or flanged type were a traditional form of weapon in Eastern Europe. This particular example seems to be larger than most others, which are generally small and apparently designed to injure lightly protected men rather than to break armour. They are an old-fashioned form of weapon developed in days before the widespread adoption of armour.

928A–C 'Gideon', silver bowl from Włocławek, Mazovia, 11th century
(Archaeological Museum, Warsaw, Poland)

The figures on this fine piece of metalwork are shown with an interesting variety of arms and armour, a variety that fits very well the known changes taking place in Polish military styles in the 11th century. Given the subject of the picture, the figures are unlikely to illustrate alien or 'pagan' arms and armour. The helmets, though relatively low-domed, lack *nasals* and seem to have mail *aventails* rather than being worn over *coifs*. As such they are probably examples of the so-called 'Great Polish' type rather than being Western-style conical helmets. One figure has a short-sleeved mail *hauberk* (B) but the other has long, close-fitting sleeves (A). This is surprising for the

11th century but might indicate contact with the more advanced cultures of Byzantium, certain steppe peoples, or even the Islamic world. It is also possible that this picture was simply copied from a piece of Byzantine art. The shields are round, either large or medium sized with *guiges* (A and B), or a small, round, convex buckler with a large boss (C). Such features also indicate traditional Slav or even Eastern influence.

929A–C Miniatures in a Polish manuscript, 11th century
(after Warner)

The date given to this unnamed manuscript is surprising considering the shape of the shields and their obvious heraldic patterns. In fact they look mid or late 12th century. Even so, they would indicate a clear and strong Western European influence both in the adoption of military styles and in the feudal concepts associated with such heraldry.

930 Seal on an unnamed document, Poland, 1220
(after Warner)

A clear distinction is made between the armour of this figure's presumed *coif* and that of his *hauberk*. The style of the seal is essentially Western, as is the figure's helmet, spear and flat-topped kite-shaped shield supported by a *guige*. His *coif* is of mail but the artist seems to be indicating that he wears a scale or lamellar *cuirass*. Although the armour looks as if it is made of scales, archaeological and other pictorial evidence makes lamellar slightly more likely.

931 Lost tomb of Peter Vlast from Vinzentkloster Church, Wrocław, Silesia, c.1270
(18th century drawing, University Library, Ms. IV, f.239, Wrocław, Poland)

The similarity between this effigy and the statues in Naumberg in eastern Germany is obvious. Duke Peter holds a long straight sword and a tall, almost completely triangular shield.

932 Seal of the Duke of Mazovia, Poland, 1343
(after Thordeman)

This is one of the most interesting sources of information concerning 14th century Polish arms and armour. The prince carries a spear, and behind his shield is a straight sword with a large *pommel*. Far more unusual is his small sleeveless lamellar *cuirass* of a type common in the Islamic world, the Mongol and post-Mongol Eurasian steppes, Russia, and parts of the Balkans. His rectangular shield is also of an unusual type that is structurally similar to the larger and later Bohemian *pavise*. Small but more trapezoid shields would be seen in 15th century Hungary, the Balkans and the Ottoman Empire, while

similar shields are seen on late 14th century memorials to Teutonic
Knights in northern Poland. Such shields, having a bulge down their
vertical axis, might have been a local Polish or western Slav
development. Roughly square shields, but without the keel-like
bulge, became popular among later 14th century German horsemen.
The prince's lamellar *cuirass* almost certainly reflects Russian or
Lithuanian influence and is quite unlike anything seen in Germany.
Mazovia was on the border with Lithuania which, under the Grand
Duke Olgiera, was now on its way to becoming the largest territorial
state in Europe. Lithuania and Poland would, in fact, unite less than
half a century after this seal was made. Lithuania's extraordinary
growth occurred in the wake of the Mongol invasions of Eastern
Europe and at a time when the Russian principalities were in a state
of fragmentation and weakness. So perhaps the appearance of
Mongol-style body armour on this seal should come as no surprise
and may reflect a temporary acceptance of Lithuanian or even
Mongol suzerainty.

933 Sword from Lutol Mokry, Gorzów, Pomerania–Brandenburg, c.1350
(probably lost in Second World War)

This weapon comes from another fluctuating frontier region where
the borders of German Brandenburg, Pomerania and Great Poland
met. The sword itself is a typical German-style 'hand-and-a-half'
weapon of the mid-14th century.

934 Sword of unknown provenance, Poland, mid-14th century
(National Museum, no.V-3457, Kraków, Poland)

Very similar to the preceding example but with thicker *quillons* and a
slightly broader blade, perhaps indicating an earlier date or local
Polish manufacture.

935 Sword from Kraków-Rakowice, Little Poland, mid-14th century
(Archaeological Museum, no.10124, Kraków, Poland)

Again a typical 'hand-and-a-half' sword of the mid-14th century.

936 Helmet of unknown provenance, probably Prussia or Cujavia, 1350–1400 (?)
(Provincial Museum, Toruń, Poland)

This is an unusual form of helmet, having some similarities with
Western European *bascinets* but being otherwise closer to the helmets
of the 13th century Ukraine. It probably represents a later
development of the latter – tall, pointed helmets, with pendant
aventails – but there is no indication of whether or not this helmet

originally had a visor. It may also be a form used by some of the troops of the greatly expanded Lithuanian state.

937 *Bascinet* from Tarnobrzeg, Sandomierz, said to have belonged to Casimir the Great, Little Poland, mid-14th century
(Wawel Cathedral Treasury, Kraków, Poland)

The so-called '*Bascinet* of Casimir the Great' is a typical mid or late 14th-century helmet. It was either of the *klappvisier* type in which a visor was hinged from the brow, or was of an earlier form in which a *bretache* (separate *nasal* or flap of mail attached to the lower part of the *aventail*) could be hooked to the brow. Both these forms were characteristic of Germany and certain other parts of Eastern Europe. The relatively small, though very corroded, brow attachment suggests a *bretache* rather than a hinged visor. The similarity between such brow-fastening *klappvisiers* and the face-masks of earlier helmets from Ukraine opens up various interesting possibilities.

Notes

1. K. Leyser, 'Henry I and the Beginnings of the Saxon Empire', *The English Historical Review* vol.LXXXIII (1968), pp.10 and 15; J. Herrmann, 'The Northern Slavs', in *The Northern World*, ed. D.M. Wilson (London, 1980), p.202.

2. E. Christiansen, *The Northern Crusades: The Baltic and Catholic Frontier 1100–1525* (London, 1980), pp.33 and 69.

3. B. Warner, *Slavonic Terms for Weapons and Armour in the Middle Ages: A Lexico-Historical Study* (M.A. thesis, London University, 1965), p.172.

4. A. Nadolski, *Broń średniowieczna z ziem polskich (Medieval Arms and Armour in Poland)* (Warsaw, 1978), pp.57–60; Warner, *op.cit.* p.137 takes an opposite viewpoint.

5. Nadolski, *op.cit.* p.59.

6. Nadolski, *op.cit.* p.58.

7. Warner, *op.cit.* pp.76–80, 137 and 172–3; Nadolski, *op.cit.* pp.57–61; A. Nadolski, 'Ancient Polish Arms and Armour', *Journal of the Arms and Armour Society* vol.IV (1962), pp.32–7.

8. Nadolski, *Broń średniowieczna, op.cit.* p.54.

9. Nadolski, *Broń średniowieczna, op.cit.* pp.61–2; Nadolski, 'Ancient Polish Arms', *op.cit.* p.32; Warner, *op.cit.* pp.175–6.

10. Nadolski, *Broń średniowieczna, op.cit.* p.60; Nadolski, 'Ancient Polish Arms', *op.cit.* p.38; Warner, *op.cit.* pp.174–6; A.N. Kirpičnikov, 'Russische Helm aus dem frühen Mittelalter', *Zeitschrift für historische Waffen- und Kostümkunde* vol.XV (1973), p.89.

11. Nadolski, 'Ancient Polish Arms', *op.cit.* p.38; Nadolski, *Broń średniowieczna, op.cit.* pp.61–2.

12. Nadolski, *Broń średniowieczna, op.cit.* p.64; B. Thordeman, *Armour from the Battle of Wisby 1361* (Uppsala, 1939), p.270.

13. G. Rausing, *The Bow, Some Notes on its Origins and Development* (Lund, 1967), pp.143–4.

14. Warner, *op.cit.* p.176.

Chapter 18

Scandinavia

The following areas are considered part of the Scandinavian military and cultural region: Denmark, Sweden, Norway, Finland, the Kingdom of the Isles (Shetland, Orkney and the Hebrides), and those North Atlantic lands colonised or possibly temporarily settled by Norse peoples, including the Faroe Islands, Iceland, Greenland and perhaps ephemeral settlements in Canada.

By the mid-11th century the great age of Viking expansion had ended and recognisable states had emerged in Scandinavia. The first of these was Denmark, which became at least superficially Christian at the end of the 10th century and, under Cnut the Great (1014–35), temporarily dominated Norway, southern Sweden and England. Norway soon retrieved its independence, but Danish rule over parts of southern Sweden lasted until the 17th century. Norway thereafter maintained a tenuous control over the Faroe Islands, the northern and western Scottish islands and the Isle of Man until the early 12th century, the Faroes, Shetlands and Orkneys remaining in Norwegian hands until the 15th century.

Although the early history of Sweden is more obscure, the state had emerged by the 11th century, Finland falling under Swedish domination by the mid-13th century. The entire Northern world, including an Icelandic state which had been independent since the early 10th century, was later united under one crown by the Union of Kalmar in 1397. Scandinavian settlements survived in south-western Greenland from the late 10th century until they disappeared in the late 14th, hardly more than a hundred years before Greenland was 'rediscovered' by Gaspar Corte-Real in 1500. It is now widely accepted that Scandinavians also reached the mainland of North America, but the scope and persistence of their contact with the New World is hotly debated.

From the 11th to 14th centuries Scandinavia itself witnessed military changes as profound as any in Europe. The warriors of the so-called Second Viking Age (late 10th/early 11th centuries) were in contact with a great many other military traditions,[1] from the Eurasian Steppes, Byzantium and the Islamic world to the 'stone-age' cultures of North America. Nevertheless, their warfare was still dominated by infantry using spears, swords and long-hafted axes well into the first half of the 12th century.[2] In Denmark a highly-structured military system had already appeared in the 11th century, where training schedules were regularised and mounted infantry played a leading role.[3] The many Anglo-Saxon refugees who migrated to Scandinavia in the late 11th and early 12th centuries[4] had no difficulty fitting into this system and may even have reinforced it. Lamellar armour might have been used in Sweden, which would indicate contact with Eastern Europe or beyond. The longbow was an important weapon, particularly in Norway,[5] though composite or reinforced wooden bows of Eastern inspiration were almost certainly also known. Such weapons remained popular among the Lapps and Finns for many centuries.[6]

The 12th to 14th centuries saw further changes. By the mid-12th century Sweden had been drawn into the mainstream of European military culture.[7] Denmark was also transformed into a reasonably typical European feudal state and, after a period of retrenchment, returned to the offensive in the Baltic during the mid-12th century.[8] Danish armies now included large numbers of cavalry,[9] and, by the 13th century, also many crossbowmen.[10] Crossbows subsequently spread throughout Scandinavia,[11] eventually becoming a central, almost mystical, feature of the *Kalevala*, Finland's national epic.[12]

Military developments on the fringes of the Northern world, in such areas as Finland, Lapland and among the neighbouring Finno-Ugrian peoples of what is now northern Russia, were, of course, chronologically behind developments in Denmark, Sweden and Norway. Harsh climatic factors also played a part, the flat bow of simple construction continuing to be used in sub-Arctic areas like Lapland where it was apparently less sensitive to low temperatures.[13] The Finns remained a tribal society without a military élite, having much in common with the Balts to their south. Like the Perms to the east they used javelins in warfare.[14] The Karelians were partly nomadic, having more in common with the Lapps,[15] though the coastal Finns were 'Europeanised' in the 13th and 14th centuries.[16] The Lapps themselves were apparently dependent on trade for all metal objects, including weapons.[17] The neighbouring Finno-Ugrian peoples of the northern Ural region also seem to have relied on trade for iron, some of which came from the far south via the Volga Bulgars.[18] The southernmost Finno-Ugrian tribes were, however, more advanced even in the 11th century, when small towns already existed in which archaeologists have recently found weapons and evidence of Christianity.

On the even more far-flung western fringes of the Scandinavian world were the *Skraelings*, or 'screamers'. This name was given by Norse settlers or explorers to all indigenous inhabitants of Greenland and North America. In reality these aboriginal peoples differed considerably among themselves, from

Eskimo hunters, through the sub-Arctic American Indians of upper Quebec and Labrador to the forest-dwelling tribes of Newfoundland, New Brunswick, Nova Scotia and New England. The unclear and much later Scandinavian written records suggest that these so-called *Skraelings*, like the most primitive Finno-Ugrian peoples, preferred iron objects, including weapons, as trade goods. There was, meanwhile, a corresponding but apparently ineffective official ban on trading such weapons with the *Skraelings*.[19]

Figures

938 **Sword-hilt with niello ornament from Leikkimati, Finland, 11th–12th centuries**
(after Nordman)

This splendidly-decorated sword is still in the 10th and 11th century Scandinavian tradition, with thick but short curved *quillons* and a basically trefoil *pommel*.

939 **Sword-found in London, probably from Denmark, 10th–11th centuries**
(London Museum, London, England)

This is a very typical Scandinavian sword. The blade tapers slightly but is clearly not a thrusting weapon. The curved *quillons* are short and thick, the *pommel* a development of the trilobate form.

940 **Sword, Scandinavia, 10th–11th centuries**
(present whereabouts unknown)

This weapon, which has been ceremonially 'killed' by heating and bending, is basically very similar to the preceding example.

941 **Decorated brow-piece of a helmet from Lokrume, 10th–11th centuries**
(present whereabouts unknown)

Decorative brow-pieces had been a feature of many early medieval European helmets but the fashion may have persisted far longer in the North. Such features could also serve to reinforce the top of a *nasal* where it met the rim of a helmet.

942 **'Danish axe' from near London Bridge, Scandinavian, 10th–11th centuries**
(London Museum, London, England)

This may be taken as a typical 'Danish axe'. Such weapons were, of course, not used by all Danes or Vikings, but they were to become associated in the popular mind with the archetypal Scandinavian warrior. Note that this original form has no upwards-sweep to the blade. Rather it has a slight downwards-sweep, which resulted in these sometimes being known as 'bearded axes'.

943 Bronze *quillons* from a Viking sword, Scandinavia, 10th–11th centuries
(London Museum, London, England)

During the 10th to 12th centuries bronze sword mounts seem to have been less rare, though still far from common, among Scandinavian peoples than elsewhere. This could reflect Eastern European influence, or might just have been a regional fashion.

944 Carved elk horn from Sigtuna, Upland, 11th century
(Historical Museum, Stockholm, Sweden)

A well-known but tiny carving from the heart of the medieval Swedish state shows a warrior wearing a conical helmet with a long *nasal*. The exaggeratedly large rivets indicate a *spangenhelm* construction. In reality the helmet would almost certainly not have been quite so pointed and was likely to have had a more curved outline.

945A–I The Lewes Chessmen, Hebridean-Norse, 1150–75
(British Museum, London, England)

The Lewes Chessmen are unique and, as a source of information for the military equipment of the 12th century Northern lands, they are unsurpassed. Various forms of helmet are shown. The most common is a straightforward one-piece conical helmet with or without a *nasal* (A, B, D, F, G and H). Four have pendant ear and neckguards, which were presumably attached by leather hinges or directly to the lining (A, B, D and H). Two seem to have flattened tops (G and H), but this might just be a result of the carver's technique. One also clearly has a rim riveted around the base of the helmet (F). Another interesting and unusual helmet (C) seems to be made from two or more sections joined horizontally and may represent a local style of *chapel-de-fer* war-hat. A mail *hauberk* may be shown once (G), and shields are of the tall, kite-shaped variety with flattened (B–C, F and H) or rounded (G) tops. A cavalry lance is shown (A), but the most common weapon is a straight sword with straight *quillons* and a large, usually nut-shaped *pommel* (E–I).

946A–B 'Massacre of the Innocents', beaten copper altar front from Broddetorp Church, West Götland, late 12th century
(National Historical Museum, Stockholm, Sweden)

This embossed metalwork has sometimes been taken as evidence that lamellar armour was used in Sweden. It may, indeed, portray lamellar, but it does so in an inaccurate manner, suggesting that the artist was using an iconographic convention. It is also worth noting that the figure in the armour is one of the 'wicked' soldiers of King Herod. Lamellar might have been known in Sweden and was almost certainly used in earlier centuries. Sweden was also in close touch with the lamellar-using regions of Eastern Europe and beyond. Nevertheless, the similarity between the supposed lamellar worn by this soldier and that given to various 'infidels' in other 12th century European art casts doubt on the Broddetorp Altar as evidence for 12th century Swedish armour.

947A–C 'Sigurd the Dragon Slayer', carved wooden doorway, Norway, 12th century
(*in situ* church, Hylestad, Norway)

The similarity between the hero's military equipment on the Hylestad carvings and that seen on the Lewes Chessmen is obvious. Here again conical helmets with *nasals* have long neckguards (B and C), and even ear-pieces (C). The shield is a tall kite-shaped type and the swords (A and C) have long straight *quillons* and round *pommels*. Even the scabbard is hung in the normal Western European manner. In fact only the pendant ear and neck defences set this man's equipment apart from that of his neighbours to the south.

948A–E Sword with inlaid decoration on the blade, Scandinavia, 11th–12th centuries
(Musée de l'Armée, no. Po. 2242, Paris, France)

The dating of this sword seems somewhat early in view of its tapering and pointed blade, long *quillons* and round *pommel* (A). The decorations on the blade (B–E) are, however, within a long-established Scandinavian tradition.

949 Reconstruction of a sword from excavated fragments, Denmark, late 11th century
(National Museum, Copenhagen, Denmark)

By the 11th century Danish weapons were already being influenced by the more advanced German styles. Some could, in fact, have been German imports. This example has the new longer, more slender *quillons* and the oval *pommel*.

950 Sword said to have been found near Lake Nipigon, Scandinavian (?), 11th–12th centuries (?)
(Royal Ontario Museum, Toronto, Canada)

The extremely corroded so-called 'Lake Nipigon sword' is one of several weapons said to have been found in eastern Canada and the north-eastern United States. Their authenticity is generally dismissed, and in fact all might have been either fakes or 'planted' by hoaxers. Yet they should not be entirely dismissed. Even disregarding the possibility of transitory Scandinavian settlements in Newfoundland and visits to the American mainland, the survival of Scandinavian colonies in Greenland well into the 14th century could provide an original provenance for at least some of these weapons. When such settlements were finally extinguished one can imagine the awe with which their iron weapons were regarded by the indigenous 'stone-age' cultures which overran them. Perhaps metal tools and weapons became totemic cult objects and might have migrated around this part of the world even if their original owners never set foot on the American mainland. Nevertheless, the 'Lake Nipigon sword' still has a peculiar-looking *pommel*, the upper part of which seems to have been lost.

951 Bronze sword-hilt from Kiviniemi, Finland, 12th–13th centuries
(after Nordman)

One of the last areas to be drawn into medieval Western European military culture was Finland, and here certain archaic technological and stylistic traditions survived for many years. This bronze hilt is a case in point. The *pommel* is very old-fashioned, and the missing *quillons* were clearly very broad. They may even have been carved from horn, as earlier seen in Poland.

952 Spearhead from Moisco, Finland (?) 12th century
(after Nordman),

Spears with wings or flanges, as here, would have been considered rather old-fashioned in many parts of 12th century Europe. On the other hand the decoration on this blade may indicate that it was more of a ceremonial standard than a weapon of war.

953 The Baldishol Tapestry, Norway, late 12th century
(Museum of Applied Arts, Oslo, Norway)

The evidence of this tapestry seems to suggest that the military equipment of Norway remained old-fashioned and backward throughout most of the 12th century. This was only to be expected in a relatively poor and rather isolated country. A horseman is here shown in a conical helmet with a *nasal* and perhaps a forward-angled crown. The helmet may also be made in two pieces, directly riveted in the Eastern European tradition. He wears a long-sleeved mail *hauberk* and *coif* but lacks *mittens* and leg armour. His shield is also of the late 11th and early 12th-century round-topped, kite-shaped variety. A round shield with a boss may be seen from the side just in front of his horse.

954 Spearhead with silvered socket from Götland, Sweden, 11th century (?)
(National Museum, Stockholm, Sweden)

Highly-decorated weapons such as this probably had ceremonial functions and might have been symbols of authority. The bulge between the socket and blade appears to be hollow and pierced.

955 Flat bow from Vibby, Sweden, undated medieval
(after Rausing)

The flat bow seems to have been popular in various parts of Northern Europe. Its name derives from the fact that the arms were thin in section (A). The bow characteristically took on an almost angled profile when drawn, as distinct from the regular curve of the normal self bow.

956 Sword, Denmark, c.1150
(National Museum, Copenhagen, Denmark)

By the mid-12th century most of Scandinavia had been drawn into the mainstream of European culture and this is clearly reflected in its weaponry. Apart from being rather slender, this splendid sword is a typical mid or late 12th-century European weapon.

957 *Great helm* from Castle of Aranaes, Sweden, c.1300
(National Historical Museum, Stockholm, Sweden)

A – reconstruction; B – actual condition. Only a few *great helms* survive and this is a good late 13th-century example. The sloping sides of the upper part of the helmet make it a midway form between the typical early flat-topped *great helm* and the later round-topped type. The lower edge of the sides and back of this helmet would not have come very far down the wearer's neck. As such it is a relatively light version, having some characteristics in common with earlier flat-topped helms with face-masks.

958 *Chapel-de-fer* war-hat, Norway, 13th century
(National Historical Museum, Stockholm, Sweden)

A very rare surviving *chapel-de-fer*, a type of helmet sometimes called a *kettle-hat* and believed to have come from Norway. Such helmets were popular throughout most of 13th century Western Europe but might have been widely used in Scandinavia at an earlier date. Early medieval sources describing Viking raiders sometimes seem to refer to wide-brimmed helmets. It is even possible that the romantic myth of the Vikings' 'winged' helmets, which later became 'horned' helmets, arose out of such *chapel-de-fer* war-hats, the broad brims of which could have been poetically described as 'wings'.

959 'Herod and the Cock' (?), carved relief, Sweden, 1130–50
(*in situ* entrance to the sacristy, Cathedral, Skara, Sweden)

Here King Herod's guards draw their swords in alarm. The weapons, though crudely carved, have straight tapering blades and relatively long *quillons*. Their hats or helmets may reflect tall pointed forms used among Slav and Baltic nations to the east and south.

960 Sword from the Gudbransdal, Norway, c.1240
(Museum and Art Gallery, Maidstone, England)

This is a typical European weapon of the time, strongly indicating that the military élite of Norway was, by the mid-13th century, equipped in much the same manner as in the rest of Western Europe.

961 War-axe, Finland, 13th century
(National Museum, Helsinki, Finland)

Another example of the survival of early forms of weapon in Finland is this decorated axe. It is a 'Danish' type, almost of the downwards-sweeping 'bearded' form. Such weapons had largely gone out of fashion in the rest of Europe by the 13th century.

962 Sword, possibly Götland, 13th century
(National Museum, Helsinki, Finland)

Although found in Finland, the style and decoration of this magnificent weapon suggests that it might have been made on the Swedish island of Götland. Götland was in many respects the hub of Baltic trade, as well as being a wealthy manufacturing centre. The style of this weapon is basically that of a typical 13th century sword, but the degree of decoration suggests that it might have been largely ceremonial.

963 Bronze hilt of a sword, Finland, 13th century
(National Museum, Helsinki, Finland)

Perhaps more typical of Finland, the hilt of this sword is all bronze and, as well as being abundantly decorated, is very archaic in form, with short, broad *quillons* and a basically trefoil *pommel*.

964 'Massacre of the Innocents', carved relief, Sweden, c.1300
(*in situ* nave of Cathedral, Linköping, Sweden)

Originally from the south door of the cathedral, this carving again shows a soldier in some kind of scale armour. Here, however, the armour looks much more realistic. Similar scale-covered coats also appear in Polish and German art; nor are they always worn by the 'wicked'. It is possible that they were genuine pieces of armour worn for the same reasons as the *coats-of-plates* that were being developed during the same period. This warrior also has a long-sleeved mail *hauberk* with *mittens*, a mail *coif*, and a round *cervellière* helmet. His tapering sword has curved *quillons* and a somewhat diamond-shaped *pommel*, the latter being a feature that is also seen in Germany.

965 **'Massacre of the Innocents', stained glass window from Eksta, Sweden, c.1270**
(National Museum of Antiquities, Stockholm, Sweden)

The armour worn by the soldiers is altogether simpler, consisting of mail *coifs*, long-sleeved mail *hauberks* without *mittens*, and full mail *chausses*. The sword, incomplete in this drawing, has a massive round *pommel* and long, straight *quillons*.

966A–C **'The Story of St Mary of Antioch', painted wooden ceiling, Hallingdal, mid-13th century**
(*in situ* wooden church, Torpa, Norway)

A–B – Guards of the Governor Olibrius; C – Sword of Olibrius. The two followers of Olibrius (A–B) probably reflect the typical armament of knights or sergeants in mid-13th century Norway. It is relatively light, consisting of broad-brimmed but apparently one-piece *chapel-de-fer war-hats*, mail *coifs*, *hauberks* and *chausses*. The shields are very large and long, probably because semi-rigid body armour had yet to become common in this region. The swords are long and straight (A–C), with long, slightly-curved *quillons*.

967A–F **Lamellar *cuirass* from a mass-grave of dead from the Battle of Wisby, Götland, c.1325–50**
(National Historical Museum, Wisby Armour no.25, Stockholm, Sweden)

A–C – reconstruction of armour as used in 1361; D – original lacing system; E–F – proposed reconstruction of armour in its original state. One of the most important armours to be found in mass graves at the site of the Battle of Wisby was this remarkable lamellar *cuirass*. The armour, as used in 1361, had been modified and reconstructed some time earlier by riveting the lamellae together and thus forming a sort of *coat-of-plates* (A–C). By then the armour might already have been half a century old. In its original state (D–F) it was a fine lamellar *cuirass* in which the individual lamellae were laced together in striking similarity to the better known lamellar armours of Eastern Europe, Asia, and the Islamic world. It may originally even have had flap-like sheets of lamellar to protect the shoulders and upper arms. The Wisby *cuirass* may have been made in some region to the south and east, areas with which Götland was in close trading contact.

968A–B **Shoulder plates from the Battle of Wisby, Götland, mid-14th century**
(National Historical Museum, Stockholm, Sweden)

Among the fragments of armour found in the Wisby graves were a number of shoulder plates from *cuirasses* or *coats-of-plates*.

969 *Coat-of-plates* from the Battle of Wisby, probably made in Flanders, mid-14th century
(National Historical Museum, armour no.7, Stockholm, Sweden)

The decoration on this *coat-of-plates* includes the arms of the Flemish Roorda family and the armour itself may have been imported from this area. It consists of notably large pieces of metal.

970A–B Reconstruction of a *coat-of-plates* from the Battle of Wisby, Götland, mid-14th century
(National Historical Museum, armour no.1, Stockholm, Sweden)

The leather foundation of this *coat-of-plates* had naturally disintegrated by the time it was excavated. This reconstruction is based on the positions in which the twenty internal iron staves, shoulder-plates and buckles were found. The result is very similar to many illustrations in early and mid-14th century art.

971A–C Spearheads, Denmark, 14th century (?)
(National Museum, Copenhagen, Denmark)

The style of these weapons suggests late 14th or even 15th-century pike heads, but such blades might have been used earlier in the 14th century.

972 Spearhead said to be from an unrecorded site in Wisconsin
(Public Museum, Milwaukee, United States)

This weapon sums up the problems and doubts surrounding several supposedly medieval weapons allegedly found in North America. Its condition is remarkably good and it was 'found' in an area of large-scale late 19th-century Scandinavian settlement. As such the spearhead, like almost all the other 'medieval Scandinavian' weapons from this part of America, is almost certainly a plant or a fake. Nevertheless, the possibility that it survived as a carefully preserved totemic object in the hands of indigenous peoples cannot as yet be totally ruled out.

973 Sword from the battle site of Nonnebjerg, Denmark, c.1340
(National Museum, Copenhagen, Denmark)

This fine though corroded sword has lost its tip. The length of the hilt also suggests that it was an early example of a 'hand-and-a-half' sword, which could be grasped by both hands to make a more powerful blow.

974A–B Crossbow bolts from Livrusttammaren, Norway, 14th–16th centuries
(after Alm)

These crossbow bolts are in a good state of repair. They have wooden flights which are twisted to make the bolt spin as it flew. Their length is just under 40 cm.

975 Axehead, Norway, 14th century (?)
(Meihaugen Museum, Lillehammer, Norway)

The thickness of the blade might indicate that it was a working tool rather than a weapon, but the protective sleeve to cover the upper part of the haft points to it being a weapon.

976 Axehead, Sweden, 14th century (?)
(West Götland Museum, Skara, Sweden)

Equally difficult to date. If it is, indeed, a weapon then its very substantial blade was probably designed to smash armour.

977A–B Painted altar front from Nes Sogn, Norway, early 14th century
(Historical Museum, Bergen, Norway)

A – The Betrayal; B – Sword in Mary's heart. This rather confused painting may show a warrior wearing a *bascinet*. He clearly has a long-sleeved mail *hauberk* with *mittens*, plus mail *chausses*. To these have been added *poleyns* for his knees and rather oddly-shaped *greaves*. This could suggest either that the artist was unfamiliar with plate armour, or that these leg defences were made of a semi-rigid material such as hardened leather. The swords (A and B) are typical of the early 14th century, having 'tear-drop' *pommels* and long, slender *quillons*.

978A–C 'Massacre of the Innocents', painted ceiling, Sweden, late 13th century
(*in situ* church, Dädesjö, Sweden)

Although one of the warriors on this painted ceiling has an up-to-date *great helm* (B), neither figure seems to have *mittens* on their long-sleeved mail *hauberks*. Both wear mail *chausses*. Shields are now smaller (B and C), flat-topped, and almost triangular.

979 'Massacre of the Innocents', stained glass window from Hablingbo, Götland, c.1350
(University Museum, Uppsala, Sweden)

Much more typical of the period are the arms and armour in a window illustrating the same subject as shown in fig.978. The swords are clearly tapering and one of them appears to have the lengthened hilt of a 'hand-and-a-half' sword. The helmets include a *chapel-de-fer* and a presumably visored *bascinet*. Plated leg-armour includes *poleyns*, *greaves* and *sabatons*, apparently worn over mail. Most attention focuses, however, on the body-armour. This is far from clear, but a distinction seems to be drawn between the mail of a *coif*, some kind of body-armour, and mail again appearing just above the hem of a tunic. The horizontal lines and dots across the body might be taken to indicate a *coat-of-plates*. Unfortunately the same pattern is seen on the presumably mail-covered arms. On balance it seems most likely that the man simply wears a long-sleeved mail *hauberk* with separate *gauntlets*. There is no indication of iron scales or plates being attached to these *gauntlets*.

980A–C **'Heraclius with the True Cross', painted wooden altar front from Nedstryn, Nordfjord, c.1300**
(Historical Museum, Bergen, Norway)

This part of a True Cross cycle again shows Norway to have been drawn into the wider European military tradition. The armour consists primarily of mail *hauberks* with integral *mittens* and *coifs*, plus mail *chausses*. All three figures have *poleyns* laced around their knees, while two also have *couters* on their elbows (B and C). The third figure (A) even has an early form of presumed *bascinet* with a hinged visor; a feature which could indicate that this painted altar front is a bit later than 1300. The horses wear *caparisons* but there is no evidence to indicate whether or not these included any form of armour beneath the cloth.

981 **'Massacre of the Innocents', carving, Götland, mid-14th century**
(*in situ* south door of the church choir, Lye, Sweden)

There is nothing exotic or alien about the equipment in this portrayal of the Massacre of the Innocents except that the armour appears very outdated . Here a warrior wears an old-fashioned flat-topped *great helm* and has a long-sleeved mail *hauberk* with *mittens*.

982A–C **'Death of St Olaf', *Flateyjarbók*, Iceland, late 14th century**
(Manuscript Institute col. 310, Reykjavik, Iceland)

Though strictly speaking dating from outside the period covered by this study, the illustrations in the *Flateyjarbók* shed an interesting light on the arms and armour of medieval Europe's most far-flung region. The warriors wear tall, conical *chapel-de-fer war-hats*. The sword (B) is a typical 14th century type with curved *quillons* and a round *pommel*. The men also wield axes that might have been included in the picture because they were mentioned in the text. Such weapons may, however, have remained popular in 14th century Iceland. Note that these axes have almost nothing in common with those supposedly found in North America.

Notes

1. P. Schreiner, 'Zur Ausrüstung des Kriegers in Byzanz, im Kiewer Russland und in Nordeuropa nach bildlichen und literarischen Quellen', *Acta Universitatis Upsaliensis, Figura* n.s. vol.XIX (1981), pp.228–31.

2. L. Musset, 'Problèmes militaires du Monde Scandinave (VII–XIIe siècles)', in *Settimane di Studio del Centro Italiano di Studi sull'Alto Medioevo* (Spoleto, 1968), pp.246, 253, 264–5 and 273.

3. A.E. Christensen, 'Denmark between the Viking Age and the time of the Valdemars', *Medieval Scandinavia* vol.I (1966), pp.33–6, 40 and 44–6; H.R.E. Davidson, *The Sword in Anglo-Saxon England* (Oxford, 1962), pp.198–202.

4. J. Shepard, 'The English and Byzantium; A Study of their Role in the Byzantine Army in the Later Eleventh Century', *Traditio* vol.XXIX (1973), pp.54–7.

5. Musset, *op.cit.* pp.251–2; G. Rausing, *The Bow, Some Notes on its Origins and Development* (Lund, 1967), pp.62–3; E. Christiansen, *The Northern Crusades: The Baltic and the Catholic Frontier 1100–1525* (London, 1980), p.65.

6. Rausing, *op.cit.* p.64.

7. Christiansen, *The Northern Crusades, op.cit.* pp.23–109.

8. Christiansen, *The Northern Crusades, op.cit.* pp.22–4 and 64–5; Musset, *op.cit.* pp.287–8.

9. Musset, *op.cit.* pp.288–90.

10. Rausing, *op.cit.* p.64.

11. Christiansen, *The Northern Crusades, op.cit.* pp.65 and 88; J. Alm, 'Europeiska armborst; En översickt', *Vaaben-historisk Aarboger* v/b (1947), pp.108, 112–14, 128–30 and 141–2.

12. F.B. Singleton, *'Kalevala' and the Historical Geography of Finland* (M.A. thesis, Leeds University, 1952), *passim.*

13. Rausing, *op.cit.* p.133; Christiansen, *The Northern Crusades, op.cit.* p.182.

14. Singleton, *op.cit.* p.111; M.J. Swanton, *The Spear in Anglo-Saxon Times* (Ph.D. thesis, Durham University, 1966), p.569.

15. Christiansen, *The Northern Crusades, op.cit.* pp.40 and 46.

16. Christiansen, *The Northern Crusades, op.cit.* p.209.

17. Christiansen, *The Northern Crusades, op.cit.* p.173.

18. R. Djanpoladian and A. Kirpičnikov, 'Mittelalterlicher Säbel mit einer Armenischen Inschrift, gefunden im subpolaren Ural', *Gladius* vol.X (1972), pp.20–1.

19. G.D. Painter, 'The Tartar Relation and the Vinland Map; an Interpretation', in *The Vinland Map and the Tartar Relation*, ed. R.A. Skelton, T.E. Marston and G.D. Painter (New Haven, 1965), pp.258–9.

Chapter 19

The Baltic Peoples

During the medieval period the modern Baltic States and certain neighbouring areas along the southern and eastern shores of the Baltic Sea were inhabited by various tribal peoples speaking Finn, Balt and Slav languages. They included the Pomeranians, Prussians, Lithuanians, Livonians, Latvians and Estonians who, for some centuries, maintained their independence from Poles, Russians and Germans. These Baltic peoples were also the target of a series of so-called Northern Crusades. Their conquest and conversion was, in fact, the reason for the creation of the Brethren of the Sword, a German military order which was amalgamated with the larger Teutonic Order in 1237–9. Although the Teutonic Order had been founded in Palestine in 1190, its greatest strength developed in the Baltic region, where it was active from 1228 until the mid-16th century.

Pomerania won its independence from Poland in 1033 but became increasingly Germanised until, as the Duchies of Slavinia and Pomerania and part of the March of Brandenburg, it was fully absorbed into the German Empire in the 13th century. The invasion of neighbouring pagan peoples by German Crusaders began in 1231, their first target being the Prussians. The ensuing wars continued well into the 14th century. Further north, present-day Estonia and Latvia had been invaded in 1203. Squeezed between these two attacks, Lithuania retained its independence and even its paganism into the second half of the 14th century. By that time, however, the Grand Duchy of Lithuania had gone on the offensive, eventually becoming the largest territorial state in Europe. Subsequently uniting with Poland in 1386 to create a vast Eastern European empire, Lithuania's paganism was only officially abolished in all areas in 1387.

Prior to these efforts at enforced conversion by German Crusaders, Poles, Danes and Russians, the pagan Baltic peoples had been tribal and backward. Though always warlike they became militarised during the 11th and 12th centuries with the appearance of mounted warrior élites.[1] Their military equipment was simple and very few men possessed armour. Weaponry was generally imported from Russia or Scandinavia, and although archery was widespread it was relatively primitive. More sophisticated weaponry was soon captured or purchased from their foes or neighbours, and the Balts also learned to copy their enemies' siege engines.[2] Nevertheless, swords were to remain rare until the 14th century, spears being by far the most common weapons.[3]

The Lett and Liv tribes of present-day Latvia had been small, weak, and previously preyed upon by their more warlike neighbours. They soon came to terms with the predominately German invaders, but the Estonians, Lithuanians and Prussians were quite a different matter.[4] Relatively rich and numerous, the Prussians adopted guerrilla tactics in their marshy and forested homeland to counter the invader's armoured cavalry and crossbows. The Lithuanians were poorer, fewer, and lived in even more inaccessible country. They had plenty of horses, however, which enabled them to develop devastating light cavalry tactics.[5] So effective were these Baltic warriors that many of the Prussian aristocracy, once converted to Christianity, were encouraged to maintain their own military traditions in the service of the Teutonic Knights. A similar process was seen later in some Lithuanian areas.[6] The German Crusaders and Military Orders were themselves, of course, equipped in typical Central European style.[7]

By the mid-14th century part of the Lithuanian élite wore full armour, probably in Western European style,[8] but the majority still fought in a traditional manner. Their military organisation may have become more sophisticated by the 13th and early 14th centuries, but the entire nation still had genuine military obligations which enabled the Lithuanian leadership to mobilise remarkably large armies of horse and foot. By now more warriors had mail, and the Lithuanians also copied both Polish and Russian military technology. Their strategy mainly rested on fast raids for cattle, slaves or booty, particularly in summer when the swamps hindered the heavy Christian cavalry. In return the Crusaders preferred to attack in winter, using the frozen rivers as highways.[9]

Following Mongol raids in the 1240s and 1250s, the Lithuanians adopted various Central Asian cavalry tactics, though using javelins and swords instead of bows, while their infantry was still armed with spears, axes and perhaps crossbows. Eastern European military influence also grew stronger, and Lithuanian arms and armour were in some ways similar to those of both Russia and the Mongols. This was particularly true of eastern Lithuania, centred upon Vilna (Vilnius) after the establishment of the *Diarchies* in 1345. This system of government meant that Lithuania was administratively divided into two regions though remaining legally one state. Eastern Lithuania soon adopted Orthodox Christianity and recruited many eastern mercenaries, including Mongols. Western Lithuania clung to its paganism for another generation but was correspondingly influenced by the Western European military technology of the Teutonic Knights.[10]

Figures

983 Spearhead from Lejabitini, Latvia, 11th–12th centuries
(National Museum, Riga, Latvia)

The peculiar outline of this blade is probably a result of burning and corrosion resulting from a 'weapon-killing' ceremony. It may originally have been similar to the weapon from Ošbirzes (fig.997).

984 Spearhead from Salapils, probably imported from
Götland, 1000–50
(National Museum, Riga, Latvia)

Once again a presumed import from the Swedish island of Götland has a distinctly angled outline.

985 Spearhead from Saaremaa Island, Estonia, 11th–12th
centuries
(Historical Institute, Academy of Sciences, Tallin, Estonia)

Spearheads with wings or lugs at the base of their blades seem rare among the non-Germanic Baltic peoples. This example might be an import from elsewhere, or it could show foreign influence. Such weapons do, however, seem to have been known in 12th-century Finland. Although culturally akin to the Estonians, the Finns were under much stronger Swedish influence.

986 Spearhead from Matkule, Kurland, 12th–14th centuries
(National Museum, Riga, Latvia)

This spearhead was made by the Kurshi people. It is an example of the weaponry used by some of Europe's last pagans in their grim fight against Teutonic Knights on the one hand and Orthodox Russians on the other.

987 Sword from Pomerania, Poland, 10th–11th centuries
(State Archaeological Museum, Warsaw, Poland)

This weapon was probably made in the Rhineland, although the *pommel* and *quillons* may have been added locally.

988 Sword from Pomerania, Poland, 10th–11th centuries
(Ethnological Museum, Łódź, Poland)

Like the previous sword from the northern part of present-day Poland, this weapon, or at least its blade, was probably made in the Rhineland.

989 Spearhead from Martina Island, Lithuanian (?), 11th–12th centuries (?)
(National Museum, Riga, Latvia)

A large number of decorated spearheads have been found in the Baltic republics. Most certainly predate the area's conquest by the German religious orders, as they are generally associated with pre-Christian burials and other rituals. The standard of metallurgical technology indicated by these weapons is very high and belies the supposed backwardness of the pagan cultures which produced them. The form of this particular spear, with its broad blade and very short socket, is, however, old-fashioned, and suggests that armour was rare.

990 Spearhead from Viltina, Estonia, 11th–12th centuries
(Historical Institute, Estonian Academy of Sciences, Tallin, Estonia)

The top of this spear blade has been bent over as part of the its ceremonial 'killing'. It would originally have been a substantial weapon, having a much larger socket than that seen in fig.989.

991 Spearhead from Salapils, probably imported from Götland, 11th–12th centuries
(National Museum, Riga, Latvia)

This highly-decorated blade is different in many ways from others found in the Baltic Republics. Its decoration suggests a Scandinavian origin, probably having come from the Swedish island of Götland.

992 Spearhead from Vegi, Latvia, 11th–12th centuries
(National Museum, Riga, Latvia)

This spear is strongly made, with a narrow blade and long socket suggesting that it might have been for use against an armoured foe.

993 Spearhead from Bunkas, Latvia, 11th–12th centuries
(National Museum, Riga, Latvia)

This blade has again been bent almost double in a 'weapon-killing' ceremony.

994 Spearhead from Markalne, Latvia, 11th–12th centuries
(National Museum, Riga, Latvia)

This decorated blade has been only slightly bent, its original shape being indicated by the dotted line. It was found in north-east Latvia and probably had a Livonian origin.

995 **Spearhead from Kazdanga, Kurland, 11th–13th centuries**
(National Museum, Riga, Latvia)

The tip of this blade has again been ceremonially turned over in a fire. Such ceremonies were characteristic of the Kurshi and other pagan peoples of present-day Latvia.

996 **Spearhead from Kurzeme, Kurland, 11th–13th centuries**
(National Museum, Riga, Latvia)

A much corroded spear also from a Kurshi site.

997 **Spearhead from Ošbirzes, Latvia, 11th–12th centuries**
(National Museum, Riga, Latvia)

This spearhead is of a different form, having an almost symmetrical leaf-shaped blade and very substantial socket.

998 **Spearhead from Turaida, Latvia, 11th–12th centuries**
(National Museum, Riga, Latvia)

A type seen throughout much of Europe. Only its pattern-welded decoration distinguishes it from spear blades seen in Scandinavia and Russia.

999 **Spearhead from Saaremaa Island, probably imported from Götland, 1000–50**
(Historical Institute, Academy of Sciences, Tallin, Estonia)

Minor details of forging suggest that this could be a Swedish import. The angled lower edge of the blade is also characteristic of Scandinavian weapons at this time, though such a style is also seen in some locally-made weapons.

Notes

1. E. Christiansen, *The Northern Crusades: The Baltic and Catholic Frontier 1100–1525* (London, 1980), pp.35–6.
2. Christiansen, *op.cit.* pp.36–7, 65 and 97; A.N. Kirpičnikov, 'Russische Helm dem frühen Mittelalter', *Zeitschrift für historische Waffen- und Kostümkunde* vol.XV (1973), p.89.
3. A. Antiens, 'The Old Arms of Basilsimsa (History of the Ventspilskaya Okrug)', *Sovietskay Venta* I (3 March 1983, Leningrad); A.K. Antiens, 'Structure and Manufacturing Techniques of Pattern-Welded Objects found in the Baltic States', *Journal of the Iron and Steel Institute* (1968), pp.565–7.
4. W. Urban, 'The Organization and Defence of the Livonian Frontier in the Thirteenth Century' *Speculum* vol.XLVIII (1973), pp.525–6 and 530.

5. Christiansen, *op.cit.* pp.102, 133 and 164–7.
6. Christiansen, *op.cit.* pp.167–8 and 202–4.
7. Christiansen, *op.cit.* p.168.
8. Christiansen, *op.cit.* pp.96–7.
9. Christiansen, *op.cit.* pp.133–4; Urban, *op.cit.* pp.525 and 528–9; A. Nadolski, *Broń średniowieczna z ziem polskich (Medieval arms and armour in Poland)* (Warsaw, 1978), p.64.
10. J. Deveike, 'The Lithuanian Diarchies', *The Slavonic and East European Review* vol.XXVIII (1949–50), pp.392–7.

Exemplary Figures

(after Angus McBride, Richard Hook, Christopher Gravett and David Nicolle)

A Second half of the 11th century (France)
B Mid-13th century (England)
C Mid-14th century (Germany)

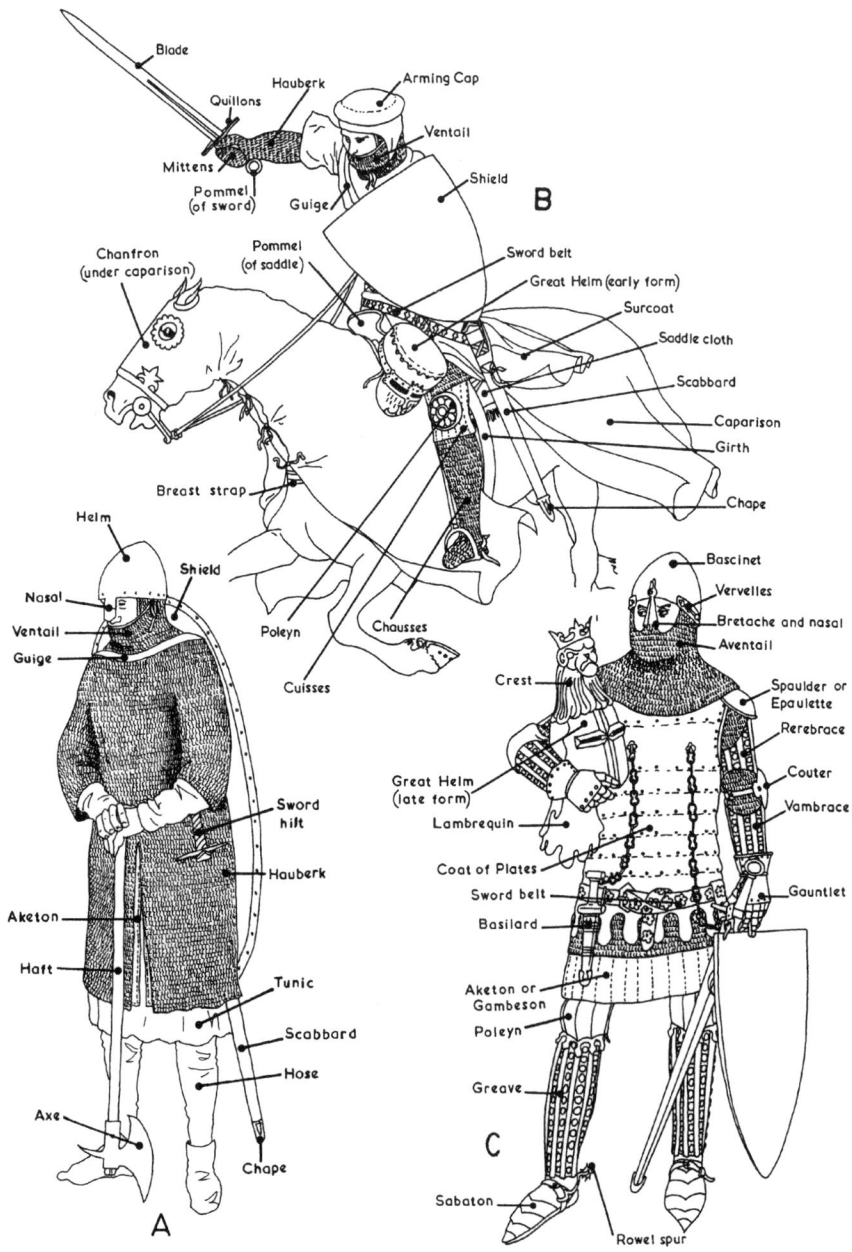

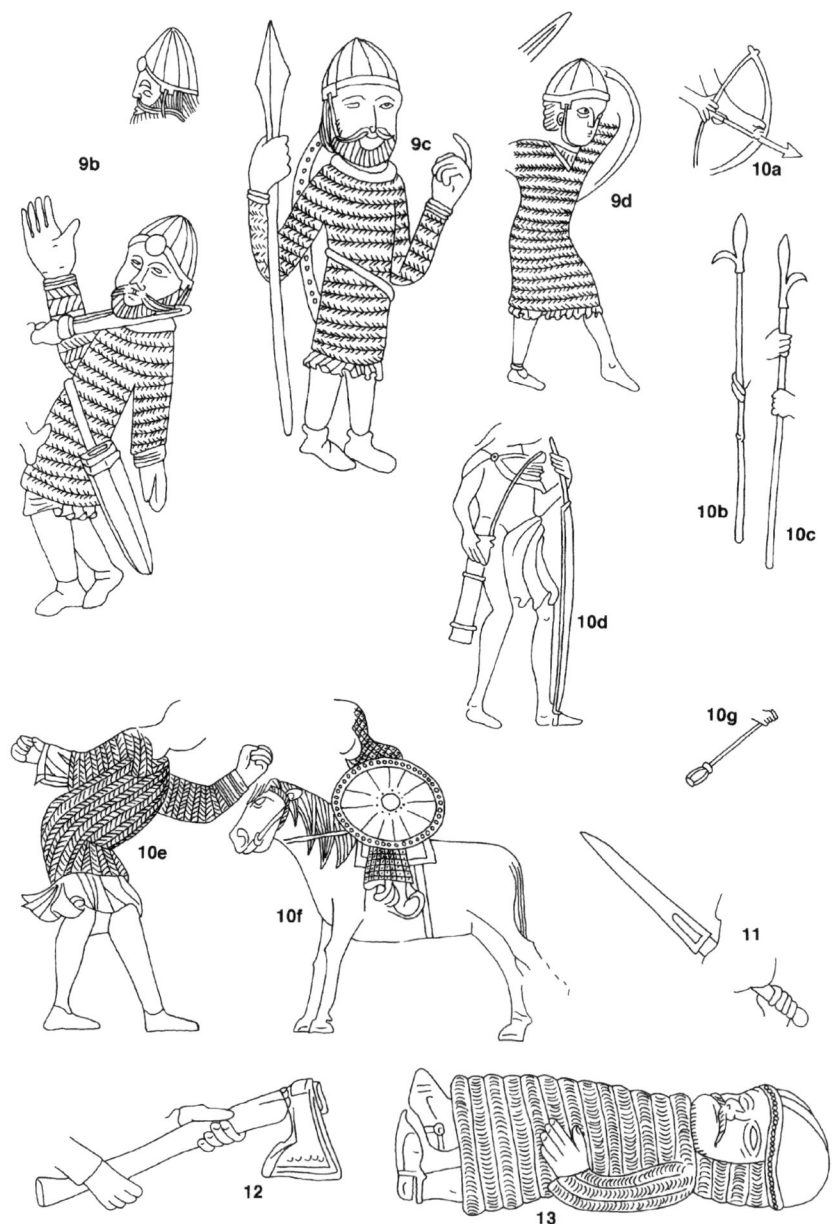

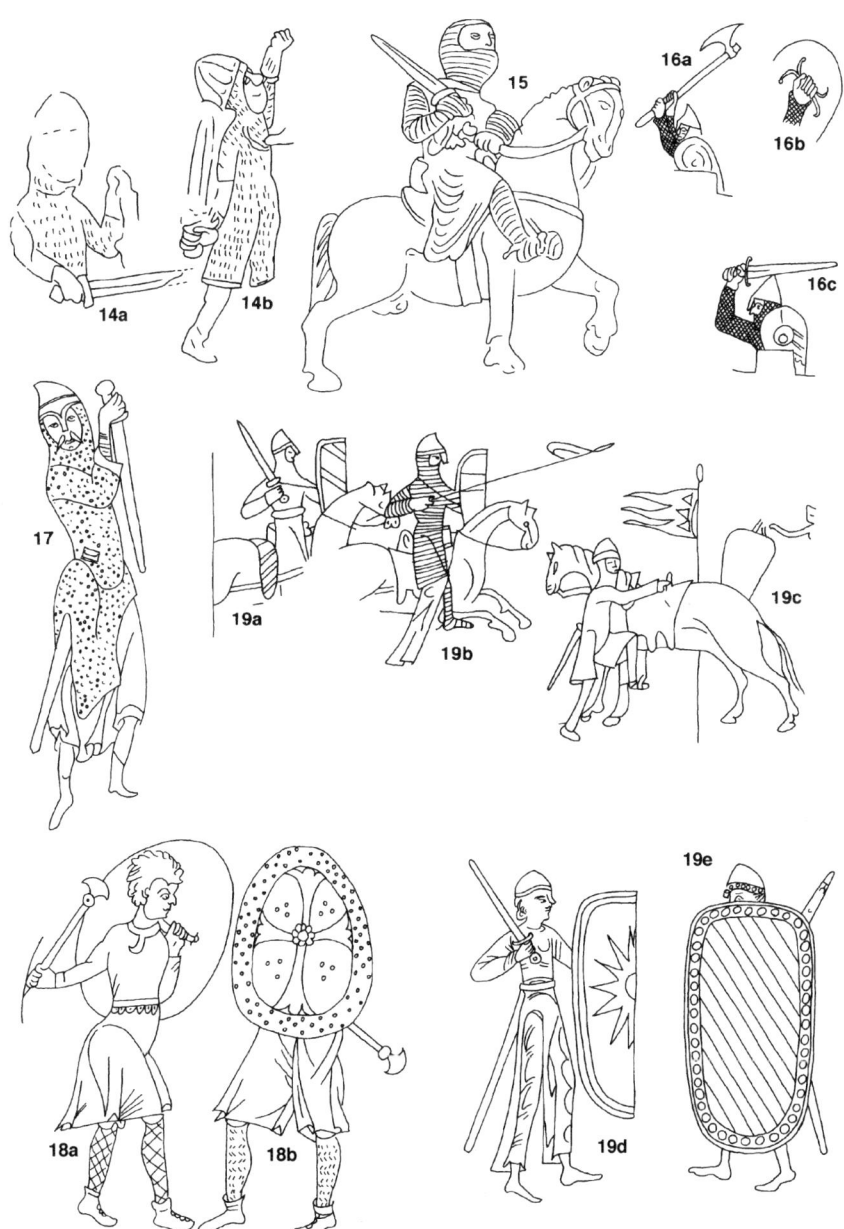

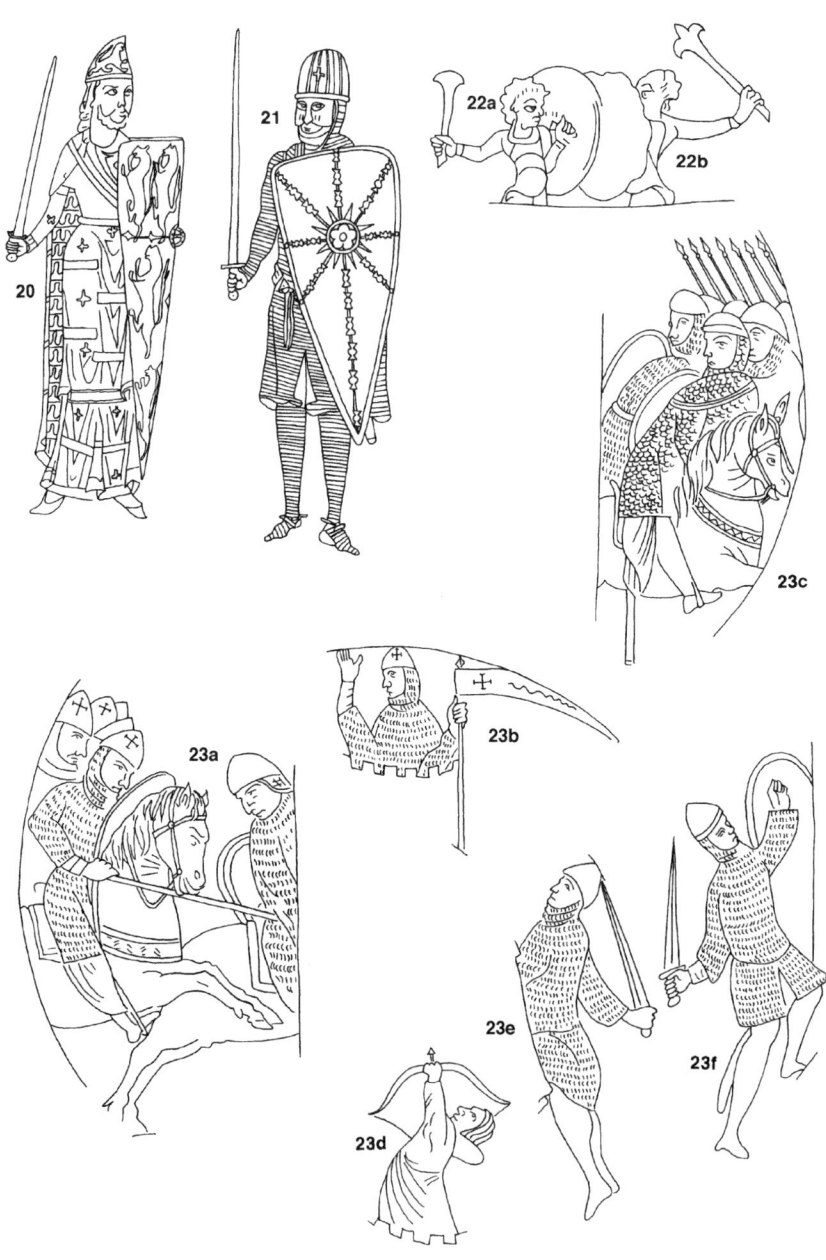

20

21

22a

22b

23a

23b

23c

23d

23e

23f

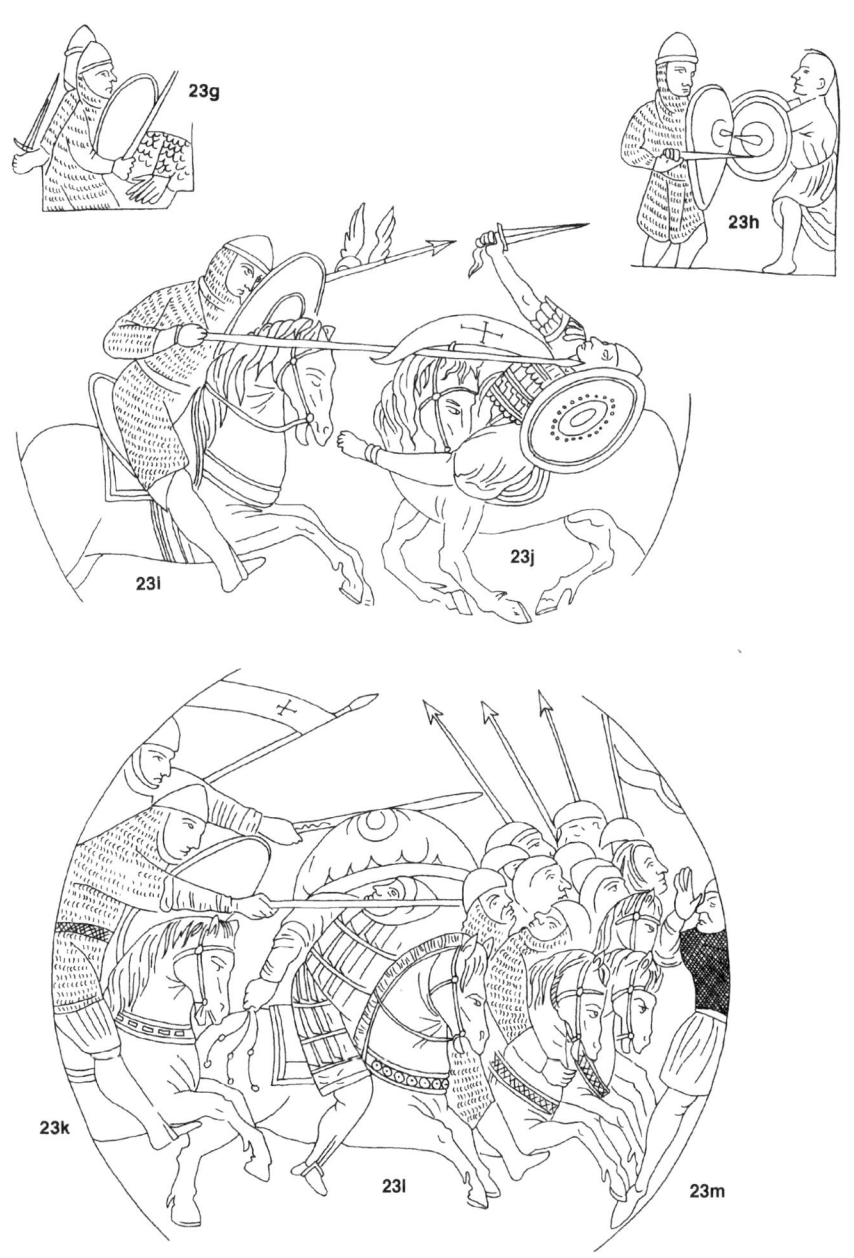

23g

23h

23i

23j

23k

23l

23m

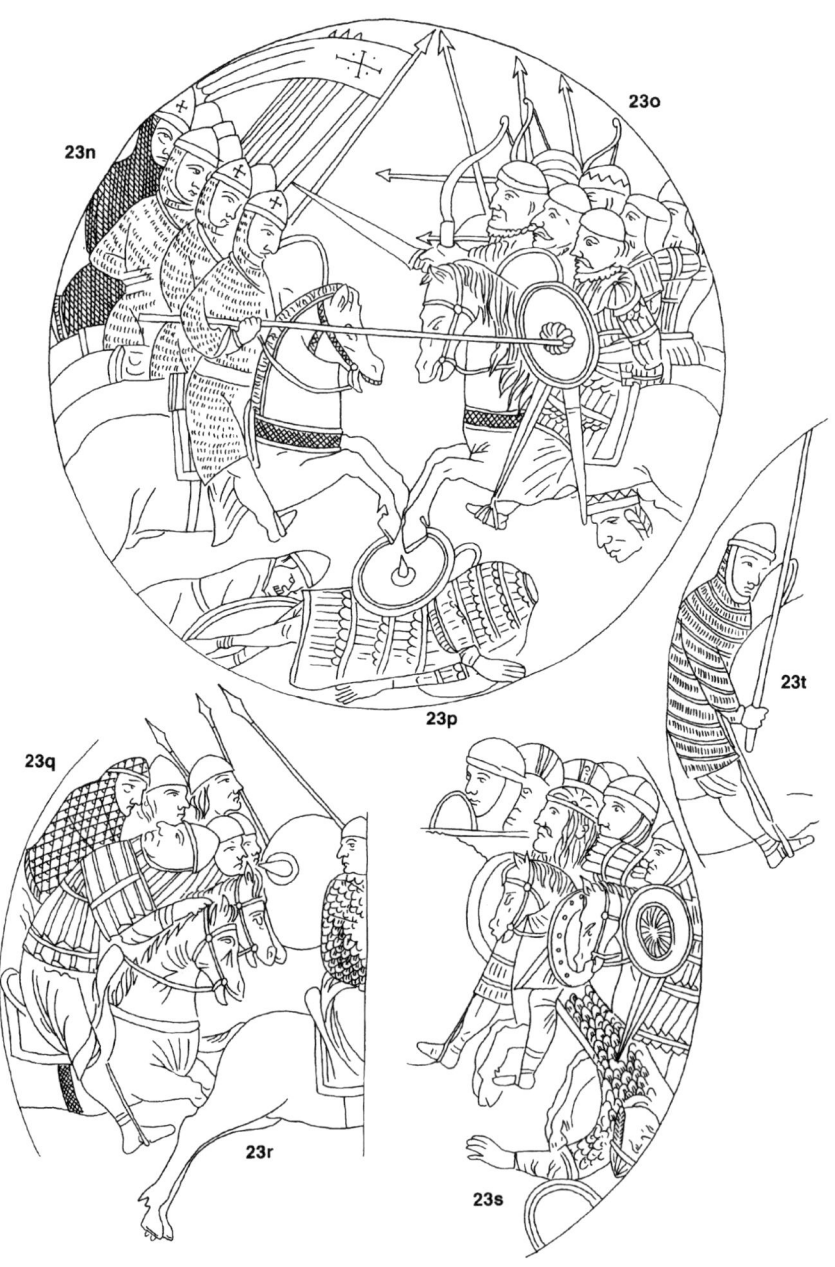

23n

23o

23p

23q

23r

23s

23t

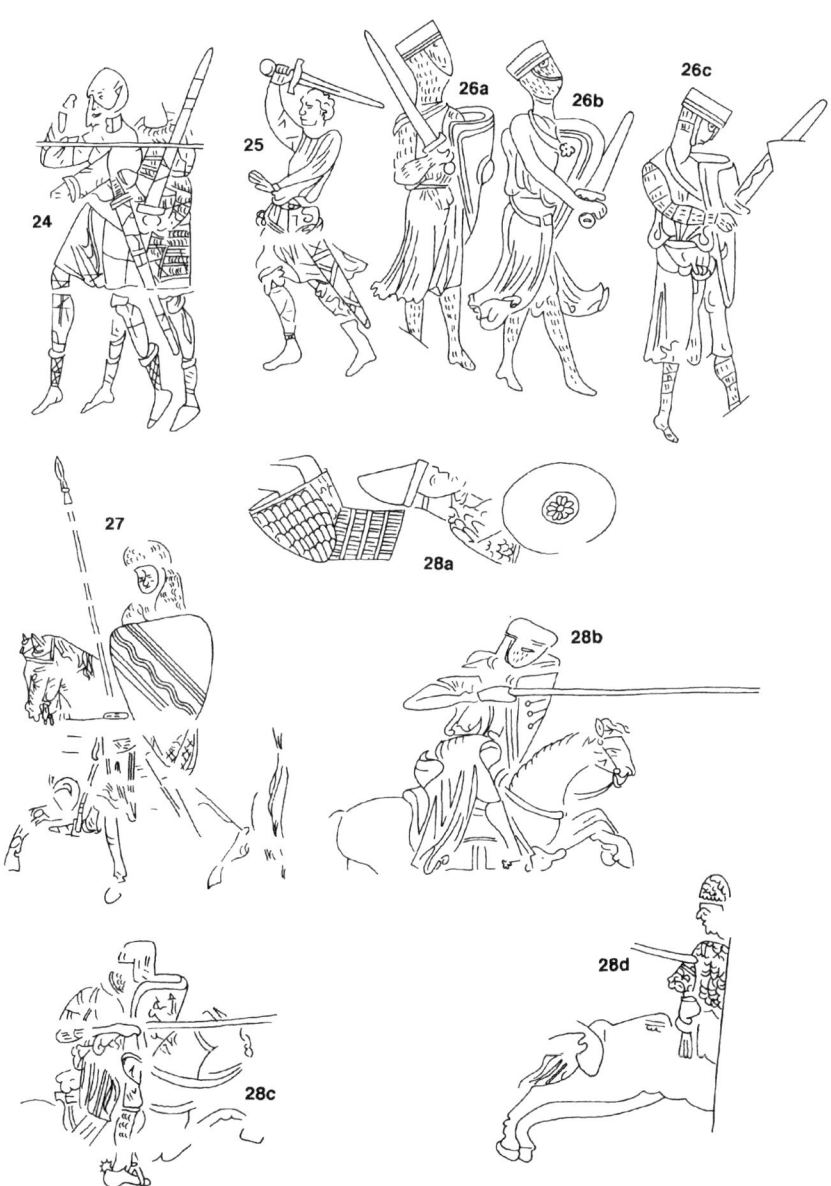

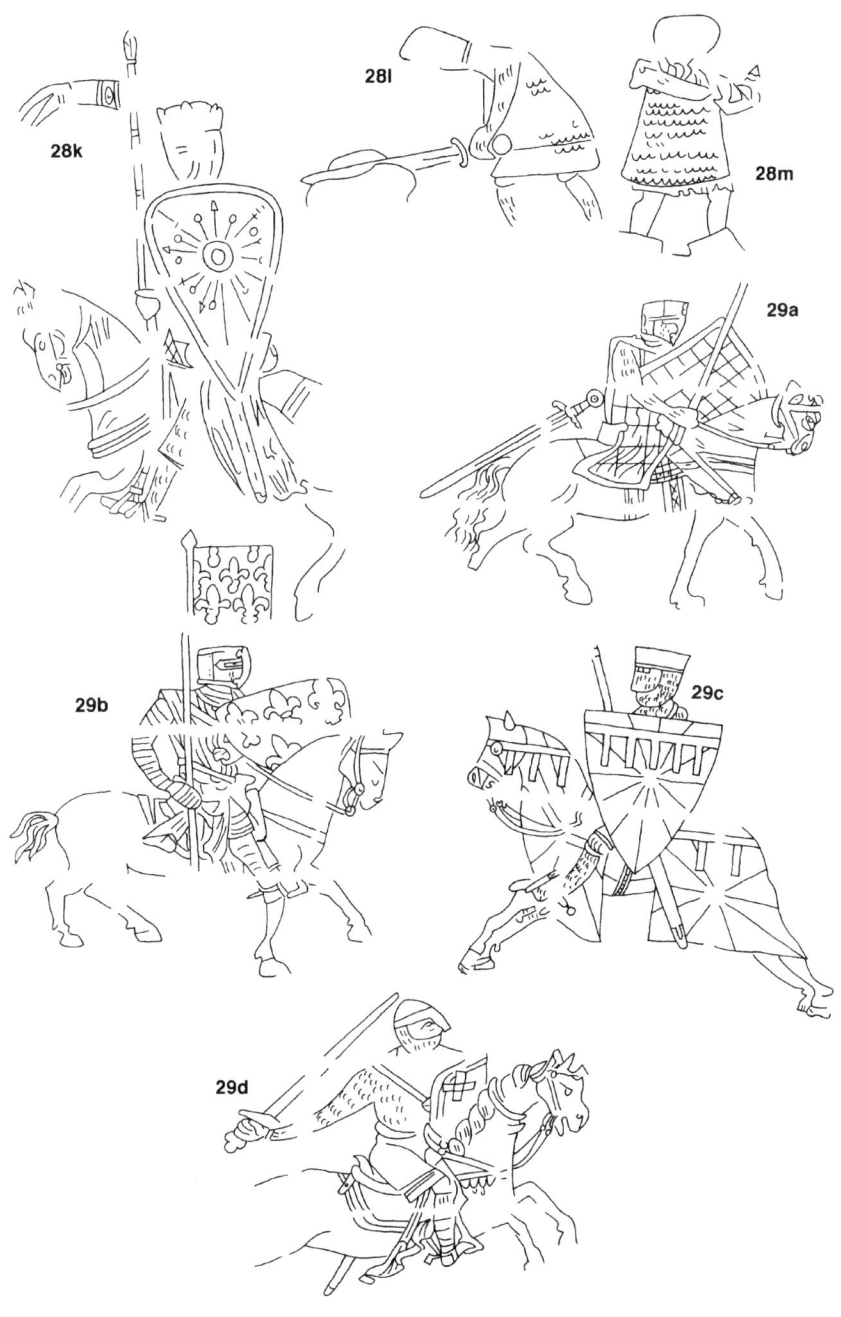

28k

28l

28m

29a

29b

29c

29d

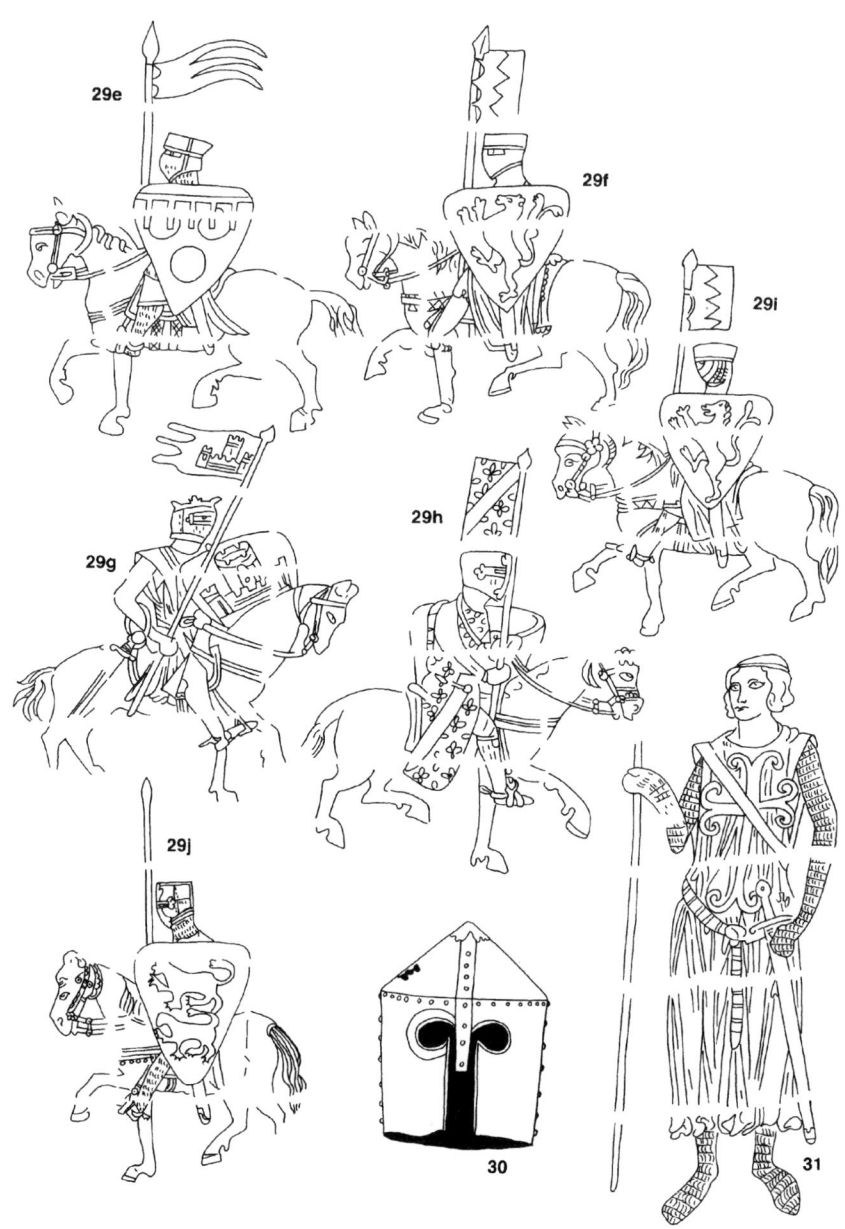

29e

29f

29i

29g

29h

29j

30

31

32a

32b

32c

33a

33b

34

35

36

37

38

39

40

41a

41b

41c

42a

42b

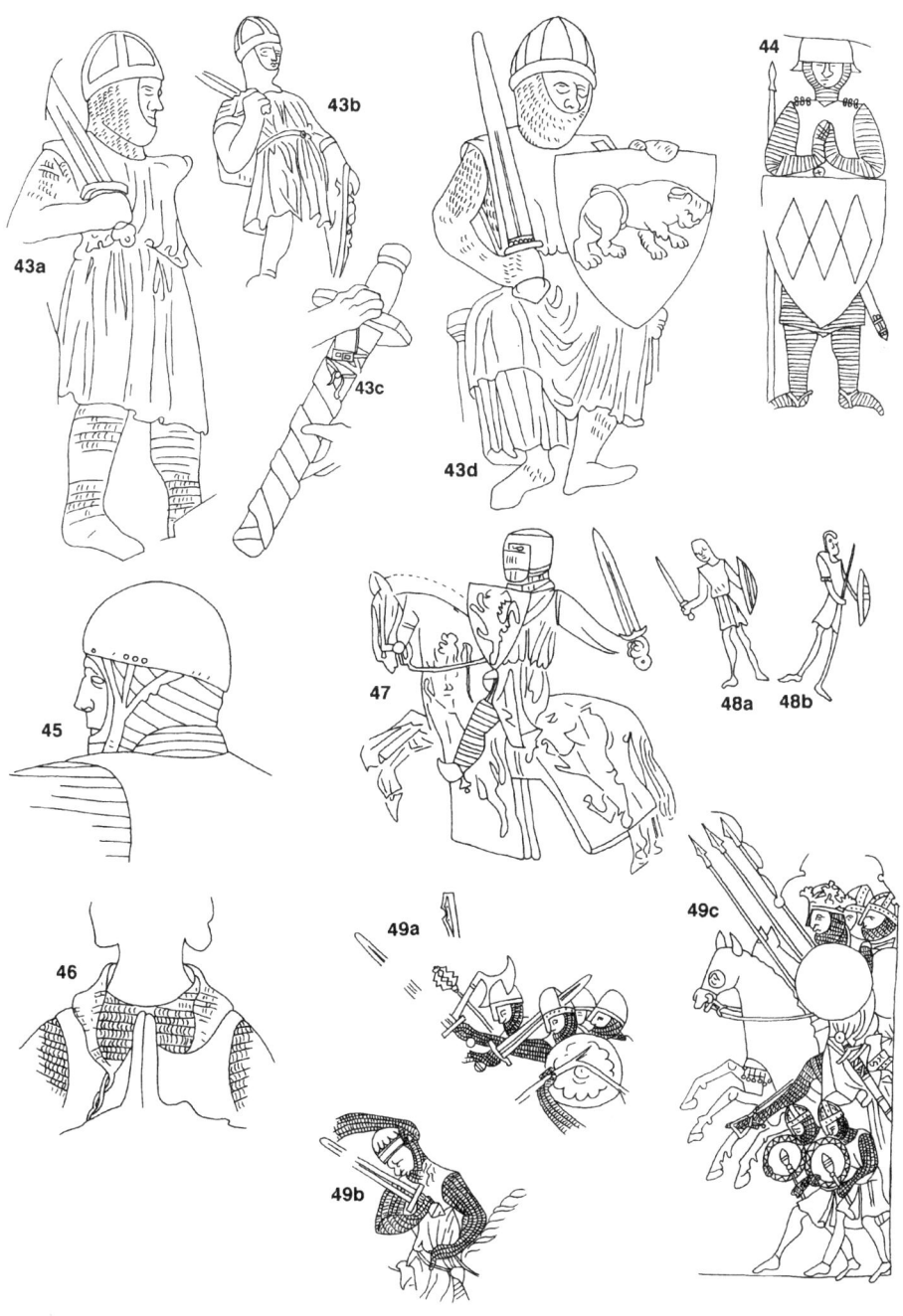

49z

49aa

49ab

49ad

49ae

49af

49ac

49ag

49ai

49ah

49aj

49am

49ak

49an

49al

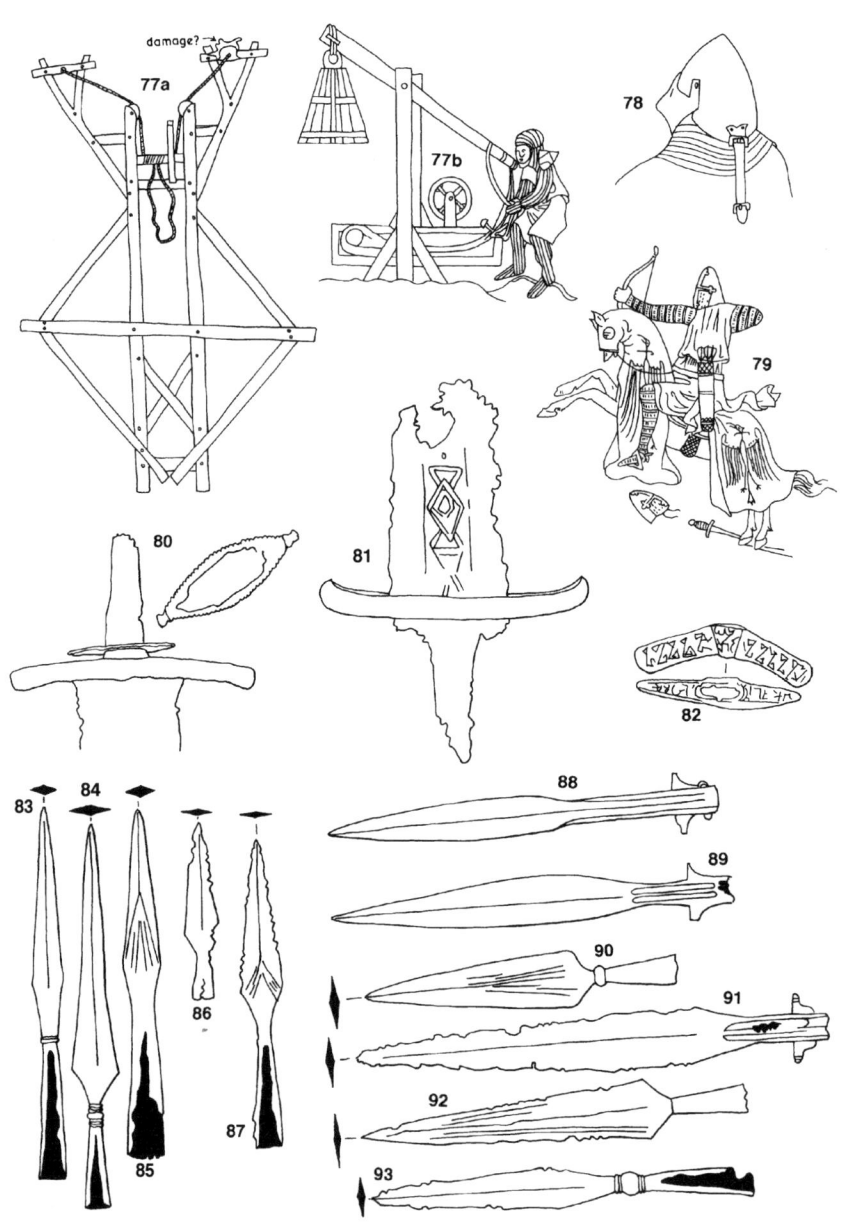

97w

97x   97y

97aa

97ab

97z   97ac

97ae

97ad   97af

97ah

97ag   97ai

97aj

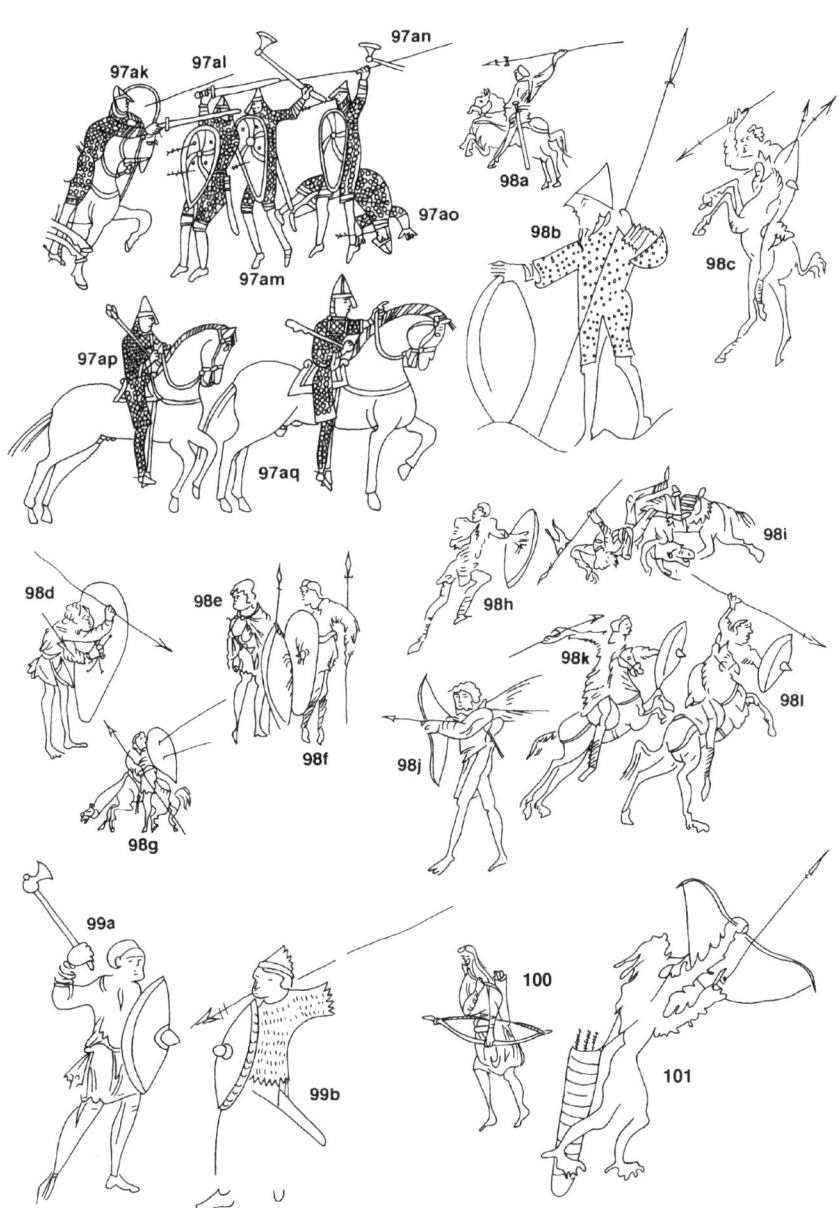

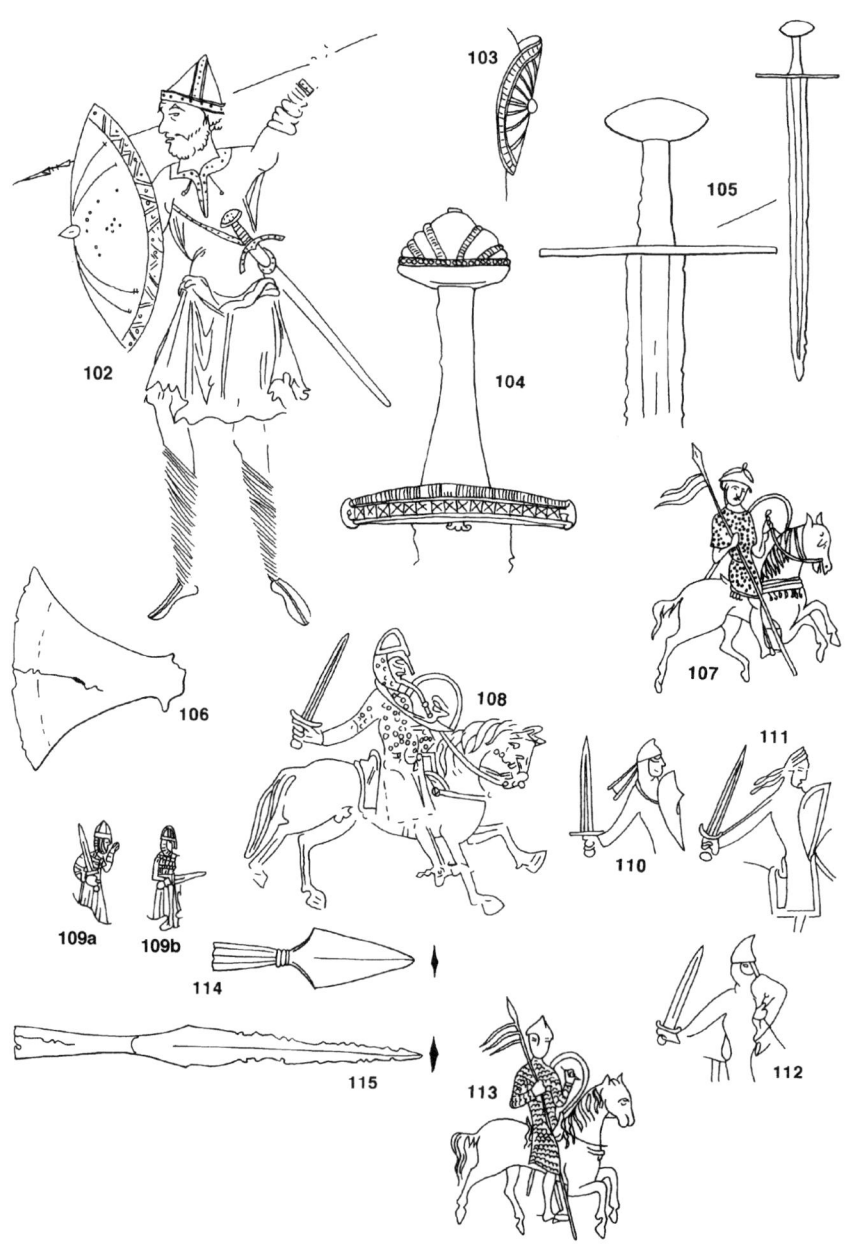

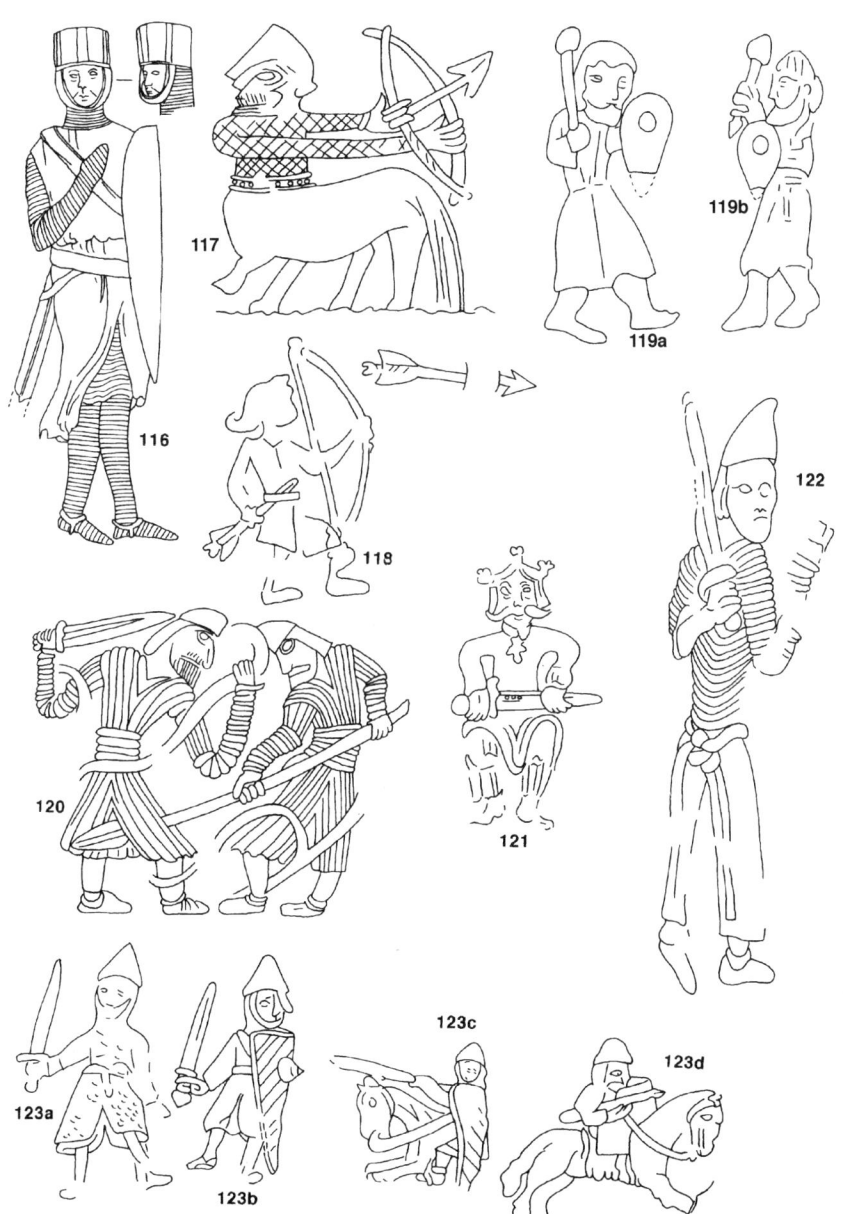

116

117

119b

119a

118

120

121

122

123a

123b

123c

123d

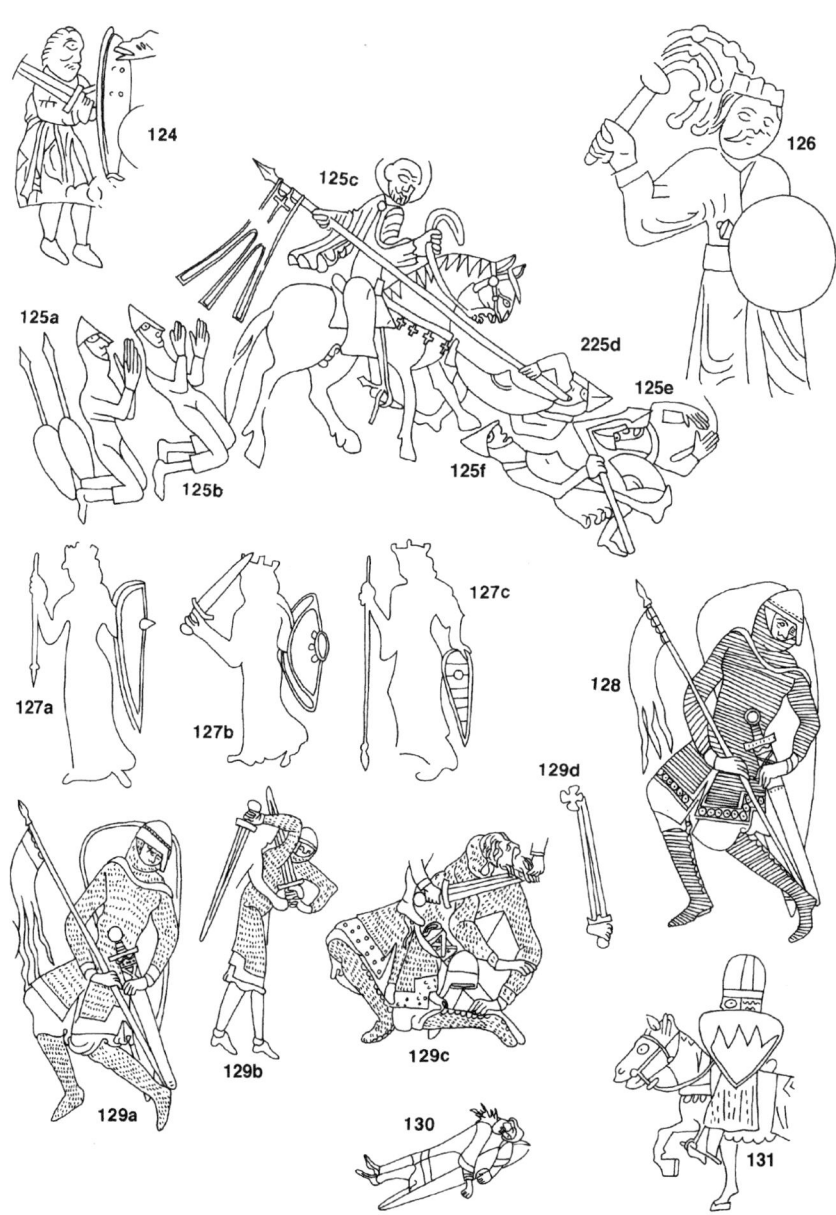

124

125c

125a

225d

126

125e

125b

125f

127a

127b

127c

128

129d

129a

129b

129c

130

131

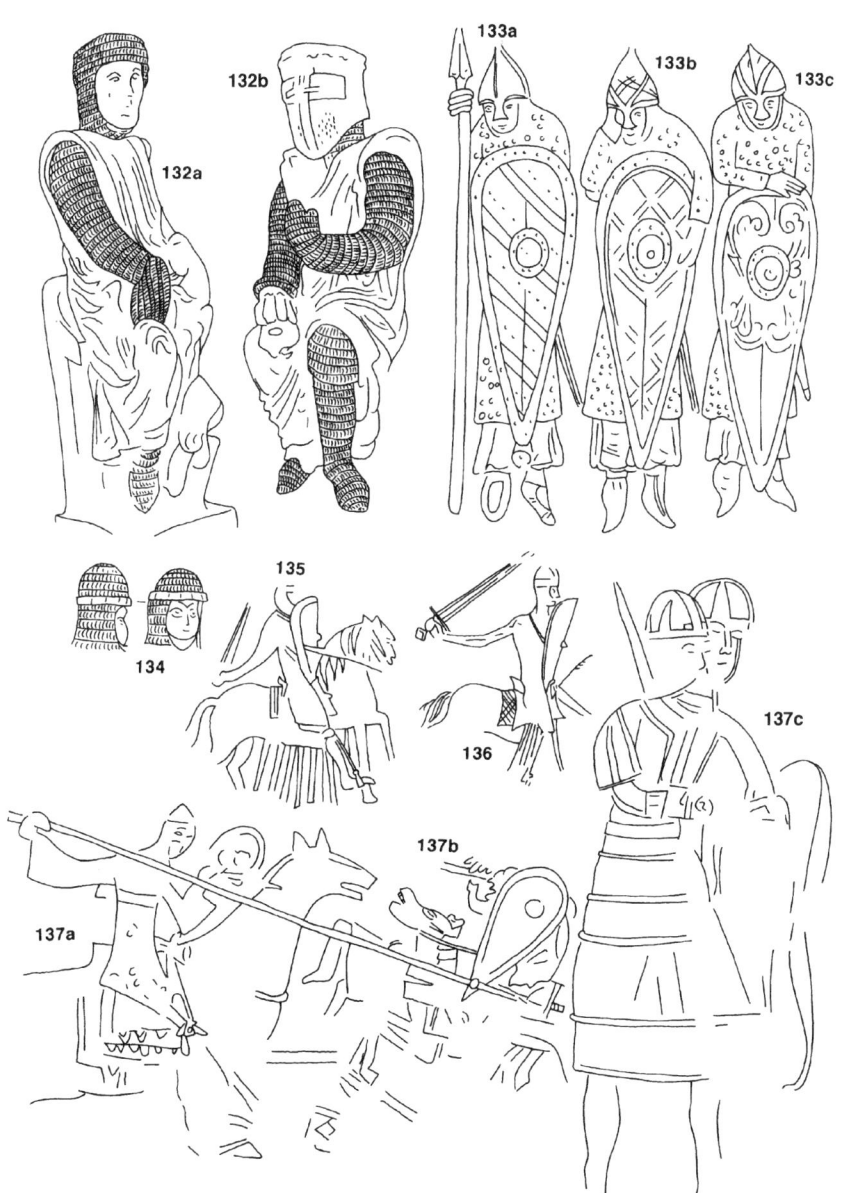

132a
132b
133a
133b
133c
134
135
136
137a
137b
137c

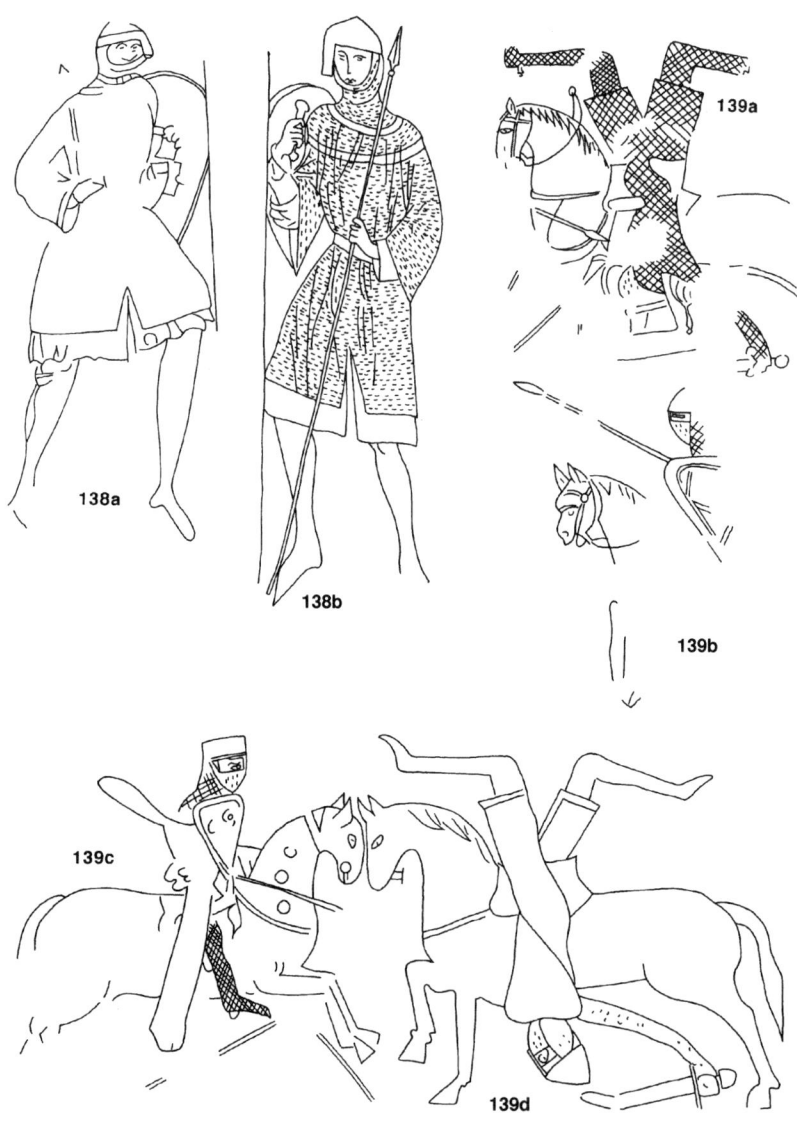

138a

138b

139a

139b

139c

139d

139e

139f

139g

139h

139k

139i

139j

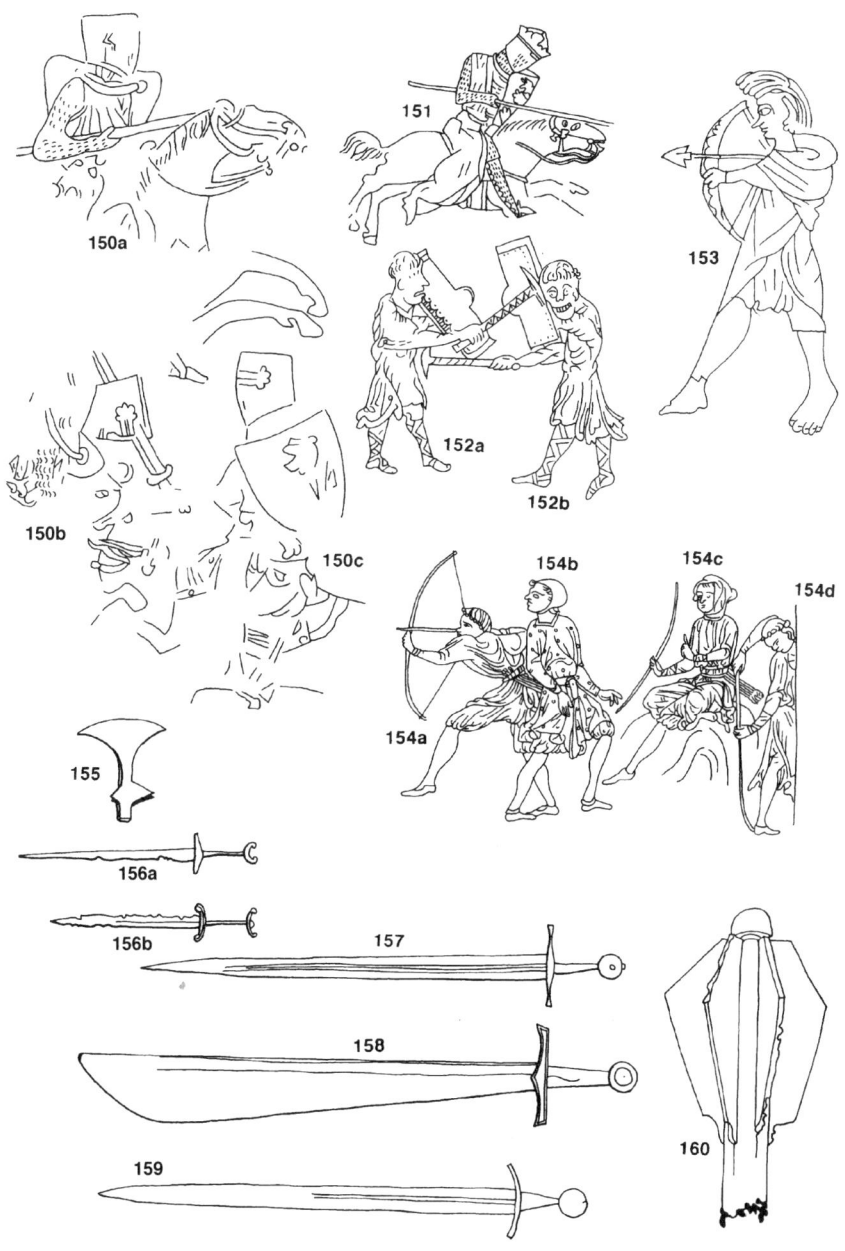

150a

151

153

150b

152a

150c

152b

154b

154c

154d

154a

155

156a

156b

157

158

159

160

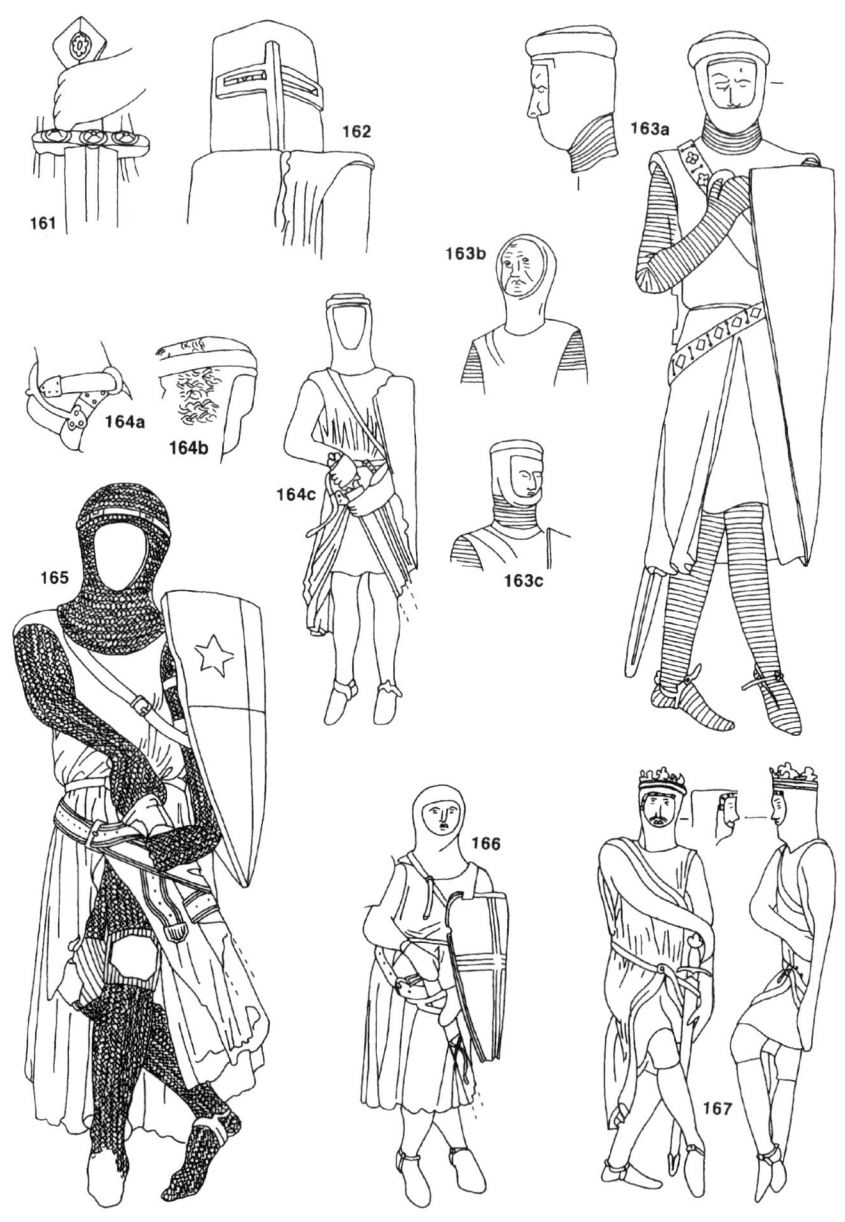

161

162

163a

163b

163c

164a

164b

164c

165

166

167

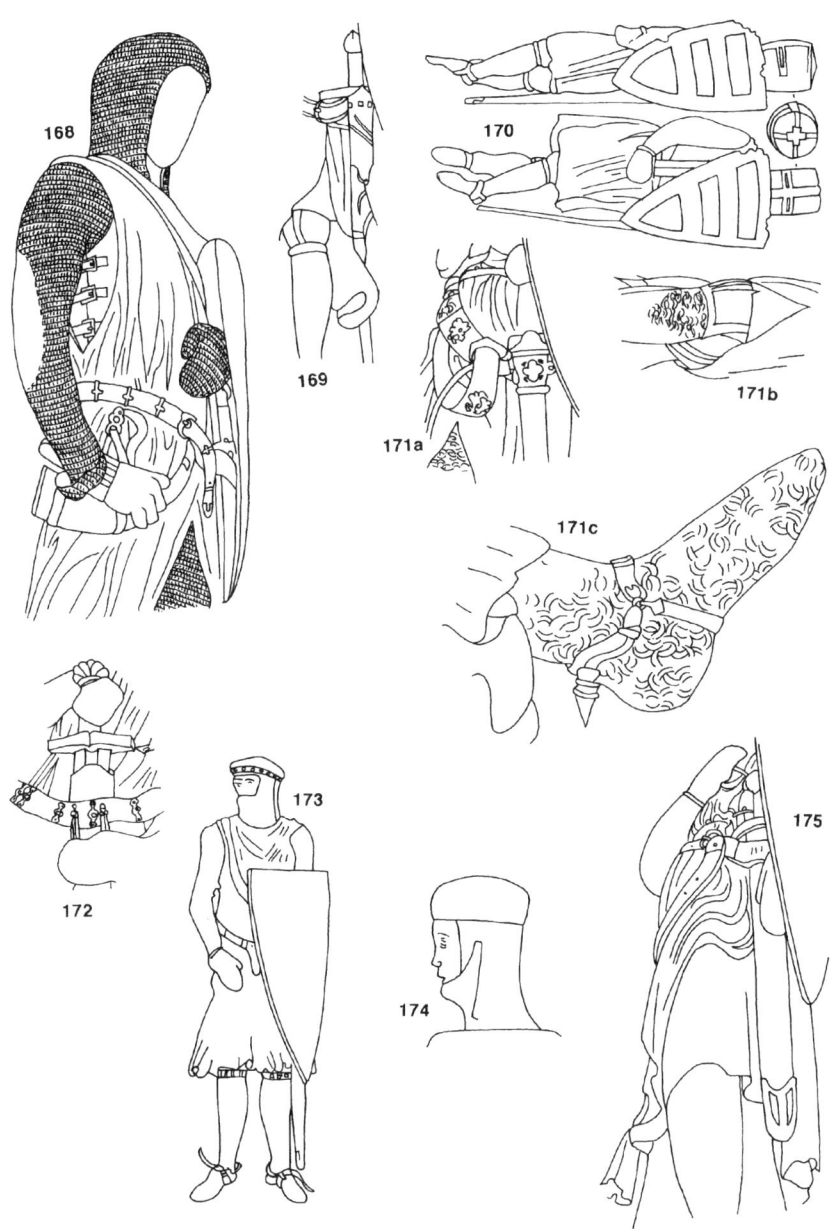

168

169

170

171a

171b

171c

172

173

174

175

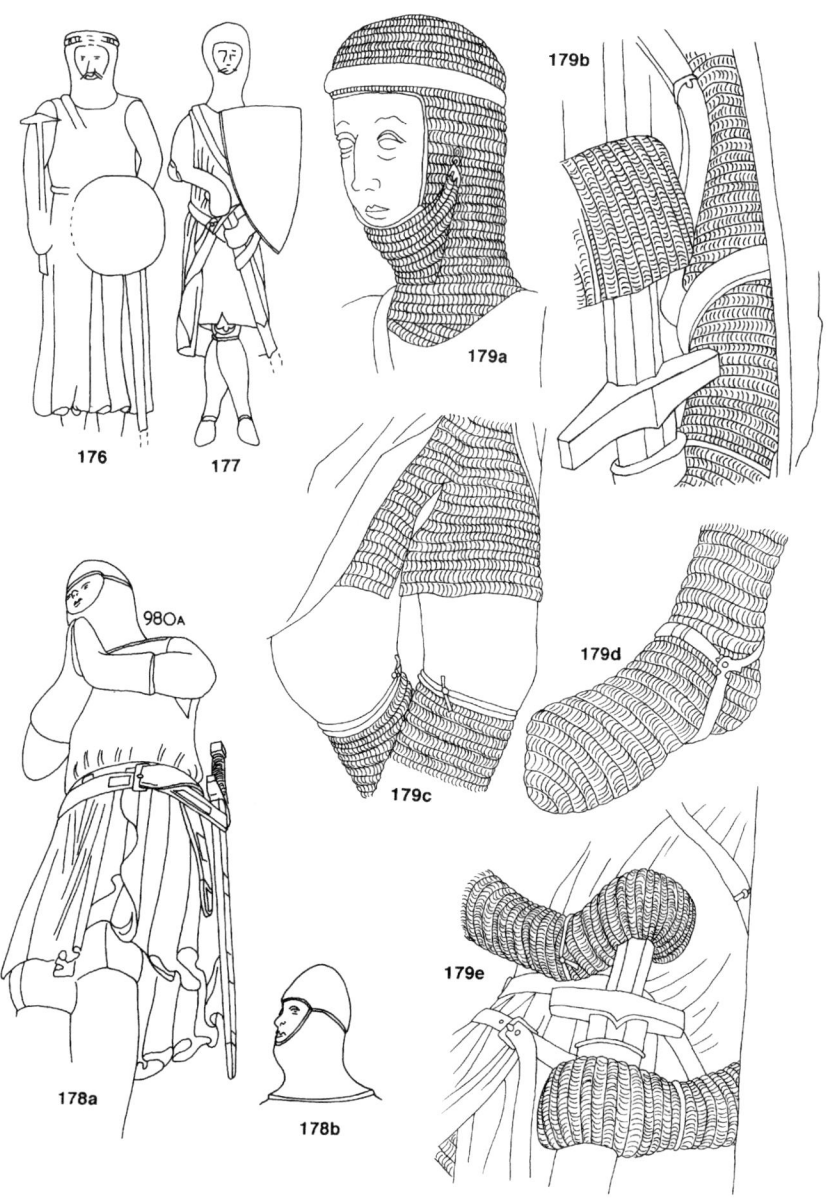

176

177

179b

179a

980A

179c

179d

178a

178b

179e

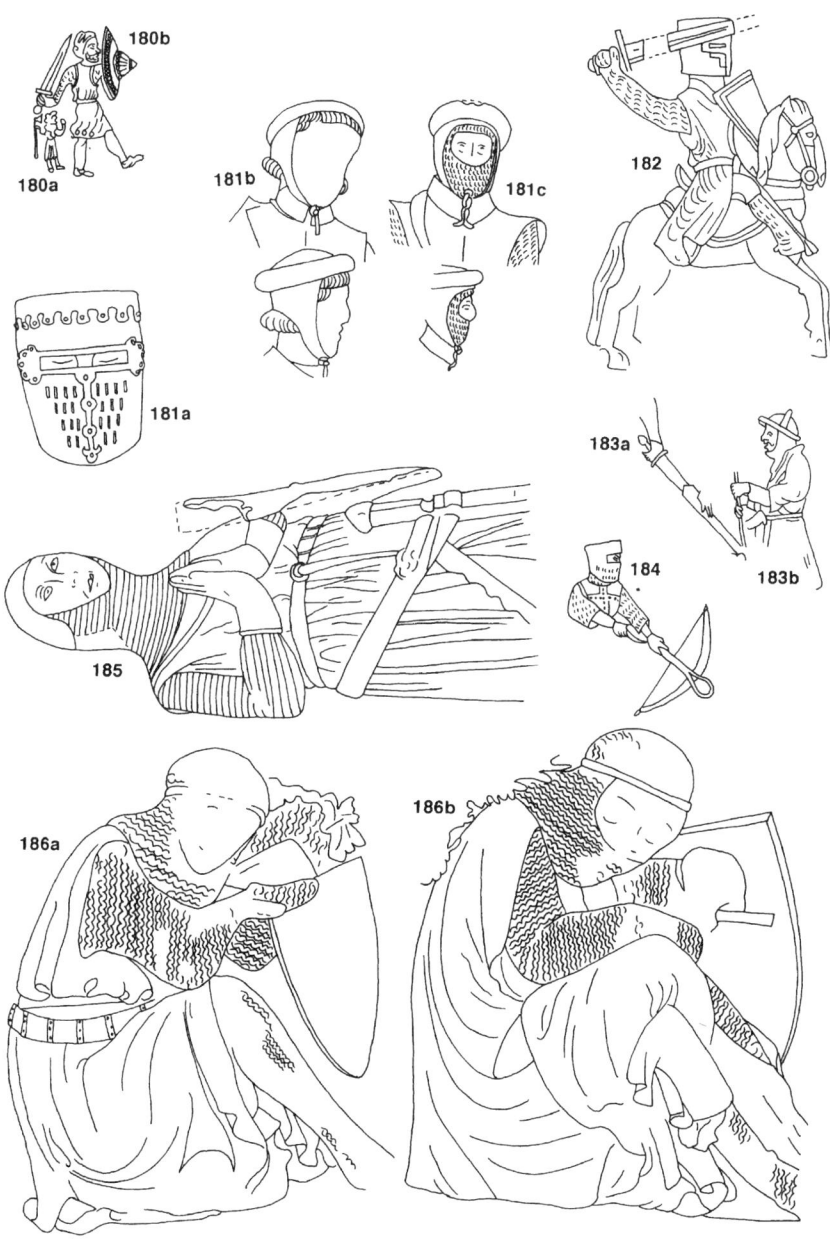

180b

180a

181b

181c

181a

182

183a

183b

184

185

186a

186b

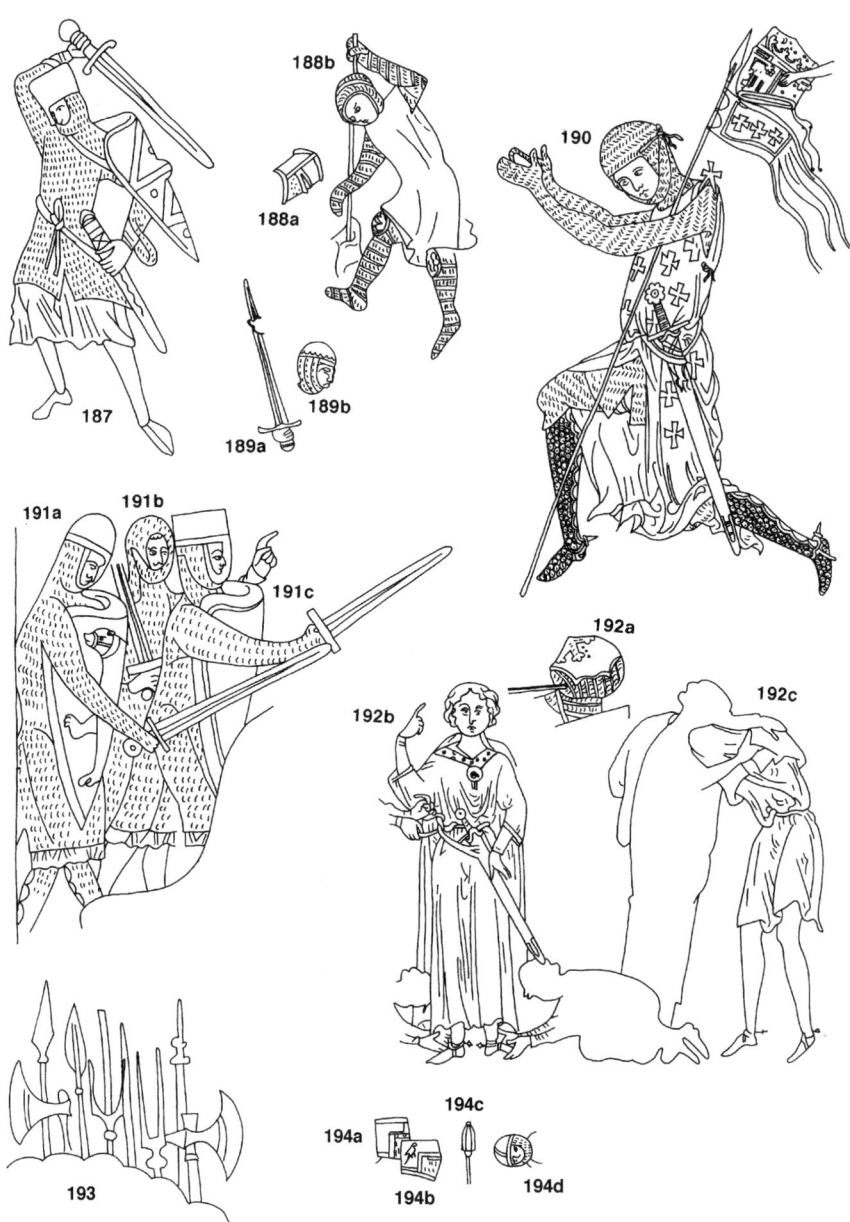

187

188a

188b

189a

189b

190

191a

191b

191c

192a

192b

192c

193

194a

194b

194c

194d

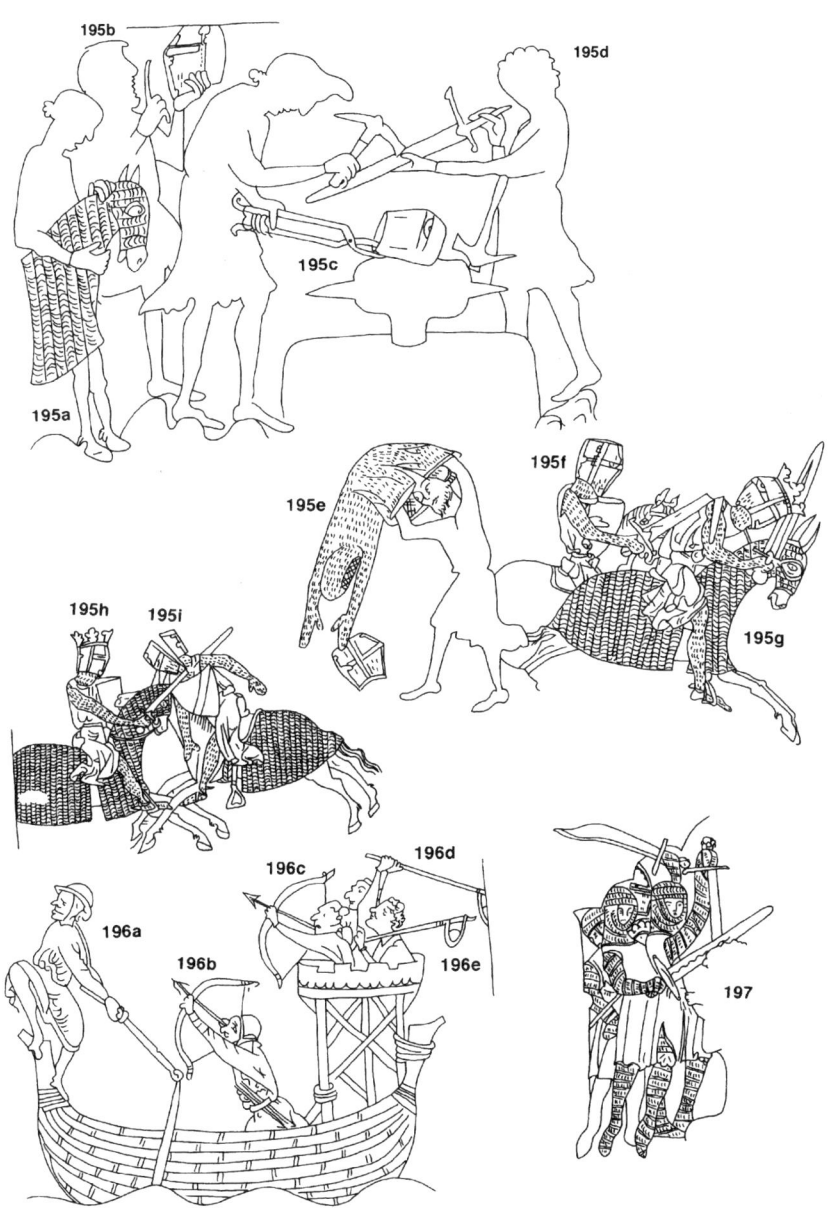

195b

195d

195c

195a

195e

195f

195g

195h 195i

196c

196d

196a

196b

196e

197

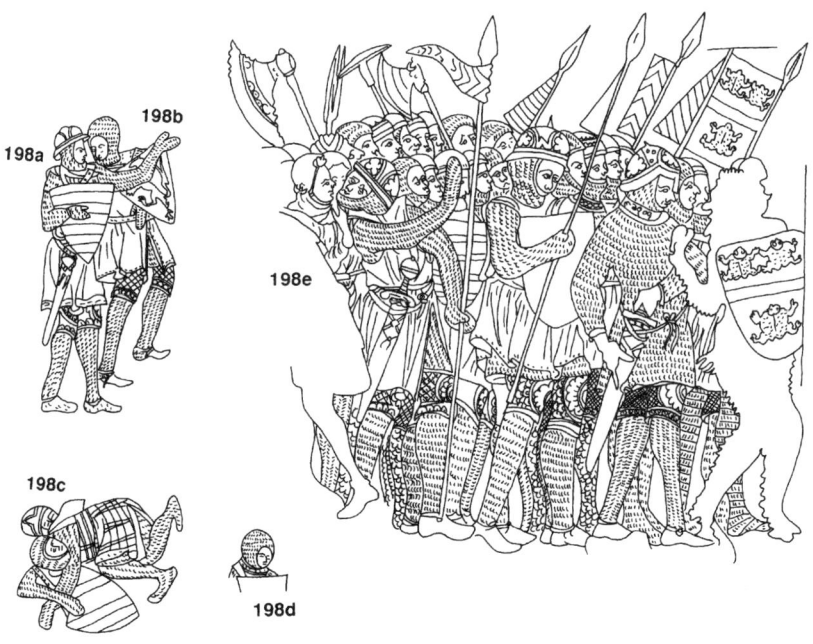

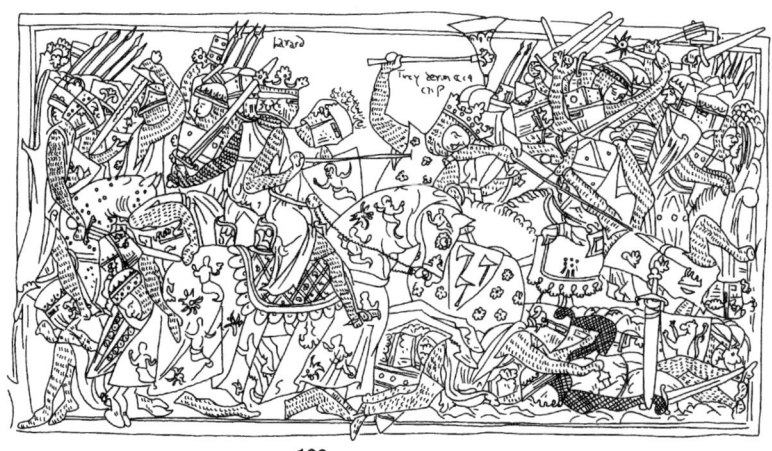

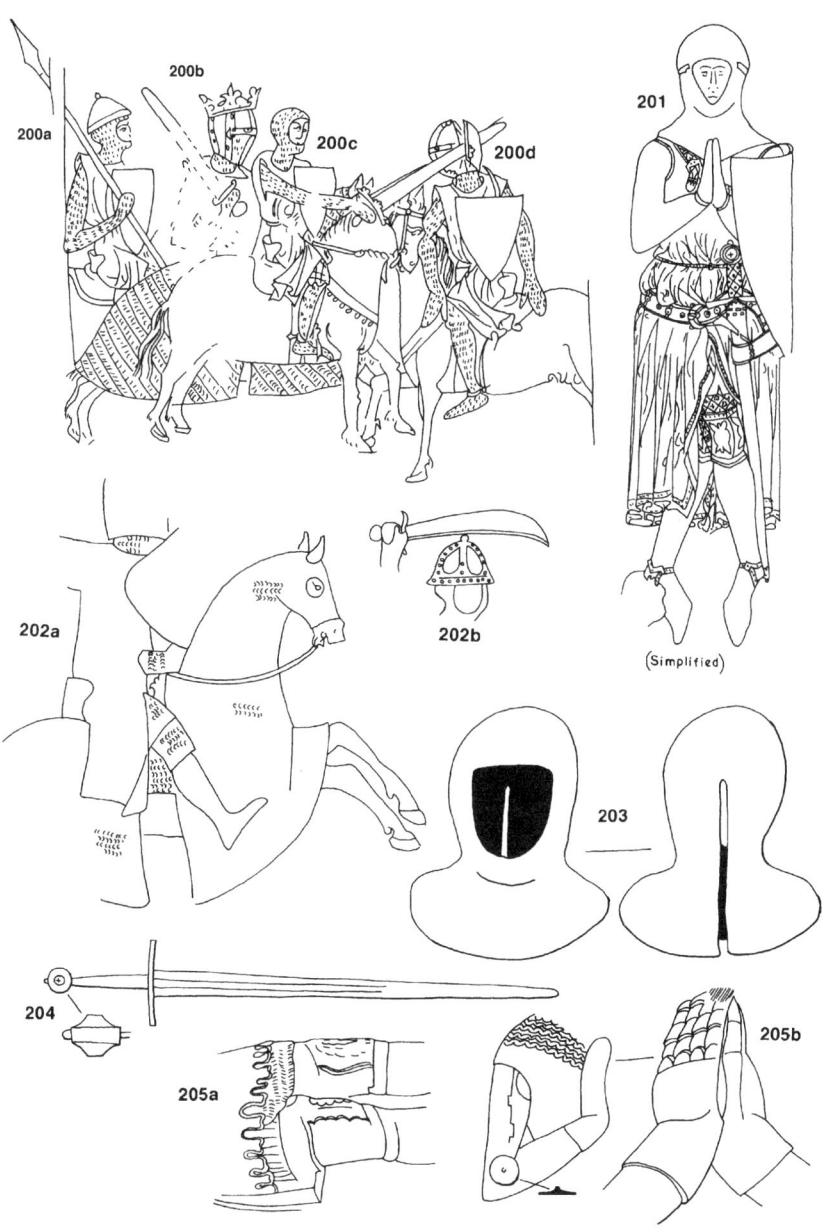

200a

200b

200c

200d

201

202a

202b

(Simplified)

203

204

205a

205b

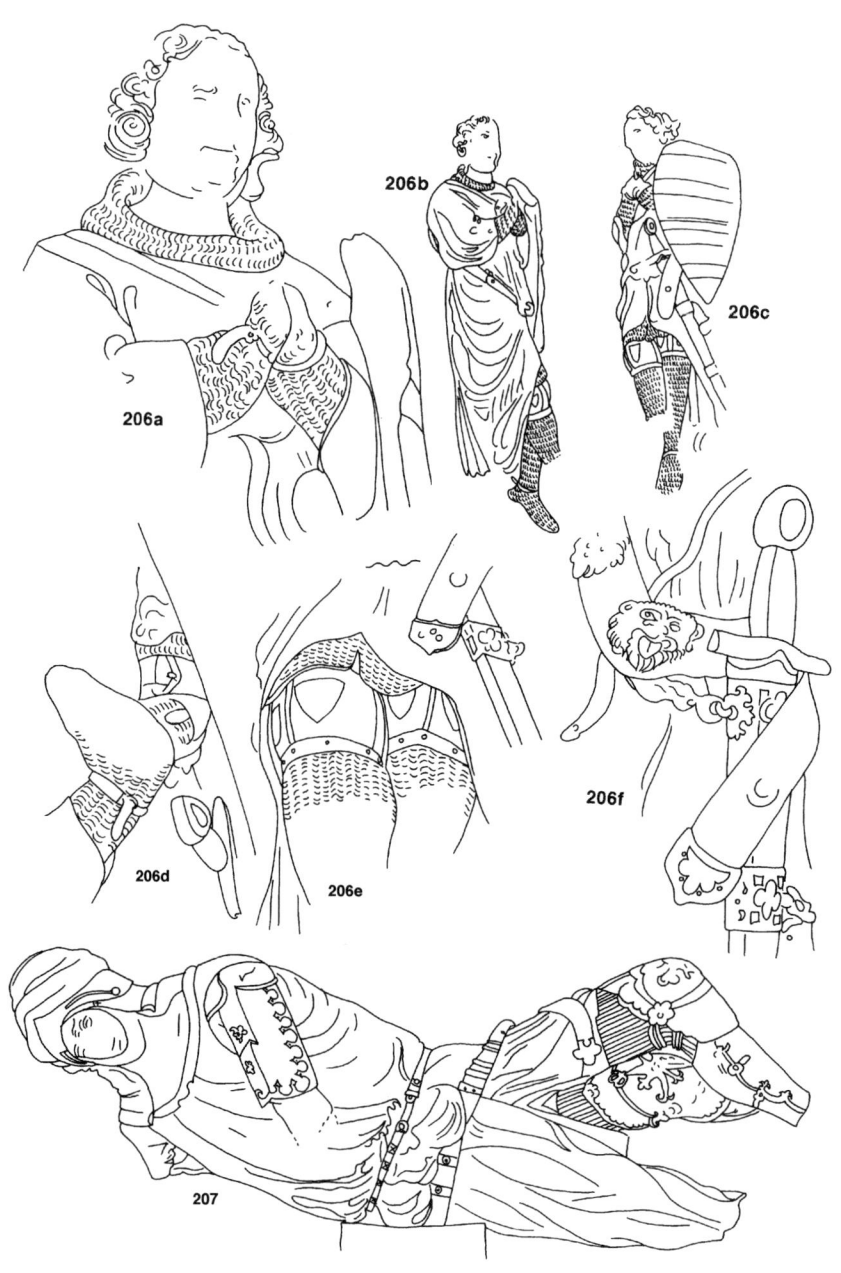

206a

206b

206c

206d

206e

206f

207

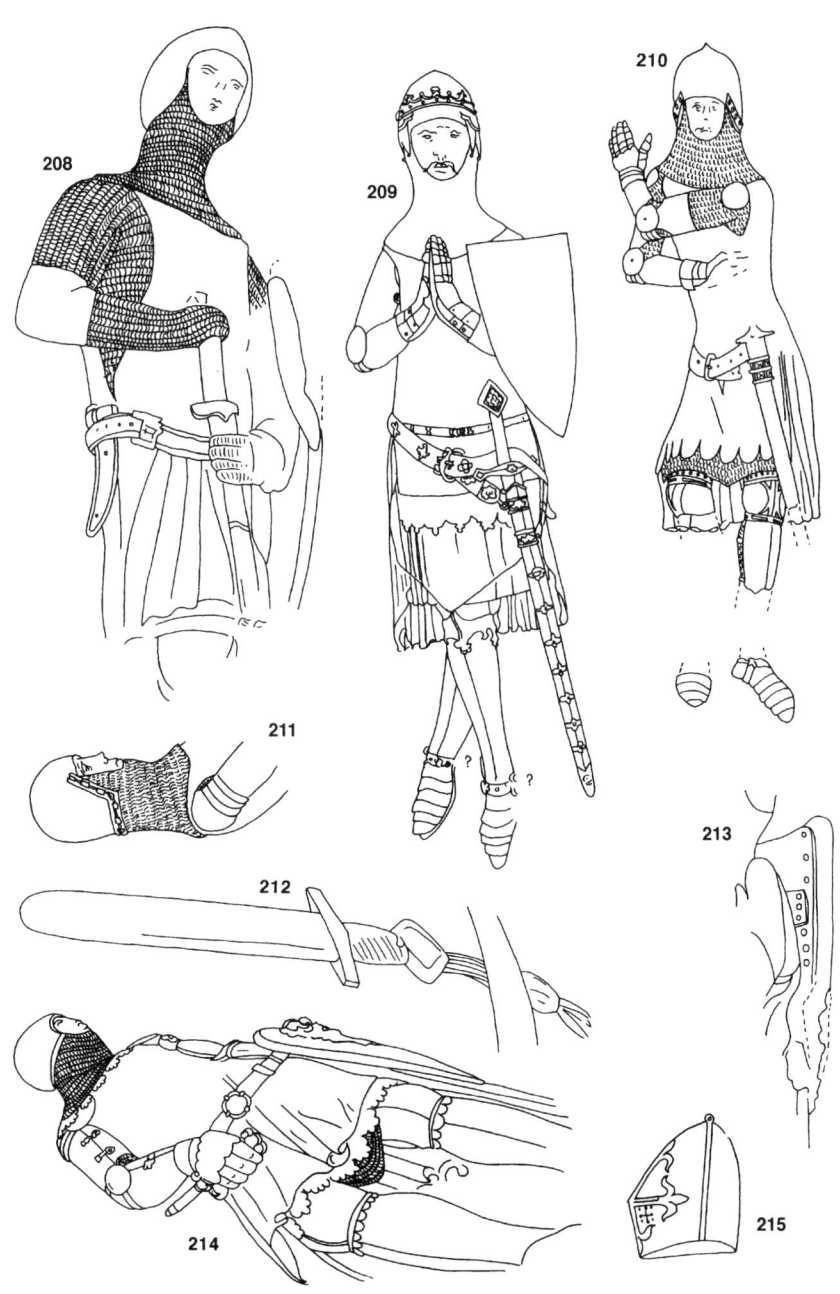

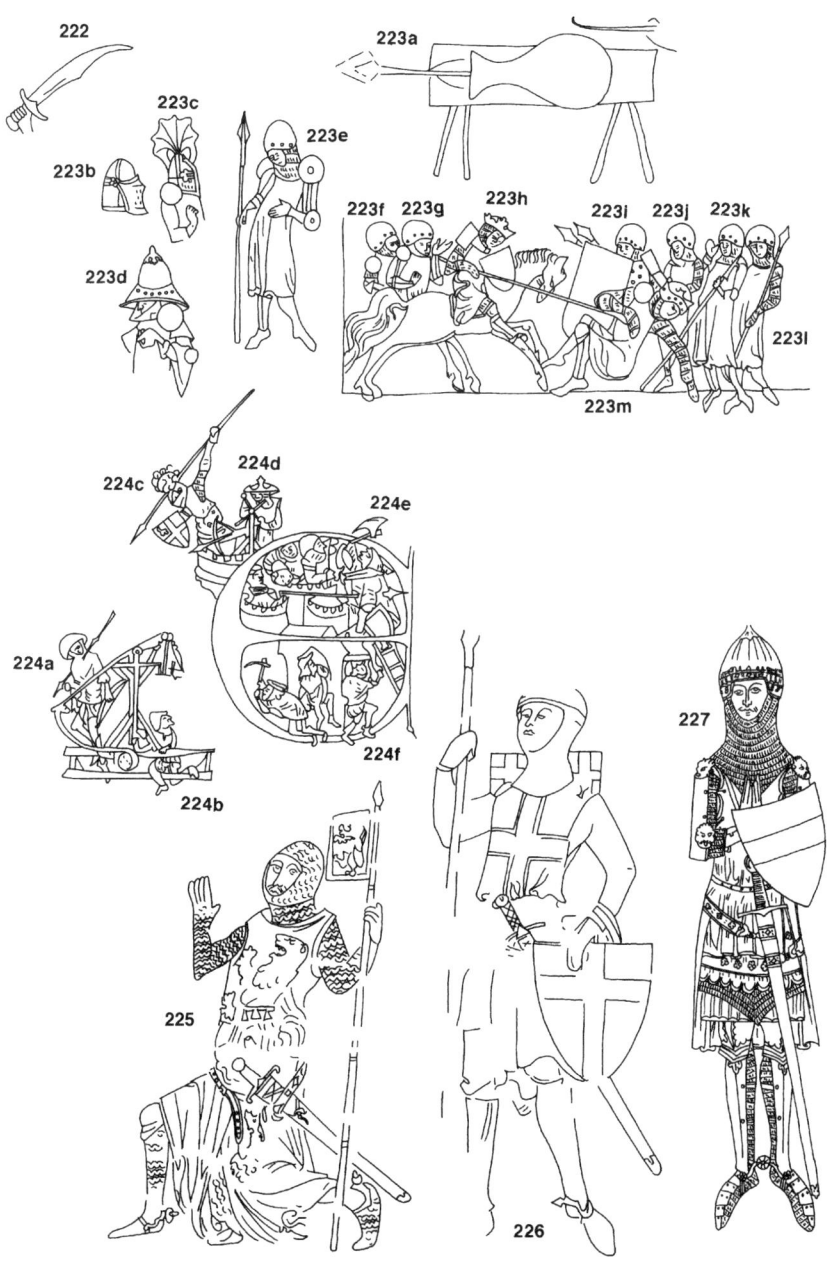

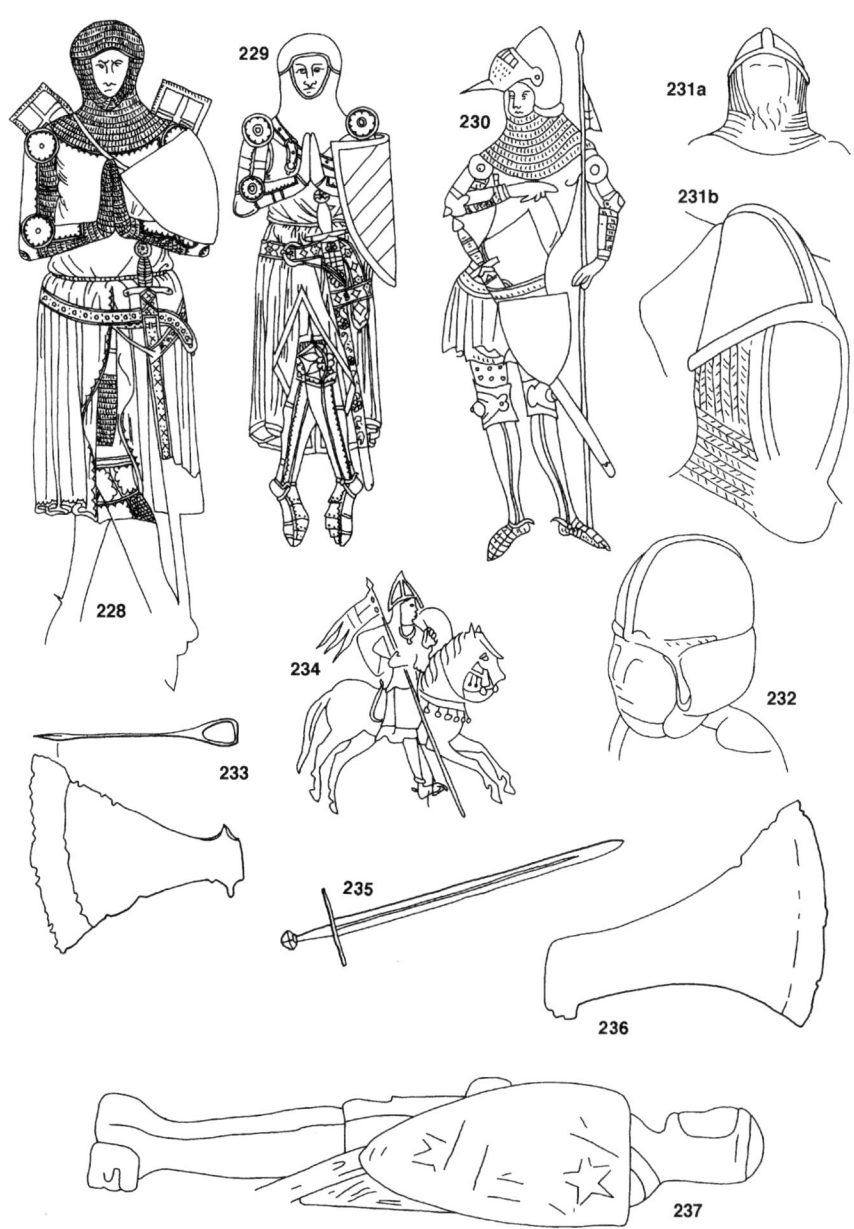

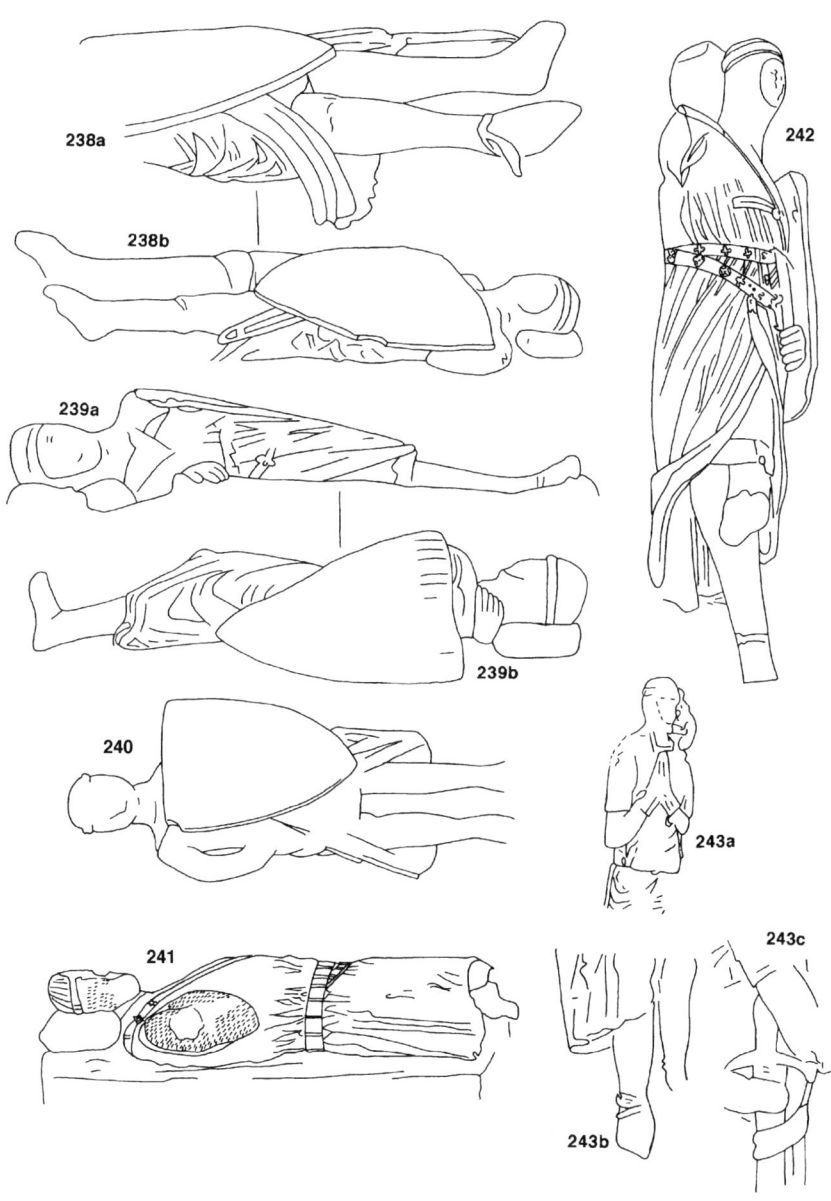

238a

238b

239a

239b

240

241

242

243a

243b

243c

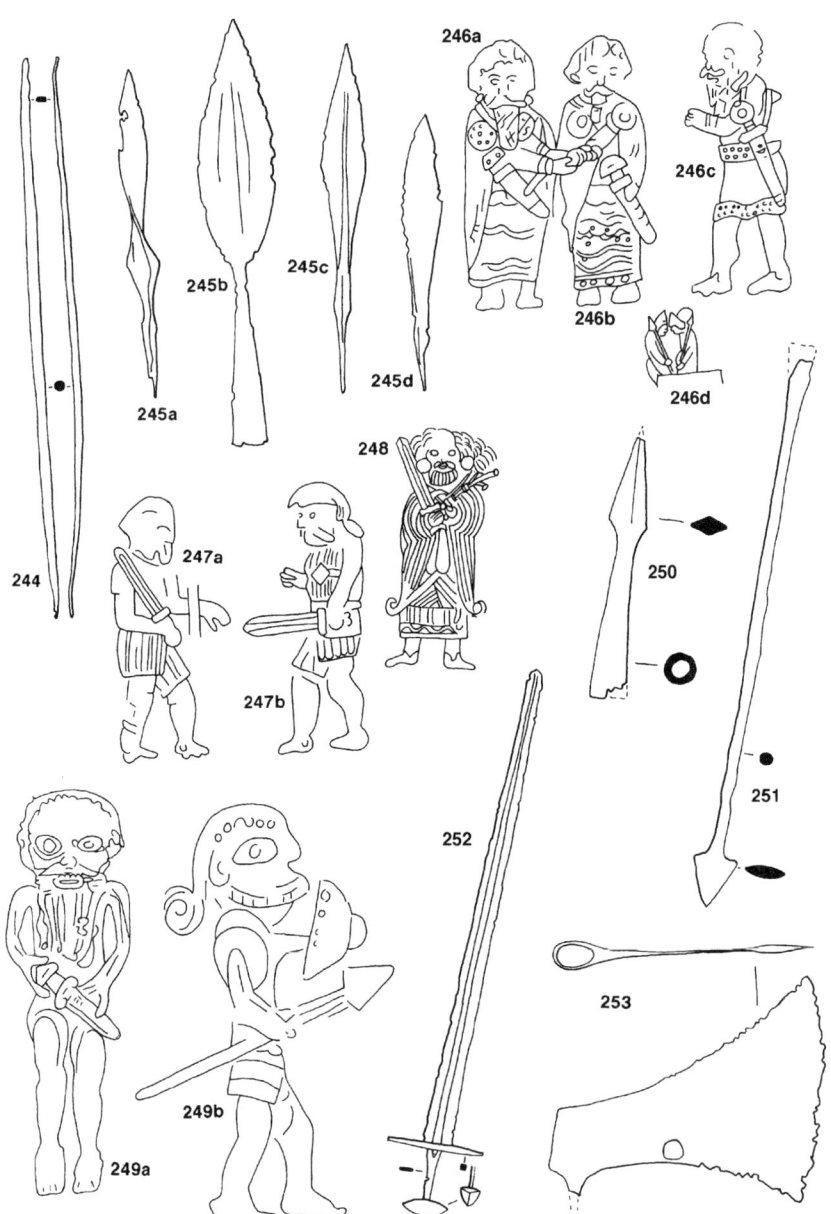

244

245a

245b

245c

245d

246a

246b

246c

246d

247a

247b

248

249a

249b

250

251

252

253

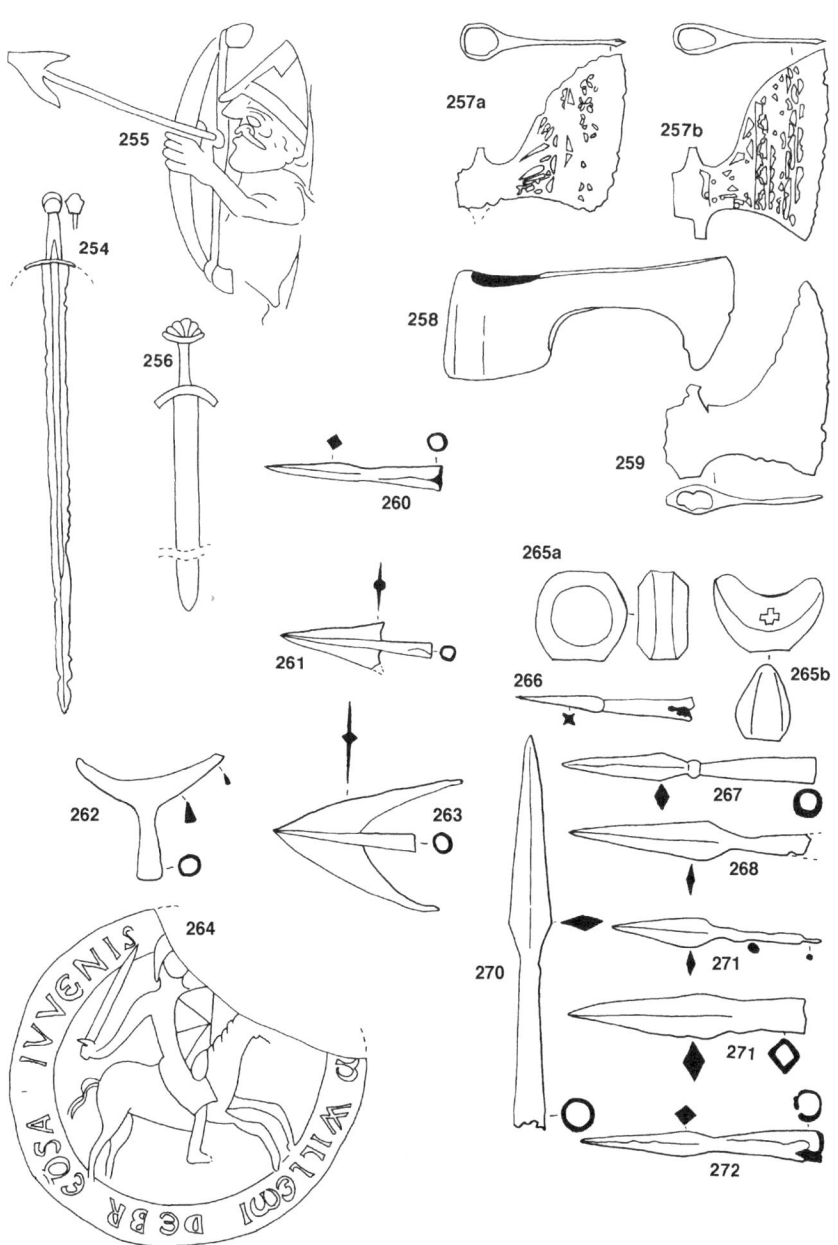

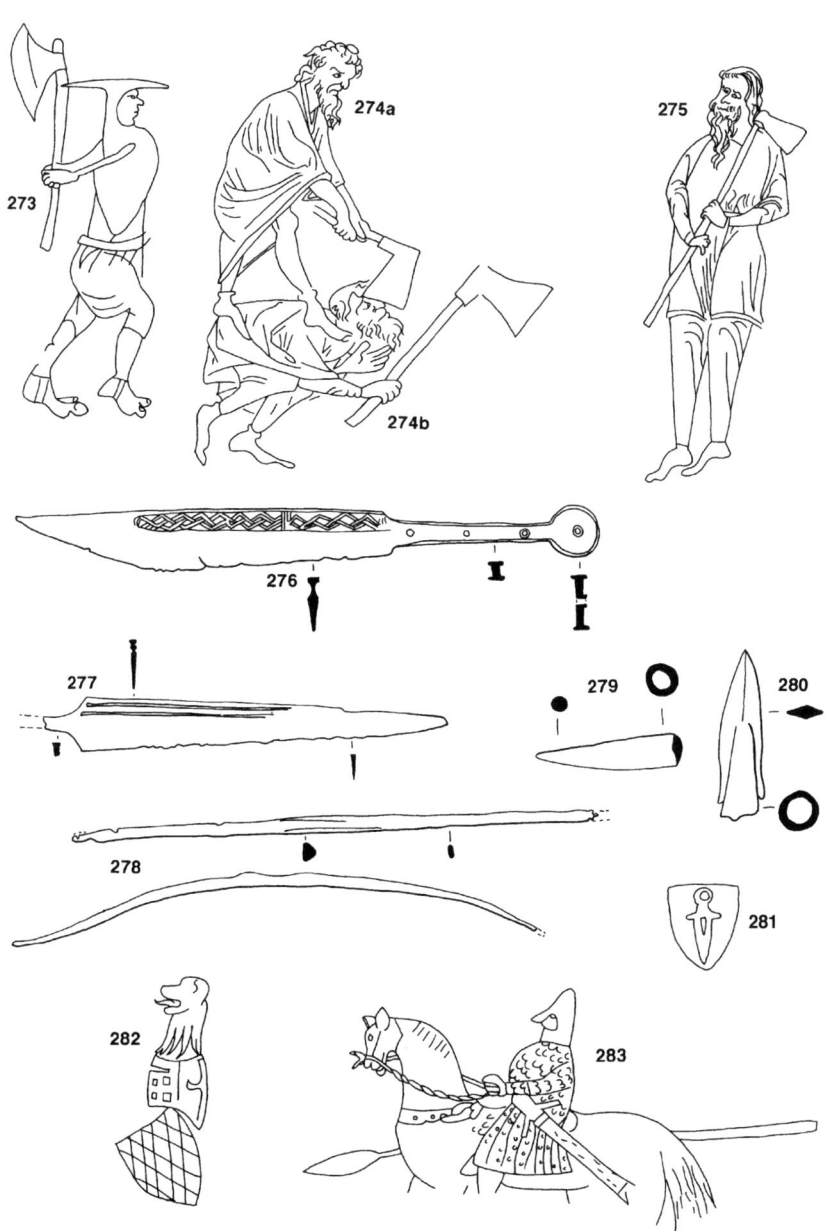

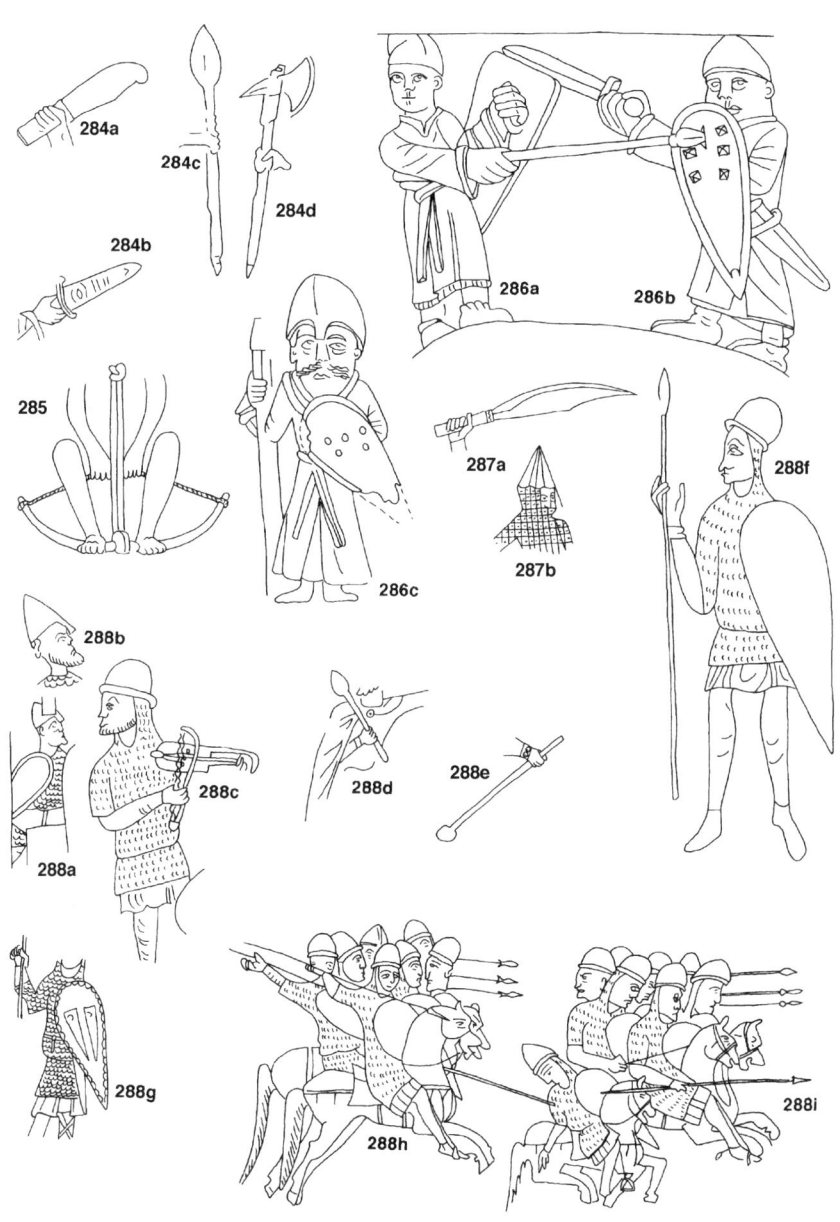

284a

284c

284b

284d

285

286a

286b

287a

287b

286c

288f

288b

288a

288c

288d

288e

288g

288h

288i

289a

289b

289c

289d

289e

289f

289g

289h

290

291b

291a

291c

291d

292a

292b

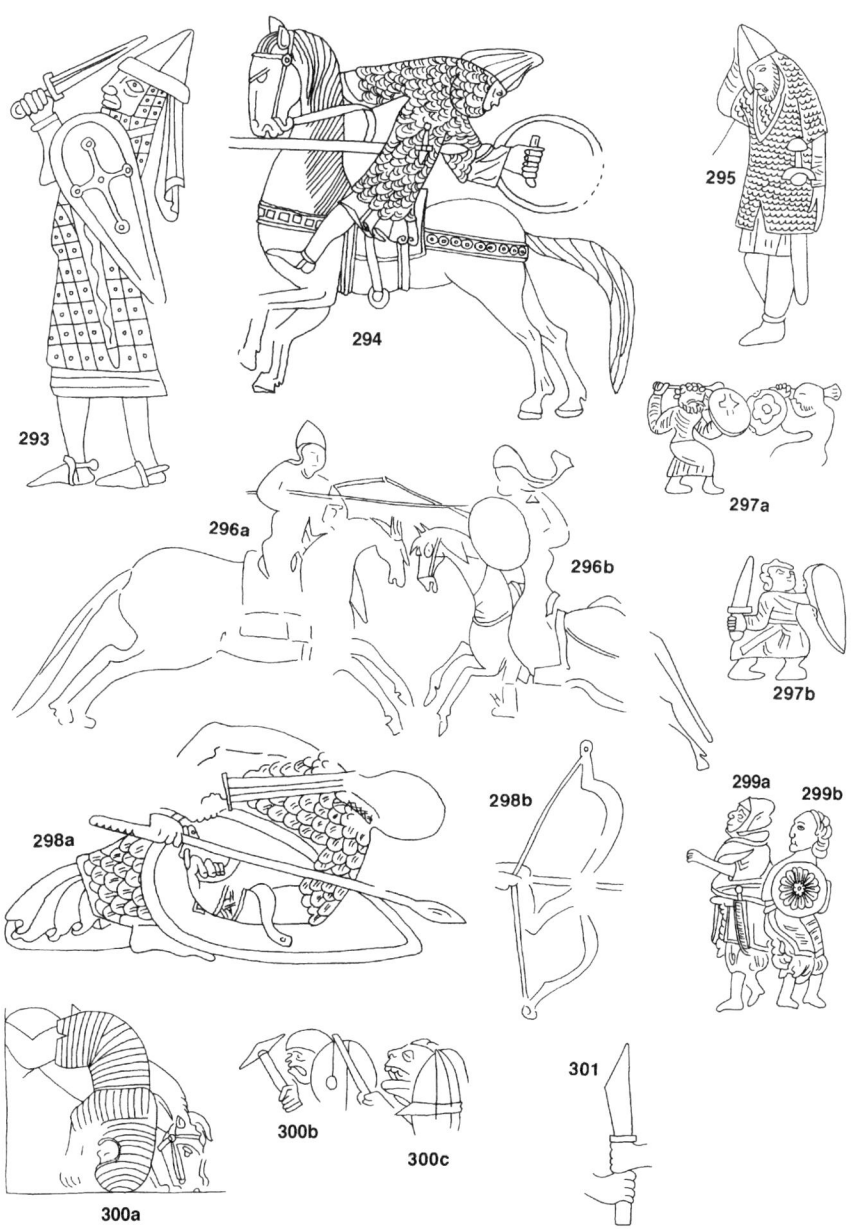

293

294

295

296a

296b

297a

297b

298a

298b

299a   299b

300a

300b

300c

301

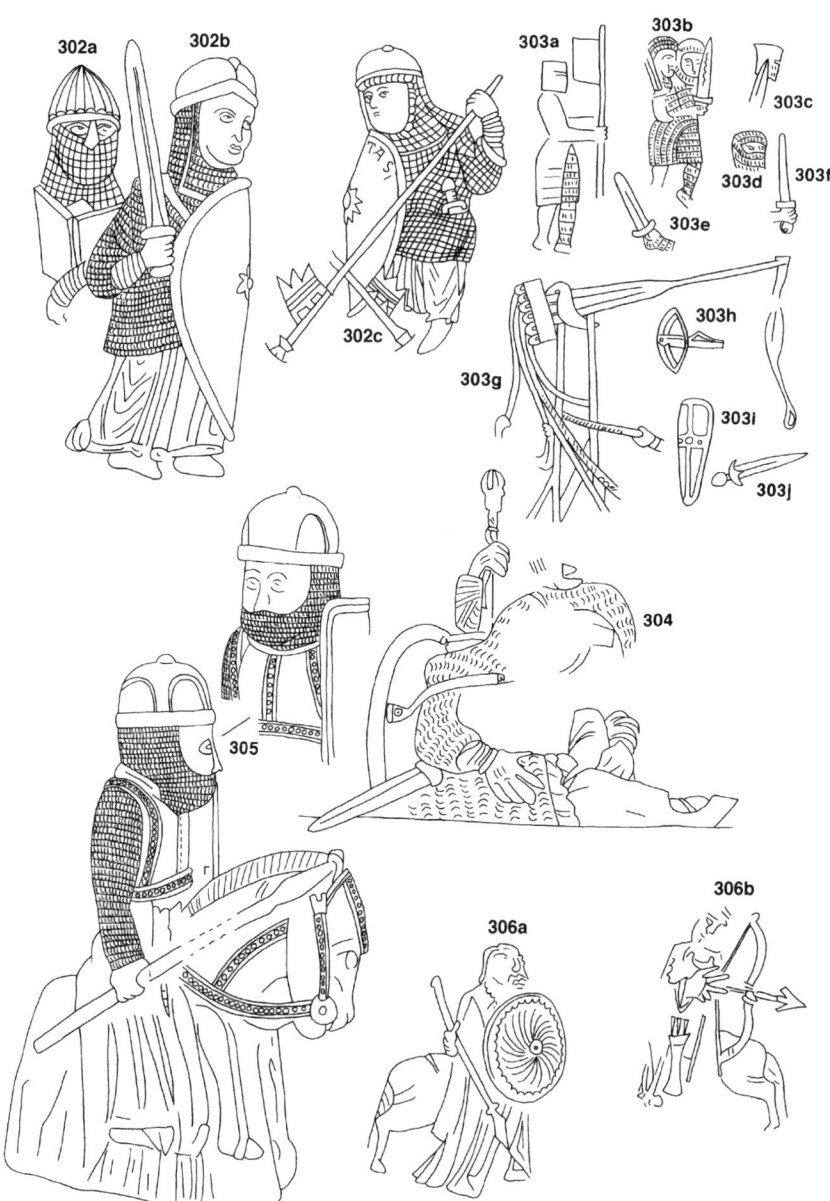

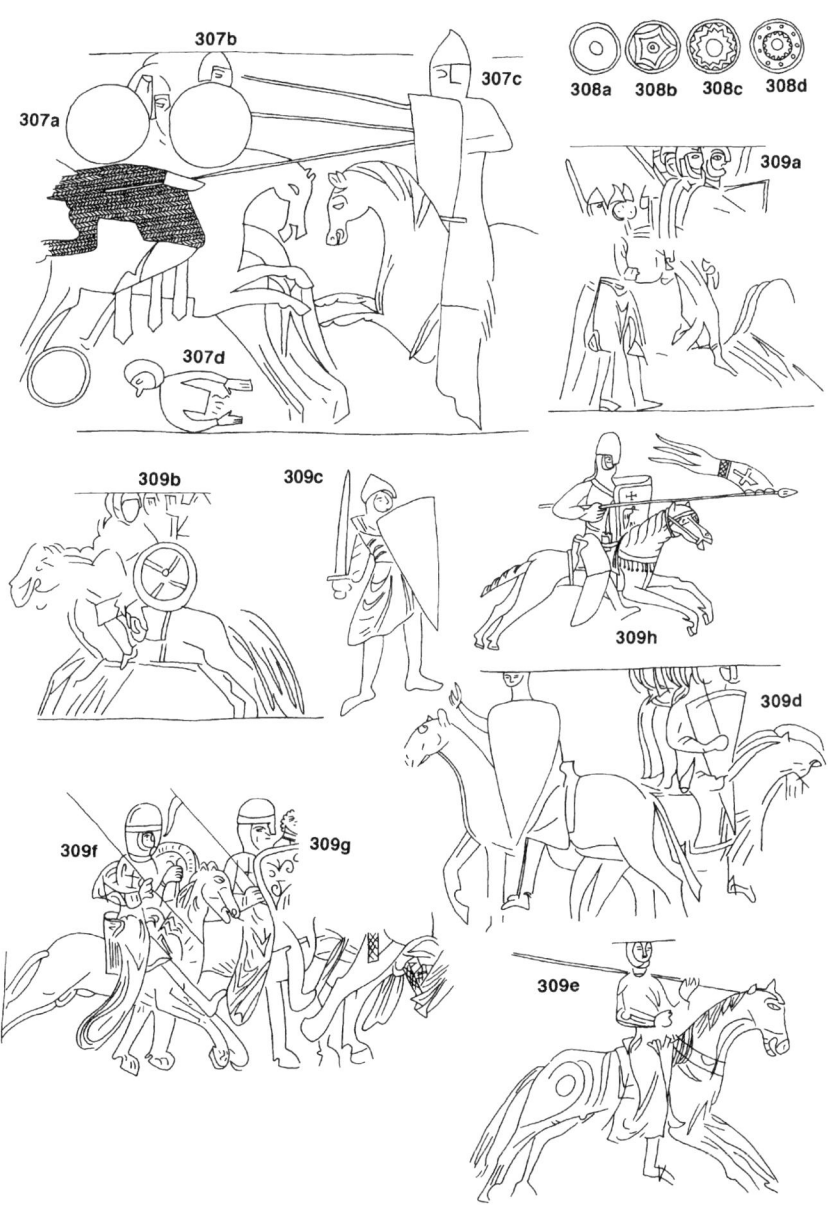

307a

307b

307c

307d

308a 308b 308c 308d

309a

309b

309c

309h

309d

309f

309g

309e

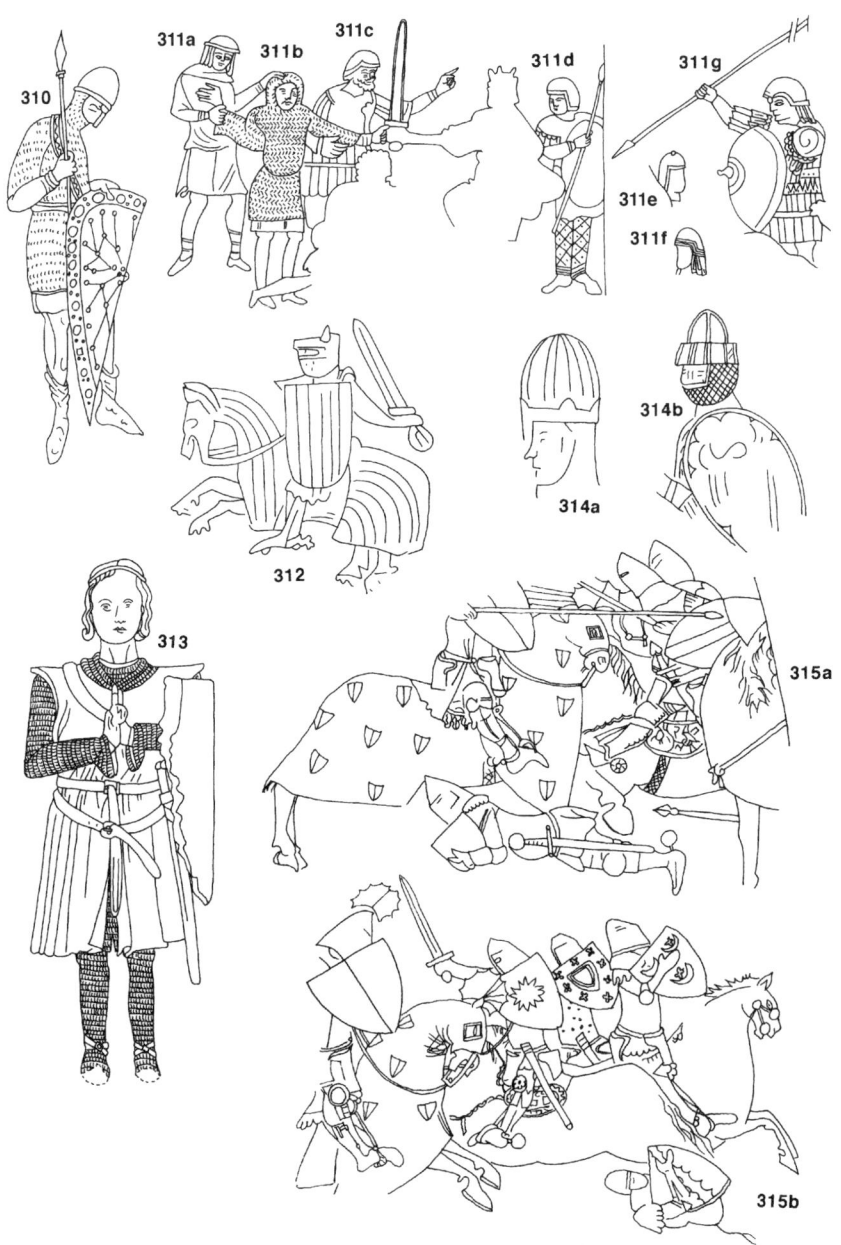

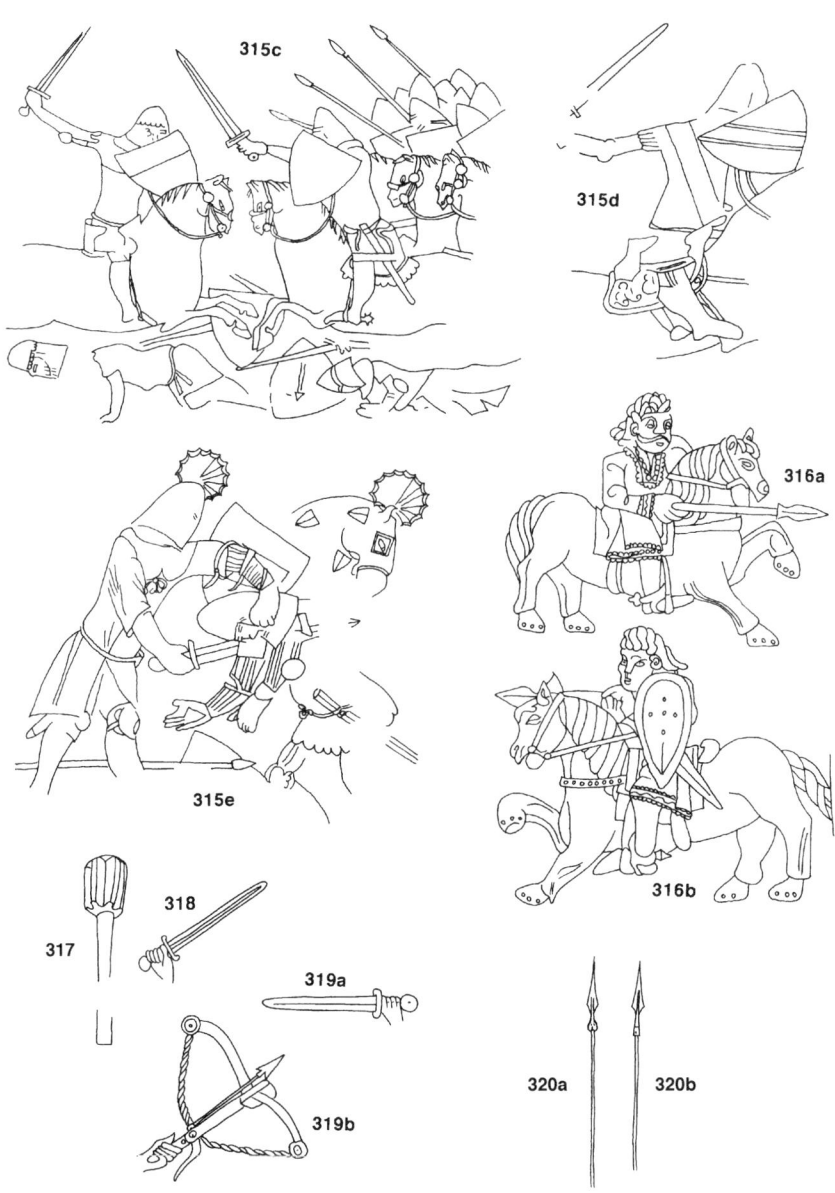

315c

315d

315e

316a

316b

317

318

319a

319b

320a

320b

321a 321b 321c 321d 321e 321f 321g 321h 321i 321j 321k 321l 321m 321n 321o 321p 321q 321r 321s 321t 321u 321v 321w 321x 321y 321z 321aa 321ab 321ac 321ad 321ae 321af 321ag 321ah

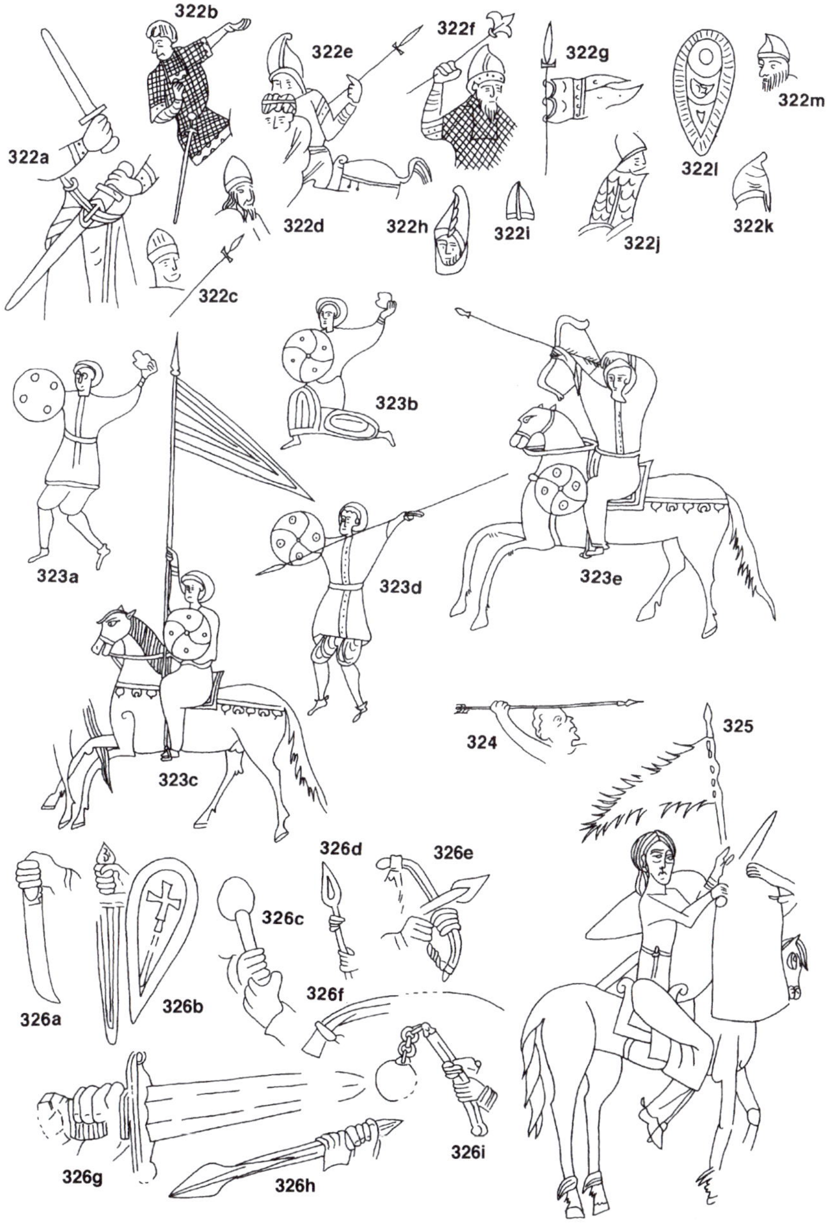

322b

322a

322e

322f

322g

322m

322d

322c

322h

322i

322j

322l

322k

323b

323a

323d

323e

323c

324

325

326d

326e

326c

326a

326b

326f

326g

326h

326i

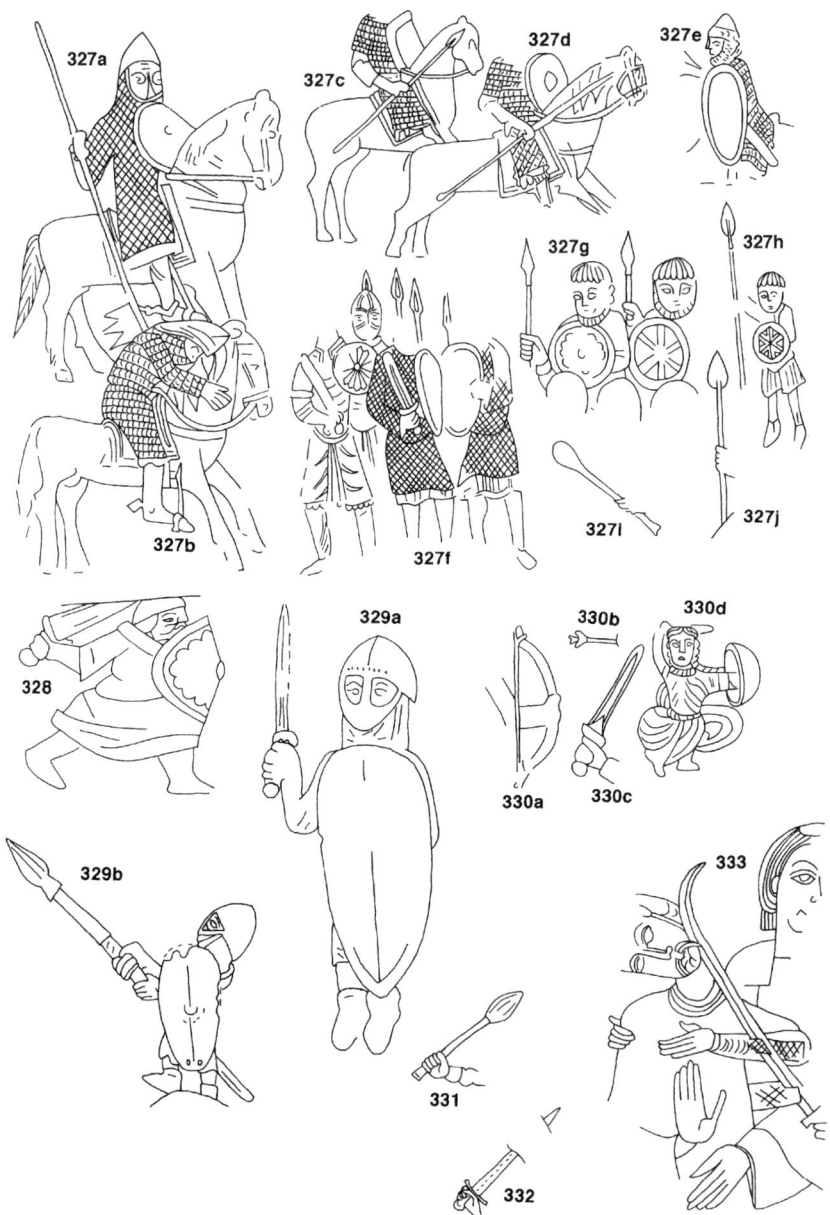

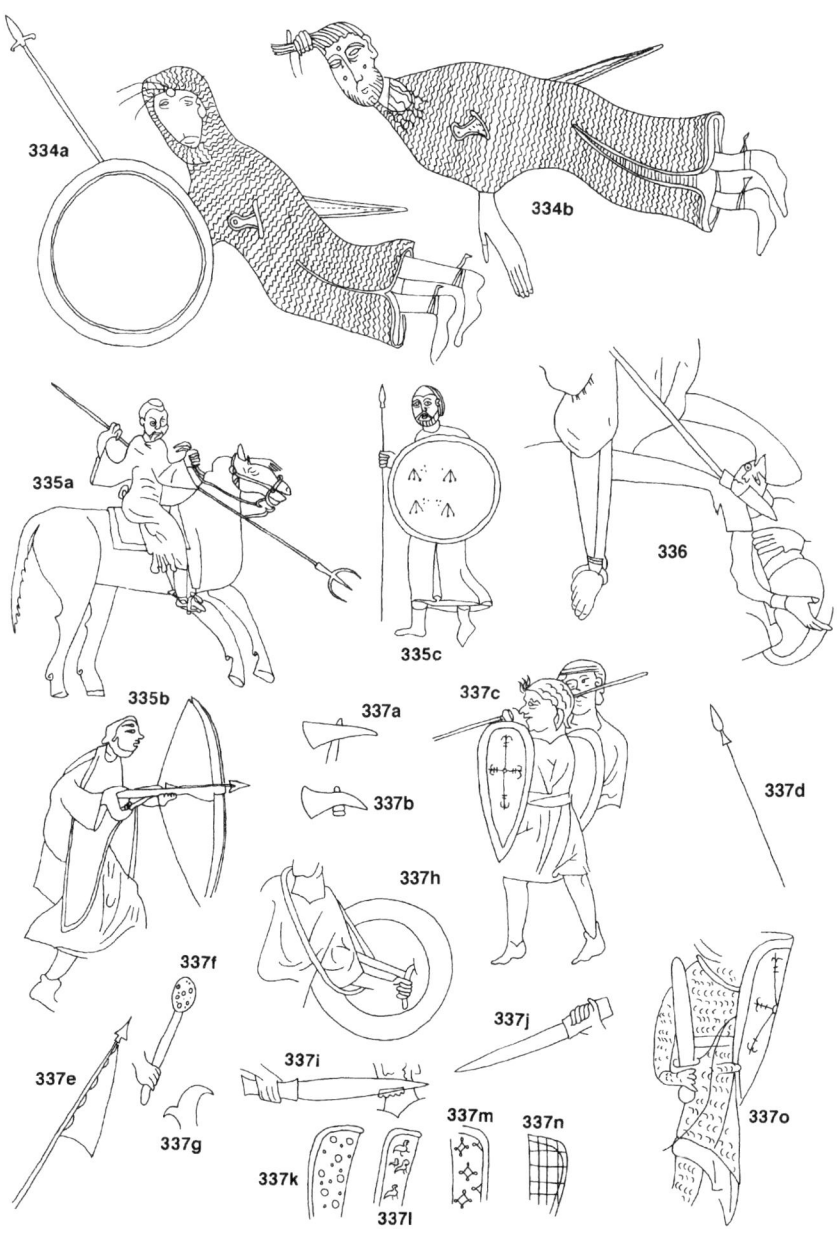

334a

334b

335a

335c

336

335b

337a

337b

337c

337d

337h

337f

337j

337e

337i

337m

337n

337o

337g

337k

337l

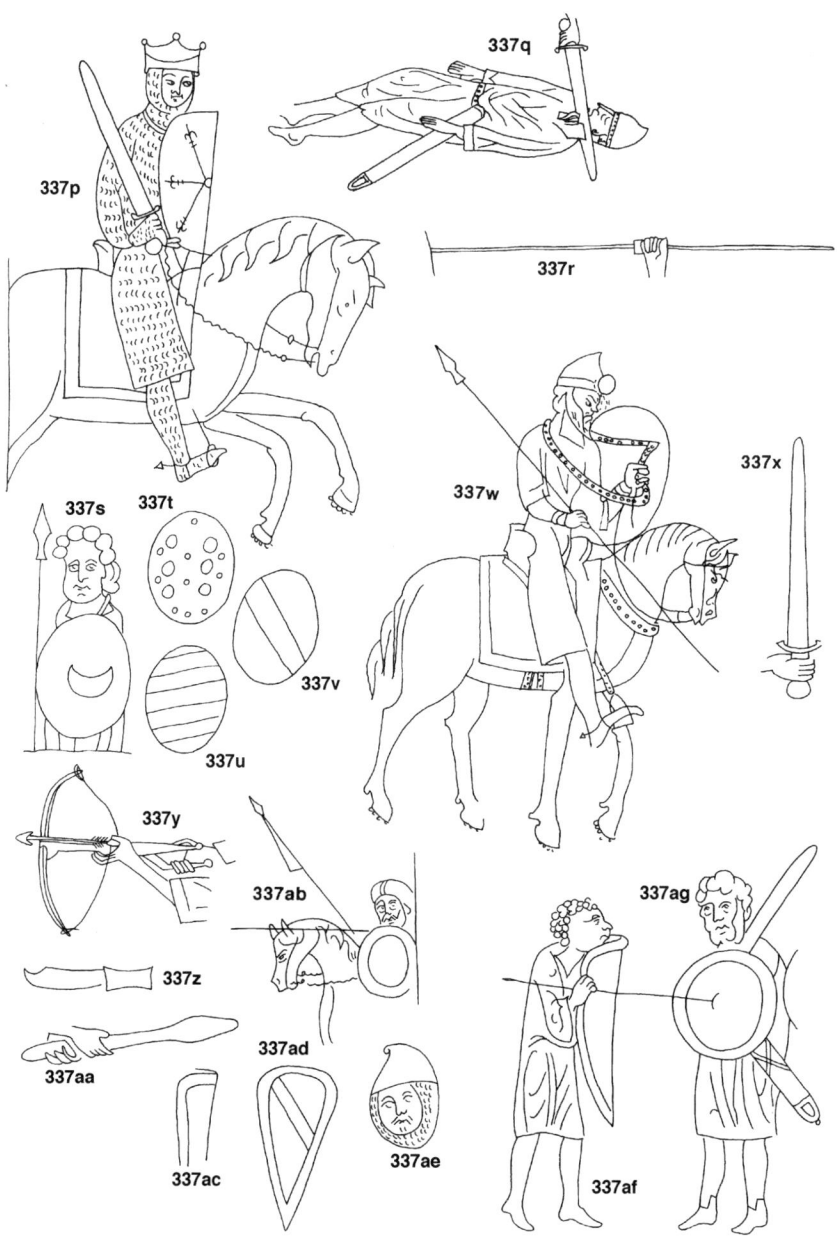

337p

337q

337r

337s

337t

337u

337v

337w

337x

337y

337z

337aa

337ab

337ac

337ad

337ae

337af

337ag

337ah

337ai

337aj

337ak

337al

337am

337an

337ao

337ap

337aq

338

339a

339b

339c

339d

339e

339f

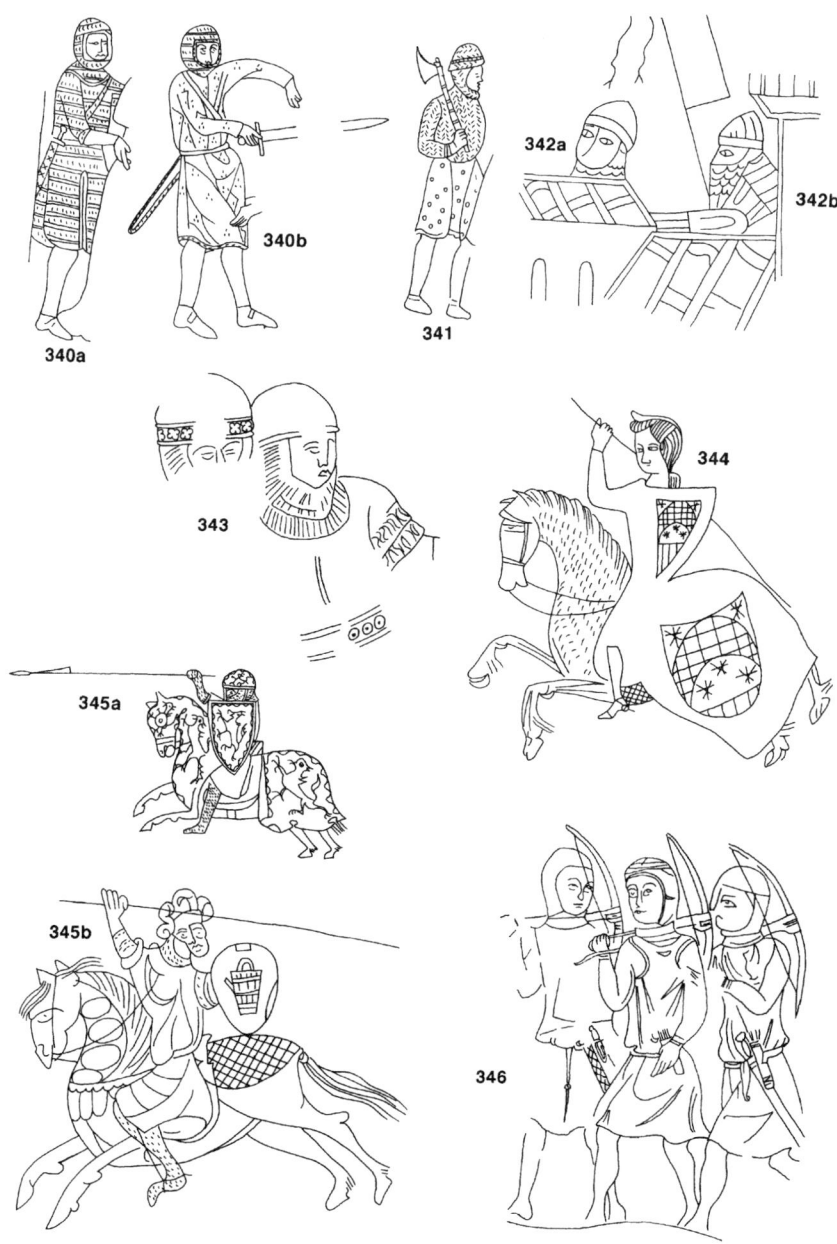

340a

340b

341

342a

342b

343

344

345a

345b

346

347a

347b

347c

347d

347e

347f

348

349

350

351

352

353

354a

354b

354c

354d

355

354e

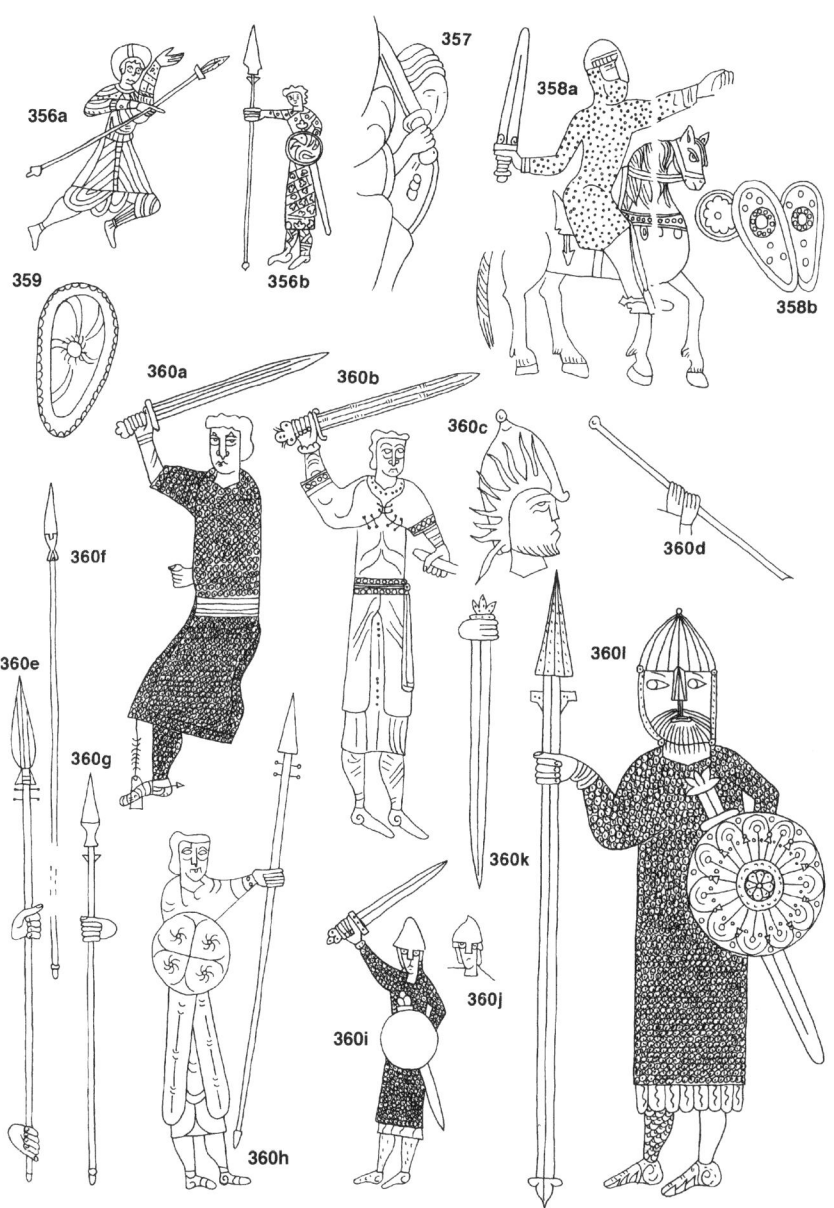

356a

356b

357

358a

358b

359

360a

360b

360c

360d

360e

360f

360g

360h

360i

360j

360k

360l

361a 361b 362 363a 363b 364 365 366 367a 367b 368a 368b 368c 369 370 371

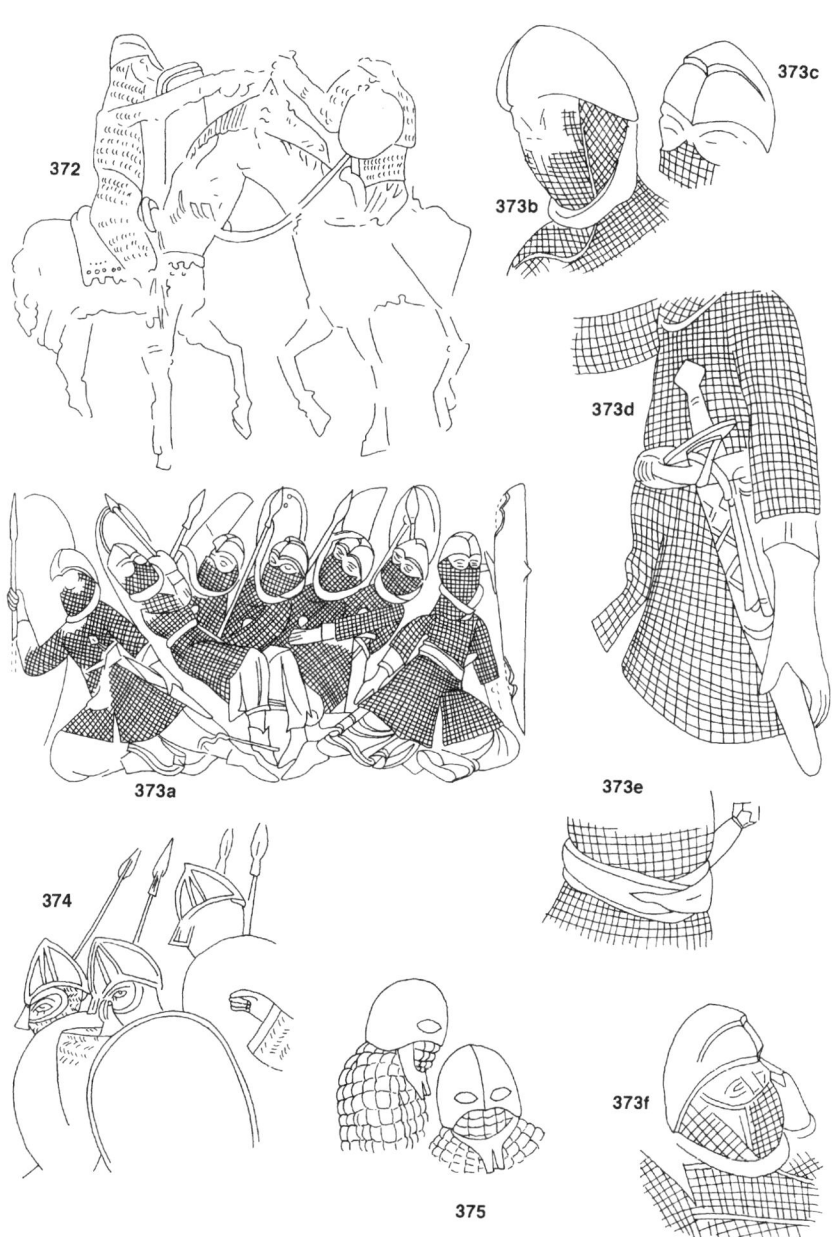

372

373c

373b

373d

373a

373e

374

375

373f

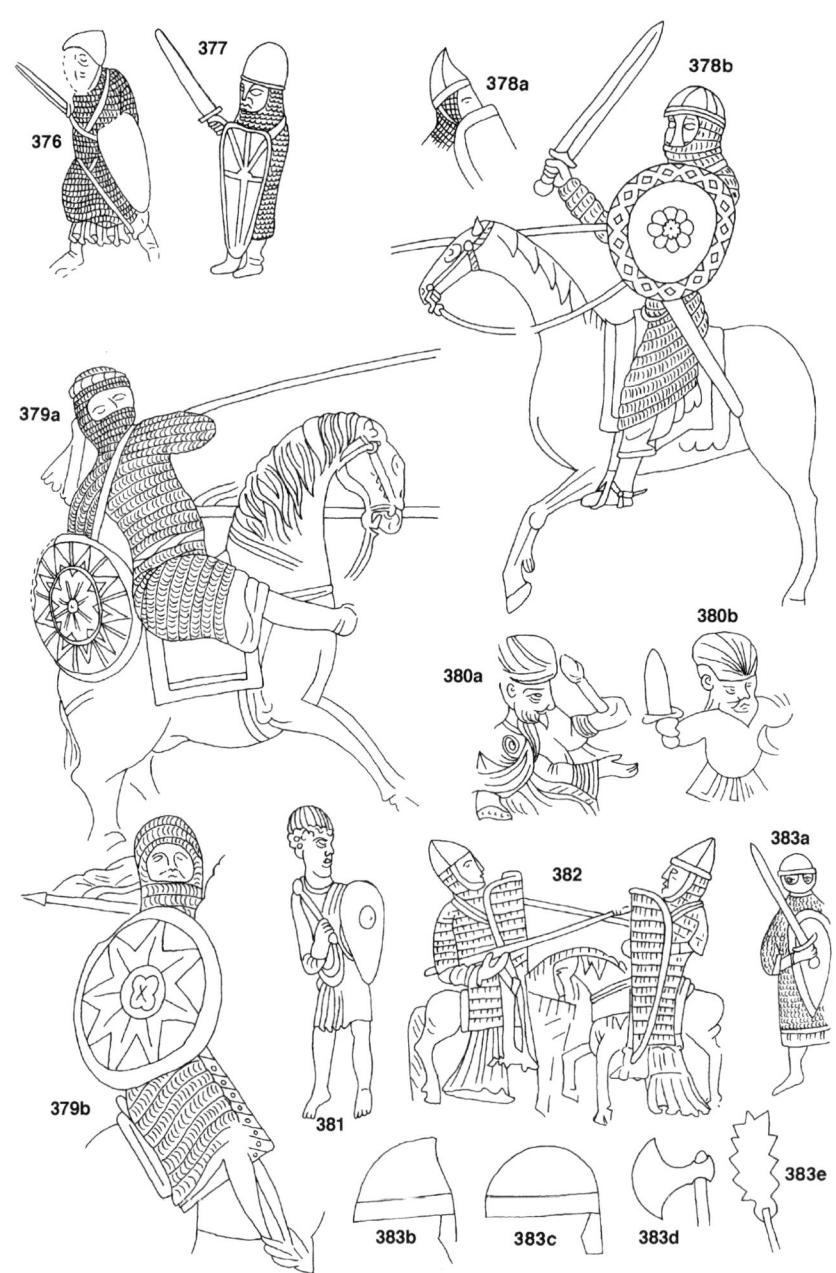

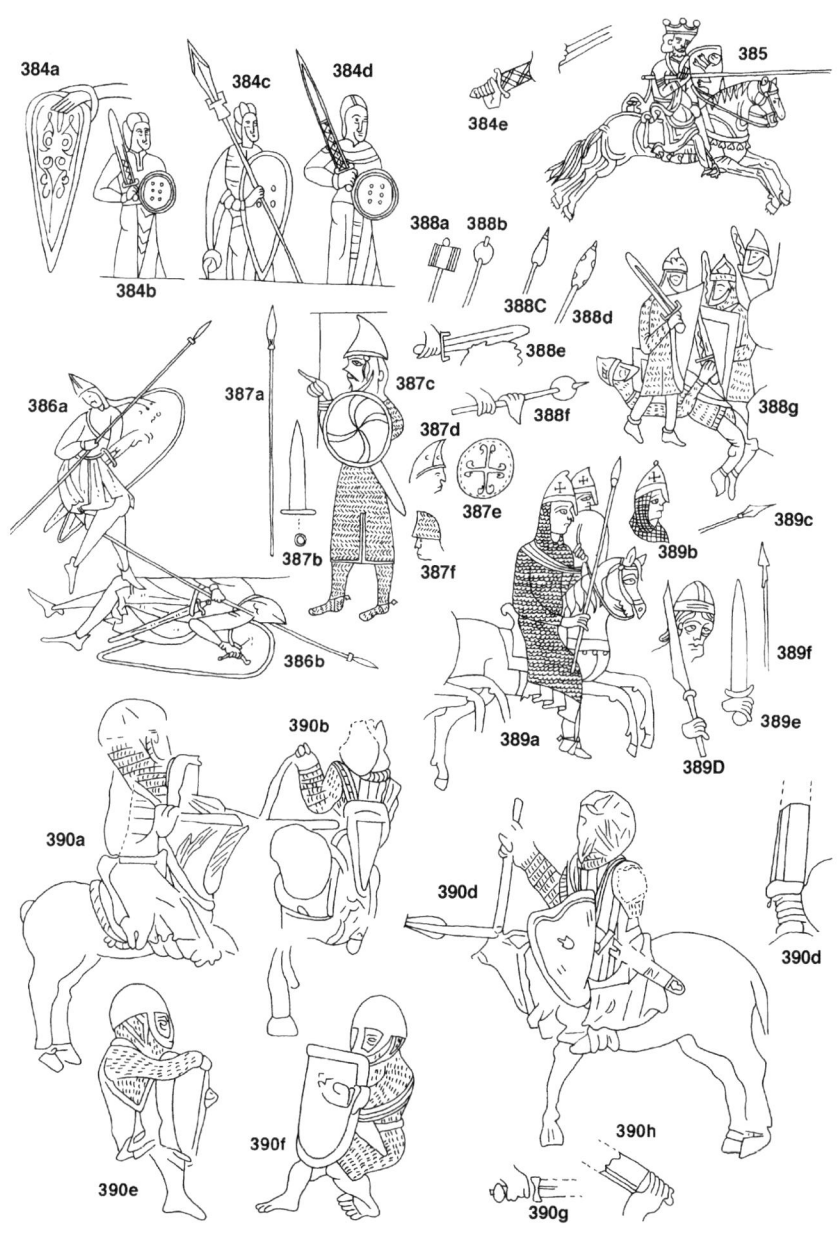

384a

384c

384d

384e

384b

385

388a   388b

388C   388d

388e

388f

388g

386a

387a

387c

387d

387e

387f

387b

386b

389b

389c

389f

389e

389a

389D

390b

390a

390d

390d

390e

390f

390h

390g

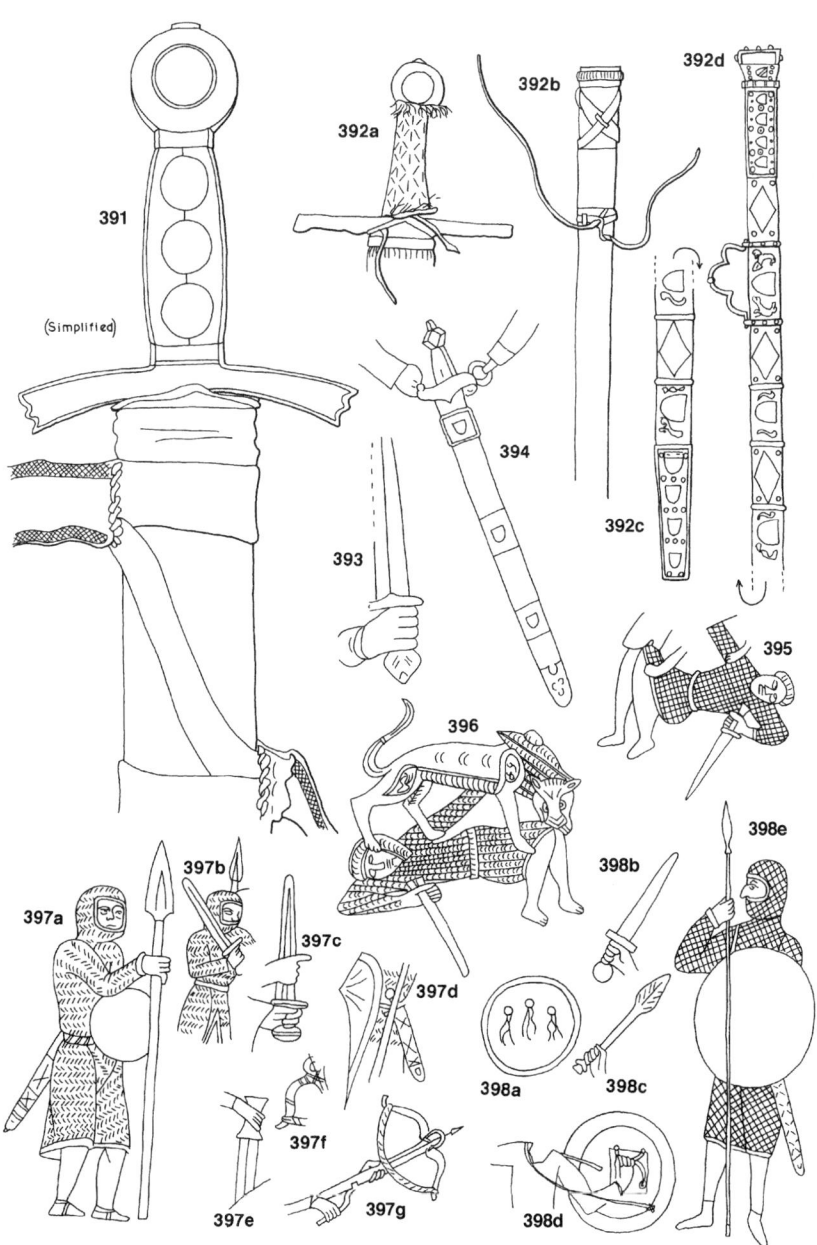

391

(Simplified)

392a

392b

392d

391

392c

393

394

395

396

397a

397b

397c

397d

397e

397f

397g

398a

398b

398c

398d

398e

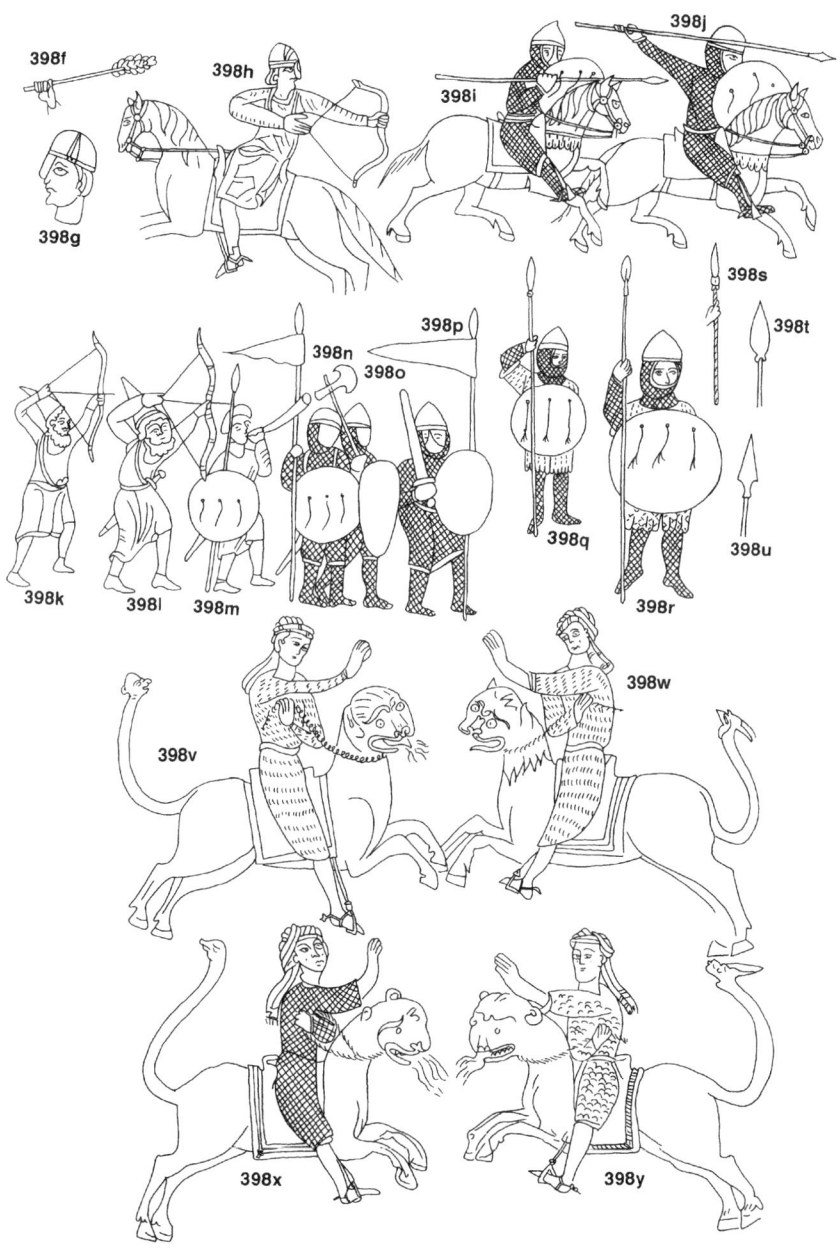

398f

398h

398j

398i

398g

398s

398n

398p

398t

398o

398k

398l

398m

398q

398r

398u

398v

398w

398x

398y

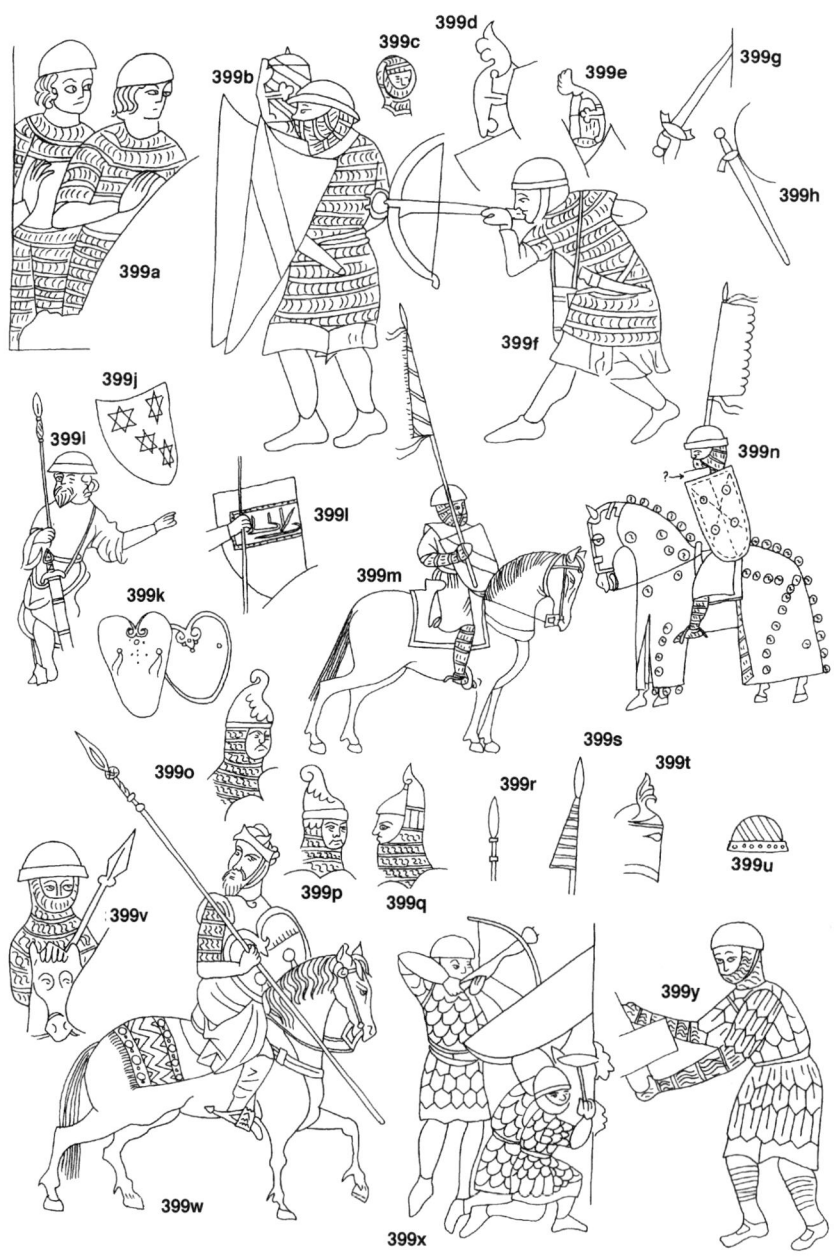

399a 399b 399c 399d 399e 399f 399g 399h 399j 399l 399l 399k 399m 399n 399o 399p 399q 399r 399s 399t 399u 399v 399w 399x 399y

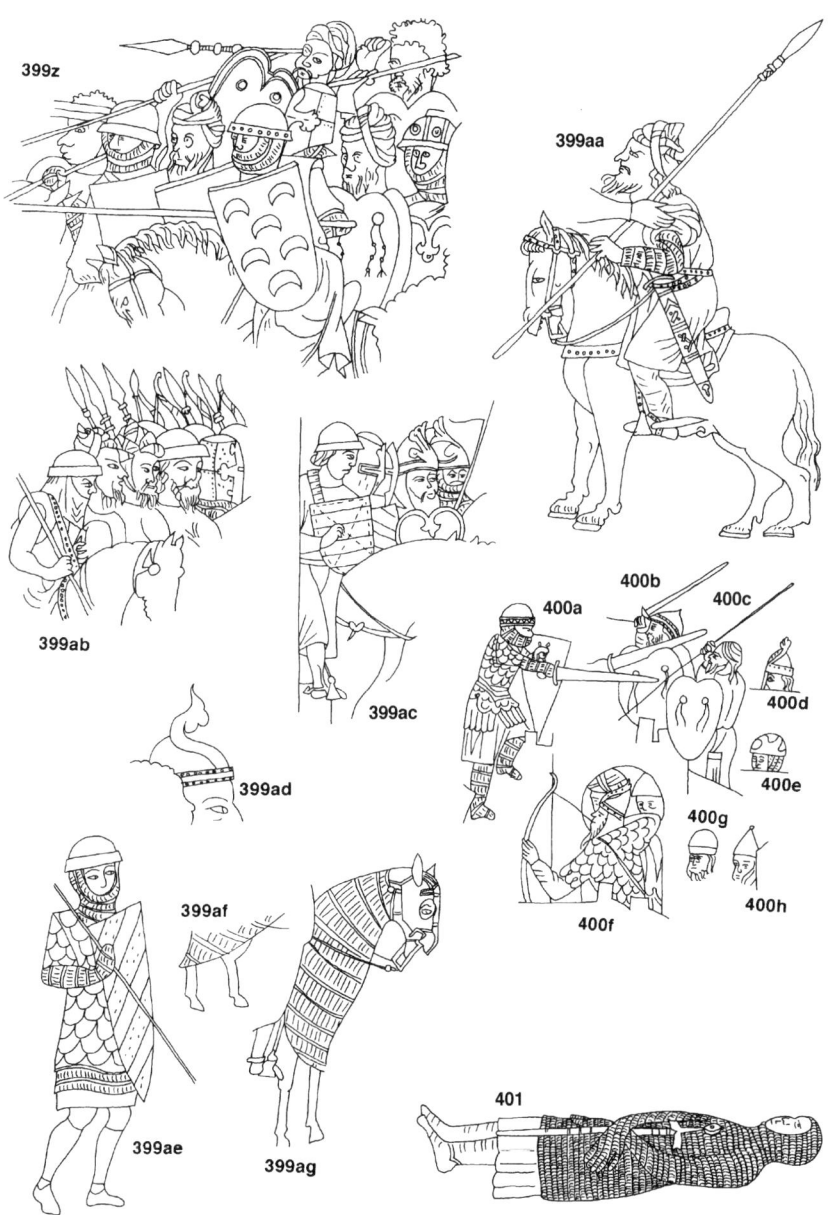

399z

399aa

399ab

399ac

399ad

399ae

399af

399ag

400a

400b

400c

400d

400e

400f

400g

400h

401

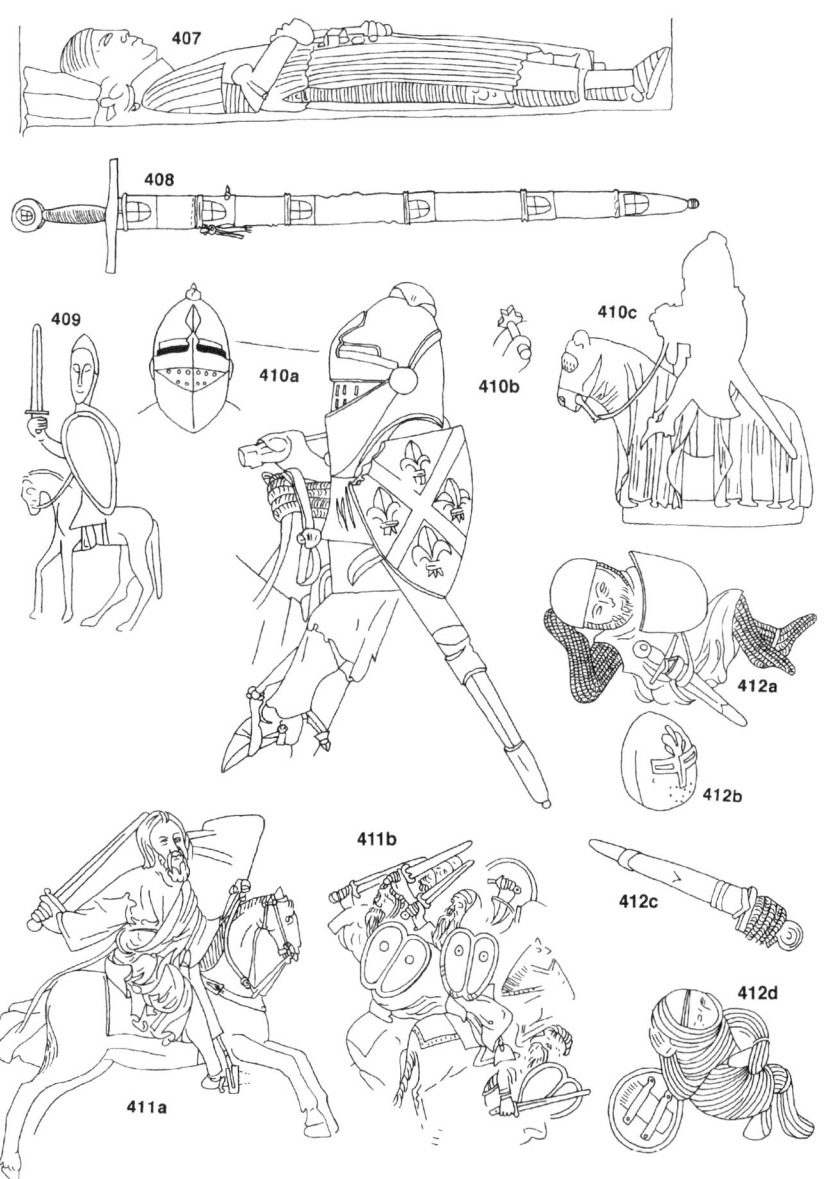

407

408

409

410a

410b

410c

412a

412b

411b

412c

411a

412d

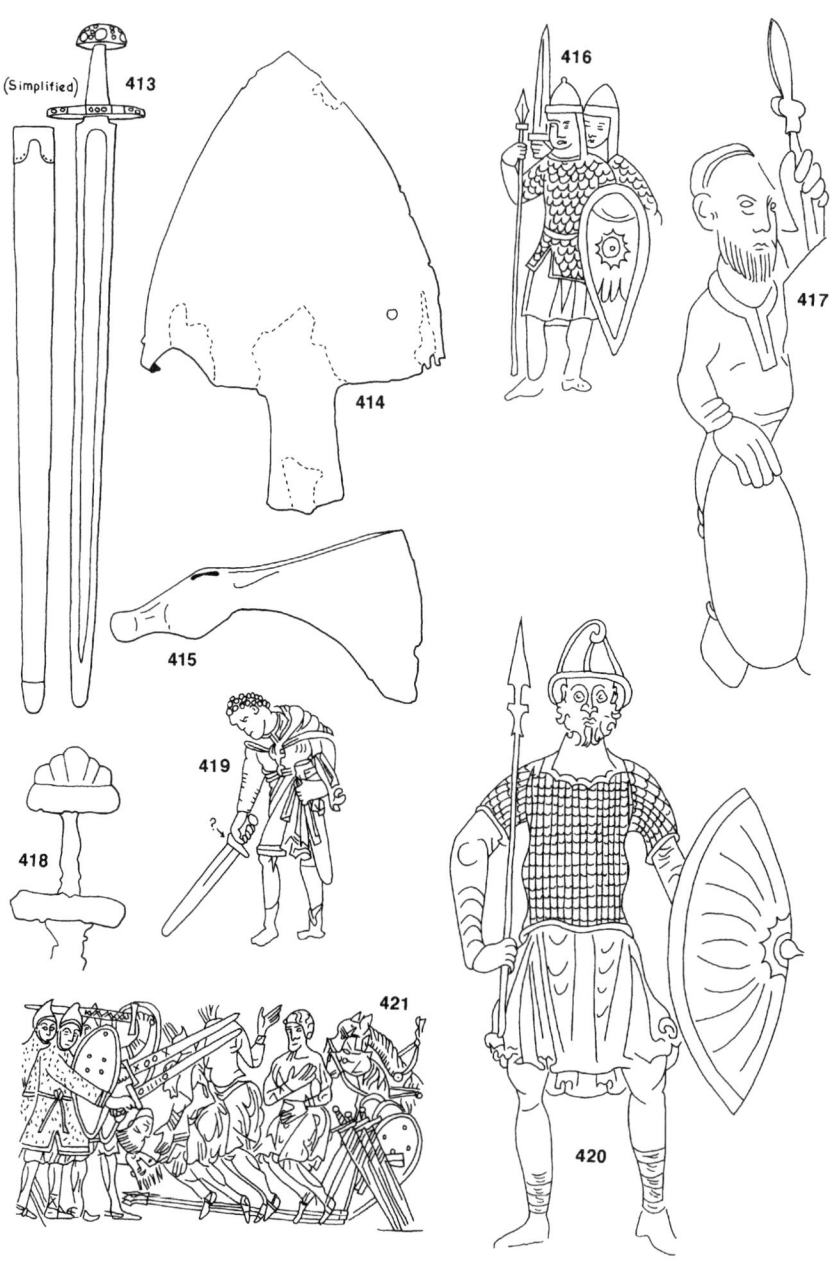

(Simplified) 413

414

415

416

417

418

419

420

421

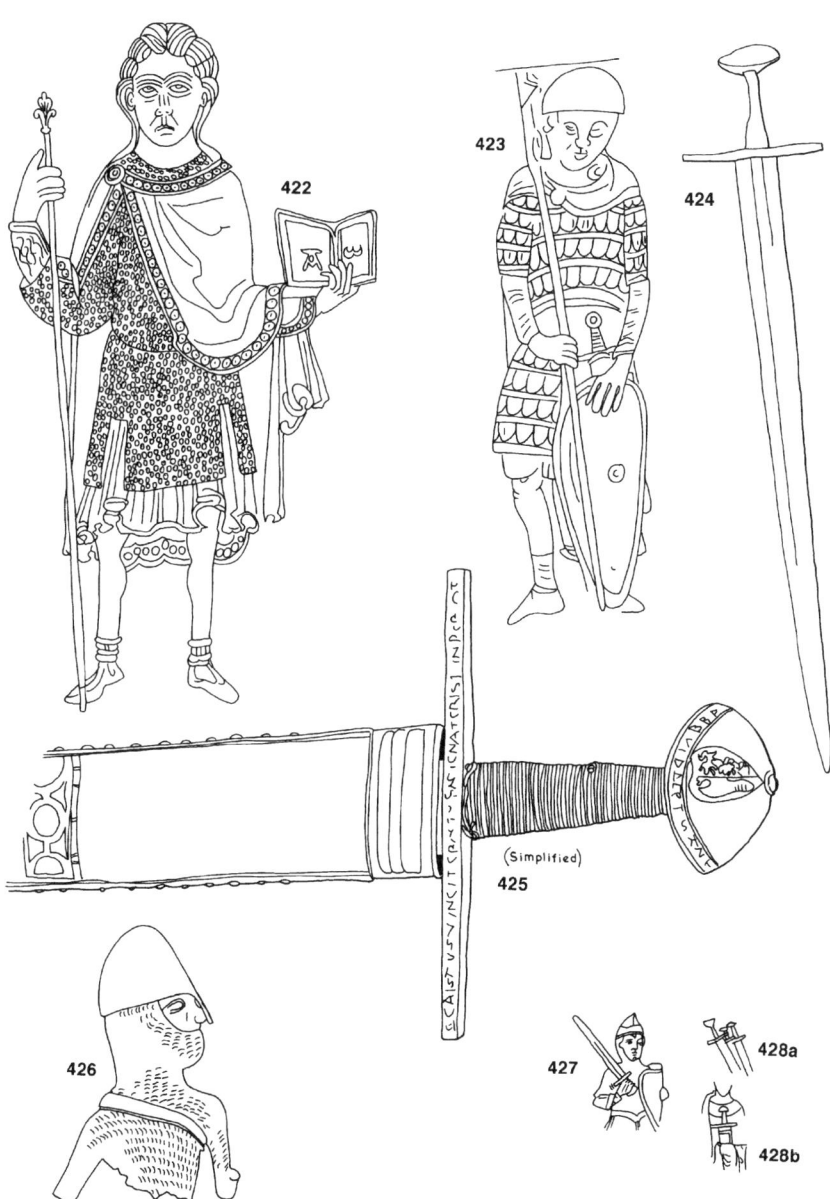

422

423

424

425 (Simplified)

426

427

428a

428b

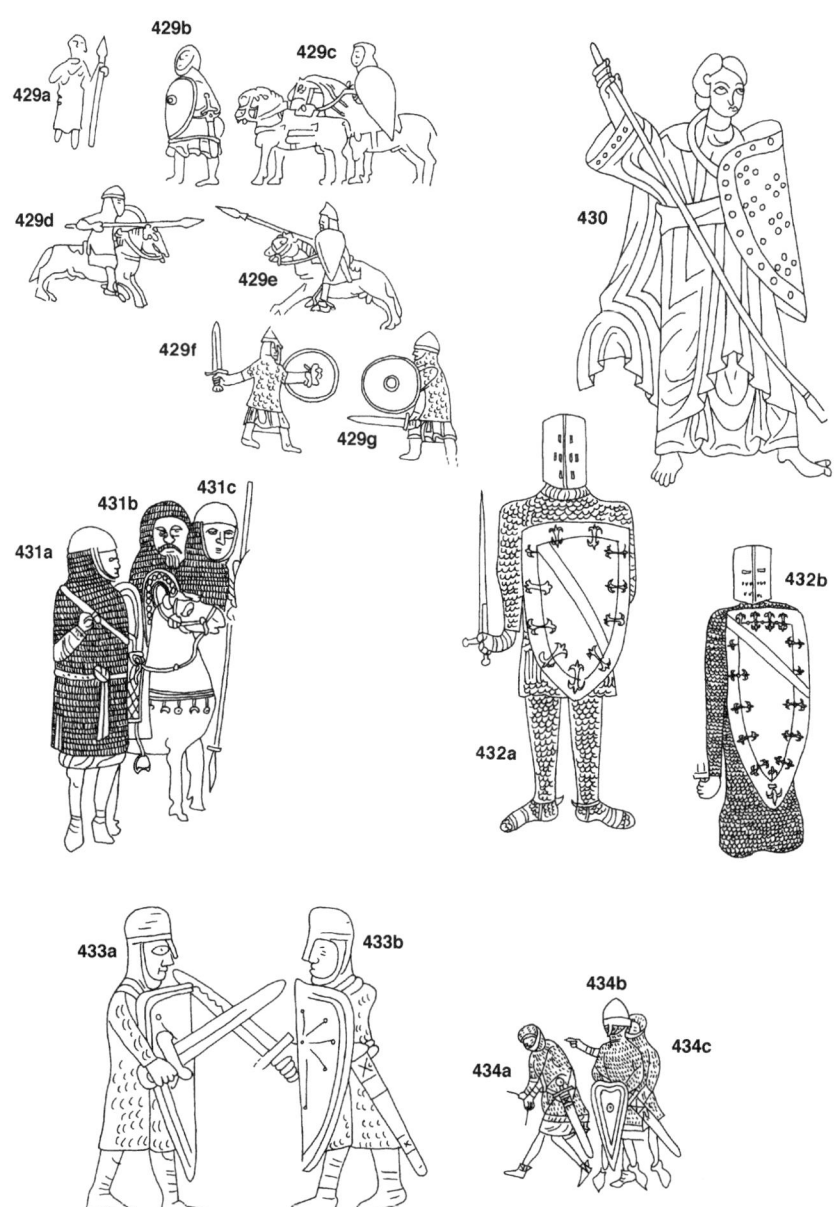

429a
429b
429c
429d
429e
429f
429g
430
431a
431b
431c
432a
432b
433a
433b
434a
434b
434c

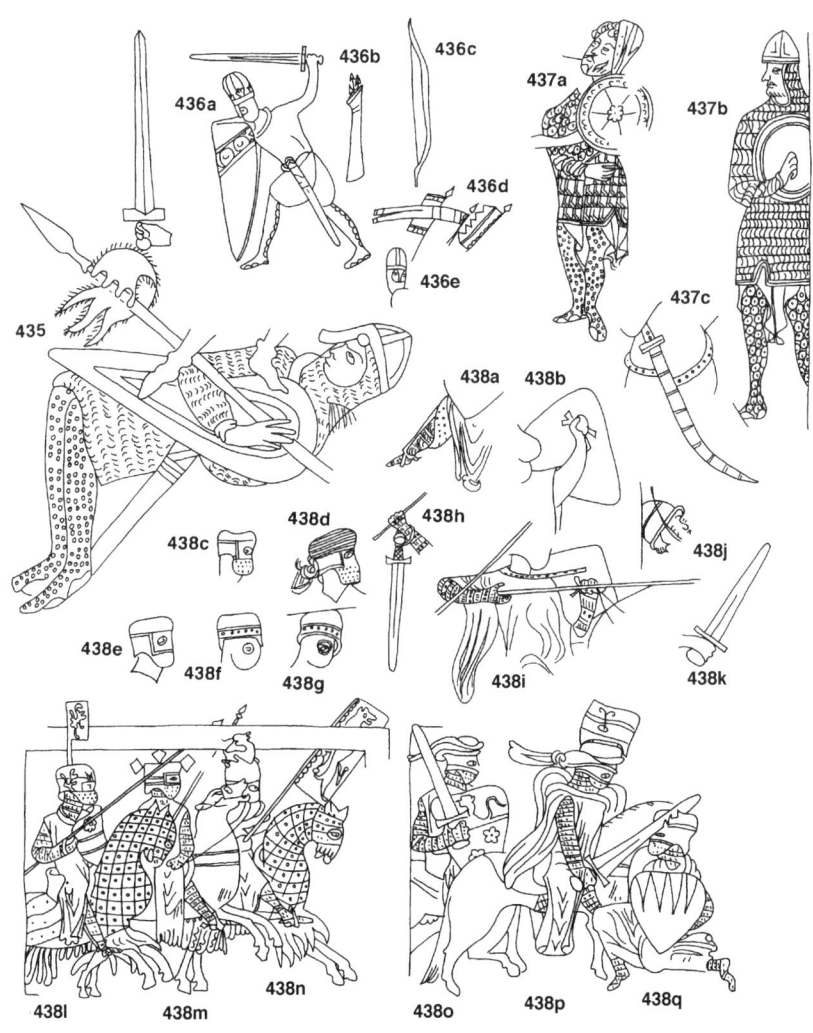

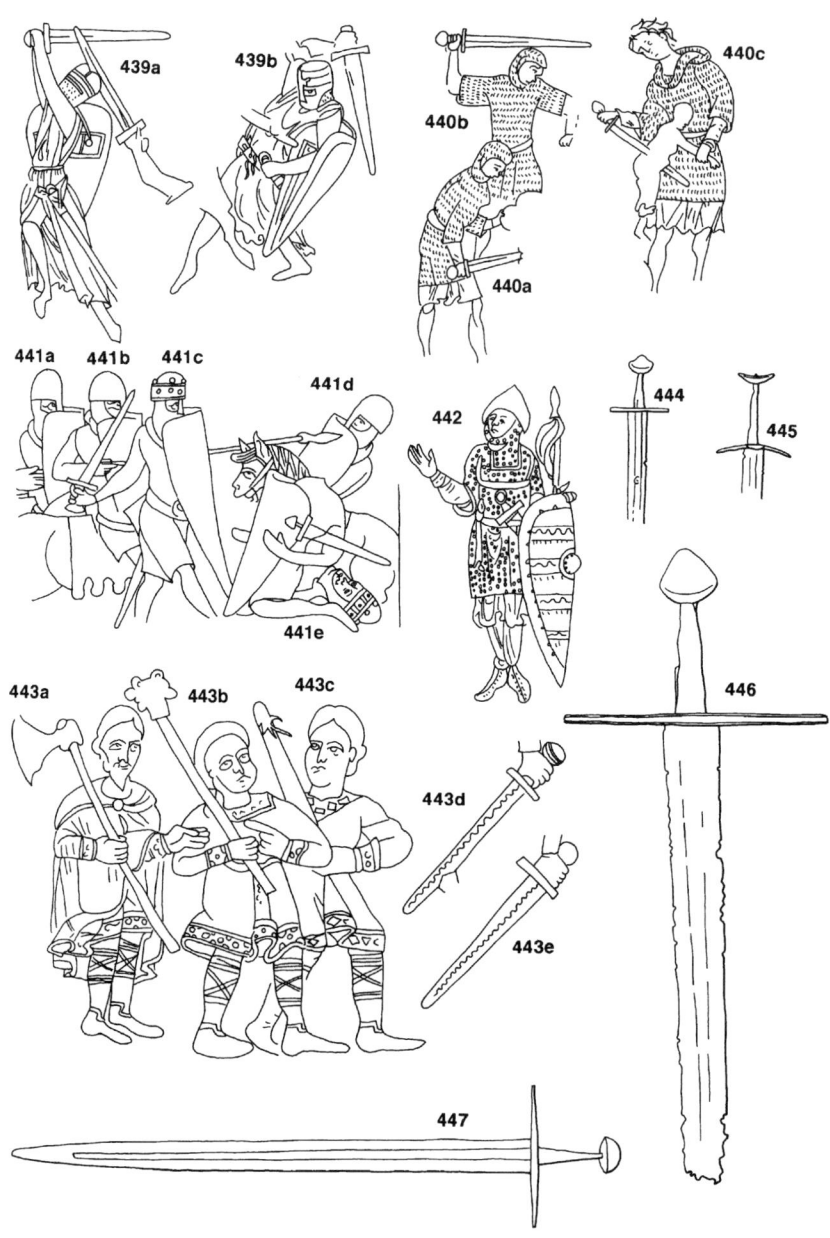

439a 439b 440b 440c 440a 441a 441b 441c 441d 442 444 445 441e 443a 443b 443c 443d 446 443e 447

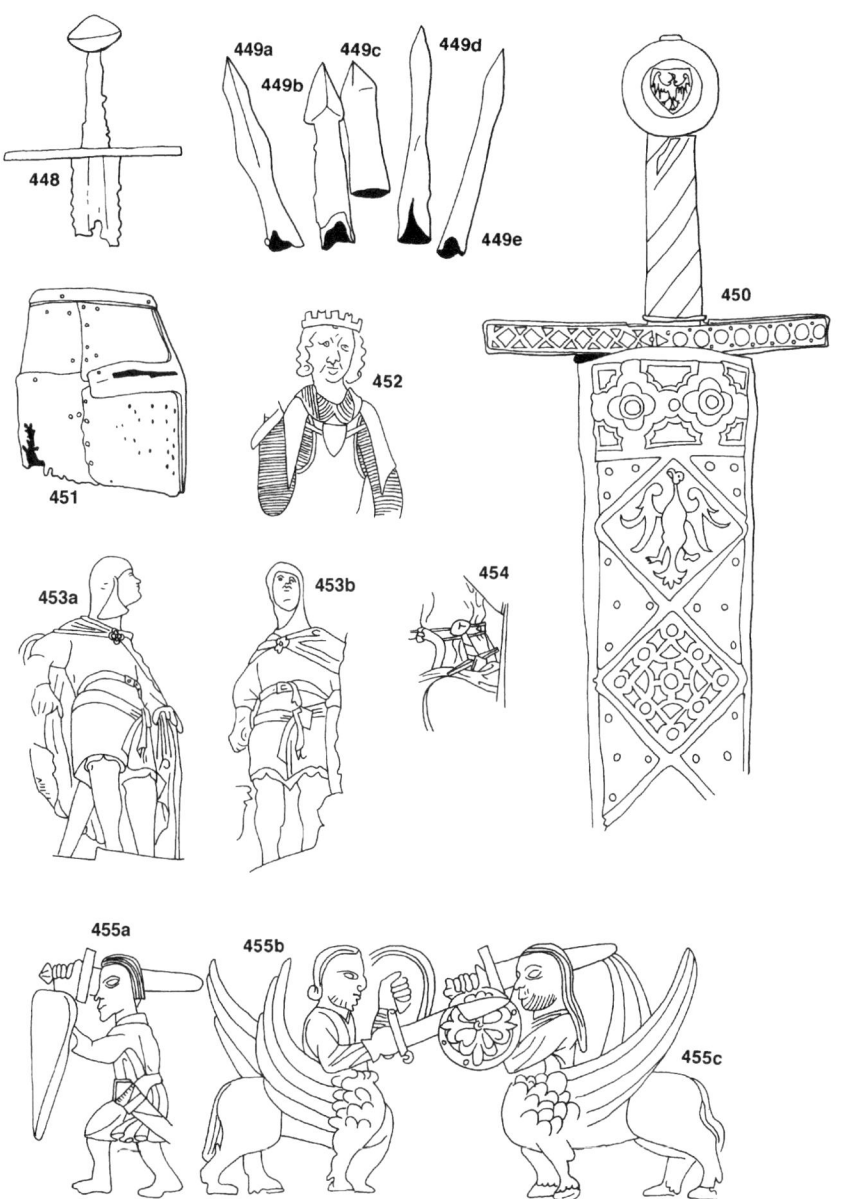

448

449a
449b
449c
449d
449e

450

451

452

453a
453b
454

455a
455b
455c

456

457

458c

458a

459

(forshortened)

460

458b

461

462a

462b

462c

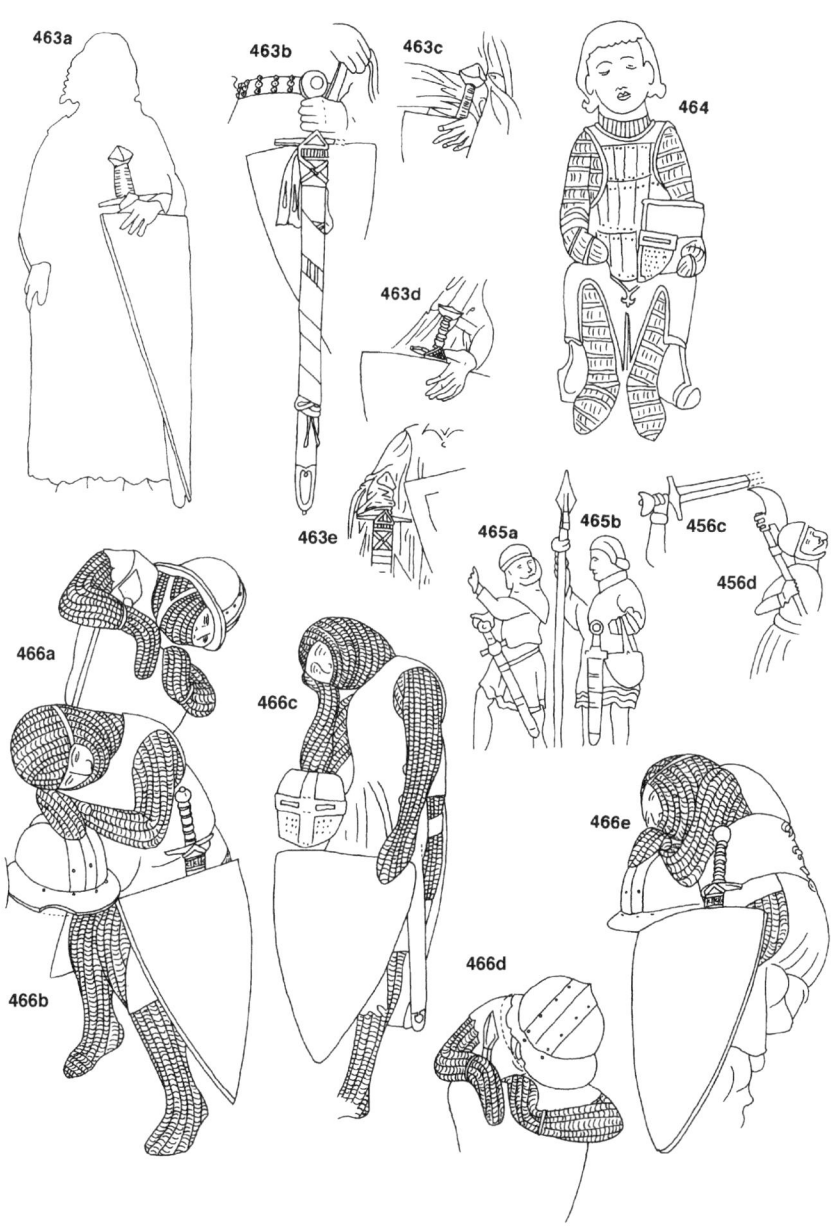

463a

463b

463c

464

463d

463e

465a

465b

456c

456d

466a

466c

466e

466b

466d

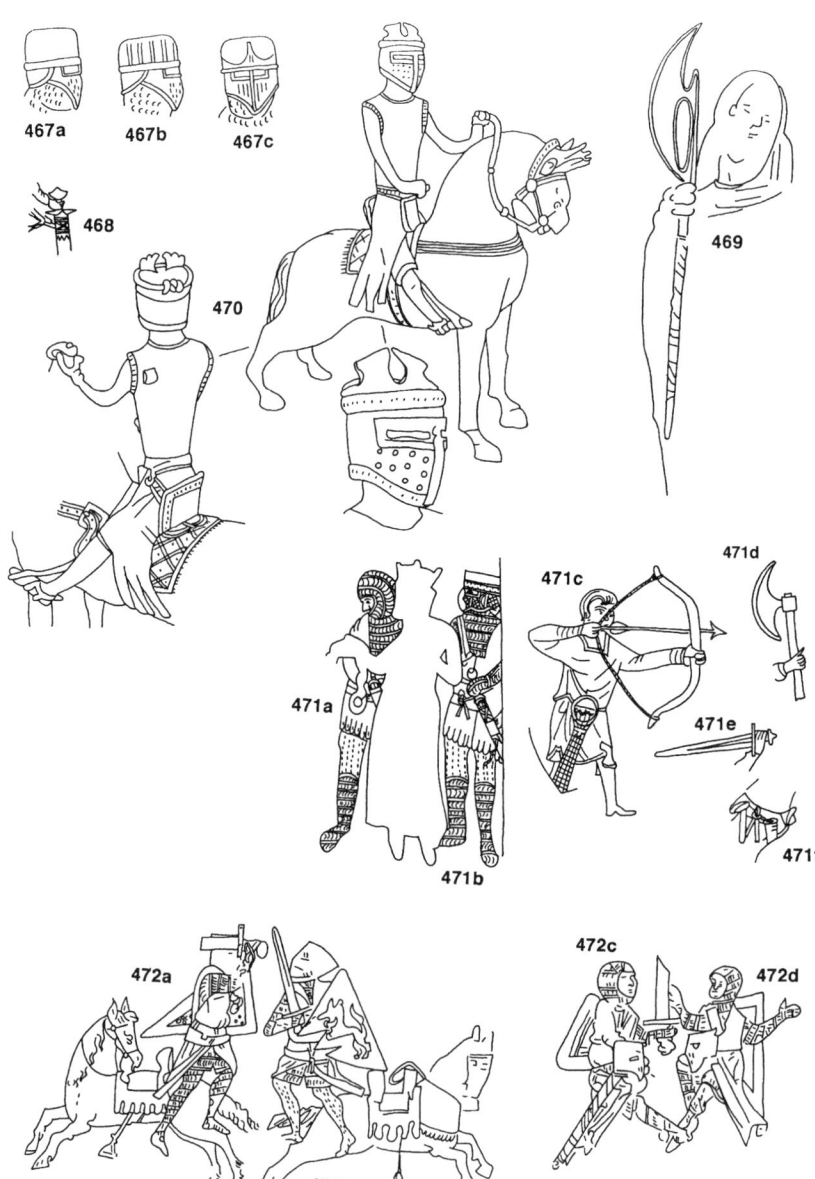

467a   467b   467c

468   470   469

471a   471c   471d

471b   471e

471f

472a   472c   472d

472b

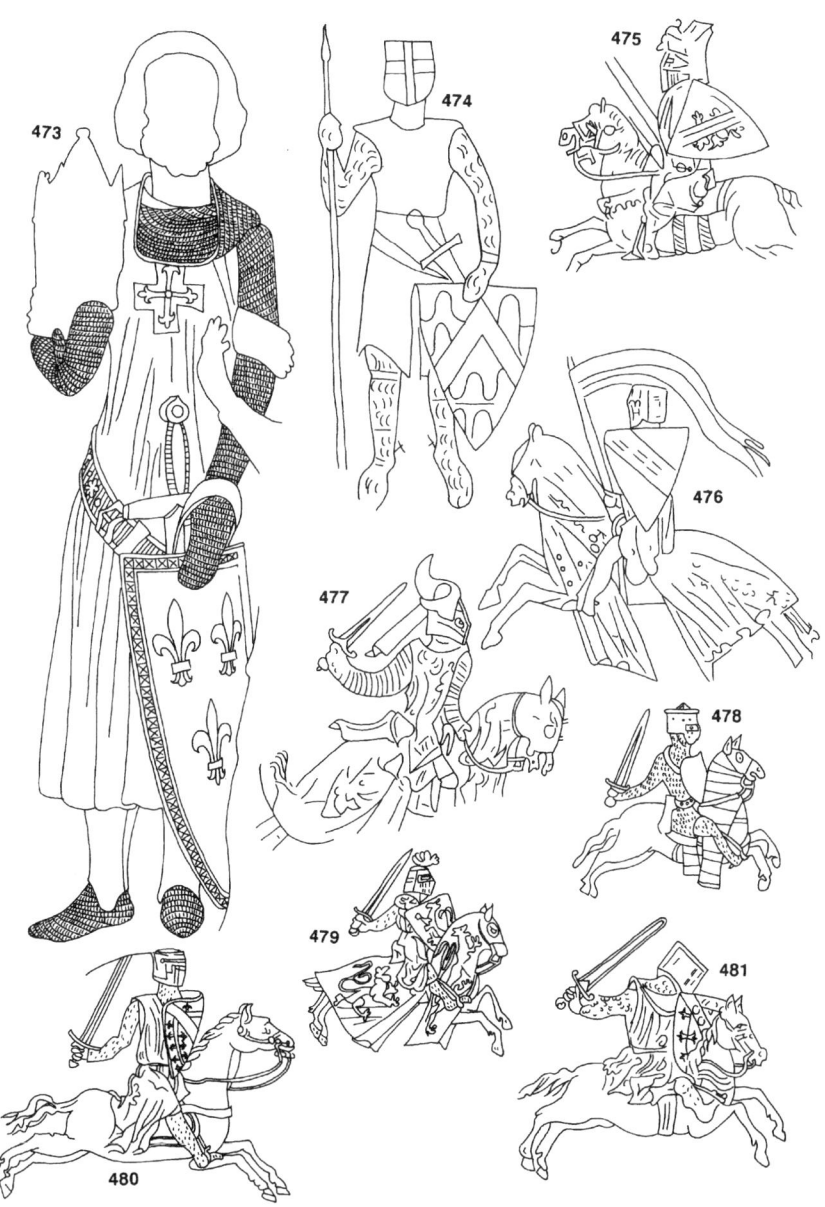

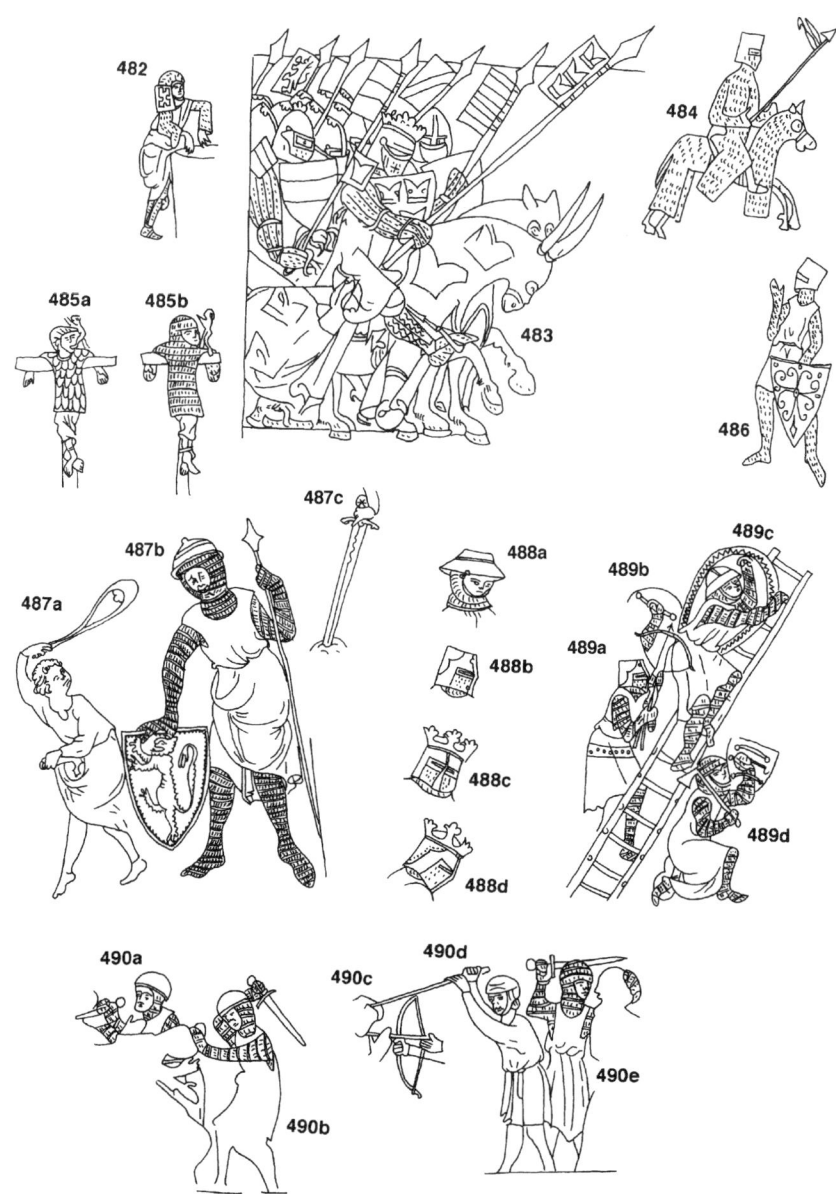

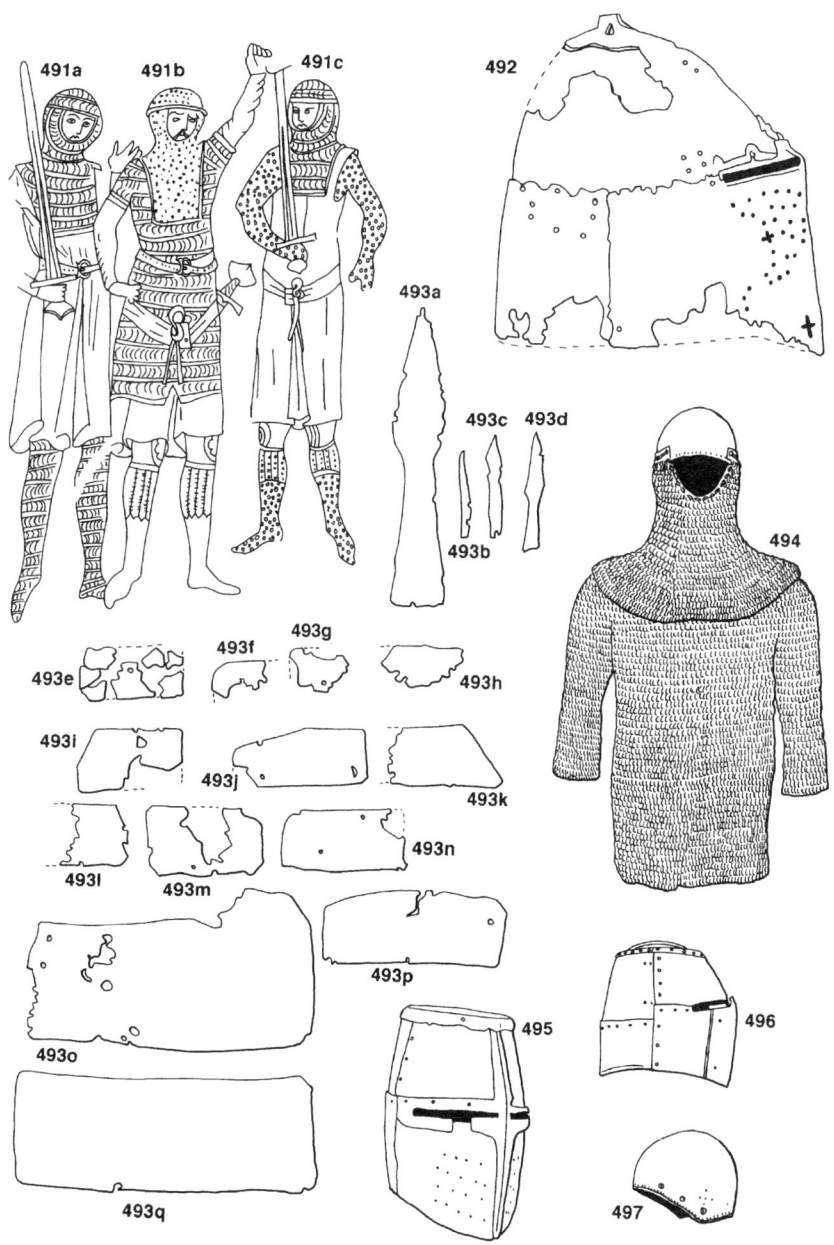

491a 491b 491c 492

493a

493c 493d

493b

494

493e 493f 493g 493h

493i 493j 493k

493l 493m 493n

493o 493p

495 496

493q 497

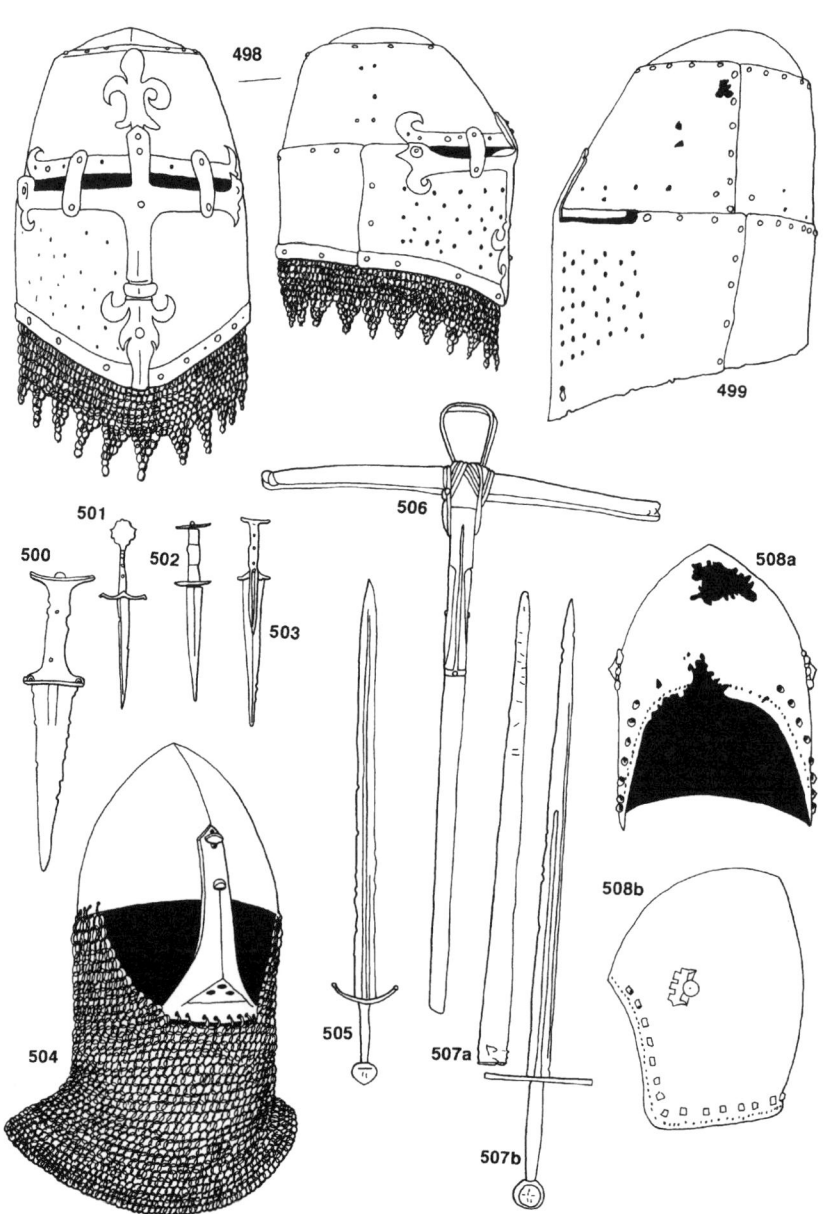

498

499

500
501
502
503

506

508a

504
505
507a
507b
508b

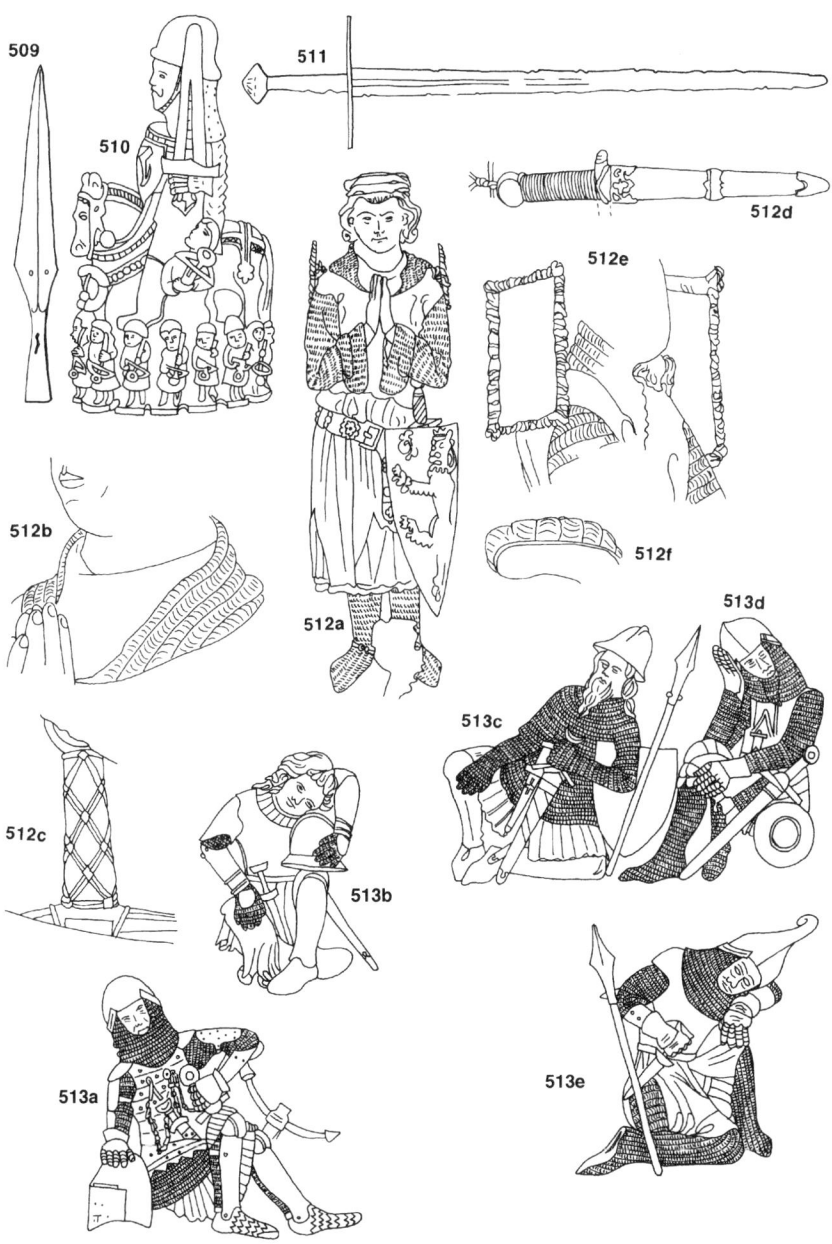

509

510

511

512d

512e

512b

512f

512a

513d

513c

512c

513b

513a

513e

514b

514c

514a

514d

515

516

517

518

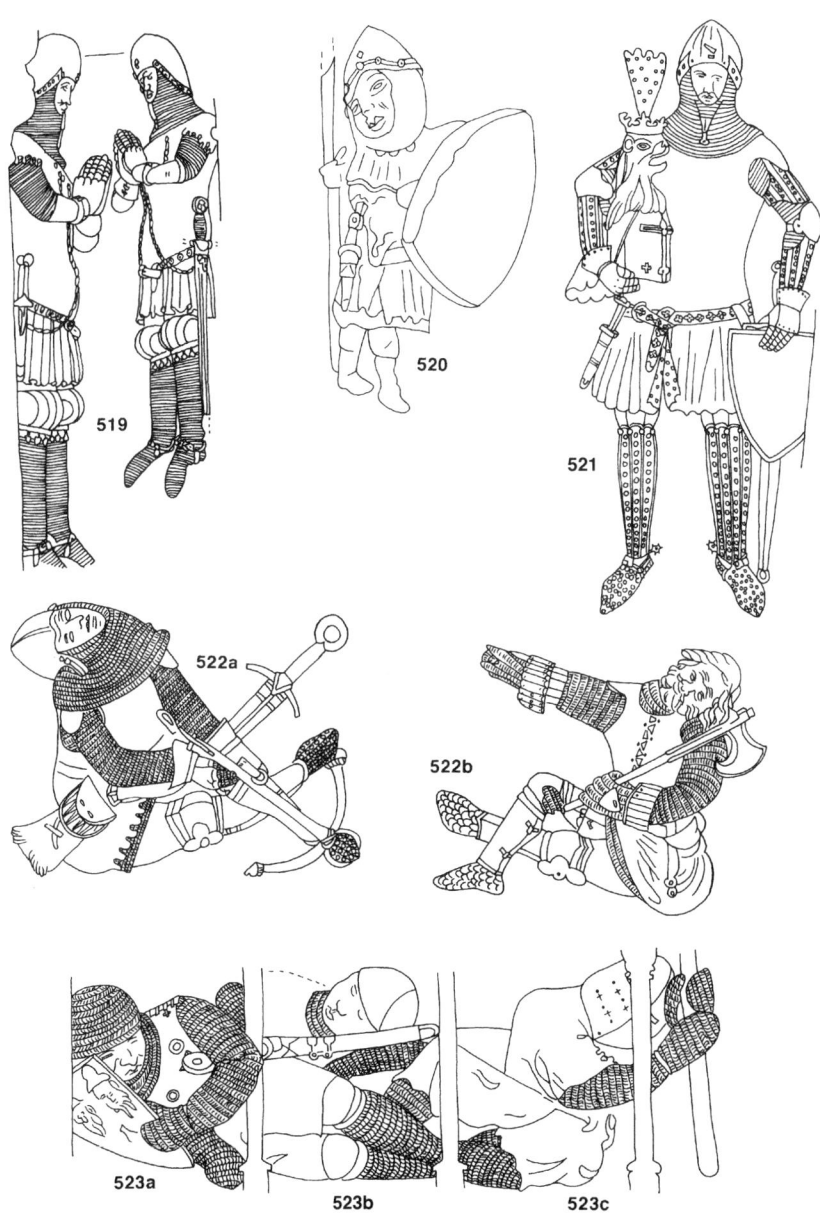

519

520

521

522a

522b

523a

523b

523c

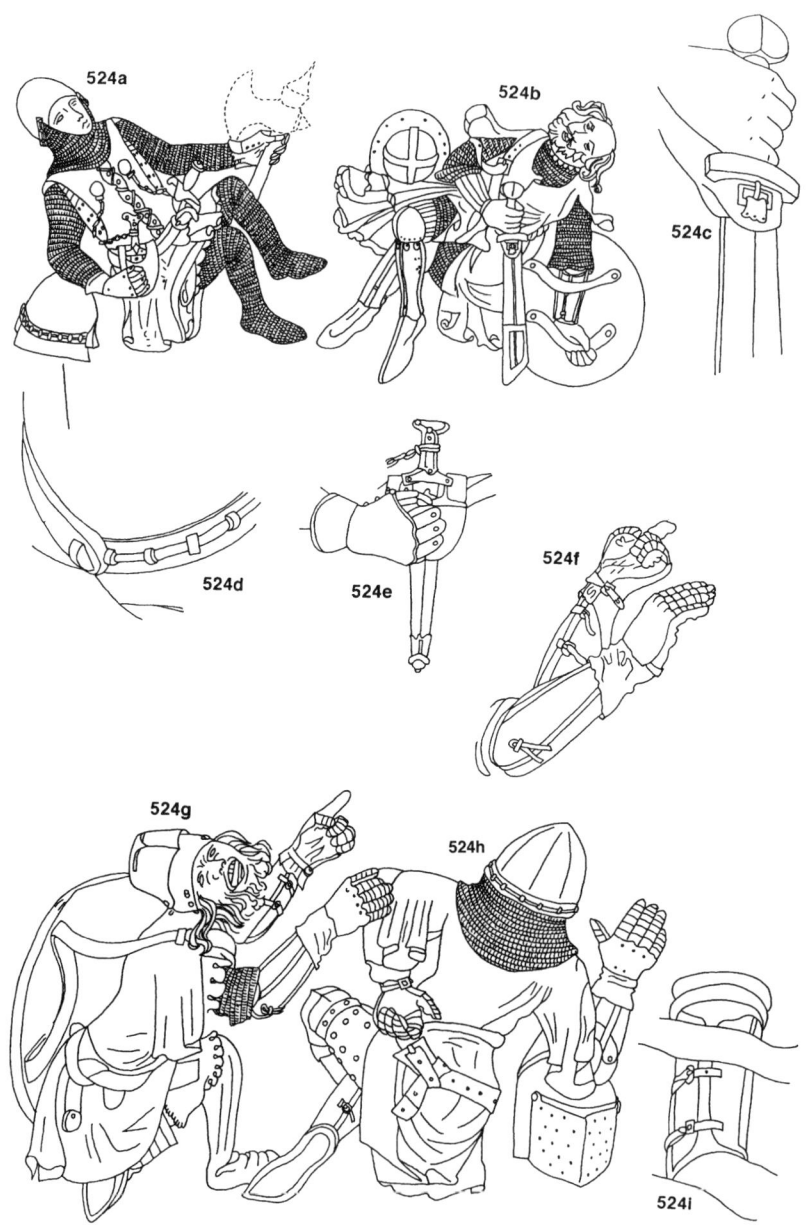

524a

524b

524c

524d

524e

524f

524g

524h

524i

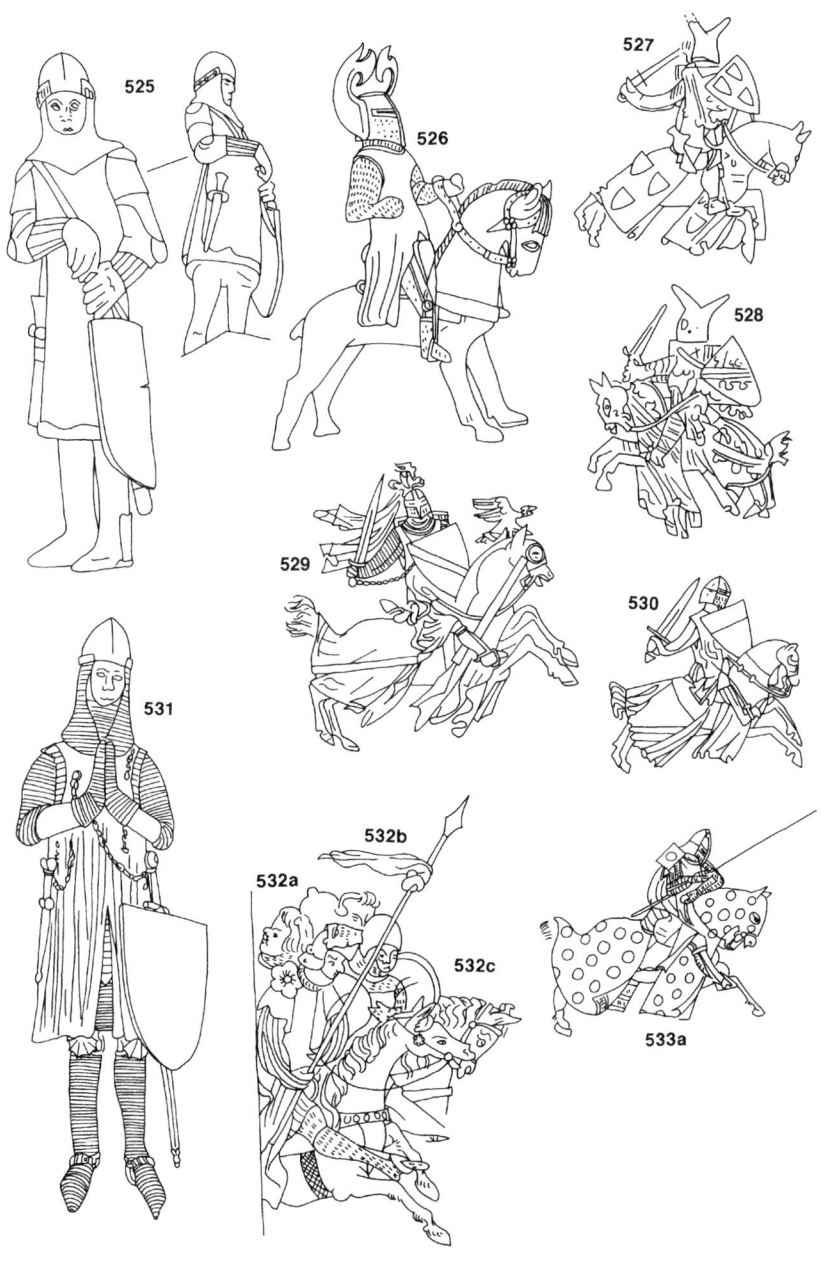

525

526

527

528

529

530

531

532a

532b

532c

533a

533b 533c 533d 533g 533e 533f 534a 534b 534c 534d 535c 535a 535b 536a 536b 537b 537c 537a 537d 538a 538b

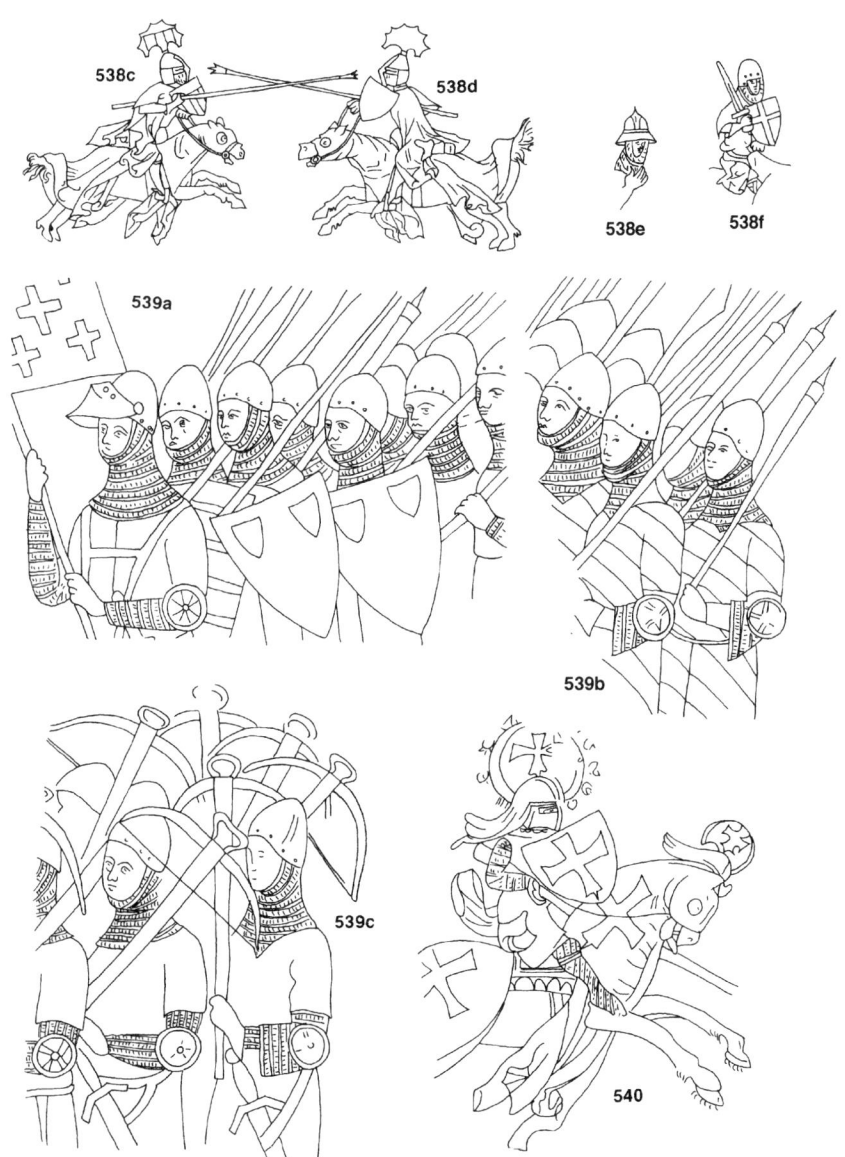

538c

538d

538e

538f

539a

539b

539c

540

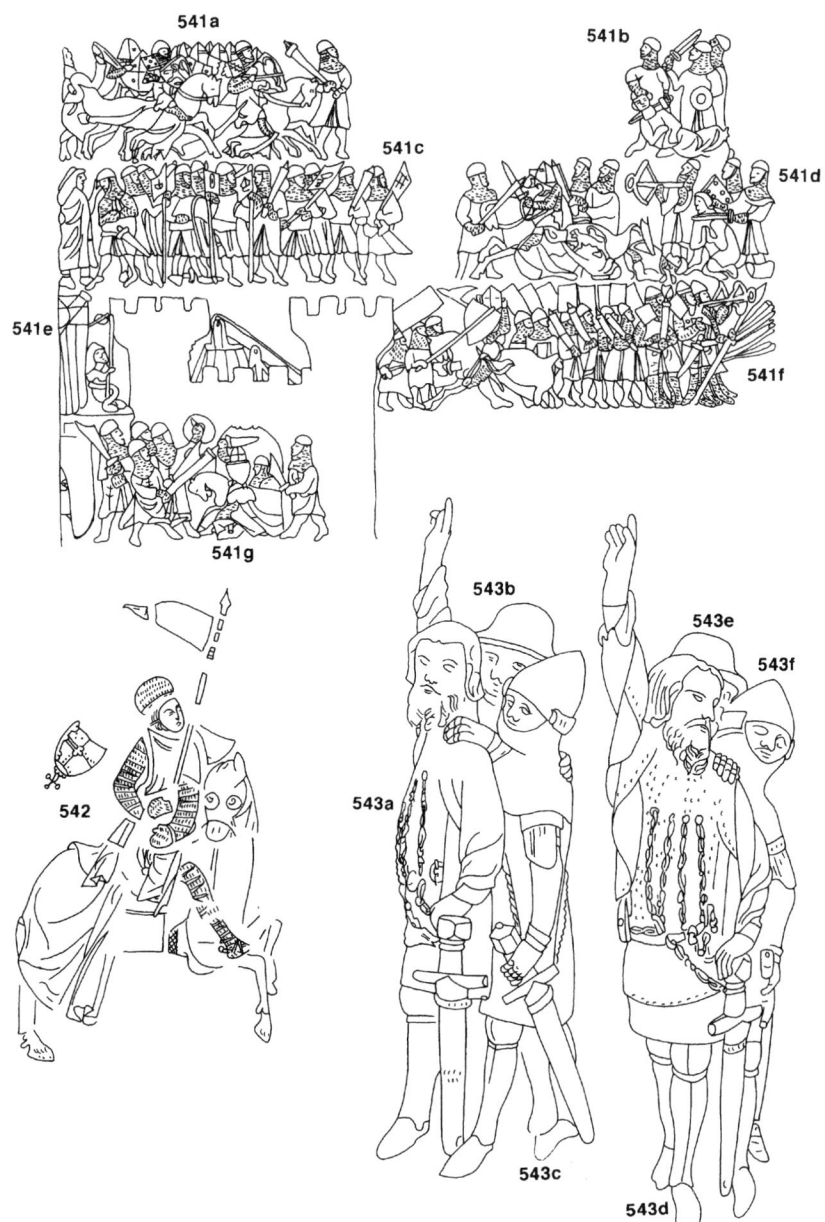

541a

541b

541c

541d

541e

541f

541g

542

543a

543b

543e

543f

543c

543d

544

545

546a

547

548

549

546b

550

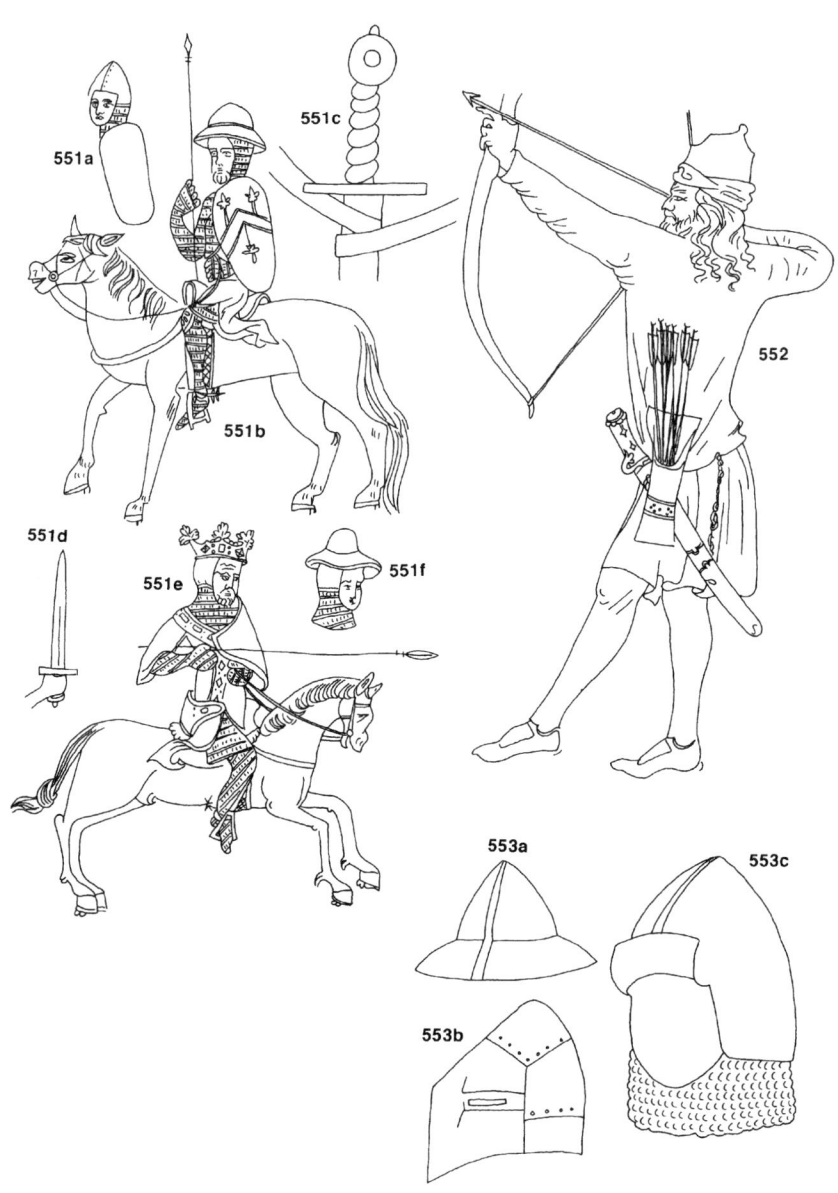

551a

551c

551b

552

551d

551e

551f

553a

553c

553b

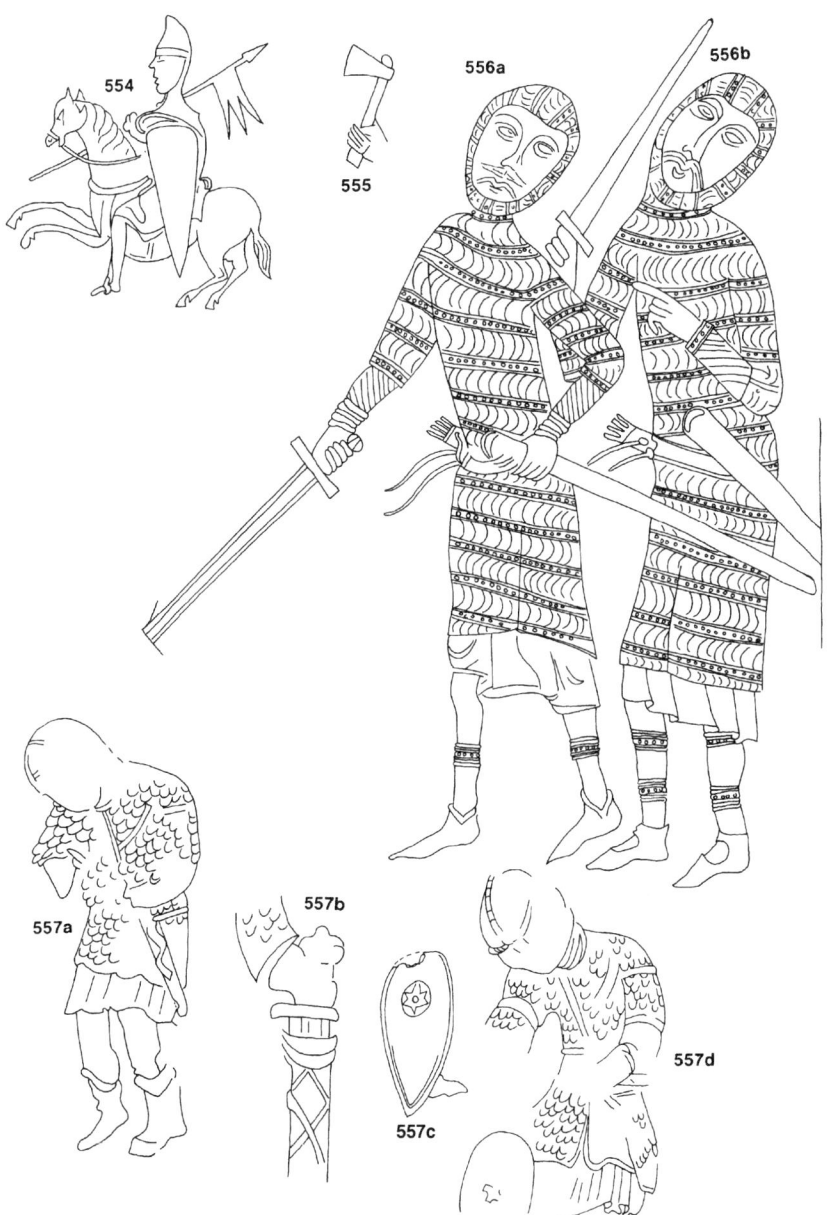

554

555

556a

556b

557a

557b

557c

557d

558a 558b 558c

559a 559b 559c 559d

560

561a 561b 561c 561d

562a

526b

562c

562d

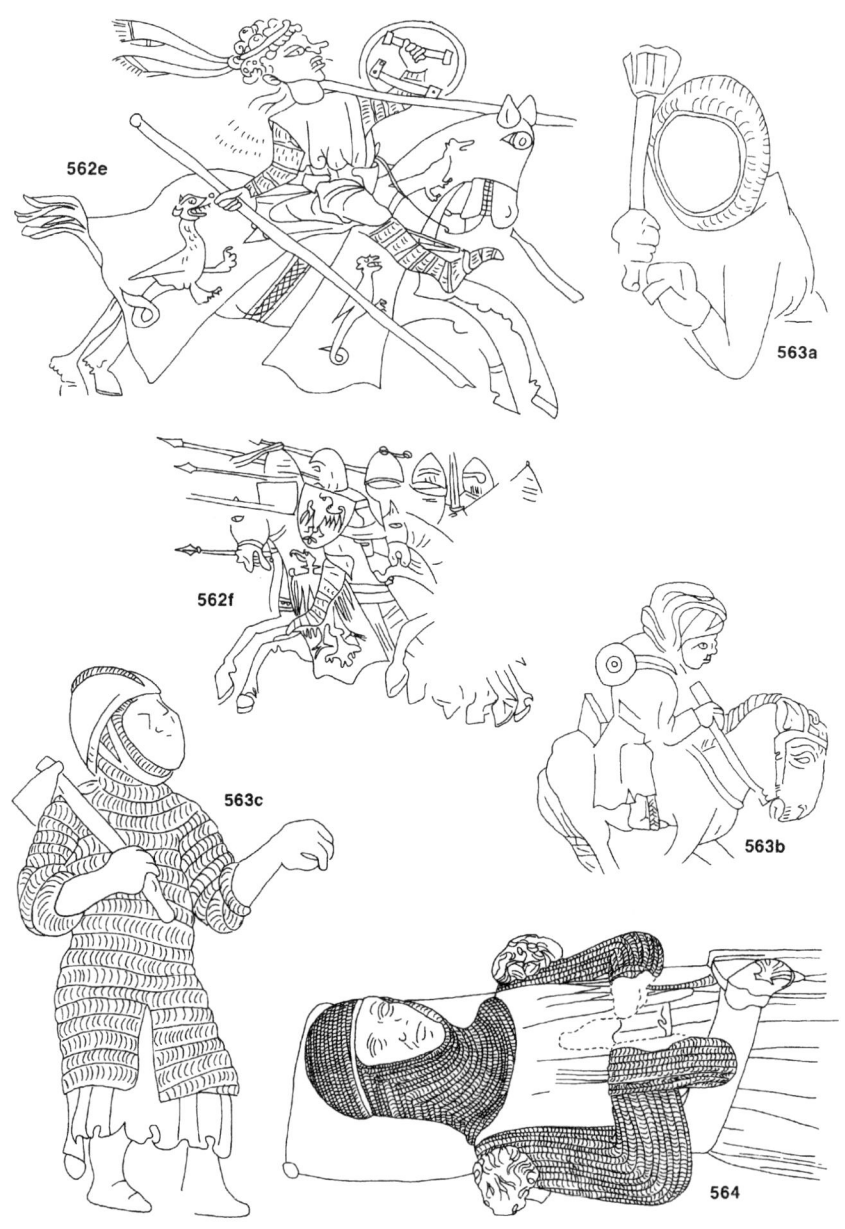

562e

563a

562f

563c

563b

564

565

566a

566b

567

568

569a

569b

570a

570b

570c

570d

570e

570f

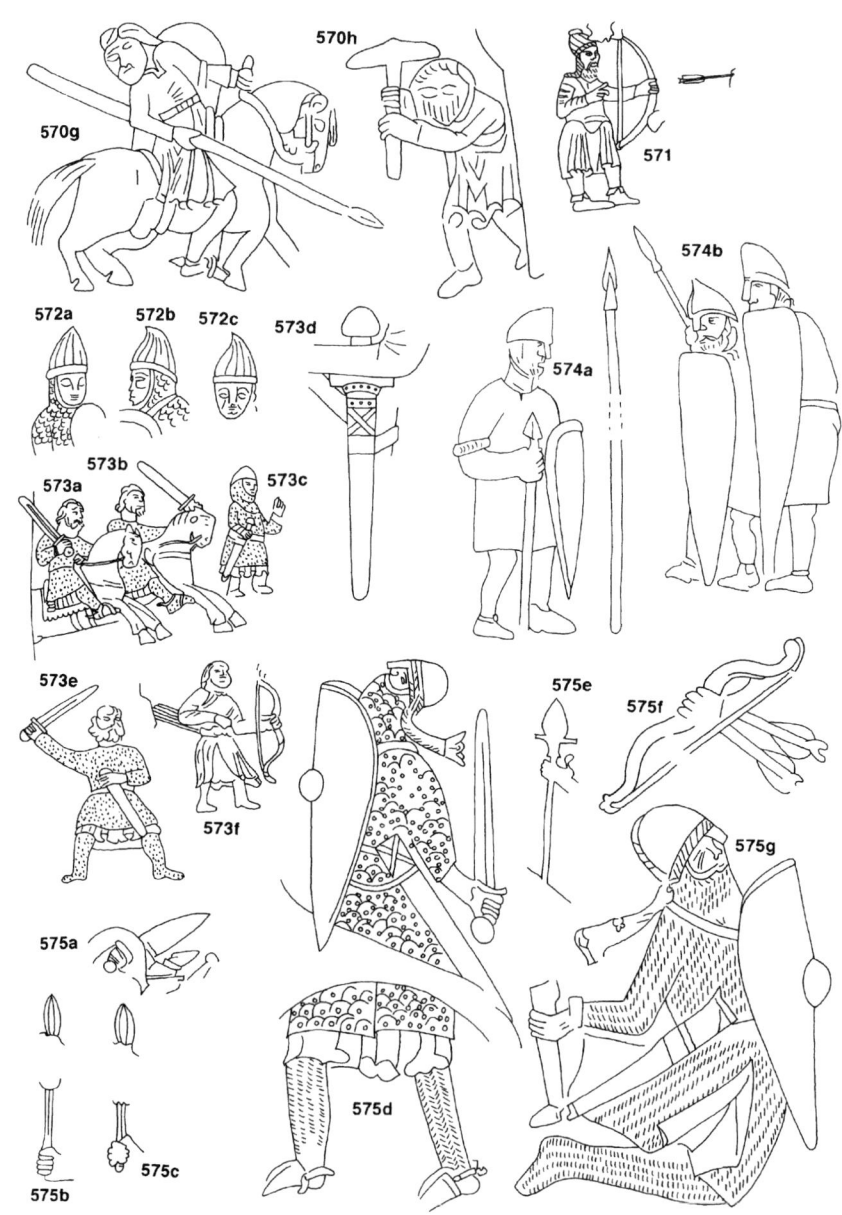

570g   570h   571

572a   572b   572c   573d   574b   574a

573b   573a   573c

573e   573f   575e   575f   575g

575a   575d

575b   575c

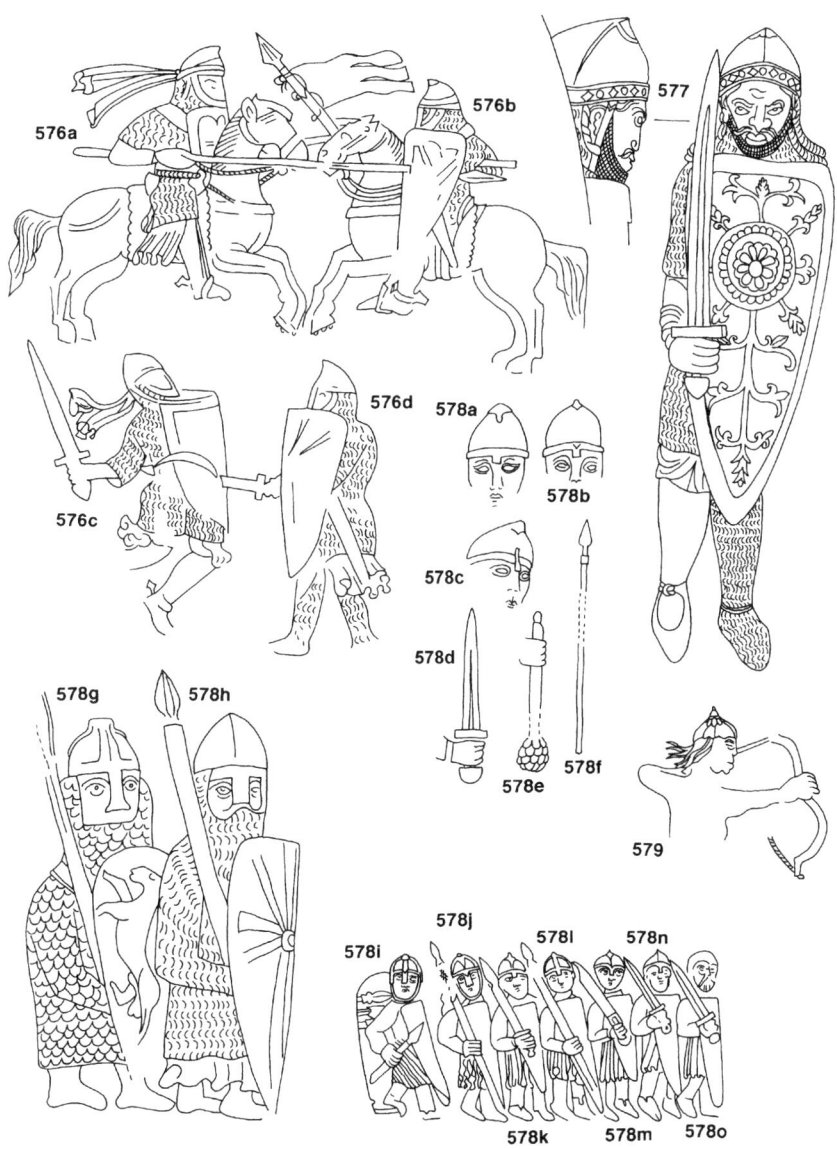

576a

576b

576c

576d

577

578a

578b

578c

578d

578e

578f

578g

578h

578i

578j

578l

578n

578k

578m

578o

579

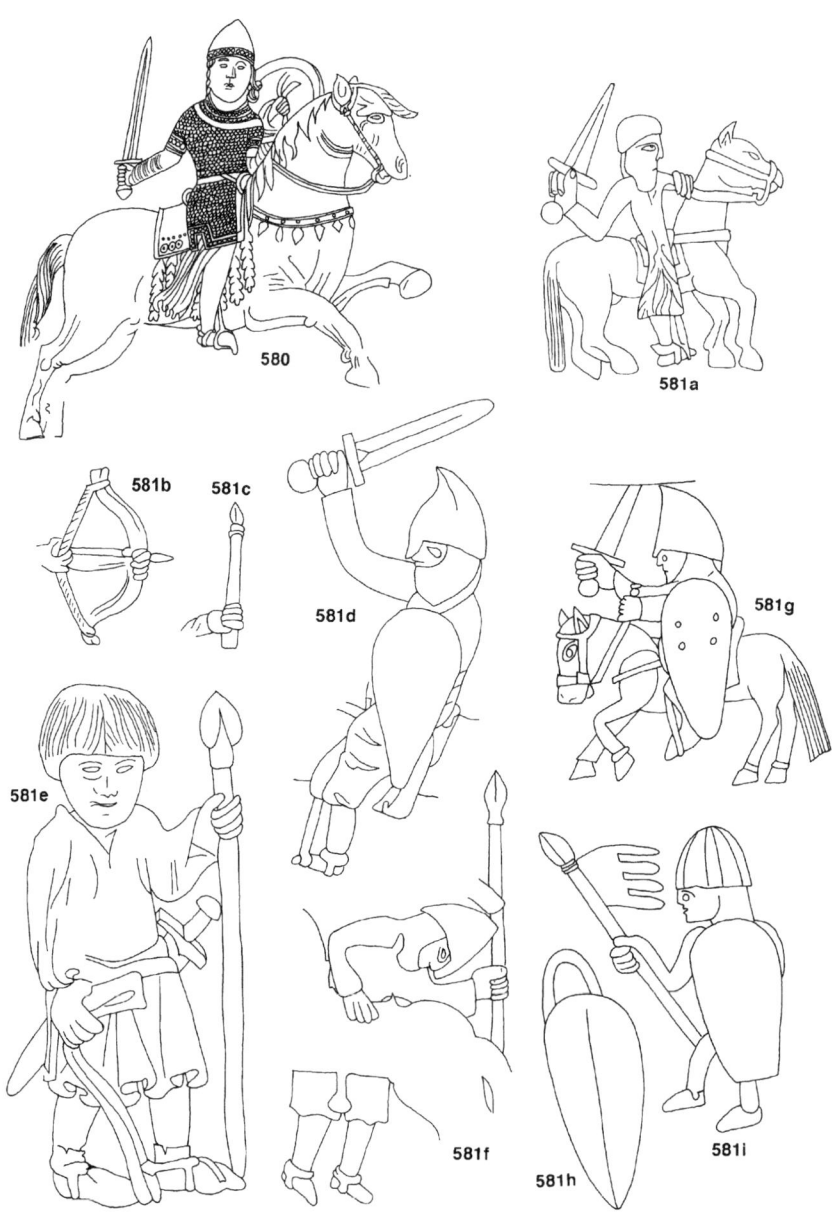

580

581a

581b   581c

581d

581g

581e

581f

581h   581i

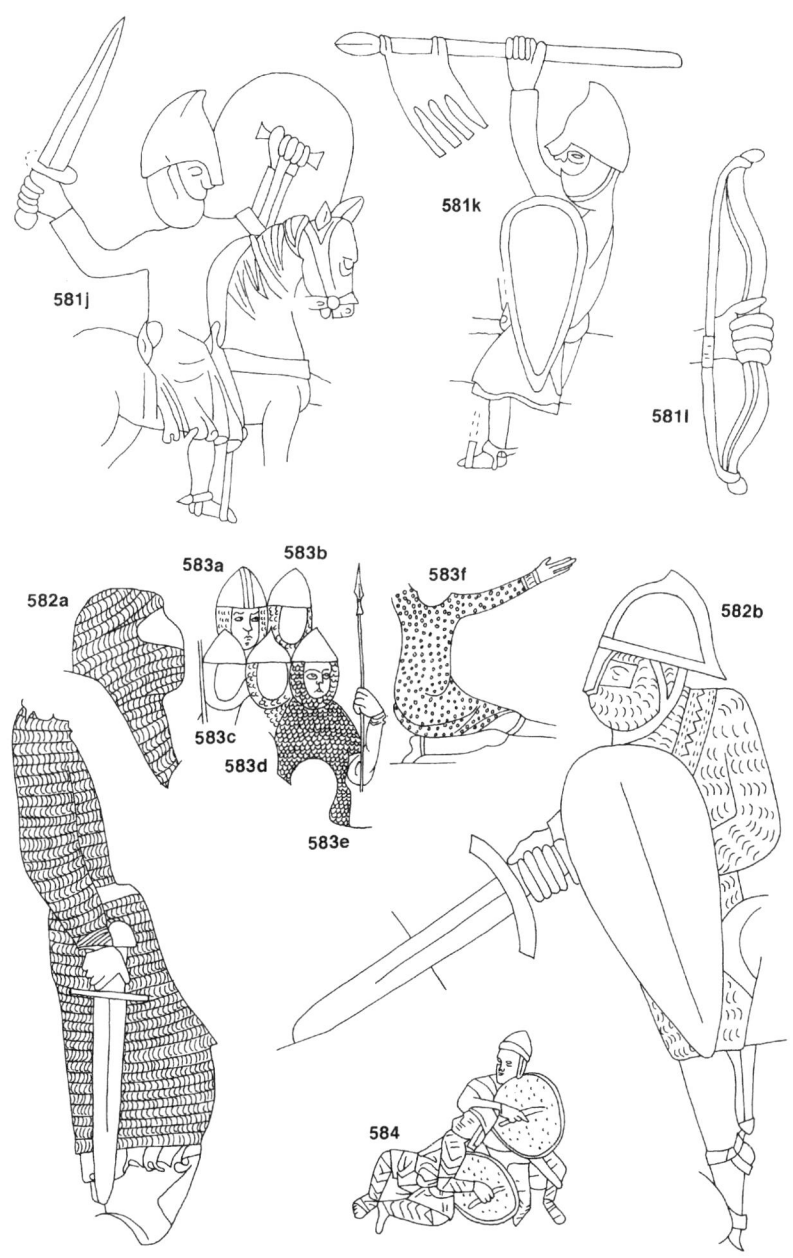

581j

581k

581l

582a

583a

583b

583f

583c

583d

583e

582b

584

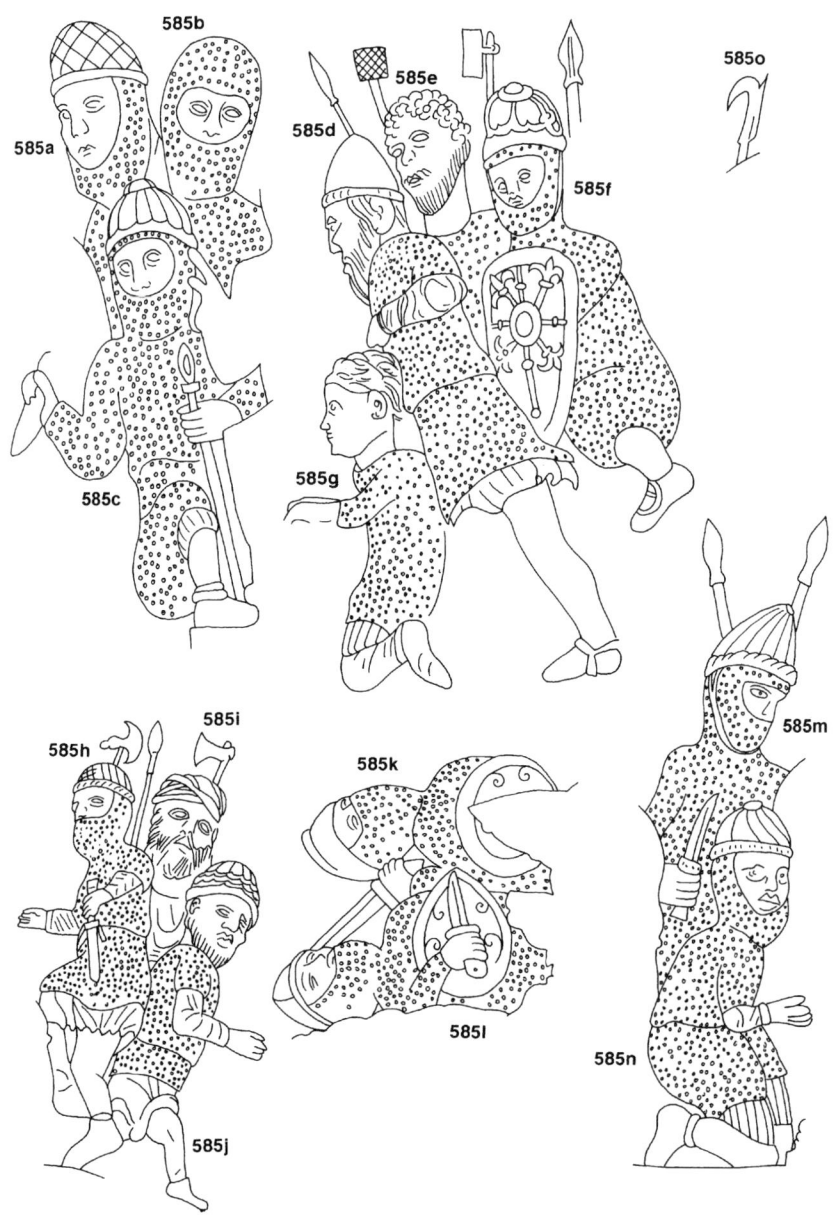

585a
585b
585c
585d
585e
585f
585g
585h
585i
585j
585k
585l
585m
585n
585o

586a

586b

586c

588

587a

587b

589

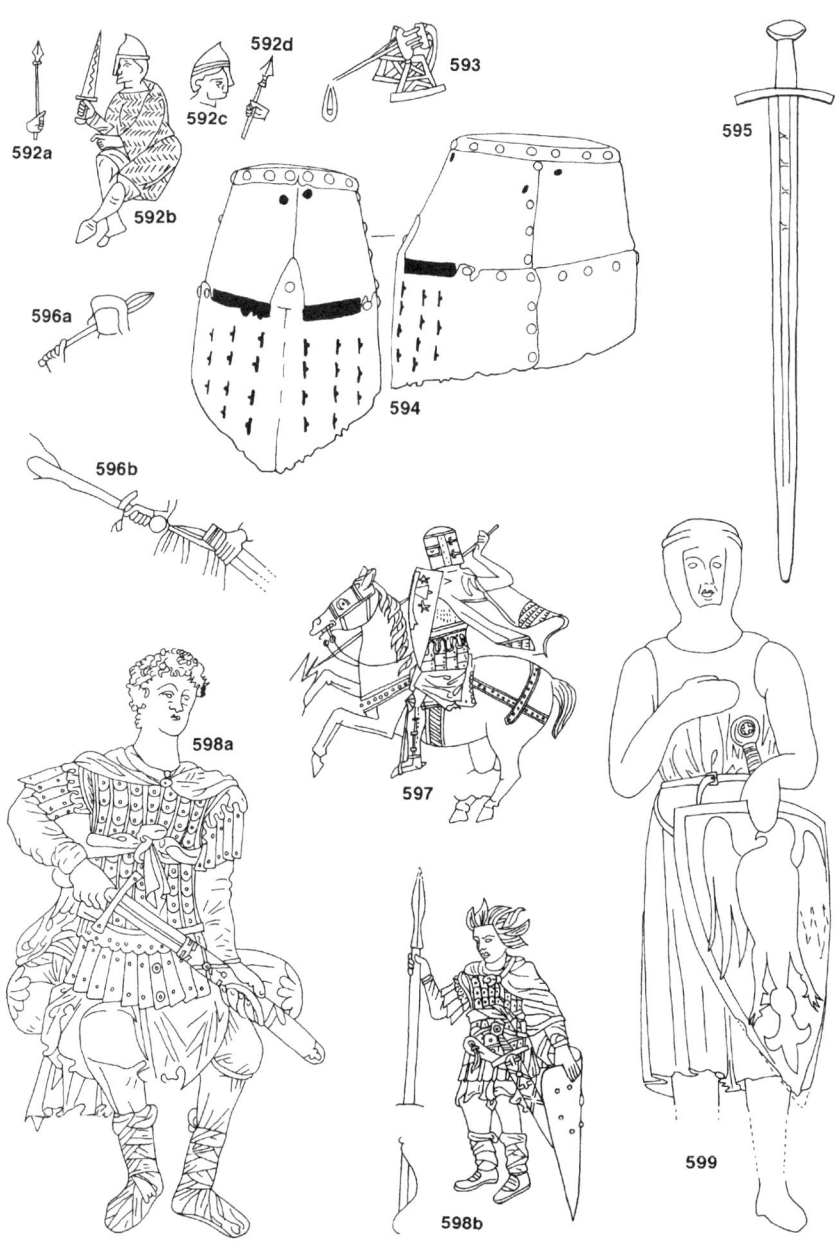

592a

592b

592c

592d

593

594

595

596a

596b

597

598a

598b

599

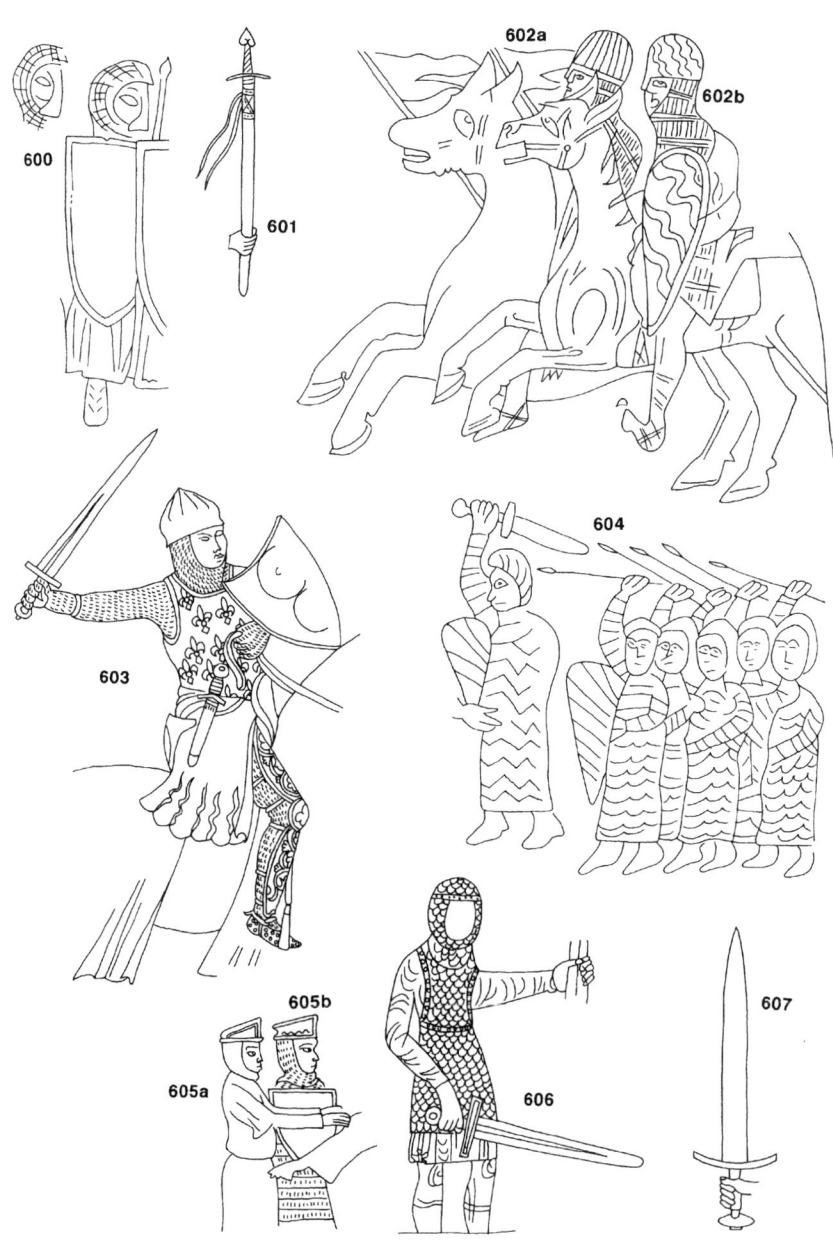

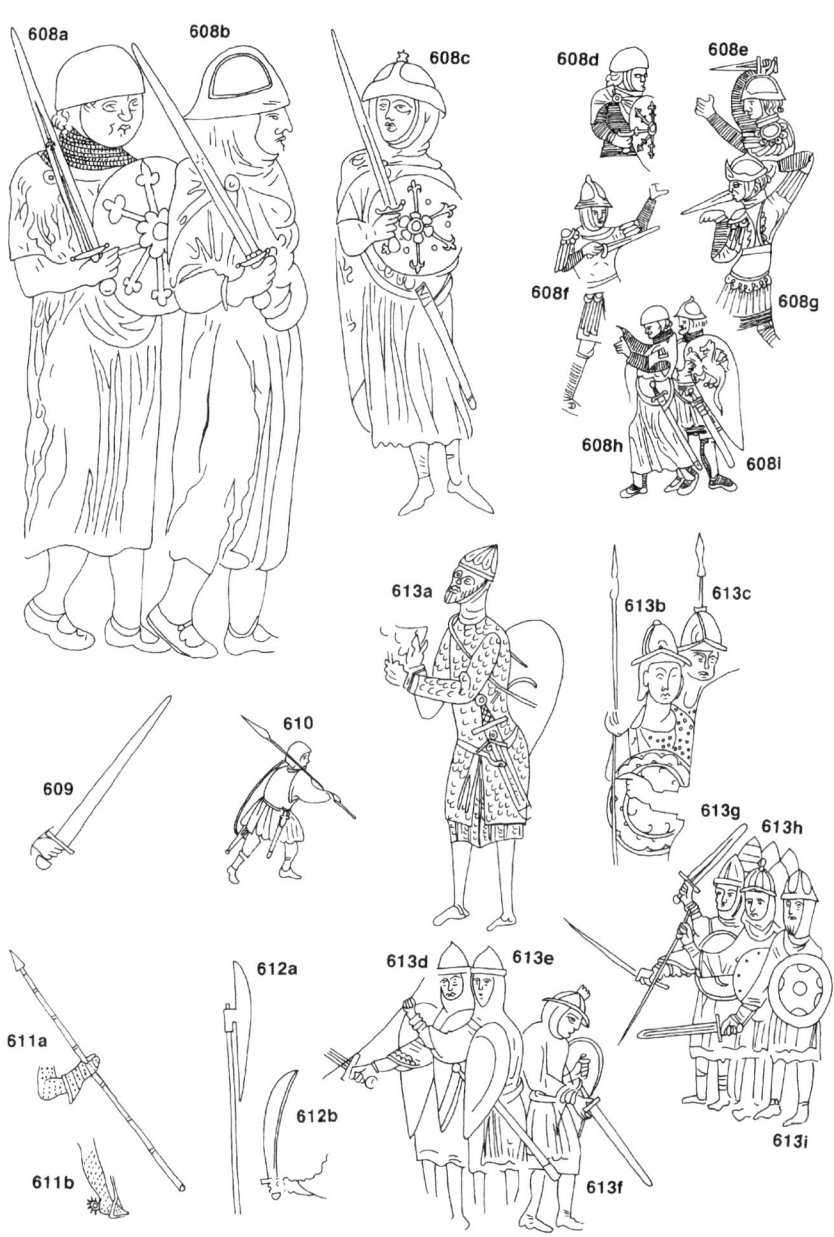

608a 608b 608c 608d 608e 608f 608g 608h 608i

613a 613b 613c 613g 613h

609 610 611a 611b 612a 612b 613d 613e 613f 613i

614a

614b

614c

614d

615

617a 617b 617c 617d

617e

616b 616c

616a 616d

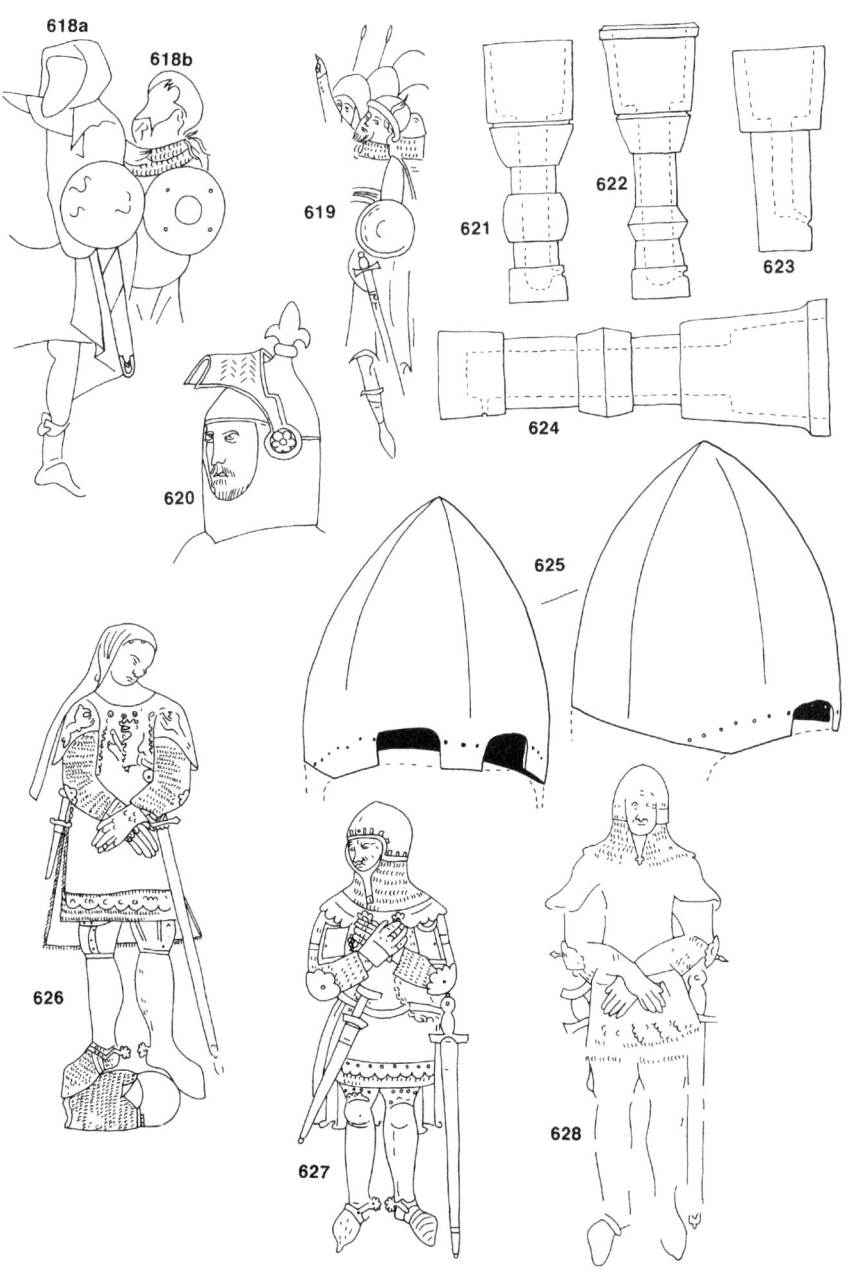

618a

618b

619

621

622

623

624

620

625

626

627

628

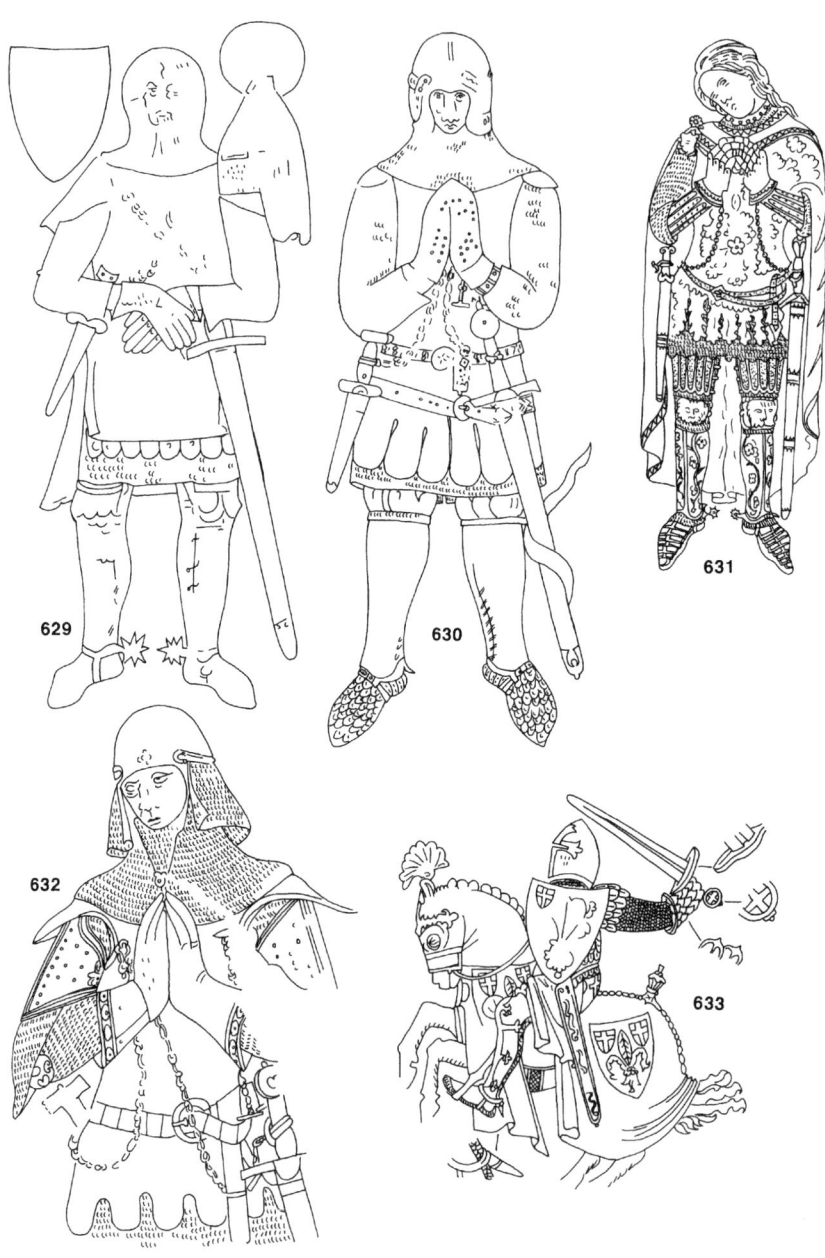

629

630

631

632

633

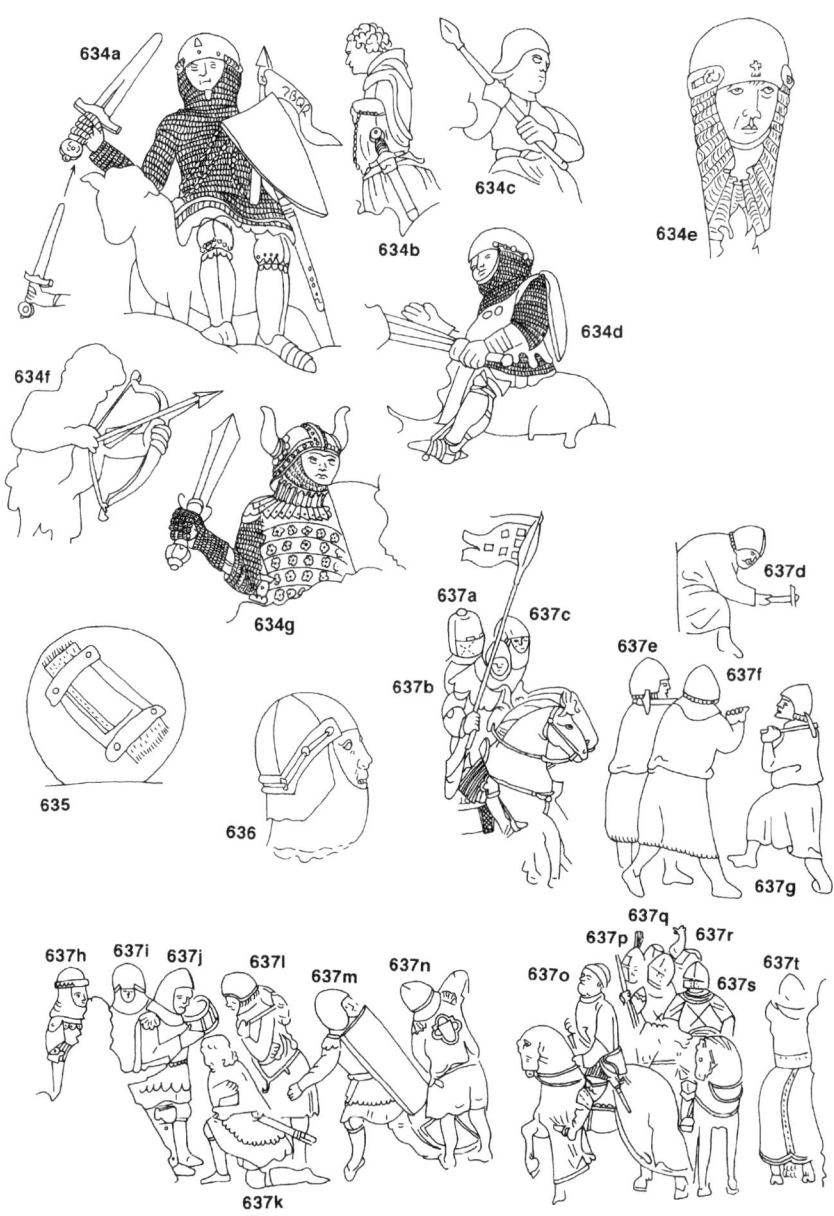

634a

634b

634c

634e

634d

634f

634g

635

636

637a

637b

637c

637d

637e

637f

637g

637h 637i 637j 637l 637m 637n 637o 637p 637q 637r 637s 637t

637k

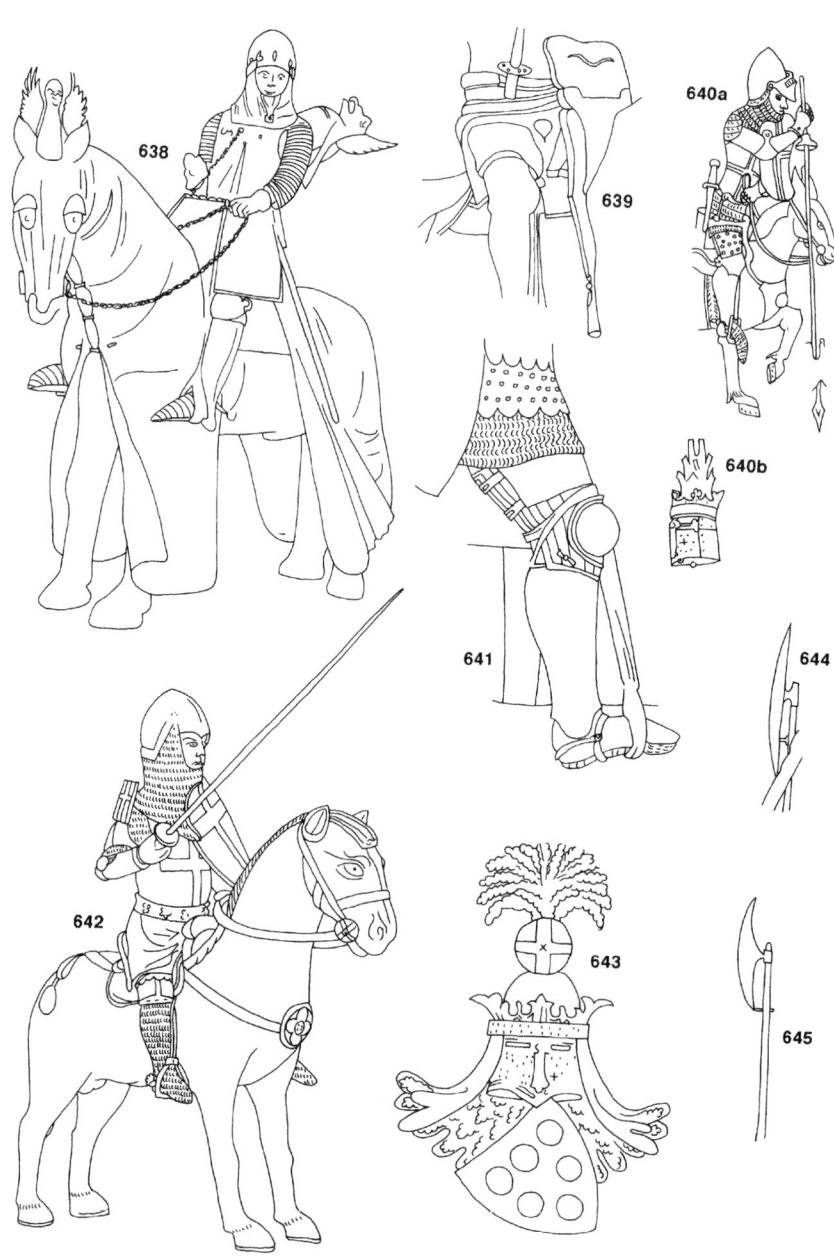

638

639

640a

640b

641

642

643

644

645

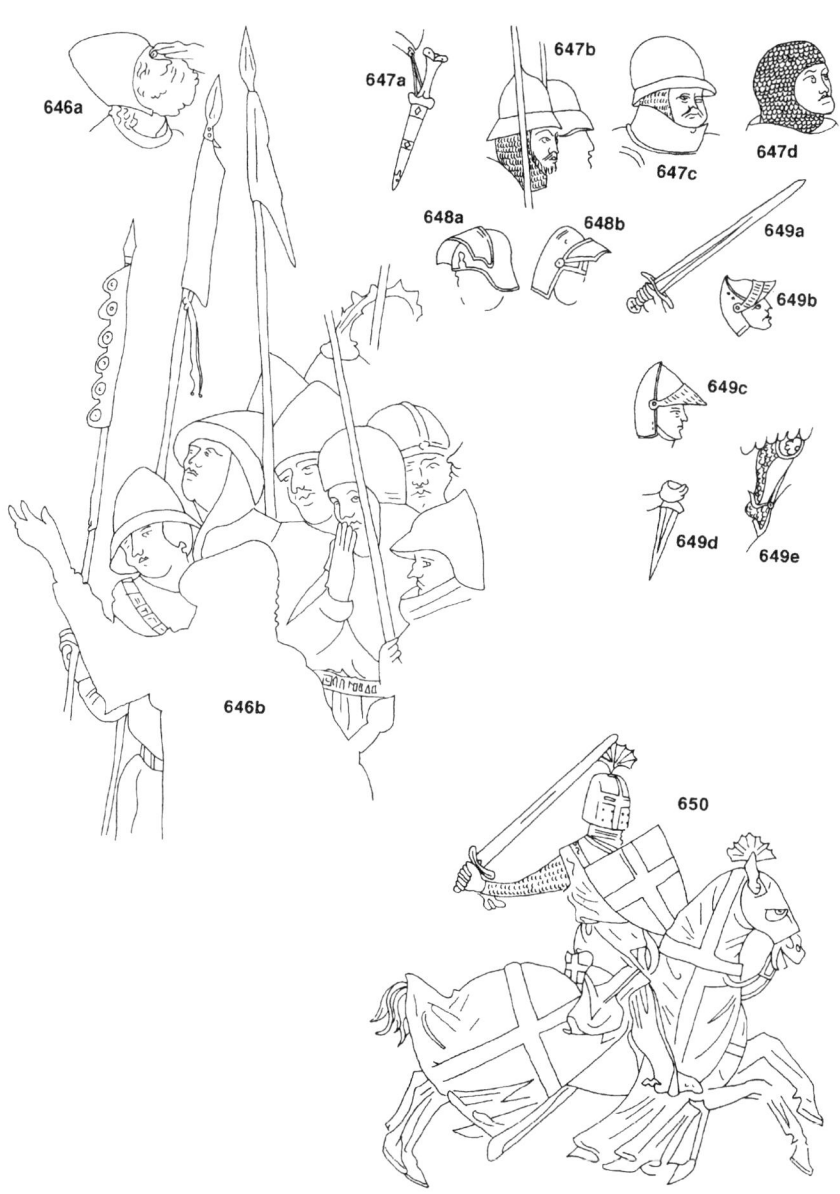

646a

647a

647b

647c

647d

648a

648b

649a

649b

649c

649d

649e

646b

650

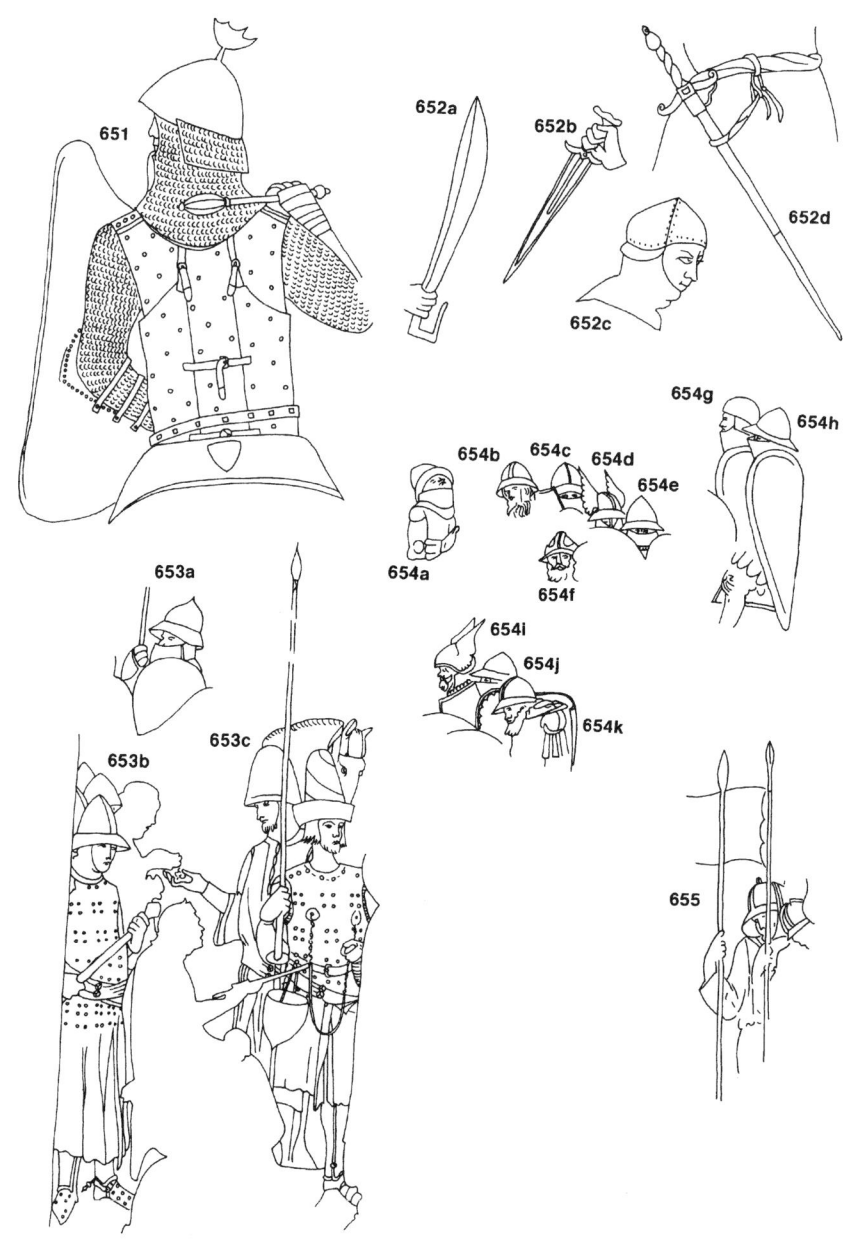

651

652a

652b

652d

652c

654g

654h

654b 654c 654d

654e

654a

654f

653a

654i

654j

654k

653c

653b

655

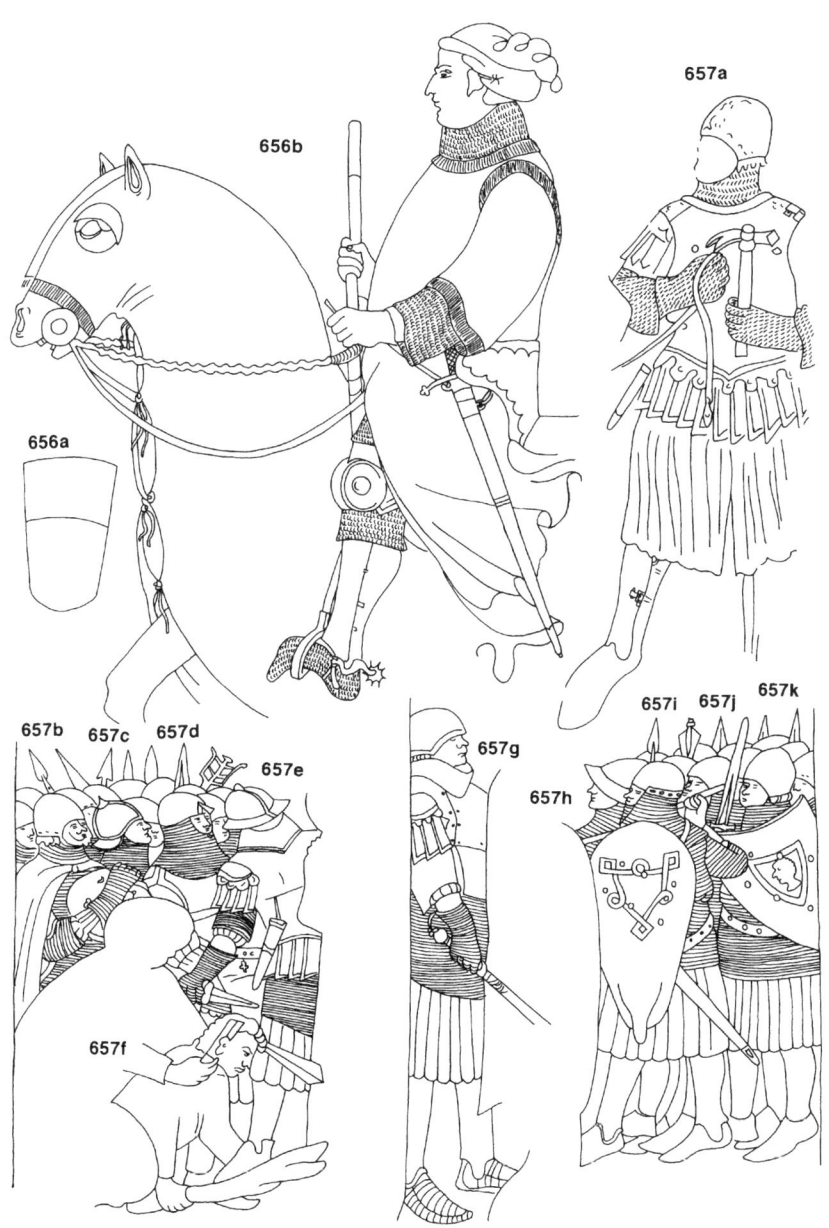

657l 657m 657n 657o 657p 657q 657r 657s 657t 657u 657v 657w 657x 657y 657z 657aa 657ab

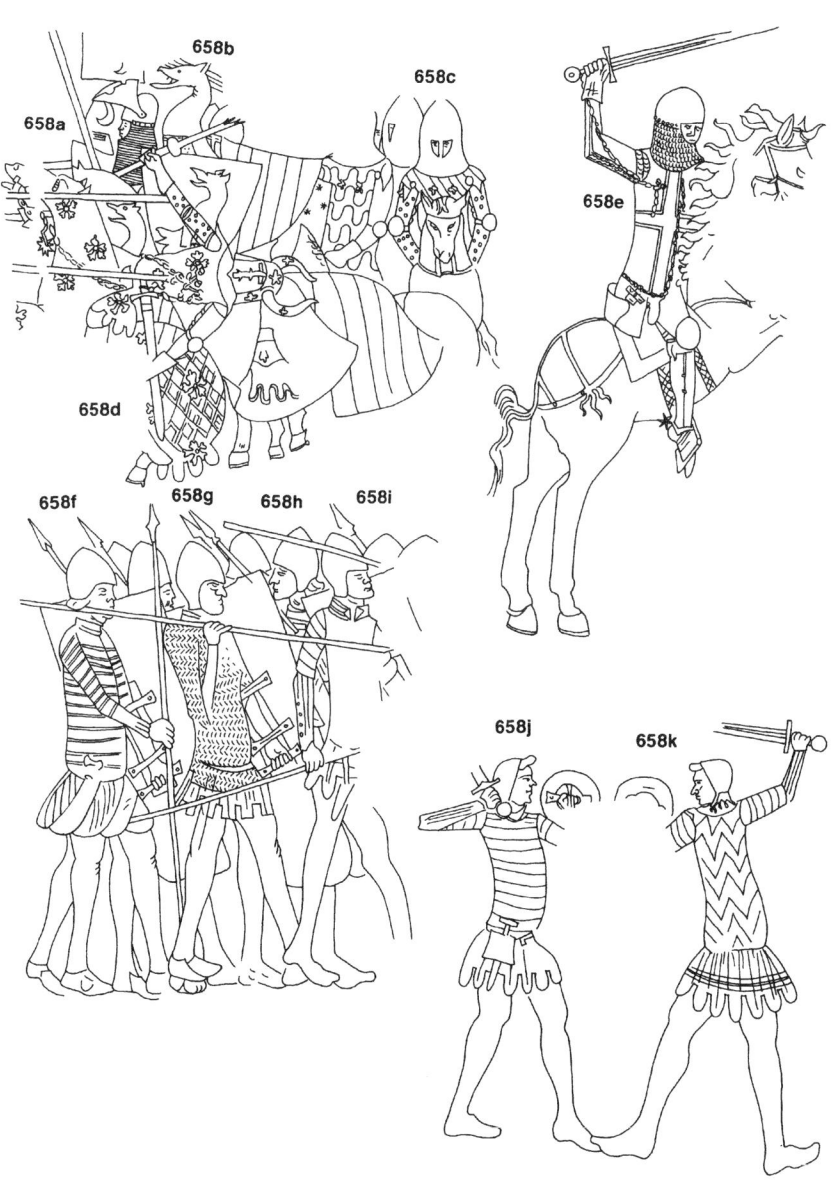

658a
658b
658c
658d
658e
658f
658g
658h
658i
658j
658k

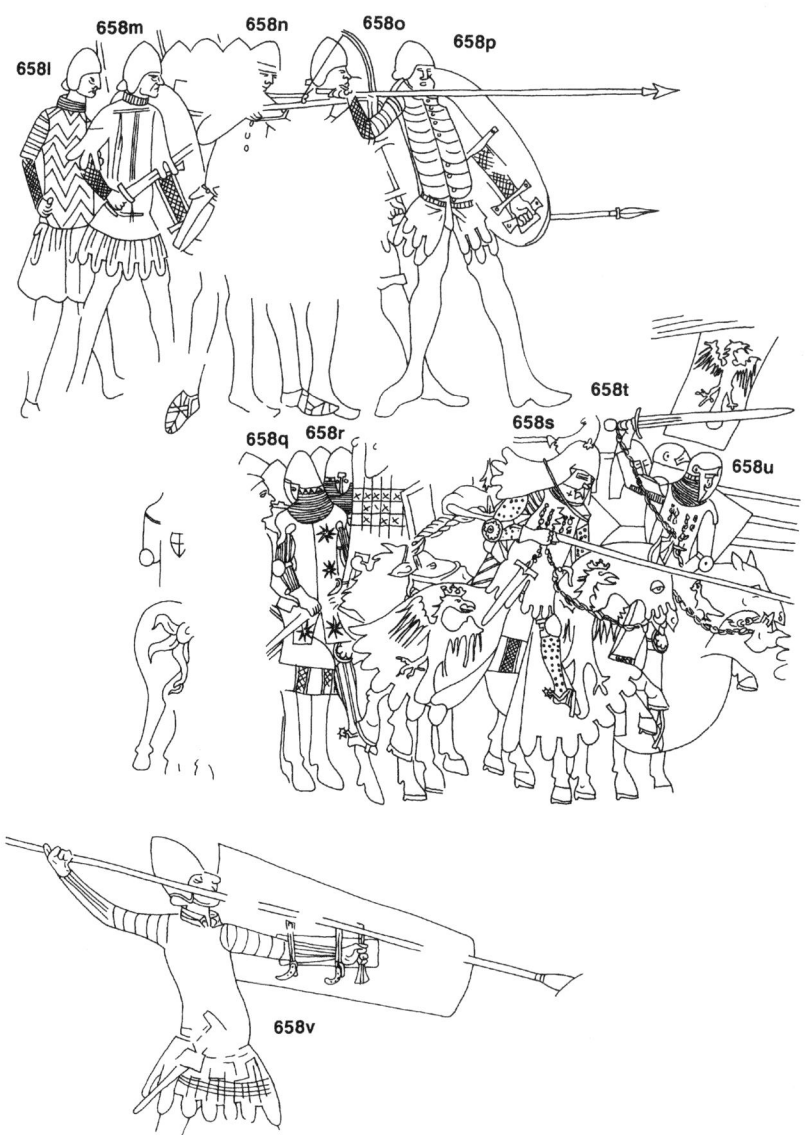

658l   658m   658n   658o   658p   658q   658r   658s   658t   658u   658v

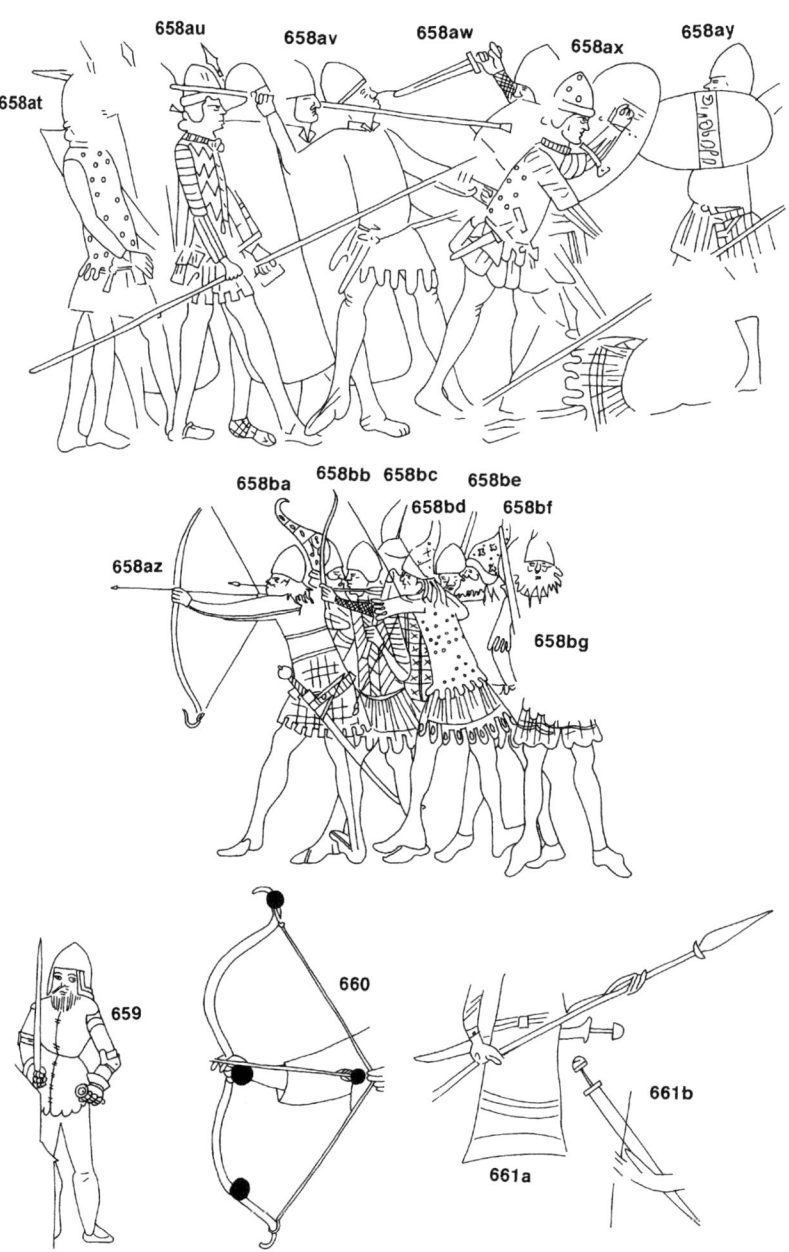

658at 658au 658av 658aw 658ax 658ay

658az 658ba 658bb 658bc 658bd 658be 658bf 658bg

659 660 661a 661b

662

663

664a

664b

665a

665b

665c

666

667a

667b

667c

667d

667e

668

669

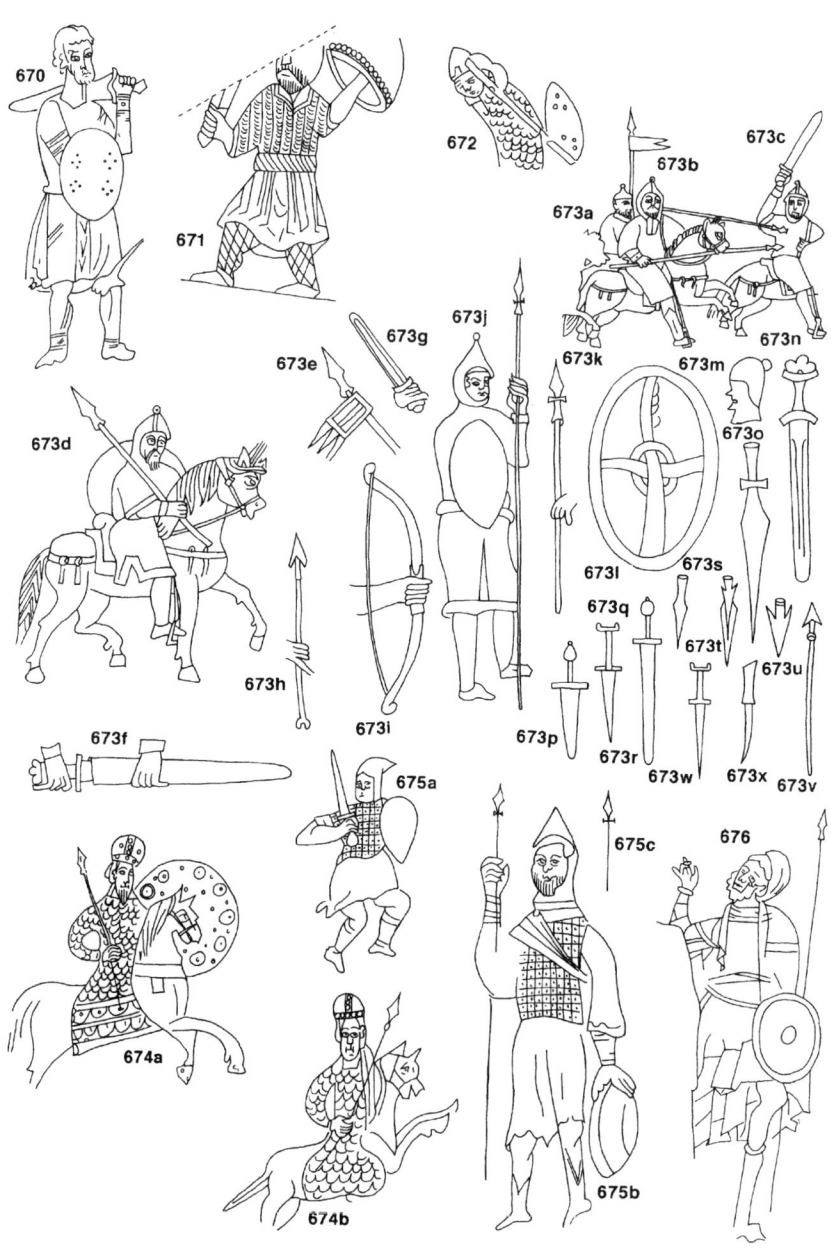

670

671

672

673a
673b
673c
673n

673d

673e

673g

673j

673k

673m

673o

673f

673h

673i

673l

673p

673q

673r

673s

673t

673u

673w

673x

673v

674a

675a

675c

676

674b

675b

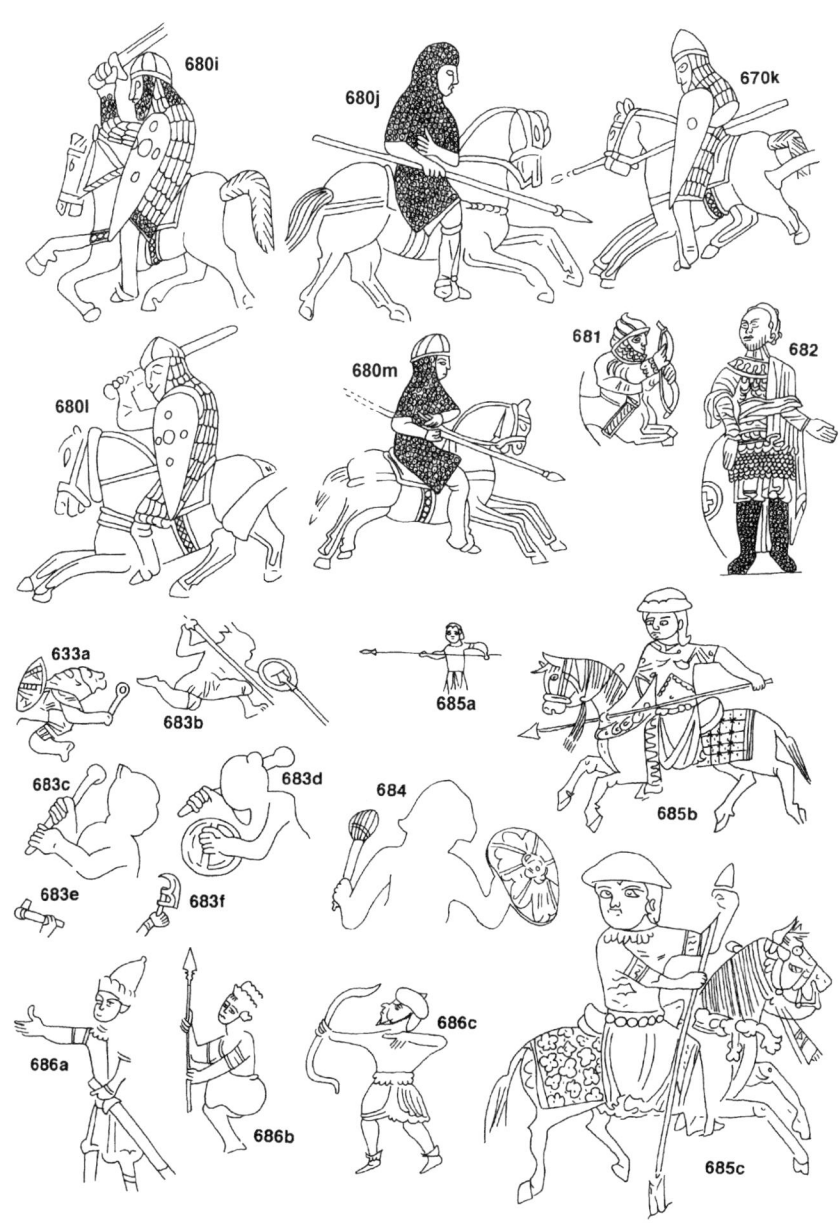

680i

680j

670k

680l

680m

681

682

633a

683b

683c

683d

684

685a

685b

683e

683f

686a

686b

686c

685c

690r

690s

690t

690u

690v

690w

690x

690y

690aa

690z

690ab

690ac

690ad

690ae

690af

690ah

690ai

690ag

690al

690ak

690am

690aj

690ap   690aq

690an

690ao

690au

690at

690ar

690as

695a   695b   695c

695d

695f   695g   695h   695i

695e

696b   696d   696e

696a   696c

695j   696f   696h   696i

696g   696j

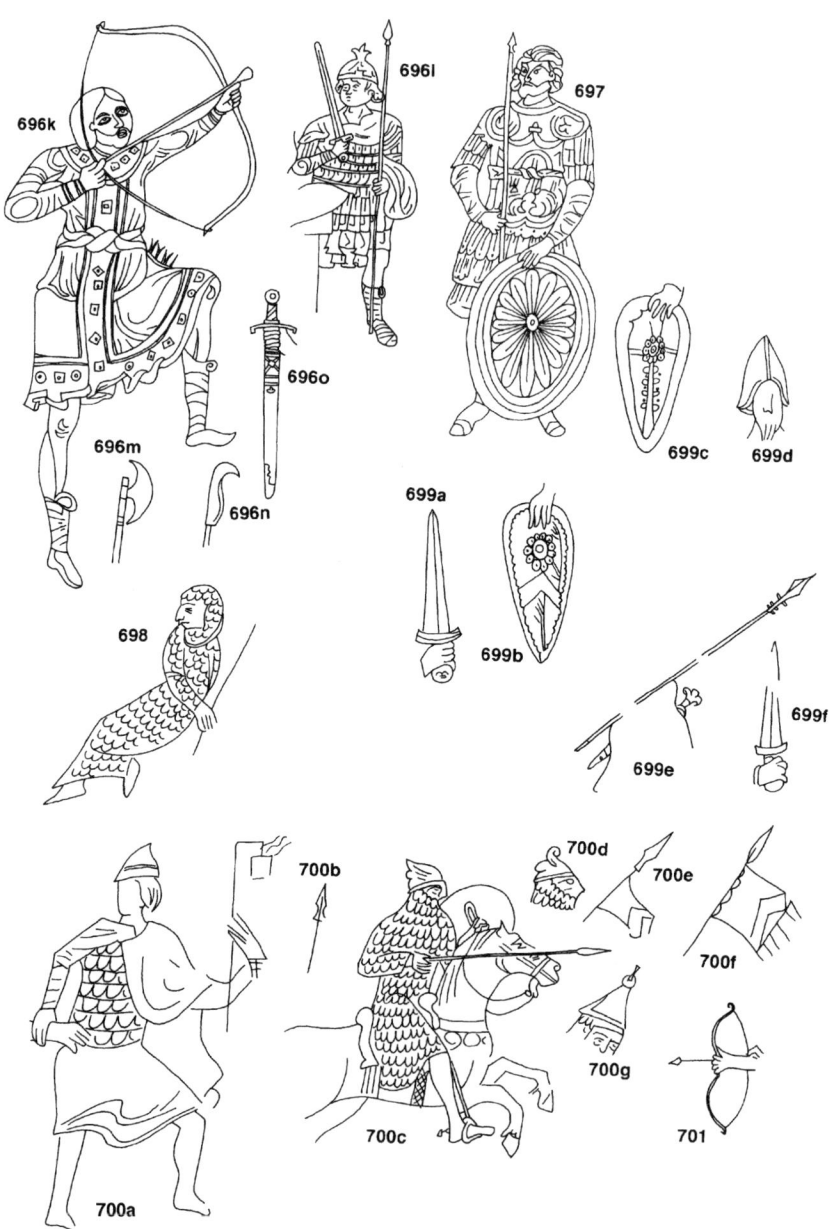

696k 696l 696o 696m 696n 697 699c 699d 699a 699b 698 699e 699f 700a 700b 700c 700d 700e 700f 700g 701

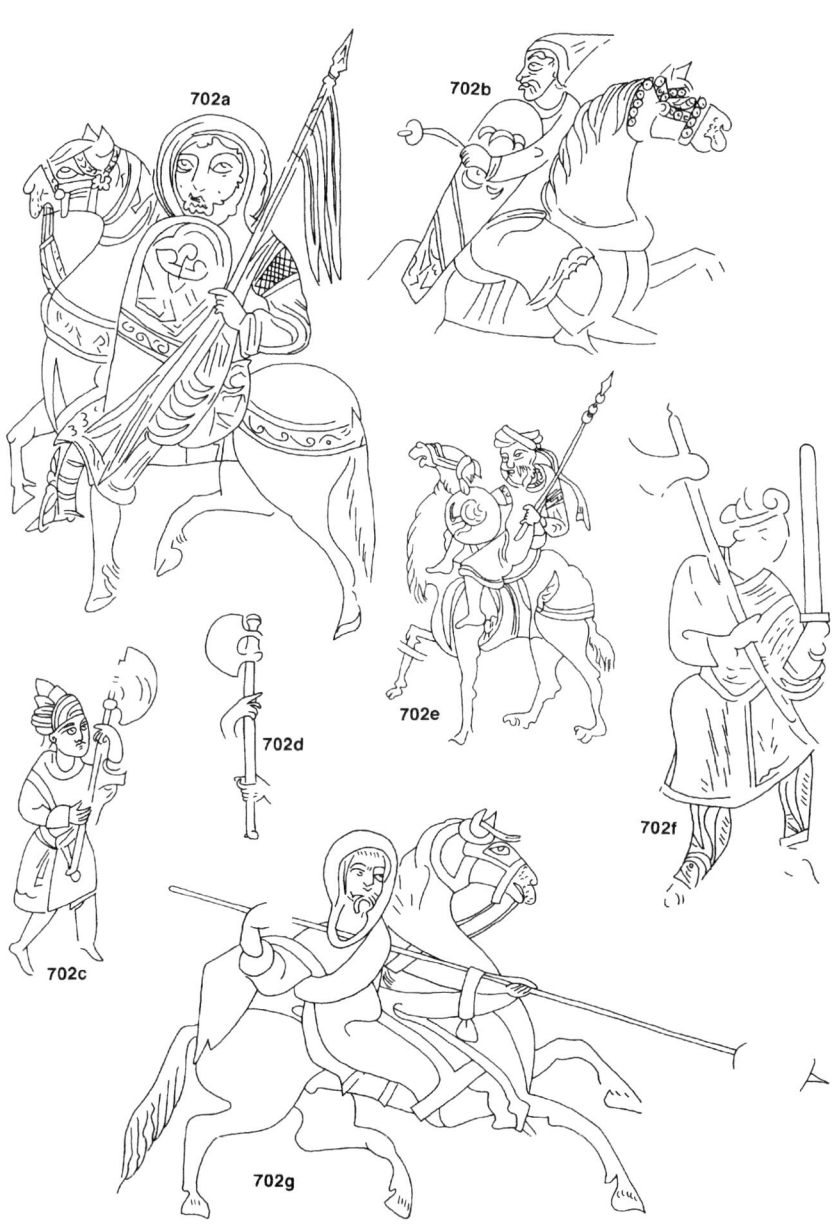

702a

702b

702d

702e

702c

702f

702g

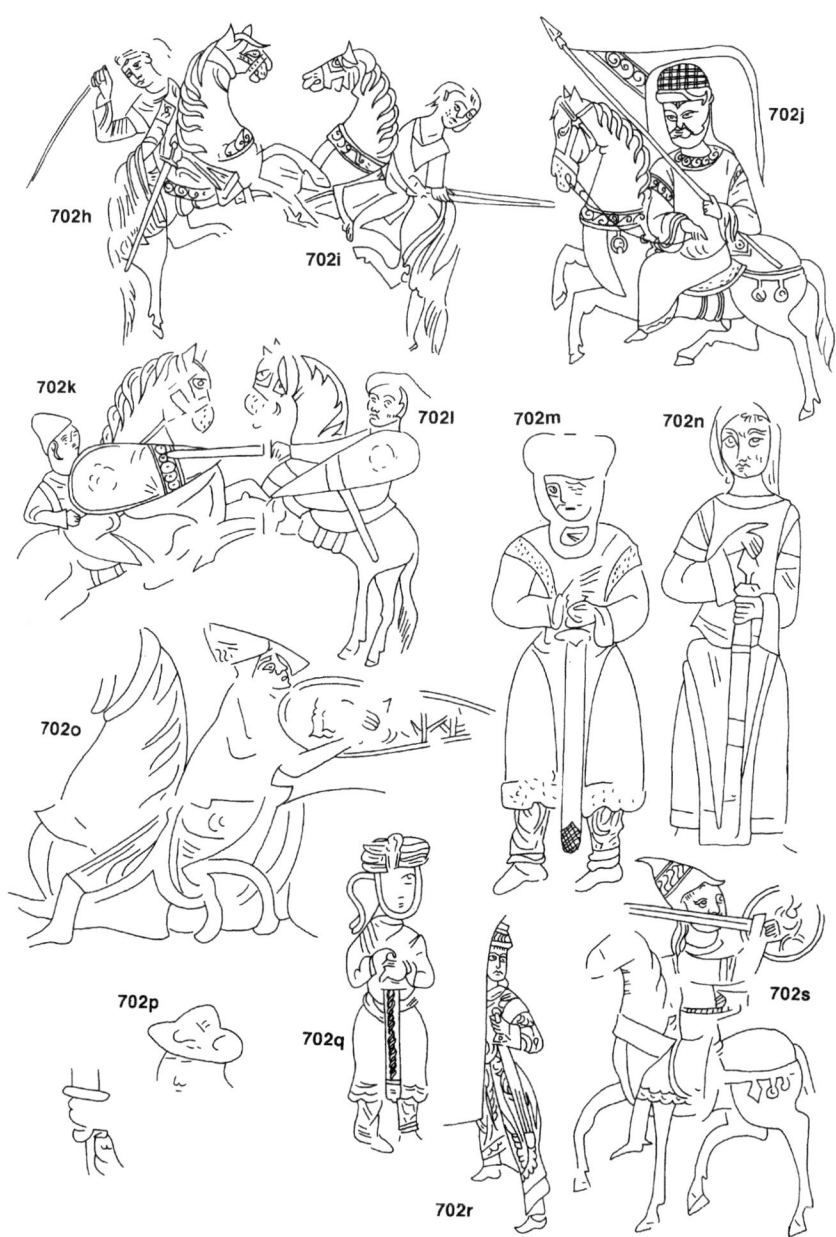

702h

702i

702j

702k

702l

702m

702n

702o

702p

702q

702r

702s

702t

702u

702w

702x

702v

702y

702z

702aa

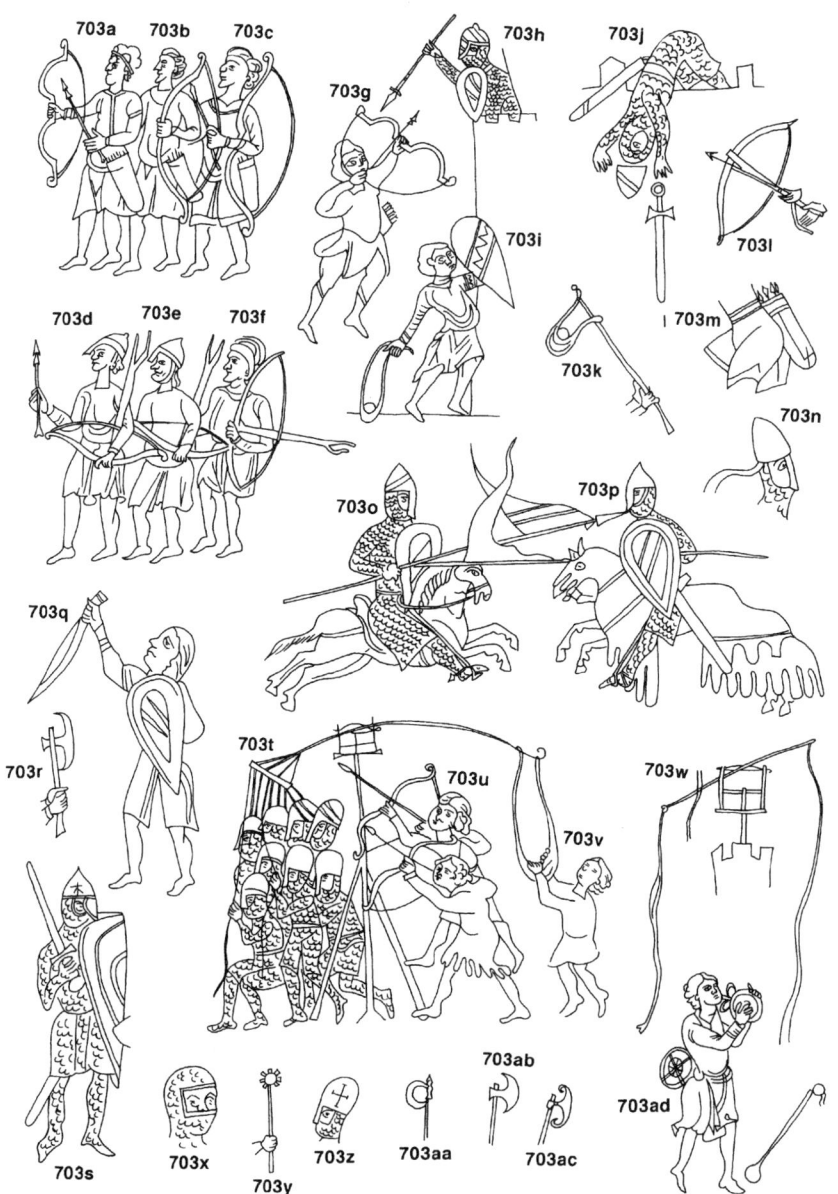

703a 703b 703c 703d 703e 703f 703g 703h 703i 703j 703k 703l 703m 703n 703o 703p 703q 703r 703s 703t 703u 703v 703w 703x 703y 703z 703aa 703ab 703ac 703ad

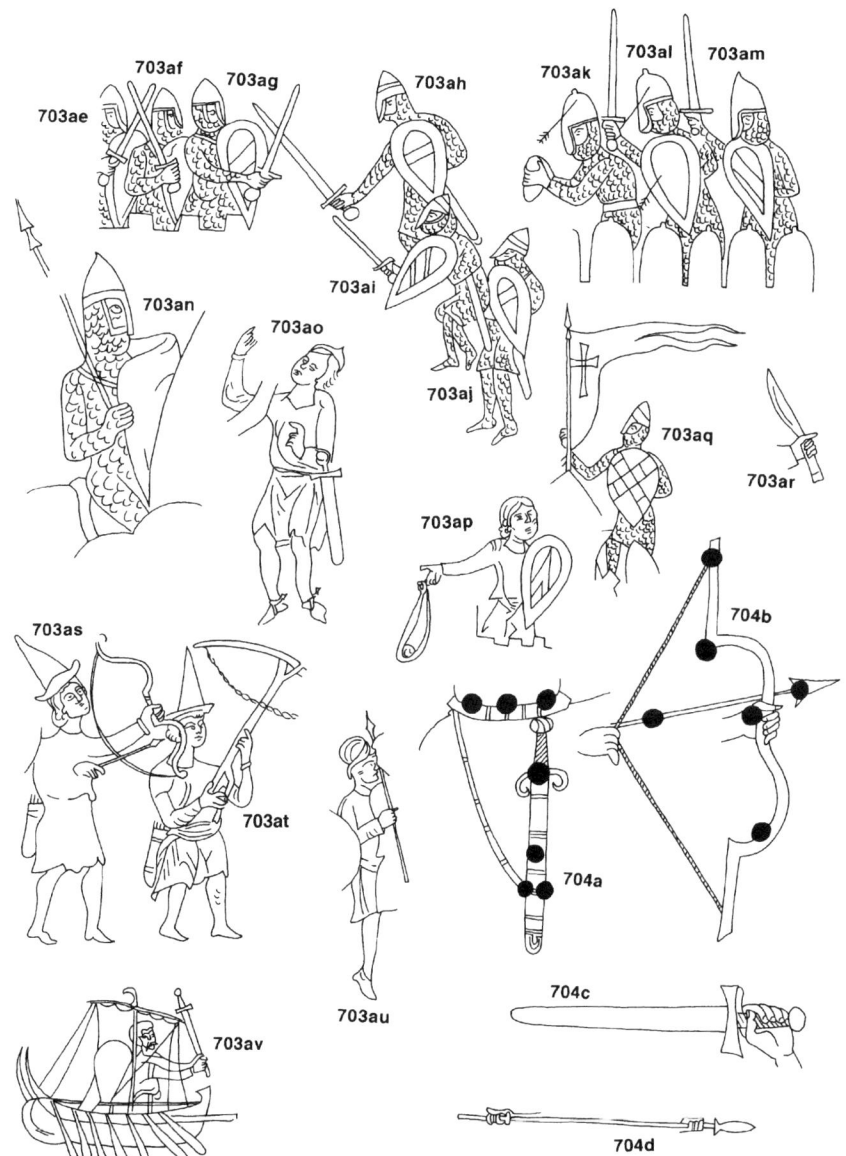

703ae
703af
703ag
703ah
703ak
703al
703am
703ai
703an
703ao
703aj
703aq
703ar
703ap
703as
704b
703at
704a
703au
704c
703av
704d

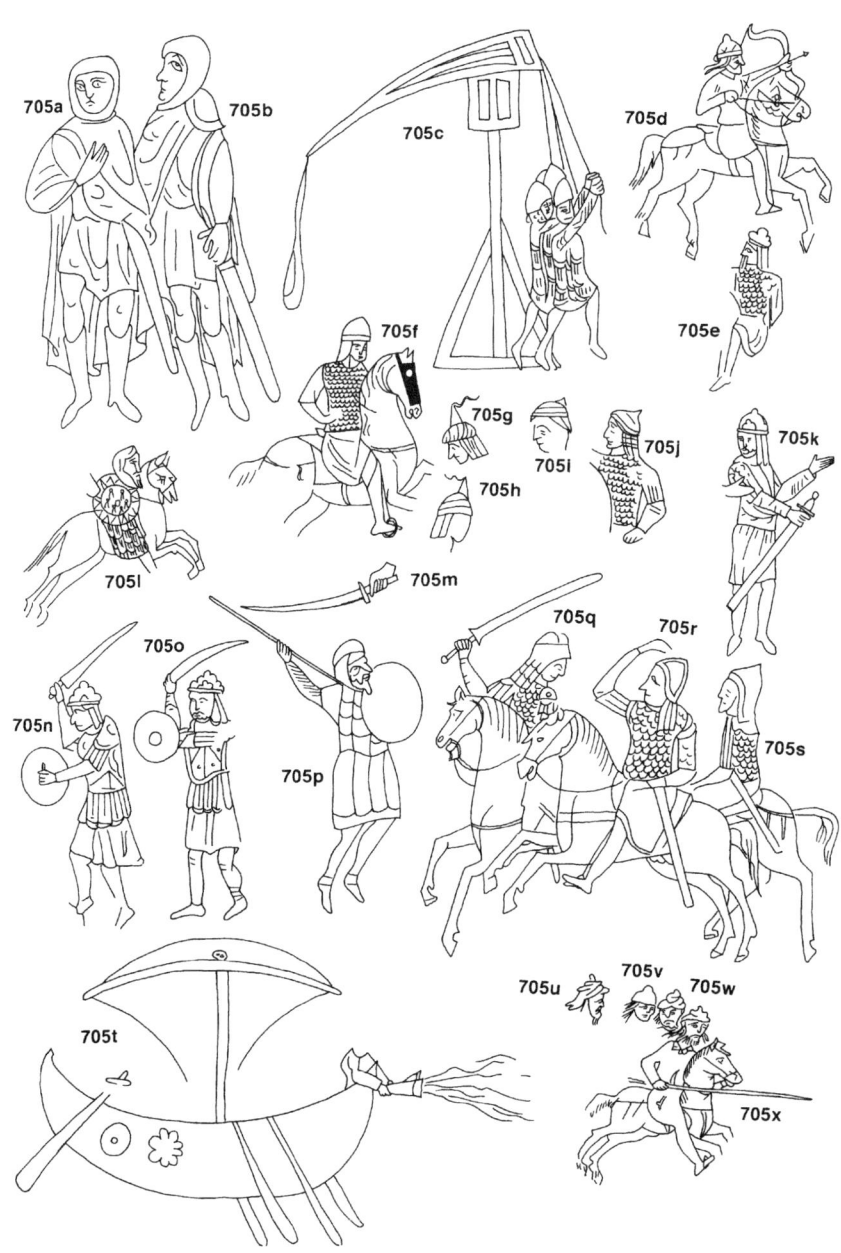

705a 705b 705c 705d 705e 705f 705g 705h 705i 705j 705k 705l 705m 705n 705o 705p 705q 705r 705s 705t 705u 705v 705w 705x

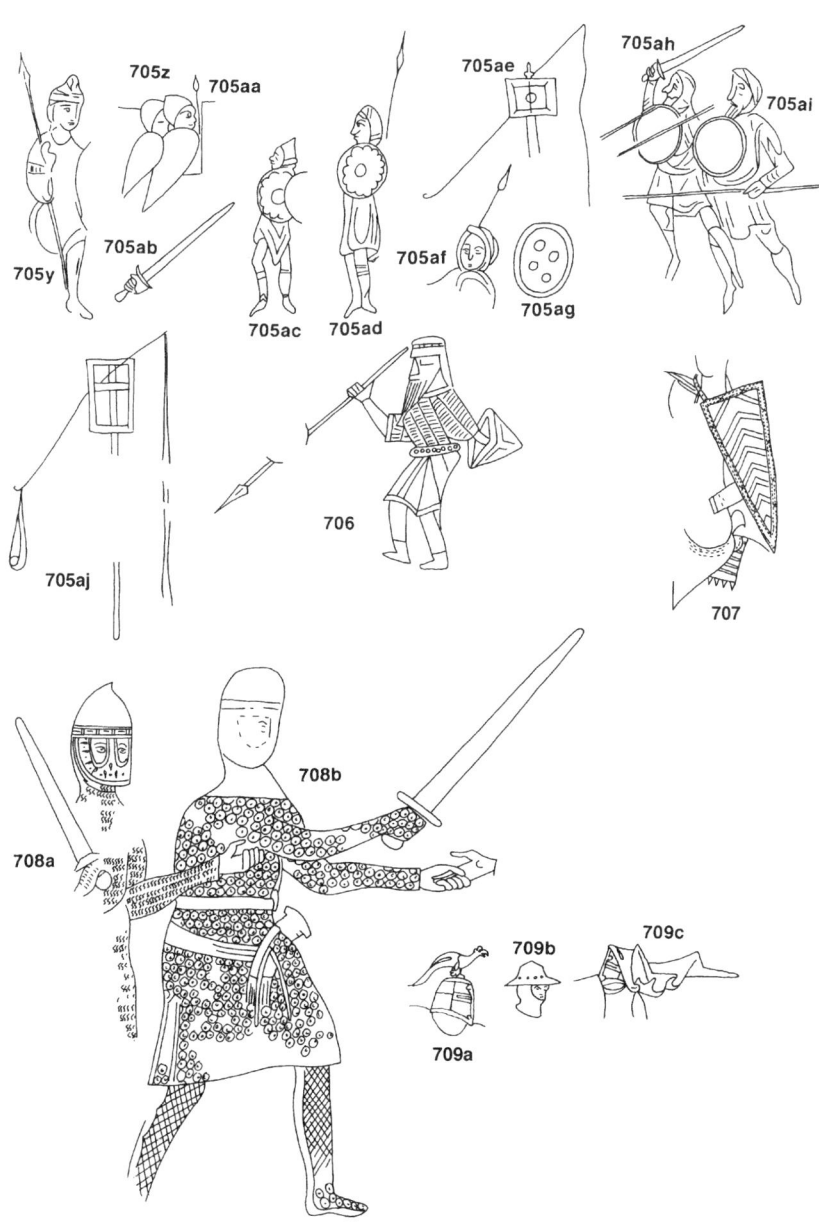

705z
705aa
705ae
705ah
705ai
705ab
705y
705af
705ag
705ac
705ad
705aj
706
707
708b
708a
709c
709b
709a

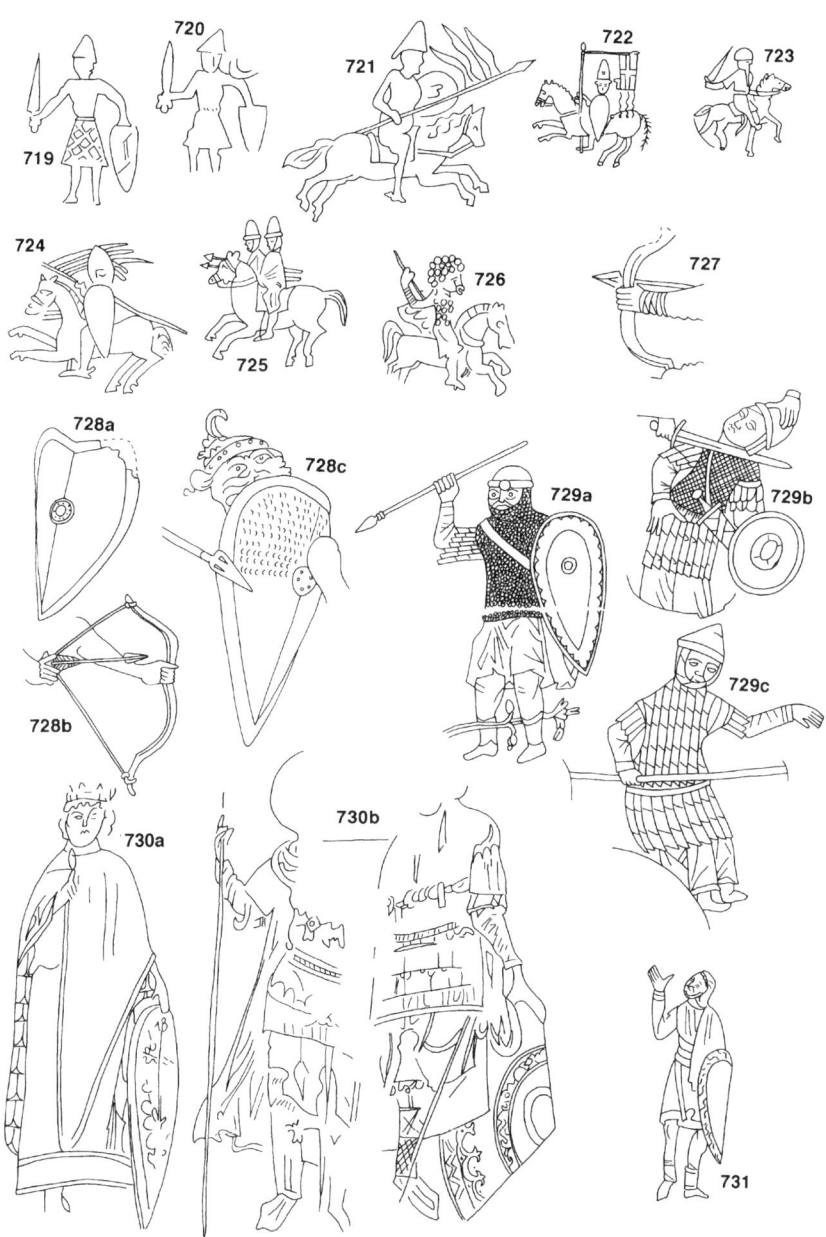

719
720
721
722
723
724
725
726
727
728a
728b
728c
729a
729b
729c
730a
730b
731

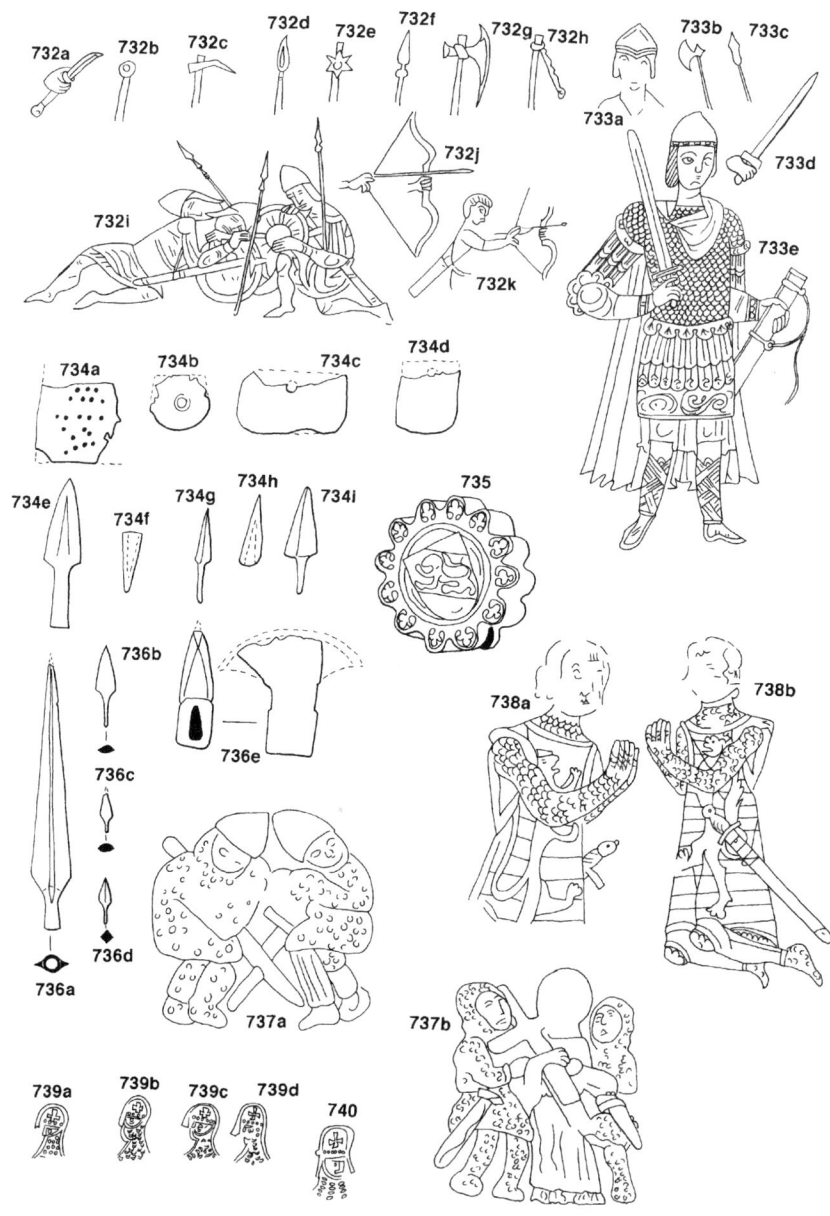

741a 741b 741c 741k 741i 741d 741e 741f 741g 741h 741j 742a 742b 742d 742e 743a 743b 742c 742f 743c 744a 744b 743d 743e 744c

745a
745b
754c
745d
745e
745f
745g
745h
745i
745j
745k
745l
747a
747b
747c
747d
747e
746a
746b
746c
746d
746e
746f
746g
746h
746i
746j
746k
746l

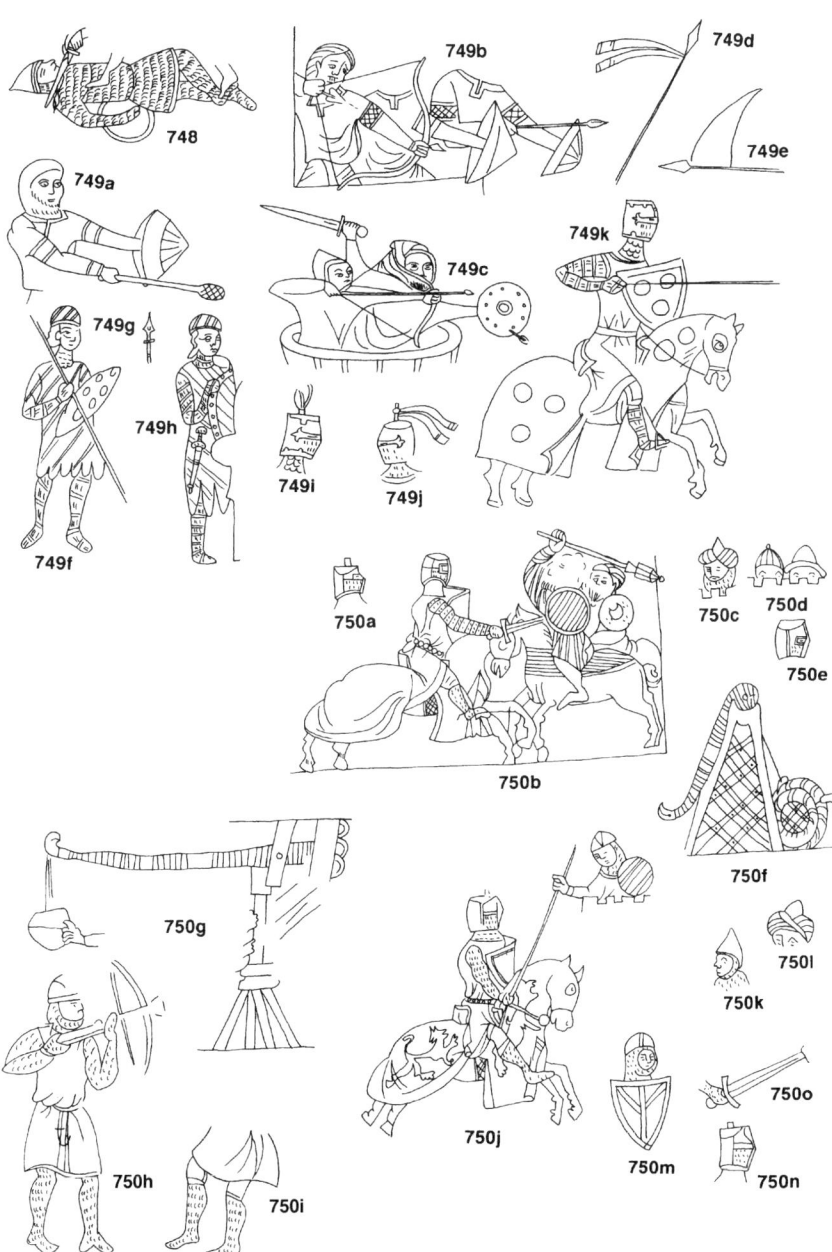

748
749a
749b
749c
749d
749e
749f
749g
749h
749i
749j
749k
750a
750b
750c
750d
750e
750f
750g
750h
750i
750j
750k
750l
750m
750n
750o

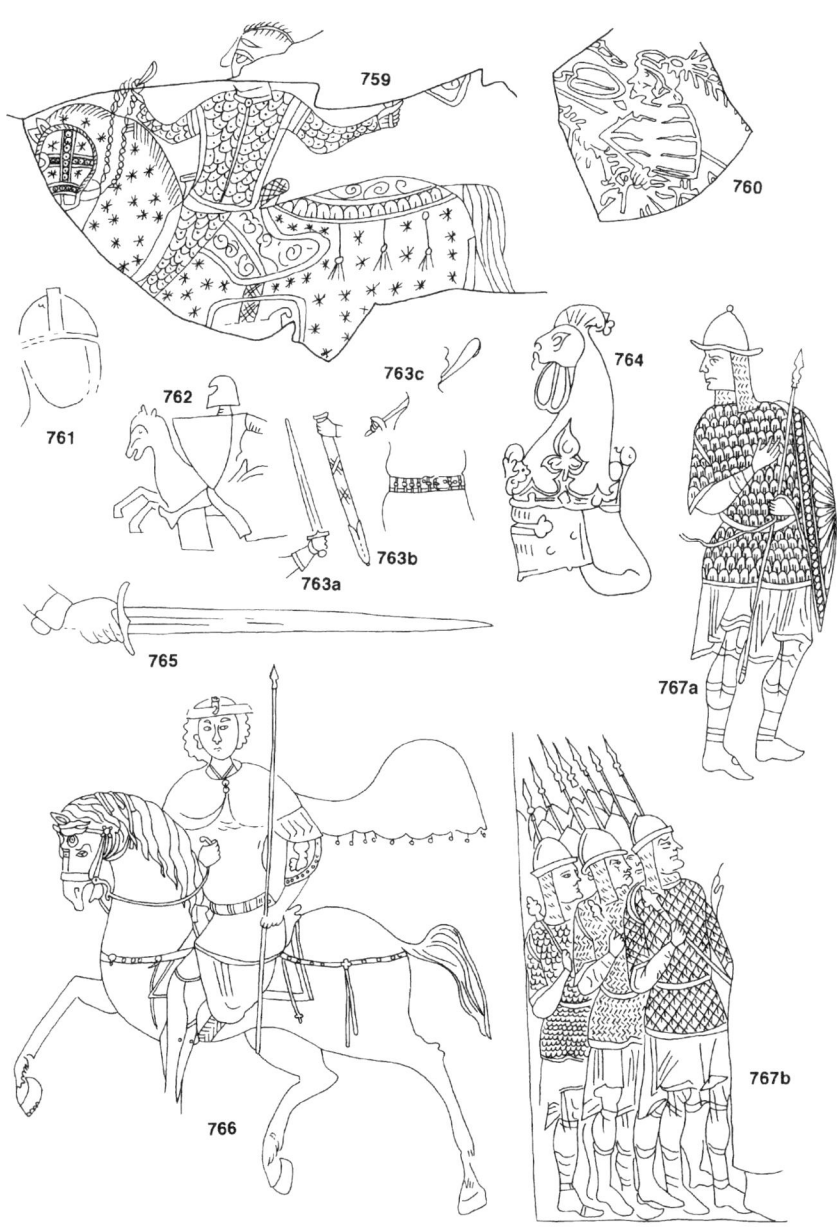

759

760

761

762

763c

763a

763b

764

765

767a

766

767b

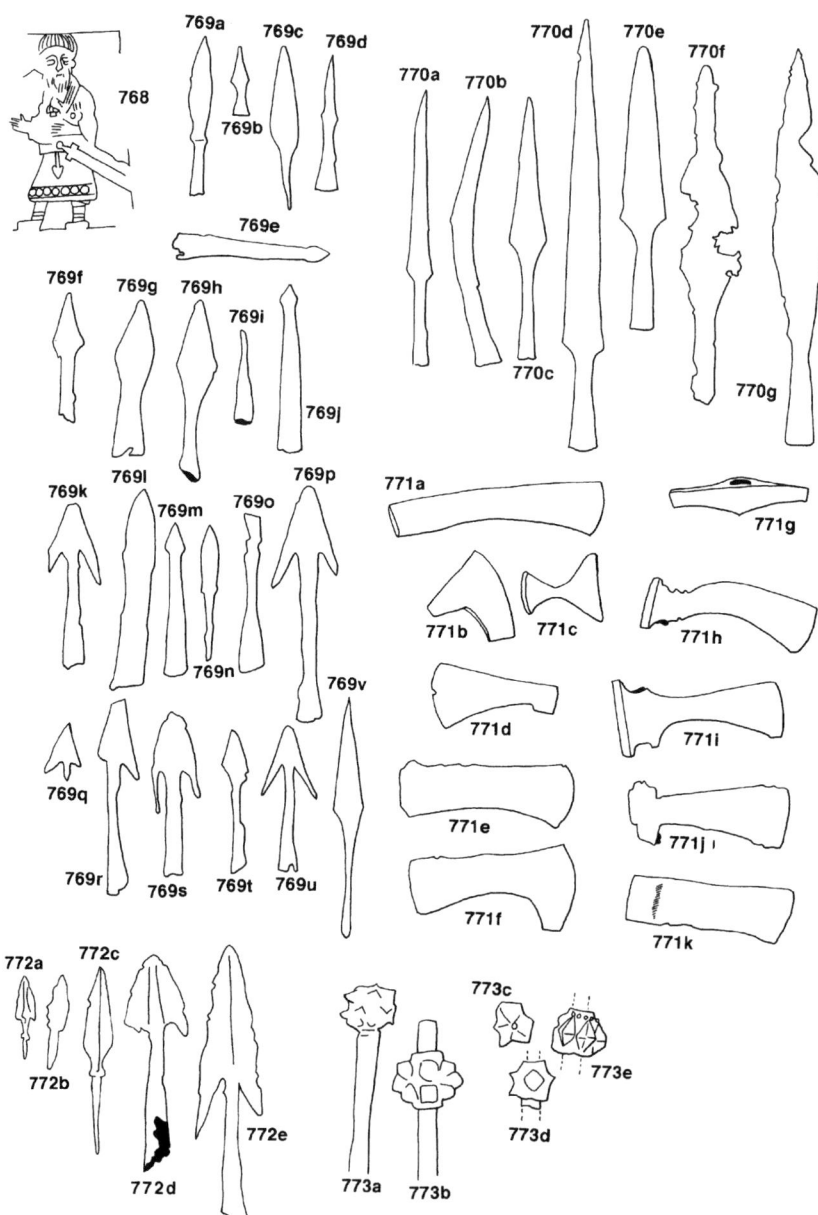

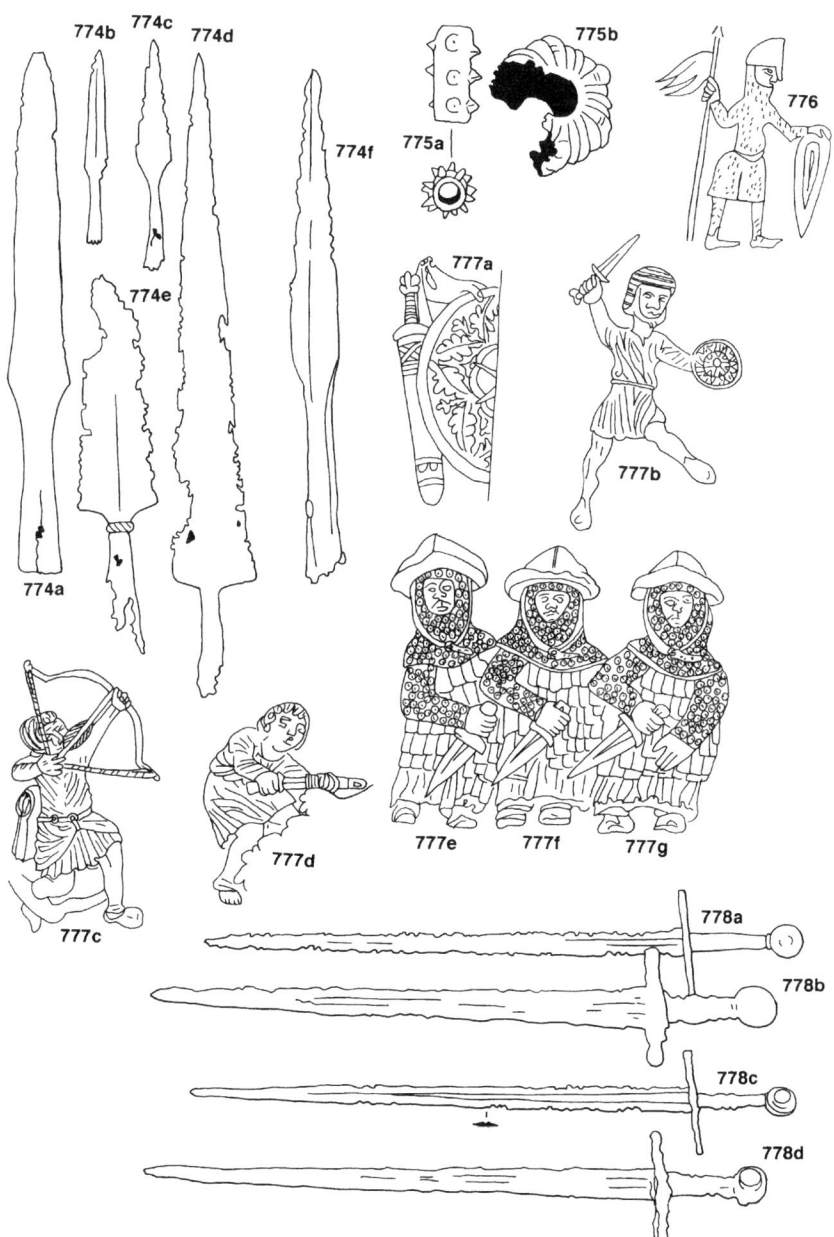

774b   774c   774d

774f

775a   775b

776

774e

777a

777b

774a

777c   777d   777e   777f   777g

778a

778b

778c

778d

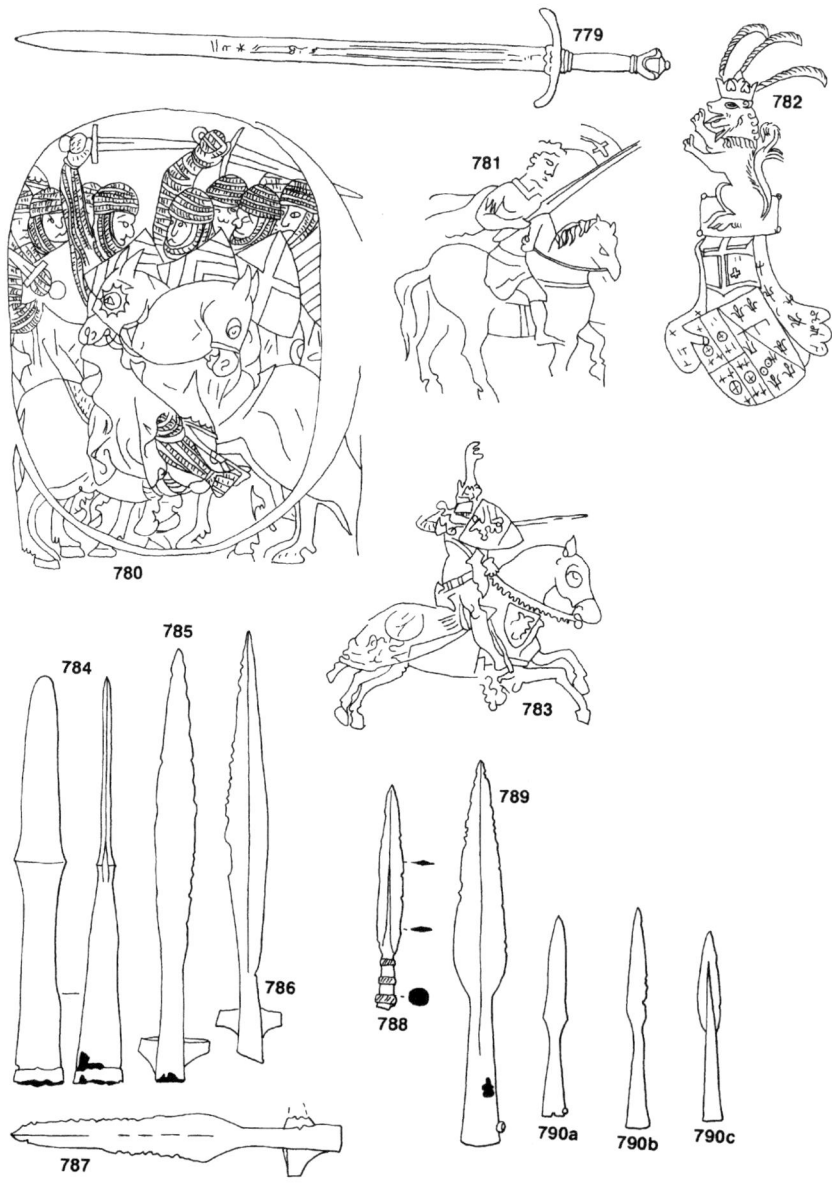

779

781

782

780

783

784

785

786

787

788

789

790a

790b

790c

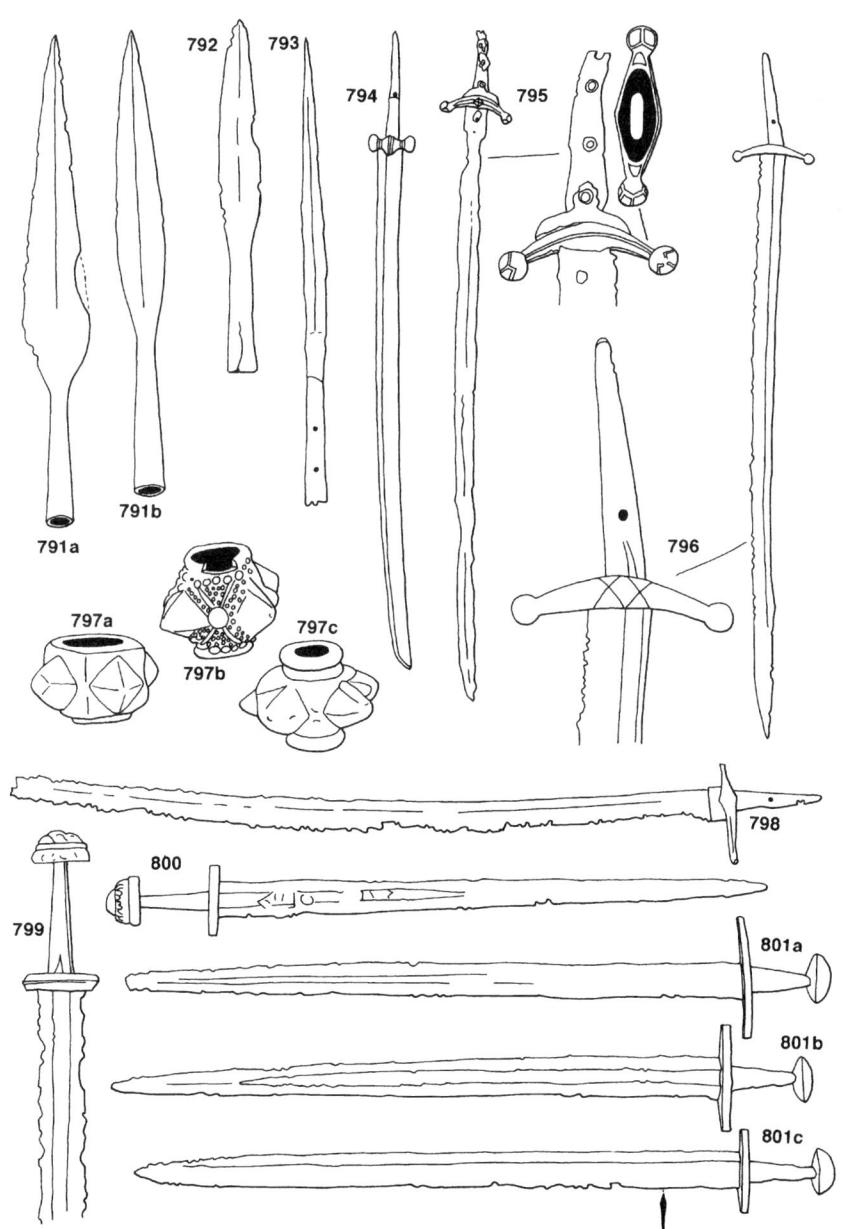

791a
791b
792
793
794
795
796
797a
797b
797c
798
799
800
801a
801b
801c

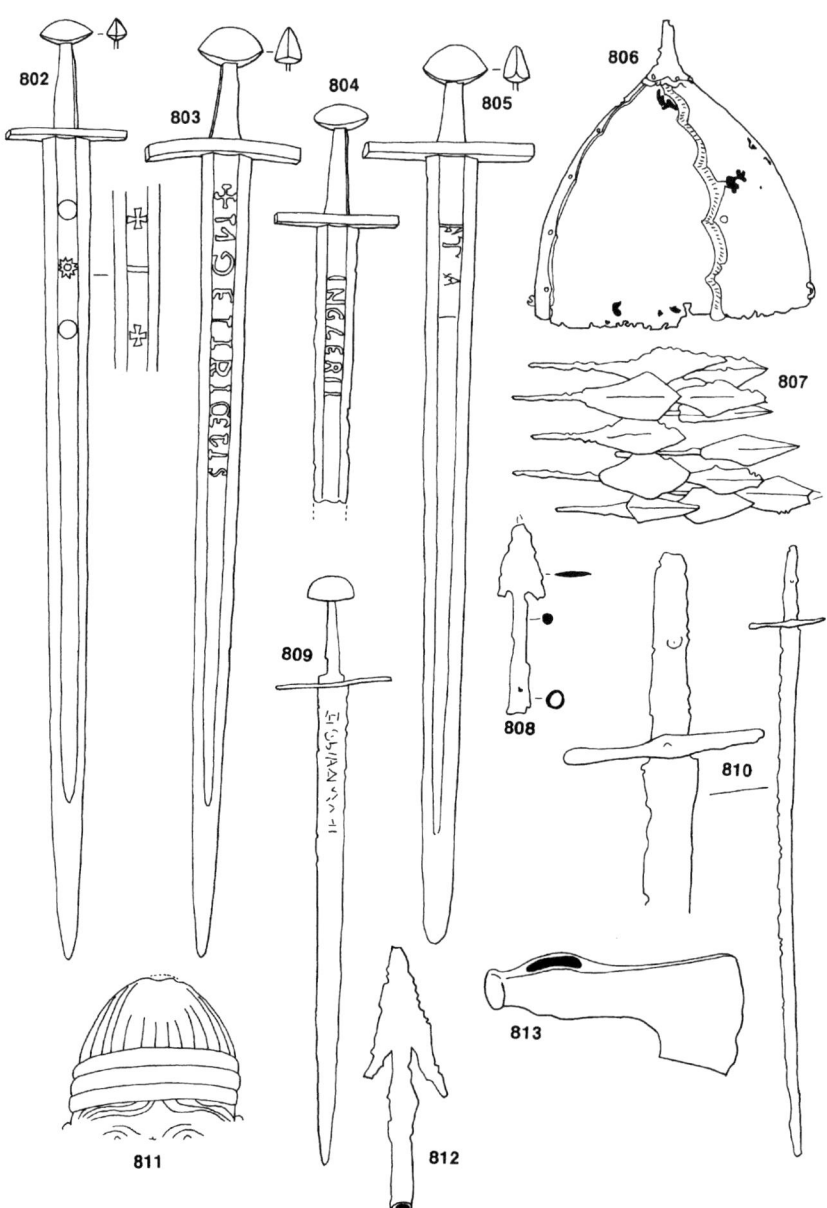

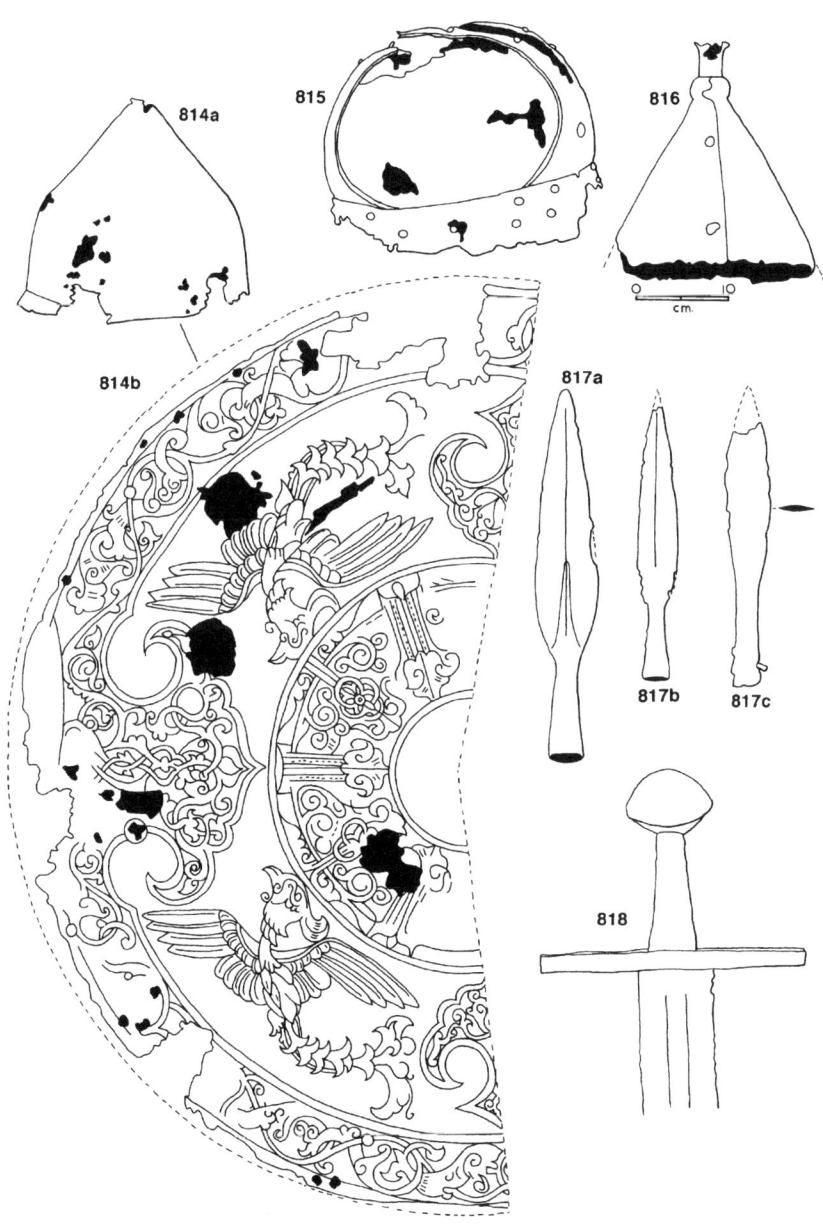

814a

815

816

814b

cm.

817a

817b

817c

818

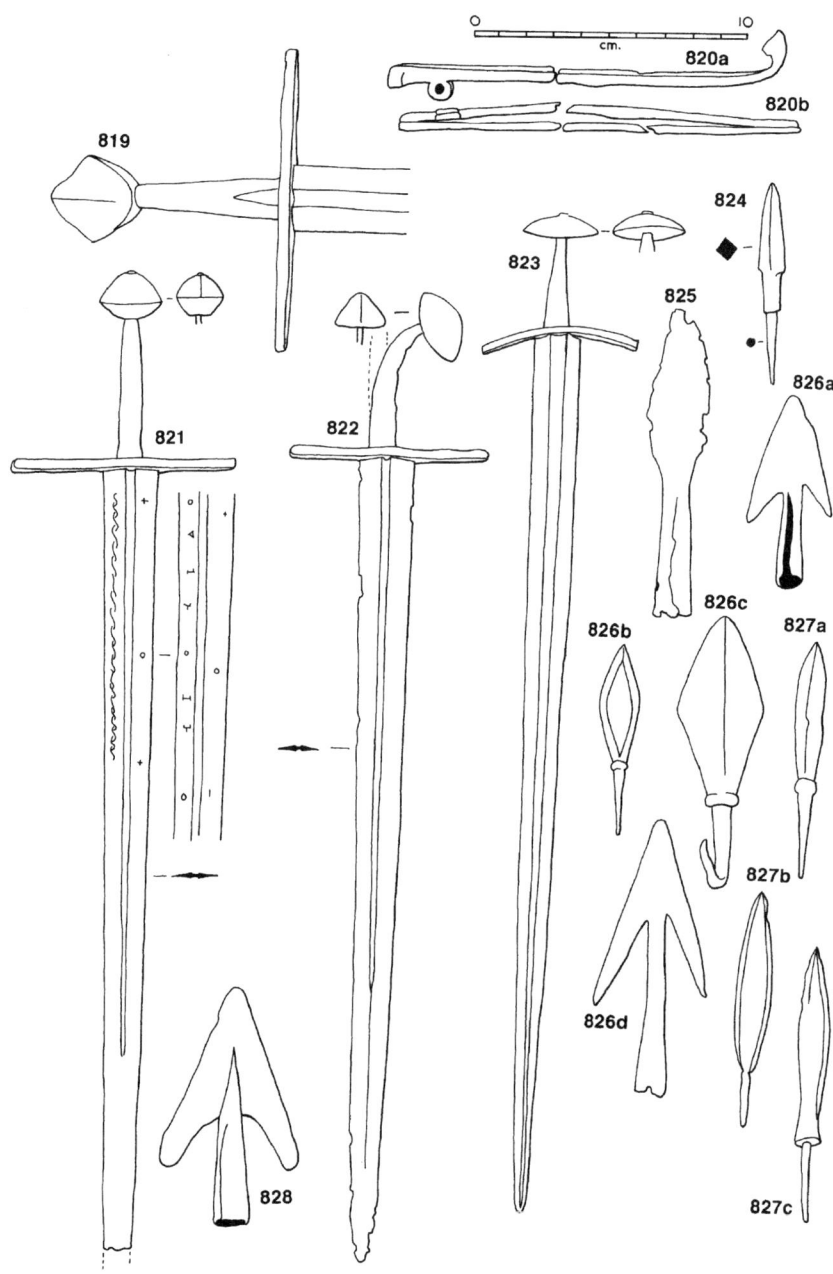

cm.

819
820a
820b
821
822
823
824
825
826a
826b
826c
826d
827a
827b
827c
828

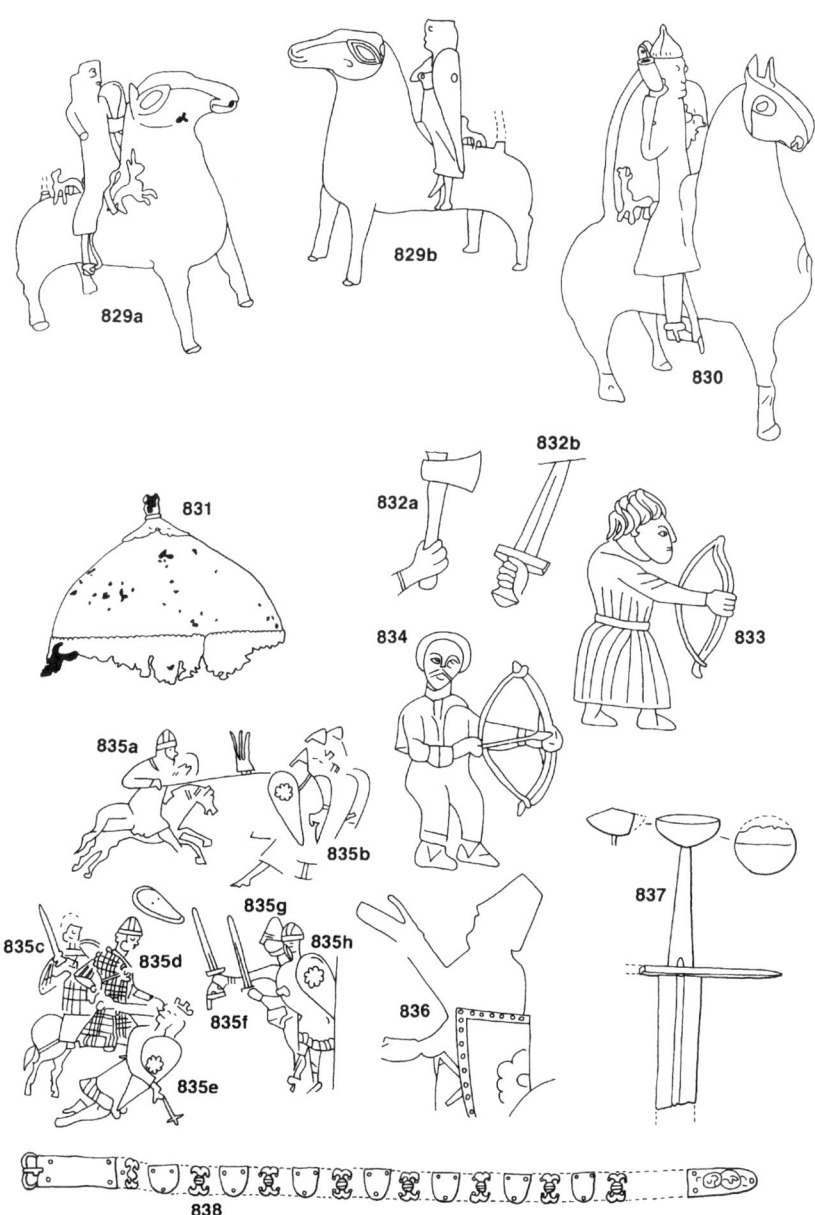

829a

829b

830

831

832a

832b

833

834

835a

835b

835c

835d

835e

835f

835g

835h

836

837

838

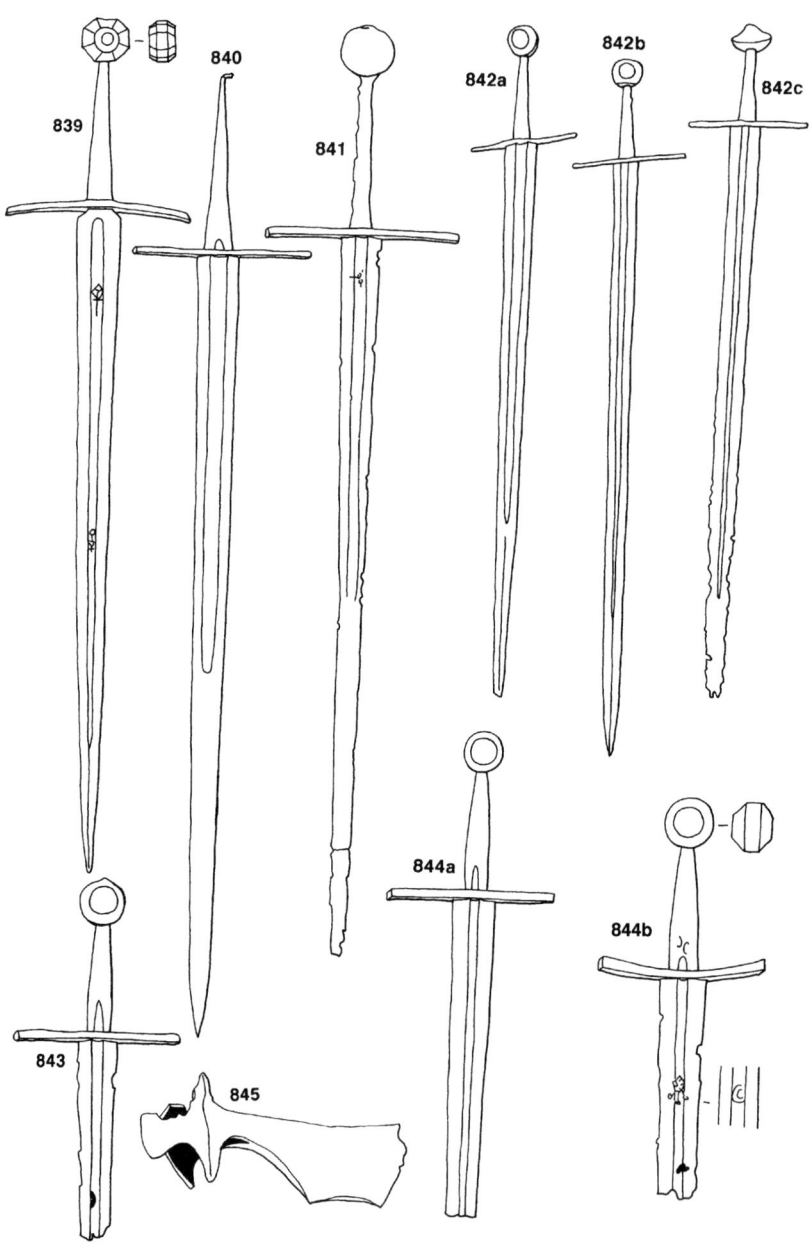

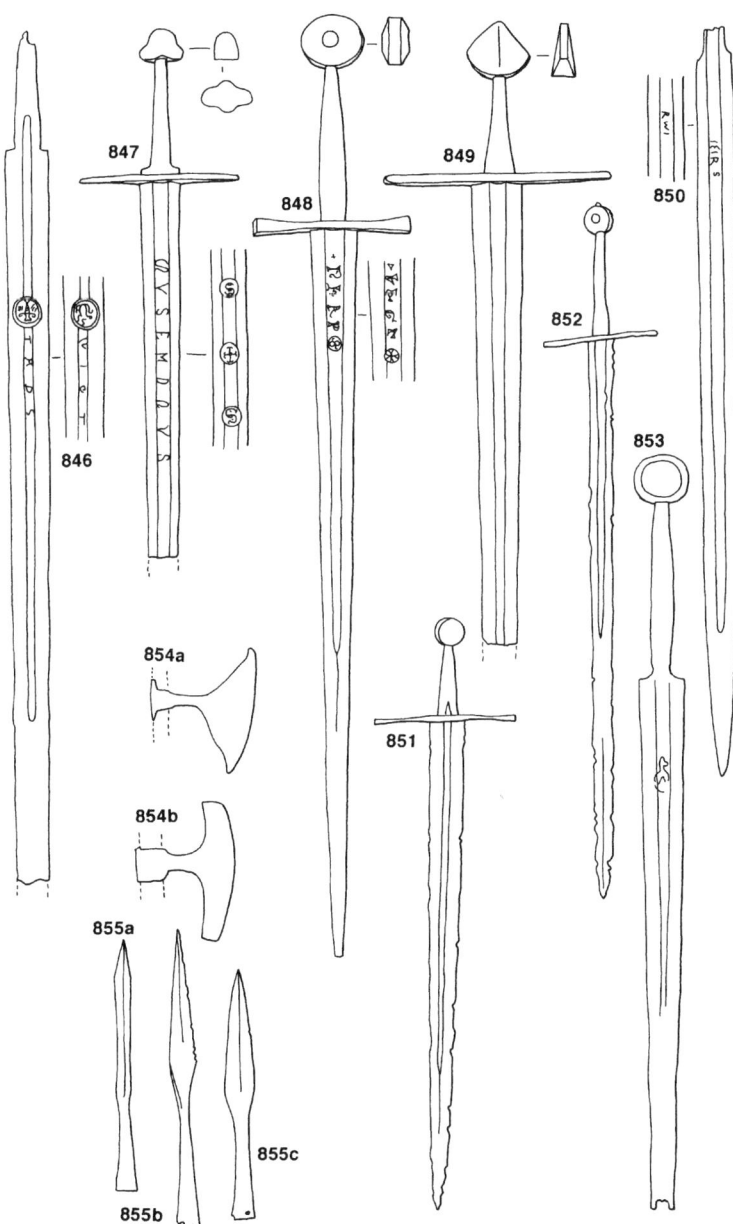

846

847

848

849

850

851

852

853

854a

854b

855a

855b

855c

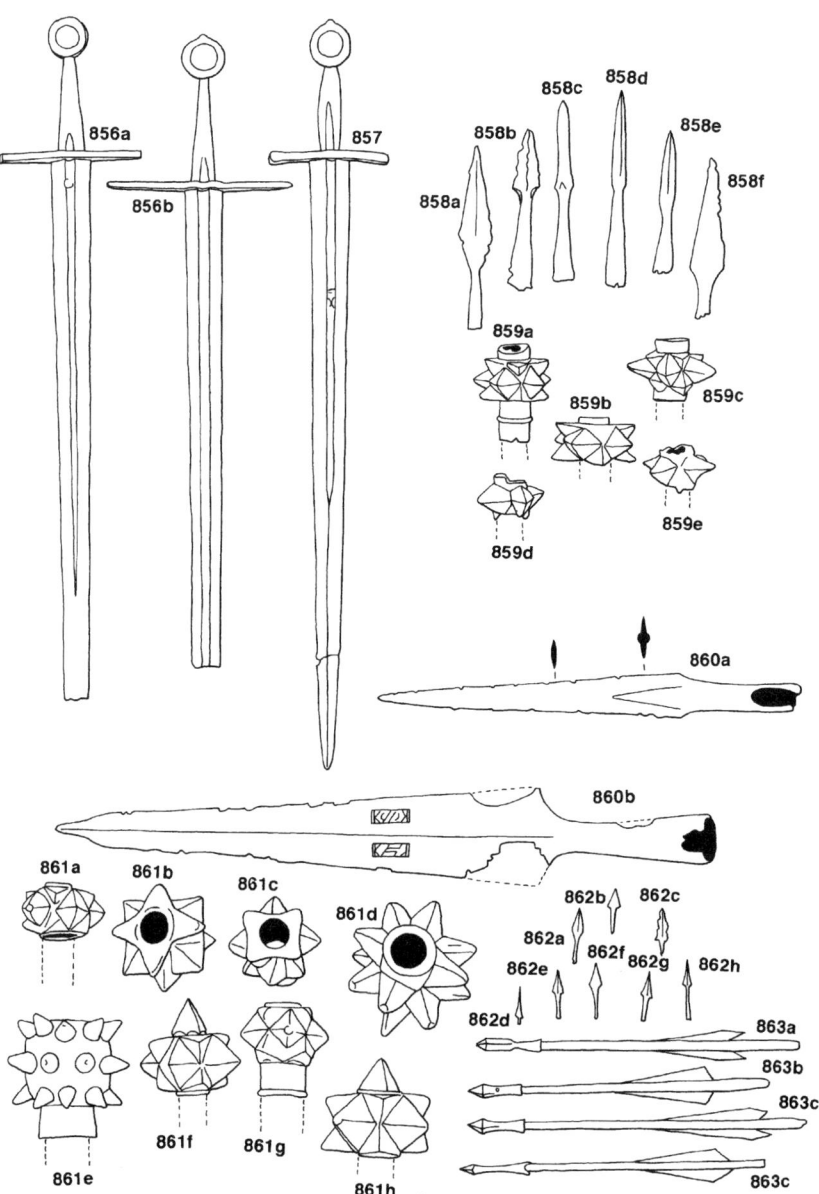

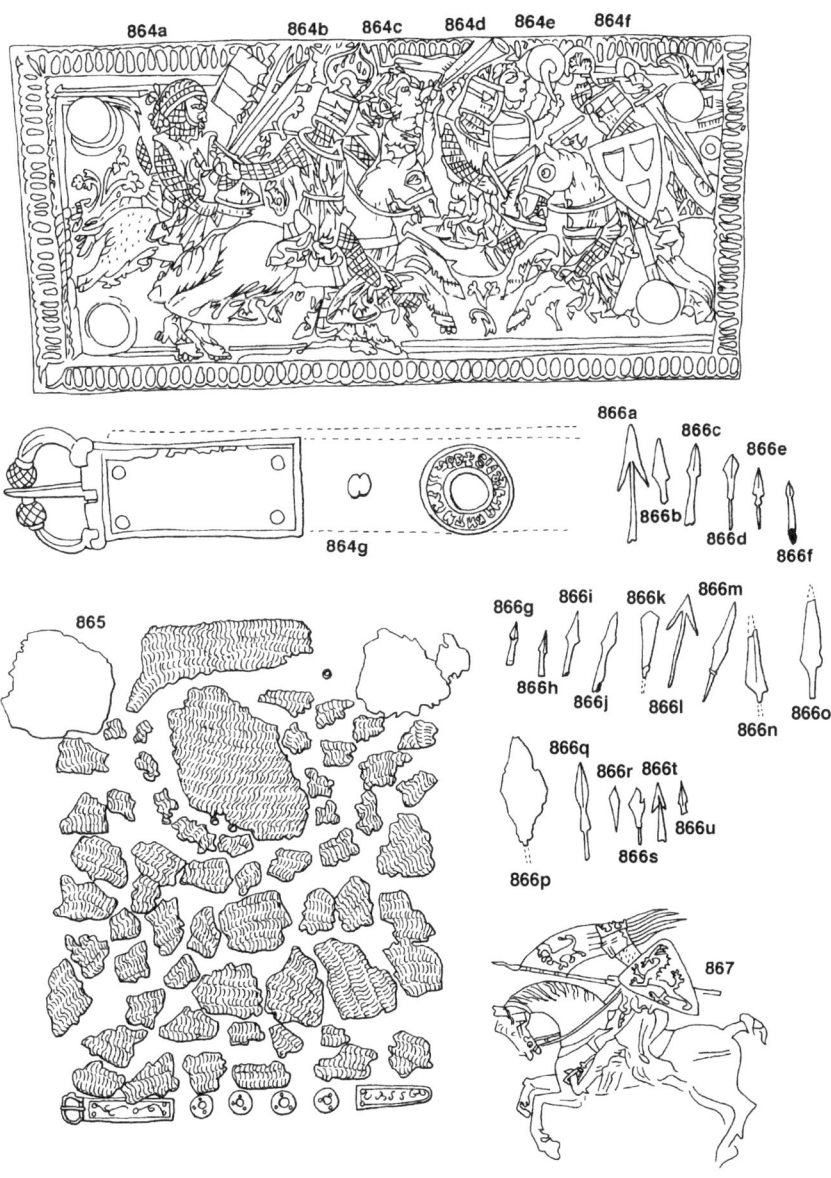

864a 864b 864c 864d 864e 864f

864g

866a 866c 866e
866b 866d 866f

865

866g 866i 866k 866m
866h 866j 866l 866n 866o

866q
866r 866t
866s 866u
866p

867

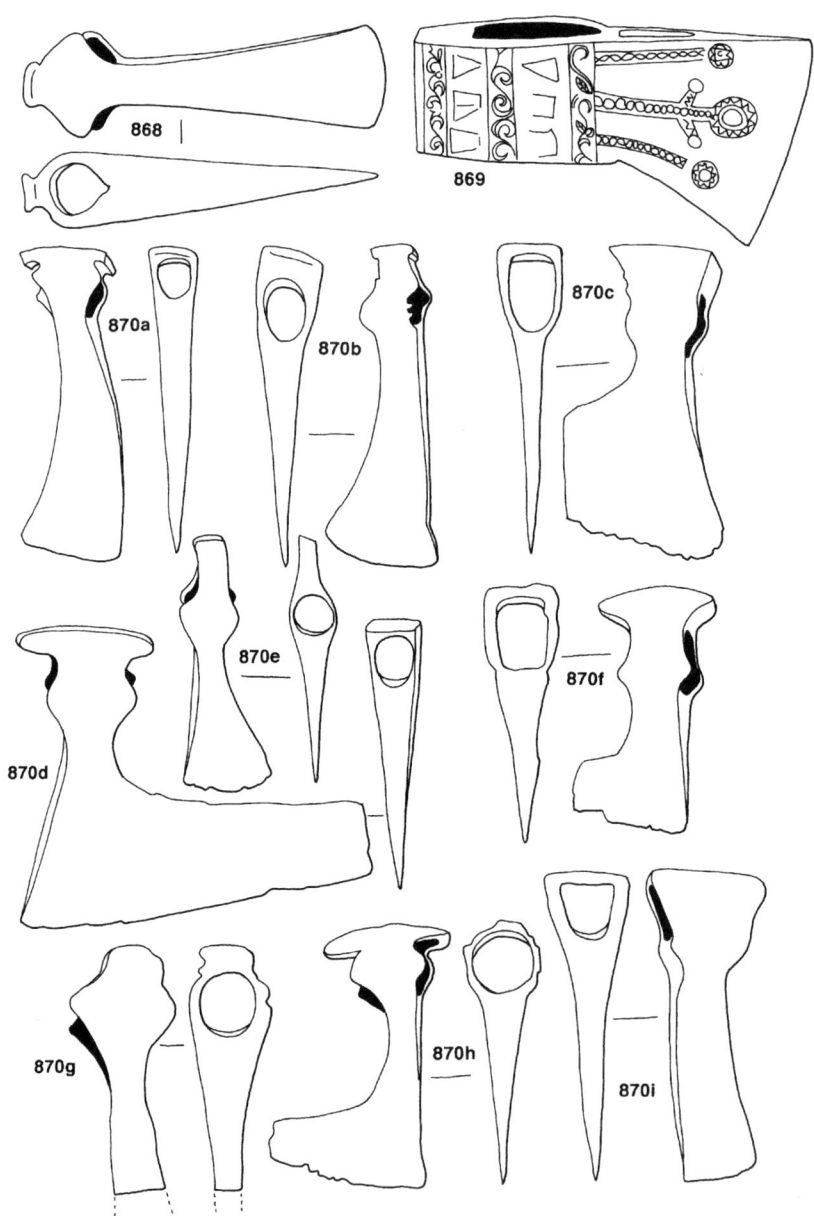

868

869

870a

870b

870c

870d

870e

870f

870g

870h

870i

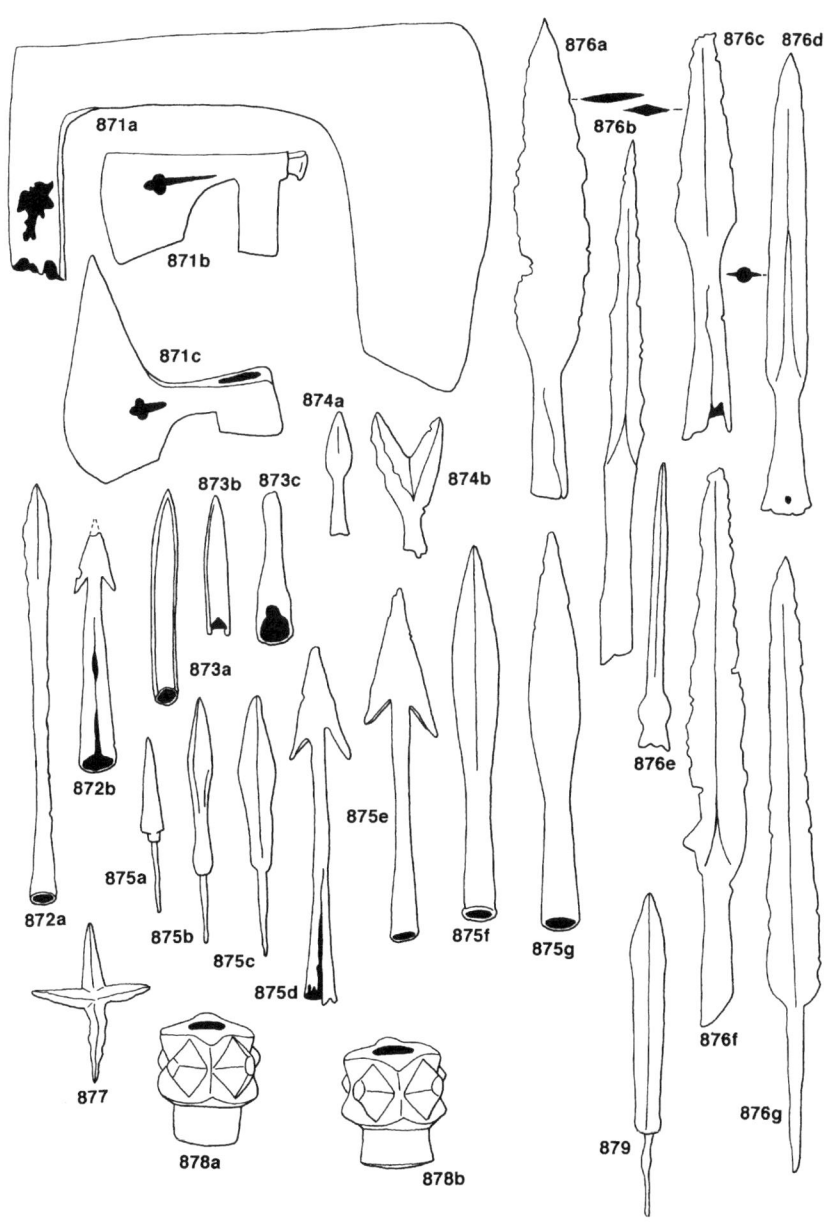

871a

871b

871c

874a

873b 873c 874b

873a

872b

875a

872a

875b

875c

875d

877

878a

878b

876a

876c 876d

876b

876e

875e

875f 875g

876f

876g

879

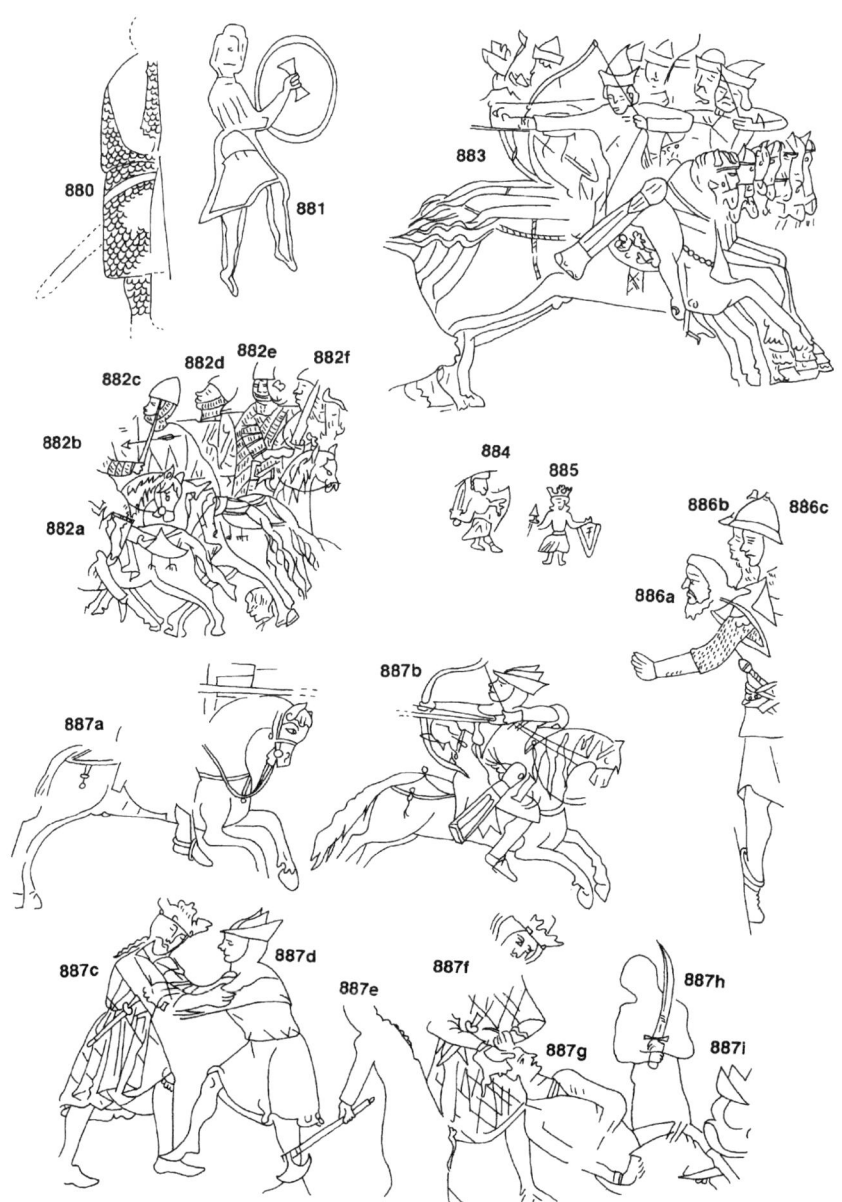

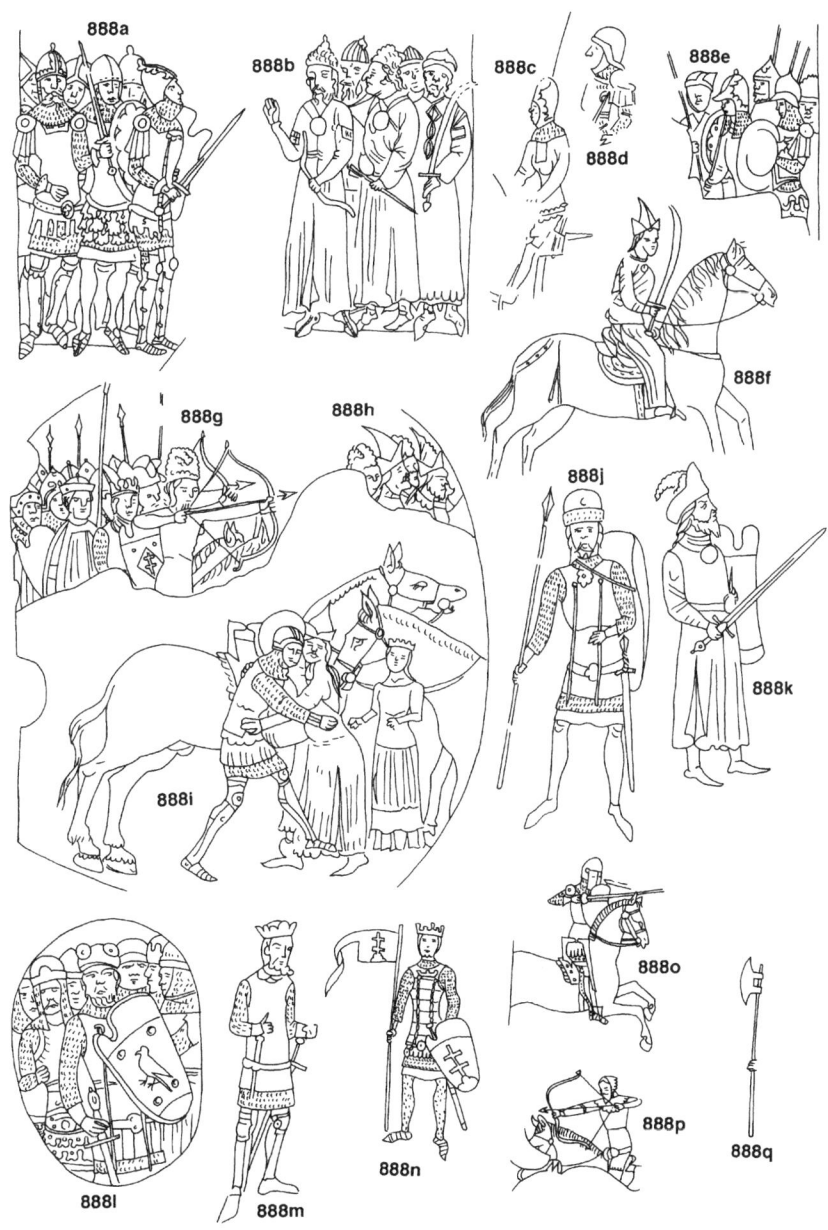

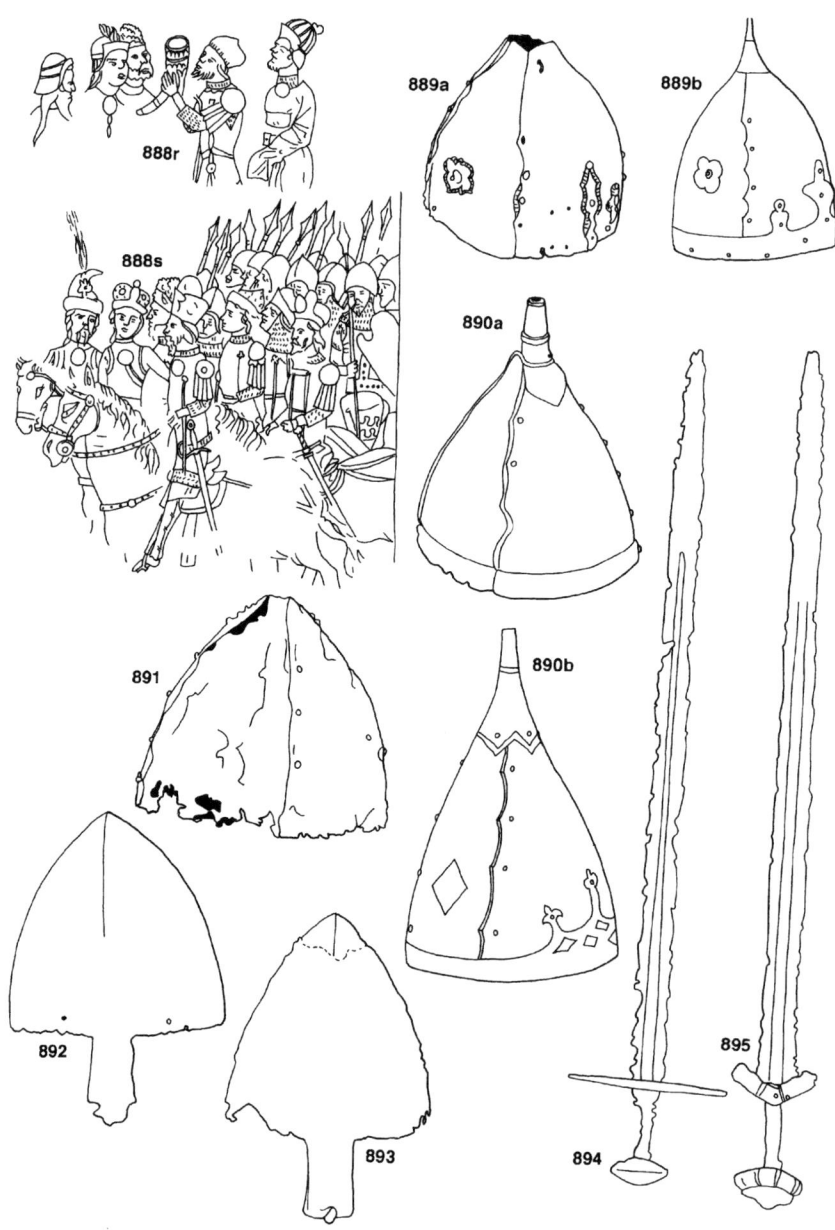

888r

888s

889a

889b

890a

890b

891

892

893

894

895

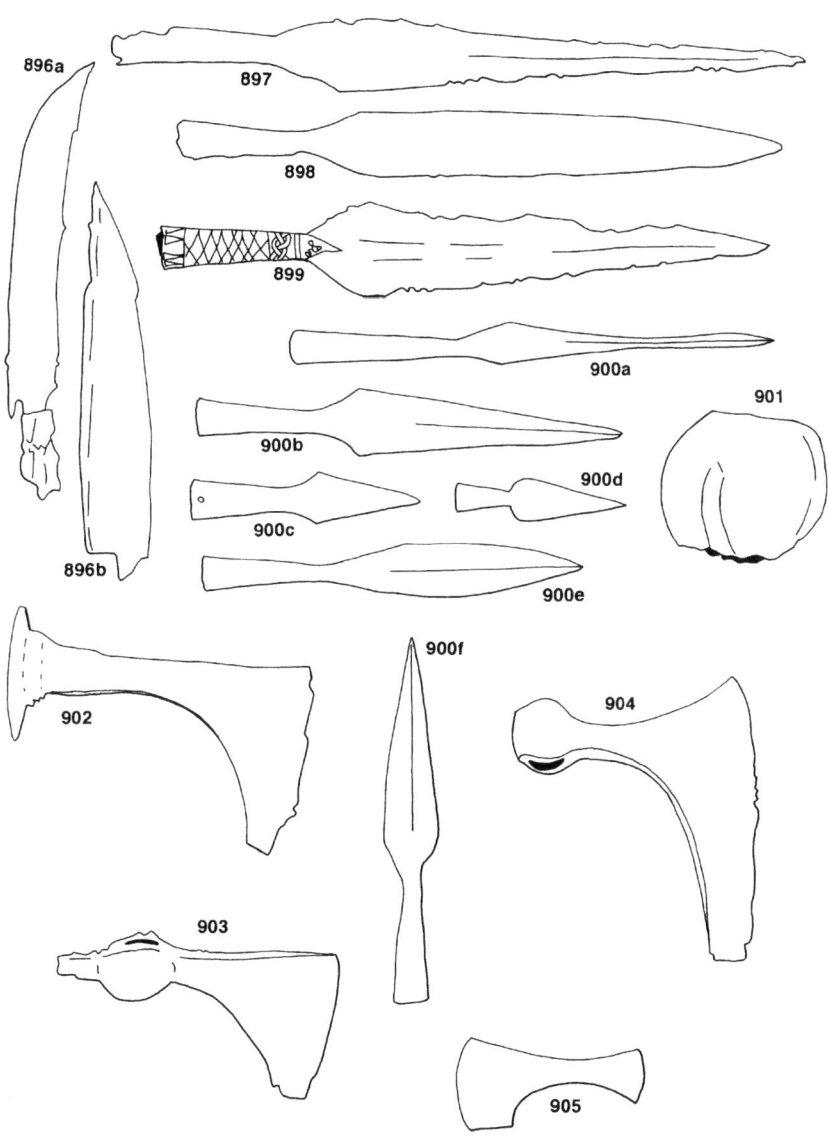

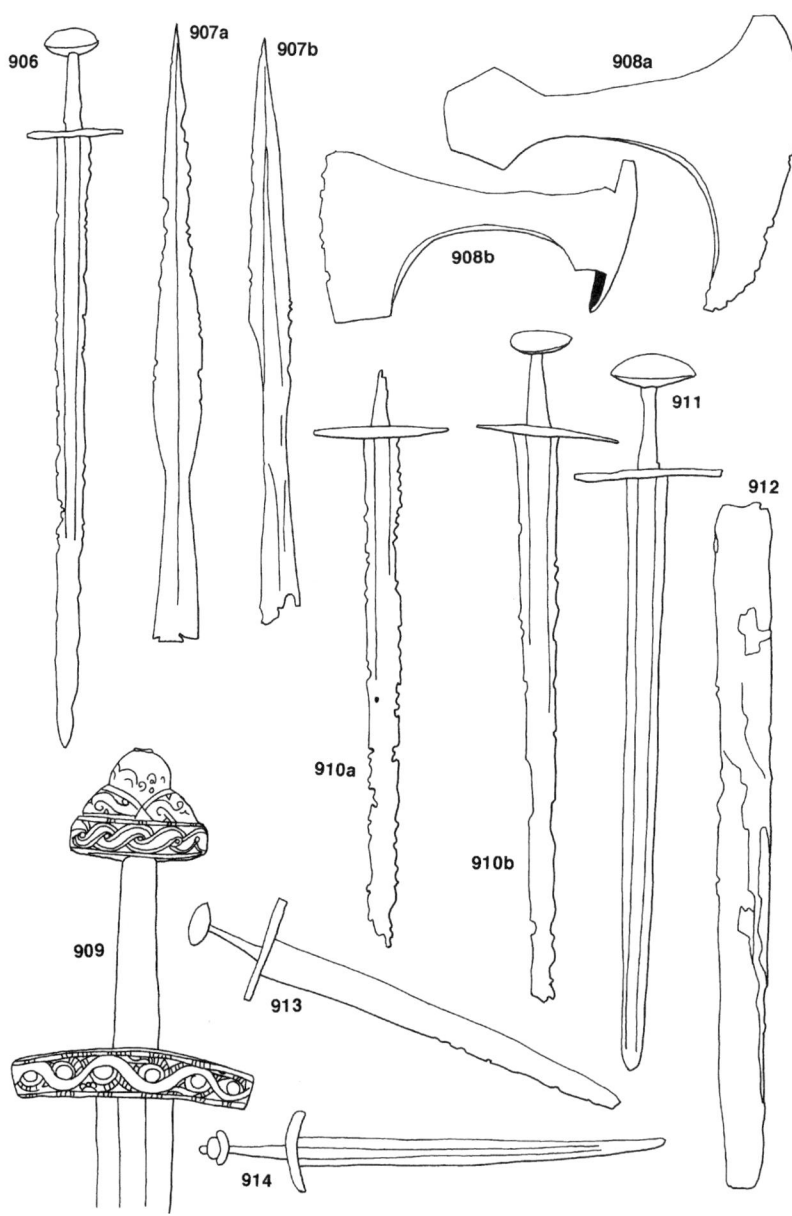

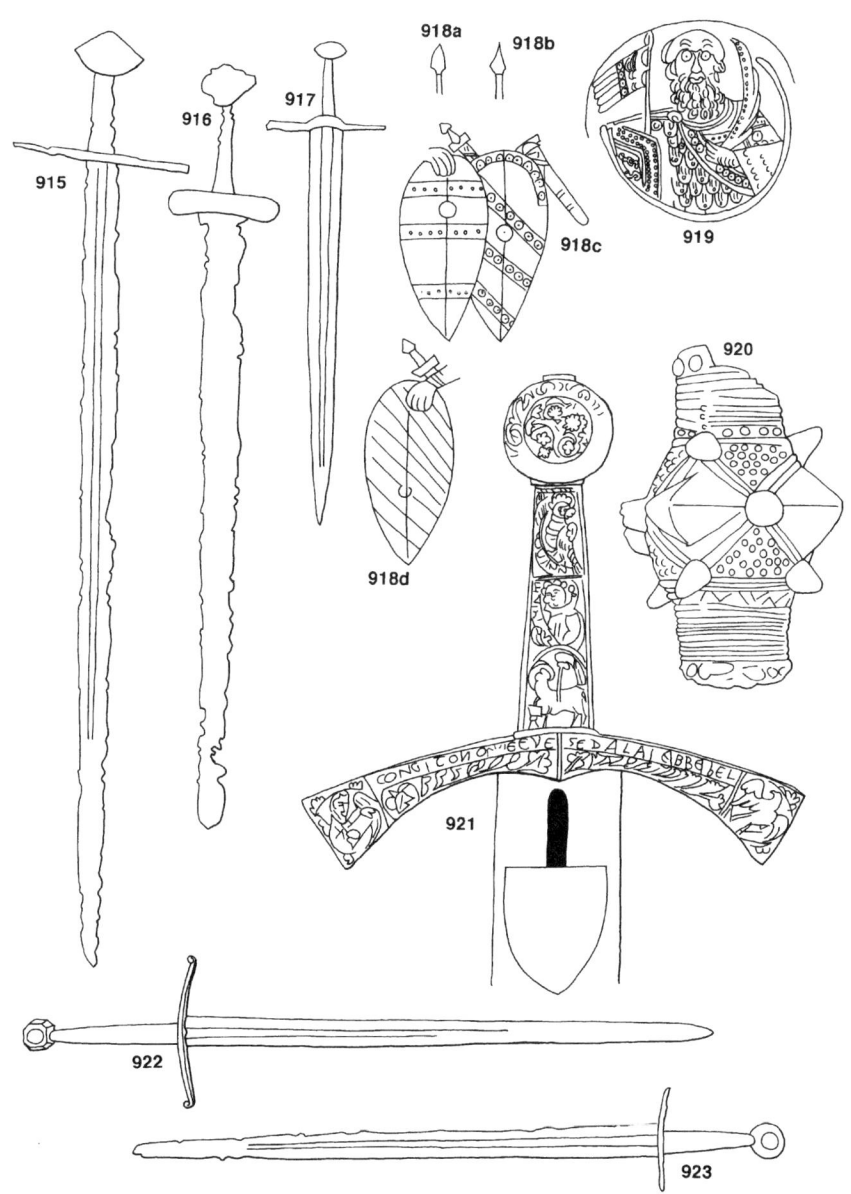

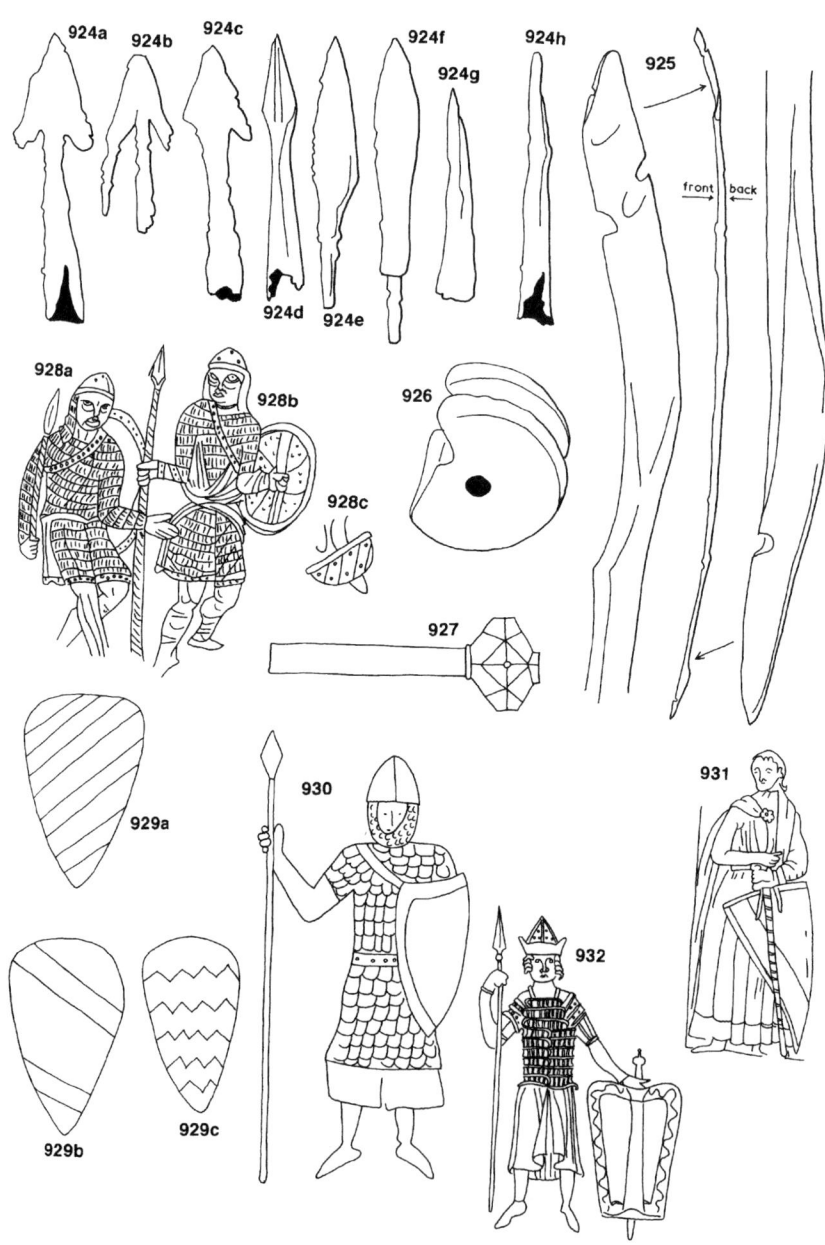

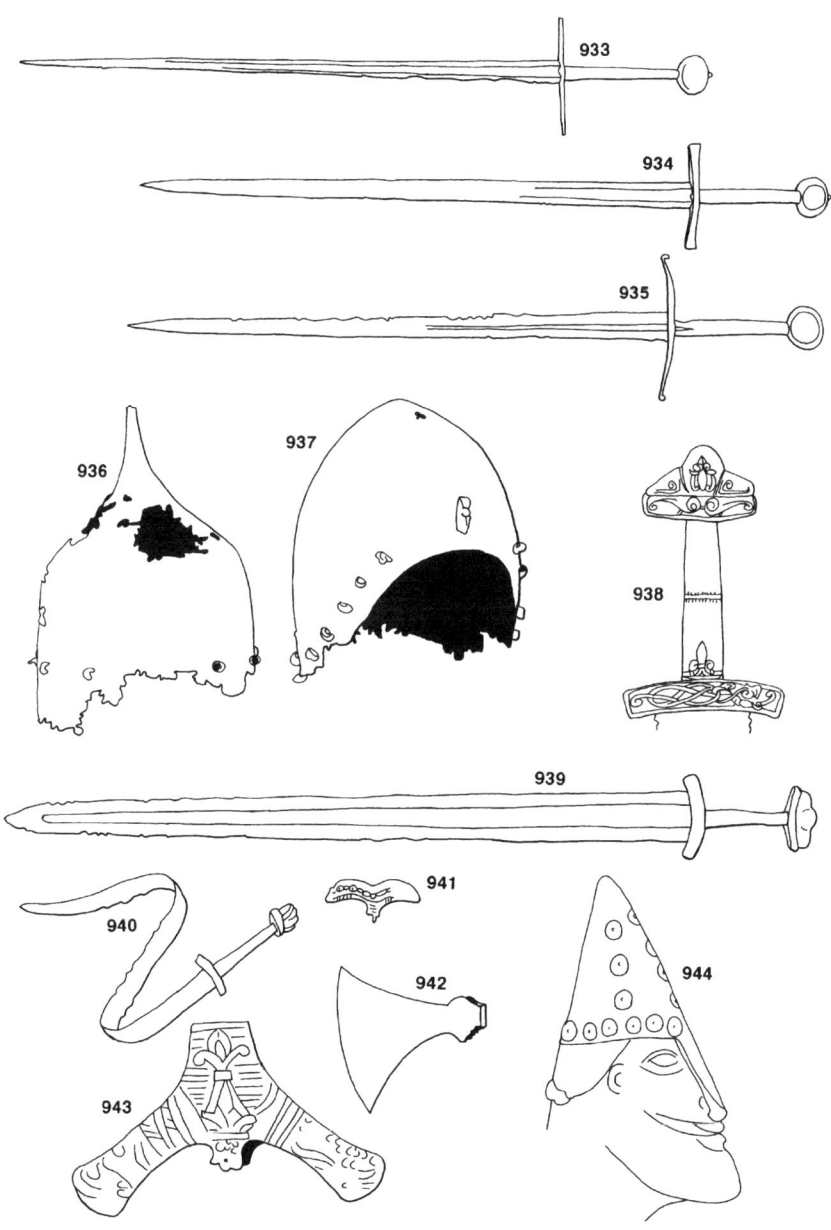

933

934

935

936

937

938

939

940

941

942

943

944

945a

945b

945c

945d

945e

945f

945g

946h

945i

946a

946b

947a

947b

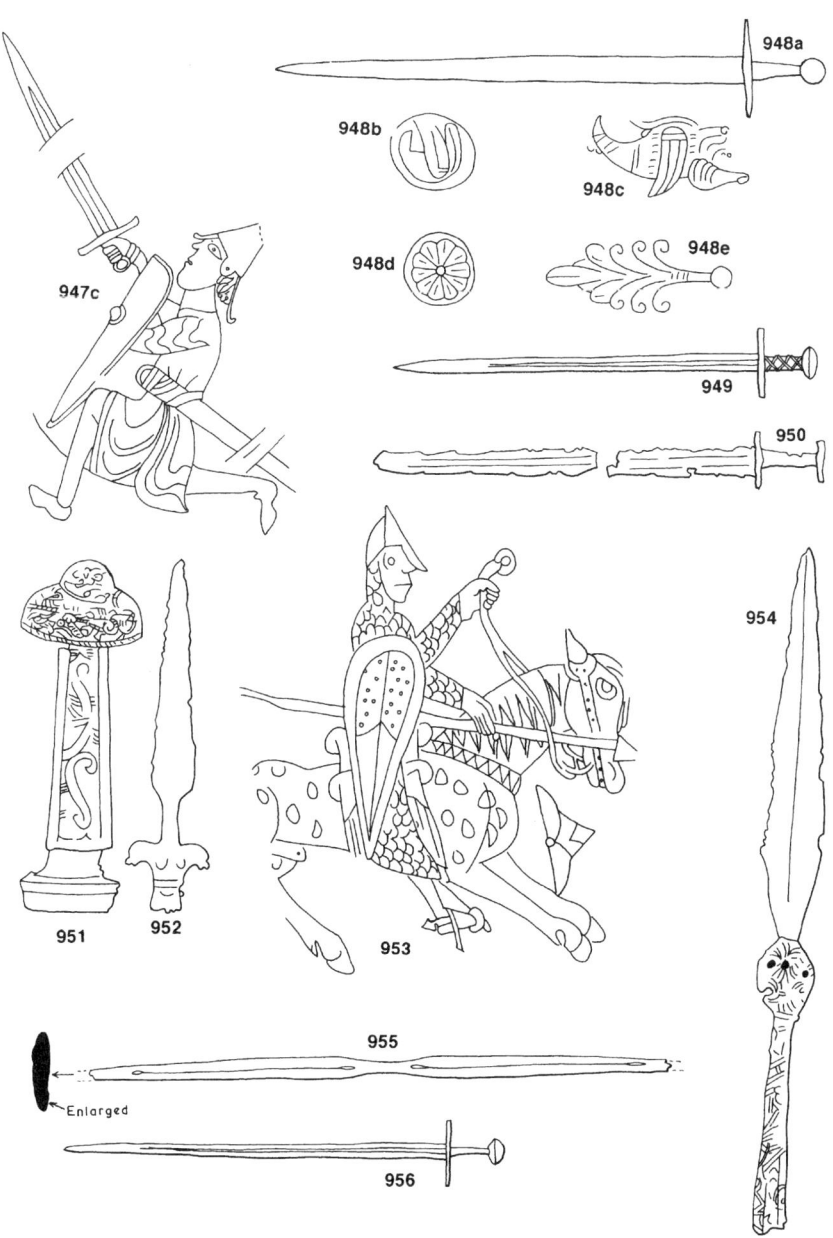

947c

948a

948b

948c

948d

948e

949

950

951

952

953

954

955

Enlarged

956

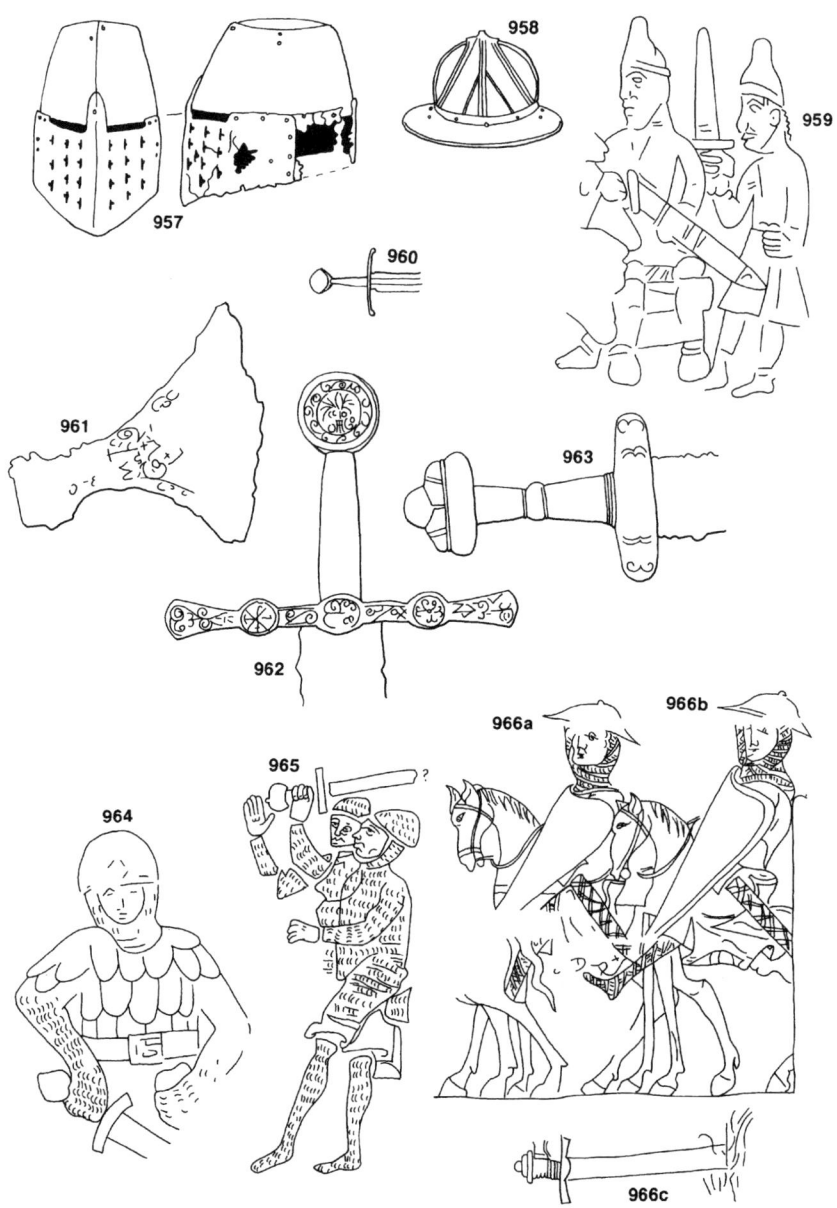

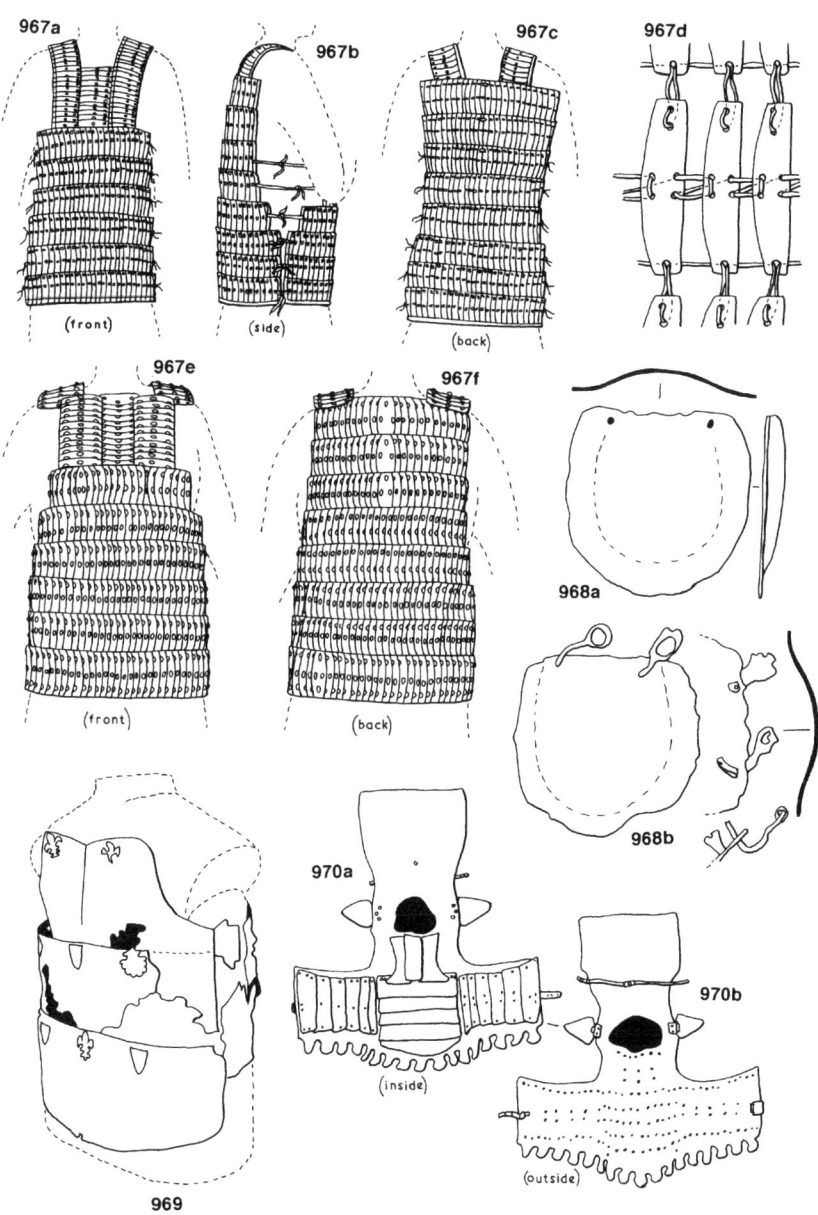

967a (front)

967b (side)

967c (back)

967d

967e (front)

967f (back)

968a

968b

969

970a (inside)

970b (outside)

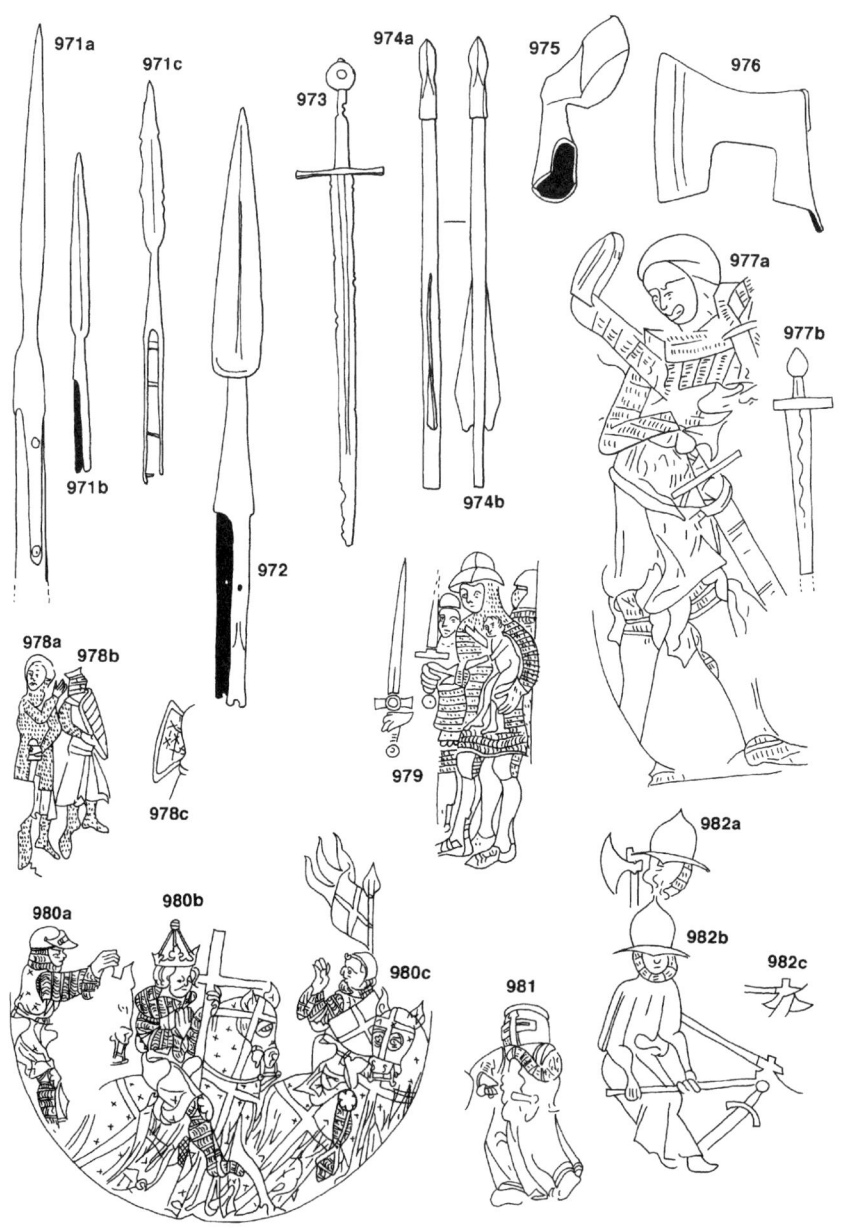

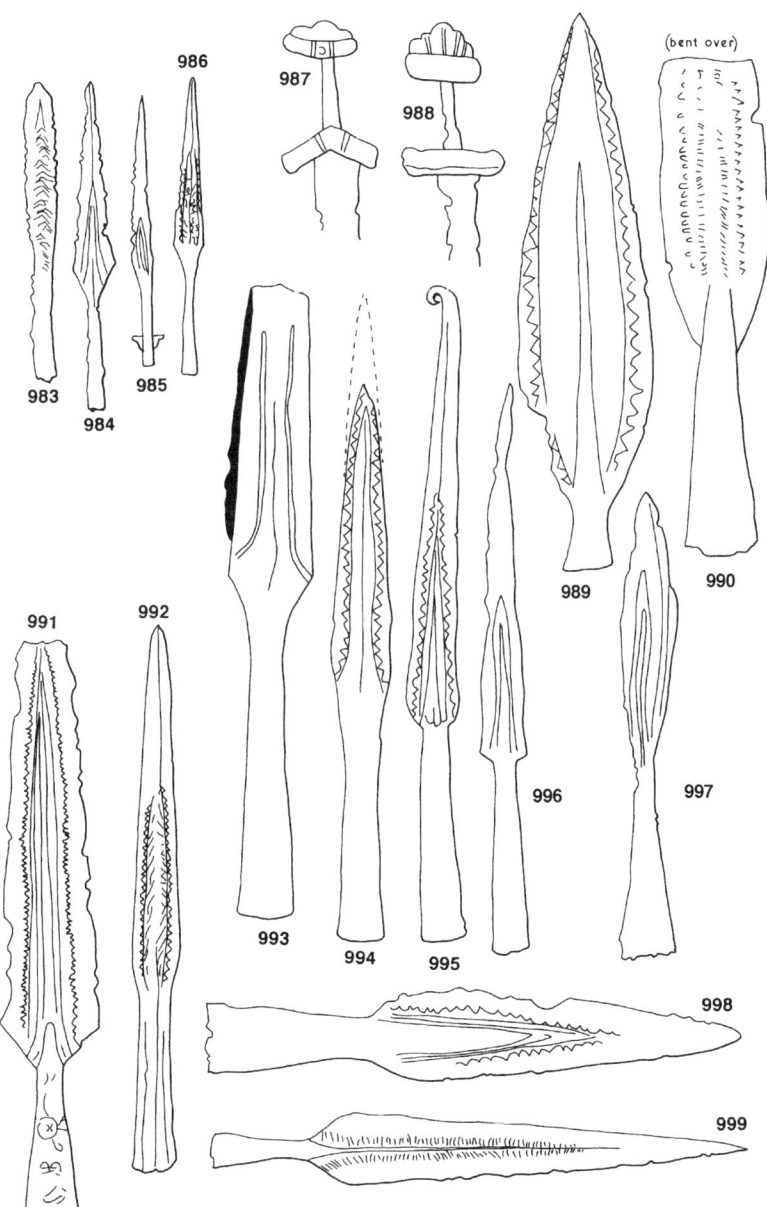

983 984 985 986 987 988 989 990 991 992 993 994 995 996 997 998 999

(bent over)

Dictionary of Terms

This Dictionary of Terms contains many of the obscure and arcane words associated with the arms and armour of the period covered in this book. It is divided into four parts:

> 1. Linguistic groupings.
> 2. List of language abbreviations.
> 3. Source abbreviations.
> 4. Dictionary of terms.

Following each term in the Dictionary, the language from which it originated is given in abbreviated form in square brackets.

Linguistic groupings

Romance languages
Catalan [Cn]
Early Italian [EI]
Medieval Latin [ML]
Occitan [Oc]
Old French [OF]
Spanish [SP]

Germanic languages
Anglo-Saxon [AS]
Flemish-Dutch [FD]
Middle English [ME]
Old Danish [OD]
Old German [OG]
Old Norse [ON]
Old Swedish [OS]
Scots-English [SE]

Celtic languages
Breton [Bn]
Cornish [Co]
Early Welsh [EW]
Irish [Ir]

Scots Gaelic [SG]

Slavic languages
Czech [Cz]
Old Common Slav [OCS]
Polish [Pl]
Serbo-Croat [SC]

List of language abbreviations
[AS]   Anglo-Saxon
[Bn]   Breton
[Cn]   Catalan
[Co]   Cornish
[Cz]   Czech
[EI]   Early Italian
[EW]   Early Welsh
[FD]   Flemish-Dutch
[Ir]   Irish
[ME]   Middle English
[ML]   Medieval Latin
[Oc]   Occitan
[OCS] Old Comman Slav
[OD]   Old Danish
[OF]   Old French
[OG]   Old German
[ON]   Old Norse
[OS]   Old Swedish
[Pl]   Polish
[SC]   Serbo-Croat
[SE]   Scots English
[SG]   Scots Gaelic
[SP]   Spanish

Source abbreviations
The majority of medieval terms referring to arms and armour appear in a great number of primary sources, as well as being referred to in numerous secondary sources. The abbreviations of these which follow most of the terms in the Dictionary are explained below. They are somewhat random and are largely a consequence of the author's continuing researches. Yet they may be taken as as a starting point for further linguistic study.

Transliteration
Transliteration from medieval versions of Roman script can cause problems and consistency is sometimes almost impossible. However, the author has endeavoured to adhere to the following patterns in this dictionary of terms:

Old French: according to A.J. Greimas, *Ancien Français* (Paris, 1980).

Occitan: according to Nelli & Lavaud, *Les Troubadours III: Le Trésor Poetique de L'Occitanie* (Paris, 1966).

Irish: according to P. Harbison, 'Native Irish Arms and Armour in Medieval Gaelic Literature, 1170–1600', *The Irish Sword* vol.XII (1976)

Old Slav languages: according to B. Warner, *Slavonic Terms for Weapons and Armour in the Middle Ages* (M.A. thesis, London University, 1965).

Alphabetical list of source abbreviations

A&M: Anon, *Arthour and Merlin*, Abbotsford Club (Edinburgh, 1838).

A&N: M. Roques, ed., *Aucassin et Nicolette, Chantefable du XIIIe siècle* (Paris, 1936).

AGG: N. Davis, J.R.R. Tolkien and E.V. Gordan, eds. *Sir Gawain and the Green Knight* (Oxford, 1967).

A Hav: W.W. Sisam, ed., *The Lay of Havelock the Dane* (Oxford, 1915).

Alc: L. Alcock, *Arthur's Britain* (London, 1971).

Alm: J. Alm, 'Europaisk armbrust: En översikt', *Vaaben-historisk Aarboger* v/b (1947).

ASR: T.A. Jenkins, ed., *La Chanson de Roland* (London, 1924).

B&C: L.G. Boccia and E.T. Coelho, 'L'armamento di cuoio e ferro nel Trecento Italiano', *L'Illustrazione italiani* vol.I, no.2 (1972).

B&G: U. Barlozzetti and M. Giuliani, 'La Prassi Guerresca in Toscana', in *Guerre e assoldati in Toscana, 1260–1364*, ed. L.G. Boccia and M. Scalini, (Florence, 1982).

Beat: J. A. Nelson, ed., 'Beatrix', in *The Old French Crusade Cycle* vol.I (Alabama, 1977).

Bee W: J. Beeler, *Warfare in England 1066–1189* (Ithaca, 1966).

Bl: C. Blair, *European Armour* (London, 1958).

Blair B: C. Blair, 'The Word "Baselard"', *Journal of the Arms and Armour Society* vol.XI, no.4 (1984).

Blair REC: C. Blair, 'The Pre-Reformation Effigies of Cheshire', *Transactions of the Lancashire and Cheshire Antiquarian Society* vols LX-LXI (1948–9).

Boc HIM: L.G. Boccia, 'HIC IACET MILES: Immagini guerriere da sepolcri toscani de Due e Trecento', in *Guerre e assoldati in Toscana, 1260–1364*, ed. L.G. Boccia and M. Scalini (Florence, 1982).

Borg: A. Borg, 'Gisarmes and Great Axes', *Journal of the Arms and Armour Society* vol.VIII (1974–6).

Brook NA: F.W. Brooks, 'Naval Armament in the Thirteenth Century', *Mariner's Mirror* vol.XIV (1928).

Chet: G.M. Myers, ed., 'Les Chetifs', in *The Old French Crusade Cycle* vol.II (Alabama, 1985).

Chev: J.A. Nelson, ed., 'Le Chevalier au Cygne', in *The Old French Crusade Cycle* vol.II (Alabama, 1985).

CL: *Chronicle of Lanercost*, in E.R. Clifford, *A Knight of Great Renown, biography of Othon de Grandson* (Chicago, 1961).

Conta: P. Contamine, *La Guerre au Moyen Age* (Paris, 1980).

Cred: A.G. Credland, 'The Blowpipe in Europe and the Far East', *Journal of the Arms and Armour Society* vol.X (1981).

De J: De Joinville, 'Histoire de St Louis', in *Historiens et Chroniqueurs du Moyen Age*, ed. A. Pauphilet and E. Pognon (Paris, 1952).

Eli: E.J. Mickel, ed., 'Elioxe', in *The Old French Crusade Cycle* vol.I (Alabama, 1977).

Fino MJ: J.F. Fino, 'Machines de jet medievales', *Gladius* vol.X (1972).

Free WB: A.Z. Freeman, 'Wall-Breakers and River-Bridgers, Military Engineers in the Scottish Wars of Edward I', *Journal of British Studies* vol.X (1971).

Gab AS: F. Gabrielli, 'Gli Arabi in Spagna e in Italia', in *Ordinamenti Militari in Occidente nell'alto Medioevo, Settimane di Studio del Centro Italiano di Studi sull'alto Medioevo* vol.XV, no.2 (Spoleto, 1968).

Gai EU: C. Gaier, 'L'evolution et l'usage de l'armament personnel defensif du pays de Liège du XIIe au XVe siècle', *Zeitschrift der Gesellschaft für Historische Waffen- und Kostümkunde* n.s.

vol.IV (1962).

Gai PO: C. Gaier, 'Le Problème de l'origine de l'industrie armuriere liègeoise au Moyen Age', *Chroniques archeologique du Pays de Liège* vol.LIII (1962).

Gaibi: A. Gaibi, 'Un raro cimelio piemontese del trecento', *Armi Antiche* (1965).

Gans A: F.L. Ganshof, 'Armature (Galbert de Bruges, ch.106, éd. Pirenne, p.152)', *Archivium latinitatis Medii Aevi* vol.XVI (1940).

Ger T: J.J. O'Meara, 'Topographia Hibernie', *Proceedings of the Royal Irish Academy* vol.LII C4 (1949).

Giu OM: M. Giuliani, 'L'organizazione militare a Firenze, fra XIII e XIV secolo', *Guerre e assoldati in Toscana, 1260–1364*, ed. L.G. Boccia and M. Scalini (Florence, 1982).

Gre: A.J. Greimas, *Dictionnaire de l'ancient Français jusqu'au milieu du XIVe siècle* (Paris, 1980).

Ha SA: J.F. Haldon, 'Some Aspects of Byzantine Military Technology from the Sixth to the Tenth Centuries', *Byzantine and Modern Greek Studies* vol.I (1957).

Hana: B.A. Hanawalt, 'Violent Death in Fourteenth and Fifteenth Century England', *Comparative Studies in Society and History* vol.XVIII (1976).

Harb 1 and Harb 2: P. Harbison, 'Native Irish Arms and Armour in Medieval Gaelic Literature, 1170–1600', Part One and Part Two, *The Irish Sword* vol.XII (1976).

Hend MT: W.S. Hendrix, 'Military Tactics in the Poems of the Cid', *Modern Philology* vol.XX (1922).

H Mc: G.A. Hayes-McCoy, 'The Gallóglach Axe', *Journal of the Galway Archaeological and Historical Society* vol.XVII (1937).

Hoff A2: Ada Bruhn de Hoffmeyer, *Arms and Armour in Spain: A Short Survey*, vol.II (Madrid, 1982).

Kell: M.L. Keller, *The Anglo-Saxon Weapon Names Treated Archaeologically and Etymologically* (Heidelberg, 1906).

Kelly: F.M. Kelly, 'Zur Entstehung des Spangenharnisches', *Zeitschrift für Historische Waffen-und Kostümkunde* n.s. vol.IV (1933).

Knud: C.A. Knudson, 'La brogne', in *Mélanges offerts a Rita Lejeune* vol.II (Gembloux, 1969).

Labou: G.C. Labouchere, 'Ein inventaris', *Oud-Ultrecht* (1933).

Lom M: M. Lombard, *Les Métaux dans l'Ancien Monde du Ve au XIe siècle* (Paris, 1974).

Magl: V. Magliolo, 'La Balestra', *Armi Antiche* I–II (1955).

MCK: A.S. Melikian-Chirvani, 'The Westward Journey of the Kazhāgand', *Journal of the Arms and Armour Society* vol.XI (1983).

Meyer RV: P. Meyer, 'Un récit en vers français de la première croisade fondé sur Baudri de Bourgueil', *Romania* vol.V (1876).

Morr: W.S. Morris, 'A Crusader's Testament', *Speculum* vol.XXVII (1952).

Morris MS: J. Morris, *Medieval Spanish Epic Style, Its Character and Development* (Ph.D. thesis, Leeds University, 1960–1).

Mot AP: G.J. Mot, 'L'arsenal et le parc de matériel a la cité de Carcassonne en 1298', *Annales du Midi* vol.LXVIII (1956).

N&L: R. Nelli and R. Lavaud, *Les Troubadours III: Le Trésor Poétique de L'Occitanie* (Paris, 1966).

Noel: R.P.R. Noel, *Town Defences in the French Midi during the Hundred Years War, c.1337–c.1453* (Ph.D. thesis, Edinburgh University, 1978).

Nor: A.V.B. Norman, *The Medieval Soldier* (London, 1971).

Nor NG: A.V.B. Norman, 'Notes on Some Early Representations of Guns and on Ribaudekins', *Journal of the Arms and Armour Society* vol.VIII (1974–6).

Oak: E. Oakeshott, *The Archaeology of Weapons* (London, 1960).

Oman AW: C.W.C. Oman, *A History of the Art of War in the Middle Ages* (London, 1924).

Pai TR: G.D. Painter, ed., *The Vinland Map and the Tartar Relation* (New Haven and London, 1965).

Pet DO: D. Petrović, *Dubrovacko Oruzje u XIV veku* (Belgrade, 1976).

Pet FB: D. Petrović, 'Fire-arms in the Balkans on the Eve and After the Ottoman Conquests of the Fourteenth and Fifteenth centuries', in *War, Technology and Society in the Middle East*, ed. V.J. Parry and M.E. Yapp (London, 1975)

Pieri SL: P. Pieri, 'I Saraceni di Lucera nella storia militare medievale', *Archivio Storico Pugliese* vol.VI (1955).

PLN: A. Pasquali-Lasagni and E. Stefanelli, 'Note di storia dell'artigliera nel secoli XIV e XV', *Archivio della Reale Deputazione Romana di Storia Patria* vol.IX (1937).

Poures: P.S. Poureshagh, *A Critical Edition of the Anglo-Norman Rhymed Translation of the Vitas Patrum Dedicated to the Templer Henri d'Arci* (Ph.D. thesis, Edinburgh University, 1977).

Pra: J. Prawer, *The Crusaders' Kingdom* (New York, 1972).

Pur: A. Puricelli-Guerra, 'The Glaive and the Bill', in *Art, Arms and Armour*, ed. R. Held (Chiasso, 1979).

R de C: Robert de Clari, 'Le Conquête de Constantinople', in *Historiens et Chroniqueurs du Moyen Age*, ed. A. Pauphilet and E. Pognon (Paris, 1952).

Rich CV: J. Richard, 'Les causes de victoires Mongoles d'après les historiens occidentaux du XIIIe siècle', *Central Asiatic Journal* vol.XXIII (1979).

Roth: H. Rothert, 'Wann und wo ist die Pulverwaffe erfunden', *Blätter für deutsche Landesgeschichte* vol.LXXXIX (1952).

RG: Robert of Gloucester, *Metrical Chronicle*, Rolls Series, Public Record Office, London.

RR: M. Roques, ed., *Le Roman de Renart* (Paris, 1955).

RT: G.R. De Lage, *Le Roman de Thèbes* (Paris, 1966).

Scal AP: M. Scalini, 'Le Armi: produzione, fruizione e simbolo nella Toscana medioevali', in *Guerre e assoldati in Toscana, 1260–1364*, ed. L.G. Boccia and M. Scalini, (Florence, 1982).

Scal DS: M. Scalini, 'Die Schutzbewaffnung bis 1500', in *Das Münchner Zeughaus*, ed. R.H. Wackernagel (Munich and Zurich, 1982).

Schr: P. Schreiner, 'Zur Ausrustung des Kriegers in Byzanz', in *Les Pays du Nord et Byzance, Acta Universitatis Upsaliensis, Figura* n.s. vol.XIX (1981).

Sm: R.C. Smail, *Crusading Warfare, 1097–1193* (Cambridge, 1956).

Smith AM: W.J. Smith, *Aspects of Military Organization in England Under King John* (M.A. thesis, University of Wales, 1950–1).

Swant: M.J. Swanton, *The Spearheads of the Anglo-Saxon Settlements* (London, 1973).

Tagl: J. Taglicht, *An Edition of the Middle English Romance 'Ywain and Gawain'* (Ph.D. thesis, Oxford University, 1963).

Thorne: P.F. Thorne, 'Clubs and Maces in the Bayeux Tapestry', *History Today* vol.XXXII (October 1982).

TOF: R.C. Johnston and D.R. Owen, *Two Old French Gauvain Romances: Le Chevalier a l'Epée and La Mule sans Frein* (Edinburgh, 1972).

Tur TD: H.L. Turner, *Town Defences in England and Wales, An Architectural and Documentary Survey AD 900–1500* (London, 1970).

Ver: J.F. Verbruggen, *The Art of Warfare in Western Europe during the Middle Ages* (Oxford, 1977).

Verb DG: J.F. Verbruggen, 'De Goedendag', *Militaria Belgica* vol.III (1977).

Verb DL: J.F. Verbruggen, 'De Kist van Oxford', *De Leiegouw* vol.XXII (1980).

Vill CC: Villehardouin, 'La Conquête de Constantinople', in *Historiens et Chroniqueurs du Moyen Age*, ed. A. Pauphilet and E. Pognon (Paris, 1952).

V Mie: Van Mieris, 'Groot Charterboek van der Graven van Holland', in *Charter van Holland* vol.II (n.d.).

Wace: see Bee W.

Wal AW: R.F. Walker, *The Anglo-Welsh Wars 1217–1267, with Special Reference to English Military Developments* (Ph.D. thesis, Oxford University, 1954).

Wal CC: D.P. Waley, 'Condotte and Condottieri in the Thirteenth Century', *Proceedings of the British Academy* (1975).

Wal O: D.P. Waley, 'Le origini della condotta nel Duecento e le compagnie di ventura', *Rivista storica italiana* vol.LXXXVIII (1976).

Warn: B. Warner, *Slavonic Terms for Weapons and Armour in the Middle Ages: A Lexico-Historical Study* (M.A. thesis, London University, 1965).

Will BT: G. Williams, *The Burning Tree, Poems from the First Thousand Years of Welsh Poetry* (London, 1956).

Will IW: G. Williams, *An Introduction to Welsh Poetry* (London, 1953).

Will PG: M.E. Williams, *An Edition of the Romance of Sir Percyvelle de Galles* (M.A. thesis, Aberystwyth, 1961).

Dictionary of terms

Abillement: [OF] general term for engine, war machine, weapon; France, 13th century (Gre).

Acesme: [OF] armoured or equipped, of a warrior; south-west France, mid-12th century (RT).

Acier: [OF] sharp tool or weapon; France, from 12th century (Gre).

Acort: [OF] hem of a mantle; France, late 12th century (Gre).

Actoune: [ME] padded *aketon* (soft armour); northern England, early/mid-14th century (Tagl).

Acuta: [ML] shields in naval warfare; Marseilles, 13th century (Brook NA).

Adarga, adagara: [SP] light leather shield; from Arabic *daraqah*; Spain, 12th–14th centuries (Hoff A2, Morris MS).

Adob: [OF] armour or military dress in general; France, late 11th century (Gre).

Adobeure: [OF] arms in general; France, 12th century (Gre).

Aesć: [AS] heavy spear, sometimes with ashen haft; England, 10th–11th centuries (Kell, Swant).

Aetgār: [AS] spear or javelin; England, 10th–11th centuries (Kell, Swant).

Aex: [AS] axe; England, 10th–11th centuries (Kell).

Afeltrer: [OF] to harness or prepare for combat; from *feltrer* ('to cover with felt'); France, late 12th century (Gre).

Afeltreure: [OF] padded part of a saddle; France, mid-12th century (Gre).

Afeutremens: [OF] either felt cloth under saddle or horse-armour, or felt caparison; France, mid/late 12th century (Beat).

Afublail: [OF] unspecified type of garment; France, late 12th century (Gre).

Agier, agie, algier, algiet: [OF] light spear or javelin, weapon to be thrown; from German *azger*; France and Norman England, late 11th–late 12th centuries (ARS, Chet, Gre).

Agroi, agrai: [OF] general term for military equipment, armour, harness; from Scandinavian *greida* ('gear'); France, late 12th century (Gre).

Aguichier: [OF] put the *guige* on a shield; France, late 12th century (Gre).

Aguillon: [OF] goad; France, late 12th century (Chet).

Aguisies: [OF] javelin or light spear; France, late 12th century (A&N).

Aisse, aze: [OF] axe, adze or hatchet used in making saddles; France, 12th–late 13th centuries (Gre).

Aisselete: [OF] shaving or splinter of wood, comparable to *ailette* worn on shoulders for heraldic purposes; France, early 14th century (Gre).

Aketon: [ME] quilted soft armour usually with sleeves, same as French *hacqueton*; differences from *gambeson* unclear; from Arabic *al-quṭn* ('cotton'); England, 12th–13th centuries (Bl, Nor).

Aketon: [OF] see *hacqueton* and *aketon* [ME].

Akton: [ME] same as *aketon*; England, mid-14th century (Will PG).

Alabarde: [OF] *halbard*, specialised form of long-hafted axe with a spike added; perhaps from Italian *alabarda*; France, early/mid-14th century (Gre).

Alamanka: [SC] sword, probably those imported from Germany; Serbia, 14th century (Warn).

Alamud: [SP] mace; from Arabic *al-ʿamud*; Spain, 11th–14th centuries (GGA).

Acube: [OF] type of tent; from Arabic *al-ku'b* ('cube'); France, late 12th century (Gre).

Alemele: [OF] blade of spear or sword, any sharp cutting weapon; France, mid-12th century (Gre).

Alesnaz: [OF] dagger, spear or pike with long triangular blade; France, 12th century (Gre).

Alesne: [OF] dart, spike, or anything that pricks; France, early 13th century (Gre).

Algarrada: [Oc and SP] type of stone-throwing machine; from Arabic *al-ᶜarrāda*; southern France, late 13th century (N&L, Hoff A2).

Algodon del perpunte: [SP] padded or quilted soft armour, same as French *aketon*; from Arabic *al-quṭn* ('cotton'); Aragón, late 13th–14th centuries (Hoff A2).

Almanganiq: [SP] mangonel; from Arabic *al-manjanîq*; Spain, 12th–13th centuries (Hoff A2).

Almajenech: [Cn] mangonel; from Arabic *al-manjanîq*; Aragón, 13th century (Hoff A2).

Almofar, almofreor, almofle: [SP] mail *coif*, usually integral part of *hauberk*; also as *almofar doblado*; from Arabic *al-mighfar*; Spain, 11th–13th centuries (GGA, Hoff A2).

Almuce: [OF] hat decorated with fur; France, 12th century (Gre).

Almucele: [OF] small hood or piece of horse-harness; France, early 14th century (Gre).

Alqueton, hoqueton: [OF] flag, usually white, or padded garment; from Arabic *al-quṭn* ('cotton'); France, early 12th century.

Alumele, alamiele: [OF] blade, generally of a sword; France, mid/late 12th century (RT, Beat).

Alve, auve, aube: [OF] band or plate joining the cantle and pommel of a saddle; France, late 11th century (Gre).

Amentum: [ML] perhaps binding around grip on haft of spear or javelin; England, 10th–11th centuries (Swant).

Amingalt, emingaut, aligot: [OF] opening or collar of a garment, or piece of garment covering the top of the chest; France, early 13th century (Gre).

Amore: [OF] blade of spear or sword, anything pointed; France, late 11th–late 12th centuries (Gre).

Anlance: [ME] probably a short spear, used by robbers; England, mid-13th century (Hana).

Ansoigne: [OF] mark, sign, pennon on a lance; same as *enseigne*; France, 11th–13th centuries (Gre).

Anste: [OF] haft of a lance; France, late 12th–early 13th centuries (Chet, Eli, Chev).

Apoieor: [OF] baton; France, 13th century (Gre).

Apointon: [OF] unspecified pointed weapon; France, 14th century (Gre).

Arbalest: [OF] crossbow used by probably mounted infantry; Crusader Constantinople, early 13th century (Vill CC).

Arbaleste, arbalestre, arsbaleste: [OF] crossbow; France and Norman England, from late 11th century (ASR, A&N, Chet, Eli, Gre).

Arbalete à tour: [OF] probably frame-mounted crossbow; same as *treuil*; France, 12th–14th centuries (Fino MJ).

Arblaste: [AS] crossbow; England, late 11th century (Kell).

Arc: [OF] hand-bow; France, southern France and Norman England, from 11th century (ASR, Beat, Poures, Gre, N&L).

Arc de cor manier: [OF] bow of horn, presumably composite construction; France and Byzantine Trabzon, late 12th/early 13th centuries (Chet, Fino MJ).

Arc turcois: [OF] presumably composite bow, but shot *quarrels* like a crossbow; also as *arc turcois de cor*; France, late 12th century (Chet).

Archegaie, azagaia: [OF] crossbow bolt or javelin shot from large crossbow; from Arabic-Berber *al-zaghayah*; France, early 14th century (Gre).

Arcon: [OF] small hand-bow; France, late 11th century (Gre).

Arcubus: [ML] hand-bow; Europe, from late 10th century.

Arcus Turquesius: [SP] general term for hand-bow, probably of composite construction; Spain, 13th–14th centuries (Hoff A2).

Arestil, arestoil, arestuel: [OF] grip of sword or lance; France, 12th century (Gre).

Arewes, arwes: [ME] arrows; England, early/mid-14th century (AGG, Tagl).

Arietes: [OF] ram used in siege warfare; France, 13th century (Gre).

Arma, armatz: [Oc] weapons in general; southern France, late 12th century (N&L).

Arma de testa: [EI] perhaps a padded *arming cap*; Dalmatia, early/mid-14th century (Pet DO).

Armadura: [Oc] armour in general; southern France, early 14th century (N&L).

Armata: [EI] quiver; Dalmatia, 14th century (Pet DO).

Armeor, armeoieor, armeoier: [OF] armourer; France, 13th century (Gre).

Armes: [ME] general term for arms and armour; England, late 13th–14th centuries (AGG, A Hav, Tagl); see also *armes* [OF].

Armes: [OF] arms in general or full set of armour and weapons; France and Norman England, late 11th–late 12th centuries (ASR, Chet, Poures); see also *armes* [ME].

Armeure: [OF] general term for armour; France, mid-12th–mid-13th centuries (RR, TOF, Beat, Gre).

Armure, armour: [ME] armour in general but particularly plate armour, usually laced on; northern England and midlands, early/mid-14th century (Tagl, Will PG); see also *armure* [OF].

Armure: [OF] general term for armour; Flanders, early 14th century (Gans A); see also *armure* [ME].

Ars: [OF] bow used by *Turcopole*; France, late 12th century (Chet).

Artillerie: [OF] an assembly of war-engines; France, late 13th century (Gre).

Artillier: [OF] gather together or make war-engines; France, 13th century (Gre).

Arvau: [EW] armour in general; Wales, mid/late 12th century (Will IW).

Arwe: [AS] arrow; England, 10th–11th centuries (Kell).

Arwev guir: [EW] armour in general; Wales, 9th–11th centuries (Will BT).

Asbergum: [ML] mail hauberk, distinct from *panzeriam*; Tuscany, early 14th century (Giu OM).

Asc: [OG] heavy spear; Germany, 10th–12th centuries (Swant).

Ascona: [SP] javelin; Navarre, 13th–14th centuries (Hoff A2).

Askr: [OS and ON] heavy spear; Scandinavia, 10th–12th centuries (Swant).

Asta, astil: [SP] probably shaft of lance; Spain, 12th–13th centuries (Morris MS).

Asta: [Oc] probably the haft of a spear or the spear itself; southern France, late 12th–early 14th centuries (N&L).

Ataces: [OF] ornamental ribbons on various objects, weapons, etc; France, late 12th/early 13th centuries (Eli).

Atcluicc: [ML] probably reference to *clogat* (Gaelic-Irish helmet); Ireland, mid-13th century (Harb 1).

Atil: [OF] armament, armour, equipment in general; France, 13th century (Gre).

Auberc: [OF] mail hauberk; also as *auberc dublier* or *auberc doublier*; France, mid/late 12th century (A&N, Beat, Chet).

Auberc jaserant, hauberc jaserant: [OF] padded and cloth-covered mail hauberk, an example described as being of scarlet, green, of cendal silk and half-silk fabric, or of green *bougerant* buckram; from Arabic *kazāghand*; France, mid/late 12th century (Beat, Eli).

Aubergel: [ME] small mail *hauberk*, probably short-sleeved, heavier than *wambassia* (soft armour); England, late 12th century (Bee W).

Aubertz: [Oc] *hauberk*, or 'armoured' in general, as in, for example, *cavals aubertz* ('armoured horses'); southern France, early 13th century (N&L).

Aunlaz: [ME] knife or dagger worn at belt; England, late 13th century (A Hav).

Ausberc: [Oc] mail *hauberk*; southern France, late 12th–13th centuries (N&L).

Ausbersh, asberch: [Cn] mail *hauberk*; Catalonia, 13th–14th centuries (Hoff A2).

Auvant: [OF] gallery of a fortification; from Latin *antevannum*; France, late 12th century (Gre).

Avant-bras: [OF] part of an armour, probably arm defences; France, late 13th century (Gre).

Avant-piz: [OF] armour protecting chest; France, early 13th century (Gre).

Aventayle: [ME] mail *aventail* attached to rim of helmet; England, mid-14th century (AGG).

Ax, axe: [ME] war-axe, sometimes synonymous with *giserne*; specifically *Denez ax* ('Danish axe'); has *bytte* (blade), *halme* (haft) and *lace* or thong, probably to put around wrist; England, late 13th–mid-14th centuries (AGG, A Hav).

Azegaya: [Sp] short-spear or javelin, mostly used by Muslims; from Arab-Berber *al-zaghayah*; Spain, 13th–14th centuries (Hoff A2).

Baccinet, bachinet, bachin, bascinet: [OF] helmet probably developed from the close-fitting *cervellière* but extended to protect the back and sides of the head, later with *aventail* and visor; Western Europe, mid-13th–14th centuries (Bl, Conta, Gai EU).

Baçilletum, bacileto, bacinetta: [ML] early form of *bascinet* with or without mail *aventail*, or *cum capirone de ferro* ('with iron cap'); Italy, mid/late 13th century (Wal CC, Wal O).

Baçinellum: [EI] *bascinet* helmet; Venice, Dalmatia and Serbia, from early 14th century (Pet DO).

Bacinet, bassinet: [Oc] *bascinet* with *capmal* (mail *aventail*); southern France, early 14th century (N&L, Noel); see also *bacinet* [SP].

Bacinet, bacineta: [SP] early form of *bascinet*, also of leather as *bacinets de cuero* and later worn with *cara* (visor) and *barbuda* (gorget, throat protection); Spain, early/mid-14th century (Hoff A2); see also *bacinet* [Oc].

Bacinum: [ML] *bascinet* helmet; Western Europe, late 13th–14th centuries (Gai EU).

Baculus: [Ml] wooden club; France and Anglo-Norman England, mid/late 11th century (Thorne).

Baculus: [EI] wooden club; Dalmatia, late 13th century (Pet DO).

Badelaire: [OF] type of short sword or dagger, possibly single edged or even curved; France, late 13th/early 14th centuries (Blair B, Gre).

Bail: [OF] iron-tipped stake or part of palisade; from Latin *baculum*; France, mid-12th century (Gre).

Balcanelle: [EI] blunted practice crossbow bolt; Dalmatia, 14th century (Pet DO).

Baldre: [OF] belt, *baldric* or part of saddle; France, mid-12th century (Gre).

Balesta à crocco: [EI] crossbow spanned by hook on belt; Italy, 13th century (Magli).

Balestas: [Oc] crossbows; also *balestas garnidas*; southern France, mid-14th century (Noel).

Balestre, baleste: [OF] siege-engine, probably a frame-mounted crossbow; from Latin *balista*; France, 12th century (Gre).

Balista, balistra: [EI] crossbow; Dalmatia, 14th century (Pet DO).

Balista à tour: [OF] large frame-mounted crossbow, perhaps spanned by a system of ratchets; also in naval warfare; Europe, 13th century (Brook NA).

Balistis: [ML] probably frame-mounted siege crossbow; also used in Mediterranean naval warfare; Europe, from late 10th century (Brook NA).

Ballestas: [SP] crossbows, small types used by horsemen; also *ballestas con estriberus* ('with loading stirrup'), *ballestas de dod pies* ('for two feet') and *ballestas de torno* (either frame-mounted or with loading winch); Spain, 13th–14th centuries (Hoff A2).

Ballista de corno: [EI] small crossbow with composite bow; used in naval warfare; Venice, mid-13th century (Brook NA).

Ballottis: [ML] cannon balls; northern Italy, mid-14th century (PLN).

Ban-beorg, ban-rift: [AS] possibly mail *chausses*; England, 10th–11th centuries (Kell).

Bandon: [OF] standard; from German *band*; France, late 11th century (Gre).

Banière: [OF] flag or pennon on a lance which is still used as a weapon; France, mid/late 12th century (Beat, Gre).

Barbe: [ME] pointed probably lower end or 'beard' of war-axe or *guisarme*; England, mid-14th century (AGG).

Barbel, barbeure: [OF] point or barb of an arrow; France, 12th century (Gre).

Barberia: [EI] large, expensive form of helmet; Genoa, early/mid-13th century (Conta).

Barbez: [ME] barbs of arrowhead; England, mid-14th century (AGG).

Barbière: [OF] form of neck protection, perhaps a raised rigid collar or stiffened mail collar worn instead of a mail *coif*; Flanders, early 14th century (Gans A).

Barbuda de ferre: [SP] large iron *gorget* worn with *bacineta* and *cara* (visor); Spain, mid-14th century (Hoff A2).

Barbuta, barbata: [EI] probably tall *bascinet*, sometimes with mail neck protection (*barbutas cum mallis*); Italy, Dalmatia and Serbia, 13th–mid-14th centuries (Pet DO, Scal AP, Wal CC); see also *barbuta* (Cz).

Barbuta: [Cz] form of deep *bascinet* helmet also popular in Italy; Bohemia, mid-14th century (Warn); see also *barbuta* [EI].

Barde: [OF] horse-armour or heavy *caparison*; possibly from Arabic *barda'ah* (saddle-cloth or pack-saddle); Crusader states, 13th century (Gre).

Barder: [OF] to cover a horse with armour; France, early 14th century (Gre).

Barres: [ME] stiffening bars on sword-belt; England, mid-14th century (AGG).

Bascuette: [ME] *bascinet* helmet, sometimes covered with decorative fabric; England, early 14th century (Blair REC).

Baselard: [ME] large dagger with triangular blade and 'H'-shaped hilt, perhaps of Swiss origin, ultimately from Basle; England, mid-14th century (Blair B); see also *baselard* [SP].

Baselard: [SP] large dagger, almost short sword; Spain, late 13th–14th centuries (Hoff A2); see also *baselard* [ME].

Basilarda: [EI] form of dagger; Italy, early 14th century (Boc HIM).

Bassinet: [OF] *bascinet*, light helmet with neck protection; France, late 12th century (Gre).

Bassinure: [OF] part of a helmet; France, mid-14th century (Gre).

Baston: [OF] baton or staff of office, or haft of lance; also *baston quare* ('four-sided'); France and Norman England, late 11th century (ASR, Chet, Poures, Gre).

Bastoncel, bastonet: [OF] staff or quarter-staff; France and Norman England, late 11th century (ASR, Gre).

Bastonier: [OF] man armed with a baton; France, early 14th century (Gre).

Batut: [SP] either mail *coif* or a small cap of mail (*batut de males de fer*); Aragón, early 13th century (Hoff A2).

Baucan, baucanissant: [OF] pennon, standard, *gonfanon*; Crusader states, late 13th century (Gre).

Bauderyk: [ME] *baldric* to carry sword; England, mid-14th century (AGG).

Baudrat: [Oc] possibly *baldric*, with *boucle* (buckle) and *notz* (knots); southern France, mid-13th century (N&L).

Baudres: [ML] pouches of hide for sling arms of *trebuchets*, etc; England, late 13th century (Free WB).

Baudrier: [OF] *baldric*, also strap to hold quiver for crossbow bolts; France, late 13th century (Conta).

Bavière: [OF] chin-strap, or bib-like piece of armour for throat; France, early/mid-14th century (Gre).

Beavor, bevor: [ME] chin or throat protection of plate, similar to *gorget*; England, from late 13th century (Bl).

Beckenel: [OG] *bascinet* helmet; Germany, late 13th–14th centuries (Gai EU).

Beffois, berfroi, boufoi: [OF] mobile siege-tower; from German *bergvrid*; France, mid-12th–early 13th centuries (RT, Eli).

Beinlinge: [OG] mail *chausses*; Germany, 14th century (Scal DS).

Beinshienen: [OG] *greaves* of iron or hardened leather; Germany, 14th century (Scal DS).

Belettes: [OF] unclear siege device of wood, literally 'weasels'; France, 13th century (Conta).

Belt: [ME] sword-belt having stiffening barres; England, early/mid-14th century (AGG, Tagl).

Bendes: [OF] probably bands of metal making the frame of a segmented helmet; France, mid/late 12th century (Beat).

Ber: [OF] point of a dart or javelin; France, 13th century (Gre).

Berceret: [OF] quiver; France, late 12th century (Gre).

Bercerie: [OF] shooting exercise with the bow; also a quiver; France, 13th century (Gre).

Berefrai: [ME] mobile siege-tower of wood; England and Scotland, early 14th century (Tur TD).

Berruier, barruier: [OF] type of helmet with chin-strap, or neck or lower face protection; France, late 12th century (Gre).

Besague: [OF] war-axe with spike at the back; from Latin *bisacuta*; France, mid-12th century (Gre).

Biail: [Ir] head of large war-axe, probably with a thrusting point; Gaelic Ireland, early 13th century (Harb 2).

Bibaldi, bideaux: [OF] perhaps daggers or short swords used by light infantry (*Almogavares*) of Aragón and Navarre; Spain and France, early 14th century (Hoff A2).

Bible: [OF] stone-throwing war-engine in the form of a 'horn'; from Latin *biblia*; France, late 13th century (Gre).

Biffe: [OF] type of very powerful but less accurate *trebuchet*, possibly with adjustable counterweight; France, late 13th–14th centuries (Conta, Hoff A2).

Bigua: [ML] base or frame of *trebuchet*; southern France, late 13th century (Mot AP).

Bijlen: [FD] probably war-axes; Flanders, late 13th century (Verb DG).

Bil: [AS] probably long-bladed axe; translated into Latin as scythe (*falcastrum*); England, 10th–11th centuries (Kell).

Bill: [ME] pickaxe; northern England, early/mid-14th century (Tagl).

Bit, bitte, bytte: [ME] blade of axe or *guisarme*; some have *barbe* ('beard'); England, mid-14th century (AGG).

Blason: [OF] shield or armorial device on shield; France, late 12th century (Gre).

Blasoun: [ME] shield having heraldic device, or the device itself; England, mid-14th century (AGG).

Bloca: [SP] boss of a shield; Spain, 12th–13th centuries (Hoff A2, Morris MS).

Boccóit: [Ir] shield bosses; Gaelic Ireland, 14th century (Harb 1).

Boce, boche: [OF] boss of a shield; France, mid-12th century (Gre).

Bocle, bocler, boucle: [OF] shield boss; France and Norman England, late 11th–late 12th centuries (ASR, TOF, Beat, Gre).

Boclere: [OF] shield having a boss; also as *escu bouclier*; France, 12th century (Gre).

Boga: [AS] bow; England, 10th–11th centuries (Kell).

Boga, bodha: [Ir] bow; Gaelic Ireland, mid-13th–14th centuries (Harb 2).

Bogan-streng: [AS] bowstring; England, 10th–11th centuries (Kell).

Bohorder: [OF] to fight with a lance or joust; from German *buhurt*; France, late 12th century (Gre).

Bohort, boort: [OF] blunted lance without a blade for friendly joust; France, late 12th century (Gre).

Boitas ferri: [ML] capstan to load *trebuchet*; southern France, late 13th century (Mot AP).

Bole: [OF] mace; France, mid-13th century (Gre).

Boljon, boldon, bolzon: [OF] large arrow or iron bar; France, 12th century (Gre).

Bolt: [ME] arrow or crossbow bolt; northern England, early/mid-14th century (Tagl).

Bombarde: [OF] siege-engine or early form of cannon; from Latin *bombus*, France, early 14th century (Gre).

Bombarde: [EI] early cannon in Florence; Italy, early/mid-14th century (B&G).

Bombardella camerata: [EI] early form of breech-loading cannon with *camerata* (powder-chamber) at base of barrel; Italy, 14th century (Gaibi).

Bombardis: [ML] probably *bombard* (cannon); northern Italy, mid-14th century (PLN).

Bord: [AS] shield; England, 10th–11th centuries (Kell).

Bordó, bordón: [Cn] long-hilted stabbing sword; Catalonia, late 13th century (Hoff A2).

Bordon, berdona: [EI] thrusting dagger; Dalmatia, early–late 14th century (Pet DO).

Bossons: [Oc] ram used in siege warfare; southern France, 13th century (Conta).

Botounz: [ME] studs, rivets or nails in the haft of an axe, probably to hold the blade; England, mid-14th century (AGG).

Boucle: [OF] shield boss; south-west France, mid-12th century (RT).

Bouertor: [ME] cloth *caparison* for horse that was probably only decorative; England, mid-14th century (AGG).

Bowes: [ME] bows; England, late 13th–mid-14th centuries (A Hav, Tagl).

Bozon: [OF] crossbow bolt; north-east France, late 12th century (TOF).

Bracamartes: [SP] single-edged *falchion* or sword used by lightly-equipped troops; Spain, 13th century (Hoff A2).

Brace: [ME] arm defences of plate, including *rerebrace* and *vambrace*; England, from mid-14th century (AGG).

Braçeiraria, braciarum, bracera, bracalium: [EI] probably *vambraces* to protect lower arm; Dalmatia, early/mid-14th century (Pet DO).

Brachia: [ML] sling-arm of *trebuchet*; southern France, late 13th century (Mot AP).

Bracuel, bracelet: [OF] armour for the arm; France, mid/late 12th century (Gre).

Brafoneras: [SP] term originally for arm defences, later used for leg-armour, mail *chausses* and *poleyns*; Spain, late 13th century (Hoff A2).

Braguers: [Oc] possibly sword-belt; southern France, early 13th century (N&L).

Braie: [OF] baggy trousers, sometimes cross-gartered; France, 12th century (Gre).

Bran, branc, brant, branz: [OF] blade, usually of sword; from German *brand*; France and Norman England, late 11th–late 12th centuries (RT, TOF, Beat).

Braň, brňe: [Cz] *hauberk*; from Old German *brunnia*; Bohemia (Warn).

Bran: [Oc] blade of sword; southern France, late 12th–early 14th centuries (N&L).

Brand, brande, brond, bront: [ME] sword-blade; England, early/mid-14th century (Tagl, Will PG, AGG).

Brand: [AS] sword or sword-blade; England, 10th–11th centuries (Kell); see also *brand* [ME].

Braquemart: [OF] short, broad, double-edged sword; France, early 14th century (Gre).

Braquet: [OF] short sword; France, 14th century (Gre).

Bras: [OF] arm, unit of length, armlet or *brassard* (small piece of armour for the arm); France, late 11th century (Gre).

Brazales, braçals: [SP] form of arm protection, possibly extended cuffs of *gauntlets* or *vambraces* of hardened leather imported from Italy; Spain and Catalonia, late 13th–mid-14th centuries (Hoff A2).

Bretasche, bretise: [ME] parapet, palisade or hurdle; England, early 13th–mid-14th centuries (Wal AW, Tagl).

Bricoles: [OF] unclear form of siege-engines; France, 14th century (Conta).

Brida: [Oc] type of *trebuchet* or *mangonel*; southern France, mid-14th century (Noel).

Brigolo, bricola: [SP] light and mobile counterweight *mangonel* mounted on a cart; Spain, 13th century (Hoff A2).

Brinie: [ME] mail *hauberk*; England, late 13th century (A Have).

Broc, broche: [OF] pointed object, pointed weapon; from Latin *brocchum*; France, 12th century (Gre).

Brogne, broigne, broine, bronie, brugne: [OF] *hauberk*, perhaps originally of scales on fabric or leather base, constructed 'in lines'; later refers to ordinary mail *hauberk*; also 'doubled' (*broigne doblière*); from German *brunja*; France and Norman England, late 11th–late 12th centuries (ASR, Chet, Chev, Knud, Gre).

Broń: [Pl] mail or less likely scale *hauberk*; from Old German *brunnja*; Poland (Warn).

Broquel: [SP] small round shield, sometimes with metal reinforcing plates added; Aragón, early 14th century (Hoff A2).

Brord: [AS] point of arrow or javelin; England, 10th–11th centuries.

Brune, brunie: [OG] *hauberk* of mail or perhaps earlier of scales of horn; Germany, 12th–14th centuries (Knud).

Brunia: [ML] mail or, less likely, scale *hauberk*; Western Europe, 8th–12th centuries (Nor, Ver).

Bruny, bryne: [ME] mail *hauberk*, may be worn with pieces of plate armour; England, mid-14th century (AGG).

Brustblech: [OG] breastplate or *coat-of-plates*; Germany, from mid-14th century (Warn).

Bruzblach: [Pl] breastplate or *coat-of-plates*; from German *brustblech*; Poland, 14th century (Warn).

Brynja: [ON] general term for mail *hauberk*; also protective coat of skin or felt; Scandinavia, 9th–11th centuries (Knud).

Brynju: [ON] armour, probably mail *hauberk*; Scandinavia, late 13th century.

Buccelarius, buchulir: [EI] small shield of common soldier; Dalmatia, mid-14th century (Pet DO).

Burde, bord: [ME] shield; northern England, early/mid-14th century (Tagl).

Burre: [OF] unspecified war-engine; France, late 13th century (Gre).

Bẏge: [AS] top of helmet; England, 10th–11th centuries (Kell).

Byrne: [AS] probably mail *hauberk*; translated into Latin as *lorica*; England, 10th–11th centuries (Kell).

Byrnie: [OF] mail *hauberk*; from German *brunja*; France and Norman England, late 11th century (ASR).

Cadrelle: [ML] crossbow bolts, in naval warfare; Marseilles, 13th century (Brook NA).

Cainture: [OF] sword-belt, also holding archery equipment of 'infidel'; France, late 12th century (Chet).

Cairels: [Oc] crossbow bolts; southern France, early 13th century (N&L).

Caithréin enmáille: [Ir] individual links of mail; Gaelic Ireland, mid-14th century (Harb 1).

Calabre, chalabre: [OF] siege-engine; also folding doors; France, late 12th century (Gre).

Calabres: [Oc] probably man-powered mangonel like French *chaable*; southern France, 13th century (Conta).

Calçes: [Sp] possibly mail *chausses* imported from Italy; Catalonia, mid-14th century (Hoff A2).

Calicas ferreis: [ML] probably *vambraces* or *rerebraces* for arms, or leg protections worn instead of *gamberuolis*; Italy, early/mid-13th century (Wal O).

Caligas: [ML] literally boots, possibly hardened leather *greaves* or padded leggings for cavalry; Tuscany, early 14th century (Giu OM).

Camail: [OF] mail hanging from rim of helmet; also mail *coif*; France, late 13th century (Gre).

Camb: [AS] top, crest or 'comb' of helmet; England, 10th–11th centuries (Kell).

Cancre, chancre: [OF] literally 'crab', descriptive term for early crossbow; France, 11th century (Den).

Candelabre: [OF] part of *elme* (helmet), made of 'fine gold', possibly descriptive term for riveted summit of helmet or of face-mask visor above the *maistre*; helmet also has *flanboiant* and *nasials*; France, late 12th/early 13th centuries (Eli, Chev).

Canivet, cnivet: [OF] small knife; from Old English *knif*; France and Norman England, late 12th century (Gre).

Cannunibus: [ML] cannon or *bombard*; northern Italy, mid-14th century (PLN).

Canon: [OF] piece of artillery, early cannon; from Italian *canone*; France, early/mid-14th century

(Gre).

Capacete: [SP] tall helmet 'in the manner of the Turks', later developed into *cabacete*; Spain, early 14th century (Hoff A2).

Çapatos: [SP] probably mail *sabatons* (foot-armour) from Italy; Catalonia, mid-14th century (Hoff A2).

Capel: [Oc] probably helmet or mail *aventail*, or mail *coif* laced on; southern France, early 14th century (N&L).

Capeline: [OF] mail *coif* or head armour; from Italian *cappelina*; France, mid-14th century (Gre).

Capellina de ferro, capiello de fierra, capillo de ferro: [SP] *war-hat* (*chapel-de-fer*) with or without large brim; also used by Muslims and may be covered with decorative cloth; Spain, 13th–14th centuries (Hoff A2).

Capello de ferro: [ML] *war-hat* (*chapel-de-fer*); Italy, late 13th century (Wal CC).

Capellum de acciario: [ML] literally 'steel cap', perhaps *cervelière* of cavalry; Tuscany, early 14th century (Giu OM).

Capellum de ferro: [ML] general term for small helmet, specifically *chapel-de-fer* (*war-hat*) of sailors; south-west France, early 13th century (Brook NA).

Capirone de ferro: [ML] probably mail *aventail* of *bacilletum* (helmet); Italy, early 13th century (Wal CC).

Čapka železna: [Cz] scale-covered cap or possibly *war-hat* (*chapel-de-fer*); Bohemia, 14th century (Warn).

Capmal: [Oc] *aventail* of *bascinet*; southern France, early 14th century (N&L).

Capmall: [Cn] mail *aventail* or *coif*; Catalonia, late 13th–14th centuries (Hoff A2).

Cappellino, capellus, cappelus de ferro: [EI] *war-hat* (*chapel-de-fer*); Italy and Dalmatia, early/mid-14th century (Conta).

Capusbon, capucha, caperuza: [SP] separate mail *coif* or mail *aventail*; Spain, late 13th–14th centuries (Hoff A2).

Capyllos: [SP] mail *coif*; Spain, 12th century (Morris MS).

Cara, careta: [SP] movable visor, usually on a *bascinet* helmet; Spain, mid-14th century (Hoff A2).

Carcais: [OF] probably quiver, of 'infidel'; France, late 12th century (Chet).

Carcasso: [EI] quiver, or bowcase for composite bow; Dalmatia, 14th century (Pet DO).

Carreaus: [OF] large arrows or crossbow bolts, probably from siege-bow, for example *grandismes carreaus* shot by Byzantines at Crusaders; Constantinople, early 13th century (R de C).

Carrel: [OF] crossbow bolt, probably with head of square sections, same as *quadrel*; France and Norman England, late 11th–mid-12th centuries (ASR, RT, Gre).

Carroccia: [EI] battle-cart used to hold banners, as well as the *martinella* (signal bell), priests and wounded men; Italy, 11th–14th centuries (Ver).

Casagan, casigan, gasigan, gasygan: [ML] fabric-covered and padded mail *hauberk*; from Arab-Persian *kazāghand*; mostly in Crusader states and Crusader Constantinople, 12th–13th centuries (Pra, MCK).

Casquete: [SP] small helmet, perhaps a *cervellière*; Spain, 13th century (Hoff A2).

Cassis: [ML] normal term for helmet; Western Europe, 11th–12th centuries (Gai EU); also large iron helmet, perhaps early form of *great helm*; England (Assize of Arms of 1181), late 12th century (Bee W).

Cassot: [SP] leather cap, perhaps with a metal frame, worn by light infantry (*Almogavars*); Aragón, 13th century (Conta).

Cathbharr: [Ir] helmet, probably segmented; Gaelic Ireland, 10th–12th centuries (Harb 1).

Cathcrois: [Ir] probably sword-belt; Gaelic Ireland, mid-14th century (Harb 1).

Cathéidedh: [Ir] general term for armour; Gaelic Ireland, mid-14th century (Harb 1).

Cauches de maille: [OF] mail *chausses*; Flanders, early 14th century (Gans A).

Cauchons [OF]: unclear form of leg protection, perhaps padded *cuisses*, used by those lacking mail *cauches*; Flanders, early 14th century (Gans A).

Causes, cauces: [OF] armoured *chausses*; also as *causes de fer* or *cauces de fer*, laced to or 'folded around' legs; France and Norman England, mid-12th–early 13th centuries (Beat, Eli, Chet).

Causone: [FD] *chausses*, probably of mail; Netherlands, late 13th century (Labou).

Celebrerium: [EI] probably *cervellière* (close-fitting helmet); Dalmatia, early 14th century (Pet DO).

Cendatz: [Oc] perhaps lance-pennon of fine cloth; southern France, late 12th century (N&L).

Cercle: [OF] part of *iaume* or *elme* (helmet), perhaps top ring or rim of flat-topped helmet, or lower rim of conical helmet; north-eastern France, late 12th century (TOF).

Cervelier, cervelière, cervellière: [OF] close-fitting helmet, originally perhaps only skull part of conical *elme* which also has *uellière* (eye-slits); France and Angevin southern Italy, late 12th–late 13th centuries (Eli, Conta, Gai EU, Gre).

Cervellera, servellera: [SP] small, close-fitting *cervellière* helmet, often worn under *almofar* (*coif*); Spain, 13th–14th centuries (Hoff A2).

Cervelleriam: [ML] small, close-fitting helmet; southern France, late 13th century (Noel).

Cervelliera: [EI] small, close-fitting *cervellière* helmet; Italy, 13th–14th centuries (Scal AP, B&C).

Cervellière: [OF] small, close-fitting helmet, sometimes worn beneath mail *coif*; originally sometimes also called *bascinet*; Western Europe, 13th–early 14th centuries (Bl); see also *cervellière* [Oc].

Cervellière: [Oc] small, close-fitting helmet; southern France, early/mid-14th century (Noel); see also *cervellière* [OF].

Cestiren: [FD] see *restiren*.

Chaable, cheable, chadable: [OF] wooden stone-throwing siege-engine, probably early form of man-powered *mangonel*; from Latin *catabela*; France and Norman England, late 11th–13th centuries (ASR, Conta, Gre).

Chapel-de-fer: [OF] literally 'iron hat', wide-brimmed helmet also called a 'war-hat'; France and Norman England, early 13th–14th centuries (Conta, Gai EU, Vill CC).

Chapelier: [OF] mail *coif*; France and Norman England, late 11th century (ASR).

Charcloie: [OF] mobile covered wooden shed to protect sappers or operators of a ram; south-western France, mid-12th century (RT).

Chat, chatte: [OF] mobile siege device in form of a shed; possibly from Latin *capsum* ('box'); France, 13th century (Conta, Gre).

Chateaux de bois: [OF] wooden siege-towers; France, 13th century (Conta).

Chats chateaux: [OF] tall form of *chat*, or towers to defend *chat* below; France, 13th century (Conta).

Chauces gambaisiees: [OF] padded or quilted *chausses*, leg armour used in foot combat; France, late 12th century (RR).

Chenel: [OF] pipe of unspecified type of weapon, perhaps early cannon; France, early/mid-14th century (Gre).

Chevece: [OF] part of a helmet, probably covering top of head; from Latin *capitia*; France, mid-12th century (Gre).

Chevillon: [OF] type of baton; France, mid-13th century (Gre).

Chledd, gledd: [EW] sword; Wales, mid/late 14th century (Will BT, Will IW).

Cibole: [OF] head of a mace; France, 13th century (Gre).

Cief: [OF] possibly a mail *coif*, having a *ventalle* across chin; France, late 12th–13th centuries (Chev).

Cinnbeirt: [Ir] unclear form of helmet, perhaps similar to *bascinet*; Gaelic Ireland, 13th–14th centuries (Harb 1).

Cirotesce: [Sp] *gauntlets*, probably partly iron; Aragón, early 14th century (Hoff A2).

Claux: [OF] nails holding blade to lance haft; France, late 12th century (Chet).

Clava: [EI] mace or club; Dalmatia, 14th century (Pet DO).

Clavain, clavière: [OF] possibly *gorget* of scales, perhaps fastened to helmet, or chest and neck protections, also described as *adoube* or *entier*; or worn under a *hauberk* of an 'infidel', perhaps reflecting Islamic lamellar *cuirass*; perhaps early form of *cuirie* (body-armour or *cuirass*); France, late 12th century (Chet, Gre).

Clavel, clavele: [OF] individual ring or link of mail; from Latin *clavellum*; France, late 12th century (Gre).

Clavel: [Oc] rivet of mail *hauberk*; southern France, late 12th century (N&L).

Claves: [ML] trigger or release of *trebuchet*; southern France, late 13th century (Mot AP).

Cleteu: [EW] sword or sword-blade; Wales, 11th–12th centuries (Will BT).

Clev: [EW] sword or sword-blow; Wales, 9th–11th centuries (Will IW).

Clice: [OF] palisade; south-west France, mid-12th century (RT).

Clipeum: [ML] shield, distinct from *tabolatum*, probably of cavalry; Italy, late 13th century (Wal CC).

Clobe, clubbe, klub, klob: [ME] wooden cudgel; also as *iryn clobe* (mace); England, late 13th–mid-14th centuries (A Hav, Tagl, Will PG).

Cloche: [OF] descriptive term for a mace; France, 12th century (Gre).

Clogat: [Ir] conical helmet with chin-strap, perhaps also brimmed as *war-hat* (*chapel-de-fer*); Gaelic Ireland, mid-14th century (Harb 1).

Cloiden, cloidhem: [Ir] sword; Gaelic Ireland, late 13th–mid-14th centuries (Harb 1).

Clypeus: [ML] large shield of a horseman; also Italian infantry in ranks; England (Assize of Arms of 1181) and Italy, late 12th century (Bee W, Oman AW).

Cniff, cnyff: [FD] large knife, example with *heft* (hilt) of ivory; Netherlands, late 13th century (Labou).

Cnilinghe, cnilinge: [FD] *poleyns* to protect knees with *wapen* (plates) added; Netherlands, late 13th century (Labou).

Cofa punta: [Oc] perhaps quilted *coif* or small helmet; southern France, late 13th century (Noel).

Cofia de armar: [SP] padded *arming cap*; Spain, 13th–14th centuries (Hoff A2).

Cofiniaus d'arain: [OF] literally 'tin containers' for *fu griois* (Greek Fire); France, late 12th century (Chet).

Coife turcoise: [OF] possibly cloth-covered or padded *coif* for an 'infidel'; France, mid/late 12th century (Beat).

Coifete: [OF] unclear form of small mail *coif* worn under a helmet; France, late 12th/early 13th centuries (Gre).

Coiffe, coife: [OF] mail coif, part of a *hauberk*; France, late 12th/early 13th centuries (Chet, Eli); see also *coiffe* [OF].

Coiffe: [OF] later form of separate mail *coif*, worn with mail *haubregon*; Flanders, early 14th century (Gans A).

Coilear: [Ir] probably mail collar or *tippet*; Gaelic Ireland, late 13th/early 14th centuries (Harb 1).

Coine, coinie, cuinie, cuinee: [OF] war-axe; Norman England, mid-12th century (Poures).

Cointise: [OF] *banderoles* or horseman's decorations; France, late 13th century (Gre).

Coissa: [Oc] possibly *cuisses* or *chausses*; southern France, late 12th century (N&L).

Coivre: [OF] quiver of an 'infidel' horse-archer; France, late 12th century (Chet).

Colafre: [SP] unclear form of siege machine; probably same as French *calabre*; Spain, 13th–14th centuries (Hoff A2).

Colaria de malia: [EI] mail collar or *tippet*; Dalmatia, late 13th century (Pet DO).

Colière: [OF] part of horse-harness; France, late 12th century (Gre); see also *colière* [FD].

Colière: [FD] perhaps stiffened collar or mail *tippet*; Holland, mid-14th century (V Mie); see also *colière* [OF].

Collare, collarium: [EI] gorget, *coif* or *aventail* of mail; Dalmatia, late 13th/early 14th centuries (Pet DO).

Coltel: [OF] small knife; France, late 12th century (Gre).

Coltell, coutell: [SP] large dagger or small sword; Spain, 13th century (Hoff A2).

Coltello: [EI] short sword, same as *corta spada*, used by Muslim ex-Sicilians of Lucera; Italy, early/mid-13th century (Pieri SL).

Conniscances: [OF] heraldic motifs; France, late 12th/early 13th centuries (Eli).

Copita: [ML] leather *chanfron*; Western Europe, late 13th century (Oak).

Coracia: [EI] *cuirass* for upper part of body, perhaps scale-lined or as a *coat-of-plates*, apparently full-length plus short sleeves; also as *unius par de coraciis* ('a pair of cuirasses') or *coracie furnite* (*cuirass* in two apparent parts); Dalmatia, early/mid-14th century (Pet DO).

Coracine: [EI] short sleeveless *coracia*, breastplate or *coat-of-plates*; Dalmatia, early/mid-14th century (Pet DO).

Coraçones: [SP] perhaps mail *hauberk* or semi-rigid *cuirass* worn beneath mail; Spain, mid-12th century (Hoff A2).

Coraziniis: [ML] probably *coat-of-plates* worn instead of *panzeria et harneriis* or *perpunto grosso*; Italy, mid/late 13th century (Wal O).

Corazza: [EI] probably semi-rigid armour with plates or scales fastened inside a leather or cloth base, ie *coat-of-plates*; also called *paio di corazze* ('pair of *cuirasses*'); Italy, late 13th–14th centuries (B&C, Scal AP).

Corda: [EI] probably single-edged dagger, perhaps slightly curved; perhaps from Turkish and Farsi *kārd*; Italy, 14th century.

Coria: [ML] leather sling or loop for *trebuchet*; southern France, late 13th century (Mot AP).

Corroies: [OF] straps inside an infantry shield, probably *enarmes*; France, late 12th century (RR).

Corta spada: [EI] short sword, same as *coltello*, used by Muslim ex-Sicilians of Lucera; Italy, early/mid-13th century (Pieri SL).

Costal: [Oc] knife or dagger, like *coutelas*; southern France, early 13th century (N&L).

Cote armeoire: [OF] armour of 'infidels', probably fabric-covered mail *hauberk* like a *jaseran*; France, mid/late 12th century (Beat).

Cote, cotte, cotel: [OF] coat or tunic, as *cote de maillier* or *cotte de mailles* (mail *hauberk*); Flanders and France (RR, Gui PO).

Cotel: [OF] type of sword used by 'infidels' as *grant cotel d'acier*, possibly single-edged or curved; France, late 12th century (Chet); see also *cotel* [Oc].

Cotel: [Oc] knife or dagger; southern France, mid-14th century (Noel); see also *cotel* [OF].

Cotiele: [OF] mail *hauberk*; France, mid/late 12th century (Beat).

Cotte de fer: [OF] probably same as *haubergeon* or *pansière*, perhaps of scales; France, 13th century (Gai EU).

Cotte gamboisee: [OF] padded or quilted *gambeson*; France, late 13th century (Conta).

Cotún: [Ir] large quilted *aketon* (soft armour) from throat to knees, worn under *luirech* (mail *hauberk*); Gaelic Ireland, mid-14th century (Harb 1).

Covertor: [ME] cloth *caparison* for horse that was probably only decorative; England, mid-14th century (AGG).

Couillarts: [OF] unclear form of siege-engine; France, early 14th century (Conta).

Cousen: [FD] *cuisses* of *iseren* ('iron'), probably splinted or of mail; Netherlands, late 13th century (Labou).

Coustiaus: [OF] small swords or large daggers, associated with *misericordes*; France, early 13th century

Couteau: [OF] dagger used in addition to or instead of sword; also associated with *misericorde*; France, early 13th century

Couteau d'armes: [OF] short sword or dagger, perhaps like Arabic khanjar or Persian *nimjah*, required by Rule of the Temple; Crusader states, mid-12th century (Conta).

Coutel, coutiaus: [OF] knife or dagger; also as *coutels cordouan* of 'infidels'; France, mid/late 12th century (RR, TOF, Beat, Chet).

Coutelace: [OF] large dagger or short sword; France, mid-14th century (Gre).

Couter, cowter: [ME] metal disc or roundel to protect the elbow, later domed; England, from late 13th century (Bl, AGG).

Couverte, couverture: [OF] saddle-cloth or decorative *caparison*; clearly as horse-armour of German Crusaders, also as *couvertures d'armes*; France, mid-12th–early 13th centuries (Beat, R de C, De J).

Covertas equi: [ML] *caparison* or horse-armour; Tuscany, early 14th century (Giu OM).

Coverture: [FD] *caparison* or padded *bard*, normally as a 'pair' but sometimes only front part mentioned; also as *paer faus coverture* (purely decorative *caparison*), or *iseren coverture* (probably mail *bard* for horse); Netherlands, late 13th century (Labou).

Cráisech, craoiseach: [Ir] spear, distinct from *ga* javelin; Gaelic Ireland, late 13th–mid-14th centuries (Harb 1).

Crestute: [EI] unclear perhaps crested helmet; Tuscany, 13th–14th centuries (Scal AP).

Crevice: [OF] possibly laminated or scale armour; from Old German *krebiz*; France, early 13th century (Gre).

Crios, cris: [Ir] sword-belt; Gaelic Ireland, mid-14th century (Harb 1).

Croc: [OF] hook, probably from a belt, to load a crossbow; from Scandinavian *krotr*; France, late 12th century (Gre).

Croix: [OF] part of a helmet, may be gilded; possibly the frame of a segmented helmet; France, late 12th century (Chet).

Cubert de fer: [Oc] unclear form of armour, probably a *cuirass*, worn with a *bascinet* by sergeants; southern France, mid-14th century (Noel).

Cuero bollido: [SP] hardened leather (*cuir-bouilli*) used in making armour; Spain, 13th–14th centuries (Hoff A2).

Cuevre, cuivre, coivre, queuvre, quivre: [OF] quiver; France, early 12th century (Gre).

Cuir: [OF] leather covering of a wooden shield; France and Norman England, late 11th century (ASR).

Cuirace, cuirie: [ME] early form of semi-rigid body armour without sleeves, only covering chest and abdomen, perhaps of *cuir-bouilli* (hardened leather); same as *quiret*; England, late 12th century (Bl, Oak).

Cuirasses: [OF] *coat-of-plates* of Navarrese and others; also in singular as *cuirasse*; France, mid-13th century (Hoff A2, Gre).

Cuirie: [OF] *cuirass*, sometimes having iron elements as *largement ferree*; France, early/mid-13th century (Kelly); also used with *haubergeon* and *bascinet* plus *aventail* by poorly-equipped men; Liège, early 14th century (Gai EU).

Cuiriee: [OF] unspecified leather garment, perhaps protective, worn under *hauberk*; France, mid-12th century (Gre).

Cuirien: [OF] chin-strap of helmet; France, early 12th century (Gre).

Cuissel: [OF] thigh armour, probably of iron or hardened leather; France, early 14th century (Gre).

Cuish, cuisse: [ME] padded or quilted armour for the thighs and knees; England, mid-13th–14th centuries (Oak, Bl).

Cuja: [SP] iron or leather pouch on right hip to support butt of lance when not in use; Spain, 13th–14th centuries (Hoff A2).

Cultello: [ML] large dagger or small sword; Italy, mid/late 13th century (Wal O).

Cultellum de ferro: [ML] sword or large dagger of cavalry or crossbowmen; Italy, late 13th century (Wal CC).

Curacie: [OF] body armour, *cuirass* in naval warfare; Marseilles, 13th century (Brook NA).

Curuéna de ballesta: [SP] early form of mace; Spain, 11th–13th centuries (GGA).

Custellerius, custellerium, custelo custelliero, cultellinus, cultellus parvus, cortellinus: [EI] dagger or short sword; also as *cultellus feritorius*; Italy and Dalmatia, 14th century (Pet DO).

Cutellos: [ML] probably small sword or large dagger; Europe, specifically England (Assize of Arms of 1252), mid-13th century (Borg, Pai TR).

Cuyrasses, *cuyraçes*: [Cn] *coat-of-plates* or scale-lined jerkin, metal elements sometimes riveted to buckskin; Catalonia, mid-13th–14th centuries (Hoff A2).

Cuyrassies: [SP] *coat-of-plates* or *cuirass*; Aragón, early 14th century (Hoff A2).

Czyn: [Pl] general term for armour; Poland (Warn).

Dagon, *dague*: [OF] large dagger; from Provençal *daga*; France, 13th century (Gre).

Darda: [EI] javelin; Dalmatia, 14th century (Pet DO).

Dardel: [OF] small javelin; France, mid-12th century (Gre).

Dardos: [ML] javelins, naval warfare; Marseilles, 13th century (Brook NA).

Darod: [AS] javelin; England, 10th–11th centuries (Kell, Swant).

Dart, *dar*: [OF] javelin; from Latin *dardum*; France and Norman England, late 11th–late 12th centuries (ASR, Chet, Poures, Gre).

Dart, *dardo*: [SP] javelin used by infantry, sometimes barbed; Spain, 13th–14th centuries (Hoff A2).

Dart, *darte*: [ME] javelin, generally for hunting; England, mid-14th century (Will PG).

Darz: [OF] javelins, probably of Venetians; Italy, early 13th century (Vill CC).

Deka: [Cz and Pl] dagger; Bohemia and Poland, 13th–14th centuries (Warn).

Đel: [AS] shield; England, 10th–11th centuries (Kell).

Delibra: [SP] unclear form of siege-engine; Spain, 13th–14th centuries (Hoff A2).

Derrivaron torres: [SP] probably mobile siege-towers; Spain, 13th–14th centuries (Hoff A2).

Destral: [OF] large axe or hatchet; France, mid-14th century (Gre).

Deueniss ax: [ME] 'Danish axe', large form of war-axe, probably rather old-fashioned; England, late 13th century (RG).

Điox: [AS] axe, heavy staff weapon, or slashing spear; England, 10th–11th centuries (Swant).

Doitie: [OF] arrow; France, end 12th century (Gre).

Donerscutte: [OG] artilleryman, literally 'thunder shooter'; Austria and Germany, early/mid-14th century (Roth).

Doublière, *doblee*: [OF] 'doubled', referring to *hauberk* possibly with two layers of mail; also to *coife doublière* and *broigne doblière*; also a *roiele* shield with three layers of leather (*de III cuirs doblee*); France, late 12th–13th centuries (Chet, Eli, Chev).

Drurye: [ME] love-token worn on or over armour; England, mid-14th century (AGG).

Dunrebussen: [OG] probably cannon; Germany, mid-14th century (Roth, Conta).

Eber-helm: [AS] probably *spangenhelm* (segmented helmet); England, from 9th century (Kell).

Ecg: [AS] edge of sword-blade; England, 10th–11th centuries (Kell).

Ecu: [EI] cavalry shield like French *escu*; Tuscany, mid-13th century (Conta).

Egisarmes: [OF] *guisarmes* of English, supposedly used at the Battle of at Hastings; France and Norman England, 11th–12th centuries (Wace, Kell).

Elm, *elme*: [Oc] helme laced on; also painted (*elme de color*); southern France, late 12th–early 14th centuries (N&L).

Elme: [OF] helmet worn over *coif*; also as *elme agu* ('pointed helmet'), or probably early *great helm* having *uellière* (eye-slits), or *elme d'acier poitevin cler* (probably one-piece steel helmet from Poitou); France, mid/late 12th century (Beat, Eli).

Elmo ferrei: [ML] helmet worn with *gorgiera* instead of *bacinetto*; Italy, mid/late 13th century (Wal O).

Empeneure: [OF] part of the arrow where the flights are fastened; France, late 13th century (Gre).

Empenon: [OF] fletched end of arrow; France, 12th century (Gre).

Enarmes, *enarme*, *enarmeure*: [OF] holding-straps inside a shield; France, mid-12th–early 13th centuries (Chet, Chev, Gre).

Engaigne, *engien*, *engin*, *enging*: [OF] siege-machine usually shooting projectiles of various kinds;

France and Norman England, mid-12th–early 13th centuries (Eli, RT, Gre).

Enheldeure: [OF] guard of sword or dagger; France, late 12th century (Gre).

Ennach: [Ir] long dagger with wooden hilt; Gaelic Ireland, mid-14th century (Harb 1).

Ense: [ML] sword; Italy, mid/late 13th century (Wal O).

Enseigne, ensegne: [OF] pennon on a lance or the lance itself with a pennon; France, from 10th century (RT, Chet, Chev, Gre).

Ensem: [ML] probably sword of militia; southern France, mid-14th century (Noel).

Ensenba: [Oc] flag or pennon; southern France, late 12th century (N&L).

Ensis: [EI] sword, probably small; Dalmatia, 14th century (Pet DO).

Entraiture: [OF] blade of sword; France, 12th century (Gre).

Entrecor: [OF] possibly sword-knot or strap to be put around wrist, or hilt of sword; France and Norman England, mid/late 12th century (TOF, Gre).

Entremain: [OF] part of an armour, possibly covering trunk of body; France, late 13th century (Gre).

Entreseigne, entreseignie: [OF] ensign or banner, or armorial *blason*; France, late 12th century (Gre).

Epaulière: [OF] light armour for shoulders, probably of mail or hardened leather, used by squires or pages with *cervellière* and iron *gorgière*; Angevin southern Italy, late 13th century (Conta).

Equis ferro tectis: [ML] descriptive term for *bard* (mail horse-armour); Flanders and Brabant, early 13th century (Gai EU).

Esbaldrei, esbaldre: [OF] *baldric* or belt; France, 13th century (Gre).

Escieles: [OF] scaling ladders; France, mid/late 12th century (Beat).

Escu, escut, escuz: [OF] shield, usually of large kite-shaped type, used by cavalry and by specialised infantry such as sappers; France and Norman England, late 11th–early 13th centuries (R de C, A&N, RR, Chet, Eli, Gre).

Escu de quartier: [OF] 'quartered shield', perhaps with cross-shaped metal reinforcing bands; France, mid/late 12th century (Beat).

Escucel: [OF] small shield supposedly one-quarter size of *escu*; France, 12th century (Gre).

Escut: [Oc] shield; southern France, late 12th–early 14th centuries (Noel, N&L).

Escut, escudos: [SP] cavalry shields; Spain, mid-12th–14th centuries (Hend MT, Hoff A2, Morris MS).

Eslingue: [OF] sling; from German *slinga*; France, end 13th century (Gre).

Espaa, espada: [SP] general term for sword, including *espadas ginetas* or *espadas moriscas* for light cavalry *jineta* tactics; Castile, 11th–early 14th centuries (Morris MS).

Espafut, pafut: [OF] large sword, but probably not two-handed in 12th century; from *spata* and *fust*; France, late 12th century (Gre).

Espalière, espallier, espallière: [OF] unclear form of shoulder-armour, or *coif* with shoulder protections, or padded soft armour worn over mail *hauberk* as required in Rule of the Temple; France and Crusader states, mid-12th–late 13th centuries (Conta, Gre).

Espatlleres: [SP] padded shoulder and upper arm defences of *perpunte* construction; Aragón and Catalonia, mid-14th century (Hoff A2).

Espaza, espeza: [Oc] sword; southern France, late 12th–13th centuries (Noel, N&L).

Espede, espee: [OF] sword; France and Norman England, late 11th–late 12th centuries (A&N, RR, Poures).

Espiel, espiet, espier, espie: [OF] spear or javelin; France, 10th–late 13th centuries (ASR, RT, A&N, Beat, Chet, Gre).

Espieut: [Oc] spear; southern France, late 12th century (N&L).

Esplente: [OF] metal blade; France, 13th century (Gre).

Espointon: [OF] pointed weapon in general; France, late 13th century (Gre).

Espringale, espringarde: [OF] war-engine, generally large frame-mounted crossbow, shooting *quarrels* with wooden or tin flights or stone or lead bullets; France, mid-13th century (Gre, Brook NA).

Estoc: [OF] short straight stabbing sword, or point of sword; France, late 12th–mid-13th centuries (Gre, Hoff A2).

Estoccadas, estocadas: [SP] pointed stabbing sword; Spain, 13th–14th centuries (Hoff A2).

Falces: [ML] probably early form of *falchion*; England (Assize of Arms of 1252), mid-13th century (Borg).

Falco, falcione: [EI] form of staff weapon, perhaps like French *faussar*, or early form of *falchion*; Italy, 13th–14th centuries (Pur).

Faldas: [SP] skirts or *cuisses* of mail from Italy; Catalonia, mid-14th century (Hoff A2).

Falsador: [EI] crossbow bolt; Dalmatia, early/mid-14th century (Pet DO).

Faltre, feltre: [OF] horse-covering beneath saddle, or felt fixed to saddle, or fastened to chest-piece (*plastron*) of horse-harness; France, early 12th century (Gre).

Fauchard: [OF] possibly straight single-edged blade mounted on short haft like an axe; England and Ireland, 13th–14th centuries (HMC).

Fauchart: [OF] large-bladed weapon or sword used by infantry; France, late 12th century (Gre).

Fauchon: [OF] early form of single-edged *falchion*, generally an infantry weapon; France, mid/late 13th century (De J, Gre).

Faus, faussal: [OF] unclear form of hafted infantry weapon, probably associated with *faussar* or later *falchion*; France, 13th century (Oak).

Faussar, fausart: [OF] unclear form of infantry weapon probably with a short haft; also as *faussar de cor* ('of horn') or as *fausart trencant* ('cutting *fausart*'); France, late 12th century (Chet).

Fenestral: [OF] probably eye-slits or face-mask of *helme*, early form of *great helm* also having *nasel* and *mentonal* (chin-strap); France, late 12th/early 13th centuries (Chev).

Fer: [OF] literally 'iron', referring to spearheads; France and Norman England, late 11th century (ASR).

Fer aceiri: [Oc] descriptive term for spear blades; southern France, late 12th century (N&L).

Fetel: [AS] sword-belt or *baldric*; England, 10th–11th centuries (Kell).

Feu ardant: [OF] probably a form of Greek Fire, apparently on arrows of 'infidels'; France, late 12th century (Chet).

Feu grigois, fu griois: [OF] 'Greek Fire'; France, late 12th century (Chet).

Fla, flan: [AS] possibly arrow or light javelin; England, 10th–11th centuries (Kell, Swant).

Flael, flaiel: [OF] flail or war-flail; from Latin *flagellum*; France, from 10th century (Gre).

Flanboiant, flanboie: [OF] crest, possibly plume-holder or piece of decorative cloth on top of a helmet also having *candelabre* and *nasal*; France, late 12th/early 13th centuries (Eli).

Flassart: [OF] bed-cloth or horse-cloth; France, 13th century (Gre).

Flece, flet, fles: [OF] arrows, some with shafts of willow; from German *flitz*; France and Norman England, late 12th–13th centuries (Chet, Eli).

Flone: [ME] arrow; England, mid-14th century (AGG).

Fodefle: [OF] stone-throwing *mangonel*; from Latin *fundibalum*; France, late 12th century (Gre).

Fodrel: [OF] scabbard; France and Norman England, late 11th century (ASR).

Fojas: [SP] *coat-of-plates* or scale-lined jerkin, called *cuyrasses* in Catalonia; Spain, late 13th–14th centuries (Hoff A2).

Fonde, fondel: [OF] sling; France, late 12th century (Gre).

Fonèvol: [Cn] probably light form of *mangonel*; Aragón, 13th century (Hoff A2).

Forche fire: [OF] perhaps imaginary trident-like staff weapon; France, late 11th century (Gre).

Fraisne, fraisnon, fraignon: [OF] literally 'ash tree', haft of lance; France, late 11th–12th centuries (Gre).

Fricia, freca: [EI] arrows; Dalmatia, 13th–14th centuries (Pet DO).

Fronda: [ML] sling of militia or levy; southern France, early/mid-13th–14th centuries (Noel).

Fuere, fuerre: [OF] sheath or scabbard; France, mid/late 12th century (TOF, Beat, Gre).

Fuoco: [EI] 'Greek Fire' used in naval warfare; Italy, late 13th century (Brook NA).

Fust: [OF] cudgel of wood or haft or spear or any wooden part of a weapon or shield; France and Norman England, late 11th century (ASR).

Ga: [Ir] javelin; Gaelic Ireland, mid-14th century (Harb 1).

Gabhla: [Ir] javelin; Ireland, 9th–12th centuries (Swant).

Gād: [AS] point of spear blade, literally 'goad'; England, 10th–11th centuries (Kell, Swant); see also *gad* [ME].

Gad, gaddes: [ME] herdsman's goad, supposedly used as weapon; England, late 13th century (A Hav); see also *gād* (AS).

Gaesa: [ME] infantry weapon, probably javelin; from Latin *gaesum*; England, 13th century (Oak).

Gaf: [Oc] unclear form of weapon, probably hooked staff weapon; southern France, mid-14th centuries (Noel).

Gafeluc, gafeluk: [AS] light javelin; from Welsh *gaflach*; England, 10th–11th centuries (Kell, Swant).

Gaflach: [EW] light javelin, a number of which may be carried in a quiver; Wales, 10th–12th centuries (Kell, Swant).

Gaigne: [OF] scabbard; from Latin *vagina*; France, 12th century (Gre).

Gal, galt: [OF] wooden haft or weapon; from German *wald*; France, late 11th century (Gre).

Galea: [ML] normal term for helmet, probably of larger type; Western Europe, 11th–13th centuries (Gai EU).

Galeus: [ML] unspecified helmet; Europe, mid-13th century (Pai TR).

Gambais, gambaisel, gambaison, gamboison, gambeson, gambison: [OF] padded garment worn beneath mail *hauberk*, probably sleeveless; possibly from Byzantine *kabadion*; France, late 11th–13th centuries (Eli, Bl, Ha SA, Nor, Vill CC; Gre).

Gambariae: [EI] arm- or leg-armour, probably mail *chausses*; Dalmatia, mid-14th century (Pet DO).

Gambax, gambeson: [SP] padded soft armour; Spain, 13th century (Hoff A2).

Gamberuolis: [ML] arm or leg defences, later worn instead of *calicas ferreis*; Italy, mid/late 13th century (Wal O).

Gambiera de ferra: [EI] *greaves* or arm-pieces, probably of plate; Dalmatia, mid-14th century (Pet DO).

Gamboison d'estoupes: [OF] descriptive term for padded armour of a Muslim in Egypt, mid-13th century (De J).

Gans de ferre: [Cn] mail or scale-covered *gauntlets*; Catalonia, late 13th century (Hoff A2).

Gant: [OF] glove or possibly *mitten* of *hauberk*; France, late 11th century (Gre).

Gant de fer: [OF] iron *gauntlet*; England, early 14th century (Conta).

Gār: [AS] javelin; England, 10th–11th centuries (Kell, Swant).

Garnizos: [Oc] full armour; southern France (N&L).

Garrixiones: [OF] unclear form of naval weapon, probably shooting or projecting missiles, or a large form of *mantlet*; Provence, mid-13th century (Brook NA).

Garrot: [OF] shaft of large arrow or crossbow bolt; France, late 13th century (Gre); see also *garrot* [Oc].

Garrot: [Oc] perhaps bolt for a large, frame-mounted crossbow, or projectile from early cannon; southern France, mid-14th century (Noel); see also *garrot* [OF]

Gavlod: [Bn] javelin; Brittany, 9th–11th centuries (Swant).

Gavaloti: [EI] type of spear or javelin; from Old French *gavrelos*; Dalmatia, mid-14th century (Pet DO).

Gavrelos: [OF] javelins used by 'infidels'; from Celtic via Old English *gafeluk*; France, late 12th century (Chet).

Gazarma: [Oc] *guisarme*, large-bladed staff weapon; southern France, mid-14th century (Noel).

Ġearwe, ġeatwe, ġetawa: [AS] general term for arms and armour; England, 10th–11th centuries (Kell).

Genellières: [OF] knee or thigh defences, associated with *gambison* and hanging 'like windows', probably padded or quilted; France, late 12th/early 13th centuries (Eli).

Gere: [ME] general term for armour; England, mid-14th century (Will, AGG).

Gescót: [AS] sling-stones; England, 10th–11th centuries (Kell).

Geserne, giserne, gisarm, gisharm: [ME] long-bladed, long-hafted axe, *guisarme*; England, late 13th–mid-14th century (AGG, A Hav, A&M).

Gew: [Co] javelin; Cornwall, 10th–13th centuries (Swant).

Gewriđ: [AS] possibly binding around haft of spear; England, 10th–11th centuries (Swant).

Ghai: [Ir] javelin; Ireland, 10th–12th centuries (Swant).

Ghiazzeriono: [EI] padded and cloth-covered mail *hauberk*, same as French *jazerant*; also as *maglia ghiazzerina*; from Islamic *kazāghand*; Italy, early 14th century (B&C, Scal AP).

Gibe, gibet: [OF] possibly hafted infantry weapon, or staff-sling, or long-hafted mace; France and Norman England, mid-12th century (Gre).

Gin: [OF] shortened form of *engin* (siege-machine); France, 13th century (Gre).

Ginoeze: [Oc] type of small helmet, perhaps *cervellière* or *bascinet* of 'Genoese' style; southern France, mid-14th century (Noel).

Gladius: [ML] general term for sword; Europe, mid-13th century (Pai TR).

Glaive, glage, glave: [OF] blade of spear, lance, or more rarely sword, on bamboo hafts in peaceful tournament in south-west France; France and Norman England, 10th–early 13th centuries (Eli, RT, Hoff A2, Gree).

Gleiue, gleyue: [ME] infantry spear; England, late 13th century (A Hav).

Glouez: [ME] gloves or *gauntlets*, can be of 'plate' metal; England, from mid-14th century (AGG).

Gocet, gosset: [OF] separate piece of armour, probably of mail, to protect the armpit, normally worn with later plate armour; France, late 13th century (Gre).

Godendac, goedendag: [FD] long-hafted mace with a thrusting spike at end, used by infantry; Flanders, 13th–14th centuries (Oak, Ver, Verb DL, Verb DG).

Godendat, godendart: [OF] heavy infantry mace with thrusting spike at end; from Flemish *godenac*; Flanders, early 14th century (Gre).

Golorones: [SP] possibly a *gorget* (neck and throat protection) from Italy; Catalonia, mid-14th century (Hoff A2).

Gonel: [Oc] type of *jupon* (tunic or soft armour); southern France, mid-14th century (Noel).

Gonele: [OF] long garment or surcoat worn over mail *hauberk*, reaching calf; France, late 12th century (Gre).

Gonella: [SP] possibly small type of mail *haubergeon*, used by *Almogavar* light infantry; Aragón, 13th century (Hoff A2).

Gonfano, gonfainos: [Oc] lance-pennon or *gonfanon*; southern France (N&L).

Gonfanon, gonfalon, gunfanon: [OF] pennon on lance; France, 11th–13th centuries (RT, Chet, Meyer RV, Gre).

Gonia, gunion: [Cn] small mail jerkin, perhaps sleeveless *haubergeon* seen among Muslims; Catalonia, late 13th–14th centuries (Hoff A2).

Gorgera, gorguera: [SP] possibly separate neck-guard, perhaps raised stiff collar of mail or large piece of plate armour around throat; Spain, mid-13th–14th centuries (Hoff A2).

Gorgeriam: [ML] probably mail *tippet, coif*, or raised semi-rigid collar; southern France, mid-14th century (Noel).

Gorgiera: [ML] probably mail *tippet* or raised collar; Italy, mid/late 13th century (Wal O).

Gorgière: [OF] mail to protect neck and upper chest, or rigid or semi-rigid *gorget* with raised collar to protect neck, worn by lightly-equipped troops with *cervellière* or *bascinet*, sometimes with *epaulière*; France and Angevin southern Italy, late 13th century (Gre, Conta).

Gormat: [Ir] helmet, possibly segmented *spangenhelm*, described as 'branching'; Gaelic Ireland, late 13th/early 14th centuries (Harb 1).

Grafe, grefe, greve: [OF] small dagger; France, mid-12th century (Gre).

Grand casque: [OF] probably a reference to the earliest form of *great helm* protecting head and face; available in France but not in Flanders, c.1160–70 (Gai PO).

Greuez: [ME] greaves, lower leg defences, may be of *stel* (steel), worn with *poleyns* and *sabatons*; England, mid-14th century (AGG).

Greve: [OF] *greave* protecting shin; France, early 14th century (Gre).

Guanti: [EI] *gauntlets*; Dalmatia, mid-14th century (Pet DO).

Guarnement: [OF] full military equipment; France and Norman England, late 11th century (ASR).

Guarnizon: [SP] armour in general; Spain, 12th–13th centuries (Morris MS).

Guasarma: [SP] long-bladed axe or *guisarme*; Spain, 13th century (Hoff A2).

Guerdas de mano: [SP] man-powered *mangonel*; Spain, late 12th/early 13th centuries (Hoff A2).

Guerites: [OF] form of wooden siege device; France, 13th century (Conta).

Guiche, guige: [OF] strap around neck to support large shield; France and Norman England, late 11th–mid-12th centuries (ASR, RT, Chet, Gre).

Guige doublee: [OF] possibly poetic reference to doubled *guige* strap; France, mid/late 12th century (Beat).

Guimple: [OF] pennon on jousting lance; France, mid-12th century (Gre).

Guir: [EW] military equipment in general, *arwev guir* (armour gear); probably from Anglo-Saxon *gere*; Wales, 9th–12th centuries (Will BT).

Guisarme, gisarme: [OF] probably long-bladed, long-hafted war-axe for infantry; perhaps from German *getisarn*; France and Norman England, mid-12th–early 13th centuries (Chet, Eli, RT, Gre).

Guivre, wivre: [OF] descriptive term for 'serpent-like' javelin or arrow; from Latin *vipera*; France, late 11th century (Gre).

Gvaev, gwaew: [EW] spear, javelin or perhaps *glaive*; Wales, 9th–11th centuries (Will BT, Swant).

Gwayw: [EW] spear or javelin; Wales, mid/late 14th century (Will BT, Will IW).

Gweith: [EW] spear or javelin; Wales, 11th–12th centuries (Will BT).

Gyldenan fetels: [AS] decorated sword-belt; England, 10th–11th centuries (Kell).

Gysarme, gisarme: [ML] *guisarme*, long-hafted long-bladed axe; England (Assize of Arms of 1252), mid-13th century (Borg, Wal AW).

Gysarum: [ML] *guisarmes*, same as Scots axe called *handhax*; Scotland, 14th century (Bord).

Haces: [OF] axes of infantry, distinct from *guisarmes*; France, late 12th/early 13th centuries (Eli).

Haces danoises: [OF] 'Danish axes', infantry axes of presumed Danish or pseudo-Viking form; France, mid/late 12th century (Beat, Chet).

Hache: [OF] war-axe; also as *hache noresche* ('Nordic axe'); France, 12th century (Gre).

Hachete: [OF] small war-axe; France, c.1300 (Gre).

Hacqueton: [OF] same as *aketon* (padded or quilted soft armour); from Arabic *al-quṭn* ('cotton'); Europe, 12th century (Ha SA).

Haeft: [AS] grip of sword; England, 10th–11th centuries (Kell).

Hakovité: [OCS] spear with wings or flanges beneath the blade; 9th–10th centuries (Warn).

Halberc: [OF] mail *hauberk*, possibly from conjectural German *halsberc*, or from Arabic *habikah* ('tightly joined together') or *hubuk* ('coat of mail'); France and Norman England, late 11th–12th centuries (ASR, Gre).

Halbercot: [OF] mail *hauberk*; France, mid-13th century (Gre).

Halbergeon: [OF] small *hauberk* used by archers; France, mid-12th century (Gre).

Halberjol: [OF] *hauberk*, apparently without a *coif*; France, mid-12th century (Gre).

Halme: [ME] haft of axe; England, mid-14th century (AGG).

Halsbeorg: [AS] probably mail *hauberk* with *coif*; translated into Latin as *thorace*; England, 10th–11th centuries (Kell).

Halsberc, halsbeite: [FD] probably mail *hauberk*; Netherlands, late 13th century (Labou).

Halsbergoele: [FD] probably mail *hauberk*; Holland, mid-14th century (V Mie).

Halsbjörg: [ON] probably mail hauberk including *coif*; Scandinavia, late 13th century.

Hand-ax: [ME] war-axe; England, late 13th century (A Hav).

Handhax: [SE] large war-axe, similar to English *guisarme*; Scotland, 14th century (Borg).

Hanepier: [OF] helmet in form of a cup, presumably domed rather than conical; France, late 12th century (Gre).

Hansac: [OF] probably short sword; from German hand-*seax*; France, late 12th century (Gre).

Hansart, hanssat: [OF] short sword or large dagger; France, 12th–13th centuries (Gre).

Hanscoen: [FD] probably simple padded *gauntlets*; Holland, mid-14th century (V Mie).

Hanste, hante, haste: [OF] haft of spear or javelin, wooden part of any staff weapon; France and Norman England, late 11th–mid-12th centuries (ASR, RT, Gre).

Harace: [OF] large shield or man-high *mantlet*, probably of reeds; Crusader states, late 13th century (Gre).

Harnage: [OF] full equipment; France and Crusader states, late 13th century (Gre).

Harnask: [FD] general term for armour; Holland, mid-14th century (V Mie).

Harnasz: [Pl] general term for full armour; from German *harnasch*; Poland, mid-14th century (Warn).

Harnays, hernays: [ME] complete armour; England, early/mid-14th century (AGG, Tagl).

Harneriis: [ML] unspecified items of armour worn with *panzeria* instead of *coraziniis*; Italy, mid/late 13th century (Wal O).

Harnois, herneis, hernos: [OF] arms, full equipment; from Scandinavian *hernest* ('provision of arms'); France, mid/late 12th century (TOF, Gre).

Harsnire, harsture: [FD] small *cervellière* worn beneath a larger helmet; Netherlands, late 13th century (Labou).

Hasegaie: [ML] weapon described as being like *gisarme*, probably from Berber-Arabic *zaghāyah* (form of short spear); also in English as *lancegay* and *archegay*.

Hauber: [ME] mail *hauberk*; northern England, early/mid-14th century (Tagl).

Hauberc, haubert: [OF] mail *hauberk*; France, mid/late 12th century (TOF, Beat, Chet, Eli, Knud).

Haubergeon, herbergeison: [OF] smaller mail *hauberk* without *manicle* (*mittens*); also possibly scale *hauberk*, or soft armour worn under mail *hauberk*; France, Norman England and Crusader states, 12th–13th centuries (Oak, Conta, Gai EU, Meyer RV, Wal AW).

Hauberghe, hawbergh: [ME] mail *hauberk*; northern England, early/mid-14th century (AGG).

Haubert: [Cn] mail *hauberk*; Catalonia, 13th century (Hoff A2).

Haubier: [OF] mail *hauberk* of largest type, distinct from smaller *haubregon*; France and Flanders, late 13th/early 14th centuries (Gans A, Gai EU).

Haubregon: [OF] lesser form of *hauberk*, lacking *coif*, distinct from *haubeir*; Flanders, early 14th century (Gans A).

Havet: [OF] hooked staff weapon; France, early 13th century (Gre).

Heaԁo-steap helm: [AS] probably one-piece conical helmet; England, 10th–11th centuries (Kell).

Hebert: [OF] javelin; France, late 13th century (Gre).

Hede: [ME] axehead or arrowhead with *poynte* and *barbes*; England, mid-14th century (AGG).

Heft: [FD] hilt or grip of *cniff* (knife or dagger), may be of ivory; Netherlands, late 13th century (Labou).

Hel, helme, heame, elme, ialme: [OF] heavy helmet, probably originally conical type but later referring to *bascinet* with mail *aventail*, with own lining, normally laced on; from German *helm*; France and

England, late 11th–mid-14th centuries (Gre, ASR, AGG, Gai EU, Tagl).

Helm: [AS] general term for helmet; England, 10th–11th centuries (Kell).

Helm, helme: [ME] large helmet, often laced in place, probably usually *great helm*; England, late 13th–mid-14th century (A Hav, Will PG).

Helm harsnire, helm harsture: [FD] large helmet, probably *great helm*; Netherlands, late 13th century (Labou).

Helt, heute, heude, heut, heu: [OF] hilt of sword or dagger; France and Norman England, late 11th/early 12th centuries (ASR, Gre).

Henča: [AS] possibly *hauberk*; England, 10th–11th centuries (Kell).

Henepier: [OF] part of a helmet, possibly referring to the entire top or the flat top of an early form of *great helm*; France, late 12th/early 13th centuries (Chev).

Hersnière: [FD] unclear form of armour for infantry militia; Holland, mid-14th century (V Mie).

Hilde-serče: [AS] literally 'battle shirt', probably mail *hauberk*; England, 10th–11th centuries (Kell).

Hilt: [AS] hilt of sword; England, 10th–11th centuries (Kell).

Hirnhaube: [OG] close-fitting *cervellière* helmet; Germany, 14th century (Scal DS).

Hoqueton: [OF] padded garment worn beneath *hauberk*; England, early 14th century (Conta); see also *hacqueton*.

Horde: [ME] point of spear or lance; northern England, early/mid-14th century (Tagl).

Hring: [AS] mail link; England, 10th–11th centuries (Kell).

Iaculis: [ML] javelins, a pair carried by Gaelic Irish; Ireland, 12th century (Ger T).

Iaume, hiaume: [OF] helmet with a nasal, laced to head; France, late 12th century (A&N, TOF); see also *helme*.

Ijzeren platen: [FD] 'iron plates' among other armour, perhaps a *coat-of-plates* or elements for a *coat-of-plates*; Flanders, late 13th century (Verb DG).

Immunicionem ferri: [ML] general term for iron armour, naval warfare; south-west France, early 13th century (Brook NA).

Irois, irese: [OF] javelin of Gaelic-Irish origin; France, early 12th century (Gre).

Jaque: [OF and Oc] short jerkin, possibly of mail or scale-lined; probably from Catalan; France and southern France, mid-14th century (Gre, Noel).

Jaquete: [OF] short-sleeved garment; France, early 14th century (Gre).

Jarse: [OF] unspecified cutting weapon; France, late 12th century (Gre).

Jaseran, jazerant, jazerenc, jaserant: [OF] fabric-covered and probably padded mail jerkin or *hauberk*; can refer to form of horse-armour; from Arabic–Farsi *kazāghand*; France and Norman England, late 11th–early 14th centuries (ASR, Cre, Beat, Chet, Meyer RV, MCK).

Joière: [OF] part of helmet or *coif* protecting cheeks; France, late 12th century (Gre).

Jube, gipe: [OF] garment worn over or under armour; from Arabic *jubbah*; France, late 12th century (Gre).

Jupeau d'armer: [OF] probably padded garment worn beneath *hauberk*, required by Rule of the Temple; Crusader states, mid-12th–13th centuries (Conta).

Juponerium: [ML] possibly padded garment used by militia; from Arabic *jubbah*; southern France, mid-14th century (Noel).

Jusarme: [OF] *guisarme*; France, late 12th century (TOF).

Kabát: [Cz] probably quilted soft armour for infantry; from Byzantine Greek *kabadion*; Bohemia.

Kalkan: [Pl] small round shield; from Turkish *qalqan*; Poland, late 14th century (Warn).

Klob, klub: [ME] see *clobe*.

Kniebuckel: [OG] knee-protecting *poleyns*; Germany, 14th century (Scal DS).

Knif, kniues, knyf, knuffe, knyues: [ME] knife or dagger, used as a weapon; England, late 13th/early 14th centuries (A Hav, AFF, Will PG).

Kniff, cnyff: [FD] large knife, example with *heft* (hilt) of ivory; Netherlands, late 13th century (Labou).

Knyf: [FD] dagger of militia infantry; Holland, mid-14th century (V Mie).

Kopie: [Cz] general term for spear; Bohemia, 10th–14th centuries (Warn).

Kopije, kopija: [Pl] spear; Poland, 10th–14th centuries (Warn).

Kopíokřídlene: [OCS] large spear with wings or lugs beneath blade; 9th–11th centuries (Warn).

Kylchwy: [EW] form of shield or buckler; Wales, 12th–13th centuries (Will BT).

Lace: [ME] probably wrist-thong of war-axe; England, mid-14th century (AGG).

Laken colier: [FD] collar or *tippet*, perhaps of padded material; Holland, mid-14th century (V Mie).

Lamerias vel coraczas: [ML] cuirass, probably *coat-of-plates*, for cavalry; Tuscany, early 14th century (Giu OM).

Lamerias: [ML] probably *coat-of-plates* worn *cum faldis spontonem*; from classical Latin but also possibly connected with Arabic *lā'mat al-ḥarb*; Italy, late 13th century (Wal CC).

Lames de fer: [OF] probable references to lamellar or scale armour of Eastern origin in Europe; 13th century (Rich CV).

Lamières: [EI] *cuirass* for chest, perhaps indicating laminated construction as a *coat-of-plates*, perhaps of hardened leather; Tuscany, mid-13th century (Conta).

Lanca: [ML] spear, specifically in naval warfare; Marseilles, 13th century (Brook NA).

Lançar: [Oc] cavalry spear; southern France, late 13th century (N&L).

Lanças, lançada: [SP] cavalry lances; Spain, mid-12th–13th centuries (Hend MT, Hoff A2, Morris MS).

Lance, lancea, lanceis: [OF] heavy spear usually couched beneath arm, *lance adobet* having pennon attached, same haft as *espie* (spear); *lances d'osiers* used in practice tournament; also *lances de sap* of fir or spruce; France, England and Ireland, from late 11th century (ASR, Ger T, Bee W, TOF, Beat, Gre).

Lancea: [EI] lance or spear; Dubrovnik, 14th century (Pet DO).

Lancegaie: [OF] javelin or short pike; France, 13th century (Gre).

Lancete: [OF] short lance; France, late 12th century (Gre).

Lancia, lanceam: [ML] cavalry spear; Italy, mid/late 13th century (Wal CC, Wal O).

Lansa: [Oc] spear used by militia; southern France, late 12th–mid-14th centuries (Noel, N&L).

Lanzelonghe: [EI] long spear or pike of infantry; Italy, early/mid-13th century (Pieri SL).

Lasbage: [ON] crossbow; Norway, 12th–13th centuries (Alm).

Launce: [ME] cavalry spear; England, mid-14th century (AGG).

Lawnev: [EW] possibly sword-blade, perhaps only poetic; Wales, 9th–11th centuries (Will IW).

Lein, llain: [EW] swords; Wales, 12th century (Will IW).

Léin: [Ir] originally a shirt, perhaps later a multi-layered soft armour; Gaelic Ireland, mid-14th century (Harb 1).

Lesche: [OF] blade of sword; France, late 13th century (Gre).

Liðere: [AS] sling; England, 10th–11th centuries (Kell).

Ligote: [OF] cord or strap inside shield; France, 12th–13th centuries (Gre).

Lluric, lluryc: [EW] general term for mail *hauberk*; from Latin *lorica*; Celtic Britain and Wales, 7th–late 13th centuries (Alc, Will BT).

Locust: [ME] reference to short arrows shot by Mamluks during fall of Acre; direct translation from Arabic *ḥusbān*, probably based on accounts by Othon de Grandson; Scotland, early 14th century (CL).

Lome: [ME] general term for weapon; England, mid-14th century (Will PG, AGG).

Lorain: [OF] harness in general, or part of horse-harness and in particular the *poitrail*; France, late 12th century (Gre).

Lorg: [Ir] club or cudgel; Gaelic Ireland, 11th–12th centuries (Harb 2).

Lorica: [ML] mail *hauberk* of large type; Europe, 8th–14th centuries (Ha SA, Bee W).

Loriga, loryga: [SP] *hauberk* of mail or possibly earlier of scales; also as *lorigas dobladas*; Muslim and Christian Spain, 10th–14th centuries (Hoff A2, Conta, Morris MS).

Lorigas de caballa: [SP] mail horse armour or *bard*; Spain, 13th century (Hoff A2).

Lorigon: [SP] possibly smaller mail *hauberk* like *haubergeon*; Spain, 13th century (Hoff A2).

Lú'irech, lúireac: [Ir] mail *hauberk*, worn over *cotún* soft armour; from Latin *lorica*; Gaelic Ireland, 7th–14th centuries (Harb 1).

Luk: [Pl] bow; Poland, 10th–16th centuries (Warn).

Lumière: [OF] probably eye-slits of large helmet; France, 12th–13th centuries (Gre).

Maca: [SP] mace; Spain, 13th–14th centuries (Hoff A2).

Mace: [ME] mace; northern England, early/mid-14th century (Tagl); see also *mace* [OF].

Mace: [OF] mace, early form having *claus d'acier* (steel studs or nails), in hands of 'infidel'; France, mid/late 12th century (Chet, Gre); see also *mace* [ME].

Macefond: [OF] stone-throwing siege-engine; Crusader states, late 13th century (Gre).

Macelote: [OF] small mace, perhaps associated with Arabic *latt* (elongated form of mace); France, 13th century (Gre).

Mache: [OF] probably mace; France, late 12th century (Gre).

Machina: [EI] siege-engines in general; Dalmatia, 14th century (Pet DO).

Macia, maca: [EI] mace, *de ferro* (of iron), *de ligno* (of wood); Dalmatia, late 13th/early 14th centuries (Pet DO).

Macle: [OF] single link of mail; France, late 13th century (Gre).

Macon: [OF] mace; France, late 12th century (Chet).

Macue: [OF] mace or cudgel used by bandit, *macue de fer* (iron mace) thrown by 'infidel'; France, late 12th century (RR, Gre).

Macuele: [OF] probably head of a mace; France, late 12th century (Gre).

Macuette: [OF] small mace; France, mid-12th century (Gre).

Maegen-wudu: [AS] wood for spear haft; England, 10th–11th centuries (Kell).

Magnos cirulos: [ML] flywheel on pulley or winch to load *trebuchet*; southern France, late 13th century (Mot AP).

Mail: [OF] mace or hammer; France, late 11th century (Gre).

Maile, maaille, maille, maux, malle: [OF] mail or mail link; France or Norman England, late 11th–late 12th centuries (ASR, RT, TOF, Beat, Chet).

Maistre: [OF] main part or 'master' of a helmet, beneath the *candelabres*, probably part of an early *great helm*; France, late 12th/early 13th centuries (Chev).

Males: [SP] mail; Spain, 13th–14th centuries (Hoff A2).

Maliokraga: [OS] probably mail *coif*; Sweden, 12th–14th centuries.

Mall: [ME] hammer or war-hammer, specialised form of mace; northern England, early/mid-14th century (Tagl).

Manches: [OF] literally 'sleeves', probably items of padded soft armour worn with *pans* and various small items of mail by least-armoured men; Flanders, early 14th century (Gans A).

Mangan: [OF] *mangonel*; France, late 13th century (Gre).

Manganilla: [SP] probably man-powered *mangonel*; Spain, 13th century (Hoff A2).

Mangas: [SP] armoured sleeves, perhaps *vambraces* or *rerebraces* from Italy; Catalonia, mid-14th century (Hoff A2).

Mangona: [EI] small *mangonel*; Dalmatia, early 14th century (Pet DO).

Mangonel, mangonele, mangouniel, mangouniaus, manonniaus: [OF] stone-throwing engine working on sling principle, early forms man-powered, probably introduced by the Avars; Europe, 12th–13th centuries (Fino MS, Beat, Vill CC, Gre).

Mangonell turques: [Cn] form of man-powered *mangonel*, probably same as 'Turkish' *manjaníq* as described in Arabic; Aragón, 13th century (Hoff A2).

Mangonnellos: [ML] *mangonel*; southern France, late 13th century (Mot AP).

Manguanels: [Oc] *mangonels*; southern France, late 13th century (N&L).

Manicis: [ML] 'of iron', *gauntlets*, probably scale-covered; Italy, late 13th century (Wal CC).

Manicle, manique, manille: [OF] armour to protect hand, probably *mittens* integral with rest of large *hauberk*; France, mid-12th century (Gre).

Manicle de fer: [OF] probably mail *mittens* of large *hauberk*, in Rule of the Temple; Crusader states and France, mid/late 12th century (Chet, Conta).

Martel: [OF] war-hammer of 'infidel', perhaps mace with zoomorphic head; France, late 12th century (Chet).

Martinet: [OF] counterweight engine to throw rocks, probably form of *trebuchet*; France, early 14th century (Gre, Conta).

Masse turquoise: [OF] mace of 'Turkish' form, probably winged or like the zoomorphic Turkish *gurz*; Crusader states, mid-12th century (Conta).

Masseam: [ML] mace or club of militia; southern France, mid-14th century (Noel).

Masseta: [Oc] small mace or club; southern France, early 13th century (N&L).

Materace, materas: [OF] javelin of an 'infidel' or a large crossbow bolt; from Arabic *mitras*; France, late 12th–13th century (Chet, Gre).

Materon: [OF] mace head; France, 13th century (Gre).

Maza, massa: [Oc] mace, or *gran maza* (large mace); southern France, late 13th/early 14th centuries (N& L).

Maza turquesa: [SP] mace of eastern Islamic form, perhaps winged or with zoomorphic head; Spain, 13th century (Hoff A2).

Meč: [Cz] straight sword; Bohemia, 10th–14th centuries (Warn).

Mēče: [AS] double-edged sword; England, 9th–11th centuries (Kell).

Mentonal: [OF] chin-strap of helmet; also possibly lower part of face-mask of an early *great helm*; France, late 12th/early 13th centuries (Chev, Gre).

Mentoner: [OF] part of early face-mask of *great helm* protecting the chin; France, 12th century (Gre).

Mes: [OF] pickaxe or axe; France, late 12th century (Gre).

Mesericorde, misericorde: [OF] slender-bladed knife or dagger, having a *cotel* blade, first recorded in hand of 'infidel', later used to dispatch the wounded; France and Crusader states, late 12th/early 13th centuries (Chet, R de C, Gre).

Messen: [FD] probably knives or daggers coming in pairs; also as a pair of *snidemessen* or *scudemessen*; Netherlands, late 13th century (Labou, Verb DG).

Miecz: [Pl] straight sword; Poland, 10th–14th centuries (Warn).

Misericordia: [SP] slender-bladed dagger associated with assassins and 'unworthy' people; Spain and Catalonia, mid-13th century (Hoff A2).

Misericordiam: [MI] dagger; France, early 13th century (Hoff A2).

Mitaine: [OF] *mitten* with separate fingers, probably integral part of *hauberk*; France, late 12th century (Gre).

Mitram ferream: [ML] probably *bascinet* helmet; Western Europe, late 13th–14th centuries (Gai EU).

Molete: [OF] pricks of a rowel spur; France, late 13th century (Gre).

Moraine, moraille: [OF] iron fastening the visor or face-mask of a helmet; from Latin *murrum*; France, mid-13th century (Gre).

More, muere, meure: [OF] point of blade of a spear or sword; France and Norman England, late 11th–late 12th centuries (Gre).

Mortaio: [EI] early form of gunpowder artillery; Italy, 14th century (Gaibi).

Mosequins: [SP] unclear form of armour, probably for the limbs and probably of mail, from Italy; Catalonia, mid-14th century (Hoff A2).

Mufflers: [ME] mail *mittens* as integral part of mail *hauberk*, or padded *mitten* as integral part of padded or quilted soft armour; England, late 12th–early 14th centuries (Bl).

Muince: [Ir] originally perhaps a decorative torque, later probably a poetic reference to a decorated mail *coif* or *aventail*; Gaelic Ireland, mid-14th century (Harb 1).

Muple: [OF] literally 'fish', type of presumably long or kite-shaped shield; France, late 13th century (Gre).

Musca, mosca: [ML] literally 'flies', slang term for crossbow bolts; Europe, from 14th century (Den).

Musekins: [OF] obscure form of armour, perhaps a raised rigid collar worn by poorly-armoured troops; Flanders, early 14th century (Gans A).

Museral: [OF] javelin of an 'infidel'; France, late 12th century (Chet).

Muserat: [OF] javelin of an 'infidel'; from Arabic *mizraq*; France and Norman England, late 11th century (ASR, Gre).

Nasal, nasel, nasuel: [OF] broad nose-protecting vertical bar from the rim of of helmet; also part of face-mask of earliest *great helm*; France and Norman England, late 11th–early 13th centuries (ASR, A&N, RT, Chev).

Nasiels: [OF] part of large *elme* (helmet) also having *flanboiant* and *candelabre*, probably part of an early face-mask type of *great helm*; France, late 12th/early 13th centuries (Eli).

Neron, nairon: [OF] composite weapon consisting of an axe and hammer, perhaps also pointed; France, early 13th century (Gre).

Nož: [Pl] large dagger or short sword; Poland, from 11th century (Warn).

Nožh: [OCS and Cz] large dagger or short sword; Bohemia, from 11th century (Warn).

Nux de torno, nose grosso de torno: [EI] release nut of crossbow mechanism; Dalmatia, 14th century

Odĕnie: [Cz] general term for armour; Bohemia (Warn).

Oeillière: [OF] part of the visor of an early form of *great helm*; France, late 12th century (Gre); see also *uellière*.

Onga: [AS] point of arrow; England, 10th–11th centuries (Kell).

Ongle: [OF] catch, hook, clasp or fastening for various pieces of armour or military equipment; France, late 12th century (Chet).

Or: [OF] edging of a shield, probably a strip of leather; France, late 12th/early 13th centuries (Chev).

Ord: [AS] possibly blade or whole spear; England, 9th–11th centuries (Swant).

Orguel: [OF] unclear siege machine, perhaps with mechanism similar to medieval muscial organ; France, late 12th/early 13th centuries (Eli).

Orle: [OF] probably metallic edging of early shield; Western Europe, 10th–11th centuries (Gai EU).

Oruzie: [Cz] general term for armour, sometimes including weapons; Bohemia, from 12th century (Warn).

Osberc, oberc: [OF] mail *hauberk* with *coif*; France and Norman England, 11th–12th centuries (ASR, Beat).

Oscĕp: [Cz] javelin or light spear; Bohemia, 12th century (Warn).

Osche: [OF] notch in bow; France, 12th century (Gre).

Paalarios: [ML] copper or iron bearings of winch to load *trebuchet*; southern France, late 13th century (Mot AP).

Paio de corazze: [EI] *pair-of-plates* or *coat-of-plates*, rigid or semi-rigid body-armour, perhaps of *cuir-bouilli*; Italy, mid-13th century (Boc HIM).

Palays, palis: [ME] palisade; England, early/mid-14th century (AGG, Tagl).

Palice, palcát: [Cz] mace; Bohemia (Warn).

Palis, paliz: [OF] palisade; France, mid/late 12th century (RT, TOF).

Pan: [OF] skirts or lower edge of *hauberk*; France and Norman England, late 11th century (ASR); also minimal form of armour for those lacking *haubier* or *haubregon*; to be worn with *manches*, *berbière, musekins, cauchons*, and *wans de maille*; possibly sleeveless mail or soft armour for the body; Flanders, early 14th century (Gans A).

Panan: [OF] barb of an arrow, or lance-pennon; south-west France, mid-12th century (RT).

Panceria, pansiere: [EI] probably a form of mail *hauberk*, or semi-rigid piece of body armour worn with a mail *hauberk*; Tuscany, mid-13th–mid-14th centuries (Gai EU, Wal CC).

Panceriam: [EI] possibly mail *hauberk* with only one *mitten* (on the sword arm); Italy, early 13th century (Morr, Wal CC).

Pancerz: [Pl] general term for body-armour; from German *panzer*; Poland (Warn).

Pancier: [OF] armour to protect the abdomen; France, early 13th century (Gre).

Pancĭer: [Cz] general term for body-armour; from Latin *panceriam* via German *panzer*; Bohemia, 12th–14th centuries (Warn).

Pane, panne, pene: [OF] leather covering of a shield, or top edge of shield; France, late 11th–mid-12th centuries (RT, Gre).

Panzeriam: [ML] body-armour, distinct from mail *hauberk* (*asbergum*); Tuscany, late 13th/early 14th centuries (Giu OM, Wal O).

Parement: [OF] long rich mantle worn over armour; France, from 10th century (Gre).

Paunce: [ME] probably *coat-of-plates* worn with mail *hauberk* and *platez* (pieces of plate armour); England, mid-14th century (AGG).

Pavesari, palvesa: [EI] tall shield of infantry, generally rectangular; Italy, mid/late 13th century (B Gui OM, Pieri SL).

Pavesium: [ML] large infantry shield or *mantlet*; southern France, mid-14th century (Noel).

Pavesius: [EI] large rectangular infantry shield, wood covered in leather, in four official sizes: large (for sentries), normal, small, and smallest (for shipboard use); Dalmatia, early/mid-14th century (Pet DO).

Paviet, pavois: [OF] large infantry shield of *pavise* type; from Italian *pavese* ('of Pavia'); France, early/mid-14th century (Gre).

Pavois: [SP] large shield for infantry; Navarre, mid-14th century (Conta).

Pece: [ME] any individual item or 'piece' of plate armour; England, mid-14th century (AGG).

Peiriers, peireira: [Oc] stone-throwing machine; southern France, early 13th century (N&L).

Pelotas de hierro: [SP] perhaps cannon balls *lancaban con fuego* ('propelled by fire'); Spain, early/mid-14th century (Hoff A2).

Pels: [OF] reference to North African leather armour, probably in 'layers' or 'lines' of scales or lamellar *granz et lungs et quarrez*; Norman England, late 12th century (Meyer RV).

Pelta: [ML] European term for small round shield; from Greek *pelta*; Crusader states, 12th–13th centuries (Sm).

Pendones: [SP] lance pennons; Spain, mid-12th–13th centuries (Hend MT, Hoff A2, Morris MS).

Pennoncel: [OF] gilded or painted heraldic device on a *targ* (shield); France, mid-13th century (De J).

Penos: [Oc] lance pennons; southern France, early 13th century (N&L).

Penzerias: [EI] probably mail *hauberk*; same as *panceria*; Venice and Dalmatia, early 14th century (Pet DO).

Perdrial: [OF] literally 'partridge', type of unclear siege-engine; France, 12th century (Gre).

Perponches: [Oc] quilted or padded soft armours; southern France, mid-14th century (Noel).

Perpunct: [ML] quilted or padded soft armour of sailors; south-west France, early 13th century (Brook NA).

Perpunte, perpunt: [SP] quilted or padded soft armour, also possibly of felt; same as French *pourpoint*; León and Castile, 10th–13th centuries (Hoff A2, Gab AS).

Perpunto grosso: [ML] large quilted or padded soft armour with iron elements, perhaps scales (*conscialibus ferreis*), worn instead of *panzeria* or *corazinus*; Italy, mid/late 13th century (Wal O).

Perrier: [OF] stone-throwing engine, probably same as *mangonel*; France and Crusader states, late 12th/early 13th centuries (RT, Beat, Eli, Vill CC, Gre).

Pestel: [OF] mace or javelin with large head; France, late 12th century (Gre).

Pestueil: [OF] javelin with large head; France, early 14th century (Gre).

Petrariae: [ML] stone-throwing engine, probably also used aboard ships; France and England, late 12th/early 13th centuries (Brook NA).

Phaetra: [EI] quiver; Dalmatia, 14th century (Pet DO).

Pharete: [OF] quiver; France, early 14th century (Gre).

Pharetris: [ML] quiver; Europe, mid-13th century (Pai TR).

Pial, piasse: [OF] axe; France, late 13th/early 14th century (Gre).

Pic: [OF] weapon of 'infidel', held in sword-belt, perhaps a war-hammer; France, late 12th century (Chet).

Picois, picon, picot: [OF] pickaxe or small javelin; south-west France, mid/late 12th century (RT, Beat, Gre).

Pignon, pignons: [OF] pennon on lance, or *barbes* on javelin head; France, mid/late 12th century (Beat, Chet).

Pikle: [ME] early form of infantry pike; England, 13th century (Oak).

Pil: [AS] javelin; from Latin *pilum*; England, 10th–11th centuries (Kell, Swant).

Pilet: [OF] javelin or crossbow bolt; France, mid-12th century (Gre).

Pisto: [SP] form of dagger; perhaps from *pitiez*, and hence associated with *misericordia*; Spain, 13th century (Hoff A2).

Pius: [OF] hafted infantry weapon or sapper's tool 'of steel'; France, mid/late 12th century (Beat).

Pizière: [OF] part of harness covering chest of horse; France, early 14th century (Gre).

Plata garnyt: [Oc] plate armour in general; southern France, mid-14th century (Noel).

Plate: [OF] plate of metal, one element of a *cuirass*; France, late 12th century (Gre).

Plate, platez: [ME] pieces of plate armour worn with *bruny* (mail hauberk), *paunce*, perhaps *coat-of-plates*; England, mid-14th century (AGG, Conta).

Plome, plomee: [OF] lead projectile or head of lead mace; France, mid-12th century (Gre).

Ploquet: [OF] small shield; France, 13th century (Gre).

Poin, poins, poing, pont, pon: [OF] literally 'fist', grip of sword-hilt or two pieces of wood around *tang* forming sword-hilt or *quillons* (crossguard) of sword-hilt; France and Norman England, 11th–12th centuries (Gre, ASR, RT, TOF, A&N, Chev, Chet).

Poitral, poitrail, poitrine, poitrier, poitre: [OF] breast-strap on harness of horse, or piece of horse-armour protecting breast of animal; France, 11th–late 12th centuries (Gre).

Poitrinier: [OF] *cuirass*; France, 13th century (Gre).

Polain: [OF] knee-armour; France, early 14th century (Gre).

Polaynez: [ME] *poleyns*, usually of metal laced around back of legs to protect knees; England, mid-14th century (AGG).

Pom, pomel, poumon: [OF] *pommel* of sword; France, 12th century (Chet, Gre).

Pomel: [ME] *pommel* on hilt of sword; northern England, early/mid-14th century (Tagl).

Porok, parak: [OCS] siege-catapult; Slav Central and Eastern Europe, early 13th–14th centuries (Warn).

Porpunte: [FD] padded or quilted soft armour, similar to *gambeson*; from French *pourpointe*; Netherlands, late 13th century (Labou).

Pourpoint: [OF] general term for quilted or padded soft armour, later including horse-armour of the same construction; France and England, 12th–14th centuries (Bl, Oak).

Pousserios: [ML] levers to turn winch while loading a *trebuchet*; southern France, late 13th century (Mot AP).

Poynt: [ME] point of an arrow or sword; England, early/mid-14th century (Tagl).

Proca: [Pl] siege-catapult; Poland, early 13th–14th centuries (Warn).

Przyłbica: [Pl] unspecified form of helmet; Poland, 14th century (Warn).

Pungiren: [FD] small knives or daggers, probably pike, later *poignard*; Netherlands, late 13th century (Labou).

Pysan, pisayn, pesane: [ME] piece of armour for neck and shoulders or upper chest, worn in addition to a *hauberk* and *ventale* or *ventail* (*aventail*), possibly originally 'from Pisa'; or perhaps raised rigid or stiffened neckpiece or *gorget* of mail or splints, or a mail *tippet*; England, mid-14th century (AGG, Will PG).

Quadrel, quarrel, quarel, querel, quariaux, quarials: [OF] crossbow bolt, probably with head of rectangular or diamond section; same as *carrel*; France and England, late 11th–14th centuries (ASR, A&N, Eli, Gre).

Quairal: [Oc] crossbow bolt; southern France, late 13th century (N&L).

Quareli quadreli: [EI] crossbow bolts; Dalmatia, late 13th–14th centuries (Pet DO).

Quartier: [OF] one sector or corner of a shield, or segment of a probably segmented helmet; France, late 11th–late 12th centuries (Beat, Gre).

Quintaine: [OF] target for lance practice, sometimes formed like a warrior with helmet, armour, shield, lance and sword; France, late 12th/early 13th centuries (Gre, Eli).

Quir boli: [OF] *cuir-bouilli* (hardened leather) for various pieces of armour, including *elme de quir boli* of an 'infidel'; France, late 12th century (Chet).

Quiral: [OF] leather covering of a wooden shield; France, late 12th century (Chet).

Quiret: [ME] same as *cuirie* or *cuirace*, probably semi-rigid body-armour of hardened leather; England, late 13th century (Oak).

Quisse: [OF] unclear but probably same as *cuisse* (thigh protection) of leather or felt, or could refer to saddle beneath thigh; France, late 12th century (Chet).

Quyssewes: [ME] probably padded or splinted *cuisses* attached to thighs with *thwongs* (thongs), worn with *poleyns*, *greaves* and *sabatons*; England, mid-14th century (AGG).

Rand-beag: [AS] rim or boss of shield; England, 10th–11th centuries (Kell).

Recors: [OF] unclear form of weapon; France, mid-12th century (Gre).

Relière: [OF] possibly a quiver for crossbow bolts; France, late 12th century (Chet).

Renge: [OF] ring holding scabbard to *baldric*; also on shield strap; France, late 11th century (Gre).

Restiren, cestiren: [FD] unknown item of arms or armour or garment worn with armour; Netherlands, late 13th century (Labou).

Ribaudekin: [FD] possible early reference to gun or cannon; Flanders, early/mid-14th century (Norm NG); see also *ribaudequin* [OF].

Ribaudequin, ribaldis: [OF] form of early cannon; England, mid-14th century (Conta, Norm NG); see also *ribaudekin* [FD].

Ringes, rynges: [ME] individual mail links of a *brinie, bryne* or *bruny* (mail *hauberk*); England, late 13th–mid-14th centuries (A Hav, AGG).

Rochet: [OF] plug on the end of a lance-of-peace used in friendly joust; France, late 12th century (Gre).

Rochet: [ML] long-hafted weapons to cut rigging, etc, in naval warfare; Marseilles, 13th century (Brook NA).

Rohatina: [Cz] heavy lance; Bohemia, 11th–15th centuries (Warn).

Rohatyna: [Pl] heavy lance; Poland, 11th–15th centuries (Warn).

Roiele: [OF] possibly a small round shield of 'three layers of leather' or of *cuirs doblee*, used by a horse-archer; also on a *guige*; France, late 12th century (Chet).

Rondele: [OF] small round shield; France, late 12th century (Gre).

Rotella: [EI] unclear form of shield; Dalmatia, late 13th–14th centuries (Pet DO).

Rouleis: [OF] palisades; France, mid/late 12th century (Beat).

Rutinc: [FD] long knife; Netherlands, late 13th century (Labou).

Ryggearmbryrsth: [OD] literally 'back crossbow', large form of crossbow used in defence of castles; Denmark, early 14th century (Alm).

Sabatounz: [ME] iron shoes or *sabatons* worn with plate *greaves* and *poleyns*; England, mid-14th century (AGG).

Sabia: [EI] curved sabre; Dalmatia, mid-14th century (Pet DO).

Safret: [OF] descriptive term for colour of mail *hauberk*; France and Norman England, late 11th century (Gre).

Sagetas: [Oc] arrows; southern France, early 13th century (N&L).

Sagittandum tonitrum: [ML] literally 'thunder arrow', probably reference to cannon or to a bolt or bullet shot from an early cannon; Germany, mid-14th century (Roth).

Sagitte: [ML] arrows; Europe, mid-13th century (Pai TR).

Saiete: [OF] arrow or arrowhead for ordinary bow; France, 12th century (Chet, Gre).

Saietele: [OF] arrow; France, 13th century (Gre).

Saiget: [Ir] arrow; from Latin; Gaelic Ireland, 12th–14th centuries (Harb 2).

Sambuque, sambuche: [OF] probably theoretical war-engine consisting of a chariot with raised platform carrying twenty men; possibly from Perso-Arabic *sandūq* ('box'); in a translation of Vegetius; France, late 13th century (Gre).

Samostřiel: [Cz] crossbow; Bohemia, from 13th century (Warn).

Samostrzał: [Pl] crossbow; Poland, from 13th century (Warn).

Saquebote: [OF] spear with curved hook to unhorse cavalry; France, early 14th century (Gre).

Saumes: [Oc] probably armament in general; southern France, mid-14th century (Noel).

Sayn, saint: [ME] sword-belt; England, early/mid-14th century (AGG, Tagl).

Scabal, sgabal: [Ir] mail *coif* or *tippet* also covering the shoulders, associated with English *pisayn*; from Latin *scapula*; Gaelic Ireland, mid-14th century (Harb 1).

Scagno: [EI] frame of frame-mounted crossbow; Dalmatia, mid-14th century (Pet DO).

Scēað: [AS] scabbard; England, 10th–11th centuries (Kell).

Scēaft: [AS] haft of spear or whole weapon; England, 10th–11th centuries (Kell, Swant).

Sceeleyder: [FD] possibly leather jerkin worn under armour; Netherlands, late 13th century (Labou).

Sceine: [Ir] small knife or dagger; Gaelic Ireland, mid-14th century (Harb 1).

Scēorp: [AS] unclear form of armour; England, 10th–11th centuries (Kell).

Schaft, schafte: [ME] shaft of arrow, or haft of spear or war-axe; England, early/mid-14th century (AGG, Tagl, Will PG).

Schanncheria, schiniera: [EI] *greaves*; Venice, Dalmatia and Serbia, early/mid-14th century (Pet DO).

Schelde, sheld: [ME] general term for shield; England, late 13th–mid-14th centuries (A Hav, AGG, Tagl, Will PG).

Schinerias sovosbergani: [ML] probably plate or hardened leather *greaves*; Italy, late 13th century (Wal CC).

Sciathroighibh: [Ir] probably *enarmes*, straps on inside of shield; Gaelic Ireland, 14th century (Harb 1).

Scinhoso, scenc gebeorg: [AS] leg-armour, perhaps mail *chausses*; England, 10th–11th centuries (Kell).

Sclopeti, sclopi: [EI] early name of hand-gun, perhaps used at Forli, end 13th century; possibly from Farsi *zabtanah* (blowpipe); Italy and Dalmatia, early/mid-14th century (Conta, Pet FB).

Scottes spere: [ME] light javelin used in hunting; England, mid-14th century (Will PG).

Scudo, scutum: [EI] ordinary term for shield, distinct from *tavolaccio*; Italy, mid-13th–14th centuries (Scal AP, Wal O).

Scuta: [OF] infantry shield, half value of *targ* shield; England, mid-12th century (Smith AM).

Scutum: [ML] general term for cavalry shield; Tuscany, early 14th century (Giu OM).

Scutum bosniensem: [EI] 'Bosnian' shield, probably rectangular or triangular with acute corners;

Dalmatia, early/mid-14th century (Pet DO).

Scutum de caravana: [EI] shield used by merchants, probably oval; Dalmatia, early/mid-14th century (Pet DO).

Scutum parvum: [EI] shield of nobility, probably kite-shaped for cavalry; Dalmatia, early/mid-14th century (Pet DO).

Scyld: [AS] shield; England, 9th–11th centuries (Kell).

Sdarga: [Ir] probably large shield, sometimes worn 'across back' probably with a *guige*; from English *targa*; Gaelic Ireland, early 11th–early 14th centuries (Harb 1).

Seax: [AS] short, single-edged sword or large dagger; England, 9th–11th centuries (Kell).

Securibus: [ML] broad-bladed axe of Scandinavian form used by Gaelic Irish; Ireland, 12th century (Ger T).

Segnal, seignal: [OF] *quillons* of a sword, sometimes 'gilded'; France, late 12th–late 13th centuries (Chet, Gre).

Segreta: [EI] close-fitting helmet, perhaps *cervellière*, to be worn under mail *coif* or larger helmet; Italy, late 13th century (Boc HIM).

Seirch: [EW] perhaps leather soft-armour; Celtic Britain and Wales, 7th–mid-12th centuries (Alc, Will IW).

Sekera: [Cz] war-axe; Bohemia (Warn).

Sele: [OF] saddle; France, late 11th century (Gre).

Senbeiras: [OC] ensigns on lances; southern France, early 13th century (N&L).

Servellarie: [ML] close-fitting helmet (*cervellière*), naval warfare; Marseilles, 13th century (Brook NA).

Sg'ath: [Ir] probably older style of traditional round shield; Gaelic Ireland, early 11th–early 14th centuries (Harb 1).

Shchit: [OCS] wooden shield; from Latin *scutum*; 10th–14th centuries (Warn).

Shelom: [OCS] general term for helmet, probably of directly riveted segmented type; from mid-12th century (Warn).

Siekiera: [Pl] war-axe; from Latin *securis*; Poland, from 11th century (Warn).

Šlap: [Cz] helmet or *coif*; perhaps from Byzantine Greek *skaplion*; Bohemia, from 12th century (Warn).

Sleg: [Ir] broad-headed spear with ashen haft; Gaelic Ireland, 11th–12th centuries (Harb 2).

Snidermessen, scudemessen: [FD] see *messen*.

Soleret: [OF] armoured shoes or mail *chausses*, in Rule of the Temple; France and Crusader states, mid-12th–13th centuries (Conta, Gre).

Sorber: [Oc] large piece of hard wood thrown by siege-engine; southern France, early 13th century (N&L).

Sorcot: [OF] *surcoat*, usually sleeveless, worn over mail *hauberk*; France, late 12th century (Gre).

Sorsele, sossele: [OF] saddle-cover or horse-blanket; France, mid/late 12th century (Gre).

Spada, spata: [EI] general term for sword, large (*magna spata* or *spada granda*) or small (*spada picula*); Italy and Dalmatia, 13th–14th centuries (Scal AP, Pet DO).

Spade schiavonesche: [EI] Balkan-style sword, possibly from Serbia; Dalmatia, mid-14th century (Per DO).

Sparth, sparthe: [ME] general term for axe but also particularly associated with Gaelic war-axes from Ireland and western Scotland (*sparthe de Hibernia*) having elongated upper 'horn' or point; from Norse *sparda* ('axe'); England, early/mid-14th century (Borg).

Spasa: [Oc] sword; southern France, late 12th century (N&L).

Spere: [AS and ME] general term for spear; England, 10th–mid-14th centuries (Kell, Swant, AGG, A Hav, Tagl).

Spingard: [EI] large frame-mounted crossbow shooting large *viretons* (bolts); same as *espringal*; Dalmatia, mid-14th century (Pet DO).

Spondière: [FD] unclear form of armour or garment for militia infantry, perhaps for chest and shoulders; Holland, mid-14th century (V Mie).

Sprēat, spreot: [AS] spear or haft of spear or heavy staff weapon; England, 10th–11th centuries (Kell, Swant).

Spret: [OG] heavy spear or staff weapon; Germany, 12th–13th centuries. (Swant).

Spriet: [FD] heavy spear or staff weapon; Netherlands, 12th–14th centuries (Swant).

Springald: [ME] large frame-mounted crossbow shooting bolts or stones; England and Scotland, late 13th–mid-14th centuries (Burl, Free WB, Tur TD).

Springallis: [ML] large frame-mounted crossbow or *springald*; southern France, late 13th century (Mot AP).

Staef-liƀere: [AS] staff-sling; England, 9th–11th centuries (Kell).

Staef-sweord: [AS] long blade on a wooden haft, probably same as German *glafe* or French *glaive*; England, 10th–11th centuries (Kell).

Staf: [ME] quarter-staff or cudgel; England, late 13th–mid-14th centuries (A Hav, AGG); see also *staf* [FD].

Staf: [FD] unclear form of hafted weapon; Holland, mid-14th century (V Mie); see also *staf* [ME].

Stálhúfu: [ON] perhaps *war-hat* (*chapel-de-fer*); Scandinavia, late 13th century.

Staue: [ME] staff or club; England, mid-14th century (AGG).

Stel, stele: [ME] general term for plate armour of 'steel', or for blade of war-axe; England, mid-14th century (AGG).

Stel-gere: [ME] general term for armour, probably referring mainly to plate armour; England, mid-14th century (AGG).

Steng: [AS] staff or quarter-staff; England, 10th–12th centuries (Swant).

Stivaletti: [EI] probably mail *chausses* to protect legs; Tuscany, mid-13th century (Conta, Giu OM).

Stocco, stocchi: [EI] slender and very pointed thrusting sword; Italy and Dalmatia, mid-14th century (Boc HIM, Pet DO).

Strāel, strāele: [AS] arrow; England, 10th–11th centuries (Kell).

Střela: [Cz] arrow; Bohemia, from 11th century (Warn).

Strzała: [Pl] arrow; Poland, from 11th century (Warn).

Sulitsa, sudlice, sulica: [OCS] javelin or large spear; Slav Central and Eastern Europe, 11th–15th centuries (Warn).

Sweord: [AS] sword; England, 9th–11th centuries (Kell).

Swerd, swerde: [ME] sword; England, late 13th–mid-14th centuries (A Hav, Tagl, Will PG).

Sythe: [ME] scythe, may be used as a weapon; England, late 13th century (A Hav).

Szczyt: [Pl] wooden shield; Poland, 10th–14th centuries (Warn).

Szlom: [Pl] general term for helmet, later referred to *bascinet* and *barbuta* types; Poland, 12th–14th centuries (Warn).

Tabart: [OF] garment worn over or beneath armour; France, late 13th century (Gre).

Tabellatio magno: [ML] large shield or *mantlet* for crossbowmen; Italy, late 13th century (Wal CC).

Tablachos: [SP] large shields for infantry; Navarre, mid-14th century (Conta).

Tablas, taulas tollidas: [SP] large leather-covered shields; Spain, late 13th century (Hoff A2).

Tabolatum, tabolaccium amplum: [ML] broad shield used by some cavalry; Italy, late 13th/early 14th centuries (Giu OM, Wal CC).

Tacle: [OF] type of shield; France, early 14th century (Gre).

Tailm: [Ir] sling; Gaelic Ireland, 11th–12th centuries (Harb 2).

Talevas, taluace: [ME] large shield, used in light infantry skirmishing; England, late 13th–mid-14th centuries (A Hav, Tagl); see also *talevas* [OF].

Talevas: [OF] large infantry shield used with sword; France, mid-12th century (RT, Gre); see also *talevas* [ME].

Taloche: [OF] small shield; France, early 14th century (Gre).

Tambre: [OF] javelin; France, early/mid-12th century (Gre).

Taran: [Pl] unspecified siege-engine; perhaps from Latin *tarantula*; Poland, mid-13th century (Warn).

Tarçeta: [EI] small shield for infantry; Dalmatia, mid-14th century (Pet DO).

Tarcois, tarquois: [OF] quiver; from Farsi *tarkash*; France, mid-12th century (Gre).

Targ, targe, targae: [OF] large shield, probably kite-shaped; twice as valuable as *scuta* shield, may have *pennoncel* of 'beaten gold', those with boss considered 'out of date' by late 12th century; also *targe roees*; perhaps from Norse *targa*; France, Norman England and Crusader states, late 11th–early 13th centuries (Gre, De J, Smith AM, ASR, RT, Beat, Chet, Eli, R de C).

Targa: [AS] shield; England, 10th–11th centuries (Kell); see also *targa* [EI] and *targa* [Ir].

Targa: [EI] cavalry shield; Dalmatia, mid-14th century (Pet DO); see also *targa* [AS] and *targa* [Ir].

Targa: [Ir] kite-shaped shield of Anglo-Norman invaders; 'English' Ireland, mid-14th century (Harb 1); see also *targa* [AS] and *targa* [EI].

Targadha, targaid: [Ir] perhaps small shield; Gaelic Ireland and Gaelic Scotland, 11th–13th centuries (Harb 1, Kell).

Targaid: [SG] small round shield; western Scotland, 11th–13th centuries (Kell).

Target: [ME] small round shield; northern England, early/mid-14th century (Tagl).

Targete: [OF] small shield; France, early 14th century (Gre).

Targiam: [ML] cavalry shield; Tuscany, early 14th century (Giu OM).

Tasselez: [ME] tassels, perhaps decorative or to tie around the wrist, on the haft of an axe; England, mid-14th century (AGG).

Tavolaccio: [ML] shield used instead of *scuto*; Italy, mid/late 13th century (Wal O).

Tavolaccio: [EI] large shield, perhaps rectangular, for infantry, like French *talevas*; Tuscany, mid-13th–14th centuries (Conta, Scal AP).

Telariae: [ML] probably a form of large siege-crossbow; England, late 12th century (Free WB).

Tesak, tesak: [OCS] single-edged short sword or dagger; Slav Central and Eastern Europe, 13th–15th centuries (Warn).

Testera: [SP] iron or leather *chanfron* (horse-armour for the head); Spain, late 13th–14th centuries (Hoff A2).

Testinia: [ML] probably iron or leather *chanfron* (horse-armour for the head); Aragón, early/mid-11th century (GGA).

Thwang: [ME] thongs around grip of club or cudgel; northern England, early/mid-14th century (Tagl).

Tinel: [OF] large mace or baton; France, late 11th century (Gre).

Tiracol: [SP] *guige* to support shield; Spain, 13th–14th centuries (Hoff A2).

Toenart, tuenart: [OF] unclear type of shield; France, mid-12th century (Gre).

Tole: [ME] weaponry in general; England, mid-14th century (AGG).

Tonitrum: [ML] general term for early artillery; Germany, mid-14th century.

Tonnoire: [OF] literally 'thunder', probably reference to gunpowder artillery; France and Flanders, mid-14th century (Roth).

Topfhlem: [OG] *great helm*; Germany, late 12th–13th centuries (Scal DS).

Topor: [Pl] war-axe; Poland, late 11th–15th centuries (Warn).

Tour: [Oc] possibly siege-tower; southern France, late 13th century (N&L).

Trabocco: [EI] counterweight *trebuchet*; Italy, 13th century (Conta).

Trabuquete, trabuquet: [SP] *mangonel*, probably counterweight type; Spain, 13th century (Hoff A2).

Trabuquetz: [Oc] *trebuchet*; southern France, late 13th century (N&L).

Trabutium, trabucium: [ML] form of *trebuchet* with fixed counterweight; Western Europe, 13th century (Conta, Fino MJ, Hoff A2).

Trebuche, trebuc, trebuchet, trebuchel, trebuchier: [OF] *mangonel*, originally referred to man-powered type but later generally reserved for counterweight form; France and Norman England, late 11th–early 14th centuries (Gre, ASR, Conta).

Trebuchet: [EI] counterweight *mangonel*; Dalmatia, early/mid-14th century (Pet DO).

Tresliz, treillis: [OF] mail; France, mid-12th century (Gre).

Treuil: [OF] probably same as *arbalete de tour* (frame-mounted crossbow); France, 13th–14th centuries (Fino MJ).

Tribok, triboke: [OG] counterweight *trebuchet* or *mangonel*; Germany, 13th century (Conta).

Triboli: [ML] *caltrops* in naval warfare; Marseilles, 13th century (Brook NA).

Tripantum: [OF] form of counterweight *mangonel* with both movable and fixed weights to give greater accuracy; from Latin; France, late 13th–14th centuries (Conta, Fino MJ).

Troqui: [OF] unspecified type of weapon or engine used in naval warfare; Genoa, mid-14th century (Brook NA).

Truaillech: [Ir] sword-scabbard; Gaelic Ireland, mid-14th century (Harb 1).

Truenos: [SP] early cannon, literally 'thunderclaps'; Andalus, mid-14th century (Col B).

Truie: [OF] literally 'sow', catapult throwing large stones; France, mid-12th–14th centuries (Gre, Conta).

Tuagh: [Ir] war-axe, probably small; Gaelic Ireland, 11th–14th centuries (Harb 2).

Tumerel: [OF] *trebuchet*; France, mid-13th century (Gre).

Turcois: [OF] quiver; from Farsi *tarkash*; France, mid-12th century (Gre).

Turno balistarum: [ML] probably frame-mounted crossbow; southern France, late 13th century (Mot AP).

Turnus: [ML] winch to load *trebuchet*; southern France, late 13th century (Mot AP).

Uellière: [OF] probably eye-slits in early forms of *elme* (*great helm*); France, late 12th/early 13th centuries (Eli, Chev).

Umbrere: [ME] movable visor of *bascinet* or later form of *great helm*; England, mid-14th century (Will PG).

Urondor: [EW] possibly unclear form of body-armour; Wales, mid/late 12th century (Will IW).

Vaginis: [ML] scabbard of sword; Europe, mid-12th century (Pai TR).

Vairescuts: [SP] shields, perhaps leather-covered, from Italy; Catalonia, mid-14th century (Hoff A2).

Varaingle: [OF] part of horse-harness; France, mid-12th century (Gre).

Venablo: [SP] javelin; Spain, 13th century (Hoff A2).

Ventail, ventaille, ventele, ventale: [OF] flap of mail forming part of integral or separate mail *coif*, drawn across chin or mouth to protect throat and lower part of face, normally laced at side of head; later referred to mail *aventail* suspended from edge of *bascinet* helmet; France and Norman England, late 11th–early 14th centuries (Gre, ASR, RT, TOF, Chet, Chev).

Ventale: [ME] mail *ventaille* of *coif*, or probably by 14th century *aventail* fastened to *bascinet*, worn with *pesane* (probably *gorget*); England, mid-14th century (Will PG).

Ventalla: [SP] mail *ventaille* on *coif*; Spain, 12th–14th centuries (Hoff A2).

Ventele: [OF] apparently referring to openings or air-holes in *great helm*; France, mid-13th century (Gre).

Verge: [OF] staff or rod, probably to beat prisoners rather than a weapon; France, late 12th century (Chet).

Vergiers: [OF] perhaps staff-weapon; also *vergiers trenchier*; England, mid-12th century (Poures).

Verniz: [OF] part of a shield; France, late 12th century (Gre).

Vignes: [OF] form of wooden siege device, perhaps scaling ladder; France, 13th century (Conta).

Vireton: [OF] crossbow bolt designed to spin in flight; France, mid-14th century (Gre).

Viretoni: [EI] large crossbow bolt; Dalmatia, mid-14th century (Pet DO).

Virga: [ML] probably horizontal pivot of *trebuchet*; southern France, late 13th century (Mot AP).

Visagière: [OF] visor, probably movable; France, early 14th century (Gre).

Visarma: [SP] long-bladed axe, *guisarme*; Spain, 13th–14th centuries (Hoff A2).

Visière: [OF] face-mask or front part of a *great helm* rather than a movable visor; France, mid-13th century (Gre).

Volet: [OF] veil or cloth floating from a helmet as a form of plume; south-west France, mid-12th century (RT).

Vooge, vouge: [OF] unclear form of pike or halbard; France, late 12th century (Gre).

Vrysoun: [ME] decorative fabric covering over a mail *aventail*; England, mid-14th century (AGG).

Wǣpen: [AS] general term for weapons; England, 10th–11th centuries (Kell).

Waffen-rock: [OG] mail *hauberk*; Germany, 11th–13th centuries (Scal DS).

Wair: [FD] lance; Netherlands, late 13th century (Labou).

Wambais, wambasia: [ME] padded or quilted soft armour, same as *gambeson*; possibly from Byzantine Greek *kabadion*; England, late 12th century (Bee W).

Wande: [ME] club or haft of mace; England, mid-14th century (Will PG).

Wans de maille: [OF] mail gloves or *gauntlets*; Flanders, early 14th century (Gans A).

Wapen: [FD] armour and weapons in general; Netherlands, late 13th century (Labou).

Wapen scoen: [FD] armoured shoes (*sabatons*); Netherlands, late 13th century (Labou).

Wapyn, wepne, weppenes: [ME] weapons in general; England, late 13th–14th centuries (A Hav, AGG, Tagl).

Wardecors: [FD] probably padded or quilted *gambeson*, or a *coat-of-plates*; Netherlands, late 13th century (Labou).

Wayelen: [FD] unclear form of armour used by militia infantry, perhaps for hands or arms; Holland, mid-14th century (V Mie).

Wede: [ME] military clothing and armour to be laced on; northern England and midlands, early/mid-14th century (Tagl, Will PG).

Wibete: [OF] type of arrow; France, mid-12th century (Gre).

Wigar: [AS] javelin or arrow; from Old Norse *vigr*; England, 10th–11th centuries (Kell, Swant).

Wigre: [OF] javelin; France and Norman England, late 11th century (ASR).

Yelmo: [SP] *great helm*; Spain, early 13th–14th centuries (Hoff A2, Morris MS).

Yrnes: [ME] general term for armour, literally 'irons'; England, mid-14th century (AGG).

Ysgwyd: [EW] form of shield; Wales, 12th–13th centuries (Will BT).

Zubbone cerbellerio: [ML] small close-fitting *cervellière* helmet of crossbowmen; Italy, late 13th century (Wal CC).

Bibliographies

A voluminous amount has been written on arms, armour, tactics, social and military organisation, and the economic basis of medieval warfare, since serious study of the subject began in the late 18th century. The following bibliographies cannot embrace all such books, articles, theses, and published and unpublished papers, but they include as large a number as possible of both well-known, readily available sources and more obscure, less readily available works. Many of the titles cover more than one aspect of the subject but have only been listed once, in the particular bibliography to which they seem primarily suited. Other works are included even though their main subject matter lies outside the scope of the book before you, because they nevertheless contain some information relevant to the subject under review.

Arms, Armour and Art

Unpublished primary sources
Carley L.K., *The Anglo-Norman Vegetius* (Ph.D. thesis, Nottingham University, 1961–2).

Published primary sources
Alberic de Besancon, 'L'Education d'Alexandre', ed. F.C.W. Vogel, in *Bartsh Chrestomathie* (Leipzig, 1875).

Alfonso el Sabio, *Las siete partidas* (Paris, 1861).
  Las siete partidas del muy noble rey Don Alfonso el Sabio, ed. G. López (Madrid, 1843–4).

Angelucci, A., *Documenti inediti per la storia delle armi da fuoco italiane* (Turin, 1869; reprint Graz, 1972).

Anon., *L'Art d'Archerie*, ed. H. Gallice (Paris, 1901).

'Assize of Arms', in *Gesta Regis Henrici Secundi benedicti Abbatis*, ed. W. Stubbs (London, 1867), pp.278–80.

'Assize of Le Mans', in *Gesta Regis Henrici Secundi benedicti Abbatis*, ed. W. Stubbs (London, 1867), pp.267–70.

Castro y Calvo, J.M., *El Arte de Gobernar en las Obras de D. Juan Manuel*, early 14th century comparative tactics (Barcelona, 1945).

Giese, W., 'Portugiesische Waffenterminologie des XIII Jahrhunderts', in *Miscelânea de Estudios en Honra D. Carolina Michaelis de Vasconcellos* (Coimbra, 1930).
  'Weffan nach den katalanischen Chronikon des XIII Jahrhundert', *Volksturm und Kultur der Romanen* vol.I (1928), pp.140–82.
  'Waffen nach den provenzalischen Epen und Chronikon des XII und XIII Jahrhunderts, Beiträge zur Geschichte der Bewaffnung Südfrankreichs im Mittelalter', *Zeitschrift für romanischen Philologie* vol.LII (1932), pp.351–405.

Waffen nach spanischen Literatur des 12 und 13 Jahrhunderts (Hamburg, 1925).

'Waffengeschichtliche und terminologische Aufschlüsse aus katalanischen literarischen Denkmälern des 14 und 15 Jahrhunderts', in *Homenage a Antonio Rubio i Lluch* (Barcelona, 1936), pp.33–67.

Unpublished secondary sources

Alexander, J.J.G., *Norman Illumination at Mont St Michel in the Tenth and Eleventh Centuries* (Ph.D. thesis, Oxford University, 1965–6).

Ayres, L.M., *The Transition from Romanesque to Gothic in English Painting and Sculpture* (B.Litt. thesis, Oxford University, 1965–6).

Borsook, E., *Principles of Mural Decoration in Fourteenth Century Tuscan Fresco Cycles* (Ph.D. thesis, London University, 1955–6).

Butler, L.A.S., *Minor Medieval Monumental Sculpture in the East Midlands* (Ph.D. thesis, Nottingham University, 1961–2).

Chevedden, P.E., *The Artillery Revolution of the Middle Ages: the Counterweight Trebuchet and the New System of Defensive Planning which it Initiated*, paper delivered at the Annual Meeting of the Middle East Studies Association (San Francisco, November–December 1984).

Corrie, R.W., *The Conradin Bible, Walters Art Gallery Ms. 152: Illustration Practices of a 13th Century Italian Manuscript Atelier* (Ph.D. thesis, Harvard University, 1985).

Dunford, P.A., *The Iconography of the Life of St John the Baptist in the Art of North and Central Italy before 1500* (Ph.D. thesis, Nottingham University, 1971–2).

Farquar, M.M., *A Catalogue of the Illuminated Manuscripts of the Romanesque Period from Rheims, 1050–1130 AD* (Ph.D. thesis, London University, 1967–8).

Gardner, C., *Freun Teuffel von Birkensee: Studies of the Tuscan Altarpiece in the Fourteenth and Early Fifteenth Centuries* (Ph.D. thesis, London University, 1975).

Garton, T.E.H., *Early Romanesque Sculpture in Apulia* (Ph.D. thesis, London University, 1975).

Geddes, J., *English Decorative Ironwork, 1100–1350* (Ph.D. thesis, London University, 1978).

Gethyn-Jones, J.E., *The Romanesque Sculpture in the Dymock Group of Churches* (M.A. thesis, Bristol University, 1965–6).

Harris, J.M., *The Development of Romanesque-Byzantine Elements in French and English Dress 1050–1180* (Ph.D. thesis, Manchester University, 1977).

Henderson, G.D.S., *Ms. K.26 in the Library of St John's College, Cambridge: A Study of the Style and Iconography of Its Thirteenth Century Illustrations* (Ph.D. thesis, Cambridge University, 1959–60).

Kauffmann, C.M., *The Illumination of Petrus de Ebulo: De Balneis Puteolanis* (Ph.D. thesis, Warburg Institute, London University, 1956–7).

Kelleher, C., *Illumination of St Bertin at St Omer, under the Abbacy of Odbert* (Ph.D. thesis, London University, 1967–8).

Margeson, S.M., *Problems of Pagan and Christian Iconography in Early Medieval Scandinavian Art, with Particular Reference to the Volsung Legend* (Ph.D. thesis, London University, 1978).

Narkiss, B., *The Illustrations of the Haggadah BM Add. Ms. 27.210 and its Relation to Other Jewish and to Christian Biblical Cycles* (Ph.D. thesis, London University, 1962–3).

Newton, P.A., *Schools of Glass Painting in the Midlands 1275–1430* (Ph.D. thesis, London University, 1961–2).

O'Reilly, J.L., *Studies in the Iconography of the Vices and Virtues in the Middle Ages* (Ph.D. thesis, Nottingham University, 1972–3).

Park, W.D., *The Romanesque Wall Paintings of Hardham Church, Sussex, with Reference to Those of the Other Churches of the Lewes Group* (M.A. thesis, Manchester University, 1975).

Robbins, E.A., *Romanesque Sculpture of Romsey Abbey* (Ph.D. thesis, London University, 1971–2).

Rodwell, C.R., *The Canterbury School of Illumination (1066–1200)* (Ph.D. thesis, Cambridge University, 1950–1).

Roe, F.E.S., *A Study of the Battle-axes, Axe-hammers and Mace-heads from England, Scotland and Wales* (M.Litt. thesis, Cambridge University, 1969–70).

Simon, D.L., *The Doña Sancha Sarcophagus and Romanesque Sculpture in Aragón* (Ph.D. thesis, London University, 1977).

    A Study of the Sculpture from San Miguel de Uncastillo in the Museum of Fine Arts, Boston (M.A. thesis, Boston University, 1973).

Stones, M., *The Illustration of the French Prose 'Lancelot' in Belgium, Flanders and Paris 1250–1340* (Ph.D. thesis, London University, 1970–1).

Swanton, M.J., *The Spear in Anglo-Saxon Times* (Ph.D. thesis, Durham University, 1965–6).

Vaughan, R., *The Relationship and Chronology of the Historical Manuscripts of Matthew Paris* (Ph.D. thesis, Cambridge University, 1954–5).

Warner, B., *Slavonic Terms for Weapons and Armour in the Middle Ages: A Lexico-Historical Study* (M.A. thesis, London University, 1965).

Wenzel, M.B., *Ornamental Motifs on Tombstones from Medieval Bosnia and Surrounding Regions* (Ph.D. thesis, London University, 1966–7).

Whittingham, J.S., *Realism in Medieval Portaiture* (Ph.D. thesis, Manchester University, 1975).

Zarnecki, J., *Regional Schools in English Sculpture in the Twelfth Century* (Ph.D. thesis, London University, 1951–2).

Published secondary sources

Abbrescia, D., 'La tombe della chiesa di S. Romano', in *Lucca, Chiesa di S. Romano* (Lucca, 1966), pp.60–7.

Achten, G., *Hildegardis-Gebetbuch, Faksimile Ausgabe*, late 12th century manuscript (Wiesbaden, 1982).

Adam-Even, P., 'Les enseignes militaires du Moyen Age et leur influence sur l'heraldique', in *Recueil du Ve Congrès international des sciences généologiques et héraldiques* (Stockholm, 1960), pp.167–94.

Adelson, H.L., 'The Holy Lance and the Hereditary German Monarchy', *Art Bulletin* vol.XLVIII, no.2 (1966).

Ahne, P., and Beyer, V., *Les Vitraux de la cathédrale de Strasbourg* (Strasbourg, 1960).

Ainaud, J., *Romanesque Painting* (London, 1963).

Alba Medea, *Gli affreschi delle cripte eremitiche pugliesi* (Rome, 1939).

Alexander, J.J.G., *Norman Illumination at Mont St Michel 966–1100* (Oxford, 1970).

Alfonso el Sabio, *Cántigas de Santa Maria (Edicion fasc'mil de Codice T.l.l. de la Biblioteca de San Lorenzo el Real de El Escorial)* (Madrid, 1979).

Alm, J., 'Europeisk armbrust: Ein översikt', *Vaaben-historisk Aarboger* V/b (1947), pp.107–255.

Andersson, A., *The Art of Scandinavia* (London, 1968).

    English Influence in Norwegian and Swedish Figure Sculpture in Wood 1220–70 (Stockholm, 1950).

Angelucci, A., *Il tiro a segno in Italia dal XII al XVI secolo, Cenni storici con documenti inediti* (Turin, 1863).

Anteins, A.K., 'Die Kurischen shombischen Lanzen spitzen mit damassierten Blatt', *Gladius* vol.VII (1968).

    Melnais Metals Latirjā (Ferrous Metals in Latvia) (Riga, 1976).

    'The Old Arms of Basilsimsa (History of Ventspilskaya Okrug)', *Sovietskaya Venta* vol.I, in Russian, (1983).

    'Structure and Manufacturing Techniques of Pattern Welded Objects found in the Baltic States', *Journal of the Iron and Steel Institute* (June 1968), pp.563–71.

Aroldi , A.M., *Armi e Armature Italiane, fino al XVIII secolo* (Milan, 1961).

Arslan, E., 'La Statua Equestre di Cangrande', in *Studi in Onore de Federico M. Mistrorigo* (Vicenza, 1951), pp.3–30.

Aubert, M., *French Sculpture at the Beginning of the Gothic Period 1140–1225* (Florence and Paris,

1929).

Le Vitrail français (Paris, 1958).

Aubert, M., *Les Vitraux de Notre-Dame et de la Sainte-Chapelle de Paris* (Paris, 1959).

Bacchi, G., *La Certosa di Firenze* (Florence, 1956).

Bailey, R.N., *Viking Age Sculpture in Northern England* (London, 1980).

Bartlett, C., and Embleton, G., 'The English Archer c.1300–1500', *Military Illustrated, Past and Present* I–II (1986).

Bauch, K., 'Anfänge des figürlichen Grabmals in Italien', *Mitteilungen des Kunsthistorischen Institutes in Florenz* vol.XV (1971), pp.227–58.

Das mittelalterliche Grabbild (Berlin, 1976).

Becksmann, R., and Waetzoldt, S., eds., *Vitrea Dedicata, Das Stifterbild in der deutschen Glasmalerei des Mittelalters* (Berlin, 1975).

Bell, C., *Twelfth Century Painting at Hardham and Clayton* (Lewes, 1947).

Beneš, F., 'Česki panovnicke peceti z let 1310–1526 (Bohemian Royal Seals)', *Muzenji z právy prozskeho kraje* vol.IV (1959).

Bergman, R.P., *The Salerno Ivories: Ars Sacra from Medieval Amalfi* (Cambridge, Mass., 1980).

Bernouli, C., *Die Skulpturen der Abtei Conques-en-Rouerque* (Basle, 1956).

Bertaux, E., 'La sculpture du XIVe siècle en Espagne', in *Histoire de l'Art*, ed. A. Micel, vol.II, no.2 (Paris, 1906), pp.670–1.

Berthelot, M., 'Histoire des machines de guerre et des arts mécanique au Moyen Age', *Annales de Chimie et de Physique* 7th ser. vol.XIX (1900), pp.289–420.

'Pour l'histoire de l'artillerie et des arts mécaniques vers la fin du Moyen Age', *Annales de Chimie et de Physique* 6th ser. vol.XXIV (1891), pp.435–521.

Bertuccioli, U., *La sala d'armi dal Palazzo ducale* (Venice, 1957).

Béthune, Baron J., *Calques des peintures murales de la chapelle de la Leugemeete, á Gand* (Gand, 1861).

Beyer, V., *La Sculpture Strasbourgeoise au XIVe siècle* (Paris and Strasbourg, 1955).

Bibliothèque Nationale, *Les manuscrits à peintures en France* (Paris, 1954–5).

Biddle, M., 'A Late Saxon Frieze Sculpture from the Old Minster', *Antiquaries Journal* vol.XLVI (1966), pp.329–32.

Bilderchronik: Chronicon pictum (Weimar-Budapest, 1968).

Biver, P., 'Tombs of the School of London at the Beginning of the Fourteenth Century', *Archaeological Journal* vol.LXVII (1910), pp.51–65.

Blair, C., *European and American Arms, c. 1100–1850* (London, 1962).

European Armour (London, 1958).

'Medieval Effigies in the County of Durham', *Archaeologia Aeliana* 4th ser. vol.VII (1930), pp.1–50.

'The Pre-Reformation Effigies of Cheshire', *Transactions of the Lancashire and Cheshire Antiquarian Society* vol.IX (1948), pp.117–47 and vol.LXI (1949), pp.91–120.

'The Word "Baselard"', *Journal of the Arms and Armour Society* vol.XI (1984), pp.193–206.

and Boccia, L.G., *Armi e Armature* (Milan, 1981).

Boase, T.S.R., *English Art 1100–1216* (Oxford, 1953).

The York Psalter (London, 1962).

Boccia, L.G., 'L'Armamento in Toscana dal Millecento al Trecento', in *Civilita delle Art Minori in Toscana; Atti del I Convegni, Arezzo 11–15 Maggio 1971* (Florence, 1973).

L'arte dell'armatura in Italia (Milan, 1967).

ed., *Dizionari terminologici, Armi difensive dal Medioevo all'Eta Moderna* (Florence, 1982).

'HIC IACET MILES: Immagini guerriere da sepolcri toscani del Due e Trecento', in *Guerre e assoldati in Toscana, 1260–1364*, eds. L.G. Boccia and M. Scalini (Florence 1982–3).

'The Xalkis Finds in Athens and New York', in *Papers delivered at the Working Sessions of IAMAM*, vol.IX (New York, 1981), pp.1–11.

and Coelho, E.T., 'L'armamento di cuoio e ferro nel Trecento Italiano', *L'illustrazione italiani* vol.I (1972), pp.24–7.

Armi Bianche Italiane (Milan, 1975).

and Rossi, F., and Morin, M., *Armi e Armature Lombarde* (Milan, 1980).

Boeckler, A., *Das Goldene Evanglienbuch Heinrich III* (Berlin, 1933).

Boeheim, W., 'Bogen und Armbrust', *Zeitschrift für Historische Waffen- und Kostümkunde* vol.I (1897–9)

Führer durch die Waffensammlung (Vienna, 1889).

Handbuch der Waffenkunde (Leipzig, 1890; Graz, 1966).

Bohigas, P., *La Illustración del libro manuscrito en Cataluña* (Barcelona, 1960).

Bonnefoy, Y., *Peintures murales de la France Gothique* (Paris, 1954).

Borg, A., 'Gisarmes and Great Axes', *Journal of the Arms and Armour Society* vol.VIII (1974–6), pp.337–42.

Borgatti, M., 'Gli Affreschi militari di Avio', *Esercito e Nazione* vol.II, no.9 (1927).

Borger, H., *Grabdenkmäles im Maingebiet vom Anfang des XIV Jahrhunderts bis zum Eintritt der Renaissance* (Leipzig, 1907).

Bosson, C., 'L'arbalète', *Les Musées de Geneve* (February 1956), p.2.

La Hallebarde (Geneva, 1955).

Bousquet, L'Abbé, *Le jugement dernier au tympanum de l'église Sainte-Foy de Conques* (Rodez, 1948).

Bravetta, E., *L'Artiglierie e le sue meraviglie dalle origine fino al nostra giorni* (Milan, 1919).

Breck, J., 'The Sepulchral Effigy of Jean d'Alluye', *Bulletin of the Metropolitan Museum of Art* vol.XXIV (1929), pp.54–5.

Brehier, L., *L'homme dans la sculpture romane* (Paris, 1927).

Le style Roman (Paris, 1941).

Brieger, P., *English Art 1216–1307* (Oxford, 1957).

Brion-Guerry, L., *Fresques romanes de France* (Paris, 1958).

Brooks, F.W., 'Naval Armament in the 13th Century', *Mariner's Mirror* vol.XIV (1928), pp.115–31.

Brückner, W., *Bilnis und Brauch, Studien zur Bildfunktion der Effigies* (Berlin, 1966).

Brun, R., 'Notes sur le commerce des armes à Avignon au XIVe siècle', *Bibliothèque de l'Ecole des Chartres* vol.CIX (1952), pp.209–31.

Brydall, R., 'The Monumental Effigies of Scotland from the Thirteenth to the Fifteenth Century', *Proceedings of the Society of Antiquaries of Scotland* (1895), pp.329–410.

Bucher, F., *The Pamplona Bibles, 1197–1200 AD* (New Haven, Conn., 1970).

Buchner, O., *Die Mittelalterliche Grabplastik in Nord-Thüringen* (Strassburg, 1902).

Buchthal, H., *The Miniatures of the Paris Psalter* (London, 1938).

Burger, F., *Geschichte des Florentinischen Grabmals von den ältesten Zeiten bis Michelangelo* (Strassburg, 1904).

Burns, R.I., 'The Medieval Crossbow as Surgical Instrument: An Illustrated Case History', *Bulletin of the New York Academy of Medicine* vol.XLVIII (1972).

Buttin C., 'Le tombeau d'Ulrich de Werdt à l'église Saint-Guillaume à Strasbourg', *Archives alsaciennes d'histoire de l'art* vol.IV (1925), pp.41–83.

Buttin, F., *Du Costume Militaire au Moyen Age et Pendant la Renaissance, Memoires de la Real Academia de Buenas Letras de Barcelona* (1971).

'La Lance et l'arrêt de Cuirasse', *Archaeologia* vol.XCIX (1965).

Cahansky, N., *Die romanischen Wandmalereien de ehmaligen Abteikirche Saint-Chef* (Bern, 1966).

Caldwell, D.H., *Scottish Weapons and Fortifications 1100–1800* (Edinburgh, 1980).

Calvert, A.G., *Spanish Arms and Armour* (London, 1907).

Carmen, W.Y., *A History of Firearms from the Earliest Times to 1914* (London, 1955).

Chamberlayne, T.B., *Laerimae Nicosienses* (Cypriot Carvings and Tombstones) (Paris, 1894).

Chamot, M., 'Early Mural Painting in France', *Apollo* vol.XIV (1931).

Cirlot, J.E., 'La Evolucion de la lanza en Occidenti', *Gladius* vol.VI (1967).

Clasen, K.H., *Die Mittelalterliche Bildhauerkunst im Deutsche-ordens Preussen* (Berlin, 1939).

Clayton, M., *Catalogue of Rubbings of Brasses and Incised Slabs, Victoria and Albert Museum, South Kensington* (London, 1929).

Cockerell, S.C., *A Book of Old Testament Illustrations* (The Maciejowski Bible, Facsimile) (London, 1927).

Coe, B., *Stained Glass in England, 1150–1550* (London, 1982).

Combe, E., and de Cosson, E.F.C., 'European Swords with Arabic Inscriptions', *Bulletin de la Société Royale d'Archéologie d'Alexandria* n.s. vol.IX, no.2 (1937).

Corrie, R.W., 'The Conradin Bible: Since de Ricci', *Journal of the Walters Art Gallery* vol.XL (1982), pp.13–24.

Cortes, J., *Museo-Provincial de Alava, Armeria* (Vitoria, 1967).

Credland, A.G., 'The Crossbow in the Far North', *Journal of the Society of Archer-Antiquaries* vol.XXVI (1983).

Crichton, G.H., *Romanesque Sculpture in Italy* (London, 1954)

Crossley, F.H., *English Church Monuments AD 1150–1550: An Introduction to the Study of Tombs and Effigies of the Medieval Period* (London, 1921).

Crozet, R., *L'Art Roman en Poitou* (Paris, 1948).
    'Nouvelles remarques sur les cavaliers sculptés ou peints dans les églises romanes', *Cahiers de civilizations medièvales* vol.I (1958), pp.27–36.

Csemegi, J., 'Az Aracsi Kö' (11th century Hungarian carving), *Archeologia Értesitö* vol.LXXXV (1958), pp.172–89.

Csillag, F., *A kardok történelmünkben* (The Sword in Hungarian History) (Budapest, 1971).

Ćurčič, V., 'Starinsko oruzie u Bosni i Hercegovini' (Old arms in Bosnia and Hercegovina), in *Glasnik Hrvatskog državnog muzeja u Sarajevu* (Sarajevo, 1943–4).

Davidson, H.R.E., *The Sword in Anglo-Saxon England* (Oxford, 1962).

Davillier, Baron C., *Recherches sur l'orfevrerie en Espagne* (Paris, 1879).

De Apraiz, A., 'La representacion de caballero en las iglesias de los cominos de Santiago', *Archivo español de arte* (1941), pp.384–96.

De Ghellinck Vaernewyck, Viscompte, *Sceaux et armoires de villes, communes, échvinages, châtellenies, métiers et seigneuries de la Flandre ancienne et moderne* (Paris, 1935).

De Gray Birch, W., *Catalogue of Seals in the Department of Manuscripts in the British Museum* (London, 1900).

De Hoffmeyer, A.B., *Arms and Armour in Spain, a Short Survey* vol.I (Madrid, 1972), vol.II (Madrid, 1982).
    'From Medieval Sword to Renaissance Rapier', in *Art, Arms and Armour*, ed. R. Held, (Chiasso, 1979)
    'Introduction to the History of the European Sword', *Gladius* vol.I (1961).
    'Middelalderens Islamiske Svaerd', *Vaabenhistoriske Aalboger* vol.VIII (1956), pp.63–80.
    Rustninger og Gamle Vaaben (Copenhagen, 1948).

De Leguina, E., *Espadas Historicas* (Madrid, 1898).

De Lucia, G., *La Sala d'Armi nel' Museo dell'arsenale di Venezia* (Rome, 1908).

De Mas-Latrie, L., 'Notes des armes existant à l'Arsenal de Venise en 1314', *Bibliothèque de l'École des Chartres* vol.XXV (1865), pp.56–66.

De May, G., *Le Costume au Moyen Age d'après les sceaux* (Paris, 1880).
    Inventaire des sceaux de l'Artois et de la Picardie (Paris, 1877).
    Inventaire des sceaux de la collection Clairambault (Paris, 1885–6).
    Inventaire des sceaux de la Flandre (Paris, 1873).

De Poerck, G., 'L'artillerie à resorts medievale: Notes lexicologiques et étymologiques', *Bulletin*

Du Cange vol.XVIII (1943–4), pp.35–49.

De Vigne, F., *Recherches historiques sur les costumes civiles et militaires des gildes et des corporations de métier, etc* (Ghent, 1847).

De Vita, C., *Dizionari Terminologici: Armi Bianche dal Medioevo all'Etá Moderno* (Ateneo di Brescia, Accademia di Scienze, Lettere ed Arti, 1983).

Dean, B., *Catalogue of European Daggers 1300–1800* (Metropolitan Museum of Art, New York, 1929).

    Handbook of Arms and Armour (Metropolitan Museum of Art, New York, 1930).

Delaporte, Y., *L'Art du Vitrail aux XIIe et XIIIe siècles* (Chartres, 1963).

    Les Vitraux de la Cathédrale de Chartres (Chartres, 1926).

Demmin, A., *Die Kriegswaffen in Ihren geschichtlichen Entwickelungen von der ältesten Zeiten bis auf die Gegenwart* (Leipzig, 1893).

Demus, O., *Romanesque Mural Painting* (London, 1970).

Denkstein, V., 'Pavises of the Bohemian Type', *Sbornik Národniho Muzea v Praze ser. A.- Histoire* vol.XVIII, nos 3 and 4 (Prague, 1964).

Deschamps, P., 'Combats de cavalerie et episodes des Croisades dans les peintures murales du XIIe et du XIIIe siècle', *Orientalia Christiana Periodica* vol.XIII (1947).

    French Sculpture of the Romanesque Period, Eleventh and Twelfth Centuries (Florence and Paris, 1930).

    'Les fresques romanes de l'église du Poncé-sur-Loire', *Congrés archéologiques de France* vol.CXIX (Maine, 1961), pp.189–94.

    La peinture en France, le haut moyen âge et l'époque romane (Paris, 1951).

    La peinture murale en France au debut de l'époque gothique de Philippe Auguste à la fin du règne du Charles V, 1180–1380 (Paris, 1963).

    'La sculpture francaise en Palestine et en Syrie', *Monuments Piot* vol.XXXI (1930), pp.94–5.

Deshoulières, F., 'Les Peintures murales de l'église de Thevet-Saint-Martin (Indre)', *Bulletin Monumental* vol.XCII (1933), p.81ff.

Di Carpegna, N., *Antiche armi dal secolo IX al XVIII gia Collezione Odescalchi* (Rome, 1969).

Dieters, F., *Die Englischen Angriffswaffen zur Zeit der Einführung der Feuerwaffen (1300–1350)* (Heidelberg, 1913).

Dillon, H., 'On Some of the Smaller Weapons of the Middle Ages', *The Reliquary* n.s. vol.I (1888), pp.2–4.

Divald, K., *Old Hungarian Art* (Oxford–Budapest, 1931).

Dodds, W., 'Crossbow Locks', *Journal of the Society of Archer Antiquaries* vol.VI (1964), pp.33–4.

Dodwell, C.R., *The Canterbury School of Illumination 1066–1200* (London, 1959).

    The Great Lambeth Bible (London, 1959).

    Painting in Europe 800–1200 (Harmondsworth, 1971).

Drobna, Z., *Medieval Costume and Weapons (1350–1450)* (London, 1958).

    and Durdik, J., and Wagner, E., *Tracht Wehr und Waffen des Späten Mittelalter (1350–1450)* (Prague, 1960).

Du Ranquet, H., *Les Vitraux de la Cathédrale de Clermont-Ferrand* (Paris, 1932).

Dufour, G.H., *Mémoire sur l'artillerie des anciens et sur celle du moyen âge* (Paris, 1840).

Durliat, M., *L'art dans le royaume de Majorque* (Toulouse, 1962).

    Arts anciens du Roussillon, peintures (Perpignan, 1954).

    La sculpture romane en Cerdagne (Perpignan, 1957).

    La sculpture romane en Roussillon (Perpignan, 1948–54).

Ellehauge, M., *The Spear Traced through its post-Roman Development* (Copenhagen, 1948).

Enlart, C., *L'art Gothique et de la Renaissance en Chypre* (Paris, 1872).

    Manuel d'archéologie française depuis les temps carolingiens jusqu'à la Renaissance, vol.III, Le Costume (Paris, 1932).

Monuments des Croisés dans le Royaume de Jerusalem (Paris, 1925–8).

Erben, W., *Der Bilderhandschrift des Petrus von Ebulo, um 1200* (Bern, n.d.).

Eri, I., 'Adatok a kigyspusztai csat ertekelesehez' (13th century clasp showing warriors), *Folia Archeologica* (1955).

Erlande-Brandenburg, A., 'Communication sur Les tombeaux de Pont-aux-Dames', *Bulletin de la société nationale des antiquaires de France* (1969), pp.93–4.

    Le Roi est Mort: Étude sur Les funerailles, Les sépultures et les tombeaux des rois de France jusqu'à la fin du XIIIe siècle (Geneva, 1975).

Evans, J., *Cluniac Art of the Romanesque Period* (Cambridge, 1950).

    Dress in Medieval France (Oxford, 1952).

Fabre, A., 'La Sculpture Provençale en Palestine au XIIe siècle', *Echos d'Orient* vol.XXI (1922).

Fau, J., *Chapitaux de Conques* (Toulouse, 1956).

Ferrani, G., *La Tomba nell'Arte Italiana dal Periodo Preromano all'odierno* (Milan, n.d.).

Ffoulkes, C.J., 'A Carved Flemish Chest at New College, Oxford', *Archaeologia* vol.LXV (1914), pp.113–28.

    'Some Aspects of the Craft of the Armourer', *Archaeologia* vol.LXXIX (1929), pp.13–28.

Filow, B., *Evangel Jean Alexandre* (Paris, 1934).

Fino, J.F., 'Le feu et ses usages militaires', *Gladius* vol.IX (1970), pp.15–30.

    'Machines de jet médiévales', *Gladius* vol.X (1972), pp.25–43.

    'Notes sur le production de fer et la fabrications des armes en France au Moyen Age', *Gladius* vol.III (1963), pp.47–66.

    'Origines et puissance des machines à balancier médiévales', *Société des antiquites nationales* n.s. vol.XI (1972).

Fiumi, E., *San Gimignano* (Florence, 1961).

Flanagan, L.N.W., 'The Gallowglass Axe', *Ulster Journal of Archaeology* vol.XXIII (1960), pp.59–60.

Fleischhauer, W., 'Spangenharnisch fund aus Burg Helfenstein', *Zeitschrift für Historisches Waffen- und Kostümkunde* n.s. vol.IV, no.2 (1934).

Flutre, L.F., 'Une arbaleste faite de cor', *Romania* vol.XCV (1974), pp.309–16.

Focillon, H., *Peintures romanes des églises de France* (Paris, 1938).

Folda, J., ed., *Crusader Art in the Twelfth Century: A volume of Ten Papers Sponsored by the British School of Archaeology in Jerusalem* (Oxford, 1982).

    Crusader Manuscript Illuminations at Saint Jean d'Acre 1275–1291 (Princeton, 1976).

    'Crusader Painting in the 13th Century', in *Acts of the 24th International Congress of the History of Art (Bologna 1979)* (1985).

Folly, V., and Perry, K., 'In Defence of Liber Igneum: Arab Alchemy, Roger Bacon and the Introduction of Gunpowder into the West', *Journal for the History of Arabic Science* vol.III, no.2 (1979), pp.200–8.

    Paler, G., and Soedel, W., 'The Crossbow', *Scientific American* (January 1985), pp.104–10.

Forestié, E., 'Hughes de Cardaillac et la poudre à canon', *Bulletin archéologique de la Société archéologique du Tarn-et-Garonne* vol.XXIX (1901), pp.93–132, 185–222 and 297–312.

Forrer, R., 'Studien material zur Geschichte der Mittelalterwaffen', *Zeitschrift für Historisches Waffen- und Kostümkunde* (1900–2).

Friedl, A., *Lekcionář Arnolda Míšenkého* (The Lectionary of Arnold of Meissen), late 13th century manuscript (Prague, 1928).

Fryer, A.C., 'Monumental Effigies made by Bristol Craftsmen (1240–1550)', *Archaeologia* vol.LXXIV (1923–4), pp.1–72.

    'Monumental Effigies in Somerset', *Proceedings of the Somersetshire Archaeological and Natural History Society* vol.LXII (1916), pp.46–85 and vol.LXVII (1921), pp.12–38.

    'Wooden Monumental Effigies in England and Wales', *Archaeologia* vol.LXI (1915), pp.487–552.

Futterer, I., *Gotische Bildwerke der deutschen Schweiz, 1220–1440* (Augsburg, 1930).

Gaibi, A., *Le Armi da Fuoco Portatili Italiane* (Milan, 1962).

'Note sulla lavorazione dei metalli in Val Sesia con cenni particolari sulla lavorazione di armi', in *Atti e memorie de Congresso di Varallo Sesia 1960* (n.d.).

'Un raro cimelio piemontese del trecento', *Armi Antiche* (1965).

Gaier, C., *Les Armes*, bibliography (Turnhout, 1979).

'L'evolution et l'usage de l'armament personnel defensif au pays de Liège du XIIIe au XVe siècle', *Zeitschrift der Gesellschaft für historische Waffen- und Kostümkunde* vol.IV (1962), pp.65–86.

'L'industrie et le commerce des armes dans Les Anciennes Principautés belges du XIIIme à la fin du XVme siècles', in *Bibliothèque de la Faculté de Philosophie et Lettres de l'Université de Liège*, vol.CCII (Liège, 1973).

'Le problème de l'origine de l'industrie armurière liègeoise au Moyen Age', *Chronique archéologique du Pays de Liège* vol.LIII (1962), pp.22–75.

and Lhoest, L., *Catalogue des armes au musée Curtius* (Liège, 1963).

Gaignières, 'Les Tombeaux de la collection Gaignières: Dessins d'archéologie du XVIIe Siècle', ed. J. Adhemar, *Gazette des Beaux Arts* vol.LXXXIV (1974), pp.1–192.

Gamber, O., *Glossarium Armorum* (1972).

'Die Mittelalterlichen Blankwaffen der Wiener Waffensammlung', *Jahrbuch der Kunsthistorischen Sammlungen in Wien* vol.LVII (1961), pp.11–31.

'Orientalische Einflüsse auf die mittelalterliche Bewaffnung Europas', *Kwartalnik historii Kultury materialnej* vol.XXI (1973), pp.273–9.

Gamble, J.D., *Battle Axes* (Providence, 1981).

Ganshof, F.L., 'Armatura (Galbert de Bruges, ch.106, ed. Pirenne, p.152)', *Archivium latinitatis Medii Aevi* vol.XVI (1940), pp.176–94.

Ganter, J., *Romanische Plastik, Inhalt und Form in der Kunst des XI und XII Jahrhunderts* (Vienna, 1948).

Gardner, A., *Alabaster Tombs of the Pre-Reformation Period in England* (Cambridge, 1940).

Medieval Sculpture in France (Cambridge, 1931).

Garton, T.E.H., *Early Romanesque Sculpture in Apulia* (London and New York, 1985).

Gaunt, G.D., and Gaunt, A.M., 'Mongol Archers of the Thirteenth Century', *Journal of the Society of Archer Antiquaries* vol.XVI (1973).

Gauthier, M.-M., *Emaux du moyen-âge occidental* (Paris, 1972).

Gelli, J., *Guida del raccoglitore e dell'armatore di Armi Antiche* (Milan, 1900; Accademica Cisalpina, 1968).

Genthon, I., *Kunstdenkmäler in Ungarn* (Budapest and Leipzig, 1974).

Gerevich, L., *Magyarorszag Romankori Emlekei* (Budapest, 1938).

Ghyszy, P., 'Über Ailettes', *Zeitschrift für Historisches Waffen- und Kostümkunde* vol.III, no.10 (1931).

Giorgetti, G., 'L'arco, la balestra e la macchine belliche', *Armi Antiche* (1964).

Giraud, J.B., *Documents pour servir à l'histoire de l'armament au Moyen Age et a la Renaissance* (Lyon, 1895 and 1904).

Goldschmidt, A., *Die Elfenbeinskulpturen aus der Zeit der Karolingischen und Sächsischen Kaiser VIII-XI Jahrhundert* (Berlin, 1914).

Die Skulpturen von Freibug und Wechselburg (Berlin, 1924).

Gomez-Moreno, M., *El Arte Romanico Español* (Madrid, 1934).

Gooses, V.P., 'Carolingian and Ottonian Influences in the Monumental Sculpture and Painting of the Eastern Adriatic', *Journal of Croatian Studies* vol.XXII (1981), pp.3–47.

Grabar, A., and C. Nordenfalk, *Early Medieval Painting from the Fourth to the Eleventh Century* (1957).

Romanesque Painting from the 11th to 13th century (1958).

Grabar, O., 'Kataphrakten, Clibenarier, Normanreiter', *Jahrbuch der Kunsthistorischen Sammlungen in Wien* vol.LXIV (1968).

Grancsay, S.V., 'The Armor of Don Alvaro de Cabrera', *Bulletin of the Metropolitan Museum of Art* (June 1952).

'A French Crusader's Sword Pommel', *Bulletin of the Metropolitan Museum of Art* vol.XXXIV (1939), pp.190–2.

'Technical Aspects of Arms and Armor', *Carnegie Magazine* (February 1954), pp.65–8.

Grand, R., *L'Art Roman de Bretagne* (1958).

Greenhill, F.A., *Incised Effigial Slabs: A Study of Engraved Stone Memorials in Latin Christendom, c.1100 to c.1700* (London, 1976).

Grivot D., and Zarnecki, G., *Gislebertus, sculptor Autun* (London, 1961).

Guerrero Lovillo, J., *Las Cántigas, estudio arquéologico de sus miniaturas* (Madrid, 1949).

Guilhermy, F., *L'abbaye de Saint Denis, Tombeaux et figures historiques des rois de France* (Paris, 1882).

Gundel, C., *Das Schlisische Tumbengrab im XIII Jahrhundert* (Strassburg, 1926).

Gunnis, P., *Historic Cyprus* (1936).

Gysin, F., *Holtzplastis vom 11 bis zum 14 Jahrhundert* (Berne, 1958).

Haenel, A.E., *Alte Waffen* (Berlin, 1920).

Hahnloser, H.R., *Villard de Honnecourt, Kritische Gesamtausgabe des Bauhüttenbuches Ms. fr. 19093 der Pariser Nationalbibliothek* (Graz, 1972).

Halpin, A., 'Irish Medieval Swords c.1170–1660', *Proceedings of the Royal Irish Academy* vol.LXXXVIC5 (1986), pp.183–230.

Hamann, R., *Die Elisabethkirche zu Marburg und ihre kunstlerische Nachfolge, Die Plastik* (Marburg, 1929).

Harbison, P., 'Native Irish Arms and Armour in Medieval Gaelic Literature, 1170–1600', *The Irish Sword* vol.XII (1976), pp.173–99 and 270–84.

Harmuth, E., 'Zur Leistung der Mittelalterliche Armbrust', *Zeitschrift für Historische Waffen- und Kostümkunde* vol.XIII (1971).

Hassall, A.G., and Hassall, W.O., *The Douce Apocalypse* (London, 1961).

Hayes-McCoy, G.A., 'The Gallóglach Axe', *Journal of the Galway Archaeological and Historical Society* vol.XVII (1937), pp.101–21.

Hayward, J.F., *The Art of the Gunmaker* (London, 1962).

Hefner-Alteneck, J.H., *Waffen* (Frankfurt, 1903).

Heimann, A., 'The Capital, Frieze and Pilasters of the Portrail Royale, Chartres', *Journal of the Warburg and Courtauld Institutes* vol.XXXI (1968), pp.73–102.

Hejdova, D., 'Der Sogenannte St Wenzels-Helm', *Zeitschrift für Historische Waffen- und Kostümkunde* (1966), pp.95–110; (1967), pp.28–54; and (1968), pp.15–30.

Held, R., ed., *Arts, Arms and Armour* (Chiasso, 1979).

Hell, V., and Hell, H., *The Great Pilgrimage of the Middle Ages: the Road to St James of Compostella* (London, 1970).

Henry, F., *Irish Art in the Romanesque Period 1020–1170 AD* (1967–70).

Heslop, T.A., 'English Seals from the Mid-Ninth Century to 1100', *Journal of the British Archaeological Association* vol.CXXXII (1980), pp.1–16.

Hewitt, J., *Ancient Armour and Weapons in Europe* (London, 1860).

Hill, D.R., 'Trebuchets', *Viator* vol.IV (1973), pp.99–114.

Hime, H.W.L., *The Origin of Artillery* (London, 1915).

Hope, W.H., 'On the Early Working of Alabaster in England', *The Archaeological Journal* vol.LXI (1904), pp.221–40.

Hope, W.H., and Robinson, J.A., 'On the Funeral Effigies of the Kings and Queens of England, with Special Reference to Those in the Abbey Church of Westminster', *Archaeologia* vol.XL, no.2 (1907), pp.517–70.

Humbert, A., 'Les fresques romanes de Brinay', *Gazette des Beaux Arts* vol.IV, no.2 (1914), p.217ff.

Humphreys, J., 'Monumental Effigies in the Churches of Worcestershire', *Birmingham Archaeological Society Transactions* vol.XXXVII (1911), pp.27–57.

Hund, J., *Irish Medieval Figural Sculpture 1200–1600* (London, 1980).

Hurtig, J.W., *The Armored Gisant before 1400* (New York, 1979).

I'anson, W.M., 'The Medievel Military Effigies in Yorkshire', *The Yorkshire Archaeological Journal* vol.XXVIII (1926), pp.345–79; and vol.XXIX (1927), pp.1–67.

Jacques, C., *Les peintures du moyen âge* (Paris, 1946).

Jalabert, D., 'Le tombeau gothique: recherches sur les origines de ses divers éléments', *Revue de l'art ancient et moderne* vol.LXIV (1933), pp.145–66; and vol.LXV (1934), pp.11–30.

James, M.R., *A Descriptive Catalogue of the Manuscripts in the Fitzwilliam Museum* (Cambridge, 1895).

> *A Descriptive Catalogue of the Manuscripts in the Library of St John's College* (Cambridge, 1913).

> *The Western Manuscripts in the Library of Trinity College* (Cambridge, 1900–4).

Janson, H.W., 'The Equestrian Monument from Can Grande della Scala to Peter the Great', in *Aspects of the Renaissance: A Symposium*, ed. A. Lewis (Austin, 1967), pp.73–85; also in *Sixteen Studies* (New York, 1973).

Jones, D., 'The Cappella Palatina in Palermo: Problems of Attribution', *Art and Archaeology Research Papers* vol.I (1972).

Juhasz, V., 'Las Pinturas de los Cruzados en la Basilica de Belém', *Terra Santa* (1950).

Kajetan, E., and Hajdu, I., *Csataképek. A magyar hadtörténclem a festészet és a grafika tükrében (Battle Pictures. Hungarian Military History in Paintings and Graphic Art)* (Budapest, 1980).

Kajzer, L., *Uzbrojenie i ubiór rijcerski w sredniowiecznej Mało palsce w swietle zrodel ikonograficznych*, with English summary (Warsaw, 1976).

Kalmar, J., *A magyar kard müveszete* (On Hungarian Swords) (Budapest, 1938).

> *Régi magyar fegyverek* (Hungarian Arms) (Budapest, 1971).

> 'Történeti Múzeum Fegyvertárának Középkori Sisakjai', *Archeologiai Értes'to* vol.LXXXV (1958), pp.191–5.

> 'Die Tschinken oder Teschener Büchse,' *Folia Archaeologica* vol.X (Budapest, 1958).

> *Die Waffen in Ungarn* (Budapest, 1942).

Karpa, O., 'Das Marburger Einzel- und Doppelgrab, Historische Grundlegung ihrer Zuschreibung', *Wallraf-Richartz Jahrbuch* vols VII–VIII (1933–4), pp.88–94.

> 'Zur Chronologie der Kölnischen Plastik im 14 Jahrhundert', *Wallraf-Richartz Jahrbuch* vols VII–VIII (1933–4), pp.53–87.

Kasanin, M., *L'Art Yougoslave des origines á nos jours* (Belgrade, 1939).

Katzenellenbogen, A., *Allegories of the Virtues and Vices in Medieval Art* (1939).

> 'The Central Tympanum at Vezelay: its Encyclopedic Meaning and its Relation to the First Crusade', *The Art Bulletin* (1944).

Kauffmann, C.M., *Romanesque Manuscripts 1066–1190* (London, 1975).

Keller, M.L; *The Anglo-Saxon Weapon Names Treated Archaeologically and Etymologically* (Heidelburg, 1906).

Kelly, F.M., 'Chain Mail', *Apollo* vol.XIV (1931).

> 'Zur Entstehung des Spangenharnisches', *Zeitschrift für Historische Waffen- und Kostümkunde* vol.IV (1933).

Kendrick, T.D., *Late Saxon and Viking Art* (London, 1949).

Knoll, G., *Das Evangelister Kaiser Heinrich III* (Wiesbaden, 1981).

Knudson, C.A., 'La brogne', in *Mélanges offerts à Rita Lejeune* vol.II (Gembloux, 1969), pp.1625–36.

Kohl, W., *Das Soester Nequambuch* (Weisbaden, 1980).

Koschorreck, W., and Werner, W., *Facsimilia Heidelbergensia Ausgewählte Handschriften der Universitätshibliothek Heidelberg, vol.I, 'Das Rolandslied des Pfaffen Konrad'* (Weisbaden, 1970)

Krasa, J., *České umění goticke* (Czech Gothic Art) (Prague, 1970).

Labouchere, G.C., 'Ein inventaris', *Oud-Utrecht* (1933), pp.50–4.

Lafargue, W., *Art Roman du Roussillon* (Lanzac, 1947).

    Les Chapiteaux du Cloître de Notre-Dame-de-Dourade (1940).

Laing, H., *Descriptive Catalogue of Impressions from Ancient Scottish Seals* (Edinburgh, 1850).

Lane, F.C., 'The Crossbow and the Nautical Revolution of the Middle Ages', in *Essays in honor of Robert L. Reynolds* (Kent, Ohio, 1969), pp.161–71.

Langlois, E., 'Le Rouleau d'Exultet de la Bibliothèque Casanatense', *Mélanges de l'École de Rome* vol.VI (1889), pp.466–82.

Larson, H.M., 'The Armour Business in the Middle Ages', *Business History Review* vol.XIV (1940), pp.49–64.

Latil, Dom A.M., *Le Miniature dell'Exultat* (Monte Cassino, 1899).

Lauer, P., *Les Enluminures romanes des manuscrits de la Bibliotéque Nationale* (Paris, 1927).

Lawrence, H., 'Military Effigies in Derbyshire', *Journal of the Derbyshire Archaeological and Natural History Society* vol.XLVI (1924–5), pp.92–107 and 137–51.

    and Routh, T.H., 'Military Effigies in Nottinghamshire Before the Black Death', *Transactions of the Thornton Society* vol.XXVIII (1924), pp.114–37.

Le Compagnie di Ventura, *Catalogo della mostra di arti figurative e armi* (Narni, 1970).

Lefrancois-Pillion, L., *Les Sculpteurs français du XIIe siècle* (1931).

    Les Sculpteurs français du XIIIe siècle (1931).

    Les Sculpteurs de Reims (1928).

Leisinger, H., *Romanesque Bronzes* (London, 1956).

Lejeune, R., and Stiennon, J., *La Légende de Roland dans l'art du moyen âge* (Brussels, 1966).

Lemoisne, P.A., *Gothic Painting in France, Fourteenth and Fifteenth Centuries* (Florence and Paris, 1931).

Lera, G., 'Ombre di Cavalieri teutonici', in *Lucca, Chiesa di San Romano* (Lucca, 1966), pp.69–73.

Lindblom, M.A., 'La peinture Gothique en Suède et en Norvège,' in *Étude sur les relations entre l'Europe occidentale et Les pays scandinaves* (L'Academie Royale des Belles-Lettres, d'Histoire et d'Archéologie, Stockholm and London, 1916).

Llanso, A.G., *Armas y Armaduras* (Barcelona, 1895).

Lockett, R.B., 'A Catalogue of Romanesque Sculpture from the Cluniac Houses in England', *Journal of the British Archaeological Association* 3rd ser. vol.XXXIV (1971), p.43ff.

Loomis, R.S., and Loomis, L.H., *Arthurian Legends in Medieval Art* (London, 1938).

Lugs, J., *Handfeuerwaffen* (Berlin, 1968).

Lüthgen, E., *Die Niederrheinische Plastik von der Gotik bis zur Renaissance* (Strassburg, 1917).

Mackeprang, M., *Jydske Granitportaler* (1948).

Macoir, G., 'La Bardiche', *Annales de la Société d'Archéologie de Bruxelles* vol.XXIV (1910), pp.299–380.

    'La Musée Royale d'Armes et d'Armures de la Porte Hal à Bruxelles', *Annales de la Société Royale d'Archéologie de Bruxelles* vol.XXXIII (n.d.).

Maffei, F. da, *Le Arche Scaligeri di Verona* (Verona, n.d.).

Maglioli, V., *Armeria reale di Torino* (Turin, 1959).

    'La Balestra', *Armi Antiche* vols I–II (1955).

Mahr, A., 'The Gallóglach Axe', *Journal of the Galway Archaeological and Historical Society* vol.XVIII (1938–9), pp.66–8.

Malatesta, E., *Armi e Armaiolo* (Rome, 1939).

Malle, L., *Le Arte Figurative in Piemonte* (Turin, n.d.).

Mango, C., and Hawkins, E.J.W., 'The Hermitage of St Neophytos and Its Wall Paintings',

Dumbarton Oaks Papers vol.XX (1966).

Mann, J., 'Armour in Essex', *Transactions of the Essex Archaeological Society* vol.XXII, no.2, pp.275–98.

'Arms and Armour', in *Medieval England*, vol.I, ed. A.L. Poole (Oxford, 1958), pp.31–7.

'Notes on the Arms and Armour Worn in Spain from the Tenth to the Fifteenth Century', *Archaeologia* vol.LXXXII (1933), pp.285–305.

'Notes on the Evolution of Plate Armour in Germany in the Fourteenth and Fifteenth Century', *Archaeologia* (1935), pp.69–97.

An Outline of Arms and Armour in England (London, 1960).

Marosi, E., *Die Anfänge der Gotik in Ungarn* (Budapest, 1984).

Martin, H., *Le miniature française du XIIIe au XVe siècle* (Paris and Brussels, 1923).

Martin, K., ed., *Studien zur Geschichte der Europäischen Plastik: Festschrift Theodor Müller* (Munich, 1965).

Martin, P., *Armes et Armures de Charlemagne á Louis XIV* (Paris, 1967).

'L'Artillerie et la fonderie à canon de Strasbourg du XIVe au XVIIIe siècle', *Armi Antiche* (1967), pp.71–90.

Martin, P., 'Wehr-, Waffen-, und Harnischpflicht der Strassburger Zünfte im 14 Jahrhundert', *Zeitschrift für Historische Waffen- und Kostümkunde* (1975), pp.102–4.

Maryon, H., 'Pattern-welding and the Damascening of Sword Blades', *Studies in Conservation* (1966), pp.25–35 and 52–60.

Matthiae, G., *Pittura Medioevale Abruzzese* (Milan, 1969).

McGuffie, R.H., 'The Longbow as a Decisive Weapon', *History Today* vol.V (1955), pp.737–41.

Mellini, G. L., *Scultori Veronese del Trecento* (Venice, 1971).

Mercer, F., *Les primitives français: la peinture clunysienne* (Paris, 1931).

Mesqui, J., *Provins: La fortification d'une ville au Moyen Age* (Paris, 1979–80).

Mesuret, R., *Les peintures murales du Sud-Ouest de la France du XIe au XIIe siècle* (Paris, 1967).

Metcalf, D.M., *Coinage of the Crusaders and the Latin East in the Ashmolean Museum, Oxford* (Oxford, 1983).

Michel, P., *La fresque romane* (Paris, 1961).

Les fresques de Tavant (Paris, 1956).

Romanesque Wall Paintings in France (1950).

Molinier, E., *Musée Nationale du Louvre, Catalogues des Ivoires* (Paris, 1896).

'Orfévrerie', in *Histoire Generale des Arts appliques à l'industrie*, vol.IV (Paris, 1901).

L'Orfévrerie religieuse et civiles du Ve à la fin du XVe siècle (Paris, 1898).

Mondadori, A., *Enciclopedia Ragionata delle Armi* (Milan, 1979).

Morosini, O., and Mormone, R., *Sculture Trecentesche in S. Lorenzo Maggiore a Napoli* (Naples, 1973).

Mot, G.J., 'L'arsenal et le parc de matériel a la cité de Carcassonne en 1298', *Annales du Midi* vol.LXVIII (1956), pp.409–18.

Müller, H., *Historische Waffen* (Berlin, 1957).

'Uber die Funde aus Burg Tannenberg', *Zeitschrift für Historische Waffen- und Kostümkunde* vol.IV, no.8 (1933).

and Kölling, H., *Europäische Heib- und Stichwaffen aus der Sammlungs des Museums für Deutsch Geschichte* (Berlin, 1981).

and Platow, G., *Gewehre, Pistolen, Revolver, Hand- und Faustfeuerwaffen vom 14 bis 19 Jahrhundert* (Leipzig, 1979).

Murbach, E., *The Painted Romanesque Ceiling of St Martin in Zillis* (London, 1967).

Musciarelli, L., *Dizionario delle armi* (Milan, 1968).

Nadolski, A., 'Ancient Polish Arms and Armour', *Journal of the Arms and Armour Society* vol.IV (1962).

ed., *Brón sredniowieczna z ziem polskich* (Warsaw, 1978).

ed., *Cmentarzysko z XI wieku w Lutomiersku pod Lodzia* (Łódź, 1959).

Polish Arms: Side Arms (Warsaw, 1974).

Polskie siły zbrojne w czasach Bolesława Chrobrego, with French summary (Łódź, 1956).

Studia nad uzbrojeniem Polskim z X, XI, XII w, with French summary (Łódź, 1954).

'Szczerbierc – The Polish Coronation Sword', *Journal of the Arms and Armour Society* vol.VI, no.6 (1969), pp.183–4.

and Głosek, W. *Miercze sredniowieczne z ziem polskich* (Łódź, 1970).

Nagy, G., 'A magyar közepkori fegyvertetröl', *Archeológia Értesitö* (1890).

Natanson, J., *Gothic Ivories of the Thirteenth and Fourteenth Centuries* (1951).

Neukam, W.G., 'Eine Nürnberger sulzbacher Plattenlieferung für Karl IV in den Jahren 1362–1363. Ein Beitrag zur Nürnberger Waffenfabrikation des 14 Jahrhunderts', *Mitteilungen des Vereins für Geschichte der Stadt Nürnberg* vol.XLVII (1956), pp.124–59.

Neuss, W., *Die Apokalypse des heiligen Johannes in der Altspanischen und altchristlichen Bibelillustration* (Munster, 1931).

Neuss, W., *Die katalunische Bibelillustration* (Bonn, 1922).

Nickl, H., *Der mittelalterliche Reiterschild des Abendlandes* (Berlin, 1960).

Ullstein Waffenbuch (Berlin, 1974).

and Pyhr, S.W., and Tarassuk, L., *The Art of Chivalry* (New York, 1982).

Nicolle, D.C., 'Armes et armures dans les épopées des Croisades', in *Les Épopées de la Croisade*, ed. K.-H. Bender (Stuttgart, 1987).

'The Cappella Palatina Ceiling and the Muslim Military heritage of Norman Sicily', *Gladius* vol.XVI (1983), pp.45–145.

'The Monreale Capitals and the Military Equipment of Later Norman Sicily' *Gladius* vol.XV (1980).

Niederle, L., *Manuel de l'antiquité Slave* (Paris, 1925).

Slovanské Starožitnosti (Prague, 1902–3).

Nielsen, K.S., 'Riddertidens våben i Danmark (Arms and Armour in Denmark in the Age of Chivalry)', *Vaabenhistoriske Aarbøger* vol.XXX (1984).

Nielsen, L., *Danmarks middelalderlige Haandskrifter* (Copenhagen, 1937).

Niox, G.L., *Le Musée de l'Armée: Arms et Armures anciennes et souvenirs historiques les plus precieux* (Paris, 1917).

Novak, R., 'Die franzosischen Waffennamen, Eine Auswahl', *Zeitschrift für Historische Waffen- und Kostümkunde* (1970), pp.68–74.

Nowakowski, A., *Uzbrojenie wojsk krzyzackick w Prusach w XIV w, i na poszatku XV w* (Armour of the Teutonic Knights), with English summary (Lodz, 1980).

Nowé, H., 'Le gisant de l'abbaye de Nieuwen Bossche à Heusden', *Revue Belge d'archéologie et d'histoire de l'art* vol.XXI (1952), pp.153–73.

Oakeshott, E., *The Archaeology of Weapons* (London, 1960).

A Knight and his Armour (London, 1961).

A Knight and his Weapons (London, 1964).

'Some Medieval Sword-pommels', *Journal of the British Archaeological Association* 3rd ser. vol.XIV (1951), pp.47–62.

The Sword in the Age of Chivalry (London, 1964).

Oakeshott, W., *The Artists of the Winchester Bible* (London, 1945).

The Mosaics of Rome (London, 1967).

Oman, C., 'An Eleventh Century English Cross', *Burlington Magazine* vol.XCVI (1954), pp.383–4.

Omont, H., 'Peintures de l'ancien Testament', *Monuments et memoires, Fondation Piot* vol.XVII (1909).

Oursel, C., *L'art roman de Bourgogne* (Dijon and Boston, 1928).

La miniature du *XII siècle à l'abbaye de Cîteaux* (Dijon, 1926).

Miniatures Cisterciennes, 1109–1134 (Mâcon, 1960).

Pächt, O., *The Rise of Pictorial Narrative in Twelfth Century England* (Oxford, 1962).

and Alexander, J.J.G., *Illuminated Manuscripts in the Bodleian Library* (Oxford, 1966–73).

Panofsky, E., *Die Deutschen Plastik des elften bis dreizehnten Jahrhunderts* (Munich, 1924).

Netherlands Painting: Its Origins and Character (Cambridge, Mass., 1953).

Tomb Sculpture (New York, 1961).

Panseri, C., 'Ricerche metallografiche sopra una spade da guerra del XIIo secolo', *Associazione italiana di metallurgia, Documenti e contributi* (Milan, 1957), pp.7–40.

Parker, E.J., 'A Twelfth Century Cycle of New Testament Drawings from Bury St Edmunds Abbey', *Proceedings of the Suffolk Institute of Archaeology* vol.XXXI (1970), p.263ff.

Pasquali-Lasagni, A., and Stefanelli, E., 'Note di storia dell'artigliera nel secoli XIV e XV', *Archivio della Reale Deputazione Romana di Storia Patria* vol.LX (1937), pp.149–89.

Patrick, J.M., *Artillery and Warfare during the Thirteenth and Fourteenth Centuries* (Utah State University Press, Monograph VIII/3, May 1961).

Payne-Gallwey, R., *The Crossbow* (London, 1903).

Pešina, J., *Česká gotické desková malba* (Czech Gothic Panel Painting) (Prague, n.d.).

Česká umění gotické (Czech Gothic Art) (Prague, 1970).

Peterson, H.L., *Daggers and Fighting Knives of the Western World* (New York, 1968).

Petrović, D., 'Un balestriere marchigiano a Ragusa nel XIV secolo', *Quaderni storici* vol.XIII (Ancona, 1970).

Dubrovačko Oružie u XIV veku (Belgrade, 1976).

'Fire-arms in the Balkans on the eve of and after the Ottoman Conquests of the fourteenth and fifteenth centuries', in *War, Technology and Society in the Middle East*, ed. V.J. Parry and M.E. Yapp (London, 1975).

'Najstariji i zapisi o graditeljima orgulja', *Zvuk* vol.XCIX (Sarajevo, 1969).

'Uloga Dubrovnika u snabdevanju srednjovekovne Bosne oružjem, XIV–XV veku', *Radovi Muzeja grada Zenice* vol.III (Zenica, 1973).

'Vatreno oružje na Balkanu uoči i posle osmanskog osvajana u XIV i XV veku', *Glasnik Cetinjskih muzeja* vol.III (Cetinje, 1970).

Piaskowski, H.J., 'Jak w XIV–XV wieku zastopiono odkuwki odlewami zeluvnymi', *Przeglad Odlewnictwa* vol.IX, no.1 (1959), pp.16–18.

'Metaloznowcze badania wczesnośredniowiecznych wyrobów zelaznych na pryzkładzie zabytkow archeologicznych z Łeczycy, Czerchowa a Buczka', *Studia z dziejow górnictwa i hutnictwa* vol.III (1959), pp.7–102.

'Metaloznawcze badania wczesnośredniowiecznych wyrobów zelaznych i zuzla z Sieradza', *Prace i Materialy Muzeum Archeolicznego i Etnograficznego w ódi* vol.VII (1962), pp.225–57.

'Metaloznawcze badania wyrobów zelaznych', in *Cmentarzysko z XI wieku w Lutomiersku pod Łódźia*, ed. A. Nadolski (Łódź 1959), pp.11–39.

'Metaloznawcze badania zabytków archeologicznych z Wycianzy, Jadownik Mokrych i Piekar', *Studia z dziejów górnictwa i hutnictwa* vol.II (1958), pp.7–98.

'Metaloznawcze badania zelaznych grotów z Zawady Lancokoronskiej, pow, Brzesko i Jarosławia', *Acta Archaeologica Carpathica* vol.IX, nos 1–2 (1967), pp.139–45.

'Technika gdánskiego hutnictwa i kowalstwa zelaznego x X–XIV wieku na podstawie badán metaloznowczych', *Gdánskie Towarzystwo Naukowe, Prace Komisji Archeologicznej* vol.II (1960), pp.51–72.

Planché, J.P., 'On the Sepulchral Effigies in Salisbury Cathedral', *The Journal of the British Archaeological Association* vol.XV (1859), pp.115–30.

Poeschel, E., *Die Romanischen Deckengemälde von Zillis* (Zurich, 1941).

Pope, S.T., *Bows and Arrows* (Berkeley, 1962).

Pope-Hennessy, J., *Italian Gothic Sculpture* (London, 1955).

Porter, A.K., *Romanesque Sculpture of the Pilgrimage Road* (Boston, 1923).

'Spain or Toulouse?' *Art Bulletin* vol.VII (1925), pp.18–19.

Poschenberg, V., *Die Schutz- und Trutzwaffen des Mittelalters* (Stuttgart and Vienna, 1938–9).

Post, P., *Das Kostüm und die ritterliche Kriegsracht in deutschen Mittelalter, von 1000–1450* (Berlin, 1939).

Kriegs-, Turnier- und Jagdwaffen vom früher Mittelalter his zum Dreissig-jührigen Krieg, Ein Handbuch der Waffenkunde (Berlin, 1929).

Prerodović, D., 'Die im Museum Altkroatischer Altertümer zu Knin (Dalmatien) befindlichen Waffen', *Zeitschrift für Historisches Waffen- und Kostümkunde* (1906–8).

'O srednjovekovnom oružja na umetničkim spomenicima Hrvatske', *Vesnik Vojnog muzej* vol.II (1955).

Priedel, H., 'Die karolingischen Schwerter bei den Westslaven', *Gandert Festschrift* (Berlin, 1959), pp.128–42.

Puig y Cadafalch, J., *L'art wisigothique et ses survivances: recherches sur les origines et development de l'art en France et en Espagne du IVe au XIIe siècle* (1961).

Puricelli-Guerra, A., 'The Glaive and the Bill', in *Art, Arms and Armour*, ed. R. Held (Chiasso, 1979).

Rackham, B., *The Ancient Glass of Canterbury Cathedral* (London, 1949).

Radocsay, D., *Gothic Panel Painting in Hungary* (Budapest, 1963).

Ragona, A., 'La ceramica della Sicilia arabo-normanna', *Rassegna delle Istruzione Artistica* vol.I, no.2 (1966).

Rausing, E., 'The Bow: Some Notes on its Origins and Development', *Acta Archaeologica Lundensia* vol.VI (1967).

Rebuffo, L., *Armature italiane* (Turin, 1959).

Rey, R., *L'Art Gothique du Midi de la France* (1934)

Les Cloîtres historiés du Midi dans l'art roman (Toulouse, 1955).

La Sculpture romane languedocienne (Toulouse and Paris, 1936).

Rice, D., *English Art 871–1100* (Oxford, 1952).

Richardson, E., *The Monumental Effigies of the Temple Church* (London, 1843).

Robertson, E., 'The Rome Casket', in *Studies in Memory of David Talbot Rice* (Edinburgh, 1975).

Rodriguez Lorento, J.J., 'The XVth Century Ear Dagger: Its Hispano-Moresque Origins', *Gladius* vol.III (1964).

Rohde, F., 'Die Abzugsvorrichtung der Frühen Armbrust und ihre Entwickelung', *Zeitschrift für Historiche Waffen- und Kostümkunde* vol.IV (1933).

'Uber die Zusammensetzung der spätmittelalterliche Armbrust', *Zeitschrift für Historische Waffen- und Kostümkunde* vol.XVI (1940).

Roques, M., *Les peintures murales du Sud-Est de la France du XIIIe au XVIe siècle* (1961).

Rorimer, J., *Medieval Monuments at the Cloisters* (New York, 1972).

Rothert, H., 'Wann und wo ist die Pulverwaffe erfunden?' *Blätter fur deutsche Landesgeschichte* vol.LXXXIX (1952), pp.84–6.

Royal Commission on Historical Monuments, *An Inventory of the Historical Monuments in London, vol.IV The City* (London, 1929).

Royer, P.-R., 'Introduction à l'étude des armes à inscriptions profanes du Musée de l'Armée, de l'apogée jusqu'aux sources (Part 2: La Renaissance et le Moyen Age)', *Revue de la Société des Amis du Musée de l'Armée* vol.LXXXIV (1980), pp.5–13.

Rumpler, M., *Sculptures romanes en Alsace* (Strasbourg, 1960).

Ruttkay, A., 'Waffen und Reiterausrüstung des 9 bis zur ersten Hälfte des 14 Jhs. in der Slowakei', *Slovenska Archeologia* vol.XXIII (1975), pp.119–216; and vol.XXIV (1976), pp.245–395.

Rygh, O., *Antiquités Norvégiennes* (1885).

Rynne, E., 'The Impact of the Vikings on Irish Weapons', *Atti del VI Congresso Internazionale delle Scienze Preistoriche e Protostoriche, Rome 1962* (Rome, 1966).

'An Irish Sword of the 11th Century', *Journal of the Royal Society of Antiquaries of Ireland* vol.XCII (1962), pp.208–10.

Salet, F., *La Madeleine de Vézelay* (Melun, 1948).

Salvini, R., *Medieval Sculpture* (London, 1969).

Sarre, F., 'L'Arte Mussulmana nel'Sud d'Italia e in Sicilia', *Archivio Storico per la Calabria e la Lucania* (1933).

Sauerländer, W., 'Tombeaux Chartrains du premier quart du XIIIe siècle', *L'information d'histoire de l'art* vol.IX (1964), pp.47–60.

Saxl, F., and Meier, H., 'Catalogue of Astrological and Mythological Manuscripts of the Latin Middle Ages', in *Manuscripts in English Libraries*, ed. H. Bober (1953).

English Sculpture of the Twelfth Century (London, 1954).

Scalini, M., 'Le Armi: produzione, fuizione e simbolo nella Toscana medioevale', in *Guerre e assoldati in Toscana, 1260–1364*, ed. L.G. Boccia and M. Scalini (Florence, 1982).

'Die Schützbewaffnung bis 1500', in *Das Münchner Zeughaus*, ed. R.H. Wackernagel (Munich and Zurich, 1982), pp.51–63.

Schapiro, M., *The Parma Ildefonsus: A Romanesque Illuminated Manuscript from Cluny and Related Works* (College Art Association, New York, 1964).

'The Romanesque Sculpture of Moissac', *Art Bulletin* vol.XIII (1931).

Schaum-Benedym, C., *Die Figürlicher Grabsteine des 14 und 15 Jahrhunderts in Hessen* (Bonn, 1969).

Scheller, H., *A Survey of Medieval Model Books* (Haarlem, 1963).

Schledermann, P., 'Eskimo and Viking Finds in the High Arctic', *National Geographical Magazine* vol.CLIX, no.5 (May 1981).

Schmidtchen, V., *Bombarden, Befestigungen, Büchsenmeister, von der Ersten Mauerbrechen der Spätmittelalters zur Belagerungsartillerie der Renaissance* (Dusseldorf, 1977).

Schneider, H., *Adel – Burgen – Waffen* (Berne, 1968).

Der Schweizerdolch (Zurich, 1977).

'Untersuchungen an mittelalterlichen Dolchen aus dem Gebiete ser Schweiz', *Zeitschrift für schweizerische Archäologie und Kunstgeschichte* vol.XX (1960), pp.91–105.

Schobel, J., *Prunkwaffen, Waffen und Rüstungen aus dem Historischen Museum Dresden* (Vienna and Dusseldorf, 1973).

Schrade, H., *Malerie des Mittelalters* (Cologne, 1958).

Die Romanesche Malerie (Cologne, 1963).

Schubert, H., 'The First Cast-Iron Cannon Made in England', *Journal of the Iron and Steel Institute* vol.CXLVI (1942), pp.131–40.

Schwarzbaum, E., 'Three Tournai Tomb Slabs in England', *Gesta* vol.XX (1981), pp.87–97.

Schwietering, J., 'Zur Geschichte von Speer und Schwert im 12 Jahrhundert', in *Philologische Schriften*, ed. F. Ohly and M. Wehrli (Munich, 1969), pp.59–117.

Scott, J.G., 'An 11th Century War-Axe in Dumfries Museum', *Transactions of the Dumfriesshire and Galloway Natural History and Antiquarian Society* vol.XLIII (1966), pp.117–20.

'Two 14th Century Helms Found in Scotland', *Journal of the Arms and Armour Society* vol.IV (1962–4), pp.68–71.

Secret, J., *Saint Jacques et les chemins de Compostella* (1955).

Seitz, H., 'La Storta – the Falchion', *Armi Antiche* (1963), pp.3–14

Blankwaffen I: Geschichte und Typenentwicklung im europäischen Kulterbereich von der prähistorischen Zeit bis zum Ende des 16 Jahrhundert (Brunswick, 1965).

Sercer, M., *Staro oružje na motki* (Zagreb, 1972).

Shetelig, H., *Viking Antiquities in Great Britain and Ireland* (London, 1940).

Simák, J.V., *Rukopisy majorátni knihovny hrabat z Nostic a Rienecka v Praze* (Prague, 1910).

Sixl, P., 'Entwicklung u. Gebr. d. Handfeuerwaffe', *Zeitschrift fur Historische Waffen- und Kostumkunde* vol.II (1900–2), p.410ff.

Škrivanić, G.A. 'Armour and Weapons in Medieval Serbia, Bosnia and Dubrovnik', *Posedna Izdanja* vol.CCXCIII (1957).

 and Petrovic, D., 'O vatre nom oružju Dubrovnika u XIV veku', *Vesnik Vojnog muzeja* vol.XVIII (1972).

Sobjejan, E., and Rubi, R., 'Espadas de Espana', *Arte Español* (1956).

Speranski, M., 'Ein bosnisches Evangelium in der Handschrift-sammlung Srečković's', *Archiv für Slavisches Philologie* vol.XXIV (1902).

Stalley, R.A., *Architecture and Sculpture in Ireland 1150–1350* (Dublin, 1971).

Steiger, A., 'Alfonso X El Sabio, Libro de acedrex, dados e tablas', *Romanica Helvetica* vol.X (1941).

Stejskal, K., *Pasionál Premýslovny Kunhutz* (The Passionale of Kunigunde Premyslide) (Prague, 1975).

 Velislav Biblia Picta (Prague, 1970).

Stenton, F., *The Bayeux Tapestry* (London, 1957).

Stone, L., *Sculpture in Britain: The Middle Ages* (Harmondsworth, 1955).

Stothard, C.A., *The Monumental Effigies of Great Britain* (London, 1817).

Stylianou, A., and Stylianou, J., *The Painted Churches of Cyprus* (Stourbridge, 1964).

Svoboda, K.M., ed., *Gotik in Böhmen* (Munich, 1969).

Swanton, M.J., *The Spearheads of the Anglo-Saxon Settlements* (London, 1973).

Swarzenski, G., *Die Lateinischen Illuminierten Mss. des XIII Jahr. in den Landen am Rhein, Main und Donau* (1936).

 Monuments of Romanesque Art: the Art of Church Treasures in North-Western Europe (London, 1967).

 Die Salzburger Malerie (Leipzig, 1903–13).

Szendrei, J., *A magyar viselet történeti fejlodése* (on Hungarian costume) (Budapest, 1905).

Tarrassuk, L., and Blair, C., eds., *The Complete Encyclopedia of Arms and Armour* (New York, 1982).

Temesváry, F., *Kunstschätze des Ungharischen Nationalmuseums, Waffenschatze, Prunkwaffen* (Budapest, 1982).

Terenzi, M., 'Armour on a Fresco in Spoleto', *Journal of the Arms and Armour Society* vol.VIII (1974).

Terret, V., *La Sculpture Bourguigonne aux XIIe et XIIIe siècles, Autun* (Autun, 1925).

Thibout, M., 'Decouverte de peintures murals dans l'église de Château-Gontier', *Bulletin Monumental* vol.CI (1942–3), pp.5–40.

 'La peinture murale en France a l'époque romane', *Cahiers d'art sacré* vol.II (1945), p.5ff.

Thomas, B., and Boccia, L.G., *Armi Storiche del Museo Nazionale di Firenze* (Florence, 1971).

 and Gamber, O., 'L'arte milanese dell'Armatura', *Storia di Milano* vol.XI (1958).

 and Schedelmann, H., *Armi e Armature Europee* (Milan, 1965).

Thordeman, B., *Armour from the Battle of Wisby 1361* (Uppsala, 1939).

 'The Asiatic Splint Armour in Europe', *Acta Archaeologica* vol.IV (Copenhagen 1933).

Thorne, P.F., 'Clubs and Maces in the Bayeux Tapestry', *History Today* vol.XXXII (October 1982), pp.48–50.

Toesca, P., 'Gli affreschi della Cattedrale di Anagni', *Le Galleries Nazionale Italiane* vol.V (Rome, 1902).

 Catalogo delle Cose d'Arte e di Antichitá d'Italia: Aosta (Rome, 1911).

Tonnelier, P.M., 'Réflexions sur les cavaliers des portraits romans', *Bulletin de la Société historique et scientifique des Deux-Sèvres* (1952), pp.225–31.

Tóth, Z., 'Fegyvertörténe tunk Szent Istványa' (on 11th century Hungarian arms), *Magyar*

Szemle (1937).

Tout, T.F., 'Firearms in England in the Fourteenth Century', in *Collected Papers* vol.II (Manchester, 1934), pp.233–75.

Tristram, E.W., *English Medieval Wall Painting in the Fourteenth* Century (London, 1955).

    English Medieval Wall Painting: The Thirteenth Century (Oxford, 1950).

    English Medieval Wall Painting: The Twelfth Century (Oxford, 1944).

    'The Roof Painting at Dädesjö, Sweden: A Note', *Burlington Magazine* (1917), pp.111–16.

Tudor-Craig, P., 'The Painted Chamber at Westminster', *The Archaeological Journal* vol.CXIV (1957), pp.92–105.

Turner, D.H., *Romanesque Illustrated Manuscripts* (London, 1966).

Tylecote, R.F., *A History of Metallurgy* (London, 1976).

Ullén, M., *Dägesjö Och Eke Kyrkor* (Stockholm, 1969).

Van Caster, E., and Op de Beeck, R., *De Grafkunst in Belgisch Limburg* (Assen, 1981).

Van Der Sloot, R., *Middeleeuws wapentuig* (Bussum, 1964).

Van Duyse, H., 'Le Costume de l'homme du Beffroi', *Inventaire archéologique de Gand* vol.III (Ghent, 1897).

Van Marle, R., *Iconographie de l'art profane au moyen âge et à la Renaissance* (The Hague 1931–2).

Van Werveke, A., 'Het Godshuis van Sint Jan en Sint Pauwel te Gent bijgenaamd de Leugemeete', *Société de Bibliophiles flamands* 4th ser. vol.XV (Gand, 1909).

Verbruggen, J.F., 'De Goedendag', *Militaria Belgica* vol.III (1977), pp.65–70.

    'De Kist van Oxford', *De Leiegouw* vol.XXII (1980), pp.163–256.

Viale, V., and Viale Ferrero, M., *Aosta: Romana e Mediovale* (Turin, 1967).

Viaud, R.P., *Nazareth et ses deux églises de l'Annonciation et de l'Atelier de St Joseph* (1909).

Villard, A., *Art en Provence* (1957).

Villard de Honnecourt, *Facsimile of the Sketch-Book of Wilars de Honnecourt, an Architect of the Thirteenth Century: with Commentaries and Descriptions by M.J.B.A. Lassus and M.J. Quicherat*, trans. and ed. R. Willis (London, 1859).

Vimont, E., 'Peintures Murales de la Cathédrale de Clermont-Ferrand', *Bulletin Archeologiques* (1901), p.44ff.

Vitry, P., *French Sculpture during the Reign of Saint Louis 1226–1270* (Florence and Paris, 1930).

Von Hefner Alteneck, J.H., *Trachten des Christlichen Mittelalters* (1840–54).

Von Schlosser, J., *The Spanish Jewish Haggadah of Sarajevo* (1898).

Von Specht, F., *Geschichte der Waffen* (Leipzig, 1872).

Wackernagel, N., *Die Plastik des XI und XII Jahrhunderts in Apulien* (Leipzig, 1911).

Wackernagel, R.H., ed., *Das Münchner Zeughaus* (Munich and Zurich, 1982).

Wagner, E., *Hieb- und Stichwaffen* (Prague, 1966).

Wallrath, R., 'Die Naumberger Stifterfiguren in der Geschichte des deutschen Stiftermonuments', *Wallraf-Richartz Jahrbuch* vol.XXVI (1964), pp.45–58.

Waterer, J.W. *Leather and the Warrior* (Museum of Leathercraft, Northampton, 1981).

Waterman, D.M., 'Excavations at Clough Castle', *Ulster Journal of Archaeology* vol.XVII (1954), pp.103–63.

Wathelet-Willem, J., 'L'épee dans les plus anciennes chanson de geste: Étude de vocabulaire', in *Mélanges offerts à R. Crozet*, vol.I (Poitiers, 1966), pp.435–49.

Watson, A., *The Early Iconography of the Tree of Jesse* (Oxford, 1934).

Wawrzonowska, Z., *Uzbroyenie i ubiór rycerski Piastów slaskich od XII do XIVw*, with English summary (Łódź, 1976).

Weckwerth, A., 'Tumba und Tischgrab in Deutschland', *Archiv für Kulturgeschichte* vol.XXXIX (1957), pp.273–308.

Weinberger, W., 'Recumbent Tomb Sculpture of a Knight in the Philadelphia Museum', *Art*

Quarterly vol.VIII (1945), p.75.

Wilinbachov, W., 'Poczatkowy okres rozwoju broni palnej w krajach Slowianskich', *Kwartalnik Historii Nauki i Technik* vol.VIII, no.2 (1963), pp. 215–35.

Will, R., *Répertoire de la sculpture romane d'Alsace* (Strasbourg and Paris, 1955).

Willems, J.F., ed., 'Keuren van Brussel,' in *Antwerpen* (Antwerp, 1827).

    ed., 'Keuren van Leuven,' *Belgisch Museum* vol.VI (Gent 1837–46), pp.294–5.

Williams, A.R., 'Methods of Manufacture of Swords in Medieval Europe: Illustrated by the Metallurgy of Some Examples', *Gladius* vol.XIII (1977).

Wilson, D.M., 'Some Neglected Anglo-Saxon Swords', *Medieval Archaeology* vol.IX (1965), pp.32–54.

Wolff, P., 'Achats d'armes pour Philippe le Bel dans la région toulousaine', in *Regards sur le Midi médiéval* (Toulouse, 1978).

Wormald, F., 'Decorated Initials in English Manuscripts, 900–1100', *Archaeologia* vol.XCI (1945).

    'The Development of English Illumination in the Twelfth Century', *Journal of the British Archaeological Association* 3rd ser. vol.VIII (1943).

    Drawings of the 10th and 11th Centuries (London, 1952).

    'An English Eleventh Century Psalter with Pictures', *Walpole Society* vol.XXXVIII (1960–2).

    'The Survival of Anglo-Saxon Illumination after the Norman Conquest', *Proceedings of the British Academy* vol.XXX (1944).

    and Pacht, O., and Dodwell, C.R., *The St Albans Psalter* (London, 1960).

Worringer, W., *L'art gothique: L'album de Villard de Honnecourt* (Paris, 1967).

Wright, G.S. 'A Royal Tomb Program in the Reign of St Louis', *Art Bulletin* vol.LVI (1974), pp.224–43.

Wünsch, C., *Ost-preussen: Die Kunst im Deutschen Osten* (Berlin, 1960).

Zarnecki, J., 'The Chichester Reliefs', *Archaeological Journal* vol.CX (1953), p.106ff.

    English Romanesque Sculpture, 1066–1140 (London, 1951).

    Later English Romanesque Sculpture, 1140–1210 (London, 1953).

    Romanesque Art (London, 1971).

Zervos, C., *Catalan Art from the Ninth to the Fifteenth Centuries* (London and Toronto, 1937).

Zygulski, Z., *Stara Bron w polskich zbiorach* (Old Weapons in Polish Collections) (Warsaw, 1982).

Military, cultural and social background

Unpublished primary sources

Anon., 'Archives of Cahors'; A.D. Edwards, ed., *A Critical Edition with a Historical Introduction, Glossary and Notes of the Archives of Cahors 1203–1270* (M.A. thesis, Southampton University, 1964–5).

Anon., 'Aye d'Avignon'; M.H. Tweedy, ed., *A Critical Edition of 'Aye d'Avignon', Chanson de Geste of the Twelfth Century* (Ph.D. thesis, Cambridge University, 1954–5).

Anon., 'Les Chetifs'; G.M. Myers, ed., *'Les Chetifs': a Critical Edition* (Ph.D. thesis, Oxford University, 1975).

Anon., 'Chronicle of William of Tyre, Continuation'; M.R. Morgan, ed., *The Old French Continuation of the Chronicle of William, Archbishop of Tyre, to 1232* (Ph.D. thesis, Oxford University, 1970–1).

Anon., 'The Destruction of Troy'; J.A. Claffey, ed., *The Destruction of Troy from Ms. Edinburgh VIII* (M.A. thesis, Dublin National University).

Anon., 'The Destruction of Troy'; J. Molyneaux, ed., *The Destruction of Troy* (M.A. thesis, Dublin

National University, 1955–6).

Anon., 'The Destruction of Troy'; J.E. Walsh, ed., *'The Destruction of Troy' from the Book of Ballymote* (M.A. thesis, Dublin National University, 1956–7).

Anon., 'Les Enfances Lancelot'; E.M. Kennedy, ed., *Les Enfances Lancelot: a Critical Edition of That Part of the Prose Romance of Lancelot du Lac Which is Commonly so Entitled* (Ph.D. thesis, Oxford University, 1951–2).

Anon., 'Gue de Burgoine'; I. Hall, ed., *Gue de Burgoine, 'Chanson de Geste', First Critical Edition of the Manuscript Harley 572 (ff.1 to 32r) of the British Museum* (Ph.D. thesis, Hull University, 1961–2).

Anon., 'Pseudo-Turpin'; I.R. Short, ed., *The Anglo-Norman Translation of the Pseudo-Turpin Chronicle by William of Briane: an Edition and Study* (Ph.D. thesis, London University, 1966–7).

Anon., 'Roland and Vernagu' A.D. Grant, ed., *An Edition of the Middle English Romances 'Roland and Vernagu, The Siege of Melayne and Duk Rowlande and Sir Ottuell of Spayne'* (Ph.D. thesis, London University, 1967–8).

Anon., 'Romain d'Aiquin'; G. Elcoat, ed., *'Le Romain d'Aiquin, Chanson de Geste', of the Twelfth Century: A Critical Edition Based on MS.2233 (fonds français) in the Bibliothèque Nationale in Paris* (Ph.D. thesis, Leeds University, 1953–4).

Anon., 'Sir Percyvelle de Galles'; M.E. Williams, ed., *An Edition of the Romance of Sir Percyvelle de Galles with a Discussion of the Continental and Celtic analogues* (M.A. thesis, Aberystwyth University, 1961).

Anon., 'The Tournament of Sorelois'; C.M. Crompton, ed., *An Edition of the Extant Version of The Tournament of Sorelois, with Introduction, Glossary and Notes* (M.A. thesis, Manchester University, 1960–1).

Anon., 'Vitas Patrum'; P.S. Poureshagh, ed., *A Critical Edition of the Anglo-Norman Rhymed Translation of the Vitas Patrum Dedicated to the Templer Henri d'Arci* (Ph.D. thesis, Edinburgh University, 1977).

Anon., 'Ywain and Gawain'; J. Taglicht, ed., *An Edition of the Middle English Romance 'Ywain and Gawain', and Introduction, Notes and Glossary* (Ph.D. thesis, Oxford University, 1963).

Broderick, G., *Chronicle of the Kings of Mann and the Isles* (M.Phil. thesis, Nottingham University, 1973–4).

Cosforth, R.H., *Provençal Poetry in Thirteenth Century Italy and Its Relations with Early Sicilian Poetry* (M.Litt. thesis, Cambridge University, 1961–2).

Feeney, B.J., *The Cartae Baronum of 1166* (M.A. thesis, Queen's University, Belfast, 1970–1).

Hill, C.M., *A Study of the 'Nef des Princes' and the 'Nef des Dames Vertueuses' of Symphorien Champier* (M.A. thesis, Manchester University, 1951–2).

Hunt, A.B., *Le Chevalier au lion: a Comparative Study of Chretien's Romance and the Medieval Translations of it* (B.Litt. thesis, Oxford University, 1971–2)

Hunter, J.A., *The Rolandslied, Willehalm and the Crusades: a Study of Their Interrelationship* (M.Phil. thesis, London University, 1979).

McCann, F., *The Development of Irish Saga or Prose Tales as Recognized in the Curriculum of the Schools of Native Learning, from 700 to 1200 AD* (Ph.D. thesis, Queen's University, Belfast, 1953–4).

McCudden, S.J.C., *Les Poésies de Guilhem Figueira, troubadour Provençal du XIIIe siècle* (Ph.D. thesis, Birmingham University, 1975–6).

Morris, J., *Medieval Spanish Epic Style, Its Character and Development, and Its Influence on Other Forms of Literature* (Ph.D. thesis, Leeds University, 1961).

Peel, C.D., *Feudal Institutions and Vocabulary in the 'Roman de Renart'* (M.Phil. thesis, Leeds University 1968–9).

Powell, B.J., *The 'Poema de mio Cid' from the Twelfth to the Fourteenth Century* (Ph.D. thesis, Cambridge University, 1977).

Price, E., *Courtly Literature and Society in Twelfth Century France* (M.A. thesis, Hull University, 1967–8).

Ryan, M.T., *The Historical Value of Giraldus Cambrensis' 'Expugnatio Hibernica' as an Account of the*

Anglo-Norman Invasion of Ireland 1166– 1185 (M.A. thesis, Dublin National University, 1966–7).

Slater, J., *An Edition of Early Scots Texts from the Beginnings to 1410* (Ph.D. thesis, Edinburgh University, 1952–3).

Walker, J.M., *The Saracens in the Thirteenth Century Chansons de Geste and Romances* (M.A. thesis, London University, 1961–2).

Published primary sources

Adam of Bremen, *The History of the Archbishops of Hamburg-Bremen*, trans. F.J. Tschan (New York, 1959).

Alfonso el Sabio, *Primera Crónica de España, que mandó componer Alfonso el Sabio y se continuaba bajo Sancho IV en 1289*, ed. R. Menéndez-Pidal (Madrid, 1955).

Ambroise, W. Hubert and J. Lamonte, eds., *The Crusade of Richard the Lion-Heart* (1942; reprint 1976).

Anderson, A.O., *Scottish Annals from English Chroniclers, AD 500 to 1286* (London, 1908).

Anon., 'Apollonius of Tyre' in *The Old English Apollonius of Tyre* (London, 1958).

Anon., 'Aucassin et Nicolette'; M. Roques, ed., *Aucassin et Nicolette, chantefable du XIIe siècle* (Paris, 1936).

Anon., 'Cantar de Mio Cid'; R. Menéndez-Pidal, ed., *Cantar de Mio Cid: Texto, Gramática y Vocabulario* (Madrid, 1956); also in *Obras de R. Menéndez-Pidal*, vol.V.

Anon., 'Chanson d'Antioch'; S. Duparc-Quioc, ed., *Chanson d'Antioche* (Paris, 1976–8).

Anon., 'Chanson d'Aspremont'; L. Brandin, ed., *Le Chanson d'Aspremont: chanson de geste de XIe siècle* (Paris, n.d.).

Anon., *Ferguut*, ed. Visscher (Utrecht, 1838).

Anon., *Fouke Fitzwarin*, ed. L. Brandin (Paris, 1930).

Anon., 'Gesta Francorum'; R. Hill, ed. and trans., *The Deeds of the Franks and Other Pilgrims to Jerusalem* (London, 1962).

Anon., 'Gormont et Isembart'; A. Payot, ed., *Gormont et Isembart, fragment de chanson de geste du XIIe siècle* (Paris, n.d.).

Anon., 'Itinerarium Peregrinorum'; K. Fenwick, trans., *The Third Crusade, Itinerarium Peregrinorum* (London, 1958).

Anon., 'King Horn'; A. Langfors ed. *Huorn le Roi* (Paris, n.d.).

Anon., 'King Horn'; M.K. Pope, ed., *The Romance of Horn* (Oxford, 1955).

Anon., 'King Horn'; W. Schofield, trans., *The Story of Horn and Rimenbild* (Modern Language Association of America vol.XVIII, 1903), p.184ff.

Anon., *King Horn*, ed. G. McKnight (London, 1901).

Anon., *King Horn*, ed. J. Hall (Oxford, 1901).

Anon., 'La Chanson de Pèlerinage de Charlemagne'; G. Paris, ed., *Romania* vol.IX (1890), pp.1–29.

Anon., 'La Chrétienté Corbaran'; P.R. Grillo, ed., *The Old French Crusade Cycle, vol.7, 'The Jerusalem Continuation: part 1, La Chrétienté Corbaran'* (Alabama, 1984).

Anon., 'La Naissance du Chevalier au Cygne'; E.J. Mickel, ed., *The Old French Crusade Cycle, vol.I: 'La Naissance du Chevalier au Cygne'* (Alabama, 1977).

Anon., 'Le Charroi de Nimes'; J.L. Perrier, ed., *Le Charroi de Nimes, chanson de geste de XIIe siecle* (Paris, n.d.).

Anon., 'Le Chevalier a l'Epée'; R.C. Johnston and D.D.R. Owen, eds., *Two Old French Gauvain Romances: Le Chevalier a l'Epée and La Mule Sans Frein* (Edinburgh, 1972).

Anon., 'Le Chevalier au Cygne'; Reiffenberg, ed., in *Monuments pour service à l'histoire des provinces de Namur* vol.IV (Namur, n.d.).

Anon., 'Le Couronnement de Louis'; E. Langlois, ed., *Le Couronnement de Louis, chanson de geste du XIIe siècle* (Paris, n.d.).

Anon., *Le Roman de Renart*, ed. M. Roques, (Paris, 1955–68).

Anon., *Le Roman de Thèbes*, ed. G.R. de Lage (Paris, 1966).

Anon., 'Les Chetifs'; G.M. Myres, ed., *The Old French Crusade Cycle, vol.II, 'Les Chetifs'* (Alabama 1982).

Anon., 'Moniage Guillaume'; W. Cloetta, ed., *Les deux rédactions en vers du Moniage Guillaume, chanson de geste du XIIe siècle* (Paris, 1906–11).

Anon., *Richard Lowenherz*, ed. K. Brunner (Vienna and Leipzig, 1913).

Anon., *Siège de Barbastre*, ed. J.L. Perrier (Paris, n.d.).

Anon., *Sir Gawain and the Green Knight*, ed. N. David, J.R.R. Tolkien and E.V. Gordan, 2nd ed. (Oxford, 1967).

Anon., *The Lay of Havelok the Dane*, ed. W.W. Sisam (Oxford, 1915).

Anon., *The Lay of Havelok the Dane*, ed. W.W. Skeet (London, 1868).

Anon., *The Liber Augustalis*, trans. J.M. Powell (Syracuse, New York, 1971).

Anon., *The Song of Dermot and the Earl*, ed. G.H. Orpen (Oxford, 1892).

Anon., 'Vie de Saint Alexis'; G. Paris, ed., *La Vie de Saint Alexis, poème de XIe siècle* (Paris, n.d.).

Anselm; R.W. Southern and F.S. Schmitt, eds., 'Memorials of Saint Anselm', in *Auctores Britannici Medii Aevi* vol.I (London, 1969).

Bello, A., *Poema del Cid* (Santiago, Chile, 1881).

Burcard; Reiffenberg, trans., 'Directorium', in 'Chevalier au Cygne', *Monuments pour service à l'histoire des provinces de Namur* vol.IV (Namur, n.d.).

Conon de Béthune; A. Wallenskold, ed., *Les Chansons de Conon de Béthune* (Helsinki, 1891; Paris, 1921).

Courtois d'Arras; E. Faral, ed., *'Courtois d'Arras', jue du XIIIe siècle* (Paris, n.d.).

David, C.W., ed., *Concerning the Conquest of Lisbon* (London, 1976).

De Belleval, R., ed., *Roles des nobles et fieffés du bailliage d'Amiens convoqués pour la guerre le 25 août 1337* (Amiens, 1862).

De Curzon, H., 'La règle du Temple', *Société de l'Histoire de France* vol.CCXXVIII (1886).

De Joinville; A. Pauphilet and E. Pognon, eds., 'Histoire de Saint Louis', in *Historiens et Chroniqueurs du Moyen Age* (Paris, 1952).

De Joinville; F. Marzials, trans., 'Histoire de Saint Louis', in *Memoires of the Crusades by Villehardouin and de Joinville* (London, 1921).

Delaborde, H.F., ed., *Oeuvres de Rigard et de Guillaume le Breton* (Paris, 1882–5).

Ebbo and Herbord; C.H. Robinson, trans., *The Life of Otto, Apostle of Pomerania* (London, 1920).

Eidelberg, S., ed. and trans., *Jews and Crusaders: The Hebrew Chronicles of the First and Second Crusades* (1977).

Enk, P.J., 'The Romance of Appolonius of Tyre', *Mnemosyne* 4th ser. vol.I (1948), pp.222–37.

Fidenza of Padua; Gulubovitch, ed., 'Liber de Recuperatione Terre Sante', *Biblioteca Biobibliografica della Terra Santa* vol.II (n.d.), p.9ff.

Foulche-Delbosc, R., 'Gesta Roderici Campidocti', *Revue Hispaniques* vol.XXI (1909), pp.412–59.

Frappier, J., *Les chansons de geste du cycle de Guillaume d'Orange* (Paris, 1955–65).

Fryde, E.B., ed., *Book of the Prests of the King's Wardrobe for 1294–5, Presented to John Goronwy Edwards* (Oxford, 1962).

Fulchres of Chartres, 'Gesta Francorum Iherusalem Peregrinantium', in *Recueil des Historiens des Croisades: Historiens Occidentaux* vol.III (Paris, 1844–95).

    F.R. Ryan, trans., *A History of the Expedition to Jerusalem 1095–1127* (1970).

Galbert of Bruges; B. Ross, trans., *The Murder of Charles the Good, Count of Flanders, by Galbert of Bruges* (New York, 1960).

    H. Pirenne, ed., *Histoire de meutre de Charles de Bon, Comte de Flandre* (Paris, 1891).

Geraldus Cambrensis, 'Expugnatio'; Stokes, ed. and trans., *English Historical Review* vol.XX

(1905).

The Itinerary through Wales and the Description of Wales, ed. W. Llewelyn Williams (London, 1908).

Opera, ed. J.S. Brewer, J.F. Dimock and G.F. Warner (London, 1861–91).

'Topographia Hibernie', ed. J.J. O'Meara, *Proceedings of the Royal Irish Academy* vol.LII C (1949), pp.113–78.

The Topography of Ireland, ed. and trans. J.J. O'Meara (London, 1982).

Gislebert de Mons, *Chronique*, ed. L. Vanderkindere (Brussels, 1904).

Giuliani, A., *Antologia della poesia italiana dalle origini al trecento* (Milan, 1975).

Gomez-Moreno, M., 'Las Primeras cronicas de la Reconquista', *Boletin Academia Historia* (1932).

Gough, H., ed., *Scotland in 1298: Documents Relating to the Campaign of King Edward the First in That Year and Especially to the Battle of Falkirk* (London, 1888).

Grabowski, K. and Dumville, D., *Chronicles and Annals of Medieval Ireland, Scotland and Wales: Studies in Textual History* (London, 1982).

Gregoire, H., 'Le Chanson de Roland de l'an 1085', *Bulletin de l'academie Royale de Belge, Classe des Lettres* 5th ser. vol.XXV (1939).

Hamaker, H.G., 'Thesauriersrek van Willem IV', in *Historsch Genootsch* n.s. vols XXI, XXIV and XXVI (n.d.).

Helmold, *Chronicle of the Slavs*, trans. F.J. Tshan, (New York, 1935).

Henry of Livonia, *The Chronicle of Henry of Livonia*, trans. J.A. Brundage (Madison, Wisc., 1961).

Jean de Mean; U. Robert, ed., *L'Art de Chevalerie* (Paris, 1897).

Jeanroy, A., *Jongleurs et Troubadours Gascons de XIIe et XIIIe siècles* (Paris, n.d.).

King, E.J., ed., *The Rule, Statutes and Customs of the Hospitallers (1099–1310)* (London, 1934).

Krey, A.C., *The First Crusade: Accounts of Eye-Witnesses and Participants* (1921).

Latham, J.D. and Paterson, W.F., *Saracen Archery* (London, 1970).

Lloyd-Jones, J., 'The Court Poets of the Welsh Princes', *Proceedings of the British Academy* vol.XXXIV (1948).

Loomis, R.S ., *Arthurian Literature in the Middle Ages* (Oxford, 1959).

Macartney, C.A., *The Medieval Hungarian Historians* (Cambridge, 1953).

The Origins of the Hun Chronicle (Cambridge, 1951).

Mathieu, M., ed., *Apulia: Guillaume de Pouille: La Geste de Robert Guiscard* (Palermo, 1961).

Matonis, A.T.E., 'Traditions of Panegyric in Welsh Poetry', *Speculum* vol.LIII (1978), pp.667–87.

Matthew Paris; J.A. Giles, trans., *Chronica Majora* (1889).

Meyer, P., 'Fragment d'un chanson d'Antioche en provençal', *Archives de la Société de l'Orient Latin* vol.II (1884), pp.467–509.

'Un récit en vers français de la première croisade fondé sur Baudri de Bourgueil', *Romania* vol.V (1876), pp.1–63.

ed., *William the Marshal* (Paris, 1891–1901).

Montalbaen; H. Hoffman von Fallersleben, ed., 'Renout', *Horae Belgicae* vol.V (Breslau, 1837).

Myers, G.M., 'The Manuscripts of the Cycle', in *The Old French Crusade Cycle, vol.1: 'La Naissance du Chevalier au Cygne'* (Alabama, 1977).

Nelli, R., and Lavaud, R., *Les Troubadours: II Le Tresor Poétiques de l'Occitanie* (Paris, 1966).

Northup, G.T., 'La Gran Conquista de Utramar and its problems', *Hispanic Review* vol.II (1934), pp.287–302.

Nuñes, J.J., *Cantigas d'amigo dos Trovadores Galego-Portugueses* (1926).

Odo de Deuil; V.G. Berry, trans., *De Profectione Ludovici VII in Orientem* (1948).

Oliver of Paderborn; J.J. Gavignan, trans., *Capture of Damiette* (n.d.).

Otto of Friesing; C.C. Mierow, trans., *The Deeds of Frederick Barbarossa* (1953).

Pope, M.K., 'Notes on the Vocabulary of the Romance of Horn and Rimel', in *Mélanges offerts à*

Ernest Hoepffner (Paris, 1949), pp.63–70.

Pütz, H.H., *Die Darstellung der Schlacht in mittelhochdoutscher Erzähldichtungen von 1150 bis zu 1250* (Hamburg, 1971).

Radulf of Caen, 'Gesta Tancredi', in *Recueil des Historiens des Croisades: Historiens Occidentaux* vol.III (Paris, 1844–95).

Raymond de Aguilers; L. Hill and J. Hill, trans., *The History of the Frankish Conquest of Jerusalem* (1968).

Robert de Clarî; P.Lauer, ed., *La Conquête de Constantinople* (Paris, n.d.).

   E.H. McNeal, trans., *The Conquest of Constantinople* (1936).

   A. Pauphilet and E. Pognon, eds., 'La Conquête de Constantinople', in *Historiens et chroniqueurs du Moyen Age* (Paris, 1952).

Roger of Hoveden; W. Stubbs, ed., 'Assize of Arms', in *Magistri Rogeri de Houedene* vol.II (London, 1868–71), pp.260–3.

Rousset, R., 'La description du monde chevaleresque dans Orderic Vitalis', *Le Moyen Age* vol.LXXV (1969), pp.427–44.

Sablonier, R., *Krieg und Kriegertum in der Chronica de Ramon-Muntaner, Ein Studie zun spätmittel-alterlichen Kriegswesen auf grunf katalanischer Quellen* (Berne, 1971).

Sandoz, E., 'Tourneys in the Arthurian Tradition', *Speculum* vol.XX (1945), pp.389–432.

Schmugge, L., *Radulfus Niger: De re militari et triplici via peregrinationis Ierosolimitane '1187/1188'* (Berlin and New York, 1977).

Schwandtner, ed., *Script. Rer. Hung.* (Vienna, from 1746).

Siebel, G., *Harnisch und Helm in der epischen Dichtung des 12 Jahrhunderts bis zu Hartemann's 'Erek'* (Hamburg, 1968).

Thorpe, M.L., 'Mastre Richard, a Thirteenth Century Translator of the 'De re militari' of Vegetius', *Scriptorium* vol.VI (1952), pp.39–50.

Turoldus; T.A. Jenkins, ed., *La Chanson de Roland* (London, 1924).

Uhlenbeck, C.C., 'Die germanischen Wörter im Altslavischen', *Archiv für Slavische Philogie* vol.XV (1893).

Van Heelu, Jan; J.F. Willems, ed., *Rijmtroniek* (Brussels, 1836).

Van Mieris, 'Groot Charterboek van der Graven van Holland', in *Charter van Holland* vol.II (n.d.).

Van Neuss, H., 'Le testament d'un bourgois armée de Hasselt', *L'Ancien Pays de Looz* V (1901), pp.27–8.

Vegetius; L. Löfstedt, ed., *Jean de Meun, Li Abregemenz noble homme Vegesce Flave René des estabissemenz apartenanz a chevalerie* (Helsinki, 1977).

   U. Robert, ed., *L'Art de Chevalerie: Traduction du 'De re militari' de Végèce par Jean de Meun* (Paris, 1897).

Villehardouin; F. Marzials, trans., in *Memoirs of the Crusades by Villehardouin and De Joinville* (London, 1921).

   A. Pauphilet and E. Pognan, eds. 'La Conquête de Constantinople', in *Historiens et Chroniqueurs de Moyen Age* (Paris, 1952).

   M. Shaw, trans., *Chronicles of the Crusades* (London, 1963).

Vogel, F.C.W., 'L'Education d'Alexandre', in *Bartsch Chrestomathie* (Leipzig, 1875).

William of Aquitaine, *Les Chansons de Guillaume IX, Duc d'Aquitaine (1071*–1127), ed. A. Jeanroy (Paris, n.d.).

William of Jumièges; J. Marx, ed., *William of Jumieges, Gesta Normannorum Ducum* (Rouen and Paris, 1914).

William of Poitiers; R. Foreville, ed., *William of Poitiers: Histoire de Guillaume le Conquerant* (Paris, 1952).

William of Ruybroek; W.W. Rockhill, trans., *Journey to the Eastern Parts of the World, 1253–55* (London, 1900).

William of Tyre; E. Babcock and A.C. Krey, trans., *A History of Deeds Done Beyond the Seas* (1943).

Williams, G., *The Burning Tree: Poems from the First Thousand Years of Welsh Poetry* (London, 1956). *An Introduction to Welsh Poetry* (London, 1953).

Unpublished secondary sources

Abulafia, D.S.H., *Commercial Relations Between the Norman Kingdom of Sicily and the North Italian Republics 1116–1191* (Ph.D. thesis, Cambridge University, 1975).

Al-Juboubi, D.A.H., *The Medieval Idea of the Saracen as Illustrated in English Literature, Spectacle and Sport* (Ph.D. thesis, Leicester University, 1971–2).

Alban, J.R., *National Defence of England 1337–89* (Ph.D. thesis, Liverpool University, 1977).

Arnold, B.C.B., *Ministeriales and the Development of Territorial Lordship in the Eichstatt Region 1100–1350* (Ph.D. thesis, Oxford University, 1971–2).

Barber, M.C., *The Grand Masters of the Order of the Temple* (Ph.D. thesis, Nottingham University, 1968–9).

Barnie, J.E., *The Ideal of the Knight in English Vernacular Romance 1330–1400* (M.A. thesis, Birmingham University, 1966–7).

Beebe, B.T., *Edward I and the Crusades* (Ph.D. thesis, St Andrews University, 1970–1).

Bollard, J.K., *Medieval English Arthurian Romances and their Celtic Analogues: a Comparative Study* (Ph.D. thesis, Leeds University, 1979).

Boulton, D'A.J.D., *The Origins and Development of the Curial Order of Chivalry 1330–1470* (Ph.D. thesis, Oxford University, 1975–6).

Careless, B.J., *The Medieval German Understanding of the Crusades* (Ph.D. thesis, St Andrews University, 1978).

Clementi, D.R., *Politics and Administration of the Mainland Provinces of the Sicilian Kingdom from 1189–1198* (Ph.D. thesis, Oxford University, 1950–1).

Critchley, J.S., *Military Organization in England 1124–1254* (Ph.D. thesis, Nottingham University, 1968–9).

Curran, D.J., *The Ui Cheannslaigh Kingship of Leinster, with Special Reference to Diarmuid Mac Murchadha, King of Leinster (1126–71)* (M.A. thesis, Dublin National University, 1966–7).

Edbury, P.W., *The Feudal Nobility of Cyprus 1192–1400* (Ph.D. thesis, St Andrews University, 1974).

Fitzgerald, B.A., *The Contacts between Britain and Ireland in the Century Preceding the Anglo-Norman invasion of Ireland* (M.A. thesis, Keele University, 1965–6).

Foster, S.M., *Some Aspects of Maritime Activity and the Use of Sea Power in Relation to the Crusading States 1096–1169* (Ph.D. thesis, Oxford University, 1978).

Gwynne, T.A., *Society in the Anglo-Scottish Border Region in the Twelfth and Thirteenth Centuries* (M.Litt. thesis, Newcastle University, 1974).

Hall, A.T., *The Employment of Naval Forces in the Reign of Edward III* (M.A. thesis, Leeds University, 1955–6).

Hall, B.E., *The Earls of Orkney-Caithness and Their Relationship with Norway and Scotland 1158–1470* (Ph.D. thesis, St Andrews University, 1970–1)

Hamdy Mahmoud, A. el H., *The Western Attitude Towards Islam Before and After the First Crusade* (Ph.D. thesis, Liverpool University, 1952–3).

Hodgetts, A.C., *The Colonies of Coron and Modon under Venetian Administration, 1204–1400* (Ph.D. thesis, London University, 1975).

Housley, N.J., *The Angevin Kings of Sicily, the Papacy and the Crusades 1254–1343* (Ph.D. thesis, Cambridge University, 1979).

Hyde, J.K., *The Last Years of the Paduan Commune c.l256–1328* (Ph.D. thesis, Oxford University, 1960).

Jackson, L.M., *The Tournament and the Evolution of a Literary Theme from French Medieval Arthurian Romance to the Works of Sir Thomas Malory* (M.A. thesis, Hull University, 1973–4).

Jurica, A.R.J., *The Knights of Edward I* (Ph.D. thesis, Birmingham University, 1975–6).

Lewis, P.N., *The Wars of Richard I in the West – a Study in the Art in the Twelfth Century* (M.Phil. thesis, London University, 1977).

Lydon, J.F., *Ireland's Contribution to the Wars of Edward I* (M.A. thesis, Dublin National University, 1951–2).

Macquarrie, A., *The Impact of the Crusading Movement in Scotland, 1095–c.1560* (Ph.D. thesis, Edinburgh University, 1982).

Martin, M.E., *Venice and the Byzantine Empire before the Fourth Crusade* (M.A. thesis, Birmingham University, 1972–3).

Matheson, L.G.S., *The Norman Principality of Capua (1058–98) with Particular Reference to Richard (1058–78)* (B.Litt. thesis, Oxford University, 1975).

McNeill, T.H., *The History and Archaeology of the Anglo-Norman Earldom of Ulster* (Ph.D. thesis, Queen's University, Belfast, 1973–4).

Nicholson, R., *The Scottish Wars of Edward III, 1327–35* (Ph.D. thesis, Oxford University, 1960–1).

Noel, R.P.R., *Town Defence in the French Midi during the Hundred Years War, c.1337–c.1453* (Ph.D. thesis, Edinburgh University, 1978).

Parker, E.J., *The Feudal Baron in the French Epic of the Twelfth Century* (Ph.D. thesis, London University external, 1951–2).

Pinsent, M.C., *The Anglo-Saxon Thegnage from 871–c.1100 with Some Comparisons with the Pre-Feudal Frankish Nobility of Service* (M.A. thesis, London University, 1951–2).

Purcell, M.P., *The Chief Instruments of Papal Crusading Policy, and Crusade to the Holy Land from the Final Loss of Jerusalem to the Fall of Acre, 1244–91* (B.Litt. thesis, Oxford University, 1968–9).

Riley-Smith, J.S.C., *The Knights Hospitallers in Latin Syria* (Ph.D. thesis, Cambridge University, 1963–4).

Singleton, F.B., *'Kalevala' and the Historical Geography of Finland* (M.A. thesis, Leeds University, 1951–2).

Skey, M.A., *Herod the Great in Medieval Art and Literature* (Ph.D. thesis, York University, 1977).

Smith, W.J., *Aspects of Military Organization in England under King John: the Foreign Mercenaries, Their Place in the Royal Armies and in Feudal Society, and Their Relationship to the Household* (M.A. thesis, University of Wales, 1950–1).

Snead, G.A., *The Careers of Four 14th Century Military Commanders Serving Edward III and Richard II in the 100 Years War* (M.A. thesis, Kent University, 1968–9).

Sommers, G.R., *Royal Tombs at St Denis in the Reign of Saint Louis* (Dissertation, Columbia University, New York, 1966).

Szur, R.C.A., *Giovanni of Ravenna and His 'History of Ragusa'* (M.Phil. thesis, London University, 1971–2).

Walker, R.F., *The Anglo-Welsh Wars, 1217–1267, with Special Reference to English Military Developments* (Ph.D. thesis, Oxford University, 1954).

Watkinson, A.E., *The King's Thegns and Serjeants in Domesday Book* (M.A. thesis, London University, 1957–8).

West, F.J., *The Justiciarship in England, 1204–1232* (Ph.D. thesis, Cambridge University, 1955–6).
The Office of Justiciar in Anglo-Norman England (Ph.D. thesis, Leeds University, 1950–1).

Published secondary sources

Abulafia, D.S.H., 'Ancona, Byzantium and the Adriatic, 1155–1173', *Papers of the British School at Rome* vol.LII (1984).
'The Norman Kingdom of Africa and the Norman Expeditions, Majorca and the Muslim Mediterranean', *Battle Conference on Anglo-Norman Studies, Proceedings* vol.VII (1984).

Ackerman, R.W., 'The Knighting Ceremonies in the Middle English Romances', *Speculum* vol.XIX (1944), pp.285–313.

Allmand, C.T., ed., *War, Literature and Politics in the Late Middle Ages: Essays in Honour of G.W.*

Coopland (Liverpool, 1976).

Amari, M., 'Su i fuochi da guerra usati nel Mediterraneo nell'XI e XII secoli', *Atti della Reale Academia dei Lincei* (Rome, 1876).

Anderson, W., *Castles of Europe from Charlemagne to the Renaissance* (London, 1970).

Anon., 'Horn Childe and the Battle of Stainmoor', *Cumberland and Westmorland Antiquarian and Archaeological Society Transactions* vol.XXXVIII (1936), pp.30–40.

Atiya, A.S., *The Crusade in the Later Middle Ages* (London, 1938).

Audouin, E., *Essai sur l'armée royale au temps de Phillipe Auguste* (Paris, 1913).

Auer, L., *Die Schlacht bei Mailberg am 12 Mai 1082* (Vienna, 1976).

Bachrach, B.S., 'The Feigned Retreat at Hastings', *Medieval Studies* vol.XXXIII (1971), pp.264–7.

'The Origins of Armorican Chivalry', *Technology and Culture* vol.X (1969), pp.166–71.

Ballesteros, A., 'La Reconquista de Murcia', *Boletin de la Real Academia de la Historia* vol.CXI (1942), pp.133–50.

'La Toma de Salé en tiempos de Alfonso el Sabio', *Al Andalus* vol.VIII (1943), pp.89–96.

Ballesteros, M., 'La Conquista de Jaén por Fernando III el Santo', *Cuadernos de historia de España* vol.XX (1953), pp.63–138.

Balon, J., 'L'organization militaire des Namurois au XIVe siècle', *Annales de la Société archéologiques de Namur* vol.XL (1932), pp.1–86.

Bandera Gómez, C., *El Poema de mio Cid: poesia, historia, mito* (Madrid, 1969).

Barash, M., *Crusader Figural Sculpture in the Holy Land* (Jerusalem, 1971).

Barlow, F., *Edward the Confessor* (London, 1970).

The Feudal Kingdom of England 1042–1216 (London, 1972).

Barlozzetti, U. and Giuliani, M., 'La Prassi Guerresca in Toscana', in *Guerre e assoldati in Toscana 1260–1364*, ed. L.G. Boccia and M. Scalini (Florence, 1982).

Barraclough, G., ed., *Eastern and Western Europe in the Middle Ages* (London, 1970).

Barrow, G.W.S., 'The Beginnings of Feudalism in Scotland', *Bulletin, Institute of Historical Research* vol.XXIX (1956).

Bates, D., *Normandy before 1066* (London, 1982).

Beeler, J., 'Castles and Strategy in Norman and Early Angevin England', *Speculum* vol.XXI (1959), pp.581–601.

'The Composition of Anglo-Norman Armies', *Speculum* vol.XL (1965), pp.398–414.

'XIIIth century Guerilla Campaign', *The Military Review* vol.XLII (1962), pp.39–46.

'Towards a Re-evaluation of English Medieval Generalship', *Journal of British Studies* vol.III (1963), pp.1–10.

Warfare in England 1066–1189 (Ithaca, 1966).

Warfare in Feudal Europe 730–1200 (Ithaca, 1971).

Bell, A., 'Notes on Gaimer's Military Vocabulary', *Medium Aevum* vol.XL (1971), pp.93–103.

Benninghoven, F., *Der Orden der Schwertbrüder* (Cologne and Graz, 1965).

Bilmanis, A., *A History of Latvia* (Princeton, 1951).

Bloch, M., *Feudal Society*, trans. L.A. Manyon (London, 1961).

Boccia, L.G. and Scalini, M., *Guerre e assoldati in Toscana 1260–1364* (Florence, 1982).

Bohigas, P., *Tractats de Cavalleria* (Barcelona, 1947).

Bökönyi, S., *History of Domestic Animals in Central and Eastern Europe* (Budapest, 1974).

Bonds, W.N., 'Some Industrial Price Movements in Medieval Genoa 1155–1255', in *Economy, Society and Government in Medieval Italy. Essays in Memory of Robert L. Reynolds*, ed. D. Herlihy, R.S. Lopez and V. Slessarev (Kent, Ohio, 1969).

Bonefant, P. and Despy, G., 'La noblesse en Brabant aux XIIe et XIIIe siècle', *Le Moyen Age* vol.LXIV (1958), pp.27–46.

Bonilla y San Martin, A., 'Las gestas del Cid Campeador', *Boletin de la Real Academia de la Historia* vol.LIX (1911), pp.161–257.

Bordonoue, G., *La vie quotodienne des Templiers au XIIIe siècle* (Paris, 1975).

Borelli de Serres, L.L., *Recherches sur divers services publics du XIIIe au XVIIIe siècle* (Paris, 1895–1909).

Bornstein and Soucek, *The Meeting of Two Worlds: The Crusades and the Mediterranean Context* (Chicago, 1981).

Borosy, A., 'A XI–XIV századi magyar lovassá grol' (on Hungarian cavalry), *Hadtörténelmi Közlemények* (1962).

Bottner, R., 'Die Wehrorganization der frühen Babenbergen im Einzelgebiet der Bezirke Melk und Scheibbs', *Jahrbuch für Landeskunde von Niederösterreich* vol.XLII (1976), pp.26–37.

Boussard, J., 'L'enquête de 1172 sur les services de chevelier en Normandie', in *Recueil de travaux offerts à Clovis Brunel*, vol.I (1955), pp.193–208.

'Les mercenaires au XIIe siècle, Henri II Plantegenet et les origines de l'armée de metier', *Bibliothèque de l'Ecole des Chartres* vol.CVI (1945–6), pp.189–224.

'Services féodaux, milices et mercenaries dans les armées en France aux X et XIe siècles', in *Ordinamenti Militari in Occidente nell'alto Medioevo, Settimane di Studi del Centro Italiano di Studi sull'alto Medioevo* vol.XV (Spoleto, 1968).

Bouteiller, H., *Histoire des milices bourgeoises de Rouen* (Rouen, 1850).

Bowsky, M.W., 'City and Contado, Military Relationships and Communal Bonds in Fourteenth Century Siena', in *Renaissance Studies in Honor of Hans Baron*, ed. A. Molho and J.A. Tedeschi (Northern Illinois University, 1971), pp.75–98.

A Medieval Italian Commune: Siena under the Nine, 1287–1355 (Los Angeles, 1981).

Bradbury, J., 'Battles in England and Normandy, 1066–1154', *Battle Conference on Anglo-Norman Studies, Proceedings* vol.VI (1983), pp.1–12.

Brooks, F.W., *The Battle of Stamford Bridge* (York, 1956).

The English Naval Forces 1199–1272 (Manchester, 1932).

Brooks, N.P., 'Arms, Status and Warfare in Late Saxon England', in *Ethelred the Unready, Papers from the Millenary Conference*, ed. D. Hill (Oxford, 1978).

Brown, R.A., 'The Battle of Hastings', *Battle Conference on Anglo-Norman Studies, Proceedings* vol.III (1980).

English Castles (London, 1976).

'The Norman Conquest and the Genesis of English Castles', *Château-Gaillard, Etudes de Castellologie médiévale (CRAM Caen)* vol.III (1966).

The Normans and the Norman Conquest (London, 1969).

The Origins of English Feudalism (London, 1976).

'The Status of the Norman Knight', in *War and Government in the Middle Ages: Essays presented to J.O. Prestwich* (Woodbridge, 1984).

Brundage, J.A., 'The Army of the First Crusade and the Crusade Vow', *Medieval Studies* (1971).

Burley, S.J., 'The Victualling of Calais 1347–65', *Bulletin of the Institute of Historical Research* vol.XXXI (1958), pp.49–57.

Burns, R.I., 'The Catalan Company and the Eastern Powers', *Speculum* vol.XXIX (1954), pp.751–71.

'Christian-Islamic Confrontation in the West: The Thirteenth Century Dream of Conversion', *American Historical Review* vol.LXXVI (1971), pp.1388–1434.

'Rehearsal for the Sicilian War: Pere el Gran and the Mudejar Counter Crusade in the Kingdom of Valencia, 1276–1278', in *XI Congresso della Coroña d'Aragón: la Società mediterranea all'epoca del Vespro* (Palermo, 1983), pp.259–87.

Byock, J., *Feud in the Icelandic Saga* (Los Angeles, 1983).

Byrne, E.H., 'The Genoese Colonies in Syria', in *The Crusades and Other Historical Essays Presented to D.C. Monro*, ed. L.J. Paetow (1928).

'Genoese Trade with Syria in the Twelfth Century', *American Historical Review* (1919–20).

Byrne, F.J., *Irish Kings and High Kings* (London, 1973).

Caggese, R., *Roberto d'Angio e i suoi tempi* (Florence, 1922–30).

Calderon, S.E., 'De la Milicia de los Arabes en España', *Revista Militar* vol.IV (Madrid, 1849).

Campbell, J., ed., *The Anglo-Saxons* (London, 1982).

Canestrini, G., *Arte militare meccanica medievale* (Milan, n.d.).
  'Documenti per service alle storie delle Milizie Italiane', *Archivo Storico Italiane* vol.XV (1851).

Cardini, F., 'La Guerra nella Toscana bassomedievale: Aspeti e dimensioni di una presenza storica', in *Guerre e assoldati in Toscana, 1260–1364*, ed. L.G. Boccia and M. Scalini (Florence, 1982).

Carile, A., *La rendita feudale nella Morea latina sec. XIV* (Bologna, 1983).
  'La signoria rurale nell'imperio latino di Constantinople 1204–1261', in *Actes du XV Congrés International d'études byzantines, vol.IV: Histoire* (Athens, 1980), pp.65–77.

Carolus-Barré, L., 'La Service militaire en Beauvaisis au temps de Philippe de Beaumanoir: L'estaigne à Gerberoy et à Beauvais (1271–1277); L'ost de Navarre (1276)', in *Actes di CIe Congrès national des Sociétés savants, Lille 1976: Section de philogie et d'histoire jusqu'à 1610, La guerre et la paix* (Paris, 1978), pp.73–93.

Carr, A.D., 'Welshmen in the Hundred Years War', *The Welsh History Review* vol.IV (1968), pp.21–46.

Carrère, C., 'Aux origines des compagnies: la compagnie catalane de 1302', in *Recruitement, mentalités, sociétés: Colloque international d'histoire militaire, Université Paul-Valery de Montpellier, Septembre 1974* (Montpellier, 1974), pp.1–7.

Carsten, F., 'Slavs in NE Germany', *Economic History Review* (1944).

Cazel, F.A., 'The Tax of 1185 in Aid of the Holy Land', *Speculum* (1955).

Centre d'Histoire Militaire, *Bibliographie d'histoire militaire belge des origines au le Août 1914 (Travaux 14)* (Brussels, 1979).

Cerone, F., *L'Opera politica e militare di Ruggiero II in Africa ed in Oriente* (Catania, 1913).

Champeval, J.B., 'Le role du ban et arrière-ban du haut Auverge', in *L'Auvergne historique, littéraire et artistique: Varia 1909–1912* (Riom, 1913).

Chazelas, A., *Documents relatifs au Clos des Galées de Rouen et aux armées de mer du roi de France de 1293–1418* (Paris, 1977–8).

Chew, H.M., 'Scutage in the Fourteenth Century', *The English Historical Review* vol.XXXVIII (1923), pp.19–41.

Cheyette, F., *Lordship and Community in Medieval Europe* (1968).

Chibnall, M., 'Mercenaries and the Familia Regis under Henry I', *History* vol.LXII (1977), pp.15–23.
  'Military Service in Normandy before 1066', *Battle Conference on Anglo-Norman Studies, Proceedings* vol.V (1982), pp.65–77.

Choc, P., *Khiha se zabývá: obdobim 850–1250v Čechách* (Prague, 1967).

Chomel, V., 'Chevaux de bataille et roncin en Dauphiné au XIVe siècle', *Cahiers d'Histoire* vol.VII (1962), pp.5–23.

Christensen, A.E., 'Denmark between the Viking Age and the Valdemars', *Medieval Scandinavia* vol.I (1966).
  The Northern Crusades, the Baltic and the Catholic frontier 1100–1525 (London, 1980).

Cilento, N., *Italia meridionale Longobarda* (Milan and Naples, 1966).
  'Le origine della signoria Capuana nella Langobardia Minore', *Istituto Storico Italiane per il Medio Evo: Studi Storice* vols LXIX–LXX (1966).

Clifford, E.R., *A Knight of Great Renown, biography of Othon de Grandson* (Chicago, 1961).

Cline, R.H., 'The Influence of Romance on Tournaments', *Speculum* vol.XX (1945), pp.204–11.

Cohn, W., *Die Geschichte der normannisch-sicilischen Flotte unter der Regierung Rogers I und Rogers II* (Breslau, 1910).

Contamine, P., 'Consommation et demande militaire en France et en Angleterre, XIIIe–XVe siècle', in *Domanda e consumi, Livelli e strutture (nei secoli XIII–XVIII), Atti della 'Sesta settimana di Studio' (27 aprile–3 maggio 1974): Instituto internazionale di storia economica 'F. Datini'* (Prato-Florence, 1978), pp.409–28.

'Crécy (1346) et Agincourt (1415): une comparison', in *Divers aspects du Moyen Age in Occident: Actes du Congrés tenu à Calais en septembre 1974* (Calais, 1977), pp.29–44.

La Guerre au Moyen Age (Paris, 1980); also as *War in the Middle Ages*, trans. M. Jones (Oxford, 1984).

Cook, D.R., 'The Norman Military Revolution in England', *Battle Conference on Anglo-Norman Studies, Proceedings* vol.I (1978), pp.94–102.

Critchley, J.S., 'Summonses to Military Service in the Reign of Henry III', *The English Historical Review* vol.LXXXV (1971), pp.79–95.

Csonkareti, K., *Hadihajók a Dunán* (Warships on the Danube from the 11th Century) (Budapest, 1980).

Csorba, C., *Varak a Hegyaljan: Tokaj-Onod-Szerence* (Fortresses of the Hegyalja, from the Mongol Conquest) (Budapest, 1980).

Curtis, E., *Roger of Sicily* (London, 1912).

D'Allessandro, V., *Politica e Socièta nella Sicilia aragonese* (Palermo, 1963).

Darkó, J., 'A magyar huszár ságeredete' (on Hungarian light cavalry), *Hadtörténelmi Közlemények* (1937).

De Boüard, M., 'Les petites enceintes circulaires d'origine medievale en Normandie', *Château-Gaillard* vol.I (1964).

De Gamma Barros, H., *Historia da administraçâo pública em portugal no sécolos XII a XV* (Lisbon, 1945–9)

De Mas-Latrie, L., *Commerce et expeditions militaires de la France* (Paris, 1880).

De Riquer, M., *Caballeros andantes españoles* (Madrid, 1967).

De Sotto y Montes, J., 'La orden de caballeria en la alta Edad media', *Revista de historia militar* vol.IV (1960), pp:39–73.

De Tourtoulon, C., *Jacme Ier de Conquérant* (Montpellier, 1863).

Décarreaux, J., *Normands, Papes et Moines en Italie meridionale et en Sicile XIe–XIIe siècle* (Paris, 1974).

Defourneaux, M., *Les Français en Espagne aux XIe et XIIe siècles* (Paris, 1949).

Del Treppo, M., 'Gli Aspetti organizzativi, economici e sociale di usa compagna di ventura', *Revista Storica Italiana* vol.LXXV (1973), pp.253–75.

Delbrück, H., *Geschichte der Kriegskunst in Rahmen der politisschen Geschichte, III: Mittelalter* (Berlin, 1923; Berlin, 1964).

Numbers in History (London, 1913).

Dellaville le Roulx, J., 'L'occupation Chrétienne à Smyrne (1344–1402)', in *Florilegum M. de Vogue* (1909), pp.177–86.

Denholm-Young, N., 'Feudal Society in the Thirteenth Century: The Knights', in *Collected Papers on Medieval Subjects* (Oxford, 1946), pp.56–67; also in *History* (1946); reprinted in *Collected Papers of N. Denholm-Young* (Cardiff, 1969), pp.83–94.

'The Tournament in the Thirteenth Century', in *Studies in Medieval History presented to F.M. Powicke*, ed. R.W. Hunt (Oxford, 1948), pp.240–68.

Deschamps, M., *Les Châteaux des Croises* (Paris, 1973).

Dessubré, M., *Bibliographie de l'Ordre des Templiers* (Paris, 1966).

Deveike, J., 'The Lithuanian Diarchies', *Slavonic and East European* Review vol.XXVIII (1950), pp.392–405.

Devos, J.-C., 'L'organization de la defence de l'Artois en 1297', *Bulletin Philologique et historique (jusqu'en 1715) du Comité des Travaux historiques et scientifiques, années 1955* (Paris, 1957), pp.47–55.

Douglas, D.C., *The Norman Achievement 1051–1100* (Berkeley, 1969).

The Norman Fate 1100–1154 (London, 1976).

William the Conqueror (London, 1964).

Duby, G., 'Dans la France du Nord-Ouest au XIIe siècle, les "Jeunes"', *Annales: Economies, Sociétés, Civilizations* vol.XIX (1964), pp.835–46.

27 Juillet 1214, Le dimanche de Bouvines (Paris, 1973); also as *La domenica di Bouvines, 27 Luglio 1214* (Milan, 1977).

The Early Growth of the European Economy: Warriors and Peasants from the Seventh to the Twelfth Century, trans. H.B. Clark (London, 1974).

Lordship and Community in Medieval Europe, trans. F.L. Cheyette (New York, 1968).

'La noblesse dans la France médievale', *Revue historique* vol.CCXXVI (1961), pp.1–22.

Duchesne, A., 'Témoins et sources de l'histoire militaire en Belgique', *Revue internationale d'histoire militaire* vol.XX (1959), pp.642–78.

and Loretti, J., 'L'histoire militaire en Belgique depuis 1959, essai bibliographique', *Revue internationale d'histoire militaire* vol.XXIX (1965), pp.514–46.

Dufourcq, C.E., *L'Espagne Catalane et le Maghrib aux XIIIe et XIVe siècles* (Paris, 1966).

Duncalf, F., 'The Peasants' Crusade', *American Historical Review* vol.XXVI (1920–1).

Durdik, J., *Husitské Vojenstvi* (including pre-Hussite background), (Prague, 1954).

Duvosquel, J.M., 'Bibliographie de l'histoire militaire en Belgique (1965–69)', *Revue internationale d'histoire militaire* vol.XXIX (1970), pp.973–1035.

Dvornik, F., *Les Slaves, Byzance et Rome* (Paris, 1926).

The Slavs, their Early History and Civilization (Boston, 1956).

École Française de Rome, *Structures féodales et féodalisme dans l'Occident mediterraneen (Xe–XIIIe siècle)* (Rome, 1980).

Eickholl, E., *Friedrich Barbarossa im Orient (Istanbuler Mitteilungen Beiheft 17*, Tübingen, 1977).

Fanning, J., 'Excavation of a Ringfort at Pollardstown, Co. Kildare', *Journal of the County Kildare Archaeological Society* vol.XV (1973–4), pp.251–61.

Fasoli, G., *Le compagne delle armi a Bologna* (Bologna, 1934).

Fauroux, F., *Recueil des actes des ducs de Normandie de 911 à 1066* (Caen, 1961).

Fawter, R., *The Capetian Kings of France* (London, 1980).

Fehr, H., 'Das Waffenrecht der Bauern im Mittelalter', *Zeitschrift der Savigny-Stiftung für Rechtsgeschichte (Ger. Abt.)* vol.XXXV (1914), pp.111–211; and vol.XXXVIII (1917), pp.1–114.

Ferrand, C.G., 'The Amount of Constantinople Booty in 1204', *Studi Veneziani* (1971).

Ferrer i Mallol, M.T., 'Mercenaris catalans a Ferrare (1307–17)', *Anuario de Estudios medievales* II (1965), pp.155–227.

Fino, J.F., *Fortresses de la France medievales* (Paris, 1970).

Fitz-Clarence, C., 'Mémoire sur l'emploi des mercenaires mahométans dans les armées chrétiennes', *Journal Asiatique* vol.XI (1827).

Fixot, M., 'Les fortifications de terre et la naissance de la féodalite dans le Cinglais', *Château-Gaillard* vol.III (1966).

Flori, J., 'Chevalerie et liturgie: Remise des armes et vocabulaire "chevaleresque" dans les sources liturgiques du IX au XIV siècle', *Le Moyen Age* vol.LXXXIV (1978), pp.147–78.

'Qu'est-ce qu'un bacheler: Etude historique du vocabulaire dans les chansons de geste du XIIe siècle', *Romania* (1975), pp.289–314.

Forey, A.J., 'The failure of the siege of Damascus in 1148', *Journal of Medieval History* vol.X (1984), pp.13–23.

Forstreuter, K., *Preussen und Russland im Mittelalter* (Königsberg and Berlin, 1938).

Fotheringham, J.K., 'Genoa and the Fourth Crusade', *English Historical Review* (1910), pp.26–57.

Fournier, G., *Les Châteaux dans la France médievale: Essai de sociologie monumentale* (Paris, 1978).

Fowler, K.A., *The King's Lieutenant: Henry of Grosmont, First Duke of Lancaster 1310–1361* (London, 1969).

France, J., 'The Crisis of the First Crusade: from the Defeat of Kerbogah to the Departure from Arqa', *Byzantion* (1970).

'The Departure of Tatikios from the Crusader Army', *Bulletin of the Institute of Historical Research* (1971).

Freeman, A.Z., 'Wall-Breakers and River-Bridgers: Military Engineers in the Scottish Wars of Edward I', *Journal of British Studies* vol.X (1971), pp.1–16.

Fuiano, M., 'La Battaglia di Civitate (1053)', *Archivio Storico Pugliese* vol.XI (1949).

Gabrieli, F., 'La Politique Arabes des Normands de Sicile', *Studia Islamica* vol.IX (1958).

Gaier, C., 'Analysis of Military Forces in the Principality of Liège and the County of Looz from the Twelfth to the Fifteenth Century', *Studies in Medieval and Renaissance History* vol.11 (1960), pp.205–61.

'Art et organization militaires dans la principauté de Liège et dans le comté de Looz au Moyen Age', *Mémoires, Academie Royale de Belgique, Classe des Lettres, des Sciences morales et politiques*, coll.8 vol.LIX, no.3 (1968).

'La cavalerie lourde en Europe occidentale du XIIe au XIVe siècle; un probleme de mentalité', *Revue internationale d'Histoire militaire* (1971), pp.385–96.

Grandes batailles de l'histoire liègeoise au Moyen Age (Liège, 1980).

Galasso, G., 'Il Commercia Amalfitano nel Periodo Normanno', in *Studi in onore di Riccardo Filangierivil* vol.I (Naples, 1959), pp.81–103.

Gallego Blanco, E., ed., *The Rule of the Spanish Military Order of St James (1170–1493)* (Leiden, 1971).

Galletti, A.I., 'La societa comunale di fronte alla guerra nelle fonti perugine nel 1282', *Bollettino della depputazione di storia patria per l'Umbria* vol.LXXI (1974), pp.35–98.

Galtier, E., 'Berrie: Arabe Barîyya', *Romania* vol.XXVII (1898).

Gautier, L., *La Chevalerie* (Paris, 1959).

Gay, J., *L'Italie Meridionale et l'Empire Byzantin* (Paris, 1904).

Le Pape Clément VI et les affaires d'Orient 1342–1352 (Paris, 1904).

Gay, V., *Glossaire Archéologique du moyen âge de la Renaissance* (Paris, 1887–1928).

Gerö, L., *Castles in Hungary* (Budapest, 1969).

Gessler, E.A., *Die Entwicklung des Geschutzwesen in der Schweiz* (Zurich, 1918).

'Die Spangenharnische von Küssnacht', *Zeitschrift für Historische Waffen- und Kostümkunde* n.s. vol.I, no.10 (1925), pp.211–15.

Die Trutzwaffen der Karolingerzeit vom VIII bis zu XI Jahrhundert (Basle, 1908).

Gibb, H.A.R., 'English Crusaders in Portugal', in *Chapters in Anglo-Portuguese Relations*, ed. E. Prestage (Watford, 1935), pp.1–23.

Gillingham, J., 'Richard I and the Science of War in the Middle Ages', in *War and Government in the Middle Ages: Essays in Honour of J.O. Prestwich*, ed. J. Gillingham and J.C. Holt (Woodbridge, 1984).

Gimbutas, M., *The Balts* (London, 1963).

Giuliani, M., 'L'organizzazione militare a Firenze, fra XIII e XIV secolo, forme de aggregazione e caratteri generali d'esercito fiorentino', in *Guerre e assoldati in Toscana 1260–1364*, ed. L.G. Boccia and M. Scalini (Florence, 1982).

Gless, K., Dorst, K., and Rathmann, E., *Des Pferd in Militärwesen* (Berlin, 1980).

Glosek, M., *Znaki i napisy mieczach sredniowiecznych w Polsce* (Warsaw, 1973).

Glover, R., 'English Warfare in 1066', *The English Historical Review* vol.LXVII (1952), pp.1–18.

Godfrey, J., *1204: The Unholy Crusade* (1980).

Golitsyn, N.S., *Allgemeine Kriegsgeschichte, part II (Mittelalter)* (Leipzig, 1874–89).

Gonzaga de Aveveda, L., *História de Portugal* (Lisbon, 1935–44).

González, J., 'Las Conquistas de Fernando III en Andalucia', *Hispania* vol.VI (1946), pp.515–631.

 Repartimiento de Sevilla (Madrid, 1951).

Gonzáles Simancas, M., 'Plazas de guerra y castillos mediovales de la frontera de Portugal', *Revista de archivos, bibliotecas y museos* 3rd ser. vols XXII–XXIII (1910).

Gonzáles Simancas, N., *España militar a principios de la Baja Edad Media* (Madrid, 1925).

Gorski, K., 'The Teutonic Order in Prussia', *Medievalia et humanistica* vol.XVII (1966).

Grassotti, H., 'Para la historia del botin y de los parias en León y Castila', *Cuadernos de Historia de España* vols XXXIX–XL (1964), pp.43–132.

Gregoire, H., and De Keyser, R., 'La Chanson de Roland et Byzance', *Byzantion* vol.XIV (1939), pp.265–316.

Grundmann, H., 'Rotten und Brabanzonen. Söldner-Heere im 12 Jahrhundert', *Deutsches Archiv für Erforschung des Mittelalters* (1942), pp.419–92.

Gualdo, G., 'I Libri delle Spese di guerra del Cardinal Albornoz in Italia conservi nell'Archivio Vaticano', in *El Cardinal Albornoz y el Collegio de España*, ed. E. Verdera y Tuello (Bologna, 1972–3), vol.I, pp.577–607.

Gutton, F., *La chevalerie militaire en Espagne: L'ordre d'Alcantara* (Paris, 1975).

 La chevalerie militaire en Espagne: L'ordre de Calatrava (Paris, 1955).

 La chevalerie militaire en Espagne: L'ordre de Santiago (Paris, 1972).

Hagenmeyer, H., *Die Kreuzzugshiefs aus dem Jahren 1088–1100* (Innsbruck, 1902)

Hagspiel, G.H., *Die Führungspersönlichkeit im Kreuzzug* (Berne, 1963).

Haleçki, O., *Borderlands of Western Civilization* (New York, 1952).

Hamilton, B., 'The Elephant of Christ: Reynald of Chatillon', *Studies in Church History* vol.XV (1978).

Hampe, K., *Der Zug nach dem Osten* (Leipzig, 1939).

Han, V., 'La culture matérielle des Balkans au Moyen Age à travers la documentation des Archives de Dubrovnik', *Balcanica* vol.III (1972).

Hanawalt, B.A., 'Violent Death in Fourteenth and Early Fifteenth Century England', *Comparative Studies in Society and History* vol.XVIII (1976), pp.297–320.

Hartwig, O., 'Eine mobilmaching in Florenze und die Schlacht von Montaperti am 4 September 1260', in *Quellen und Forschungen zur ältesten Geschichte der Stadt Florenze* (Halle, 1880).

Harvey, S., 'The Knight and the Knight's Fee in England', *Past and Present* vol.XLIX (1970), pp.3–43.

Hatem, A., *Les Poèmes épiques des croisades: Genèse, historiaté, localization – Essai sur l'activité litteraire dans les colonies franques de Syrie au Moyen Age* (Paris, 1932).

Hatto, A.T., 'Archery and Chivalry: A Noble Prejudice', *The Modern Language Review* vol.XXV (1940), pp.40–54.

Hay, D., 'Booty in Border Warfare', *Transactions of the Dumfriesshire and Galloway Natural History and Antiquarian Society* 3rd ser. vol.XXXI (1954), pp.145–66.

 'The Division of Spoils of War in Fourteenth Century England', *Transactions of the Royal Historical Society* 5th ser. vol.IV (1954), pp.91–109.

Hayes-McCoy, G.A., *Irish Battles* (London, 1969).

Hendrix, W.S., 'Military Tactics in the Poem of the Cid', *Modern Philology* vol.XX (1922), pp.45–8.

Herde, P., 'Die Schlacht bei Tagliocozzo: Eine historische-topographische Studie', *Zeitschrift für bayerische Landesgeschichte* vol.XXV (1962), pp.679–744.

Hewitt, H.J., *The Horse in Medieval England* (London, 1983).

 The Organization of War under Edward III, 1338–62 (Manchester, 1966).

Hill, D., ed., *Ethelred the Unready: Papers from the Millenary Conference* (Oxford, 1978).

Hill, J.H., and Hill, L.L., *Raymond IV, Count of Toulouse* (Syracuse, New York, 1962).

Hill, R., 'Crusading Warfare: a Camp-Follower's View', *Battle Conference on Anglo-Norman Studies, Proceedings* vol.I (1979).

Hollister, C.W., *Anglo-Saxon Military Institutions on the Eve of the Norman Conquest* (Oxford, 1962).

'The Annual Term of Military Service in Medieval England', *Medievalia et Humanistica* vol.XIII (1960), pp.40–7.

'The Five-hide Unit and the Old English Military Obligation', *Speculum* vol.XXXVI (1961), pp.61–74.

'The Knights of Peterborough and the Anglo-Norman Fyrd', *The English Historical Review* vol.LXXVII (1962), pp.417–39.

The Military Organization of Norman England (Oxford, 1965).

'Normandy, France and the Anglo-Norman regnum', *Speculum* vol.LI (1976), pp.204–42.

'The Significance of Scutage Rates in Eleventh and Twelfth Century England', *The English Historical Review* vol.LXXV (1960), pp.577–88.

Holt, J.C., 'The Introduction of Knight Service into England', *Battle Conference on Anglo-Norman Studies, Proceedings* vol.VI (1983), pp.89–106.

Housley, N.J., 'King Louis the Great of Hungary and the Crusades, 1342–1382', *Slavonic and East European Review* vol.LXII (1984), pp.192–208.

'The Mercenary Companies, the Papacy and the Crusades 1356–1378', *Traditio* vol.XXXVIII (1982).

Howarth, S., *The Knights Templar* (London, 1982).

Huici Miranda, H., *Las grandes batallas de la Reconquista durante los invasiòns africanas* (Madrid, 1956).

Iorga, N., *Notes et extraits pour servir à l'histoire des Croisades* (Paris, 1899).

Philippe de Mézières (1327–1405) et la Croisade au XIVe siècle (London, 1973).

Jackson, W.H., *Knighthood in Medieval Literature* (London, 1982).

Jäger, G., *Aspekte des Krieges und der Chevalerie im XIV Jahrhundert in Frankreich, Untersuchungen zu Jean Froissart's Chroniques* (Bern, 1981).

Jamison, E., *Admiral Eugenius of Sicily* (London, 1957).

'The Norman Administration of Apulia and Capua', *Papers of the British School at Rome* vol.VI (1913).

'Some Notes on the Anonymi Gesta Francorum with Special Reference to the Norman Contingent from South Italy and Sicily in the First Crusade', in *Studies presented to M.K. Pope* (Manchester, 1939).

Jarousseau, G., 'Le guet, l'arrière-guet et la garde en Poitou pendant la guerre de Cent Ans', *Bulletin de la Société des Antiquaires de l'Ouest* (1965), pp.159–202.

Jeffrey, G.H., *Cyprus under an English King* (London, 1978).

John, E., 'The End of Anglo-Saxon England', in *The Anglo-Saxons*, ed. J. Campbell (London, 1982).

Johns, C.N., 'Excavations at Pilgrims' Castle, Atlit (1932–33): Stables at the southwest of the suburb', *Quarterly of The Department of Antiquities of Palestine* vol.V, no.1 (1935), pp.31–60.

Johrendt, J., *Milites und Militia im 11 Jahrhundert, Untersuchung zur Frühgeschichte der Rittertums in Frankreich und Deutschland* (Nuremburg, 1971).

Jolliffe, J.E.A., *Angevin Kingship* (London, 1966).

Jones, C.M., 'The Conventional Saracen in the Songs of Geste', *Speculum* vol.XVII (1942), pp.201–25.

Joris, A., 'Remarques sur les clauses militaires des privilèges urbains liègeois', *Revue belge de Philologie et d'Histoire* vol.XXXVII (1959), pp.297–316.

Kedar, B.Z., ed., *Outremer: Studies in the History of the Crusading Kingdom of Jerusalem Presented to Joshua Prawer* (Jerusalem, 1982).

Keen, M.H., 'Chivalry, Nobility and the Man-at-Arms', in *War, Literature and Politics in the Late Middle Ages: Essays in Honour of G.W. Coopland*, ed. C.T. Allmand (Liverpool, 1976).

Kimball, E.G., 'Serjeantry Tenure in Medieval England', *Yale Historical Publications, Miscellany* vol.XXX (1936).

Kiraly, B., and Rothenberg, G., eds., *War and Society in East Central Europe* (New York, 1983).

Knusset, R., *Die deutschen Italienfahten 951–1220 und die Wehrverfassung* (Göttingen, 1931).

Kohler, C., ed., 'Deux projects de croisade en Terre Sainte composés à la fin du XIIIe et au debut du XIVe siècles', *Revue de l'Orient Latin* X (1903–4).

Komata, D., 'Forteresses hautes-médiévales albanais', *Ilyria* vol.V (n.d.).

Kosiary, E., *Woyny no Baltyku X–XIXw* (Warfare in the Baltic) (Gdansk, 1978).

Krollmann, C., *The Teutonic Order in Prussia* (Elbing, 1938).

Kurth, F., 'Der Anteil niederdeutscher Kreuzfahrer an den Kämpfen der Portugiesen gegen die Mauren', *Mittheilungen des Instituts für österreichische Geschichtkunde* vol.VIII (1911), pp.131–59.

La Monte, J.L., *The Feudal Monarchy in the Latin Kingdom of Jerusalem* (1932).

Labande, E.R., *Histoire de l'Europe Occidentale XIe–XIVe s.* (London, 1973).

Lacarra, J.M., 'La Conquista de Zaragoza por Alfonso I (18 diciembre 1118)', *Al Andalus* vol.XII (1947), pp.65–96.

    Vida de Alfonso el Batallador (Saragossa, 1971).

    'Les villes-frontières dans l'Espagne des XIe–XIIIe siècles', *Le Moyen Age* vol.LXIX (1963), pp.202–22.

Lambert, E., *L'architecture des Templiers* (Paris, 1955; reprint, 1978).

Lameyre, A., *Guide de la France Templière* (Paris, 1975).

Lamma, P., *Comneni e Staufer: Richerche sui rapporte fra Bisanzio e l'Occidente nel secolo XII* (Rome, 1955).

Latrie, M., *Histoire de Chypre* (Paris, n.d.).

Le Croix, P., *Military and Religious Life in the Middle Ages and the Renaissance* (New York, 1964).

Le Maho, J., *La Motte Seigneuriale de Mirville (XIe–XIIe s.)* (Rouen, 1984).

Le Patourel, J., *The Norman Empire* (Oxford, 1976).

Legge, M.D., 'The Lord Edward's Vegetius', *Scriptorium* vol.VII (1953), pp.262–5.

Lévi-Provençal, E., 'Une Heroïne de la Résistance Musulmane en Sicile au debut du XIIIe Siècle', *Oriente Moderna* vol.XXXIV (1954).

Lewis, A.R., *Medieval Naval and Maritime History AD 300–1500* (University of Indiana Press, 1983).

    Naval Power and Trade in the Mediterranean AD 500–1100 (Princeton, 1951).

    The Northern Sea, Shipping and Commerce in Northern Europe, AD 300–1100 (Princeton, 1958).

Lewis, N.B., 'An Early Indenture of Military Service, 27 July 1287', *Bulletin of the Institute of Historical Research* vol.XIII (1935), pp.85–9.

    'The English Forces in Flanders, August–November 1297', in *Studies in Medieval History presented to F.M. Powicke*, ed. R.W. Hunt (Oxford, 1948), pp.310–78.

    'The Recruitment and Organization of a Contract Army, May to November 1337', *Bulletin of the Institute of Historical Research* vol.XXXVII (1964), pp.1–19.

    'The Summons of the English Feudal Levy, 5 April 1327', in *Essays in Medieval History presented to Bertie Wilkinson*, eds. T.A. Sanquist and M.R. Powicke (Toronto, 1969), pp.236–49.

Leyser, K., *Medieval Germany and Its Neighbours* (London, 1982).

Linder, K., *Dawno wojsko Polskie w Illustracji* (Warsaw, 1955).

Lomax, D.W., 'Las Milicias cistercienses en el reino de León', *Hispania* vol.XXIII (1963), pp.29–42.

    La Orden de Santiago (1170–1275) (Madrid, 1965).

Lombard, M., 'Arsenaux et bois de marine dans la Mediterranée (VIIe–XIe siècle)', in *Le navire et l'economie maritime du moyen âge au XVIIIe s. principalement en Mediterranée (Actes II e Coll.*

internat. d'Histoire maritime, Paris 1957) (Paris, 1958), pp.53–99.

Les Métaux dans l'ancien Monde du Ve au XIe siècle (Paris, 1974).

Lopez, R., and Raymond, I., *Medieval Trade in the Mediterranean World* (1955).

Lot, F., *L'Art Militaire et les armées au Moyen Age, en Europe et dans le Proche-Orient* (Paris, 1946).

Loud, G.A., 'The Church, Warfare and Military Obligation in Norman Italy', *Studies in Church History* vol.XX (1983), pp.31–45.

'The Gens Normannorum – Myth or Reality?' *Battle Conference on Anglo-Norman Studies, Proceedings* vol.IV (1981).

'How Norman was the Norman Conquest of Southern Italy?', *Nottingham Medieval Studies* vol.XXV (1981).

Loyn, H.R., *The Norman Conquest* (London, 1982).

Lucas, A.J., 'Irish-Norse Relations: Time for a Reappraisal?' *Journal of the Cork Historical and Archaeological Society* vol.LXXI (1966), pp.62–75.

Luchaire, A., *Les communes françaises a l'époque des Capétiens directs* (Paris, 1890).

Luttrell, A., *Latin Greece, the Hospitallers and the Crusades 1291–1400* (London, 1982).

Lydon, J.F., 'The Hobelar: an Irish Contribution to Medieval Warfare', *The Irish Sword* vol.II (1954), pp.12–16.

'An Irish Army in Scotland, 1296', *The Irish Sword* vol.V (1962), pp.184–9.

'Irish Levies in the Scottish Wars, 1296–1302', *The Irish Sword* vol.V (1962), pp.207–17.

The Lordship of Ireland in the Middle Ages (Dublin, 1972).

Mackenzie, W.M., *The Battle of Bannockburn: a Study in Medieval Warfare* (Glasgow, 1913).

'The Real Bannockburn, June 23–24 1314', *Transactions of the Glasgow Archaeological Society* n.s. vol.VI, no.l (1910), pp.80–102.

Mallett, M., *Mercenaries and their Masters: Warfare in Renaissance Italy* (London, 1974).

Mályusz, E., 'A magyar köznemessegkialulása', *Századok* (1942).

March, U., 'Die holsteinische Heeresorganization im Mittelalter', *Zeitschrift der Gesellschaft für Schleswig-holsteinische Geschichte* vol.XCIX (1974), pp.95–139.

Martin, J.L., 'Originer de la Orden Militar de Santiago (1170–1195)', *Anuario de Estudios medievales* vol.IV (1967), pp.571–90.

Martin, P., 'Quelques aspects de l'art de la guerre en Alsace au XIVe siècle', *Revue d'Alsace* vol.LXXXVIII (1948), pp.108–23.

Mayer, E., *Historia de las instituciones sociales y politicas de España y Portugal durante los siglos V a XIV* (Madrid, 1925).

Mayer, H.E., *The Crusades* (Oxford, 1972).

Kreuzzüge und Lateinischer Osten (London, 1983).

'Latins, Muslims and Greeks in the Latin Kingdom', *History* (1978).

'Le service militaire des vasseaux de Jérusalem a l'étranger et le financement des campagnes en Syrie du nord et en Egypte du XIIe siècle', *Memoires de l'Académie des inscriptions et belles-lettres* n.s. vol.V (Paris, 1984).

McNeal, E., 'Fulk of Neuilly and the Tournament of Ecry', *Speculum* (1953).

Meier-Welcker, H., 'Das Militärwesen Kaiser Friedrichs II, Landes Verteidigung, Heer und Flotte im sizilischen 'modellstaat'', *Revue internationale d'Histoire Militaire* (1975), pp.9–48.

Meissner, G ., *Das Kriegswesen der Reichsstadt Nordhausen (1299–1803)* (Berlin, 1939).

Melville, M., *La Vie des Templiers* (1951).

Menager, L.-R., *Amiratus – L'Émirat et les Origines de l'Amirauté (XIe–XIIIe siecles)* (Paris, 1960).

Hommes et Institutions de l'Italie Normande (London, 1981).

Menendez-Pidal, R., *La España del Cid* (Madrid, 1956); also as *The Cid and his Spain*, trans. H. Sutherland (London, 1934).

Mens, A., 'De Brabanciones of bloeddorstige en plunderzieke avonturies (XII–XIIIe eeuw)', in *Miscellanea historica in honorem Alberti de Meyer*, vol.I (Louvain and Brussels, 1946), pp.558–70.

Michel, P., 'Les defenseurs des châteaux et les villes fortes dans le Comtat Venaissin', *Bibliothèque de l'Ecole des Chartres* vol.LXXV (1915), pp.315–30.

Milleken, E.K., *Archery in the Middle Ages* (New York, 1967).

Miller, E., *War in the North: The Anglo-Scottish Wars of the Middle Ages* (Hull, 1960).

Miller, W., *The Latins in the Levant: A History of Frankish Greece (1204–1566)* (1908).

Mollat, M., 'Problèmes navals de l'histoire des Croisades', *Cahiers de Civilizations Medievales* vol.X (1967), pp.345–59.

Monreal y Tejada, L., *Ingenieria Militar en la Cronicas Catalanas* (Barcelona, 1971).

Monroe, D.C., 'A Crusader: Foucher de Chartres', *Speculum* (1932).

'Letters of the Crusaders written from the Holy Land', *Translations and Reprints from the Original Sources of European History* vol.I, no.4 (1902).

Monti, G.M., *La Espansione mediterranea del mezzogiorno d'Italia e della Sicilia* (Bologna, 1942).

Montu, C., *Storia dell'artigliera italiana* (Rome, 1934).

Mor, C.G., 'La difesa militare delle Capitaneta ed i confine della regionale al principio del secolo XI', *Papers of the British School in Rome* vol.XXIV (1956), pp.29–36.

Morris, C., 'Villehardouin and the Conquest of Constantinople', *History* (1968).

Morris, J.E., *Bannockburn* (Cambridge, 1914).

Morris, W.S., 'A Crusader's Testament', *Speculum* vol.XXVII (1952).

Musset, L., 'Problèmes militaires du monde scandinavie (VIIe–XIIe siècle)', in *Ordinamenti militari in Occidente nell'alto medioevo, Settimane di Studio del Centro Italiano di Studi sull'alto Medioevo* (Spoleto, 1968), pp.229–91.

Musset, L., *Les invasions: le second assault contre l'Europe chrétienne (VIIe–XIe siècle)* (Paris, n.d.).

Navel, H., 'L'enquête de 1133 sur les fiefs de l'évêché de Bayeux', *Bulletin de la Société des Antiquaires de Normandie* vol.XLII (1939), pp.5–80.

Nesbitt, J.W., 'The Rate of Marching of Crusading Armies in Europe', *Traditio* vol.XIX (1963), pp.167–81.

Neu, H., *Bibliographie des Templer-Ordens, 1127–65* (Bonn, 1965).

Newark, T., *Celtic Warriors 400 BC–1600 AD* (London, 1986).

Nicholson, R.L., *Edward III and the Scots: The Formative Years of a Military Career, 1327–35* (Oxford, 1965).

'The Siege of Berwick, 1333', *The Scottish History Review* vol.XL (1961), pp.19–42.

Tancred: A Study of His Career and Work (Chicago, 1940).

Noguier, L., 'Enceinte murale de Béziers a l'époque gallo-romaine et au moyen-âge', *Bulletin de la Société archéologiques, scientifique et littéraire de Beziers* 2nd ser. vol.VII (1873), p.274ff.

Nordman, C.A., 'Nordiske Ornamentik in Finlands Järna-alder', *Nordiske Kultur* vol.XXVII (1931).

'Vapnen in Nordens Forntid', *Nordiske Kultur* vol.XII/B (1943), pp.59–61.

Nørlund, P., *Gyldne Altre* (1926).

and Lind, E., *Danmarks romanske Kalkmalerier* (1944).

Norman, A.V.B., 'An Early Illustration of Body Armour', *Zeitschrift für Historische Waffen- und Kostümkunde* vol.XVIII (1976), pp.38–9.

The Medieval Soldier (London, 1971).

'Notes on Some Early Representations of Guns and on Ribaudekins', *Journal of the Arms and Armour Society* vol.VIII (1974–6), pp.234–42.

Noyé, G., 'Le château de Scribla et les fortifications normandes du bessin de Crati', *Società potere e populo nell'eta de Ruggero II (III Giornate normanno-suevi, Bari 1977)* (Rome, 1979).

Ó'Corrain, D., *Ireland before the Normans* (Dublin and London, 1972).

O'Neill, B.H.StJ., *Castles and Cannon* (Oxford, 1960).

Oerter, H.L., 'Campaldino, 1289', *Speculum* vol.XXXIII (1968), pp.428–50.

Oman, C.W.C., *A History of the Art of War in the Middle Ages* (London, 1924).

Orpen, G.H., *Ireland under the Normans* (London, 1911–12).

Otten, C., 'Les Pisans en Egypte et à Acre dans la seconde moitée du XIIIe siècle: documents nouveaux', *Bolletino storico pisano* vol.LIII(1983), pp.163–90.

Otway-Ruthven, J., 'Knight Service in Ireland', *Journal of the Royal Society of Antiquaries of Ireland* vol.LXXXIX (1959), pp.1–15.

Packard, S.R., 'The Norman Communes under Richard and John, 1189–1204', in *Anniversary Essays in Medieval History by Students of Charles Homer Haskins* (Boston and New York, 1929), pp.231–53.

Padrutt, C., *Staat und Krieg im alten Bünden* (Bern, 1965).

Painter, G.D., *The Vinland Map and the Tartar Relation* (New Haven and London, 1965).

Painter, S., 'Castle Guard', *The American Historical Review* vol.XL (1934–5), pp.450–9.

Paoli, C., *La battaglia di Montaperti* (Siena, 1869).

'Le Cavallate fiorentine nei secolo XIII e XIV compilato sui documente dell'Archivio fiorentino', *Archivio Storica Italiano* 3rd ser. vol.II (1865).

ed., *Il libro di Montaperti* (Florence, 1889).

'Rendiconto e approvazioni de spese occorse nell'esercito fiorentino contro Pistoia nell maggio 1302', *Archivio Storico Italiano* 3rd ser. vol.VI, no.2 (1867).

Parisse, M., *La noblesse Lorraine, XIe–XIIIe siècles* (Lille, 1976).

Pauler, G., 'Néhány szo hadi viszonyainkról a XI–XIII században', *Hadtörténelmi Közlemények* (1888).

Peres, D., *Como nasceu Portugal* 5th edn. (Porto, 1959).

Perlbach, M., ed., *Die Stataten des deutschen Ordens* (Halle, 1890).

Pescador, C., 'La caballeria popular en León y Castilla', *Cuadernos de Historia de España* vols XXXIII–XXXIV (1961), pp.101–238; vols XXXV–XXXVI (1962), pp.56–201; and vols XXXVII–XXXVIII (1963), pp.88–198.

Peters, E., ed., *Christian Society and the Crusades 1198–1229* (1977).

Pieri, P., 'Alcune Quistioni sopra la fanteria in Italia nel periodo comunale', *Rivista Storica Italiana* vol.XLV (1933), pp.411–14.

'Federigo II di Suevia e la guerra del suo tempo', *Archivio Storico Pugliese* vol.XIII (1960), pp.114–31.

'Milizie e capitani di ventura in Italia nel Medio Evo', *Atti del Reale Accademia Peloritano di Messina* vol.XL (1937–8).

'I Saraceni di Lucera nella storia militare medievale', *Archivio Storico Pugliese* vol.VI (1953), pp.94–101.

Poole, A.L., *Medieval England* (Oxford and New York, 1958).

Postan, M.M., 'Economic Relations between Eastern and Western Europe', in *Eastern and Western Europe in the Middle Ages*, ed. G. Barraclough (London, 1970).

Powers, J.F., 'The Origins and Development of Municipal Military Service in the Leonese and Castilian Reconquest 800–1250', *Traditio* vol.XXVI (1970), pp.91–111.

'Towers and Soldiers; the Interaction of Urban and Military Organization of the Militias of Medieval Castile', *Speculum* vol.XLVI (1971), pp.641–55.

Powicke, F.M., 'Distraint of Knighthood and Military Obligation under Henry III', *Speculum* vol.XXV (1950), pp.457–70.

'The General Obligation of Cavalry Service under Edward I', *Speculum* vol.XXVIII (1953), pp.814–33.

Military Obligation in Medieval England: A Study in Liberty and Duty (Oxford, 1962).

Prawer, J., *The Crusaders' Kingdom* (New York, 1972).

Histoire du royaume latin de Jérusalem, 2 vols (Paris, 1969–70).

'The Nobility of the Feudal Regime in the Latin Kingdom of Jerusalem', in *Lordship and Community in Medieval Europe*, ed. F. Cheyette (1968).

'The Settlement of Latins in Jerusalem', *Speculum* (1952).

Prestwich, J.O., 'War and Finance in the Anglo-Norman State', *Transactions of the Royal Historical Society*, 5th ser. vol.IV (1954), pp.19–43.

Prestwich, M., *The Three Edwards: War and State in England 1272–1377* (London, 1981).

'Victualling Estimates for the English Garrisons in Scotland During the Early Fourteenth Century', *English Historical Review* vol.LXXXII (1967), pp.536–43.

Prince, A.E., 'The Army and Navy', in *The English Government at Work, 1327–1336, vol.1: Central and Prerogative Administration*, ed. J.F. Willard and W.A. Morris (Cambridge, Mass., 1940), pp.332–93.

'The Payment of Army Wages in Edward III's Reign', *Speculum* vol.XIX (1944), pp.137–60.

'The Strength of English Armies under Edward III', *English Historical Review* vol.XLVI (1931). pp.353–71.

Pryor, J.H., 'Naval Architecture of Naval Transport Ships: a Reconstruction of Some Archetypes for Round-hulled Sailing Ships,' *Mariner's Mirror* (1983), pp.171–292 and 363–86.

Queller, D.E., ed., *The Latin Conquest of Constantinople* (1971).

Querol y Roso, L., *Las milicias valencianas desde el siglo XIII al XV* (Castellón de la Plana, 1935).

Raleigh-Radford, C.A., 'The Later Pre-Conquest Boroughs and their Defences', *Medieval Archaeology* vol.XIV (1970), pp.83–103.

Rasi, P., *Exercitus italicus e Milizie cittadine nell'alto medioevo* (Padua, 1937).

Rassow, P., 'La confrad'a de Belchite', *Anuario de historia del derecho español* vol.III (1926), pp.200–26.

'Zum byzantinisch-normanischen Krieg 1147–1149', *Mitteilungen der Institut für österreich Geschichts Forschung* vol.LXII (1954), pp.213–18.

Rathgen, B., *Das Geschütz im Mittelalter* (Berlin, 1929).

Razin, A.E., *Geschuchte der Kriegskunst, II: Die Kriegskunst der Feudalperiod des Krieges* (Berlin, 1960).

Reinaud, M., and Fave, *Histoire de l'Artillerie, du Feu Grégois, des feux de guerre et des origines de la poudre à canon* (Paris, 1845).

Richard, J., *The Latin Kingdom of Jerusalem* (Oxford, 1979).

'Les Navigations des Occidentaux sur l'ocean indien et la mer caspienne (XIIe–XVe siècles),' in *Sociétés et compagnies de commerce en Orient et dans l'ocean indien*, ed. M. Mollat (Paris, 1970), pp.353–63.

Riley-Smith, J.S.C., *The Feudal Nobility and the Kingdom of Jerusalem 1174–1277* (London, 1973).

The Knights of St John in Jerusalem and Cyprus 1050–1310 (London 1967).

'Peace never established: the case of the Kingdom of Jerusalem', *Transactions of the Royal Historical Society* 5th ser. vol.XXVIII (1978), pp.87–102.

Ritchie, R.L.G., *The Normans in England before the Norman Conquest* (Edinburgh, 1948).

The Normans in Scotland (Edinburgh, 1954).

Robson, J.A., 'The Catalan Fleet and Moorish Sea-Power (1337–1344)', *English Historical Review* vol.LXXIV (1959), pp.386–408.

Rodgers, W.L., *Naval Warfare under Oars* (Annapolis, 1967).

Romeiss, M., 'Die Wehrverfassung der Reichsstadt Frankfurt am Main im Mittelalter', *Archiv für Frankfurts-Geschichte und Kunst* (1953), pp.5–63.

Ross, D.J.A., 'L'Originaté de Turoldus: le maniement de la lance', *Cahiers de Civilizations Médiévale* vol.VI (1963).

Roth, R., *Histoire de l'archerie* (Paris, 1964).

Rousset, P., 'Note sur la situation du chevalier a l'époque romane', in *Literature, Histoire, Linguistique, Recueil d'études offerts á Bernard Gagnebin* (Lausanne, 1973), pp.189–200.

Rubia y Lluch, A., 'La companya catalana soto el comandament de Teobald de Cepoy (1307–1310)', in *Miscellania E. Prat de la Riba* (Barcelona, 1923), pp.219–70.

Rubinstein, N., ed., *Florentine Studies* (London and Evanston, 1968).

Runciman, S., *The Families of Outremer: The Feudal Nobility of the Crusader Kingdom of Jerusalem*

1099–1291 (1960).

A History of the Crusades (London, 1971).

Russell, P.E., *The English Intervention in Spain and Portugal in the Time of Edward III and Richard II* (Oxford, 1955).

Salch, C.L., Burnouf, J., and Fino, J.F., *L'Atlas des Châteaux Forts en France* (Strasbourg, 1980).

Salvemini, G., *I balestrieri del Commune di Firenze* (Bologna, 1967).

La dignita cavalleresca nel Commune di Firenze (ed altri scritti) (Milan, 1972).

Sander, E., 'Der Belagerungskrieg im Mittelalter', *Historische Zeitschrift* vol.CLXV (1941), pp.99–110.

Sanders, I.J., *Feudal Military Service in England* (London and New York, 1956).

Sarton, G., *Introduction to the History of Science* (Baltimore, 1947–8).

Sastre Santos, E., 'El martirologio de Uclés y los origines de la Orden de Santiago', *Hispania Sacra* vol.XXXIV (1982), pp.217–52.

Sauvageot, A., *Les Anciens Finnois* (Paris, 1961).

Saxtorph, N.M., *Krigsfolk tilalle tider* (Warriors of all Times) (Copenhagen, n.d.).

Schlight, J., *Monarchs and Mercenaries: A Reappraisal of the Importance of Knight Service of Norman and Angevin England* (Bridgeport, Conn., 1968).

Schlumberger, G., *Renaud de Châtillon, Prince d'Antioch seigneur de la terre d'Outre-Jourdain* (Paris, 1898).

Schreiner, P., 'Zur Ausrustung des Kriegers in Byzanz, dem Kiever Russland und Nordeurope nach bildlichen und literarischen Quellen', in *Les Pays du Nord et Byzance, Actes du Colloque nordique et internationale de byzantinologie tenu à Upsal 20–22 avril 1979: Acta Universitatis Upsaliensis Figura* n.s. vol.XIX (1981), pp.215–36.

Schultze, J., 'Die Bürgliche Dienst- und Wehrpflicht in der Mark Bandenburg', *Jahrbuch für die Geschichte Mittel- und Ostdeutschland* vol.XXIII (1974), pp.270–80.

Semaan, K., *Islam and the Medieval West: Aspects of Intercultural Relations* (Albany, 1980).

Sennhause, A., *Hauptmann und Führung im Schweizer Krieg des Mittelalters* (Bern, 1965).

Setton, K.M., *Catalan Domination of Athens, 1311–1388* (London, 1975).

ed., *A History of the Crusades* (London and Wisconsin, 1962– in progress).

Simms, K., 'Warfare in the Medieval Gaelic Lordships', *The Irish Sword* vol.XII (1975), pp.98–108.

Simon, E., *The Piebald Standard: A Biography of the Knights Templars* (Boston, 1959 and 1976).

Škrivanić, G.A., 'Borbe oko Zadra (1105, 1202 i 1345/46) godine: Les combats de Zadar', *Vesnik, Vojni muzej* vols XIII–XIV (Belgrade, 1968), pp.59–80.

Smail, R.C., 'Art of War', in *Medieval England*, ed. A.L. Poole (Oxford and New York, 1958), vol.I, pp.128–67.

'Crusaders' Castles in the Twelfth Century', *Cambridge Historical Journal* (1951).

Crusading Warfare, 1097–1193 (Cambridge, 1956).

Smith, F., 'Über die florentinische Wehrmacht im Jahre der Schlacht von Montaperti (1260)', in *Delbrück Festschrift* (Berlin, 1908).

Soldevila, F., *Els Almogávers* (Barcelona, 1952).

Spahiu, H., and Komata, D., 'Shurdhah (Sard): La cité Albanaise médiévale fortifiée', *Iliria* vol.III (n.d.).

Sprandel, R., *Das Eigengewerbe im Mittelalter* (Stuttgart, 1968).

Sprömberg, H., 'Die Feudale Kriegskunst', in *Beiträge zur belgisch-niederländischen Geschichte* (Berlin, 1959), pp.30–55.

Stenton, F.M., *The First Century of English Feudalism 1066–1166* (Oxford, 1932).

Sternfeld, R., *Ludwigs des heiligen Kreuzzug nach Tunis, 1270, und die Politik Karl I, von Sizilien* (Berlin, 1896).

Stotten, P., 'Wandlungen und Gebrauchs der Kriegswaffen im Mittelalter', in *Die Entwicklung der Kriegswaffen und inhre Zusammenhang mit der Sozialordnung*, ed. L. Von Wiese (Cologne, 1963), pp.118–33.

Strayer, J.R., 'Knight Service in Normandy in the XIIIth century', in *Anniversary Essays in Medieval History by Students of Charles Homer Haskins* (Boston and New York, 1929), pp.312–27.

Szendrei, J., *Ungarische kreigsgeschichtliche Denkmäler* (Budapest, 1896).

Tabacco, G., 'Il regno italico nei secoli IX–XI', in *Ordinamenti militari in Occidenti nell'alto medioevo, Settimane di Studio del Centro Italiano di Studi sull'alto Medioevo* vol.XV, no.2 (Spoleto, 1968), pp.763–90.

Taylor, A.J., 'Three early castle sites in Italy: Motto Camastra, Sperlinga and Petralia Soprana', *Château-Gaillard* vol.VII (1974).

Thompson, A.H., 'The Art of War to 1400', in *Cambridge Medieval History* vol.VI (London, 1929).

Tomasi, G.L., *Ritratto del Condottiero* (Turin, 1967).

Topping, P., *Studies in Latin Greece AD 1205–1715* (London, 1977).

Torres, A.P., 'Contribución al estudio del ejército en los estados de la Reconquista', *Anuario de Historia del Derecho Español* vol.XV (1944), pp.205–351.

Tóth, Z., 'A hadakozónép', in *Magyar Müvelödéstörténet* vol.I (Budapest, n.d.).

'A hadviselés átalakuláas', in *Magyar Müvelödéstörténet* vol.II (Budapest, n.d.).

'A huszárok eredetérol' (on Hungarian cavalry), *Hadtörténelmi Közlemények* (1934).

'A huszárok eredethagyománya 1937', *Hadtörténelmi Közlemények* (1938).

'A kigyóspusztai csat jelentösege', *Turul* (1933).

'A közepkor magyar katonája', *Pannonia* (1940).

Tuchmann, B., *A Distant Mirror, the Calamitous 14th Century* (London, 1979).

Turner, H.L., *Town Defences in England and Wales: An Architectural and Documentary Survey AD 900–1500* (London, 1970).

Tuulse, A., *Castles of the Western World* (London, 1958).

Ubieto Areta, A., 'La guerra en la Edad media según los fueros de la linea del Tajo', *Saitabi* vol.XVI (1966), pp.91–210.

Urban, W., *The Baltic Crusade* (De Kalb, Il., 1975).

'The Organisation of Defence in the Livonian Frontier in the Thirteenth Century', *Speculum* vol.XLVIII (1973), pp.525–32.

Uri, S.P., 'Het tournooi in de XIIe en XIIIe eeuw', *Tidtschrift voor Geschiedenis* vol.LXXIII (1960), pp.376–96.

Vale, J., *Edward III and Chivalry: Chivalric Society and its Context 1270–1350* (London, 1982).

Van Luyn, P., 'Les milites dans la France du XIe siècle, Examen des sources narratives', *Le Moyen Age* vol.LXXVII (1971), pp.5–51 and 193–238.

Van Winter, J.A., 'Cingulum militae. Schwertleite en miles-terminologie als spiegel van veranderend menselijk gedrag', *Tijdschrift voor Rechtsgeschiedenis* vol.XLIV (1976), pp.1–92.

Verbruggen, J.F., 'L'art militaire en Europe occidentale du IXe au XIVe siècle', *Revue internationale d'Histoire militaire* (1953–5), pp.486–96.

The Art of Warfare in Western Europe during the Middle Ages (Oxford, 1977).

'Het leger en de vloot van de graven van Vlaandered vanafhet outstaan tot in 1305', *Verhandelingen van de Koninklijke Vlaamse Academie voor wetenschappen lettered en schonekinsten van Belgie, Klasse der letteren* vol.XXXVIII (Brussels, 1960).

'De historiografie van de Guldensporslag', *De Leiegouw* vol.XIX (1977), pp.245–72.

'De militaire dienst in het graafschap Vlaandered', *Tijdschrift voor Rectgeschiedenis* vol.XXVI (1958), pp.437–65.

De slag der gulden sporen, Bijdrage tot de geschiedenis van Vlaanderens vrijheidsoorlog 1295–1305 (Antwerp and Amsterdam, 1952).

'La tactique militaire des armées des chevaliers', *Revue du Nord* vol.XXIX (1947), pp.161–80.

1302 in Vlaanderen: De Guldensporslag (Brussels, 1977).

'Vlaamse Gemeentelegers tegen Franse Ridderlegers in de 14de en 15de Eeuw', *Belgisch Tijdschrift voor Militaire Geschiedenis* vol.XXIV (1981), pp.359–82.

Verdera y Tuello, E., ed., *El Cardinal Albornoz y el Collegio de España* (Bologna, 1972–3).

Von Wiese, L., ed., *Die Entwicklung der Kriegswaffen und ihre Zusammenhang mit der Sozialordnung* (Cologne, 1953).

Waley, D.P., 'The Army of the Florentine Republic from the Twelfth to the Fourteenth Century', in *Florentine Studies*, ed. N. Rubinstein (London and Evanston, 1968), pp.70–108.

'Combined Operations in Sicily, AD 1060–78', *Papers of the British School at Rome* vol.XXII (1954).

'Condotte and Condottieri in the Thirteenth Century', *Proceedings of the British Academy* (1975), pp.337–71.

'Le origini della condotta nel Duecento e le compagnie di ventura', *Rivista Storica Italiana* vol.LXXXVIII (1976), pp.531–8.

'Papal Armies of the Thirteenth Century', *The English Historical Review* vol.LXXII (1957), pp.1–30.

Warlop, E., *The Flemish Nobility* (Courtrai, 1975–6).

Webster, K.G.T., 'The Twelfth Century Tournament', in *Kittredge Anniversary Papers* (Cambridge, Mass., 1913), pp.227–34.

Werner, K.F., 'Heeresorganisation und Kriegsführung im deutschen Königreich des 10 und 11 Jahrhunderts', in *Ordinamenti Militari in Occidente nell'alto Medioevo, Settimane di Studio del Centro italiano di Studi sull'Alto Medioevo* vol.XV, no.2 (Spoleto, 1968), pp.791–843.

White, G.H., 'The Household of the Norman Kings', *Transactions of the Royal Historical Society* 4th ser. vol.XXX (1948), pp.133–4 and 151–2.

White, L., 'The Crusades and the Technological Thrust of the West', in *War, Technology and Society in the Middle East*, ed. V.J. Parry and M.E. Yapp (London, 1975).

Medieval Technology and Social Change (Oxford, 1962).

Wienand, A., ed., *Der Johanniter Orden: Der Malteser Orden: Der ritterliche Orden des hl. Johannes vom Spital zu Jerusalem: seine Aufgaben, seine Geschichte* (Cologne, 1970).

Wieruszowski, H., 'The Norman Kingdom of Sicily and the Crusades', in *A History of the Crusades, vol.II, The Later Crusades 1189–1311*, ed. K.M. Setton (London, 1962), pp.3–42.

Willard, J.F., and Morris, W.A., eds., *The English Government at Work, 1327–1339, vol.1: Central and Prerogative Administration* (Cambridge, Mass., 1940).

Wilson, D.M., ed., *The Northern World* (London, 1980).

Wolff, P., *Commerces et marchands de Toulouse (vers 1350–vers 1450)* (Paris, 1954).

Wormald, F., 'Bloodfeud, Kindred and Government in Early Modern Scotland', *Past and Present* vol.LXXXVII (1980), pp.54–97.

Yewdale, R.B., *Bohemund I, Prince of Antioch* (1924).

Yver, J., 'Les châteaux-forts en Normandie', *Bulletin de la Société Antiquaires de Normandie* vol.LIII (1955), pp.28–115.

Zachariadou, E.A., 'The Catalans of Athens and the Beginnings of the Turkish Expansion in the Aegean area', *Studia Medievali* 3rd ser. vol.XXI (1980), pp.821–38.

Zachariadou, E.A., *Romania and the Turks (c.1300–c.1500)* (London, 1985).

Zöllner, W., *Geschichte der Kreuzzüge* (Berlin, 1979).

Index